THE LOST CRUSADE

America in Vietnam

THE LOST CRUSADE

AMERICA IN VIETNAM

By Chester L. Cooper

With a Foreword by Ambassador W. Averell Harriman

DODD, MEAD & COMPANY, NEW YORK

ISBN 0-396-06241-5

Library of Congress Catalog Card Number: 79-135539

Printed in the United States of America
by The Cornwall Press, Inc., Cornwall, N. Y.

For Orah, who knows why

Acknowledgments

There have been many books written on the American involvement in Vietnam (and there will be many more). If my own adds knowledge or insight, it will be in no small measure due to the efforts of those who worked with me. Mrs. William Corson and Mrs. Marjory Pickard provided valuable over-all advice on content and kept the enterprise moving when my own energies flagged. Mrs. Corson, a most imaginative and persevering researcher, prospected and mined vast lodes of source material. The bibliography, chronology and index were prepared by her. Mrs. Pickard gave every line of the manuscript the favor of her discerning editorial eye and the manuscript as a whole the benefit of her discriminating sense of organization and order. Mrs. Christine Yoshida and Mrs. Carolyn Phelan cheerfully carried the burden of typing from conception to delivery. The book could not have been done without these devoted colleagues.

The entire manuscript was reviewed and improved upon by Daniel Davidson, friend and ex-colleague. Among the host of busy men who gave generously of their time and advice and who deserve more than the perfunctory "thanks" that this format allows were: McGeorge Bundy, William Bundy, Joseph Buttinger, Mark Chadwin, Leo Cherne, Wesley Fishel, Averell Harriman (whose Foreword graces the book), Paul Kattenberg, General

Charles Lanham, Edward Lansdale, Ben Read, Maxwell Taylor and Vu Van Thai.

To my wife, Orah, whose good humor and patient help stood me in good stead through endless hours and many drafts, and to my daughters, Joan and Susan, whose solicitude and understanding toward what sometimes must have seemed an act of madness, I owe much.

I need hardly say that the story I tell is my own. My colleagues and those I interviewed may well have told it differently and bear no responsibility for my views, my errors or my omissions. The research for this book was supported from a Ford Foundation grant made available to the Institute for Defense Analyses. However, though they were generous and understanding, they played no part, nor sought any, in the conclusions of this study.

CHESTER L. COOPER

Foreword

by Ambassador W. Averell Harriman

This survey of the full course of the United States involvement in Vietnam reflects Chester Cooper's long and unique experience with Asia and Vietnam. He is the only man I know who was a member of the United States Delegation to the 1954 Geneva Conference on Indochina, the 1954 Conference in Manila which established SEATO, the 1961–62 Geneva Conference on Laos and the 1966 Summit Conference in Manila. In 1964 McGeorge Bundy asked him to serve as the Assistant for Asian Affairs on the White House Staff.

In the spring of 1966 he was granted a one-year leave of absence to devote his time to research and writing on international affairs. Although I had already been involved, it was about the same time that President Johnson gave me the specific responsibility to bring about negotiations for a settlement and follow every lead or opening that might appear. Prior to that time there had been public discussion of whether every lead had been carefully followed through. The President asked me to make sure that no opportunity, no matter how tenuous, was neglected.

In undertaking this assignment I turned to Chet Cooper for assistance. I had had the benefit of his wise counsel during the difficult negotiations for a Laotian settlement in 1962. After some hesitation, he set aside his work on what I assume would have been an earlier version of this book and became, not only my Special Assistant for Vietnam Negotiations, but also my entire staff for them. He performed his duties with extraordinary initiative, originality, devotion, and, fortunately, a never-failing sense of humor. He remained with me until October of 1967 and after that time continued to serve as a valued consultant. It is Chester Cooper's background that makes this book such a valuable contribution amidst the ever-growing literature on Vietnam.

Mr. Cooper's thorough research on the early history of the United States relationship to Indochina adds significantly to the historical record, even when the book discusses matters in which he was not personally involved. For example, his chapter on President Roosevelt's intention to refuse to permit the French to return to Indochina at the end of World War II is the most thorough account with which I am familiar. I was particularly interested in that chapter, because I still vividly recall President Roosevelt's statement in my presence on more than one occasion that the French should never be allowed to return to Indochina. If Roosevelt had lived to carry out his ideas and if the states of Indochina could have emerged from World War II as free and independent nations, a great deal of suffering by many peoples might have been avoided. The chapter on Diem's appointment as Prime Minister also contains much new information.

A particularly valuable aspect of this book is the author's honesty. To the best of his ability he has tried to re-create what happened as he saw it. When he was wrong, he does not hesitate to admit it. Indeed, if anything, he does not indicate how often he was right.

The Lost Crusade is a most distinguished and important book on the history of United States involvement in Vietnam. It is a fascinating account and sheds light on critical questions about how we got to where we are. It should be read by all those interested in the problem.

How long a period must pass before a government official may write appropriately about his official experiences is always a difficult question. In the case of Vietnam it can be sincerely argued that the subject is of such vital and continuing importance that the facts should be made available to permit the public to make a more informed judgment. I express no judgment on the question. I was consulted neither about the decision to write this book nor on its contents. It is Chet Cooper's account. I write this foreword as a grateful colleague and admirer of Mr. Cooper but not as an indication that I either agree with or know the basis of all his reports, comments, or personal reactions.

There are some who are naïve enough to think that only members of anti-war groups and their supporters worked for peace. This book is an account by one of the most tireless of that dedicated group within government who devoted their energies to attempting to bring about a peaceful settlement. Chester Cooper is one of the unsung heroes in the battle for peace.

Contents

Contents

America in Vietnam

THE LOST CRUSADE

America in Vietnam

I

The Decade of Vietnam

The historian of the year 2000 writing his "Survey of the United States in the Twentieth Century" may well characterize the 1960s as the "Decade of Vietnam." Certainly to most of us who have groped our way through these years the war in Vietnam was the most critical international problem and, together with civil rights, the most divisive domestic issue. Vietnam deeply influenced American relations with every important country; it embittered our national politics; it tore apart the fabric of our society. The future historian may shed light on why the Saigon Government, assisted unstintingly by the most powerful nation in the world, was not able to dispose of the ragtag Viet Cong and its major ally North Vietnam, a country of 16 million people. But to us the confrontation has been bewildering and frustrating—especially frustrating. The emotional quotient has been high among all involved Americans—government officials, Women Strikers for Peace, war correspondents, Congressmen, and military men. Chasing around the steaming landscape after Viet Cong who were there one moment and gone the next, working out yet another pacification plan with yet another Prime Minister, sitting in Paris trying to negotiate a settlement with suspicious allies and stubborn enemies was enough to try the soul of the most philosophical GI or the most patient Ambassador or the most resilient President. It is constructive to suggest that we draw back and examine our experience in Vietnam more dispassionately, but calm objectivity will not come easily.

A student of American history since World War II may conclude that an epic combination of fate, accident, and conscious decision led us to the Decade of Vietnam, but to most Americans the terrible problem of Vietnam seemed to have crept up on us. Yesterday we had a few military advisers there; suddenly there were hundreds of thousands of combat troops. Yesterday we were helping an ally fight off a few thousand rebels; suddenly we were engaged in a war against regular Communist forces, a war that has spread to neighboring countries as well.

The historian may observe that the threat to the Government of South Vietnam became most urgent just about the time that a new Administration was preparing to take over in Washington—an Administration determined to press ahead with "counter-insurgency assistance" for its hard-pressed ally. When Vice President Lyndon Johnson visited Vietnam in May, 1961 he assured President Diem, obviously with President Kennedy's approval, that "The United States is . . . conscious of its responsibility and duty, in its own self-interest as well as in the interest of other free peoples, to assist a brave country in the defense of its liberties against unprovoked subversion and Communist terror." [1] In the autumn of 1961 President Kennedy sent General Maxwell Taylor to Vietnam on what was to be only the first of a long series of "fact-finding" missions. On Taylor's recommendation Kennedy substantially augmented the number of American military "advisory" personnel in Vietnam, although he rejected suggestions that their mission be expanded to include a combat role. In early 1962 a Military Assistance Command was established to direct the activities of the few thousand American military advisers then in Vietnam. By the end of 1964 the number of American military personnel had increased to about 23,000 men. And then half way through the Decade, in 1965, the United States launched bombing attacks on North Vietnam, introduced B–52 strategic bombers, and opened a new chapter in the saga of American involvement in Vietnam that led to the eventual deployment of more than a half million American troops.

For most of the Vietnam Decade, Americans, as part of their breakfast routine, have been treated to promises or threats of "progress," "corner-turning," "stalemates," "Dien Bien Phus," "reverse Dien Bien Phus," "pull-outs," "sell-outs," and finally (one hopes), "Vietnamization." Large portions of statistics were served up to support claims of success or to document charges of stalemate: classrooms built, schools destroyed; miles of road open, villages still isolated; improved effectiveness of the Vietnamese Army, large-scale desertions from the Vietnamese Army; kill ratios; villages pacified, village chiefs kidnapped. To make all this more digestible, the statistics had been reduced to colored maps and bar charts and graphs galore.

But every Administration in Washington during the Decade had finally to come to grips with the realization that most Americans did not understand or did not believe or did not give a damn about the claims and counter-claims. Americans developed an immunity to numbers related to the Vietnam war. What made an impact was not how many enemy troops in Vietnam had been killed or captured, but how many Americans had been killed or drafted; not how many classrooms had been built in Quang Tri or Pleiku, but how many could have been built in Washington or Boston; not the graph showing an upward trend in weapons lost by the Viet Cong, but the graph showing an upward trend in cost-of-living in New York and Kansas City.

*   *   *

Questions as to whether the United States or any particular Administration was right or wrong in Vietnam—premature or tardy, too soft or too tough at any particular point in time—are interesting and relevant. But they are not crucial. Vietnam is not an area isolated and insulated from events and trends in the rest of the world. And the Decade of Vietnam is not an experience shared only by miserable Vietnamese and tortured Americans. Our involvement in Vietnam has gone well beyond Vietnam itself, beyond it in terms of area and beyond it in terms of time.

The outcome of the war will be important in determining the future of Vietnam, but more important to the United States, it will have a profound influence on America's future international role. In that light it is all the more significant that the explanations of why we became involved in Vietnam have been superficial, confusing, and perhaps even misleading. Did we commit ourselves, as Presidents Eisenhower, Kennedy, Johnson, and Nixon have often said, solely to give the South Vietnamese a "free choice"? If so, we have also implicitly undertaken a major commitment to provide this service to a host of other deprived peoples. Did we get involved, as Secretary Rusk and others have frequently and emphatically stated, to protect our own national security? If so, we should select more carefully those areas where our vital interests are more obviously at stake. Did we spend billions of dollars and more than 45,000 American lives to "Stop China"? If so, we chose the wrong place, for even a clear-cut military victory in Vietnam would not "stop" China if Peking decided to "go." Sooner or later China will have to be dealt with in another way through some political arrangement between Washington and Peking. There are 800 million Chinese and a "solution" other than a political one would be disastrous, not only for the Chinese but for the Vietnamese and all the rest of us.

American involvement in Vietnam did not emerge full-blown in the dawn of the 1960s. Despite campaign rhetoric, the course of history does not end and then begin anew with every change of Administration in Washington. The beginnings of our involvement go back to the years of World War II, and a critical turning point confronted us in the mid-1950s.

The Geneva Agreements of 1954 provided only a brief respite for the troubled and weary peoples of Vietnam. They and their Laotian neighbors soon again became caught up in a struggle that went well beyond their borders and their ken. Vietnam became the scene of not only a military and political battleground between Saigon and Hanoi, but of a confrontation between the two systems that Moscow and Washington represent. Both the Russians and the Americans probably would have given a lot to have Vietnam and Laos fade quietly away; failing that, both would probably have preferred a compromise settlement (although not necessarily the same compromise settlement) to a continuation of the fighting. But Great Powers are vulnerable as well as powerful; their options are limited, and in this situation their initiatives have been constricted by two insignificant but troublesome protégés.

Americans, as they listen to the newscasts, often find the problems that confront them at home as a consequence of Vietnam, and in Vietnam itself, almost beyond forbearance. In our own concern and frustration, it may be of some small solace to realize that the Russians too have cause to be concerned and frustrated. In the course of Soviet involvement with distant, virtually unknown comrades, they found that strains had increased with the one country they now fear most—the People's Republic of China. And to compound their worries, a political settlement of the war, which would ease Soviet–American relations, may further strain the Soviet–Chinese bond. Vietnam became not only a focus of American–Soviet confrontation, but of Sino–Soviet confrontation as well.

In the aftermath of the events in Geneva during 1954, Vietnam became a Great Power crossroads. Once in, the United States could not simply walk out; nor was it easy for the USSR to renege on its commitment to Hanoi. And despite the advocates of more robust military measures against North Vietnam, the war against Hanoi could not have been stepped up to the point where the Hanoi regime itself was placed in jeopardy; Washington, wisely, wished to avoid direct confrontation with Peking and Moscow. The war was fought savagely, frequently ineffectually, and with a tremendous cost in blood and treasure. Historians may well acknowledge that ultimate American aims in Vietnam were much too modest to warrant the efforts expended to realize them.

One of the great issues that will long be debated is whether, if we had known in 1954 what we knew in 1970 (or in 1965 or 1960), we would have been drawn into Vietnam in the first place. In retrospect it seems clear that our original commitment to Vietnam in 1954 was in response to what was then a felt national interest, but our involvement in scale and cost eventually outran any requirements we may have felt we had to preserve a non-Communist regime in Saigon. After all, we have learned to accept, however grudgingly, a Communist regime in Havana ninety miles from our own border. Even if we emerge with "honor" or "dignity," how many Americans, including Americans holding high positions in the White House, Pentagon, or State Department, would choose to intervene in Vietnam if the choice had to be made over again? We had allied ourselves with a "non-government." Can even a Great Power afford that?

The fruits of Vietnam (win, lose, or draw) are likely to be sour, not only for America but for many other countries who have, or thought they had, an American "commitment." We may be able to demonstrate that we honored our commitment to Vietnam, but will the American people, at least in this generation, rush to honor others? Will this war, which had been justified as a demonstration of American concern for international order, lead to a new form of American isolationism? In the light of South Vietnam's experience, will other threatened small nations seek American "protection," or will they prefer to passively succumb to Communist pressure?

This is one of the crucial questions. Its answer will shed light on the role and destiny of the United States over the next decade and perhaps beyond. In trying to engage with this fundamental problem we must resign ourselves to the fact that there are only two knowns, neither of which is very helpful: the first is that the United States will remain a Great Power; the second is that virtually nothing else can be predicted with a high degree of confidence. Irving Kristol is right, I think, when he says, "because we are a Great Power, we are a 'committed nation' without knowing what our commitments precisely are. Our commitments are necessarily defined, to a considerable extent, by circumstance and contingency." [2]

The United States as a Great Power today has different international and national values, problems, objectives, and aspirations than the Soviet Union has as a Great Power. And the international responsibilities and national priorities of France and England in past decades provide little guidance for us now or over the years ahead. But because of our far-flung interests, the Soviet Union and the United States have some things in common. Foreign Ministers from every country in the world, for example, must be regarded and treated as personages of consequence by the Soviet Foreign Minister and the American Secretary of State. That Cambodia, a country of some 6 million people, broke relations with the United States was a source of greater concern to Washington in 1965 than it would have been many years ago. That the Congo, a country of approximately 16 million people, refused to recognize the USSR was more annoying to Moscow in 1967 than it would have been three decades ago. Perversely enough, prestige and pride are more important to Great Powers than to small—Great Powers want to be loved or at least respected, small powers don't have to give a damn. Great Powers have a harder time these days than they used to; our friends in London, Paris, and Tokyo should show Moscow and Washington somewhat more compassion than is their wont.

                    *   *   *

National interests, national prestige, and national security are not the only elements that have dominated Washington's and Moscow's view of the world since the end of World War II. Superimposed on these traditional elements of foreign policy has been a sometimes vague, sometimes sharply defined, sense of mission and ideology; the "system," as well as the "national interest," is at stake. The sounds of Cold War have been muted in recent years, but one need not strain too hard to hear them still. The decision of a ballet dancer to renounce the East for the West, or a decision by a college professor to pull up his roots in the West for the East, continues to send audible murmurs of wrath or amusement through the propaganda and policy establishments in Moscow and Washington. This persistent sense of mission has provided spice to diplomatic receptions, but it has also complicated American and Soviet foreign relations and has introduced grave risks in confrontations between any two countries of the world in which either Washington or Moscow, or both, have staked an interest.

The American experience in Vietnam has provided successive Administrations in Washington with a bitter amalgam of all these ingredients—Great Power confrontation, national interests, and national prestige. Since 1954 the problem faced by each President in Vietnam (and Laos) has been to reduce the dangers of confrontation with the Soviet Union and China, while pursuing what were perceived to be American interests. Complicating this problem has been a felt need to preserve that frequently elusive coin of foreign exchange, "national prestige." The question of "prestige" has had an intangible but significant influence on decisions to move step by step up the ladder of increasing military involvement, and it has substantially complicated the problem of disengagement.

To the intelligent bystander outside government the issue of "prestige" may seem trivial compared to the importance of an American withdrawal from Vietnam. To him it is a matter of the utmost urgency to get out—and to get out soon. The Man from 1600 Pennsylvania Avenue must also wish to get out—and get out soon. But to him the "prestige" factor is by no means trivial. On this issue may ride his ability to exert influence short of using brute force to protect American interests in some other place at some other time. On it too may ride his ability to contain or outflank the jingoist right-wing elements in the United States and maintain a strong moderate center—a matter in which even those American liberals who argue that we should get out of Vietnam "regardless of the consequences" have a considerable stake.

The point has been made that President Kennedy took his lumps at the Bay of Pigs in the early spring of 1961 and yet the power of the United States on the world stage was left intact. Possibly so. But there are some close observers who say that Kennedy's foreign policies, including his approach to Berlin, Vietnam, and Laos, were strongly influenced by his first confrontation with Nikita Khrushchev in Vienna later in the spring of 1961.[3] The Russian Premier's harsh and rigid response to Kennedy's overtures was at least in part a result of the American disaster in Cuba. The President felt impelled to prove to the Soviet leadership that the United States would not buckle under pressures from Moscow.

The point has also been made that Moscow seemed no worse

off for having suffered a tremendous blow to its prestige during the Cuban Missile Crisis of 1962. Possibly so. But Khrushchev was tossed onto the political garbage heap for this "adventure," and the new Soviet leadership felt the need to embark on a major reappraisal of its foreign policy and military strategy and to build up its missile and naval capabilities—this despite the fact that the population of the Soviet Union was kept very much in the dark about the debacle in Cuba.

What, then, are the realistic choices for the United States in Vietnam? Whatever they may be, they would not seem to include simply packing our gear and leaving, however attractive that may appear to be in the short run. It should not be difficult to understand why any President would want desperately to close out the American involvement in Vietnam on the basis of a negotiated political settlement in which *both* sides had made significant compromises. And if there is to be a withdrawal without a negotiated settlement, it is understandable that a President would hope to disengage, if not with the cloak of victory, with at least the seventh veil and a fig leaf. Unless something of political consequence is left behind in Vietnam, even a Communist Government put into office through a free election, the consequences for the United States are likely to be grave: a right-wing backlash in 1972; an over-reaction on the part of the Administration to other international crises in an effort to "prove" itself; a sense of general disillusionment and malaise leading to a popular revulsion against any international commitments, even those involving foreign economic assistance. Americans, Vietnamese, and the world in general will be better off if, somehow, the last chapter of our involvement could be closed with "honor," "dignity," or "face," however these shopworn clichés are defined.

That France ignominiously withdrew from Vietnam and Algeria and yet emerged with the tri-color flying high is not necessarily a relevant precedent. France was fighting the last great battle in a lost war—colonialism vs. nationalism. And, with deference to the aspirations of Charles de Gaulle and others, France is not a Great Power and has not been one since 1940. Her international commitments are not taken seriously—if in fact they exist at all outside of Western Europe. The United States is a Great Power and does have solemn commitments which must be regarded seriously by both friends and enemies. International peace and order can be achieved, but it cannot be achieved by turning a deaf ear to pleas by friends whose security is endangered by hostile forces. Nor can peace and order be conditioned on an American readiness to beat down every threat to the status quo. The key can probably be found in a credible, demonstrated American readiness to guard against clear-cut threats to our own national security and to fulfill carefully defined, legitimate international obligations.[4]

But this key will always be an elusive one. The concept of "national security" and the content of "international obligations" are more difficult to pin down as they apply to the United States than to say, Denmark or Canada or Japan. Official documents list scores of countries that are described as being of "critical" importance to American security for political, economic, or strategic reasons. Some of these countries are included in solemn defense treaties, some in less formal or specific arrangements, and some in none at all. But in an era when nuclear warfare hangs like a persistent black cloud over every clash of interest between the Great Powers, it is obvious that criteria for establishing national interests and for undertaking military commitments must be very different from the days when Britannia Ruled the Waves or even from the early post-World War II period when serious strategists talked about a Pax Americana.

The dilemma for present-day American strategists is to relate such considerations as "strategic importance" to our expanding industrial and military technology, to the higher risks to our society in the event of war, and to the mood of the American people. All those factors lead to a higher threshold for judging an interest as "critical" and a much more discriminating approach toward international military commitments. By this token there are probably now not more than a handful of international interests that are so critical as to warrant any President risking nuclear war. But this does not mean there are not a host of other interests, some now readily identifiable, some not now foreseen or even foreseeable, which the United States as a Great Power will find itself striving to preserve or attain. Some can be managed through ambitious economic assistance projects, cultural and educational exchanges, and population control programs. Others may require instead, or in addition, military assistance in the form of training and equipment. Still others may push dangerously close to actual military involvement. The array of priorities and the mix of ingredients in our international commitments will vary with time and circumstance.

President Nixon seems ready to subject our complex of post-war American interests, obligations, and commitments to careful re-examination. Costs, risks, and competing domestic requirements probably would have dictated such an appraisal in any case, but it is clear that the present mood of the American people is now one that would have forced any but the most insensitive Administration to take a hard new look. And for this at any rate, we have our passage through the Decade of Vietnam to thank.

❀   ❀   ❀

For much of the journey it seemed that we and our fellow passengers, the South Vietnamese Government, were going in the same direction, headed for the same intermediate—if not ultimate—destination. The defeat of the Viet Cong and the restoration of peace and stability was what we at least told each other was our goal. In the course of time, and as the trip became more expensive, Washington announced that it might not wish to go all the way: we would get off when the South Vietnamese people were able to choose, without interference, the direction they wished to go and whom they would like to take them there. But if our traveling companions from Saigon heard us, they paid little attention. They would decide on the destination for the people of South Vietnam, and they would take them there.

Although there were some signposts along the way that indicated that we and our fellow passengers were approaching a parting of the ways, we both felt that somehow one of us could convince the other to stay aboard. But in 1968 we reached the fork in the road. At the Hotel Majestic in Paris our ways parted.

From then on it appeared that the Americans had to go it alone or seek some other traveling companions.

Southeast Asia has been blessed with ample food and generous portions of other forms of natural wealth. The region is peopled with quiet, easy-going folk who worship an ancient and understanding deity and who take a tolerant, bemused view of the busy and brash civilization of the West. By all measures Southeast Asia should have been a happy, prosperous corner of Asia. And yet most of the area has been troubled for most of this century. In particular Vietnam, a country of 30 million people, with an ancient history and impressive resources, has gone through the agonies of Great Power colonialization, occupation, pacification, confrontation, and now "Vietnamization." It may take generations of tranquility and therapy before the Vietnamese society recovers from the trauma of recent decades.

The American involvement in South Vietnam was launched in the high tide of lofty rhetoric and noble purpose. It was felt that the people there should be provided a mantle of American encouragement and assistance to enable them to construct a democratic society in the face of dark and hostile forces on their borders. As time went on and as the Communist threat became real and dangerous, American involvement grew and took on increasingly moralistic and self-righteous overtones. It took on the quality of a crusade. But somehow, perhaps very soon in its inception but apparently too late to change, the leaders took a wrong turning. The captains and the footsoldiers did what was expected of them, but they were lost. One wonders whether Gibbons' comment on the medieval crusades may not apply to our own: "The lives and labors of millions . . . would have been more profitably employed in the improvement of their native country."

The roots of evangelism lie deep in American diplomatic history. At the close of the nineteenth century, American thrusts into the world outside were justified to ourselves and explained to others by high moral preachments. The occupation of Cuba, Puerto Rico, and the Philippines provided the United States with naval bases, trading advantages, and strategic toeholds in the Caribbean and the Pacific. But before we could savor those first tasty fruits of our new imperialist role, we had to sugar them with a sticky coating of humanitarianism, sentimentality, and righteousness. We were on God's side. And we've stayed there in all our foreign adventures since. When we weren't fighting the heathen, we fought others to save (and hopefully convert) him.

Our expanding global interests and the periodic threats to these interests have not been enough in themselves to rouse the American people from their enthusiastic pursuit of happiness at home. Before our country could be stirred into robust action to meet challenges from abroad, the issues at stake had to be put into the lofty and stark context of Good vs. Evil. Until relatively recently, however, the soaring hortatory slogans were trumpeted forth in tandem with an actual clash of arms. With the advent of the Cold War, they became a standard motif in our political rhetoric. President Truman rang all the changes in his special message to Congress on March 12, 1947 when he requested aid to Greece and Turkey: "We shall not realize our objectives . . . unless we are willing to help free peoples to maintain their free institutions and their national integrity against aggressive movements that seek to impose upon them totalitarian regimes . . . . it must be the policy of the United States to support free peoples who are resisting attempted subjugation by armed minorities or by outside pressures . . . . we must assist free peoples to work out their own destinies in their own way." And this, as Hans Morgenthau notes, was the beginning of the postwar "anti-Communist crusade." [5]

Dwight Eisenhower gave this crusade its formal baptism in his Presidential acceptance speech to the 1952 Republican convention. ". . . you have summoned me . . . to lead a great crusade —for freedom in America and freedom in the world." Although his Administration was less zealous in deed than in word, the crusading spirit, embodied especially in the pronouncements of Secretary of State John Foster Dulles, became a fundamental element in American foreign policy during the rest of the decade. It was in 1954 that the groundwork was laid for the mighty confrontation to come between the hosts of Freedom and Democracy and the hordes of Asian Communism.

In the subsequent decade the holy war of words was transformed into the sounds of battle. And we hear them still. We know now that the crusading armies will not be defeated, but neither will they be victorious. The crusade itself has been lost in the forests of unobtainable objectives and the swamps of weary disillusionment: a Communist regime will remain in North Vietnam and the Communists will not be purged in South Vietnam; "wars of liberation" will sputter and probably ignite elsewhere; Communist China will be no more "contained" in 1970 than it was in 1960.

For Americans the lost crusade in Vietnam may well be the last crusade. This is probably just as well. Americans have become wiser and more sophisticated about the world; American foreign policy will have to be based more on an appeal to reason and self-interest than to emotion and righteousness. The crusade in Vietnam thus may provide us with something of value after all.

What follows in these pages is a description of our crusade in Vietnam from the time that we first decided to launch it. It is in no sense a definitive record of the period, nor does it pretend to be the official history of even those events in which I played a peripheral or direct role. Important events and personalities have been glossed over, and less important, perhaps even trivial incidents have been included. This may present an exaggerated picture of my own role for good or ill in the development of American policy toward Vietnam, but that was not my purpose. Rather, I wished to share some of my experiences, concerns, and conclusions about a brief span in history and a part of the world in which I have found myself involved for over twenty-five years.

The war in Vietnam grinds nearer each day to a close—or at least to American disengagement. The modalities of how we extricate ourselves seem important to us now, but in terms of the direction of American policy even in the near future, it is much more important to examine some of the lessons we can draw from our lost crusade. Some of my own thoughts on that are contained in the concluding chapters of this book. But I must admit at the outset that I have no nostrums and no ready answers. It may be useful, however, to raise some questions.

II

The Colonial Legacy

I arrived in Geneva one winter's day in late March, 1954 and literally watched the city slip into spring. From the moment I stepped from the plane under gray, sulking skies, until I found refuge in the overheated hotel lobby, a cold wind pursued me. But the next morning I was awakened by the trundling of gardeners' carts on their way to the plant beds on the Isle de Rousseau; swans had suddenly appeared on the new green lake; the sun was pale and weak to be sure, but it was definitely in its place; hotel porters had transformed the sidewalk into a carnival of brightly painted tables and chairs. Spring had come to Geneva overnight. This was my first day in Switzerland, my first exposure to a full-scale International Conference. All this, and spring too, was very heady.

I had expected to find Geneva a cosmopolitan city, but that first day made me feel that Washington was an isolated, provincial town. Chinese, Russians, Koreans, Indians seemed to be everywhere. And strolling through the halls of the Palais des Nations, window-shopping along the Quai, or sipping cognac in the Old City were the central figures of the conference—the graceful and diminutive Indochinese, who seemed very much at home in French-speaking Geneva. The Laotians, Cambodians, and the non-Communist Vietnamese were nattily dressed in the latest French mode. The Viet Minh delegation were turned out in ill-fitting, new, blue serge suits and sandals; they looked uncomfortable and self-conscious in probably the first suits, shirts, and ties they had worn in many years—perhaps the first ever for the younger among them.

I had seen some Indochinese during the war when I was in Southwest China—"Annamites" they were called—but in their big straw hats and loose-fitting black pajamas they had seemed very different from those who were wandering around Geneva that spring. For most Americans, from the Secretary of State to the Marine Guard, the Vietnamese in Geneva were the first they had ever seen. And for most of the Vietnamese, we were probably the first Americans they had laid eyes on. In a sense, then, we discovered Vietnam in 1954. Several Secretaries of State, many regiments of Marines, and I were to see millions of Vietnamese before the Geneva Conference and its aftermath had run its course.

Captain John White, a seagoing Yankee peddler, seems to have been the first American to visit Vietnam. He sailed into Saigon harbor well over a century ago looking for a profitable deal or two. Symbolically enough, the only items in his cargo for which he could find a ready market were weapons, uniforms, and books. A shortsighted man, Captain White felt that Saigon offered little opportunity for long-run profits and left in somewhat of a hurry. He did not bother to return. Twelve years later, in 1832, a Mr. Roberts attempted to establish regular trade between America and Indochina. Roberts, like Captain White, enjoyed the sights of exotic Saigon but found business opportunities lacking. He too sailed away, never to come back.

Although a fairly brisk exchange of goods and services had developed between the United States and Indochina by 1914, it was not until the late twenties that a regular steamship service was inaugurated between the West Coast and Saigon. Within a few years American goods became a common sight throughout Indochina. In 1932 our Consul in Saigon could report (in a style that would be frowned on by present-day desk officers), "It is indeed pleasant for an American when motoring . . . to stop at a little hamlet . . . for a light repast, and to find in the inevitable

Chinese shop . . . rows of familiar brands of California fruits and fish which . . . may be eaten with American crackers. About one out of five automobiles . . . are American. . . . The clerks . . . are pounding away on American typewriters. . . . It is no longer a novelty . . . to see American tractors."[1]

Aside from trade representatives, the Americans who had any contact with Indochina were largely those drawn there as a result of the colony's energetic tourist campaign. An Indochinese travel brochure published in its own special brand of English in 1938 must have whetted the appetite of many jaded travelers who had done the Grand Tours of Europe and the Holy Lands: "A fact worth mentioning and very significant of the quiet state of mind of the Indochinese populations, is that travelers can move about unarmed in the remotest corners of the country in absolute safety, by night as well as in broad daylight. On certain tracks which take you for long hours in the jungle you will probably watch at distant places, a few bamboo and straw huts, a camp in the forest, some hunters with their primitive weapons so effective in their hands; you will always see, especially during the night, some wild beast much surprised to be disturbed on its estate. But if there happened a trouble at your motor car or if you got stuck in the mud, it would be surprising that the natives of the neighborhood should let you [sic] without assistance."

But all was not entirely well in terms of French attitudes toward Americans, despite the Consul's ebullient report and the cozy descriptions in the travel folders. At the official level in Indochina there was growing resentment at American efforts to replace French influence in China's Yunnan Province, which bordered Indochina. Its capital, Kunming, was the terminus of the Indochina railroad. The resentment was based in part on the competition of American Protestants with the French Catholic missionaries and later on the growing importance of Kunming as the base for the Flying Tigers, the American volunteer air force organized under General Claire Chennault to assist Chiang Kai-shek's government against the Japanese invaders.

In Indochina itself the French had no reason to complain about the size of the American presence during the prewar years.

There were, to be sure, some American business representatives, a few traveling salesmen, and a handful of tourists, but the official American representation was practically nonexistent. Through the decade of the thirties the United States had one consul and a vice consul posted in Saigon to cover the entire area of Vietnam, Laos, and Cambodia. By 1940 the State Department had assigned a consular officer to Hanoi. On the eve of Pearl Harbor we had a total consular staff of four; a year after the war ended we were represented by one consul and two vice consuls. But in any case it was not the American presence that was to threaten French control and influence in Indochina; there was a much graver threat close to hand.

*   *   *

The Japanese began their occupation of Indochina by stages starting in mid-1940, with hardly a shot fired. Even if the French had chosen to resist Japanese demands, it would have been evident to Paris, and almost certainly to Tokyo, that they had pathetically meager resources to do so. France had only one cruiser and a handful of lesser ships to patrol Indochina's 1,200 miles of coastline. Its army was basically a glorified police force and it had virtually no air force. If the French were to offer more than token resistance against an invader, they needed help from outside Indochina. France was unable to spare one ship or one platoon from the metropole; the British could provide only diplomatic assistance; the United States was still determinedly neutral. The only offer of material aid came from Chiang Kai-shek, who proposed that Chinese troops be sent into Indochina to buttress the French forces there, but this was turned down by France's Vichy Government. The French then began a series of deals with the Japanese, until by the end of the war they had lost every vestige of influence over the course of events.

On June 19, 1940 the French Ambassador in Tokyo was told to inform his government of the Japanese demand that the Indochina border be closed to all shipments of strategic goods to China and that a Japanese control group be permitted to monitor this agreement. This was accompanied by conspicuous movements of

Japanese troops toward the China–Indochina border and by naval
maneuvers in the Gulf of Tonkin. In a desperate effort to resist
the ultimatum, the French Governor General in Hanoi cabled his
colleague in Washington asking urgently for indications of possible American assistance. The French Ambassador had a disappointing session with Under-Secretary Sumner Welles. According
to French sources (no American corroboration is available),
Welles reminded the Ambassador of the American desire to contain the war in Europe and noted that we did not wish to go to
war against Japan. Welles' personal advice was that the French
should give in to the Japanese demands. They did so.

American public opinion the cause

Within weeks the Japanese made yet another demand. On
August 2 Tokyo insisted on the right to cross Tonkin (the north-
eastern provinces of Indochina) and occupy French airfields.
Again the French Ambassador to Washington appealed for help.
Again he was told that although the United States was committed
to maintaining the status quo in the Far East, it would have to
confine its actions to the diplomatic sphere. But Tokyo had no
interest in either the status quo or diplomacy. On the 22nd of
September Japanese troops moved across the border of Indochina
and in quick succession captured two towns. The French took the
hint, and the Japanese got French blessing to establish three air
bases and to station units at the port of Haiphong.

Having taken its stance, or rather non-stance, the United
States proceeded to indulge in vigorous hand-wringing. "It seems
obvious," Secretary of State Cordell Hull said on September
23, 1940, "that the *status quo* [in Indochina] is being upset and
that this is being achieved under duress. The position of the
United States in disapproval and in deprecation of such procedures has repeatedly been stated." The Department spokesman
went on to say, somewhat defensively, that the United States
Government "has not at any time or in any way approved the
French concessions to Japan." [2]

Whether Welles did, in fact, encourage the French to embark
on the long path of accommodation, we were destined to pay a
heavy price as a consequence of the French concessions. In July,
1941 the Japanese, with the permission of the Vichy Government

and on the pretext that Japan was in danger of being "encircled," moved armed forces into Indochina. Neither the still-neutral United States nor the hard-pressed British could do much more than wag a finger—despite the obvious threat this movement posed for the American position in the Philippines and the British positions in Singapore and Malaya. To be sure, President Roosevelt on July 24 made a desperate effort to forestall the Japanese occupation. He volunteered his good offices to bring about the "international neutralization" of Indochina and later of Thailand, provided the Japanese would not introduce military forces into Indochina, or, if they had already done so, would withdraw. Sumner Welles has described the Japanese move as "the last overt danger signal." A few days later all Japanese assets in the United States were frozen.

On August 2, 1941 Welles, then the Acting Secretary, told the press that the agreement between the French and Japanese "virtually turns over to Japan an important part of the French Empire. . . . Under these circumstances this Government is impelled to question whether the French Government at Vichy in fact proposes to maintain its declared policy to preserve for the French people the territories both at home and abroad which have long been under French sovereignty. This Government, mindful of its traditional friendship for France, has deeply sympathized with the desire of the French people to maintain their territories and to preserve them intact." [3]

Tokyo waited until August 6 before making a reply to the President's neutralization proposal. Among other provisions, the Japanese note asked for the removal of all restrictions on U.S. trade with Japan, the suspension of U.S. military actions in the Southwest Pacific, and the good offices of the United States in achieving a negotiated settlement of the Sino–Japanese war. The note stated that after a settlement between China and Japan, Japanese troops would be removed from Indochina. Finally Japan asked that the United States recognize Japan's special position in Indochina even after the withdrawal of Japanese troops. The Secretary of State informed Tokyo two days later that the Japanese note was not responsive to the President's proposal and was not acceptable.

In mid-August President Roosevelt and Prime Minister Winston Churchill held their now-famous Atlantic Conference. Among their decisions was an agreement against any new Japanese aggression. The Japanese were informed of this decision upon the President's return to Washington, but they were not impressed. The Emperor's troops poured into Indochina until the very eve of the war. On December 6 President Roosevelt made a final appeal to Hirohito to pull his troops out of Indochina and so assure "peace throughout the whole of the South Pacific area." On the night of the seventh, Japanese troops occupied Hanoi, and on the following day the French were presented with yet another ultimatum.

The Japanese reaped tremendous dividends from their modest investment in Indochina. They were able to seal off China's southern border and force the Allies to resort to the costly alternatives of hazardous airlifts and long overland convoys over the two tortuously-constructed truck routes—the Burma and Ledo roads. They had virtually unharassed use of Vietnamese ports and harbors for transshipping strategic raw materials, military supplies, and manpower between Japan and Southeast Asia. They had control over Indochina's rubber, minerals, and rice. They had convenient air bases for operations against China and Southeast Asia. They had an important and relatively secure link in the chain of countries from Korea to Indonesia which, they envisioned, would comprise a Greater East Asian Co-Prosperity Sphere. And, since the French took care of the routine housekeeping problems, they had all the advantages and few of the disadvantages of full-scale occupation, at least in the early years of the war.

To add to Tokyo's sense of well-being and optimism with respect to the future, the people of Indochina in general, and of Vietnam in particular, had lost confidence in the omnipotence of their Western rulers. Indeed in the initial stages of the Japanese take-over many Vietnamese looked to Tokyo as providing a long-sought opportunity to gain complete independence. There were, in fact, many Vietnamese nationalists who for years had been given refuge and assistance in Japan. However, the Japanese turned out to be just another in a series of foreign invaders and oppressors.

Although for all practical purposes Indochina was lost to the Allied cause on the very eve of Pearl Harbor, it was not completely forgotten. The Chinese in particular had it very much in mind, in no small part because the Japanese occupation created tremendous logistic difficulties for Chiang's forces. But over and above this immediate interest, the Chungking government had longer-range aspirations with respect to Indochina. As the Chinese looked forward to the postwar world, a French-free Indochina under some form of Chinese hegemony must have seemed a very attractive prospect. The warlords of neighboring Yunnan and Kwangsi Provinces appeared to have even more specific and personal designs; to them the possibility of postwar economic concessions was very appealing and many of their actions toward Vietnam (Laos and Cambodia were pretty much overlooked) during and immediately after the war seemed to be directed to this end.

The Viet Minh (as the Viet Nam Doc Lap Dong Minh Hoi, or League for the Independence of Vietnam, has subsequently been called) was founded in May, 1941 in Chingsi, a small town in China's Kwangsi Province which served at the time as a center of refuge for many leaders of the outlawed Indochinese Communist Party (PCI). Although the Viet Minh was formed as a united front under the aegis of the PCI, its membership included representatives from other Vietnamese nationalist parties and groups, as well as the PCI. Its short-term purpose was to defeat the Japanese invaders through close collaboration with the Allies; its long-term objective was to achieve Vietnam's independence. It is interesting to note the frequent mention of the United States in the Viet Minh declaration of 1941. "All the Indochinese people . . . beg the great powers and, above all the United States for assistance in their movement. . . . They implore the United States to come to their aid in the fight against Japanese fascism by granting them the means, *viz*: munitions, advisers and instructors."

missed opportunity

Nguyen Ai Quoc * (who later took the name of "Ho Chi Minh," which means "He Who Enlightens") served as the first Secretary General of the Viet Minh. He remained in South China for several months where he concentrated on training cadres. Sometime later in 1941 Quoc slipped back into Tonkin's northern provinces and then in July, 1942 decided to return to China to seek further support for the Viet Minh from Chiang's government in Chungking. Posing as a Chinese journalist complete with business cards and identity papers, he crossed the border into China. For reasons which are still obscure, Quoc was arrested by the warlord of Kwangsi Province as a "French spy" and as a "Communist." He spent the next thirteen months in Chinese jails. In the meantime the Kwangsi warlord had set up his own anti-French, pro-Chinese political group of Vietnamese nationalists who would be loyal to his private designs on Indochina. But this group, the "League of Vietnamese Revolutionary Parties," was unable to provide the necessary intelligence on Indochina. It became clear that only the Viet Minh with its more solid and better organized network of agents could do that. Quoc reportedly contacted the warlord from his prison cell and expressed his willingness to cooperate with the "League." Quoc was soon released from jail. There are shadowy accounts to the effect that this took place without the prior knowledge of Chiang. (The Office of Strategic Services may have played a role in this operation, but if so, there is no record of it.)

* Nguyen Ai Quoc was born in 1890, the son of a poor but scholarly and intensely nationalistic father and a peasant mother. That name is also an alias meaning "Nguyen the Patriot." His real name was "Nguyen That Than," which means "Nguyen Who Will Be Victorious." At 21 Quoc left Vietnam, serving as a cabin boy aboard various ships having ports of call in France, North Africa, England, and the United States (he reportedly spent some time in New York and Boston). In 1914 Quoc arrived in London where he worked at the Carlton Hotel under the famous chef Escoffier. Three years later he moved to Paris, eking out an existence as a retoucher of photographs but, more importantly, making contact with various European socialists and other leftist-oriented political activists. In 1919 Quoc turned up at the Versailles Conference in a rented cutaway and attempted to present the claims of the Annamese patriots for Vietnam's freedom. In a memorandum to U.S. Secretary of State Robert Lansing, Quoc wrote: "We count on your great kindness to honor our appeal by your support when ever the opportunity arises." Quoc was rebuffed. In 1920 he joined the newly-created French Communist Party, and from then on he devoted his life to the achievement of Vietnamese independence.

It was at this point that Nguyen Ai Quoc changed his name to "Ho Chi Minh," either to mask his earlier Communist affiliation or to escape the immediate notice of Chungking, or both. Despite the understanding with the Chinese Nationalists, relations between the Vietnamese Communist Viet Minh and Chungking were almost immediately characterized by mutual suspicion and by jockeying for control over the modest resistance and intelligence activities the Nationalists were conducting in Vietnam. The ineffectual, clumsy groping of Chungking proved no match for the efficient and strongly-motivated efforts of the Viet Minh, and Ho was soon to pursue an independent course.

The French were neither unaware of nor unconcerned about these activities. The Free-French mission in Kunming was attempting through its own network of French and Vietnamese agents to keep abreast of developments in Vietnam. Their lot was not an enviable one. Chinese officials, both at the National Government level in Chungking and at the virtually independent Yunnan Provincial level, made no secret of their unwillingness to see Vietnam returned to the French. Throughout the war the activities of the French mission were carefully watched and circumscribed, first by the Chinese and later also by the Americans in the China Theater.

Sometime in early 1944 it must have become evident to the French, the Chinese, and the Vietnamese resistance movement itself that the Americans were becoming interested and active in matters concerning Indochina. All of these groups recognized that only the Americans could provide the necessary transport and communications equipment to supply a resistance and espionage activity in Vietnam. They were also aware that as the war progressed into late 1944 and the United States forces moved island-by-island closer to the mainland, there was a growing American interest in the possibility of an invasion of Indochina. The need for an intelligence and a behind-the-lines resistance movement was becoming increasingly more urgent and obvious.

By early March, 1945 the Japanese were sufficiently alarmed over evidence of Gaullist sentiments among the French in Vietnam and concerned over reports of a possible American invasion to assume direct control over Indochina. In a coup on March 9 they imprisoned French officials, key businessmen, and as many French troops as they could get their hands on. In an effort to consolidate the defense of Indochina against expected Allied landings, the Japanese pulled their garrisons out of the wild country along the China border. This gave both the OSS and its Viet Minh agents an opportunity, which they quickly exploited, to filter into the northern part of Vietnam.

The exact, or indeed the approximate, date when the OSS first became actively engaged in working with resistance groups in Indochina is not clear. Cordell Hull reports that when an OSS proposal to assist such groups was forwarded to the President on October 13, 1944, he was told by Roosevelt, "we should do nothing in regard to resistance groups . . . in relation to Indochina. You might bring it up to me a little later when things are a little clearer." [4] But from my own OSS experience in the area I learned that the OSS was nothing if not a freewheeling organization, especially in such out-of-the-mainstream places as Southwest China. It is not unlikely that even while Roosevelt was pondering the question, OSS agents had already been in contact with Ho. Certainly there had long been considerable interest in the intelligence that the various resistance groups could bring out of Indochina, and it is not unreasonable to assume that efforts were made to help the flow along. Ho himself is reported to have made four secret visits to the OSS Headquarters in Kunming in late 1944 and early 1945 seeking arms and ammunition in exchange for intelligence and other services. He finally succeeded in getting six pistols and a few rounds of ammunition.[5] But Ho would not have wandered down that dark, muddy road on the outskirts of town unless some OSSer in the field (possibly in Kwangsi Province where Ho seemed to have a special relationship with the local warlord) had directed him, or even personally guided him. Surely neither Chinese nor French intelligence officers would have tried to establish a working relationship between the Vietnamese resistance and the Americans. It is probably a safe bet that some energetic OSS sergeant (perhaps a Wall Street lawyer, shipping magnate, or college professor in real life) had been working up a deal with Ho for many months prior to Hull's October exchange with Roosevelt.

Although U.S. officers in the field were told to "do nothing" in regard to Indochina, when the Japanese struck in March, 1945 General Chennault, Commander of the Fourteenth Air Force in China, immediately sent help to the retreating French forces, making arrangements to drop in ammunition, food, and medical supplies. But according to General Chennault:

> . . . orders arrived from Theater Headquarters stating that no arms and ammunition would be provided to French troops under any circumstances. I was allowed to proceed with "normal" action against the Japanese in Indochina provided it did not involve supplying French troops.
>
> . . . [General Albert C.] Wedemeyer's orders not to aid the French came directly from the War Department. Apparently it was American policy then that French Indochina would become a mandated territory after the war and not be returned to the French. The American government was interested in seeing the French forcibly ejected from Indochina so the problem of postwar separation from their colony would be easier.
>
> . . . I carried out my orders to the letter, but I did not relish the idea of leaving Frenchmen to be slaughtered in the jungle while I was forced officially to ignore their plight.[6]

Washington's restrictions against providing arms and equipment to the French were reversed in about mid-June, but the OSS obviously was given permission to help the Viet Minh considerably earlier. In April Admiral William Leahy succeeded in obtaining "the President's agreement that American aid to the Indochina resistance groups might be given provided it involved no interference with our operations against Japan."[7] By May a small number of OSS personnel had been parachuted into Ho Chi Minh's headquarters in northern Tonkin. The primary mission of this group was to establish arrangements for assisting downed Allied air crews to escape the clutches of the Japanese.

The Americans lived and worked closely with Ho and his followers, and for several months there was a flourishing exchange of views and ideas. It was through the OSS radio that Ho first contacted the French in Kunming with respect to the forthcoming negotiations about Vietnam's postwar future. According to one OSS officer, Ho sought his advice on framing the Viet Minh's declaration of independence. (The actual declaration begins with the familiar "All men are created equal. They are endowed by their Creator with certain unalienable rights, among these are Life, Liberty and the pursuit of Happiness.")

But Ho was not only talking, he was fighting. Under the leadership of a young man named Giap, the Viet Minh resistance groups armed themselves from stocks the French had left behind and with captured Japanese weapons. These supplies were augmented by arms dropped to them by the Americans. By August Ho's influence extended across northern Tonkin and southward to the Delta provinces. His American associates and comrades-in-arms were duly and justifiably impressed.

The actual amount of aid given to the Viet Minh by the OSS is still a matter of doubt. It was probably not very large, but it did have a very important psychological effect—both at the time and subsequently. Ho Chi Minh was able to claim that the Viet Minh was part of the Allied war effort against the Japanese—and that it had American support in its early efforts to achieve Vietnamese independence. But over and above the actual supplies and equipment given to the Viet Minh, there were OSS officers actually leading and training Viet Minh guerrillas in the last months of the war.

1st Foreign Advisers

         ❀   ❀   ❀

On the heels of the Japanese takeover, General Charles de Gaulle began to assert French interest in participating in, if not actually taking charge of, the liberation of Indochina. On March 14 he announced that the resistance forces there were operating under the policies and the direction of Paris. If there were no French forces in the Far East Theater it was, he said, because the Allies had been withholding the necessary transport. At issue, he clearly implied, was a coup by the Japanese occupiers against the constituted *French* administration and the Japanese would have to be forced to surrender their control to the *French*.

Some posturing as SVN generals

But this was not quite the way the United States saw the future course of events. Indeed as early as February, 1944 Washington was beginning to do some postwar planning with respect to the administration of enemy-occupied areas in Southeast Asia. Indochina presented an especially tricky problem, because the United States did not recognize either the Government of France at Vichy or the government in exile. In a memorandum from the Department of State to the White House on February 17, the Department noted that the Civil Affairs Division of the War Department needed guidance on the extent to which it was American policy to plan on using French troops and nationals in regaining control over and subsequently administering Indochina. In passing on the White House guidance to the War Department, the Director of the Office of European Affairs noted that "The President orally expressed the view to Mr. Stettinius [Under-Secretary of the Department of State] that no French troops whatsoever should be used in operations in Indochina. He added that in his view the operation should be Anglo–American in character and should be followed by the establishment of an international trusteeship over the French colony. With regard to the question of international trusteeship, this Government has as yet made no approach to other Governments for the purpose of ascertaining their views." [8] This is the first official inkling of American wartime policy toward the future role of the French in Indochina, although as early as July, 1941 Admiral Leahy told the French orally that "if Japan was the winner, the Japanese would take over French Indochina. And if the Allies won, we would take it." [9]

An even more cryptic and provocative clue to American postwar policy was a message from the White House to the military planners in late 1944. In essence Roosevelt's note to the Pentagon said, "Keep your hands off Indochina." FDR experts feel that Roosevelt was signaling his intent to develop within the White House postwar policy for this area.

In November of 1944 General Wedemeyer reported that as part of an apparent French effort to restore colonial rule, the French had established a mission in India which was preparing to infiltrate into Indochina. General Wedemeyer asked for guidance.

Indochina had been declared by the Combined Chiefs of Staff to be in the Chinese Theater, and all operations there were supposed to be under his cognizance. Wedemeyer presumably was also aware of an increasingly active French mission much closer to both his own Headquarters and Indochina itself—a French military group based in Kunming in Yunnan Province. On the day following the receipt of Wedemeyer's report the President asked Patrick Hurley, the American Ambassador in Chungking, to inform the General that his policy guidance would have to await American consultation with the Allies at a forthcoming Combined Staff Conference. The President asked Hurley to shed any light he could on British, French, and Dutch plans with respect to their colonies in Southeast Asia, but the Ambassador was apparently unable to discover anything worth reporting. Nor were the American Joint Chiefs of Staff any the wiser with respect to our Allies' intentions in Southeast Asia during this period. When Roosevelt set off for the Yalta Conference at the beginning of February, 1945 he was armed only with general reports that the French had vague plans to send troops to Indochina.

Distracted

The British had had ample warning of Roosevelt's train of thought with respect to the postwar administration of Indochina. In late March, 1943 Foreign Secretary Anthony Eden visited Washington. Roosevelt raised the question of a trusteeship for Indochina, as well as for the Japanese-mandated islands in the Pacific. There is no record of Eden's reaction at that time, but early in the following January the British Ambassador, Lord Halifax, came to see Secretary of State Hull. He noted that the British had heard from various sources that President Roosevelt had told the "Turks, Egyptians and perhaps others" that "Indochina should be taken away from the French and put under an international trusteeship." Hull replied that he "knew no more about the matter than the Ambassador." [10] Halifax was obviously and understandably anxious to get a more accurate reading than Hull was able to provide. He went directly to the President. Roosevelt, reporting on this meeting to Hull, said he had told the Ambassador "quite frankly that it was perfectly true that I had, for over a year, expressed the opinion that Indochina should not go back to

France. . . . France has had the country . . . for nearly one hundred years, and the people are worse off than they were at the beginning." Roosevelt told Hull that he saw "no reason to play in with the British Foreign Office in this matter. The only reason they seem to oppose it is that they fear the effect it would have on their own possessions. . . . They have never liked the idea of trusteeship because it is . . . aimed at future independence . . . the case of Indochina is perfectly clear. France has milked it for one hundred years. The people of Indochina are entitled to something better than that." [11]

It was not long after this session with Halifax that the issue of the French return became a practical rather than a hypothetical one. It took the form of whether French troops should participate in military operations for the liberation of Indochina. The question was raised by the British in the late summer of 1944. The matter soon became more urgent for Washington upon receipt of reports that the French were in contact with the British High Command in Southeast Asia. On November 3 the President instructed Hull that no American representatives in the Far East were to make any "decisions on political questions with the French mission or anyone else." [12] And on January 1, 1945 Roosevelt was even more emphatic: "I still do not want to get mixed up in any Indochina decision," he told the Secretary. "It is a matter for postwar. By the same token, I do not want to get mixed up in any military effort toward the liberation of Indochina from the Japanese. You can tell Halifax that I made this very clear to Mr. Churchill. From both a military and civil point of view, action at this time is premature." [13] The role, if any, that the French were to assume when Allied forces returned to Indochina plagued the relations between the Americans and British, as well as the French, until the end of the war.

Although Roosevelt apparently intended to raise the trusteeship idea at Yalta, it seems clear that the matter was never formally discussed—neither Churchill nor Eden refers to it in his account of the Conference (or indeed in any other connection). It was, however, a subject of bilateral American–Soviet concern. On February 8 Roosevelt, Averell Harriman, and Charles Bohlen *playing Stalin vs Churchill*

met with Stalin and Molotov. The official transcript reveals that Roosevelt told Stalin he "had in mind a trusteeship for Indochina." He added that the British did not approve of this idea. They wished to give Indochina back to the French, since they feared that Roosevelt's proposal might affect the restoration of British rule over Burma.

Stalin told Roosevelt the British had lost Burma during the war because they had placed their reliance on French control of Indochina, and he doubted that the British would be able to provide protection for Burma in the future. Somewhat enigmatically Stalin added that he thought Indochina "was a very important area." Roosevelt then gave Stalin a short course in anthropology and history. He noted that the Indochinese were people of small stature, like the Javanese and Burmese, and were not warlike, and France had done nothing to improve the lot of the natives since she had had the colony. He told Stalin that de Gaulle had asked for ships to transport French forces to Indochina. "Where was de Gaulle going to get the troops?" Stalin asked. De Gaulle said he would find the troops, Roosevelt replied, when the United States turned up with some ships. Up to the present, however, there were no available ships.[14]

Whatever in fact did transpire at Yalta with respect to Indochina was either a carefully-held secret or soon forgotten. The Yalta Protocol on Trusteeship gives no hint that Indochina was considered:

> It was agreed that the five nations which will have permanent seats on the Security Council should consult each other prior to the UN Conference on the question of territorial trusteeship.
>
> The acceptance for this recommendation is subject to its being made clear that territorial trusteeship will only apply to (a) existing mandates of the League of Nations; (b) territories detached from the enemy as a result of the present war; (c) any other territory which might be voluntarily placed under trusteeship; and (d) no discussion of actual territories is contemplated at the forthcoming UN conference or in the preliminary consultations, and it will be a matter for subsequent agreement which territories within the above categories will be placed under trusteeship.

On his way home from Yalta, Roosevelt shared his hopes and forebodings with three newspapermen who were accompanying his party, and he remarked that he had been worrying about the return of French rule to Indochina "for two whole years." He confessed that he had raised the question with Chiang Kai-shek in November, 1943 at Cairo and again later that same month with Stalin at Teheran. His proposal was that a trusteeship for Indochina be established. "Have a Frenchman, one or two Indochinese, and a Chinese and a Russian . . . and maybe a Filipino and an American—to educate them for self-government." Both Stalin and Chiang "liked the idea." The problem was that the British, when they finally registered on the issue, did *not* like it.[15]

At the Cairo Conference, according to a Chinese Government account, Chiang told Roosevelt that "China and the United States should endeavor together to help Indochina achieve its independence after the war. . . . The President expressed his agreement." And at Teheran, Stalin told FDR that "he did not propose to have the Allies shed blood to restore Indochina, for example, to the old French colonial rule. He repeated that France should not get back Indochina and that the French must pay for their criminal collaboration with Germany. The President said he was one hundred percent in agreement with Marshal Stalin and remarked that after 100 years of French rule in Indochina, the inhabitants were worse off than they had been before." Roosevelt later recounted this conversation to Secretary of State Edward Stettinius. According to Stettinius' notes, ". . . at Teheran the President raised the question with Stalin, who said that Indochina should be independent, but was not yet ready for self-government. He said that the idea of a trusteeship was excellent. When Churchill objected, the President said, 'Now look here Winston, you are outvoted three to one.'"[16]

For several months Hurley was kept in the dark with respect to any decisions made at Yalta and indeed, with respect to Washington's views on Indochina. Finally he could contain himself no longer. As he recounted it many years later, on May 11 he sent a telegram to the Secretary of State "indicating that it would be helpful to me . . . if the Department would telegraph . . . the substance of the Yalta decision in regard to Indochina." He got his answer a week later: "No Yalta decision relating to Indochina known to the Department." [17]

Elliott Roosevelt provides some interesting sidelights on his father's views on the subject of Western colonialist policy in Asia. Having accompanied his father to the Casablanca Conference in January, 1943, he recounts several conversations he had with him then. FDR remarked that "The English mean to maintain their hold on their colonies. They mean to help the French maintain *their* hold on *their* colonies. Winnie is a great man for the status quo. He even *looks* like the status quo, doesn't he?" FDR thought that after the war France should "be restored to a world power, then to be entrusted with her former colonies, as a trustee. As trustee she was to report each year on the progress of her stewardship. . . ." Independence would be extended to colonies "after the United Nations as a whole have decided that they are prepared for it." Following a meeting with de Gaulle, Roosevelt told his son that de Gaulle "made it quite clear that he expects the Allies to return all French colonies to French control immediately upon their liberation. . . . I'm by no means sure in my own mind that we'd be right to return France her colonies *at all, ever,* without first obtaining in the case of each individual colony some sort of pledge, some sort of statement of just exactly what was planned, in terms of each colony's administration." When Elliott questioned his father about how the United States could talk about not returning the colonies to their former rulers, FDR remarked, "The Japanese control [Indochina] now. Why was it a cinch for the Japanese to conquer that land? The native Indochinese have been so flagrantly downtrodden that they thought to themselves: Anything must be better than to live under French colonial rule! . . . Don't think for one moment, Elliott, that Americans would be dying in the Pacific tonight, if it hadn't been for the shortsighted greed of the French and the British and the Dutch. Shall we allow them to do it all, all over again? . . . When we've won the war, I will work with all my might and main to see to it that the United States is not wheedled into the position of accepting any plan that will further France's imperialistic ambitions, or that will aid and abet the British Empire in *its* imperial ambition." [18]

Shortly after he returned from Yalta, President Roosevelt told one of his advisers that French Indochina "should be taken from France and put under a trusteeship." Then after a slight hesitation he added, "Well, if we can get the proper pledge from France to assume for herself the obligations of a trustee, then I would agree to France retaining [Indochina] with the proviso that independence was the ultimate goal." [19]

Roosevelt's trusteeship idea died hard. A month or so after the President had returned from Yalta, Ambassador Hurley and General Wedemeyer were in Washington to discuss, among other matters, the liberation of Indochina. The President admonished Wedemeyer to pay careful attention to French and British political activities in that area and to assist them only in activities directly related to military operations against the Japanese. Wedemeyer told the President that "there were not many [French troops] there" and that he had been turning down requests for arms and equipment from the French general in charge. [20]

While Hurley and Wedemeyer were in Washington a message came from Churchill noting that there had been some difficulties between Wedemeyer and Britain's Admiral Lord Louis Mountbatten in regard to activities and operations in Indochina. Churchill proposed that he and Roosevelt direct the Combined Chiefs of Staff to arrange for a "full and frank exchange of intentions, plans and intelligence between Wedemeyer and Mountbatten as regards all matters of mutual concern." [21]

The President told Churchill on March 22 that he understood both commanders were independently conducting air operations and intelligence missions in Indochina. This, he felt, was wasteful and could lead to dangerous confusion. He suggested that all operations, "regardless of their nature," be coordinated by Wedemeyer and asked Churchill to apprise Mountbatten of this. Wedemeyer stopped off at Mountbatten's headquarters on his way back to Chungking. Acting on the basis of the oral directive Roosevelt had given him, he told Mountbatten that he could support only those British and French operations that were directed against the

Japanese and were not designed to foreclose the options with respect to the postwar government of Indochina. When he left he had the definite impression that Mountbatten understood that the British should clear with him any operations they might conduct in Indochina.

But Mountbatten had a different impression. When on April 11 Churchill finally replied to Roosevelt's proposal, he apparently incorporated Mountbatten's understanding of the agreement he had recently made with Wedemeyer. In his note to President Roosevelt Churchill said, ". . . it is essential not only that we should support the French by all the means in our power, but also that we should associate them with our operations into their country. It would look very bad in history if we failed to support isolated French forces in their resistance to the Japanese . . . or if we excluded the French from participation in our councils as regards Indochina." Churchill included in the letter to Roosevelt the instructions he had forwarded to Mountbatten. These were considerably at variance with the Roosevelt–Wedemeyer version and, apparently, also with Wedemeyer's conception of what Mountbatten had agreed to. "You may conduct," Churchill told Mountbatten, "from whatsoever base appears most suitable the minimum pre-occupational activities in Indochina which . . . your forces require. It is essential, however, that you should keep General Wedemeyer . . . continually informed. . . ."

Churchill's letter was to be the last communication between him and Roosevelt. His note arrived in Washington on the eve of Roosevelt's death. It was left to President Truman to try to put the understanding straight, and the urgency with which Truman regarded the matter is indicated by the fact that he replied to Churchill's letter on April 14, virtually within hours of assuming office. Truman told Churchill of his understanding of the Wedemeyer–Mountbatten agreement. According to this, Mountbatten "would notify Wedemeyer when he desired to conduct an operation in Indochina and that the operation would not be conducted until approval was given by the Generalissimo [Chiang Kai-shek]. . . . If the proposed operation . . . could not be integrated with

China Theater plans, then Mountbatten agreed he would not undertake it." [22]

This basic misunderstanding was bound to lead to trouble. And it soon did. By May, Wedemeyer and Mountbatten were in open disagreement. Mountbatten informed Wedemeyer that he intended to fly twenty-six sorties into Indochina to support French guerrilla activities. Wedemeyer insisted that the French Government had agreed to place all French guerrilla groups in Indochina under Generalissimo Chiang Kai-shek. Wedemeyer went on to say that as the Generalissimo's Chief of Staff he had to insure that the equipment furnished the French was used to fight the Japanese and not for the purpose of re-establishing political control over the Vietnamese. Mountbatten ignored Wedemeyer's message and proceeded to move ahead with the supply missions. Wedemeyer was outraged and wired Mountbatten that "your decision to conduct these operations without the Generalissimo's approval is a direct violation of the intent of our respective directives." Wedemeyer and Hurley seized on this incident to attempt to seek more specific guidance from Washington. In Wedemeyer's message to the Joint Chiefs of Staff he reminded them that he did not have "sufficient information available to coordinate or evaluate the operations Mountbatten is now undertaking and I cannot carry out the explicit instructions of the President. . . ." [23]

Hurley was even more blunt in a message to the Secretary of State on May 28. "Attention is called to the fact that Lord Louis [Mountbatten] very recently requested . . . a large increase in lend-lease supplies that will enable him to defeat the Roosevelt policy in Indochina and reestablish imperialism in that area." Putting his finger squarely on the root of his problem (and possibly the root of many even more serious problems to follow), he noted that while he and Wedemeyer had been given guidance by President Roosevelt in their various *conversations,* "we in this theater have never received a written directive on the political policy of the United States in Indochina." He concluded his message by what, through hindsight at least, seems a very mild and not unreasonable request: "It would clarify the situation in Asia for all of us if we could be given: (1) a definite Indochina

policy, and (2) a definite policy on Hong Kong * or if we could
be directed to follow the Roosevelt policy in both areas." [24]

The Department duly noted Ambassador Hurley's views and
on June 10 cabled that "the President . . . fully appreciates the
difficulties in which you and General Wedemeyer may be placed
on account of the lack of specific directions. . . . The President has
asked me to say that there has been no basic change in the policy
. . . and that the President's present policy is as follows: . . . as a
result of the Yalta discussions the trusteeship structure . . . should
be defined to permit the placing under it of such of the territories
taken from the enemy in war as might be agreed upon at a later
date. . . . The position . . . has been confirmed in conversations
which are now taking place in San Francisco. . . . Throughout
these discussions the American delegation has insisted upon the
necessity of providing for a progressive measure of self-government for all dependent people. . . . Such decisions [sic] would
preclude the establishment of a trusteeship in Indochina, except
under the French Government. The latter seems unlikely. Nevertheless, it is the President's intention at some appropriate time to
ask that the French Government give some positive indication of
its intention in regard to the establishment of basic liberties and
an increasing measure of self-government in Indochina before
formulating further declarations of policy. . . ." The telegram went
on to say that the Joint Chiefs were prepared to consider "on
their own military merits" offers of French assistance in the Pacific and, for those operations which were approved, would provide the French whatever was needed on the condition that
resources were not diverted from priority operations elsewhere.[25]

Neither Hurley nor Wedemeyer could be described as phleg-
matic or easy-going. One wonders how they received the message
that there had been "no basic change" in policy with respect to
Indochina in the several months since Roosevelt's death and
Hull's retirement. In 1951 Hurley minced no words about what he
thought had transpired. He told the Senate Committees on Armed
Services and Foreign Affairs that President Roosevelt had told

---

* Hurley was worried about British policy toward Hong Kong, as well as
French policy toward Indochina.

him in March, 1945 that at the San Francisco Conference "there would be set up a United Nations trusteeship. . . . In the San Francisco Conference China seemed to have stood with Russia for the kind of . . . trusteeship . . . that President Roosevelt favored. . . . The American delegation . . . seemed to support the theory of imperial control of colonies . . . these seem to indicate a change in the American policy. . . . There is a growing opinion throughout Asia that America favors imperialism rather than democracy. . . . If America is not opposed to imperialism in Asia, it is in conflict with the Roosevelt policy." [26]

The shift in American policy from President Roosevelt's notion of trusteeship can probably be dated around the time of the San Francisco Conference (April 25 to June 26). On May 8 Secretary of State Stettinius informed France's Foreign Minister Georges Bidault, "the record is entirely innocent of any official statement of [the U.S.] government questioning, even by implication, French sovereignty over Indochina." The Secretary later recounted, "Bidault seemed relieved . . . that he received renewed assurances of our recognition of French sovereignty over that area." [27] Immediately after the Conference the State Department transmitted to the War Department a policy paper dealing with the postwar situation in Asia. With respect to Indochina, "The United States recognizes French sovereignty over Indochina. It is, however, the general policy of the United States to favor a policy which would allow colonial peoples an opportunity to prepare themselves for increased participation in their own government with eventual self-government as the goal." [28]

People who were close to Roosevelt during this period and were familiar with his style of operation are not surprised that his ideas for the postwar administration of Indochina died with him. It was not that Truman or the Secretary of State consciously decided against pursuing Roosevelt's trusteeship plan—either as a unilateral American policy or through the new United Nations. The problem was that at the time there was nothing very much to go on. Roosevelt himself probably had not reached a firm decision on Indochina's future. He tended to postpone final decisions until the last possible moment, discussing variants of and alternatives to any line of policy with virtually anyone who would listen. In any case, if he had made up his mind he would not have confided his thoughts to the State Department. He felt that State officials were "too pro-Vichy" and did not trust them.

In retrospect, then, it is not clear whether American policy on the postwar administration of Indochina, as it began to evolve in the spring of 1945, represented a shift from Roosevelt's ideas or was the result of queries, doubts, possibly even alternative arrangements that Roosevelt himself had set in train. What does seem clear is that sometime between the Conferences at Yalta and San Francisco the idea of an international trusteeship for Indochina was suffering from neglect. And in the few weeks between San Francisco and Potsdam it perished. And yet even after Potsdam the idea seemed to exhibit occasional—if weak—heartbeats. For example, the American mission that was established in Hanoi after the Japanese surrender was apparently operating on the assumption that Indochina would ultimately come under a United Nations Trusteeship. Although the Americans in the mission recognized the occupation authorities that had been set up after the Japanese surrender, they were guided in their relationships with them by their understanding that final administrative arrangements would not be worked out until after the first meeting of the United Nations. By late September, however, Washington informed the American mission that, although the idea of a United Nations Trusteeship had not been definitely dropped, steps were to be taken to "facilitate the recovery of power by the French." [29]

See Fall
for French
resentment

*   *   *

And so died, finally and irrevocably, the Trusteeship issue. Some would say that it had actually been killed months before in a deal between Churchill and Roosevelt. The deal—if there was a deal—gave the United States major influence over Japan, China, and the Western Pacific in exchange for predominant British influence in South Asia.

Whether there was such a deal—and available records do not reveal one—it is evident that at San Francisco there were only bland and general references to colonial territories and their eventual independence. And at Potsdam the immediate postwar administration of Indochina was divided between the British and the Chinese—with the British prepared at the earliest opportunity, and the Chinese in due course and reluctantly, to facilitate the return of French control.

In any case, the sympathies of the Americans—OSSers, Civil Government teams, and liaison officers—were clearly on the side of the Vietnamese nationalists in the first several weeks following the Japanese surrender. This attitude probably reflected more an ideological affinity for colonial peoples trying to obtain their independence than it did a conscious attempt to follow any actual or assumed policy with respect to a trusteeship. Jean Sainteny, the Free-French Major who during the war had been in touch with Ho on the question of French–Vietnamese postwar relationships, described the American attitude during August and September of 1945 as "infantile anti-colonialism, which blinded almost all of them." [30] (When I first met Jean Sainteny more than two decades after the war, he still carried some psychological scars from this early postwar experience.) Sainteny was miffed at the Americans, and not without reason. The OSS officers who had been working with the Viet Minh since March were impressed with the courage, dedication, and the national aspirations of Ho and his small band of guerrillas. Together with those OSSers who came to Hanoi immediately after V–J Day to arrange the release of American PWs, they made no secret of where their sympathies lay as between the Vietnamese and the French. Nor did the regular American Army officers who, as we have seen, thought they were the vanguard of an international trusteeship arrangement. Nor did the American correspondents who, for example, reported that "after the war, American sympathies appeared to lean strongly toward the Vietnamese nationalists led by Ho. . . . Ho Chi Minh at that time was still touched by the glamour of his wartime association with anti-Japanese guerrilla operations under the direction of the OSS. . . . About all that most Americans then in Indochina knew of Ho was that he had been on 'our side' while the French Vichyite regime in Saigon was collaborating with the enemy. . . ." [31]

Sainteny found his movements in Hanoi carefully circumscribed by the Viet Minh and the Japanese. French civilians and troops continued to be under virtual confinement well after the Japanese surrender, and the Americans reportedly did little or nothing to assist the French to re-establish their authority. More than that, in their conversations with the French and with the Viet Minh, in their official reporting back to Washington, and in their news commentary, they did much to encourage Ho and his followers to believe they could count on American support in their efforts to achieve independence.

But both the American manifestations of support, however unofficial they may have been, and the Vietnamese nationalists' expectations of help from Washington, however naive they may have been, flickered out by the end of 1945. Indeed for those Vietnamese who observed the return of the French troops, armed with American weapons and dressed in American uniforms, the postwar American policy was abundantly clear by the early autumn.

At the war's end Vietnam was swept by a surging wave of nationalism. And the Viet Minh, as the most active and aggressive of the national resistance groups, picked up wide support throughout the country. Recognizing that, whatever the ultimate form of American policy toward independence, he was unlikely to receive any early support from Washington and that time was working against him, Ho acted quickly. His intention was to present the British forces, who were arriving to occupy the area south of the 16th parallel, and the Chinese, who were to administer Vietnam north of that line, with a fait accompli. Viet Minh forces took over Saigon and Hanoi (with at least the tacit help of the Japanese) within hours of Japan's surrender. The British, with the help of recently-released French troops, regained control of Saigon; but the Chinese were apparently acquiescent, or at least resigned, to continued Viet Minh control of the northern capital. Indeed it was from this position of strength that the Viet Minh soon began their long but unsuccessful series of negotiations with the French.

As for the Americans, they hung around for a while and then quietly left. Nothing more was to be heard in Washington pronouncements about independence or trusteeship. Our official interest was manifested by the presence in Saigon and Hanoi of a few junior Foreign Service officers.

*   *   *

I tend to date my first direct experience with the Vietnam problem from the moment I set foot in Geneva in 1954. But the tale of our wartime experience with Indochina itself evokes memories of a much earlier exposure. Soon after the war I witnessed a moment in the history of Vietnam that has troubled me for years.

The troopship that was taking me home from China was slowly slipping out of the Colombo harbor after a brief refueling stop. The hot Ceylonese September sun was beating down and the air was still. There was a general sense of relaxation and lassitude as the thousands of troops on board settled down for the long trip home. And then suddenly we were aware of another ship, as crowded with soldiers as our own, steaming close by. It was flying the Union Jack. A roar of recognition, fellowship, goodwill, rose from each ship. And then a strange silence. "Where you goin'?" a Cockney voice demanded over the short distance of intervening water. "Home!" came the answer from a thousand GIs. "Where y'all headed?" boomed a GI hanging on a stanchion nearby. "Vietnam!" was the answer from a battalion of Britishers. "My God," the sergeant standing next to me at the rail whispered, "the war started for them six years ago and they can't go home yet!" But his thoughts, as well as mine, were sharply cut off by a leather-lunged neighbor. Over the two hundred yards of water, over the Pacific and Atlantic Oceans, over the years of danger endured and overcome, came the final American pronouncement: "Limey bastards!!" The ships moved apart—ours headed west, the British ship north.

In my more moody moments, as I brood about how the United States ever got involved in Vietnam, I am inclined to dismiss the turgid exegeses of the historians and the facile descriptions of the politicians and lay the whole explanation to the reaction of an angry God on that hot September morning in the waters off Colombo.

III

Passing the Baton

In the first year or so after the defeat of the Japanese, the United States declined the invitation of Ho Chi Minh to join him in the journey from French Indochina to Independent Vietnam. We were uneasy about our would-be traveling companion and uncertain as to whether we could agree on either the ultimate destination or the route. Some time later we were eager to embark on a more limited, albeit hazardous trip from French Indochina to Free, more-or-less Independent Vietnam. But because of the costs and dangers, we sought other like-minded partners to join us. When it was clear that we would have to make the journey accompanied only by an already travel-sick and bankrupt friend, we decided to stay home—at least for a while.

*   *   *

Looking back over the period of World War II, it is hard to find any precise articulation of American policy toward Indochina. It is a moot question as to whether there actually was a policy. President Roosevelt, as we have seen, brooded about and, on occasion, raised the possibility of some form of international arrangement as an alternative to the re-establishment of French colonial rule. But Roosevelt's policy—if it actually was a policy—was never

43

"staffed out," never put forward in detail, never incorporated—
so far as one can tell—in any official White House document.

The State Department role is shrouded in mist. The official
then in charge of South East Asia recalls that trusteeship was
"official policy" and that he prepared several planning documents
on this idea for the White House. On the other hand, another
official who was working on the Indochina desk during this period
was unaware of any planning documents prepared in the Department or of any White House guidance. He described the trusteeship issue as an "idea or aspiration," rather than a policy, and
seriously doubted that President Truman knew anything about it
when he succeeded Roosevelt. Both men agree that the French
Desk, which then had paramount influence, would have smothered
the idea in the Department if trusteeship for Indochina had been
seriously discussed after Roosevelt's death.

If Roosevelt had lived to press his views during the critical
period of late 1945 and 1946, events in Indochina might have
taken a different course. But apparently few high officials in Washington knew of Roosevelt's concern about the restoration of French
colonial rule. Averell Harriman recounts that Roosevelt felt there
was a pro-French bias among State Department officials and
therefore was reluctant to take them into his confidence on the
Indochina problem. Except for Cordell Hull, who resigned in November 1944, and the Hurley–Wedemeyer team, which had no
responsibility for the formulation of policy, no one privy to the
President's idea felt interested enough to push it after strong
French and British opposition became apparent. In the end trusteeship for Indochina died of under-exposure and mal-nourish-
ment shortly after Roosevelt's death. When General de Gaulle
visited Washington in late August, 1945 he was told by President
Harry Truman that the United States "offers no opposition to the
return of the French Army and authority in Indochina." [1] In
de Gaulle's view the collapse of Japan effectively removed "the
American veto which had kept us out of the Pacific. Indochina
from one day to the next became accessible to us once again." [2]

On the eve of his departure from Washington or perhaps during his visit, de Gaulle had received a dramatic and prophetic

appeal from Vietnam. The key paragraphs of this message could well have been written by Ho Chi Minh. In fact, the appeal was from Emperor Bao Dai. If de Gaulle knew of the message during his discussions with Truman, he almost certainly did not reveal its contents to the President:

> I am addressing myself to the people of France, the country of my youth. I am also addressing myself to its head and liberator, and I want to speak as a friend rather than as a Head of State.
>
> You have suffered enough for four disastrous years not to understand that the Annamese people with 20 centuries of history and a glorious past behind them no longer want and no longer can tolerate any domination or any foreign administration.
>
> You would understand better if you could see what is happening here, if you could sense the desire for independence which runs to the bottom of every heart and which no human force can curb. Even if you should manage to reestablish a French administration here, it would no longer be obeyed; each village would become a nest of resistance, each former collaborator an enemy and your officials and your colonials themselves would demand to leave this asphyxiating atmosphere.
>
> I beg you to understand that the only way to safeguard French interests and the spiritual influence of France in Indochina is to openly recognize the independence of Vietnam and renounce all ideas of reestablishing sovereignty or any form of French administration.
>
> We could so easily understand each other and become friends if you would drop this claim to become our masters again.
>
> Making this appeal to the well-known idealism of the French people and to the great wisdom of their leader, we hope that the peace and joy which are sounding for all the people of the world will be equally assured for the inhabitants of Indochina, whether natives or foreigners.

President Truman was also the recipient of a message from Bao Dai, which the Emperor had sent on the 20th in the knowledge that de Gaulle and Truman were to meet and in the vain hope that his two appeals would somehow influence the course of their discussion. To President Truman he wrote:

Knowing that the head of the provisional government of France is going to confer with you on the future of Indochina, I have the honor to inform you that the various states of Indochina have already proclaimed their independence and are determined to preserve it.

As far as the Vietnamese people are concerned, we do not consider the French as enemies; we respect them and their economic interests, but we are opposed with all of our forces to the reestablishment of French sovereignty over the territory of Vietnam under whatever regime it would be.

The colonial regime no longer conforms to the present course of history. A people such as the Vietnamese people who have a two-thousand year old history and a glorious past cannot accept remaining under the domination of another people.

The French people must yield to the principle of equity which the powerful American nation has proclaimed and defends. France must recognize this with good grace in order to avoid the disaster of a war breaking out on the territory of our country.

Our people have already suffered a great deal from a war which is just coming to an end without our having participated in it. Therefore, our people demand to take part in the building of a just peace in the world.

I will be extremely grateful to you to please transmit this message to the governments of Britain, China and Russia.

I beseech you, Mr. President, to kindly accept my thanks and those of my people for the assistance which, for the sake of justice and humanity, you will be able to kindly furnish to us.

Although Indochina has been in the spotlight of the world's stage since 1954, it was very much in the wings as far as the United States was concerned during 1945. Japan surrendered sooner than most American policy planners anticipated and left the United States and Allied Forces little time to turn from problems of a postwar Europe to the largely ignored problems of a postwar Southeast Asia. In Potsdam, for example, General George Marshall, virtually on the eve of V–J Day, proposed that Admiral Mountbatten accept two French Divisions in his Southeast Asia Command, but he told Mountbatten that because of transport difficulties, "it would probably be the *late spring of 1946* before he could expect to get them." [3]

Even more significant to the eventual shape of postwar Southeast Asia than high-level innocence of how soon we would confront the problems of victory in the Far East, was the understandable priority given to Japan itself. Washington had tried earlier
to make clear to the British (and engaged in some acrimonious
exchanges to press the point) that it regarded all of Indochina as
part of the China Theater under the command of Chiang Kai-shek
and his American Chief of Staff, General Wedemeyer. But in July
the Administration virtually begged the British to take over responsibility for part of Indochina. In the joint U.S.–British military talks at Potsdam, General George Marshall suggested that
the British take responsibility for the southern part of Indochina
(south of the 15th parallel—later revised to the area south of the
16th parallel) and emphasized that "it would be a great advantage . . . if the transfer . . . could take place at an early date.
General MacArthur is fully occupied with operations to the northward and it would a considerable benefit to him if he could be
relieved of these responsibilities as soon as possible." [4] It would
be the American task to bring Chiang along on this arrangement,
and it was left to the British to inform the French.

Compounding the problems of the interested parties—the
Americans, British, French, Chinese, the Vietnamese themselves,
and even the Japanese—was the lack of precision as to what was
meant by "responsibility" for the two zones of Indochina. *

In the event, American post-surrender policy toward Indochina was not formulated; it was a passive acquiescence to the
interpretation of the Potsdam agreement by the British, French,
and Chinese. Furthermore, the American position on ex-colonial
territories at the first UN meeting in San Francisco was so bland
that President Truman and Secretary of State Stettinius, even if
they shared Roosevelt's forebodings about the return of French
rule, could do no more than act as spectators to the game that
was soon to go on in Indochina. In early October Washington

---

* To obfuscate the problem even more, Roosevelt drew no distinction between the three separate areas within Indochina—Vietnam, Laos, and Cambodia.
He treated the whole area as one ethnic and political entity.

made its official views known in a telegram to American diplomats abroad: "US has no thought of opposing the reestablishment of French control in Indochina and no official statement by US Govt has questioned even by implication French sovereignty over Indochina. However, it is not the policy of this Govt to assist the French to reestablish their control over Indochina by force and the willingness of the US to see French control reestablished assumes that French claim to have the support of the population of Indochina is borne out by future events." [5]

The State Department's Director of the Office of Far Eastern Affairs, John Carter Vincent, remarked in a speech on October 20, 1945 that the situation in Southeast Asia "has developed to the liking of none of us. . . ." The United States "does not question French sovereignty in that area . . ." but hopes "an early agreement can be reached between representatives of the governments concerned and the Annamese . . . it is not our intention to assist or participate in forceful measures for the imposition of control by the territorial sovereigns, but we would be prepared to lend our assistance, if requested to do so, in efforts to reach peaceful agreements. . . ." [6]

By January, 1946 the British passed on their responsibilities lock, stock, and barrel to the French. The Chinese Nationalists, encouraged by Americans then in Hanoi, handed over the northern zone to Ho Chi Minh and left him to work out his own destiny with the French. In exchange for the evacuation of the Chinese troops, the French agreed to relinquish extra-territorial rights in China, sell the Yunnan railroad to the Chinese Government, provide a free port at Haiphong, and allow merchandise originating in or destined for China to be transshipped tax and duty-free. French troops reoccupied the northern part of Vietnam in early March, 1946.

Preoccupied with problems of postwar Japan, European recovery, Soviet troublemaking from Iran to Germany, and reconversion of the U.S. economy, it would have been surprising if Washington had concerned itself with events in Southeast Asia. To the extent there was any interest in this area, it was confined to the Indonesian struggle against the Dutch, which broke out in

1946, and the uprisings of the Huks in the Philippines that occurred in 1948. Indochina was a forgotten area, and it would be the Chinese (under Mao Tse-tung this time) who were later to remind us of it.

In retrospect this was a lost opportunity. We entered the postwar era with considerable influence over the future of Vietnam. Although virtually all of our military forces were farther north in Japan and Korea, Wedemeyer's position as Chiang's Chief of Staff could have given us a major role at least in that part of Indochina north of the sixteenth parallel. And we had, however transitory and self-serving it may have been, the goodwill of the leaders of the Viet Minh—and perhaps some influence over them as well. Thus on September 2, 1945, "Vietnamese Independence Day," a young man named Vo Nguyen Giap paid tribute to the "particularly intimate relations" with China and the United States, "which it is a pleasant duty to dwell upon. . . ."[7] The Viet Minh was counting on the United States to come to its support—at least by putting pressure on France to grant Vietnam's independence. Encouraged by some OSS officers and a few American journalists, the Viet Minh leaders sent long, formal letters to President Truman. The letters were ignored and the United States remained officially neutral. Viet Minh appeals to the UN, transmitted by OSS officers, were also ignored.

By the end of 1945 all American liaison and military government groups had been removed from Hanoi. A solitary Vice-Consul was the only American representative. But worse was to follow from the point of view of the Viet Minh leadership—and from the point of view of all Vietnamese nationalists of whatever persuasion. The French soldiers who soon poured into Vietnam were virtually indistinguishable in their uniforms and equipment from American troops. To the Vietnamese this signaled a major change in American policy and an ominous threat to their aspirations for independence; the brave words contained in Roosevelt's Four Freedoms, and American war aims in general, clearly did not apply to them. Even General MacArthur was outraged: "If there is anything that makes my blood boil, it is to see our Allies in Indochina and Java deploying Japanese troops to reconquer the little people we promised to liberate. It is the most ignoble kind of betrayal." [8]

If Roosevelt's trusteeship idea had had the understanding and support of the men in Washington who were to make the key decisions of mid-1945, would subsequent events have been altered? Could the fighting have been avoided? Could the Viet Minh have been induced to broaden its base and create a genuinely nationalist party? Would Americans have had the will and ability to hold the fort until a trusteeship arrangement could be worked out in the fledgling United Nations? Would the British have yielded to determined pressure by the United States for such a trusteeship? And what about trusteeships for Malaya, Indonesia, and Burma? These are interesting but not very helpful questions. The residue of American policy in Indochina during late 1945 and early 1946 left a permanent stain. The unfulfilled expectations of American support for their independence movement affected the attitudes of Vietnamese intellectuals and the political elite of both North and South Vietnam and influenced the course of events for the succeeding twenty-five years. Our subsequent claims that we were in Vietnam to help the people exercise their "free choice" seems ironic to those with long memories.

*   *   *

The Potsdam decision to divide Indochina into two zones at the sixteenth parallel lasted less than a year. By the summer of 1946 both the British and the Chinese had left Vietnam, and the French who took their place were confronting an independent republic proclaimed and headed by Ho Chi Minh. Negotiations between the two sides in early 1946 resulted in the "March 6 Agreement," which provided that France recognize the Democratic Republic of Vietnam as "a free state with its own government, parliament, army and finances, forming part of the Indochinese Federation and the French Union." The agreement promptly broke down (Vietnamese would say because of French chicanery, but there is probably some blame for the Vietnamese to share). In November there was a major clash between French and Viet Minh forces in Haiphong when a French cruiser bombarded that city, resulting in 6,000 casualties. By the end of the year the two sides were at war—a war that was to continue for another eight years.

The United States kept largely aloof from Indochina during this period. More surprisingly, so did England. Even under a Labour Government that gave independence to one British possession after another, London made no move and raised no voice against the French attempt to resist the tide of nationalism that was sweeping Asia. Indeed the British reportedly provided French troops in Indochina with almost £20,000 worth of military equipment between the end of the war and mid-1947,[9] possibly in connection with their own efforts to counter a clearly defined Communist threat to Singapore and Malaya.*

The Russians too pretty much kept their counsel with respect to Indochina, although they were making rude noises and troublesome moves elsewhere. Neither in their propaganda nor in the UN did Ho get much Soviet help. Moscow expected that the French Communist Party would establish itself in a French government, and the French Communist Party line was that Vietnam should achieve its independence within the framework of the French Union. One Viet Minh leader told Harold Isaacs that he expected no help from the Soviet Union. "The Russians are nationalists for Russia first and above all. They would be interested in us only if we served some purpose of theirs. Right now, unfortunately, we do not seem to serve any such purpose."[10]

Even the Indians, who professed to be the model for and mentor of ex-colonial peoples, did not give the Viet Minh much support. Pandit Nehru was philosophically attuned to the developing situation in Indochina and was frustrated by his inability to offer assistance. "We have watched British intervention in Indochina with growing anger, shame and helplessness that Indian troops should thus be used for doing Britain's dirty work against our friends who are fighting the same fight as we."[11] Nevertheless, at

* The struggles in Vietnam and Malaya had many things in common, but there was one major difference—a difference that played a critical role in each outcome: the British had promised unequivocal independence to their territories and were fighting to preserve that independence; the French refused to make such a commitment and were fighting to preserve their colonial power.

the Inter-Asian Relations Conference, held in New Delhi in March, 1947, Nehru told the Vietnamese delegation that "India was not prepared to risk a war with France by extending physical support to Vietnam." [12]

Perhaps the starkest contrast between Washington's lassitude with regard to developments in Vietnam and its reaction to other postwar eruptions of nationalism was provided by the Indonesian struggle against the Dutch. Large American investments in Indonesian rubber and oil industries were largely responsible for the intense U.S. interest in the outcome of that struggle. There was, to be sure, a period of American hesitation because of the large reservoir of sympathy the Dutch had in the United States—considerably more than the French had because of the bitter aftertaste of Vichy. But in the end we came out foursquare for Indonesian independence, and by late 1948 we were putting substantial pressure on The Hague and giving material and moral support to the Indonesians. *

                              *   *   *

The American attitude toward the emerging situation in Indochina can probably be best explained by considering the developments in Europe rather than in Southeast Asia. The Soviet Union, through its support of the European Communist parties, and

---

* During the period of official Washington hesitation over how to deal with the Dutch–Indonesian struggle, an American businessman took matters into his own hands. Representatives of the Indonesian Nationalists came to Washington to seek American financial assistance in early 1947 but met with no success. Mr. Matthew Fox, a freewheeling and imaginative movie executive, provided them with a generous loan in exchange for a virtual monopoly over Indonesian trade to and from the United States. In the early and uncertain period of the Indonesian revolution, Fox was practically the only source of Western help. When victory seemed assured, the Indonesians, with the encouragement of the United States Government and American companies with prewar ties to Indonesia, quickly dismissed Fox.

I had known Fox during the war and had seen him several times in the immediate postwar period, but the first inkling I had of his involvement in Indonesia was when his contract with the Indonesians crossed my desk. He later recounted that when he was sick and bored in the hospital, a friend brought in some Indonesian visitors "with unpronounceable names." He "liked their looks" and, even more, their stories of vast resources of tin, copra, oil, and rubber. Although it would be many months later before he could find Indonesia on the map, he called his bank and closed the deal "then and there." Or so he said.

through more overt and ominous political and military moves, was threatening the stable and democratic Western Europe that had been the goal of American postwar planning. In our concept of a new postwar Europe, France loomed very large. Germany was numb, the Low Countries were prostrate, and Italy was recovering slowly and, moreover, confronting a strong Communist party. But France seemed to have a sense of purpose and direction. The Monnet Plan, designed to make France economically independent by 1950, had gotten off to a promising start, in no small measure due to the impetus given it by the American aid program.

French attempts to preserve their empire in Asia, as distasteful as they were to American liberals, were of little concern to the policymakers and planners in Washington. The Soviet and local Communist moves of the early postwar years made the choice seem to be one between the evils of Communism and colonialism. Increasing evidence that the Viet Minh was Communist-dominated put the Indochina war in the same category as the Malayan insurgency. (Indonesia was different, because Indonesian nationalists had fought and beaten the Communists among them.) If the French were not on the side of the angels in Indochina, they seemed, to the extent anyone in Washington thought about the question in 1946 and 1947, to be backing the lesser devil. Adding to the hesitancy about interjecting American views in Indochina was a fear that any Washington meddling might cause the downfall of the frail Third Force Government and lead to a government headed again by the difficult and unpredictable de Gaulle or the dangerous and predictable Communists.

Thus Washington was fully engaged in a game of high stakes in Europe and had to watch with a mixture of anxiety and helplessness the contest being waged in Indochina. There was little the Administration was able to do to affect the outcome.

The American attitude toward Indochina was summed up by General Marshall in early 1947 when he was Secretary of State. He hoped, he said in February, that "a pacific basis of adjustment of the difficulties could be found." [13] Marshall's statement revealed as much by what he omitted as by what he said. There was actually little that the United States could do, or at least was prepared to do, to assure a "pacific basis of adjustment." We could not lend our "good offices," because we had burned our bridges with the Viet Minh, and because too we were not willing to exert pressure to assure that both sides observed the March 6 Agreement. Except for occasional expressions of hope, we paid very little notice, officially or in our press, to the events of Indochina. By design or default, we adopted a hands-off approach. Our attention was diverted elsewhere.

The foreign policy goals the United States set for itself in the early postwar years revolved around converting Germany and Japan into stable democracies and reconstructing the economies of the liberated nations (France, Greece, and the Low Countries). In Europe these goals were to be achieved in cooperation with our major wartime allies, Great Britain and the Soviet Union. In the Far East, however, the situation was much less clear-cut. England and France were much too involved with their confused colonial problems, the Chinese Nationalists had all they could do to cope with their own troubles with the Communists, and the Soviet Union was playing it very cool.

The immediate postwar era was characterized by misgivings about the Soviet Union, and by 1946 Washington began to re-examine its policy towards Moscow. Doubts had already emerged during the war; they were reinforced by the conflict over the repatriation issue in Germany and by Soviet actions in Eastern Europe. In late 1946, following Soviet pressures on Iran, Turkey, and Greece, the specter of Soviet expansionism in Europe became a matter of grave concern. From early 1947 Washington was almost totally immersed in re-examining its European strategy and policy in the light of one disillusioning experience after another with the Soviet Union.

France, with American assistance, began to assume a major strategic role in Europe, but the situation was by no means encouraging. The French economy was still shaky, and even more worrisome was the increasing strength of the French Communist Party; in the 1946 elections the Communists could claim 25 percent of the popular vote and important posts in the government. The United States was underwriting French power, but Washington was reluctant to influence French policy in Indochina; we needed French support in the Western Alliance. Washington felt comfortable about its policy because of Paris' assurances that steps were being taken that would lead to the eventual independence of Indochina. We were duped, it is now apparent, by the French Government and misled by the influential French desk of a European-oriented Department of State.

It was not until the Chinese Communists took over the China Mainland in October of 1949 that Washington once more paid much attention to any area in the Far East other than Japan and China itself. Although American efforts were first engaged in trying to salvage Chiang Kai-shek's regime, and later in repulsing a North Korean attack on the Republic of Korea, the problem of Indochina became an increasingly insistent claimant.

* * *

Among the royalty displaced in the aftermath of World War II was the Emperor of Vietnam. The drama that accompanied the comings and goings of the kings of Europe tended to overshadow the saga of Bao Dai, the last Emperor to occupy the throne held by generations of the Nguyens of Hue. Even when he came to our notice in the early 1950s, the pathos of the Vietnamese people as a whole tended to reduce the saga of Bao Dai to just another sad and futile episode in Vietnam's search for peace and independence.

Like so many of our experiences with Vietnam, the Bao Dai incident is replete with frustration and futility. American efforts to induce the French to give Bao Dai (in the name of the Vietnamese) enough independence to establish himself as a nationalist counterweight to Ho Chi Minh were misunderstood and resented by the French and, in any case, were largely unsuccessful. Our efforts to induce Bao Dai to exercise whatever authority and prestige he possessed to unite the Vietnamese people behind non-Communist nationalism were misunderstood and resented by the Vietnamese and were also largely unsuccessful.

Dean Acheson graphically described the dilemma of the Truman Administration. In an interview in 1969 he agreed with a suggestion that Washington "came to the aid of the French in

Indochina, not because we approved of what they were doing, but because we needed their support for our policies in regard to NATO and Germany." According to Acheson "The French blackmailed us. At every meeting when we asked them for greater effort in Europe they brought up Indochina and later North Africa. . . . They asked for our aid for Indochina but refused to tell me what they hoped to accomplish or how. Perhaps they didn't know. They were obsessed with the idea of what you have you hold. But they had no idea how to hold it. . . . They wanted nothing to detract from French control. We urged them to allow more and more scope to the political activities of the Vietnamese. They did not take our advice. I thought it was possible to do something constructive with Bao Dai—not much, but something." [14]

At the end of the war with Japan, Bao Dai stayed on in Hanoi as an adviser to Ho Chi Minh. He accepted the rank of a common citizen and played his new role quietly and with grace—for six months. Then shortly after the signing of the March 6 Agreement, he was sent on a mission to Chungking, the exact nature of which is not clear. Instead of returning to Hanoi, he went from Chungking to Hong Kong where he remained in self-imposed, luxurious exile for three years. As agreement between the French and the Viet Minh became less and less likely, Bao Dai became an important figure to the government in Paris—and to the non-Communist nationalists in Vietnam. Only he, it seemed, could provide a counterweight to Ho Chi Minh. In the fall of 1947 a strong movement was launched in Vietnam to get Bao Dai to return as head of a more-or-less (less rather than more, as it turned out) independent government. In early December 1947, after many weeks of bargaining and maneuvering, Bao Dai signed an agreement which went well beyond Paris' original draft, although it still disappointed the more ardent of the Vietnamese nationalists.

The role of the United States in the evolution of the awakened French interest in Bao Dai is uncertain, but William Bullitt, the American Ambassador to France during World War II, may have been the channel, if not the actual marriage broker, between the

French Government and the Emperor. Bullitt had visited Indochina in October, 1947 and from there went on to Hong Kong to
see Bao Dai. He then went to Paris where he met with some
important French officials, and early in 1948 he paid yet another
visit to Bao Dai in Geneva. In December, *Life* magazine published an article by Bullitt which, while advocating that the
French "permit the non-Communist nationalists of Vietnam to
prepare complete political, economic and military organizations
for control of the country," studiously avoided mentioning the
name of Bao Dai.[15]

One French writer makes an extravagantly angry case that
American meddling with Bao Dai was largely responsible for the
inability of the French to put Indochina to rights. "When the
French set about manufacturing Vietnamese Independence this
Americanism sprang most energetically to life. It had begun in
Hong Kong where every day the United States consulate had advised Bao Dai (on the French proposals): 'Don't weaken. Refuse.'
And when Bao Dai accepted nevertheless, shutting himself away
in Dalat with his neurasthenia and his debauchery, there was a
kind of explosion of outbidding in Saigon: Americans of every
kind whispered to Vietnamese of every kind, 'Ask for more. Don't
give in. Don't let yourselves be swayed by the French: they have
just been waiting for their moment and they are trying to get out
of their difficulties by disguising their colonial problem as anti-
Communist.' It worked one hundred percent against the French.
By every means, and above all by the use of dollars, the Americans built themselves up a following." [16]

The French obviously hoped to be able to give Bao Dai enough
of the trappings of independence to induce him to return to
Vietnam, but they were unprepared to give him enough to attract
nationalist support away from Ho. For his part Bao Dai was unwilling to settle for less than Ho was demanding. In June, 1948,
after months of fruitless talk, a provisional central government of
Vietnam was established, headed by the weak and ineffectual
General Xuen. It was not taken seriously, and it did not deserve to
be. Bao Dai remained in Hong Kong, and few Vietnamese of any
stature associated themselves with the provisional government.

By the end of 1948 Paris began to court Bao Dai in earnest. The French had been having trouble enough coping with the troops of Ho Chi Minh, but Mao's armies were now making ominous progress in China, and it was evident that the Viet Minh would soon have a friendly and powerful neighbor on their northern border. The need for developing a strong and energetic non-Communist alternative to the Viet Minh became increasingly urgent, even to the most unregenerate officials in Paris. A series of intensive negotiations culminated on March 8, 1949 in what was to become known as the "Elysée Agreement." Although the Agreement had still to be ratified by the French Assembly, Bao Dai was satisfied and set about, at long last, to return to Vietnam. He arrived in late April, after a three-year exile, and installed himself in his hunting lodge at Dalat to await official French ratification. This came in early June, and Bao Dai then formally entered the contest against Ho Chi Minh for the support and allegiance of the Vietnamese people.

Bao Dai's return was scarcely noticed in the United States. The State Department contented itself with a bland comment: "The United States Government hopes that the agreements on March 8 between President Auriol and Bao Dai, who is making sincere efforts to unite all truly nationalistic elements within Vietnam, will form the basis for the progressive realization of the legitimate aspirations of the Vietnamese people." [17] Our attention was riveted on the worsening plight of Chiang Kai-shek, and it would be many more months before we would focus on the events in Indochina.

*   *   *

For the first two years or so of the struggle against the French, Ho hoarded his strength against the day when he could move strong regular forces directly against French units. During this period the main burden of the fighting fell on Viet Minh local militia and regional forces equipped with a hodgepodge of simple weapons. As a consequence, the French tended to underestimate the true strength of the Viet Minh—a mistake that was to prove costly as hostilities moved beyond the level of guerrilla warfare. By late 1949 Viet Minh troops were being trained and equipped in the Chinese provinces bordering Indochina. By 1950 the Viet Minh had a regular army numbering 60,000 organized into five divisions, equipped with the first installment of Chinese- and Russian-supplied weapons.

Liu Shao-chi signaled Peking's interest in the fortunes of the Viet Minh in the fall of 1949, months before Peking actually recognized the government of Ho Chi Minh. "The war of national liberation in Viet Nam," Liu said, "has liberated 90 percent of her territory. . . . The national liberation movement . . . will never stop short of complete victory." [18] A Chinese military mission reportedly visited the Viet Minh headquarters in December, 1949 to study its requirements for military assistance. Ho Chi Minh went to Peking the following April and was successful in getting tangible Chinese Communist help in the form of guns and mortars. Within a few months of Ho's visit the French were reporting heavier firepower and high morale in the Viet Minh units.

The Viet Minh, emboldened by the support of the Chinese Communists, went on a major but abortive offensive in 1950 and 1951. Their tremendous losses made it clear that a return to guerrilla warfare was necessary. But despite their mauling by the French, the Viet Minh had secured control of a large part of northern Indochina and had established lines of communication directly to supply bases in Communist China.

The actual amount of Chinese aid given to the Viet Minh will probably never be known. Some observers have estimated it as ranging from an average of 10-12 tons per month in 1951, to 400- 600 tons per months in 1954. When the battle of Dien Bien Phu began in 1954, the flow was estimated to have risen to 1,500 tons per month, and by June it had reached a peak of 4,000 tons. Petroleum products and ammunition comprised 75 percent of Chinese aid; arms and medical and signal equipment constituted the remaining 25 percent.[19] By and large, however, the Viet Minh relied on an amalgam of crude weapons made in their own arsenals, those turned over or appropriated from wartime Japanese stocks, and those captured from the French. To this was added American equipment left behind in China by the Nationalist

armies. (Some of the latter was probably still in use by the North
Vietnamese and Viet Cong forces as late as 1965.)

With Mao Tse-tung's victory and with Chinese Communist
forces deployed along the northern borders of Laos and Vietnam,
Washington stirred out of its lethargy. The war between the
French and the Viet Minh had taken on an entirely new character
—it became an integral part of the struggle between the "Free
World" and "International Communism." The lines were drawn
between Peking and Moscow, on the one hand, and Washington
on the other.

In January, 1950 China, quickly followed by the Soviet Union,
recognized the government of Ho Chi Minh. If anything else had
been needed to remove the French–Viet Minh war from the sordid
ranks of a Colonialist–Nationalist struggle into the elevated status
of a confrontation between the Free World and the Communist
Bloc, this was it. Secretary of State Acheson viewed this action as
removing "any illusions as to the 'nationalist' nature of Ho Chi
Minh's aims and revealing Ho in his true colors as the mortal
enemy of native independence in Indochina." [20] The French cause
was now one Americans could support with something more than
General Marshall's hope that "a way could be found" to resolve
the difficulties peaceably. But first the French had to provide at
least some aura of independence to the Bao Dai Government.
This was apparent even to the foot-dragging National Assembly.
The Minister for France Overseas put the case succinctly: "It is
evident," he said in mid-January, "that as long as Parliament does
not recognize this independence, no foreign and friendly state will
be disposed to recognize [Vietnam, Laos, and Cambodia]. . . ." [21]
After ten months of delay France ratified the agreements to provide nominal independence for Laos, Cambodia, and Vietnam.

American recognition of Bao Dai on February 7, 1950 followed
on the heels of the French ratification. The State Department
noted that "this recognition is consistent with our fundamental
policy of giving support to the peaceful and democratic evolution
of democratic peoples toward self-government and independence." [22] Several weeks later Ambassador Loy W. Henderson
clarified the United States' position in a speech to the Indian

Council of World Affairs: "The United States is convinced that the Bao Dai Government . . . reflects more accurately than any rival claimants to power in Viet Nam the nationalist aspirations of the people of that country . . . any movement headed by a Moscow-recognized Communist such as Ho Chi Minh must be in the direction of subservience to foreign states, not in that of independence or self-government. My Government felt, therefore, that Bao Dai offered more opportunity to the Viet Namese people to develop their own national life than a leader who, in accordance with his political creed, must obey the orders of international communism." [23]

The years that followed were to see an agonizing struggle, sometimes on the surface, sometimes below it, between Saigon and Paris and between Washington and Paris to make meaningful and perceptible progress in the "evolution . . . toward self-government and independence." American recognition of Bao Dai was almost immediately accompanied by military and economic aid. The military assistance was given directly to the French; the economic aid, after some hesitation by Washington and considerable resentment by the French, went directly to the Bao Dai Government.

* * *

The Mutual Defense Assistance Act, approved by Congress in October, 1949, was the instrument for providing military assistance to the newly-formed NATO, to Greece and Turkey, and to Iran, the Republic of Korea, the Philippines and Nationalist China. During the first year of the Act, France was granted about $20 million of military aid. While the terms of the Act required that "assistance furnished . . . shall be subject to agreements . . . designed to assure that the assistance will be used to provide an integrated defense of the North Atlantic area," the French were able, by virtue of American assistance, to transfer military equipment from their own stocks in Indochina. Washington's protestations that the United States was not aiding Paris in order to restore colonial rule in Indochina, but rather to rebuild the strength of Western Europe, had a hollow ring to the Vietnamese, especially since much of the French equipment sent to Indochina was American surplus left behind in 1945.

On May 8, 1950 the pretense was dropped. At a meeting in Paris, Secretary of State Dean Acheson announced that American aid would now be given to the French for direct use against the Viet Minh. "The [French] Foreign Minister and I have just had an exchange of views on the situation in Indochina and are in general agreement both as to the urgency of the situation in that area and as to the necessity for remedial action. . . . The United States recognizes that the solution of the Indochina problem depends both upon the restoration of security and upon the development of genuine nationalism and that United States assistance can and should contribute to these major objectives. The United States Government, convinced that neither national independence nor democratic evolution exist in any area dominated by Soviet imperialism, considers the situation to be such as to warrant its according economic aid and military equipment to the Associated States of Indochina and to France in order to assist them in restoring stability. . . ."[24]

Altogether, between early 1950 and the end of the war in the spring of 1954, the United States supplied the French with $2.6 billion of military materiel—about 80 percent of the cost of the French military effort. During the same period the Bao Dai Government was given $126 million in direct economic, military and technical assistance by Washington. The extent of American help was well known to the leaders of the Viet Minh, and is probably still part of the mystique of the North Vietnamese leaders. To Ho Chi Minh and his colleagues the Viet Minh victory in 1954 was not only against the French armies but also against the arsenal and treasury of the United States. One American observer provided a bitter summing up of the American policy: "Washington kept hold of the hand of French colonialism as it disappeared down the drain."[25]

*   *   *

The outbreak of the Korean war on June 25, 1950 gave further respectability to American assistance to the French efforts against the Viet Minh. With the Viet Minh now overtly supported by Moscow and Peking, the fighting in Indochina was transformed from a seedy, backwater colonialist-nationalist struggle to a major international contest between the Free World and Communist ideologies. The United States now knew where it stood. And lest there was uncertainty about it, the increasing shrillness of Senator Joseph McCarthy and the "Who-Lost-China?" witch-hunt strengthened the Administration's determination.

Shortly after his decision on June 27, 1950 to aid the Republic of Korea, President Truman announced that "The attack upon Korea makes it plain beyond all doubt that Communism has passed beyond the use of subversion to conquer independent nations and will now use armed invasion and war. . . . I have similarly directed acceleration in the furnishing of military assistance to the forces of France and the Associated States in Indochina and the dispatch of a military mission to provide close working relations with those forces." [26] The first shipments of American military materiel to Vietnam were air-lifted to Saigon in July. In August a Military Assistance Advisory Group (MAAG) was sent to Indochina with instructions to turn over this materiel directly to the French and to avoid direct contacts with the Cambodians, Laotians, and Vietnamese.

*   *   *

The Eisenhower Administration took office at a time of international tension and domestic trauma. Communist influence abroad seemed to be expanding everywhere, particularly in Asia. Senator Joseph McCarthy was at the apex of his power and was soon running rampant, not only over the entire Executive Branch but over American foreign policy.

The most immediate concern of the new Administration was the fulfillment of Eisenhower's promise to settle the Korean war as soon as possible. While he was prepared to discuss a peace settlement with the North Koreans and Chinese with respect to Korea, Eisenhower felt the need to demonstrate a posture of firmness toward Communism in the rest of Asia. He became, as we shall see, desperately concerned lest the French follow his Korean

More French resentment [handwritten margin note]

example, especially since Indochina was regarded as an important element in Washington's determination to contain Communist China. American bombers, transport aircraft, tanks, and large quantities of small arms, ammunition, and medical supplies poured into Indochina even before the Korean armistice. With the Communists blocked from moving south of the 38th parallel in Korea, the Administration regarded Indochina as the next area in which to contain Peking's outward thrust.

The intentions of a Republican Administration had been signaled by John Foster Dulles two years before Eisenhower took office. ". . . there is a civil war [in Indochina] in which we have, for better or worse, involved our prestige. Since that is so, we must help the government we back. Its defeat, coming after the reverses suffered by the Nationalist Government of China, would have further serious repercussions on the whole situation in Asia and the Pacific. It would make even more people in the East feel that friendship with the United States is a liability rather than an asset."[27]

Within days after he took over the Department of State, Dulles began to articulate the "Domino Theory." In a nationwide broadcast he said, "If they [the Soviets] could get this peninsula of Indochina, Siam, Burma, Malaya, they would have what is called the rice bowl of Asia. . . . And you can see that if the Soviet Union had control of the rice bowl of Asia that would be another weapon which would tend to expand their control into Japan and into India. . . ."[28] In his State of the Union Message on February 2, 1953 President Eisenhower emphasized the importance of the American stake in Indochina. He referred to the war in Korea as "part of the same calculated assault that the aggressor is simultaneously pressing in Indochina and Malaya. . . ."[29]

*   *   *

In the meantime it was increasingly clear that the French were no longer fighting a ragtag band of guerrillas but a large, well-armed, highly trained regular army. The war had taken an ominous and, as it turned out, a definitive turn. Nothing the French could do would redress the balance. The armistice in Korea, signed in late

July, 1953, relieved China of supplying its forces there, and by the summer heavier and more sophisticated weapons and equipment were in the hands of the Viet Minh. The dilemma faced by the French is described by Melvin Gurtov in terms that evoke our own dilemma a decade later. "When France began using Vietnamese troops and receiving more American aid following the Korean War, the Chinese in turn stepped up their own aid program just enough to re-establish l'equilibre. When French fortunes rose, so did Chinese aid; the Indochina campaign eventually became a crude game in which the French could never permanently regain the high ground." [30]

Same as later

By the end of 1952 virtually all of North Vietnam outside the Tonkin Delta was under Viet Minh control. In early April of 1953 General Giap undertook a major offensive against Laos and succeeded in overrunning about 20,000 square miles of the countryside. By the first of May, Giap's armies were on the outskirts of the Laotian royal capital of Laung Prabang. Instead of seizing control of the capital, however, the Viet Minh faded back into the jungles and then proceeded to occupy the Province of Sam Neua, in the northeast part of Laos, where they established the "Resistance Government of Pathet Lao" (a high card which they retained and played very successfully during the Geneva Conference a year later). The Viet Minh invasion dramatized French military weakness not only to Laos, but to Cambodia and Vietnam as well.

Additional frictions between the three Associated States and Paris were caused by French devaluation of the piaster in early May, 1953. None of the governments of the Associated States was told in advance of this action. The effects in Indochina, not only in economic terms, but also in terms of reminding the governments how little independence they had, stimulated pressures for a major review of relationships between the Associated States and France. The coincidence of these pressures, plus the replacement of the French Commander-in-Chief in Indochina and a change in government in Paris (in which Joseph Laniel took over as Prime Minister and Georges Bidault as Foreign Minister), resulted in a

French offer in early July to review their relations with each of the three Associated States.

The French note of July 3 was loose enough to satisfy the hard-liners, who favored a continuation of French control in Indochina, and the liberal and left-wing groups, who were in favor of incorporating Indochina into a French-style "commonwealth." In due course and with some modifications, Laos agreed to the French proposal. Cambodia bargained hard for additional concessions, but nothing conclusive was worked out. In Vietnam, discussions were not only inconclusive but bitter. While non-Communist nationalists welcomed the French decision to modify relations with Vietnam, they rejected Bao Dai's equivocal stand; in September a Nationalist Congress in Saigon issued a manifesto sharply criticizing the French and also, by indirection, Bao Dai. A second Congress, handpicked by Bao Dai, was convened in mid-October, but once again Vietnamese participation in the French Union was rejected.

The October Congress provided a catalyst for a change of mood in France. Wide sectors of French opinion recognized that concessions had been made to Bao Dai that went beyond Ho Chi Minh's demands eight years before and that, in addition, the war in Indochina had changed from one in which the French were attempting to reassert their former control to one in which they were carrying the major burden against Communist aggression. Nonetheless, the French Government was reluctant to turn to the UN or to other countries, particularly the United States, for direct assistance in the struggle. If they internationalized the war, the French reasoned, they would damage their prestige and their prospects for attaining even a modest degree of influence in Indochina. Moreover, Paris was more concerned about participating effectively and directly in the defense of Western Europe than in holding the line against Communist expansion in Asia.

The fact that the fighting in Korea had been brought to a close and that the Americans were making terms with the Communist enemy there, made it all the more tempting for the French to try to work out the best arrangement they could with the Communists in Indochina.* Speaking before Parliament in October, 1953 Premier Laniel said: "I must repeat in the clearest and most categorical fashion that the French Government does not consider the Indochinese problem as necessarily requiring a military solution. No more than the Americans in Korea do we demand an unconditional capitulation of the adversary in Korea in order to discuss with him. No more than the United States does France make war for the sake of war, and if an honorable solution were in view, either on the local level or on the international level, France, I repeat, like the United States in Korea, would be happy to welcome a diplomatic solution of the conflict." [32]

This, then, was what President Eisenhower faced during his first year of office. Despite his own and Secretary Dulles' forebodings of the consequences of a Communist victory in Indochina, it was becoming clear to the President that the United States would be unable to change the course of events in Vietnam short of a large-scale injection of American forces. By the summer of 1953 Washington was torn between the need to keep the French fighting on whatever basis and its inability to convince the French to do what seemed necessary to engage the loyalty and support of the Vietnamese themselves. Superimposed on this was the desire of the Administration to establish the European Defense Community, an enterprise which required not only the participation but the energetic cooperation of the French Government.

There was widespread unrest in France and an increasingly desperate military situation in Indochina. France's major new thrust against the Viet Minh (the "Navarre Plan") had already shown signs of weakening, and the French position at Dien Bien Phu was particularly ominous. The Administration in Washington was confronted with a stark choice: it would either have to provide immediate, massive aid (almost certainly including Ameri-

* Bernard Fall has a titillating revelation about a Washington–Paris understanding about these negotiations. "Although it has not been admitted publicly that the two allies exchanged formal agreements guaranteeing that neither would conclude a peace without the other, it has nevertheless been admitted by highly reliable French sources (and, at least once, mentioned before an American Congressional committee) that the United States exerted strong pressure upon France not to pursue peace feelers extended by the Viet Minh in 1952." [31]

can forces) to the French, or it would have to resign itself to having Paris seek negotiations at any price. It is worth quoting Eisenhower's description of his dilemma at some length. It has a familiar ring to anyone involved in the Vietnam problem a decade later.

The situation confronting the United States in our hope of finding ways to help the French effectively was complicated. The most obvious and least risky method was to provide material aid, and we were already giving this. . . . This kind of aid was being sent in as rapidly as French capacity to absorb it permitted. . . .

. . . if three basic requirements were fulfilled, the United States could properly and effectively render real help in winning the war. The first requirement was a legal right under international law; second, was a favorable climate of Free World opinion; and third, favorable action by the Congress.

Regarding the legal right, the course was clear. Any intervention on the part of the United States would scarcely be possible save on the urgent request of the French government, which request would have to reflect, without question, the desire of the local governments.

. . . We carefully examined methods and procedures calculated to win the approbation of most of the Free World. One method would have been for the three Associated States of the French Union to go to the United Nations. . . . Another would be to confine United States intervention to participation in a coalition, including Britain, the ANZUS powers, and some of the Southeast Asian nations. While we recognized that the burden of the operation would fall on the United States, the token forces supplied by these other nations, as in Korea, would lend real moral standing to a venture that otherwise could be made to appear as a brutal example of imperialism. This need was particularly acute because there was no incontrovertible evidence of overt Red Chinese participation in the Indochina conflict.

Another consideration . . . was the type of forces which might be employed. . . . I could not at that moment see the value of putting United States ground forces in Southeast Asia.

One possibility was to support the French with air strikes . . . on Communist installations around Dien Bien Phu. There were grave doubts in my mind about the effectiveness of such air strikes on deployed troops where good cover was plentiful. Employment of air strikes alone to support French forces in the jungle would create a double jeopardy; it would comprise an act of war and would also entail the risk of having intervened and lost. Air power might be temporarily beneficial to French morale, but I had no intention of using United States forces in any limited action when the force employed would probably not be decisively effective.[33]

Washington was likely to get little help from the British, who were just beginning to see some progress in reconstructing their economy and in the long war they had been fighting in Malaya. Eisenhower was clearly opposed to having the United States mount a solo rescue operation through the introduction of American ground or even air forces.

It was under these inauspicious circumstances that the Foreign Ministers of the Soviet Union, the United Kingdom, France, and the United States assembled in Berlin in late January, 1954 to discuss the future of Germany, Austria, Korea, and the Far East. According to Eisenhower, Bidault knew that he had to return to Paris with a commitment that Indochina, as well as Korea, would be discussed at Geneva in the spring if the Laniel government was to stay in power. "Molotov was fully aware of the political pressures on . . . Bidault to achieve a settlement in Indochina." The Americans had an important stake in the survival of the Laniel government. "We were convinced," Eisenhower said, "that no succeeding government would take a stronger position . . . on the defense of Indochina, or in support of the European Defense Community." Nonetheless, Secretary Dulles "attempted to discourage Bidault from overanxiety to negotiate. . . ."[34]

Despite Dulles' advice to Bidault and his promise that American military assistance to French forces in Indochina would continue, Bidault desperately sought assurances on early negotiations for Indochina. The situation in Vietnam was deteriorating daily, especially in the Dien Bien Phu area, and pressures on the Laniel government in Paris were building up. Bidault's position augured ill for France's bargaining position. He "found himself in the position of practically pleading with Molotov for the inclusion of Indochina on the Geneva agenda."[35]

In early 1954 President Eisenhower had established a group to examine the desirability and feasibility of sending American ground forces to Indochina. At about the same time he designated Lt. General John W. O'Daniel as the chief of the U.S. Military Advisory and Assistance Group in Vietnam to coordinate the American military aid efforts there.

Congress was by now exhibiting a queasy feeling about American intervention, especially on the heels of the costly Korean war. Even such stalwarts as Senators Stennis and Russell expressed concern. On February 10 Eisenhower wired Dulles (then in Berlin) ". . . certain legislators have expressed uneasiness concerning any use of American maintenance personnel in Indochina. They fear that this may be opening the door to . . . [the] introduction of American troops. . . . There is no ground whatsoever for assuming that we intend to reverse or ignore U.S. commitments made to French. . . . General O'Daniel's most recent report is more encouraging than given to you through French sources. I still believe that the two things most needed for success are French will to win and complete acceptance by Vietnamese of French promise of independence as soon as victory is achieved." [36]

Faced with Congressional reluctance to permit even American maintenance personnel to assist the hard-pressed French forces, sharp differences within the Administration and the military establishment on the relative effectiveness and desirability of American air and/or ground support, a restive mood in France, and a disintegrating military situation in Indochina, the Administration was engaged throughout February and early March in a continuing reappraisal of the American position with respect to Indochina and all of Southeast Asia. The forthcoming Geneva Conference was a matter of grave concern in Washington and the prospect of Americans negotiating with the Chinese Communists was especially worrisome to the hard-liners. Senator Knowland labeled the Conference a possible "Far Eastern Munich" and had "substantial misgivings" about the United States sitting down with the Chinese Communists to discuss peace in Indochina.[37] The Secretary of State, in his report to the nation on the Berlin Conference, tried to put the problem in a reassuring light; China would come to Geneva "not to be honored by us, but rather to account before the bar of world opinion." [38]

A few days later Secretary Dulles and Admiral Arthur W. Radford, then Chairman of the Joint Chiefs of Staff, met with Congressional leaders to test the water for a Joint Resolution authorizing the President to use American ground forces. After the meeting Dulles reported to the President that "Congressional support would be contingent upon meeting three conditions:

"(1) United States intervention must be part of a coalition to include the other free nations of Southeast Asia, the Philippines, and the British Commonwealth.

"(2) The French must agree to accelerate their independence program for the Associated States so there could be no interpretation that United States assistance meant support of French colonialism.

"(3) The French must agree not to pull their forces out of the war if we put our forces in." [39]

Dulles suggested that the President personally intervene with Churchill to induce the British to join the U.S., France, and others in a military effort to prevent the Communists from overrunning Indochina. Eisenhower agreed. Churchill replied three days later: the British would be ready to discuss the matter with Secretary Dulles in London on April 12. Eisenhower concluded that "the British had little enthusiasm for joining us in taking a firm position and it seemed clear that the Congress would not act favorably unless I could give assurances that the British would be by our side." [40]

Any remaining illusions that Washington may have had about the French maintaining a position of strength as the Geneva Conference approached had been dispelled by France's Chief of Staff, General Paul Ely, who visited Washington in late March on his way back from an investigation of the situation in Indochina. The General made it clear that the Navarre Plan held little prospect of success and that the French were in desperate military straits. Ely's conversations in Washington probably had a definitive effect on American policy. Major American intervention would now be necessary if the situation was to be saved, but the Administration was determined not to take unilateral action. Dulles took a tough line on this issue by the end of March: "the U.S. feels that the possibility [of a Russian and Chinese Communist takeover of Indochina] should not be passively accepted but should be met by united action." [41]

In response to Churchill's invitation Dulles left for England on April 11. In London he broached the idea of a 9-power conference in Washington to discuss "united action," to take place prior to the opening of the Geneva Conference on April 27. Dulles sent Eisenhower an optimistic message—the British might be more willing to take united action in Indochina than had appeared earlier. But if Dulles had given an accurate report, London quickly reversed its position. It was clear that the British were reluctant to do anything that might provoke the Communists prior to the convening of the Geneva Conference. The idea of a pre-Geneva Washington conference was dropped.

Dulles then went on to Paris. From there he sent Washington a dolorous account of the situation in Dien Bien Phu. According to the French, the only way that the situation could possibly be saved was by a massive American air intervention. Bidault indicated that while he had always opposed any internationalization of the war, at this last critical moment he was willing to accept such an intervention. In Bidault's view British participation was not important, since London was unable to make a meaningful contribution.

In the anxious days of mid-April, 1954 when the fate of Dien Bien Phu hung in the balance, threatening and bellicose remarks made by Secretary Dulles, Admiral Radford, and Vice President Nixon gave rise to rumors that the United States might use an atomic bomb in an effort to relieve the French garrison. The fact that two American aircraft carriers equipped with atomic weapons were ordered into the Gulf of Tonkin at the time lent credibility to these rumors. Richard Nixon's critics have recently promoted him to the position of chief advocate, but John Foster Dulles actually deserves the number one spot. Dulles' oft-repeated but generalized views on "massive retaliation," and his reiteration in late 1953 and early 1954 that overt Chinese Communist intervention against the French would have "grave consequences which might not be confined to Indochina," implied the use of air and sea power and provided a doomsday note to warnings emanating from Washington.

Richard Nixon was neither as verbose nor as fierce in his public statements as Secretary Dulles. Although he did hint at the possibility of American intervention, he neither mentioned nor implied the use of atomic weapons. According to *The New York Times,* Nixon told the American Society of Newspaper Editors on April 17 that "The United States as a leader of the free world cannot afford further retreat in Asia. It is hoped the United States will not have to send troops there, but if this Government cannot avoid it, the Administration must face up to the situation and dispatch forces."

The Eisenhower Administration remained genuinely reluctant to commit ground forces to Indochina despite Nixon's reference to "troops." Moreover, there is little evidence that bombing, let alone atomizing, the besiegers of Dien Bien Phu was given serious consideration by the President. Years later in a TV interview, Eisenhower said, "Well, I couldn't think of anything probably less effective than in a great big jungle area and with a besieged fortress, trying to relieve it with air force. I just can't see how this could have been done unless you were willing to use weapons that could have destroyed the jungles all around the area for miles and that would have probably destroyed Dienbienphu itself, and that would have been that." [42]

It may well be true that American sea-based aircraft would have been used, possibly even with atomic weapons, if Chinese Communist armies had moved South. But the Chinese did not cross the Indochina border. Perhaps Peking felt the Viet Minh could accomplish its objectives without help from Chinese ground forces. Perhaps the leaders of the Viet Minh actively opposed the introduction of Chinese armies into Indochina. Perhaps Dulles' threats were taken seriously.

While Dulles was in Paris the French position at Dien Bien Phu became even worse. Dulles cabled Eisenhower on April 23

Ridgeway [handwritten marginal note]

No! Viet Minh would not have wanted Chinese troops [handwritten marginal note] that the "situation at Dien Bien Phu is desperate. . . . Only alternatives . . . are [a] massive B–29 bombing . . . or [a] request for cease fire. . . ." Dulles reported that he told Bidault that the use of B–29s, which the French had suggested, "seemed . . . out of the question under existing circumstances" but that he would inform Washington of Bidault's request. "Bidault," said Dulles, "gives the impression of a man close to the breaking point." Later the same evening Dulles cabled that, "The situation here is tragic. . . . There is, of course, no military or logical reason why loss of Dien Bien Phu should lead to collapse of French will, in relation both to Indochina and EDC.*. . . Dien Bien Phu has become a symbol out of all proportion to its military importance." [43] Eisenhower recounts that he immediately telephoned Bedell Smith (then Under-Secretary of State) about the French request for direct intervention and "agreed that Foster's position should stand unchanged. There would be no intervention without allies." [44]

Dulles saw Eden in Paris that weekend and reported to him that the United States would not intervene with American forces in Indochina without British agreement to participate. Eden flew back to London on April 25 to report to Churchill, who decided that no unified action could be taken until every effort had been made to resolve the Indochina situation through negotiation.

"Thus," said President Eisenhower, "the Geneva Conference could not have begun or been conducted under worse conditions." [45]

* European Defense Community.

IV

Blueprint for a House of Cards:
Geneva, 1954

Like Shakespeare's whining schoolboy, the American delegation "crept like a snail unwillingly" to Geneva. Eisenhower and Dulles had been fighting a rear guard action against the conference for months, hoping that somehow the whole unpleasant affair would go away. But when the bell sounded the Americans knew they had to be there if only to participate in the Korean phase of the conference. This may well have been the first time since V–J Day that Washington felt it had completely lost the diplomatic initiative.

John Foster Dulles was hardly an ebullient personality even under the most salubrious circumstances. His arrival in Geneva on that gray April day lent little joy to the cheerless Hotel du Rhone or to the oppressive mood of the senior members of the American delegation. Before leaving Washington, Dulles had made a last brave effort to set a proper tone for the months ahead by expressing the hope that "the aggressors would come to the conference in a mood to purge themselves of their aggression." [1]

But the "aggressors" came to Geneva in anything but a supine mood. From the moment they emerged from their planes grinning and waving, it was evident that China's Chou En-lai and North Korea's General Nam Il were ready to undertake major diplomatic offensives rather than to lie prostrate before the American Secretary of State. The Viet Minh delegate, Pham Van Dong, was neither a smiler nor a waver, and his grim and caustic demeanor gave little promise that he had traveled all the way to Geneva for the purpose of purging himself.

It was my task in Geneva to provide the principal American delegates with such "back room" services as current-analyses, short-term projections, and longer-term profundities on matters relating to Asia in general and Korea and Indochina in particular. To assist me in these endeavors I was assigned a staff of two experts—a lady whose specialty was something called "Content Analysis of Communist Propaganda" and a gentleman whose metier was translation into or out of ten languages. The lady practiced her black art for a few days and then, by mutual agreement, turned to typing as a more useful contribution toward settling Asian problems. The gentleman was a man of many parts and skills. I found his knowledge of the local cafes and boites to be inexhaustible and reliable; he could lip-read Russian; he was impeccably dressed. But I discovered that he was sending his dirty shirts back to his Alexandria laundress through the diplomatic pouch. Then there were only two of us.

Even before I boarded the plane for Geneva I had been given my first chore: Was there really a Ho Chi Minh—or more precisely, was the original Ho Chi Minh still alive? This seems amusing now, but no one thought so then. Ho had not been seen for a long time; there were reports that he had died several years before; there were rumors that some vague and benign old man with a wispy beard was being used to keep alive Ho's image until the successor leadership felt more secure. If he was alive, had he once again disappeared into some dark crevice of the world?

I satisfied myself and, more importantly, my platoon of superiors that Ho was not only very much alive but very much in charge. Mission accomplished, I turned my attention from the corridors to the plenary Conference Room of the Palais des Nations. The atmosphere there was somber—even mournful. The Conference Room floor was crowded with delegates and advisers. The balconies and bleachers were packed with staff members, functionaries, and assorted experts. The Chinese delegation alone numbered close to two hundred.* The American and Russian delegations added up to more than one hundred each.

Photographs taken at the opening session show that—except for a few old-time diplomatic hams, who at the sight of a photographer automatically bared their teeth in professional smiles, and the Palais staff, who dated back to the League of Nations days and who had learned that nothing was ever as serious as it seemed —the large and handsome room was devoid of a smiling face. And for a perfectly good reason—there was nothing to smile about.

Korea was first on stage, but Indochina kept peeking out of the wings. Except for the Koreans themselves, the Geneva Conference on Korea was an anticlimax. The ceasefire had already been arranged, and there was little expectation that any substantial progress could be made on a political solution. There were, of course, the expected and dutiful exchanges of charges and counter-charges as to who had started the war, but no one really thought much more could be done. A certain amount of spice was provided by the attempts of the huge American delegation to pretend that the even huger Chinese delegation did not exist—and vice versa. Attempts to observe the mutual policy of non-recognition were not made any easier by the fact that the senior American and Chinese delegates carried a major burden of the negotiations. Moreover, many Chinese and Americans had known each other in earlier incarnations. Early in the proceedings I found myself alone in an elevator with a young Chinese I had known from my college days. He was now an "American expert" in Peking's Foreign Ministry. Neither of us spoke, but as we looked at each other we began to smile and then to laugh. By the time we arrived at the conference floor we were convulsed. As the door opened we hastily recovered our composures and studiously avoided looking at each other from that moment on.

The whole atmosphere, both inside the Palais and in Geneva itself, had a poignant, ironic flavor. Here was lovely, sunny, elegant, shining, sparkling, rich, capitalist Geneva. And here were

*It was common gossip that Peking was using the conference as a training camp for members of the expanding Chinese Communist diplomatic corps.

young Chinese and North Koreans and Viet Minh—and even Russians—who had never set foot in the West, who had experienced
years, perhaps decades of war and privation, who had been taught
that the West was decadent and sordid. But where in Geneva
were the exploited poor? Where were the horrible slums, the beg-
gars, the starving orphans? The security officers of the Communist
delegations were not unaware of the dangers of these stark and
troubling contradictions. "Outings" were arranged, evening classes
were held, "buddy systems" organized, check-ins and check-outs
insured. There was a moment when the system almost broke
down. My young daughters were playing in a park by Lake Leman
one Sunday afternoon in May when several members of the
Viet Minh delegation strolled by. They stopped to pick up the
girls' errant ball, threw it gently back, joined the children's laughter when the ball was wildly returned. For several minutes Joan,
Susan, and Ho Chi Minh's delegation were absorbed in the vital
task of generational and international communication. Then the
gentlemen recognized my wife and me sitting nearby. The game
was over; they walked away. Fresh air was at a premium even in
Switzerland.

The somber atmosphere at the Palais had a more tangible
and immediate cause than the social embarrassment that arose
from the niceties and ploys of international relations. The French
were in Geneva to admit defeat, to surrender what was once a
rich empire to people they had not very long before referred to
as *les jaunes*—and all the other delegations, friends, foes, and
neutrals alike, knew it. The Americans were there, sulking, wrig-
gling, agonizing—and all the other delegations knew that too. The
Chinese were there hoping to use Geneva as a launching platform
from which to move into the international orbit. The Russians
were there more because of their interest in Europe than their
concern about Asia. The British, having already given up most of
their empire, having their own troubles in Malaya, and anxious to
persuade the French to concentrate once more on Europe, were
interested in almost any kind of solution that could provide some
degree of stability in Indochina. The Indians were there to boost
Delhi's prestige as the leader of the unaligned world by perform-

ing a middleman and brokerage function. And the Vietnamese were there—Communist and non-Communist—to preserve as best they could their bargaining positions against each other and against erosion and ravages by Big Power Deals. Hanging over the conference was the burning, macabre question of whether the garrison at Dien Bien Phu could ward off disaster until the French could strike a deal in Geneva.

*   *   *

As the Korean discussions drew to a close on the seventh of May, an usher unobtrusively delivered a note to M. Bidault, the French Foreign Minister. Bidault turned pale as he took the note, he turned green as he read it: "DBP Fini." The French had put their blue chips on Dien Bien Phu. The loss of the garrison would be "critical," and so, although there were still large and powerful French forces fighting in Indochina, Paris knew it had lost the war.

contrast with Diem view, see fn 1

On May 9, when the Indochina discussions began, the French entered the Palais naked of bargaining power. Bidault had earlier confessed to Eden that his hand consisted of "a two of clubs and a three of diamonds." [2] Premier Laniel was operating on a day-to-day lease, and the military and political situation in Indochina was clearly beyond retrieval. Only a fortuitous set of international circumstances, plus a strange congruence of diverse and common national interests, would permit France and the non-Communist Vietnamese to emerge from Geneva with a negotiated rather than a dictated settlement. And that is what happened.

Not long after the conference on Indochina began in earnest, I warned Washington that when the procedural questions were settled (the demand by the Communists that the insurgent groups of Laos and Cambodia be represented) and the discussions had advanced to settling the future of Indochina, there would be considerable differences not only between the Communists and the Western powers but among the Western powers themselves. It was clear at this early point in the conference that the Western powers were by no means in agreement.

The beginning of the Indochina phase of the conference was

McCarthy & Nixon strike again

accompanied by growing American suspicion and anxiety. French desperation to achieve an immediate ceasefire and the British readiness to help the process would have troubled the Americans in any case. But with Congress still seeking scapegoats for the "loss of China," the Administration was obviously anxious to avoid having to justify a major Communist diplomatic victory in Southeast Asia. Added to this was the gnawing recognition that the Administration could hardly claim either a major military or political victory in Korea, especially in the light of the tremendous casualties we had suffered.

One secret effort to hedge against a diplomatic defeat at Geneva leaked a few days later and caused considerable bitterness among the French and the British, as well as apprehension among the other delegations. On May 12 the French had privately asked the U.S. what steps the Americans would take in the event that no agreement could be reached with respect to a satisfactory ceasefire arrangement.[3] The request was obviously motivated by French recognition that their bargaining power to achieve an immediate ceasefire—without accompanying time-consuming and costly political arrangements—was practically nil. The American/French conversations were reported in the *New York Herald Tribune* and the *Christian Science Monitor* on May 15th, much to Eden's annoyance and Laniel's chagrin. After the press leak a representative of Laniel's government made public a statement indicating that the Americans would be ready to intervene in Indochina if the conference broke down or if the French requested such intervention beforehand.[4]

Experienced observers might have been able to detect some prior warning of the Administration's concern about the possible outcome of the conference from a speech Secretary Dulles made in Washington on May 7. After taking some pains to remind the world that American participation in the conference in no way implied recognition of Communist China, Dulles discussed at some length the problem of Southeast Asia. Four separate references were made to the grave consequences that would follow Communist control of the area. He emphasized the need for "united action" among all interested countries of the Free World to ensure the continued freedom of the threatened nations in the area. The speech concluded with a veiled warning to the negotiators in Geneva: "The present conditions [in Indochina] do not provide a suitable basis for the U.S. to participate with its armed forces . . . but we would be gravely concerned if an armistice or ceasefire were reached at Geneva that would provide a road to a Communist takeover and further aggression." [5]

Just a few days later at a press conference (May 11), Dulles seemed resigned to an unfavorable resolution of the Indochina conflict. "It's true," he said in answer to a question, "that at Geneva we have so far not achieved the unification of Korea, nor does it seem likely that we will achieve the unification of Indochina under the conditions of freedom and peace. We never thought that there was a good chance of accomplishing those results." [6]

On May 14 Molotov broke with an important line of argument that had been advanced by the Viet Minh on May 10th and which the Chinese Communists had supported on May 12th. The issue was a critical one, since it involved the composition of the group that would supervise the ceasefire. Pham Van Dong, with a shrill assist from Chou En-lai, had demanded that the supervisory commission be made up of representatives of the two belligerents —the French and the Viet Minh. Molotov's proposal that the commission be made up of representatives of "neutral countries" went a long way to meet the insistence of General Bedell Smith, who now headed the American delegation, that the supervisory group have an international composition. This was a significant concession, and it probably was advanced only after some acrimonious discussions among the Russian, Chinese, and Viet Minh delegations.

It is hard to explain Molotov's partial abandonment of the Viet Minh on this issue. Perhaps after Dulles' speech of May 7 he felt uncertain and uneasy about Washington's intentions, concerned that the U.S. might do something desperate in Indochina unless visible progress could be made at Geneva.

The meeting of the 14th was the last plenary session for three weeks. The forum of the discussions shifted to a series of more than twenty restricted sessions that were to continue off and on throughout the remainder of the Conference.

On the day before the restricted sessions began, General Smith met privately with Emperor Bao Dai in a small resort town across the French border. The Emperor stressed his opposition to any partition arrangement, and Smith was clearly impressed with Bao Dai's arguments. At about the same time he received new instructions from Washington which gave him considerable latitude to withdraw from the Conference or to limit the American role to that of an observer if, in his judgment, the negotiations were leading to a diplomatic defeat for the West. The meeting with Bao Dai and the new instructions from Washington combined to produce a hard, even rigid, American approach throughout the remainder of the Conference. Indeed the restricted sessions had hardly gotten under way when Smith, apparently worried that secret agreements would be reached that the Administration would find hard to explain to Congress or the American people generally, asked the British and French to terminate the restricted sessions and resume the open plenary meetings. Eden and Bidault were convinced that only through restricted meetings could progress be made, and they greeted Smith's request with consternation. Bidault based his case for continued restricted sessions on the grounds that his government would fall if the American request were put before the Conference. Smith yielded, and there were twelve restricted meetings before the next plenary session was held on the 4th of June.

When the delegates met for their first private session on May 17, there were two basic issues to be resolved. The first was the question of whether Laos and Cambodia should be considered separately from or together with Vietnam. For the non-Communist countries, and especially for Laos and Cambodia, this was a critical issue. The Communists wanted a blanket settlement for Indochina as a whole, hoping thereby to exploit the military situation in Vietnam in order to exact political concessions, not only in Vietnam, but in Laos and Cambodia as well. Indeed virtually all of the discussion in the first three restricted sessions was devoted to procedural questions with respect to Laos and Cambodia. Despite Eden's private efforts to break the impasse, this issue was to remain in deadlock for many more days.

The second major issue was whether a ceasefire should precede discussion of the political elements of a settlement, or whether military and political problems should be dealt with in a single package. The Viet Minh had maintained the military initiative, and the Communists felt that by postponing a ceasefire they could improve their bargaining position on the political issues. In any event, Molotov, and then Pham Van Dong, agreed fairly quickly that a ceasefire should be worked out as soon as possible, although the modalities for the ceasefire arrangements took many meetings to resolve.

An interesting, perhaps crucial by-product of the first restricted session was the agreement reached by the French and the Viet Minh to establish a working group to arrange for the evacuation of wounded from Dien Bien Phu. Colonel de Brebisson and Colonel Ha Van Lau were to work out the plan. These two men subsequently dealt with the details of the ceasefire, and they probably contributed more to the final work of the Conference than all the senior delegates and their entourages. We shall meet Colonel Lau again in Paris at yet another conference in 1968.

After many days of haggling on the Cambodia and Laos issue, Pham Van Dong finally agreed on May 24 that the Conference could begin with the question of ceasefire arrangements for Vietnam. Then the delegates would talk about Cambodia and Laos. On the 29th Eden succeeded in gaining unanimous agreement to the following proposal for getting the technical military talks started:

In order to facilitate the early and simultaneous cessation of hostilities it is proposed that:

(a) Representatives of the two commands should meet immediately in Geneva and contacts should also be established on the spot.

(b) They should study the dispositions of forces to be made upon the cessation of hostilities, beginning with the question of regrouping areas in Vietnam.

(c) They should report their findings and recommendations to the Conference as soon as possible.[7]

Despite general agreement on this procedure, it quickly became evident that there were many major hurdles to be crossed before the Conference could agree on the political aspects of the ceasefire: Pham Van Dong acknowledged that the first problem was to stop the fighting, and he supported the British proposal for immediate direct contacts between the two military commanders to arrange the ceasefire; but the fundamental problem was that of Vietnamese independence and unity. Any arrangement for withdrawal zones in connection with a ceasefire should be regarded as provisional only. "Independence and unity," he said, "could be attained through general elections."

There were others who were even more disturbed than Pham Van Dong at the implications of "withdrawal zones." The representatives from Laos and Cambodia were concerned that the sudden evidence of unanimity with respect to Eden's proposal would carry them along in dangerous directions leading to partition of their own countries. They hastily stressed that Eden's proposal and Pham Van Dong's remarks with respect to military regrouping should apply only to Vietnam. Bao Dai's representative, with considerable prescience, argued that withdrawal zones would inevitably lead to the partition of Vietnam and this his government could not accept. The Americans too were disturbed. Smith reiterated the U.S. position that foreign forces (i.e., the Viet Minh) should be withdrawn from Cambodia and Laos rather than "regroup" within those countries. He warned the conferees that the United States would reserve the right to judge whether the recommendations of the military experts prejudiced the American position with respect to the political independence of Vietnam, Laos, and Cambodia. In short, while the American delegation was not opposed to the British proposal, Smith did not want to imply that it accepted it.

Smith may have been responding to an overnight, private message from Washington (he gave no inkling to the delegation of having received one), or he may have been acting on the instruc-

tions he had received two weeks before. In any case, Smith had
decided to "preserve his options" and not get too deeply committed in advance to the outcome of discussions in which the
Americans would have no participant. He therefore adopted a
holding action.

Apparently Eden had no advance warning of General Smith's
new line. He referred to it as a "very far-reaching American reser-
vation. It surprised me, since there had been no hint of it last
night." This was not the end of Eden's problems with Smith that
afternoon, for "right at the end Bedell Smith suddenly said he
wanted to make his reservations public." [8] Eden decided not
to release his own proposal to the press so that Smith would not
feel required to publicize his reservations.

To put the final touch on what must have been a very difficult
day, late on the evening of the 29th Eden received a phone call
from Paris indicating that the French and Americans had agreed
on "some plan apparently for intervention in Indochina." Eden
interpreted Smith's view as a sign that "Washington must . . . be
losing patience with our negotiations. . . . the Americans seem
deeply apprehensive of reaching any agreement, however innocu-
ous, with the Communists. Their delegation had recently been
expressing concern about the contacts which they believed to be
taking place between the French and Viet Minh delegations, and
seemed to fear that they would make a deal of their own. . . .
There were signs, too, that the bogey of intervention was once
again with us. Sir Gladwyn Jebb [British Ambassador to France]
reported from Paris on May 31 that the United States had practically reached agreement with France on the conditions for intervention, should the Conference fail. Bidault confirmed to me
on the same day that, if no agreement were to be reached at
Geneva, American help was contemplated to the extent of three
divisions." [9]

Although Eden and Smith were old friends and both
were polished professionals, it was impossible to keep the American–British difficulties from being public knowledge. Despite
Eden's plea, the unenthusiastic American reception of Eden's
proposal of May 29 had been leaked to the press. The British, for

their part, were unable to hide their exasperation and frustration with the Americans. Thus on the first of June *The New York Times* reported: "Advance predictions that the Far East Conference would impose terrific strains on British–United States relations have been borne out." According to the *Times,* members of the British delegation were shocked at Smith's reservations to Eden's proposal. The British felt, the *Times* said, that "the entire episode reflects a split within the U.S. delegation or else between the delegation and the State Department. The British make the pointed comment that they want a settlement without a war and ask what the U.S. wants."

In accordance with Eden's proposal, a military commission was organized and met for the first time on the first of June. Colonels de Brebisson and Lau worked out the key understandings with respect to the withdrawal zones, which in turn became the basis for the partition of Vietnam.

With the military subcommittee working on problems of regroupment, the next issue to be confronted was the matter of supervision of the ceasefire. For two weeks the delegates wrestled with the question of the composition of the supervisory commission. The roots of the difficulty went deeper than the discussions at Geneva or the situation in Indochina—they extended to the very core of the Cold War. Both sides professed that the commission should be "neutral." The problem arose in reaching an agreement between the Russians and the Americans as to just what "neutrality" meant and which countries or combinations of countries would meet the requirements of "neutrality."

Smith laid down three conditions for effective supervision: the countries represented must be truly neutral; the system cannot depend only on the good faith of the opposing parties; and the members of the commission must have unrestricted geographic access. Smith made it quite clear that the U.S. did not consider Communist countries as "neutral" and indeed was suspicious of the international alignment of those non-Communist countries that might fit the Soviet definition of "neutral." During this period I worked my way through mountains of newspaper and radio material looking for Communist definitions of neutrality. Eventually

I found one, in the official Hungarian press: a neutral nation was one which, though not Communist, agreed with the Communist position on all important points.

As an example of the sort of "neutral commission" the Russians had in mind, the Soviet spokesman proposed that it be comprised of India, Poland, Czechoslovakia, and Pakistan. He took sharp issue with Smith that Communist countries could not be considered neutrals. It was no coincidence that Smith's ulcers began to act up shortly afterward.

In an effort to bridge the gap, Eden advanced the general proposition that any control group, regardless of its composition, would have to be responsible to a broader international body if it were to be effective; it could not have a life of its own. In Eden's view the United Nations should designate the control group, and then have ultimate responsibility for it. But the UN format was obviously not acceptable, since neither the Viet Minh nor the Chinese Communists were members.

Molotov summarized his position by supporting Eden's contention that any supervisory group should operate under the general aegis of a more formal international body. He took pains to deny any differences between himself and Pham Van Dong on the question of the supervisory commission. (Dong had earlier argued for a commission made up of belligerents.) Molotov then proposed two supervisory bodies: one would be made up of the belligerents, and the other would be composed of neutral countries organized along the lines of the Korean Neutral Nations Supervisory Commission. While neither one would be subordinate to the other, the Neutral Nations Supervisory Commission would be the more important. Molotov's proposal was so obscure and complicated that it left most of the delegates gasping. In the end the delegates settled for Eden's basic concept (out of which emerged the amorphous arrangement whereby the British and Russian co-chairmen provided a rather leaky umbrella of international authority and responsibility for the work of the supervisory group).

Eden's troubles were to multiply during the first half of June. The Conference was not only running into difficulty on the question of neutrality, but it had to face up to the fact that no progress whatsoever had been made on procedures for dealing with Laos and Cambodia. Eden was in despair. He felt that the Conference was close to breaking down. "French reluctance, American apprehension, Chinese suspicion and maybe ambition, were combining to bring the Conference to a standstill." [10] The tactics of the American delegation were now reflecting new instructions from Washington. Stimulated in part by the fall of the Laniel Government on June 12, Eisenhower and Dulles were becoming increasingly impatient. "We decided," Eisenhower later recalled, "that it was best for the United States to break off major participation in the Geneva Conference. The days of keeping the Western powers bound to inaction by creating divisions of policy among them in a dragged-out conference were coming to an end." [11]

But like the silent movie heroine Pauline, the Conference was rescued from the brink of disaster. Two last minute concessions from the Communists did the trick. On the 15th Molotov told Eden that he was prepared to soften his stand on both the Laos–Cambodia and the control group issues. On the 16th he noted that, while the Soviet Union did not subscribe to the view that the situations in Laos and Cambodia were different from that of Vietnam, they were sufficiently unique to warrant special treatment. He repeated his formula for a supervisory commission that would include Poland and Czechoslovakia, but he went on to propose the possibility of a commission made up of three countries—India, Poland, and Indonesia or some other Asian country.

Chou En-lai saw Eden privately on the morning of the 16th and said he was ready to make several concessions to the Western point of view. And indeed he did. Later that day, in his most moderate speech of the Conference, Chou acknowledged that the situations in Laos, Cambodia, and Vietnam were not completely alike, and the Conference should recognize the special problems in Laos and Cambodia. He proposed that representatives of the military commands meet and discuss a ceasefire in Laos and Cambodia, as they were now doing for Vietnam. He recognized that Cambodia and Laos should be given the means for defending themselves and, further, that foreign troops would have to be withdrawn from those countries under international supervision.

Pham Van Dong, obviously aware in advance of Soviet and Chinese plans to present a more moderate face to the Conference, proposed direct negotiations between representatives of the two commands of Laos and Cambodia. Reversing his earlier position, he acknowledged that the situations in those two countries were different from that of Vietnam and therefore the solution would have to be different.

Bedell Smith could hardly contain his surprise and satisfaction. He told his fellow delegates that the Chinese spokesman's remarks were moderate and wise and that he was prepared to give the Chinese proposal serious consideration. In retrospect the Communist concessions of mid-June do not appear substantial, but they were extremely well-timed; Chou, by breaking the deadlock on the issue of Laos and Cambodia, probably saved the Conference from collapse. But the optimism that had been generated was dispelled by the tough line taken at the next session by Assistant Secretary Walter Robertson, sitting in for Bedell Smith who was ill with an ulcer attack. Reversing the tone, and perhaps even the content, of Smith's remarks of a day or two before, Robertson told the Conference that the U.S. was unable to accept Chou En-lai's proposal on the grounds that it was imprecise.

This latest American intervention once again clouded the prospects for agreement. Robertson had confirmed the general suspicion that the Americans were anxious to see the Conference remain stalled—or even to fail. Eden described Robertson's remarks as "a violent and wholly unexpected attack on the Chinese proposals. . . . This did not fit in with anything the Americans had told me, nor with Bedell Smith's description of the Chinese offer at an earlier session." [12] Even the delegates from Laos and Cambodia, who had thus far been sympathetic with the American position, stated their readiness to accept Chou's proposal as a basis for armistice talks. The delegates agreed to pause and regroup.

❀   ❀   ❀

The events in Geneva during the critical days of mid-June were closely related to developments then taking place in Paris. Perhaps the Communists realized they had played out their hands on the Laos–Cambodia issue and on the composition of the international supervisory commission, but the timing of their concessions must have been influenced, in part at least, by the change of government in France.

Shortly before the Laniel Government fell on June 12, Pierre Mendes-France had urged direct negotiations with Ho Chi Minh and had opposed American military intervention in Vietnam. In a session of the National Assembly on June 10, he called for a complete change in the government's policy "to make it sure that France's aim is not the intervention of the United States, but an honorable end of the terrible conflict which has lasted for eight years. . . . France should play for a straightforward peace with the Vietminh." [13] A week after he took over the Government, Mendes-France announced his deadline for a settlement—if agreement were not reached within 30 days (that is, by July 21, he threatened to resign.* Although this was a colossal bit of theatrics, it turned out to be effective. For different reasons most of the key delegations at Geneva—Communist and non-Communist alike—did not want to take their chances on whoever would succeed Mendes-France.

Molotov, especially, had high hopes for a French Government under Mendes-France—hopes that went beyond a settlement of the Indochina war. The Russians had been trying desperately to forestall the organization of a European Defense Community (EDC) that would include West German troops, and French participation in such a Community was a critical element in the American or British decision to move ahead. London and Washington had been putting considerable pressure on the Laniel Government to obtain French agreement. Laniel had been stalling for many months, because he did not feel he had the necessary support in the Assembly, although he continued to hold out the prospect of ultimate French approval. The Soviet leaders may well have calculated that under the new left-of-center government the

---

* The progress and understandings reached in the Brebisson–Lau conversations may have given Mendes-France sufficient encouragement to gamble his government's future on his ability to force the Conference to a successful conclusion within thirty days after his investiture.

EDC could finally be killed off, and that it would be wise to demonstrate to the French Assembly that Mendes-France could get a satisfactory settlement in Geneva. There has been speculation that a deal was actually made between Mendes-France and Molotov to trade off the EDC for a favorable settlement in Indochina.

Another factor that may have influenced the nature and timing of the Communist tactics was the continuing uncertainty about American policy. There was ample evidence in June that Washington was regarding with considerable satisfaction the prospect of the imminent collapse of the Geneva talks and was preparing another strong political offensive to enlist its allies in a program of "united action" against the Communists of Southeast Asia. American, French, British, Australian, and New Zealand military staff officers were already discussing this contingency.

*   *   *

Much of the work was now being done by the military subcommittees, and the senior delegates left Geneva on June 20th for consultations with their governments. The military reports were to be completed within three weeks, and the delegates indicated that if those reports warranted discussion they would all be prepared to return to Geneva. Although the Conference continued at a lower level of representation and at half-speed, important discussions were going on between the military representatives of France and Laos and Cambodia, on the one hand, and France and the Viet Minh on the other. It was here that the specific withdrawal zones were being determined.

The three-week hiatus of the Conference was marked by intense diplomatic activity in several key capitals. Eden stopped off in Paris on his return to London. Mendes-France told Eden that, in view of the American and Vietnamese attitudes, he was not optimistic about the possibility of meeting his commitment to achieve a settlement by July 21st. Eden then urged Mendes-France to have an early meeting with Chou En-lai and with Pham Van Dong. Mendes-France agreed to do this, although in a press conference a day or two later he denied that he would be seeing Dong.[14]

Mendes-France did, in fact, meet with Chou En-lai on the 23rd in Bern. Chou reaffirmed his readiness to see Laos and Cambodia treated separately, and he informed the new French Premier of Communist China's intention to recognize the two royal governments. While Chou insisted that regrouping zones for the Pathet Lao should be arranged, he said that "Viet Minh forces which had penetrated Laotian territory would be able to be withdrawn after the armistice." [15] Mendes-France was told that the Chinese did favor large regrouping zones in Vietnam. It was agreed that bilateral talks between the French and the Viet Minh would be the best way to make progress in the negotiations.

On his return to London, and shortly before he and Churchill were to depart for Washington, Eden made a speech to the House of Commons that was to plague him and to exacerbate the already strained relations between the Americans and the British. He said he hoped it would be possible to work out for Southeast Asia some "reciprocal arrangement in which both sides take part, such as Locarno." [16] (The Locarno Pact was essentially a series of agreements whereby the European powers undertook to guarantee mutually the peace in Western Europe following World War I.) In addition, obviously in anticipation of his talks in Washington, he hoped there would be some sort of NATO-type arrangement for Asia. While the two systems would operate separately, he thought they need not be inconsistent. The reference to "Locarno" produced an immediate and unfavorable reaction in the U.S. Since the original Locarno conference had worked out arrangements by which Germany could enter the League of Nations after World War I, the conclusion was immediately drawn that Eden was floating a somewhat similar scheme to bring China into the UN. [17]

Dulles had announced the Churchill–Eden visit on June 15, shortly before the important Communist concessions in Geneva. His frustrations with the Conference were evident: "it looks now as though the Geneva Conference either will be terminated or recessed or perhaps reduced to a lower level of negotiation." [18]

It was hoped the American–British "Summit" meeting would clear up the serious misunderstandings and eliminate the friction that had developed over the past several months in connection with Southeast Asia. But Eden's House of Commons speech produced the worst possible mood music for the trip. Eden and Churchill must have been under no illusions as to the effect of Eden's remarks on American opinion. Influential members of both the House of Representatives and the Senate proclaimed that Eden was challenging American policy in the Far East.

Obviously the mere reference to Locarno could not in itself have created such a stir. To an America that had hardly recovered from the bloody and costly war in Korea, Eden seemed much too ready to yield to Communist demands in Asia. The "China Lobby," for which Senator William Knowland and Congressman Walter Judd were ardent spokesmen, was at the height of its influence.* Over and above this, Senator Joseph McCarthy was tearing the country apart in his quest for the heads of those ho thought were "soft" on Communism. Eden's untiring and conspicuous efforts at Geneva to achieve a settlement that, in the light of France's desperate military position, would necessarily involve Western concessions were regarded by many Americans as appeasement. The events in Geneva in mid-June had aroused concern in many quarters, probably including the White House and Department of State, that some agreement with the Communists might actually emerge. American policymakers were torn between the fear that the United States would have to intervene militarily in Indochina to help the French continue the war, and the hope that the Conference would collapse so that the war could continue and the Viet Minh be defeated.

Despite the unpleasant offstage noises that accompanied the American–British talks, Eden put a good face on his visit to Washington. His first talk with Dulles was "encouraging." He noted that his reference to a "Locarno" for Southeast Asia had "raised a storm of outraged protest in the United States. . . . I had to persuade the Americans that Locarno was not a dirty word.

* The "China Lobby" was a group of conservative and influential Congressmen and businessmen, primarily Republicans, who maintained strong pressures during the early 1950s for the support of Chiang Kai-shek and the containment of Communist China.

After our talks I was satisfied that the American Administration not only understood what it meant but seemed to like the idea." According to Eden, Dulles "accepted that nothing short of intervention with ground forces could restore the situation in Indo-China, and also seemed ready to countenance the partition of Vietnam...." [19]

Eden and Dulles worked out for transmittal to Mendes-France the minimum terms the Americans and British were prepared to accept as the negotiations went into the final stages. An armistice agreement would have to preserve the integrity of Laos and Cambodia and assure the withdrawal of Viet Minh forces; preserve the southern half of Vietnam; permit Laos, Cambodia, and the non-Communist part of Vietnam to maintain non-Communist governments and adequate forces for internal security; include the possibility of ultimate peaceful reunification of Vietnam; permit the transfer of persons from zone to zone in Vietnam; and provide for effective international supervision.

Despite the optimistic tone of Eden's account, the Eden–Churchill visit did little to dispel American doubts about the wisdom of continued participation in the Geneva Conference. In part this attitude was a reflection of the mood of Congress. Thus at the end of June twelve members of the House Foreign Affairs Committee told Eisenhower that Eden's proposal for a non-aggression treaty with Asian Communists was equivalent to a guarantee of Communist expansion in Asia. The Congressmen warned Eisenhower that, unless they were assured Eden's proposal would be repudiated by the Administration, Congress would have to re-examine the whole concept of mutual security. Furthermore, the House of Representatives passed an amendment to the Mutual Security Act to the effect that "no part of the funds appropriated . . . shall be used on behalf of governments which are committed by treaty to maintain Communist rule over any defined territory of Asia." [20]

*   *   *

The Administration decided not to send a senior delegate to Geneva when the Conference resumed on July 12th. The prospect of not having a senior American representative during the closing phase of the Conference troubled both Eden and Mendes-France. They felt that unless the Americans were present it would be difficult to get a meaningful and satisfactory settlement, and if the armistice were to be stable and long-lasting, the United States would have to participate in its guarantees.

The French Ambassador called on Secretary Dulles in an effort to persuade him or Under-Secretary Smith to return to Geneva. Dulles stood fast, however, stating that neither he nor Smith would return to Geneva unless there was "some evidence of Communist goodwill." In desperation, Mendes-France asked Dulles to come to Paris for discussions with him and Eden. Dulles left for Paris forthwith, but before leaving he cautioned that his trip was "without prejudice to the previously expressed position that neither I nor Under-Secretary Smith have at the present time any plans for going to Geneva." [21]

Mendes-France was able to convince Dulles that he would strive to meet the minimum conditions Eden and Dulles had set a fortnight before in Washington. On his return to Washington, Dulles stressed that the talks in Paris "brought about an understanding about Indochina much more complete than has heretofore existed. . . . We have found a formula of constructive allied unity which will have a beneficial effect upon the Geneva Conference. And it carries no danger that the United States will abandon its principles." [22] Dulles then announced that General Smith would return to Geneva to participate in the final stages of the Conference.

The hiatus between June 20 and July 12 that produced some anxious moments for several world statesmen, also provided me with some cliff-hanging experiences. With Smith back in Washington and the Conference in low gear, I decided to drive to Salzburg for a short holiday. I left my itinerary with the delegation in Geneva and my principals in Washington. As I was driving over the Alps, however, I got caught in a blinding snowstorm and had to slither my way down the first valley I could find. The only accommodations available were in a small "Alkohol-Frei" pension. The mountain passes were closed for several days, and I, in my lightweight slacks and sport shirt, had a dreary, cold, and abstemious several days. When the telephone service finally was restored, I called Geneva and discovered that calls had been placed along my expected route in order to summon me back. Fortunately I had some photographs of both the snow and my accommodations to verify a story that would otherwise have been treated with skepticism.

❋   ❋   ❋

When the delegates once more took their seats it was abundantly clear that, in spite of the long and dreary days of speechmaking and private negotiations that had taken place through the spring and early summer, the Conference was not even close to agreement on major issues, nor would it even have a draft document to address. Most of the work had yet to be done. And the clock was ticking away toward Mendes-France's deadline on July 21. Much of the actual negotiation during the final moments was conducted personally and privately among the chief delegates; it will probably never be possible to reconstruct the understandings, implicit or explicit, that were reached in these tête-à-têtes. Formal meetings were virtually dispensed with—except for one restricted session on the 18th of July and the final plenary meeting on the 21st.

The week of July 10 was marked by a frenetic series of meetings between the French and the Communist Delegations. Although the French and Viet Minh military staff talks had worked out the concept of withdrawal zones, the decision on the precise location of the demarcation line had been left to the senior delegates. This was now the basic issue to be resolved as Mendes-France scurried from one secret meeting to another. The French demanded that the line be drawn at the 18th parallel; the Viet Minh insisted on the 13th. Pham Van Dong was apparently under considerable pressure from both Chou and Molotov since as the days went by he successively relaxed his demands; on July 13 he told Mendes-France that he would accept a line at the 16th parallel. The French remained adamant on their original demand, and it was not until July 20 that Molotov, standing over a map of Indo-

"Illegit" governments

china with Eden, Chou, Dong, and Mendes-France, suggested that all agree on the 17th parallel.[23] And that was how "North Vietnam" and "South Vietnam" were born.

Virtually throughout this period General Bedell Smith, though in Geneva, remained aloof from the actual discussions. During the final days of the Conference he either had, or only said he had, an acute attack of ulcers and confined himself to his hotel suite. The American Delegation was insulated and isolated from what was going on, except for what crumbs of information we could pick up from better-informed friends and colleagues in other delegations. Smith himself was in close touch with developments, primarily through phone conversations with Eden. But the General was in an even more forbidding mood than usual during this period, and it was a courageous man who attempted to mix a solicitous call at Smith's bedside with a quest for information.

The most dramatic moments of a conference that had more than its share of drama came, appropriately enough, in its closing hours. July 21 was Mendes-France's deadline. Some of the principals may have been skeptical that the French Premier would follow through on his threat to resign if no agreement had by then been reached. But all the delegations were ready, each for its own reason, to make one heroic, Wagnerian effort to reach the finish line before midnight July 20th. Agreement had already been reached on Vietnam—although Bao Dai's delegation had indicated that it would disassociate itself from the accords. Arrangements for Laos had also been agreed upon. By the evening all that remained was to obtain the approval of the Cambodian Delegation for its part of the agreement.

The Cambodian Delegation was unimpressed by Mendes-France's personal problems or by vague, pontifical references to "international considerations." It held out stubbornly for every one of its demands. A French friend later recounted how in the small hours of July 21 the French and the Russians were trying to clear up the last of the Cambodian problems. The clock in the room had been symbolically set back, but there was no denying that dawn was beginning to break. Molotov, who apparently found himself admiring the Cambodian's determination and courage, was being extremely patient. With the hours slipping by, the Cambodians moved from sentence to sentence of their armistice agreement. "Is that all?" Molotov would ask the Cambodians as they successfully argued their way through a paragraph. "Yes," said the Cambodians, and all present gave a sigh of relief. "But," said the Cambodians, "we have several more points in the following paragraph." These too were eventually disposed of. "Now is that all?" said Molotov. "Yes," said the Cambodians—a general sigh of relief—"but we have several more points in the following paragraph."

On the afternoon of July 21 champagne corks popped in the Delegates Lounge of the Palais des Nations. The deadline had been met; the world had weathered another crisis. But few of the delegates or their phalanxes of assistants were in a festive mood. Indeed, except for the fact that the shooting in Vietnam had stopped, there was little reason to be cheerful. The final declaration promised to accomplish little more than give international blessing to the independence of Laos and Cambodia and establish two political entities in Vietnam. It was not signed by any of the delegations, and it was opposed by the two most directly affected—the non-Communist and Communist Vietnamese representatives. And to cast yet a deeper pall over the occasion, the United States, in a unilateral statement, disassociated itself from the declaration, although it promised to abide by it in substance. The portents were not as good as the champagne.

❖   ❖   ❖

The Viet Minh delegates must have left Geneva bitter and disappointed. They had been pressing for a partition line well south of the 17th parallel and, in any case, certainly hoped to have the ancient capital of Hue included in their zone; this was denied them. They wanted a commitment of early elections throughout Vietnam, confident that they would soon be able to gain control over the whole country; the agreement called for a period of two years before elections (and in fact these elections were never held). They hoped to secure for the Pathet Lao an autonomous sovereign area in northern Laos; Mendes-France, in his private talk with Chou En-lai, had disposed of that.

One can sympathize with the grim Bidault, the hard-pressed Mendes-France, the patient Eden, and the confused Molotov as they tried to divine American tactics and strategy with respect to the negotiations in Geneva and the fighting in Indochina.

For Eden, especially, the Geneva Conference was obviously a tremendous strain. "I was continually producing proposals, because if I did not we stuck fast. On the other hand, we were constantly being criticized for doing so, particularly in the American press. . . . I had been compelled to adopt the role of intermediary between the Western powers and the Communists. My activities in this respect were open to every kind of misrepresentation. I was concerned about their effect on Anglo–American relations. . . . I had never known a conference of this kind. The parties would not make direct contact and we were in constant danger of one or another backing out of the door." [21]

On the day following the agreement President Eisenhower took a pessimistic view, but he expressed the hope that the results of Geneva would "lead to the establishment of peace consistent with the rights and the needs of the countries concerned." Bedell Smith, on his return to Washington, took issue with those members of Congress who were denouncing the agreement as an appeasement of the Communists. He acknowledged that the Geneva Accords had some aspects which were unsatisfactory, but he was "nevertheless convinced that the results were the best that we could possibly have obtained in the circumstances. . . . I would like to point out too that when we analyze and discuss the results of Geneva that diplomacy has rarely been able to gain at the conference table what cannot be held on the battlefield." [25]

In commenting on the American role at Geneva, William Bundy, Assistant Secretary of State, noted that, "We played a critical backstage role . . . keeping alive the possibility of U.S. military intervention. Many observers at the time believed this played a crucial part in inducing the Soviets, Communist Chinese and Hanoi to settle for a temporary division of Viet Nam and an independent Cambodia and Laos." [26] Mr. Bundy gives the Eisen-

hower Administration too much credit for conscious policy planning. A more likely explanation for the American position was
that the Administration itself was in a state of confusion as it tried
to maneuver between many diplomatic shoals and obstructions:
an unpromising military situation in Indochina and a weak diplomatic situation in Geneva; powerful Congressional pressures for
armed action against the Communists, and the felt need for the
containment of Communist China; the desire to preserve the
Laniel Government, compounded by deep anxiety with respect to
French intentions toward the European Defense Community.

Perhaps the most unclear aspect of the whole Conference was
that involving the partitioning of Vietnam at the 17th parallel.
The decision, as we have seen, evolved from the arrangements
agreed upon by relatively junior French and Viet Minh officers to
facilitate the separation of the two military forces. The American
and both Vietnamese delegations had a prescience that the "withdrawal zones" would take on much greater significance as political
zones, but the pressures to reach an agreement were such that
their reservations were ignored or swept away. If the other major
powers at the Conference, the British, French, Soviet, and Chinese Communists, thought very much about the ultimate implications of splitting Vietnam at the 17th parallel, they probably
chalked up Vietnam, with Korea and Germany, as another "divided country" which, sooner or later (probably much later)
would somehow be reunified.

The concept of partition was not, of course, launched as a full-
blown surprise before an innocent American delegation. Discussion of partition possibilities had taken place in Washington even
before the Conference had started. On the eve of Secretary Dulles'
departure for Geneva, for example, Senator John F. Kennedy
made a major speech on the Senate floor in which he noted that
the American delegation would be likely to confront "two basic
alternatives." One was to persuade the French to continue the
war. This would require vast American military and economic
assistance, which Kennedy felt would be "dangerously futile and
self destructive." The other "is a negotiated peace, based either
upon partition of the area . . . possibly along the 16th parallel; or

based upon a coalition government in which Ho Chi Minh is represented." Either partition or coalition, Kennedy felt, would eventually result in "domination by the Communists." Neither alternative, Kennedy reminded the already downcast Secretary of State,
was attractive.

What finally emerged from Geneva was indeed not very attractive. The "Agreements" were a hasty, slap-dash potpourri containing a few lofty principles. They had a predictably short life
expectancy, if only because the three players, the governments of
Hanoi, Saigon, and Washington, made an early decision that the
game was not worth the candle. Such pious platitudes as "observing the principles of Geneva" are good political slogans but bad
policy. If there is to be a lasting political solution for Vietnam,
clearly the Geneva Agreements, while still containing some useful
provisions, will have to be carefully examined in the light of the
experience in Indochina during the years since 1954.

V

Forging a Double-edged Sword:
Manila, 1954

Little time was wasted between the final ceremonies at Geneva and preparations for the conference that would attempt to resuscitate Dulles' idea of "united action." The delegates had not yet packed their bags when President Eisenhower put the world on notice that "The United States is actively pursuing discussions with other free nations with a view to the rapid organization of a collective defense in Southeast Asia in order to prevent further direct or indirect Communist aggression in that general area." [1] A few days later, Walter Robertson, the Assistant Secretary of State for Far Eastern Affairs, in a speech to the American Legion, was characteristically blunt about the Geneva Accords and the urgency for a Southeast Asia defense organization. "It would be an understatement to say that we do not like the terms of the ceasefire agreement just concluded. . . . What is of the first importance now is to prevent further Communist expansion—first by arousing Asia's unwitting masses to an awareness of the ruthless enslavement which threatens them, and second by the rapid organization of a collective defense pact in Southeast Asia." [2]

I had barely returned to Washington when I was told to leave immediately for Manila and departed in such a hurry that I was forced to spend many days in the damp tropical climate encased

Domino beginning?

in the cellophane-like, primitive wash-and-wear clothing I had been wearing in Geneva.

The Defense Treaty and the Southeast Asia Treaty Organization (SEATO) that emerged from the Manila Conference were the tangible result of Secretary Dulles' long-sought goal of collective security for Asia. This had been an elusive objective for Dulles even before he became Secretary of State. In a trip during the winter of 1951 Dulles, serving as the head of a mission to Tokyo for talks with the Japanese on the proposed treaty of peace, explored the possibilities of banding Asian countries together for a common defense against Chinese Communist expansion. "That effort failed," he said, "at that time in the sense that we were not able to put together a collective security arrangement of any large proportions, and we ended with a series of separate pacts—one with Japan, one with Australia and New Zealand (ANZUS), and another with the Philippines." [3] Writing in 1952 Dulles dwelt on the difficulties of enlarging the Asian grouping to go beyond the ANZUS, Japanese, and Philippine security pacts. One of the reasons for not adopting a single treaty, as opposed to three separate ones, was the reluctance of the Australian, New Zealand, and Philippine Governments to enter into any security arrangements with Japan. Furthermore, as Dulles stated, it was "not at this time practicable to draw a line which would bring all the free peoples of the Pacific and East Asia into a formal mutual security area." Moreover, Dulles felt, "the United States should not assume formal commitments which overstrain its present capabilities and give rise to military expectations we could not fulfill, particularly in terms of land forces." Dulles, however, did not regard these Pacific treaties as final, and the door was left open for other arrangements for the future." [4]

From the time Dulles originally set forth on his Far East mission in 1951 to the moment when the SEATO Treaty was signed three years later, the concept of collective security went through many variants. It was conceived in the wake of the Communist attack against Korea, and it was hoped that it would bring together the non-Communist countries of Asia, the United States, and those major European allies with interests in the area. When this proved difficult, Washington resorted to piecemeal treaty arrangements with a few countries that felt some form of alignment with the United States, rather than neutrality, offered the best hope of protection against the Chinese.

This sufficed until the French military position in Indochina began to deteriorate in early 1953. At this point the idea of collective security was transformed into the sharper, more dynamic concept of "united action." Thus in April of that year the President called on the countries of the area to organize for "united action for the defense of South East Asia." He cited the Communist aggressions in Korea and in Southeast Asia as "threats to the whole free community to be met by united action." [5] As the months went by it became increasingly clear that by "united action" the Eisenhower Administration meant international military intervention in Indochina. The pressure for this continued until the eve of the Geneva Conference.

But as anxious as the Administration was to stave off a French military defeat in Indochina and a diplomatic defeat in Switzerland, it was hamstrung by Eisenhower's firm personal opposition to any form of unilateral American military intervention, by British reluctance to participate even in discussions on "united action" while there was a prospect for negotiated settlement, and by French reluctance to permit the war to be "internationalized."

The early spring of 1954 was marked by frenetic efforts in Washington to plug the dikes holding back Communist expansion in Asia. After all, the Republican Administration had come to power to the chant of "Who Lost China?" and had now settled for less in Korea than many of its hard-liners would have liked. There were overtones of desperation in Eisenhower's and Dulles' approach to the Communist threat to Southeast Asia. A Geneva Conference on Indochina was clearly unavoidable, and last-minute attempts were still being made to avert a French defeat because of the consequences such a defeat would have for the Western diplomatic bargaining power. At the same time the Administration seemed resigned to a Communist victory in Indochina and was making hasty plans to develop programs and vehicles for "united action" or "collective security" in order to forestall further Communist expansion in Asia.

In late March Secretary Dulles called for "united action" to provide a strong and effective counter to Communist—particularly Chinese Communist—aggression in the area, and, as we have seen, in early April President Eisenhower made a major effort to induce the British to join with the Americans in organizing a regional grouping for the area. In his letter to Churchill he reminded him of the "gallant fight" the French were waging at Dien Bien Phu, and noted that "the situation there does not seem hopeless. . . . But . . . I fear that the French cannot alone see the thing through. . . . It is no solution simply to urge the French to intensify their efforts. And if they do not see it through and Indochina passes into the hands of the Communists the ultimate effect on our and your global strategic position with the consequent shift in the power ratios throughout Asia and the Pacific could be disastrous . . . the situation in Southeast Asia requires us urgently to take serious and far-reaching decisions. . . . I can understand the very natural desire of the French to seek an end to this war which has been bleeding them for eight years. But . . . there is no negotiated solution of the Indochina problem which in its essence would not be either a face-saving device to cover a French surrender or a face-saving device to cover a Communist retirement. The first alternative is too serious in its broad strategic implications for us and for you to be acceptable. . . . Somehow we must contrive to bring about the second alternative. . . . the best way to put teeth in this concept [united action] and to bring greater moral and material resources to the support of the French effort is through the establishment of a new, ad hoc grouping or coalition composed of nations which have a vital concern in the checking of Communist expansion in the area. I have in mind in addition to our two countries, France, the Associated States, Australia, New Zealand, Thailand and the Philippines. The United States government would expect to play its full part in such a coalition. . . . The important thing is that the coalition must be strong and it must be willing to join the fight if necessary. I do not envisage the need of any appreciable ground forces on your or our part. . . ." [6]

Churchill's reply was brief and not very enthusiastic. However, he indicated that his government would discuss the question of united action with Secretary Dulles in London. It was clear that the British were unwilling to proceed with any arrangements for "collective security" or "united action" until after the Geneva Conference. Churchill's lukewarm response posed a serious dilemma for Eisenhower: the British seemed unlikely to join in any Asian security arrangement, but unless they did the Administration's plans were likely to be rebuffed by Congress.

The British attitude toward the American proposal was to prove a source of friction between Secretary Dulles and Foreign Minister Eden for many months. According to Eden, "The issue of intervention continued to dog us during the opening stages of the Conference." No sooner had he arrived in Geneva than Dulles accosted him on the issue of "united action." "I told him once more," Eden recounts, "that if a settlement were achieved at the conference, the United Kingdom would be prepared to join in guaranteeing it. If the Conference failed, we would be ready to examine the situation afresh, but we were not willing to take part in armed intervention now." He gave Dulles a memorandum which set forth his views on Southeast Asian defense. The essence of Eden's position was that the problem of Communism in Asia went well beyond military containment; it involved a very substantial political commitment. Moreover, any military grouping would require the support of as many Asian countries as possible, including neutral countries. In order to get this wide support "we must prepare the ground carefully for what is, in any case, intended to be a lasting defense organization, not a hastily contrived expedient to meet the present crisis." [7]

Throughout May and early June the British tried to make clear that they were willing to consider some form of Asian defense organization but wanted to make haste slowly. They were obviously anxious to avoid alienating Asian neutrals—especially India—who were hoping some meaningful agreement would emerge from the Geneva Conference.

Dulles continued to press for united action throughout May. He also continued to conceive of united action as involving substantial and ready forces. He stressed that the military containment of China was the raison d'être for the whole enterprise. In a press conference on May 11th, he pointed out that commitments involved in any defense treaty should be of "such a character that if they were openly challenged we would be prepared to fight. . . ." When asked if the concept of an Asian defense alliance was designed to meet the situation in Indochina or the problems of Asia in general, Dulles said "the purpose . . . is to save Southeast Asia, to save all of Southeast Asia if it can be saved; if not to save essential parts of it. . . . As the nations come together, then the 'domino theory,' so-called, ceases to apply. And what we are trying to do is create a situation in Southeast Asia where the domino situation will not apply." [8] On May 25 Dulles qualified his idea of the terms under which the United States would participate in the military defense of territory in Asia: "We are not prepared to go in for a defense of colonialism. We are only going to go in for a defense of liberty. . . . We don't go in alone; we go in where the other nations which have an important stake in the area recognize the peril as we do. We go in where the United Nations gives moral sanction to our action." [9]

In early June, perhaps because of his concern about the deteriorating situation in Asia, Dulles put forward a somewhat more modest goal for a Southeast Asia defense organization than the one he had proposed a month earlier. When asked by the press what the objectives of the united action would be, Dulles responded, "The objective would be to retain in friendly hands as much as possible of the Southeast Asian peninsula and island area. Now the practicability varies from time to time. What was practical a year ago is less practical today. The situation has, I am afraid, been deteriorating." [10]

Thus, months before the Manila Conference, the United States had begun to scale down its ambitious objectives for a Southeast Asia defense organization. From late spring onward Secretary Dulles had been pointing to the difficulties of organizing an effective defense alliance. By late July Dulles expressed doubts as to whether Laos, Cambodia, and South Vietnam could be eligible for membership in the defense pact—this despite the fact that the concept of "united action" was originally based on the threat to the Indochinese states. The British, for their part, had no doubts on this score whatsoever; they felt that the membership of Laos, Cambodia, and Vietnam would be inconsistent with understandings that Eden had reached with Chou En-lai with respect to the neutrality of the Indochinese states. Eden felt, however, that any defense pact worked out for Asia generally could provide for safeguarding the neutrality of Indochina.

The pressures on the British to come to grips with the question of a Southeast Asia defense arrangement were reflected in Eden's speech to the House of Commons on June 23rd. There, as we have seen, he tried to bridge the gap between the American conception and the British view. He put forward two propositions —the ill-starred Locarno arrangement designed to guarantee a Geneva settlement and which would include Peking as one of the guarantors, and a "NATO-type of arrangement" for Southeast Asia which would represent an alliance of non-Communist countries to prevent further aggression in that area. Eden noted with some satisfaction his success in averting the "precipitate action" which, by implication at least, the Americans had been advocating. In the end, however, Dulles' view prevailed. After the Churchill–Eden visit to Washington in late June, Eden told Dulles that the Southeast Asia pact should be "limited to those powers willing to undertake specific commitments for military action, in the event of a renewed Communist aggression" (thereby cutting out the neutrals and those less able or willing to commit military forces), and "that the United Kingdom was willing to examine the possibilities of this latter arrangement at once." [11] These views were later transmitted to Paris.

The Administration lost no time in working out the modalities for the earliest possible organization of a Southeast Asia defense pact. A joint American–British committee was organized to work out the broad outlines of such a treaty. Hardly had Churchill and Eden left Washington when, on June 30th, our partners in ANZUS were asked to participate in the planning and this group soon "agreed on the need for immediate action to bring about the early establishment of collective defense in Southeast Asia—an area in which the three participating countries are all vitally concerned." [12]

In short order the broad outlines of the treaty were discussed with representatives of the Philippines and Thailand. Thus many weeks before the conference was convened at Manila, there was substantial agreement on the basic treaty provisions and on many of the detailed issues. A key element of these preliminary discussions was Washington's insistence that no American forces could be maintained on the Asian Mainland. In part this reflected the competing requirements of major American military commitments in Europe and elsewhere in Asia; in part it stemmed from Eisenhower's determination to avoid American ground forces being involved on the Asian Mainland. But regardless of the reason, the constraint Washington placed on the use of American ground forces resulted in a substantially weaker treaty than Dulles had been advocating not long before. It also cast some cloud of doubt over subsequent claims by the Johnson Administration that American commitments under the treaty justified the deployment of American combat forces to Vietnam.

*   *   *

The actual meeting in Manila on September 6, 1954 came as an anti-climax to the advance fanfare and the prior working sessions. Assembled in the Malacanang Palace were representatives of the United States, the United Kingdom, France, Australia, New Zealand, Pakistan, Thailand, and the Philippines to assist in the delivery of a weak and unpromising child—the Southeast Asia Collective Defense Treaty organization. Efforts, primarily by the British, to get a wider Asian representation had failed; other Asian countries were reluctant even to send observers. Thus the group that met and the organization that was established had only two bona fide representatives of Southeast Asia—the Philippines and Thailand.

In his opening statement Secretary Dulles once again reminded the conferees that their purpose was to establish a collective security arrangement for Southeast Asia. He acknowledged that the countries represented could not possibly "match the vast

land, Pakistan, Thailand, and the Philippines to assist in the de-
and pointed out that it would be "self-destructive" for the nations
there to try to "maintain or support formidable land-based forces
at every danger point." "In so far as the United States is concerned," he said, "its responsibilities are so vast and so far-flung
that we believe that we serve best by developing the deterrent of
mobile striking power, plus strategically-placed reserves." Many
countries directly concerned with the treaty area were not present
in Manila. "Among these are Cambodia, Laos and Viet-Nam. . . .
I hope that we shall be able to throw over them some mantle of
protection." [13]

Each of the countries that had sent representatives to Manila
probably had its own motivation for participating in the Conference. The British were more concerned about the guerrillas they
were fighting in Malaya than they were about overt Chinese aggression in Southeast Asia, and apparently they hoped that
SEATO would be of some assistance to their counter-insurgency
forces. Eden himself had little interest in the Conference. He did
not attend and his memoirs devote a scant two pages to the
proceedings.

During the summer of 1954 the French still had hopes that
they could preserve some degree of economic and political influence in Vietnam. To assure this, however, they needed more
robust American guarantees of support for the Geneva Agreements than had been emanating from Washington. If a French
signature on a collective security treaty for Southeast Asia was
the price of such an American guarantee, the government of
Prime Minister Mendes-France was ready to pay it. But the
French had additional reasons for going to Manila. Prospects
for French participation in the European Defense Community had
dwindled after the Geneva Conference. On August 30 the whole
enterprise in which Washington had set such great store was killed
by the French Assembly. Clearly Paris had some fence-mending
to do in Washington, and its association with Dulles' Asian security pact was part of that operation.

Pakistan was at least as much interested in the possibility of
using SEATO assistance in the event of war with India as it was

in containing Communist aggression in Southeast Asia. The Philippines was undoubtedly attracted by the economic and military aid that its association with the treaty organization would bring but, for its part, could make only a marginal military contribution. Moreover, since Manila had already signed a mutual defense treaty with Washington, the Philippines gained little in terms of additional security by the broader agreement. Australia and New Zealand were staunch advocates of the collective security concept. Although they were tied to the United States through the ANZUS treaty, they regarded SEATO as an earnest demonstration of American interest in a "forward defense" strategy in Southeast Asia. Thailand, worried about further encroachments from North Vietnam, probably had the strongest interest in the treaty. As of now, SEATO amounts to little more than a bilateral U.S.–Thai agreement.

Well before the conference had begun its formal deliberations, Dulles' concept of "united action" had eroded to the more passive one of "collective security." And even this became more and more pallid until, by the time the Manila conferees finished their deliberations, what finally emerged was a pastel version of the bright and bold picture Eisenhower and Dulles had painted six months before. Very few of the countries, with the possible exception of Australia and New Zealand, had any stomach for an arrangement that would arouse hostility among the unaligned countries of Asia, let alone attempt an ambitious and provocative program for the containment of Communist China.

The final wording of the treaty contained much of the boiler plate that had become standard in most regional security agreements. It provided that each of the signatories recognize that aggression against any country in the treaty area would threaten its own security and, consequently, would "act to meet the common danger"; in case of threats other than by armed attack the parties would consult immediately on measures for common defense, but no action would be taken except at the invitation or with the consent of the government concerned; a council was established that would meet at any time for consultation; the treaty area included "the general area of Southeast Asia, including also the entire territories of the Asian Partners"; the signatories agreed to maintain and develop their individual and collective capacity to resist attack and "subversive acts from without"; the treaty was to remain in force indefinitely.

An important element of the Treaty was a protocol designating Cambodia, Laos, and South Vietnam as areas to which the military and economic provisions of the treaty applied.

One issue not resolved was the basic difference between the position of the United States and the rest of the participants on whether the pact should be directed in particular against "*Communist* aggression" or simply against "aggression." As a compromise a separate American declaration was appended to the effect that aggression and armed attack under the terms of the Treaty applied only to "Communist aggression." [14] Pakistan continued to maintain, however, that the terms of the treaty covered Indian actions against Pakistan and, at a later date, argued that Indian aggression was equivalent to Communist aggression.

The Chinese Communists directed a stream of invectives against the Manila Conference. According to Peking, the "imperialists" were once again girding themselves to interfere militarily on the Asian Mainland, and the United States in particular was attempting to upset the Geneva Accords. Both Peking and Moscow characterized the Treaty as an "aggressive move." But Peking did not confine itself to propaganda. While the Manila Conference was in session, the Chinese initiated the most serious crisis in the Taiwan Strait since they had taken over control of the Mainland. Indeed on the very evening the Philippine Government was hosting a grand fiesta for the delegates, a courier from our Embassy came to the palace ballroom with a message for Dulles: the Communists were bombing the Offshore Islands and Taiwan itself was in imminent danger of attack.

*   *   *

Despite the brave oratory in the conference and the high-sounding phrases of the treaty, realists in Washington recognized that SEATO was primarily a morale building exercise, and in the last analysis both the conference and its treaty organization were frail instruments for either the military containment of China or as a bulwark against Communist subversion.

Since its organization SEATO has done little more than hold periodic meetings and engage in ineffectual and frequently academic planning efforts. It has met faithfully each year and usually has had weighty and consequential matters on the agenda. But the discussions are rarely reflected in any important actions. SEATO's headquarters, much to the despair of the more activist members, has tended to concentrate on such amiable and lofty pursuits as art exhibits and educational activities. Two of its members—Pakistan and France—have, for all practical purposes, resigned, and the rest rely heavily on their bilateral arrangements with the United States (NATO, in the case of the United Kingdom) for whatever assistance they expect in the event of subversion or attack. To the extent SEATO has served any useful purpose, it has acted as a clearinghouse for the exchange of information on subversion, has established military training programs and exercises for member countries, and has provided the Foreign Ministers of some of the signatory powers with an opportunity for a periodic exchange of views. Even this, however, is small change, since the Foreign Ministers of the Philippines, Thailand, Australia, New Zealand, and the UK have other opportunities for exchanging views with the United States. Over the past decade, SEATO's annual meetings have lasted only a day or two, and the business at hand has been pretty much pro forma.

The war in Vietnam salvaged SEATO from the international junk heap. From time to time the United States explained that American intervention in Vietnam had been made under the terms of the SEATO treaty. This, of course, was nonsense. Other than the United States, the major troop-contributing country was South Korea, which is not a member of SEATO. Commitment of Filipino and Thai troops to Vietnam was made only after the U.S. agreed to pay a high price for each soldier deployed. Three of the SEATO countries—the UK, France, and Pakistan—not only refused to send forces to Vietnam but, in the case of France and Pakistan at least, have criticized the intervention.

SEATO evokes Mark Twain's final judgment of a ragtag and

bobtail group of Confederate volunteers he helped organize at the beginning of the Civil War: "But, really, what was justly to be expected of them? Nothing, I should say. That is just what they did."

What the Manila Conference did accomplish was to put the United States squarely into the Southeast Asian picture. It was a commitment, albeit one considerably less robust than was originally conceived, to involve the United States in the security and economic development of the countries in that area—a part of the world which until 1954 had been pretty much left to the British and the French. Part and parcel of the American organization of the Manila Conference was a Washington decision to involve the United States much more directly in Vietnam.

VI

Birth of a Non-Nation

It was barely spring, but the air on that April day in 1963 was hot and wet, and the endless cups of tea did little to stem the rivers of perspiration. I had been sitting in a low, uncomfortable chair all morning fighting against falling into a complete stupor. My opponents in this struggle were the droning electric fans and the monotonous, uninterrupted stream of French emerging from Ngo Dinh Nhu. I felt as if I were on a merry-go-round, slipping off and climbing back on at various points but never really getting anywhere. I was being given a cram course in Elementary Strategic Hamlets, and after the first twenty minutes had already been subjected to more than I wished to know. Every now and then I stole a furtive glance at Nhu's mammoth desk that all but hid its occupant behind a veritable mountain chain of dossiers and files. Nhu must have been so well organized that he could spare several hours for a visitor, or so completely behind in his work that another few hours made no difference. The latter explanation turned out to be the correct one; the peaks and valleys of paper maintained the same topographical contours for months at a time.

At about noon Nhu stood up to indicate that the three-hour, one-man show was over. Lunch at Ambassador Nolting's air-conditioned house provided but a brief respite, for I had a two o'clock appointment with President Diem.

After lunch I returned to the Presidential Palace and in due course was ushered to a small, dreary anteroom. The ubiquitous fan, a few chairs, a low, round table stacked high with packages of cigarettes, and—to my horror—a large pot of tea were the only furnishings. I assumed that I would be conducted into the President's office, but in a few minutes Diem himself appeared. I had a strange sensation that Diem was only vaguely aware of another presence in the room. His handshake was as robust as a butterfly's caress, and he barely acknowledged the greetings I forwarded to him from various officials in Washington. I wondered whether he had a clue as to who I was and why I wanted to see him. It occurred to me that he may have been subjected to so many visitors from Washington that he took the routine for granted and, like a jukebox, automatically thumped out the same old tunes in the same old way. It turned out, however, that Diem was well briefed on who I was and that I was there to make an inventory of his assets and liabilities.

Diem seemed an unworldly, almost spiritual figure. Small, round, glossy, he looked like a porcelain Buddha in a white suit. I was sweating and rumpled, but he seemed untouched and unsoiled by either the heat or the pressures of office. There was no sign of perspiration, every hair was in place, his white suit was immaculate. He looked as if he spent his life in a sterilized air-conditioned incubator—as perhaps he did. The only aspect of the man that seemed out of character was his compulsive smoking. The ashtray in front of him soon became piled with still-burning butts, and the ethereal quality of the whole experience was intensified as Diem became enshrouded in swirls of smoke. He constantly switched from American to French to Vietnamese cigarettes, seeming to derive some sensual pleasure from this innocent promiscuity.

His monologue was more rambling and less focused than Nhu's. I was first treated to an interminable exposition of the history, sociology, geography, and anthropology of Vietnam; he then skidded onto another conversational expressway and dealt at great speed with the current state of affairs. His remarks were salted and peppered with the use of *n'est-ce pas?*—"This hamlet is in unfriendly territory, *n'est-ce pas?"*—"two weeks, *n'est-ce pas?"* He exuded optimism about the progress being made both in urban and rural areas and about his own political situation. According to Diem the people in the rural areas were simple children, his children, and they loved him like a father; American journalists who spent their time sitting in Saigon bars were spreading gossip, falsehoods, and canards. They were obviously sympathetic to the Communists (*n'est-ce pas?*); the teahouses were full of parasites and ambitious but lazy would-be politicians who should not be taken seriously.

Was he trying to convince me or himself? Probably me. He seemed already convinced—and why shouldn't he have been, since he scarcely ventured out of the Palace and had to rely for his information on sycophants and frightened underlings?

Diem had—or seemed to have—a vast number of facts, or at least details, at his fingertips, and he seasoned his long and rambling flow of words with references to the completion of a particular strategic hamlet and to the number of kilometers of a particular road that had been opened the day before. On these occasions he turned to a map and jabbed his finger at the hamlet or road he was talking about (or maybe it was any road or hamlet the smoke was so thick, my glasses were so steamed up, and the map was so cluttered, he could have been using an Esso road map of New York State and I would have been none the wiser).

I tried to listen carefully to what he was saying, but I had the same sensation as earlier in the day with brother Nhu—hopping on or falling off the merry-go-round at various points in his discourse. My spasms of daydreaming gave me some feeling of guilt when I sat down later that night to send Washington an account of my day at the Palace. But I felt confident, on the basis of the long stretches when I was concentrating, that neither Diem nor Nhu was likely to have said anything very important during my moments of numbness. I checked a few of the details Diem had cited and found some to be true, some not. Perhaps he was imagining some of the aspects of progress he was referring to; perhaps he had been misinformed by his subordinates. In the event, I was able to construct only a two-page telegram to record the sum total of seven hours of conversation with the President and his brother.

My visit to the Presidential Palace followed many weeks of travel throughout Vietnam. During that time I visited scores of strategic hamlets, covered most of the provinces of the country, was initiated into a Montagnard tribe, and spoke to probably a hundred American and Vietnamese military and civilian officials. During late 1962 and early 1963 there were disturbing differences between the official reporting on the situation in Vietnam and the reporting of the press. Neither Ambassador Frederick Nolting nor General Paul Harkins seemed able to communicate with the American correspondents or to reconcile their own optimism with the forbodings of serious trouble that characterized the press accounts. But the reason for doubts in Washington went well beyond this. There was concern about Diem's ability to attract meaningful popular support and to motivate the people in the countryside. There was worry about divergencies within the Saigon Mission itself; there was uneasiness about faltering GVN programs; and there were gnawing doubts about Diem's ability to maintain control despite, or perhaps because of the harsh methods used by the government in general and the Ngo Dinh Diem family in particular. The growing influence exerted by Nhu and Madame Nhu on what appeared to be an increasingly isolated and ineffectual President was worrying many officials in the White House and elsewhere. In short, Washington was convinced that something had to be done, but was uncertain about what, if anything, could be done. I was not the first person sent to Vietnam to explore the question, "Can we win with Diem?"—nor was I the last.

I returned to Washington full of quandries. I was by no means sure that I had had enough exposure to the relevant problems, or of my ability to interpret what I had seen. There had been, typically, many explanations for any given situation. I heard one account from an American reporter, another from a high-level officer in the political section of the Embassy, a third from a CIA man, a fourth from an Army Major in the field, and a fifth and sixth and seventh from various Vietnamese officials. Perhaps they were all right with respect to one aspect or another, and just possibly, because of their particular biases or interests, all of them were wrong. I was disturbed not only by the Kafkaesque sessions with Nhu and Diem, but even more by my conviction that they were divorced from what was going on outside of Saigon. I was unable to make any firm judgments as to whether the Vietnamese people would be better off generally, and more able to cope with the Communist threat, if Diem were replaced.

In looking back I think my doubts reflected a sense that the Americans could do little if anything about Diem. We had virtually no leverage in Saigon short of threatening to get out altogether; nor did we even have much meaningful influence. How, in fact, could one get rid of Diem? His legal term of office extended until 1966, and there was little evidence that he would voluntarily withdraw before that time. Even if he chose to do so, it was becoming clear that Nhu was ready to take his place. Indeed, there was already gossip that Nhu intended to replace Diem by a Palace coup some time in the immediate future. But Nhu presented even worse problems than Diem. How then could we replace Diem and block Nhu unless the Vietnamese themselves took the initiative? There were, then, two questions not one that had to be addressed: Could we "win with Diem," and what would we do if we could not "win with Diem"?

I had had some exposure in the past to American efforts to find a knight in shining armor to replace an undesirable or ineffectual ruler, and I had no faith in our ability to identify, and then to install, a regime in Saigon that would be more effective in its dealing with the Viet Cong, have more popular support, and be generally more satisfactory to the United States than the present one. My report was probably much more equivocal than my sponsors expected, although it included some measures the United States might take to increase its influence on Diem and Nhu or, at a minimum, to restore meaningful communications between the Embassy and the Presidential Palace. But I was still tortured by the emotional impact of my session with Diem. The man was living in his own world, and this gave me a vague sense of impending doom that clouded all my recommendations. When one high official asked whether Diem "still had all his marbles," I replied that, "if I were Diem's mother I would be seriously worried."

Events in Vietnam moved quickly, and the question of Diem's future was soon to become academic.

         ❊   ❊   ❊

Much has been written about Diem—his early life, his experience under the French and later under the Japanese, and the events that surrounded his rise to power. But to recreate the drama of the early American involvement in Vietnam, we must become familiar with the principal character in the case, Ngo Dinh Diem himself, and we must try to reconstruct the American role in his emergence as Prime Minister in the early summer of 1954.

In 1953 Ngo Dinh Diem was a virtual recluse in Catholic monasteries in the United States. In 1954 he became Prime Minister, and a year later he was President of South Vietnam. In 1963 he was murdered by an officer in the army of the Government of Vietnam. The saga of the rise and fall of the man Denis Warner calls "The Last Confucian" has been told and retold in many forms and permutations. For angry men who wish to ascribe devious and dark motives to Presidents Eisenhower, Kennedy, and Johnson, the story turns on how Diem used and was used by important American Catholics, "hawky" professors and writers, and anti-Communist liberals. It is said that the Central Intelligence Agency had, from a very early moment, "fingered" Diem as its chosen instrument in Vietnam. Thus Sanford Gottlieb, Executive Director of the National Committee for a Sane Nuclear Policy, traces the American sponsorship of Diem back to early 1953 when, after a meeting of the Association of Asian Studies in late March and early April of 1953, the CIA asked for a copy of a speech that Diem had made. The Agency's interest in Diem's speech convinced Mr. Gottlieb and others that the Eisenhower Administration (and by extension, the Kennedy and Johnson Administrations as well) was actively promoting Ngo Dinh Diem to take over Vietnam as long as a year before the Geneva Conference. In more lurid accounts of Diem's elevation others, such as Robert Scheer, have written how an insidious combination of Cardinals, capitalists, and cold warriors catapulted Diem from the cloister to the palace.[1]

The implication we are to draw from these accounts is that the Americans shoved Diem down the throats of both the Vietnamese Nationalists and the French, who in early 1954 were looking for a leader to head a non-Communist government in Vietnam. According to this theory, the Vietnamese were induced, bluffed, or virtually blackmailed into accepting him; Emperor Bao Dai was helpless and supine. It may be, of course, that the full story of Diem's rise to power will never be known. He and some of his closest associates are not alive to tell the story; other witnesses or participants, such as Bao Dai and ex-Foreign Minister Georges Bidault, remain mum; and yet others appear to have only fragmentary accounts or faulty memories of the events between December, 1953 and June, 1954. I will not vouchsafe that my own account is either complete or entirely accurate. It does, however, reflect the firsthand accounts of a few of the active participants—Vietnamese, American, and French—and may shed some light on the American role in the Diem Saga.

One of the curious aspects of the Vietnamese struggle for independence has been the readiness on the part of ardent anti-French nationalists to take up residence in France. For some, particularly those close to Bao Dai, France provided an amiable atmosphere in which they could practice their professions (primarily in the fields of law, medicine, and engineering) and their children could pursue an education. For others, especially the non-Communist members of the Viet Minh, France was a refuge; they were unwelcome throughout both Viet Minh and French-controlled areas of Vietnam. When the fight against the French was approaching a climax in late 1953 and early 1954, a large number of Vietnamese were living in Paris. They comprised a heterogeneous and fractionalized community, frustrated by their inability to exert meaningful influence on the course of events in Vietnam, and guilty about being expatriates. Some were Catholics and conservatives, some were Communists, some were apolitical, opportunistic Francophiles. All tended to be what one Vietnamese described as *strategistes aux affaires du commerce*. The opponents of Bao

Dai were especially frustrated—caught as they were between the French and Vietnamese ruling groups. Scheming and plotting were rife. But among these expatriate Vietnamese were some genuine nationalists.

One such patriot was Dr. Nguyen Nhoc Bich. By profession Bich had been an engineer—a graduate of France's prestigious Ecole Polytechnique. He was a consequential and revered figure. His father was one of the founders of a branch of the Cao Dai sect, and his family had long been highly respected in the southern part of Vietnam, particularly in the area of Ben Tre Province. Bich had joined the Viet Minh because he was convinced there was a chance for non-Communist nationalists to band together with the Communists in a broad coalition to establish a genuinely free and independent Vietnam. Bich, as well as many other educated, non-Communist nationalists, was influenced by the French political tactic of alliances between moderate and Communist groups to achieve short-range objectives. The problem in Vietnam, however, was that the non-Communist nationalists had no significant political base of their own and were either swallowed up or destroyed by the Viet Minh's well-organized, politically aggressive Communist leadership.

As commander of the Viet Minh forces in the Delta during the late 40s, Bich became one of the most popular local heroes. During 1946 the Viet Minh hierarchy became concerned that Bich might pose a threat to the aims of the Viet Minh in the southern part of Vietnam, and by the end of that year Ho apparently decided that Bich had served his purpose in the Delta. He was "invited" to move North to become a member of the Viet Minh political and military headquarters in Hanoi. Bich was reluctant to leave his command, not only because of his desire to continue the fight against the French, but also because he felt uneasy about leaving his base of power. Nonetheless, he made his way north via the nationalist underground to Hanoi.

A day or two before Bich was to report to the Viet Minh headquarters, the French discovered his hiding place near Hanoi. Since he was on the French "most wanted" list, he was subjected to an intensive and unpleasant interrogation. He had no doubt that summary execution was next on the program. In desperation he wrote to the "Old Boy" association of graduates of the Ecole Polytechnique. It was the old school tie that saved Bich's life; the bonds of this most elite of educational institutions made brothers even of enemies. Whether the Viet Minh had actually betrayed him to French agents is not known for certain, but Bich always suspected that this was how he had been discovered. In any case, he sensed that he would be in great danger if he reported to the Viet Minh, and he quickly took advantage of the French offer to spirit him and his wife out of Vietnam. On his arrival in France, Bich embarked on a new career in medicine. When he discovered some time later that he had cancer of the throat, he spent the rest of his life using himself as a guinea pig for his study and research.

After the Four Powers agreed at Berlin on February 18, 1954 to hold an international conference on Vietnam, Dr. Bich and other Vietnamese non-Communist nationalists pressed the French for complete independence. This was finally and grudgingly granted on April 28. As the weeks passed and it became increasingly apparent that the French faced certain military defeat, the quest for independence developed into an anxious search for a nationalist leader who could provide the Vietnamese people with a non-Communist alternative to Ho Chi Minh. A group of Vietnamese intellectuals began to meet regularly in Paris to discuss various possible candidates. While the group was by no means united in its views, it reached early common agreement that Bao Dai could not provide the necessary inspiration or leadership and that a strong Prime Minister was needed.

At an early point in the deliberations Bich was regarded as a leading possibility for the Prime Minister's post because of his almost mystical appeal to millions of Vietnamese. But many in the Paris group, especially the conservative members, found Bich's style too rigid and idealistic. Moreover, he was immersed in his medical research and lacked political experience. And so Bich was rejected.

Ngo Dinh Diem was the favorite candidate of the conservative Catholics, but was regarded generally as an honest and hardened nationalist, with a brilliant academic record and practical experience in government. Diem's youngest brother, Ngo Dinh Luyen, was an active participant in the Paris meetings and saw to it that Diem's name was very much in the foreground. The efforts of Diem's supporters were further assisted by the maneuvers of brother Ngo Dinh Nhu in Saigon.

Diem left the United States for Europe in May, 1953. He stayed at the Benedictine monastery of Saint Andre-les-Bruges in Belgium and used his new quarters as a base to lobby on his own behalf among the Vietnamese community in France. Diem first met with the Paris group early in the spring of 1954 and, according to one person present, made a "very bad impression." Bich walked out after one exposure to Diem and refused to associate himself with any of the subsequent deliberations. One member of the group reported that Diem was "obscure" and "murky" and that his ideas were "obsolete." He remembered feeling that Diem was "stupid." And of course Diem talked "incessantly." Despite all this, however, Diem had strong supporters and even those who were lukewarm or even opposed to him had no strong alternative candidates to put forward.

The American role in the selection process seems to have been, at most, indirect and unofficial—at least prior to Diem's arrival in Paris. The implication that Diem was an official American protégé as early as 1953 does not square with the pro-French bias that dominated American Indochina policy during this period. While Diem had made contacts with many Americans and was apparently highly regarded by them during 1952 and 1953, his official contacts seemed to be confined to Democrats—a curious act of oversight, at least during 1953 when there was a Republican administration. In any case, Diem was unable to get American assistance for his trip to Europe in pursuit of power.

Diem's two years of voluntary exile in the United States were not, as might be inferred from some accounts, spent in wheeling and dealing among the rich and great. He lived in Maryknoll Seminaries in Lakewood, New Jersey and Ossining, New York where he meditated and did some writing. Upon occasion, he emerged from behind the cloistered walls to address some obscure

scholarly forums or to make a trip to Washington. He was taken
in hand by a few professors concentrating on Southeast Asia, in
part because he was regarded as a thoughtful and interesting
Vietnamese nationalist, and in part too because he was one of the
few "real, live" Vietnamese around and therefore an interesting
specimen to put on display.

Justice William O. Douglas gave Diem a boost in 1953: "Ngo
Dinh Diem . . . is a hero in Central and North Vietnam, with a
considerable following in the south too. . . . Ngo Dinh Diem is
revered by the Vietnamese because he is honest and independent
and stood firm against the French influence. There are few officials in the Vietnamese government who have that reputation." [2]
Aside from Douglas, Diem's only consequential contact in Washington was Senator Mike Mansfield, whom he met once or twice.
He was brought to the attention of Ambassador Joseph Kennedy
and he met Cardinal Spellman, but Spellman paid little attention to him until after he became Prime Minister. To the extent
that official Washington knew of him (and of Bich), it was
through the efforts of Professor Milton Sacks of Brandeis University, who in the early fifties was a junior member of the State
Department.

According to one Vietnamese who was studying at Cornell
while Diem was cloistered at Maryknoll, Diem was actively seeking support from other Vietnamese in the United States for his
eventual return to Vietnam. Diem spent a great deal of time writing "beautifully typed chain letters" in which he asked for views
and opinions on the political future of Vietnam. He also sponsored informal get-togethers of Vietnamese Catholic students,
admonishing them to "get ready to return to Vietnam" and hinting
of rewards in exchange for their support.

The moment of decision with respect to Diem took place
shortly before the fall of Dien Bien Phu. Adding to the urgency
of selecting a new Prime Minister was the universal desire to get
rid of the present Prime Minister Buu Loc, who was a cousin of
Bao Dai. It was evident to all Vietnamese nationalists and even to
Bao Dai that Loc would be totally incapable of pulling together
a non-Communist government after the Geneva Conference.

At this point it was abundantly clear that the French had lost all hope of salvaging their political and economic position in Vietnam and, further, that a settlement of the thorny problems involved in a cessation of hostilities could be obtained only at the price of a partitioned country, along the models of Korea and Germany. The French, according to a Vietnamese familiar with the bargaining over the choice of a Prime Minister, were "gently pushing" the candidacy of Tran Van Huu, but Bao Dai would have none of it. Tran Van Huu had been a weak, pro-French Prime Minister in the early 1950s, and Bao Dai realized that he was not the man to lead the Vietnamese into independence. Such French leftists as Francois Mitterand then suggested Buu Hoi. Although he was a member of the Imperial family, Buu Hoi had close contacts with Ho's government and during the late '40s and early '50s had served as an unofficial intermediary between Ho Chi Minh and the French. Bao Dai rejected this choice also, perhaps as much because Hoi was not a politician by occupation as because of his close association with the Viet Minh. (In fact the French felt so strongly about Hoi that they continued to tout him as the logical Prime Minister, even after Diem had taken the post, and there are reports that when Mendes-France was in the U.S. in late 1954 he tried to promote Hoi's fortunes.[3])

It was at this point that Bao Dai began to look favorably upon suggestions that Ngo Dinh Diem get the imperial nod. The key figure in the negotiations was not some shadowy American, nor a member of the Ngo clan, but Nguyen Dê, who since 1932 had been Bao Dai's Chef de Cabinet. Dê, a successful businessman in Indochina prior to World War II and an adviser to the Viet Minh delegation at Fontainebleau, was a highly cultivated man with excellent connections in Vietnamese commercial and intellectual circles and in the international business and diplomatic community. He had had close personal relationships with Diem since childhood, and like Diem he was a Catholic. Dê embarked on what one knowledgeable Vietnamese has described as a "rescue operation" to disassociate Bao Dai from the French-controlled governments of the pre-Geneva period. Bao Dai may have been ready to settle on Diem in any case, but Dê apparently was at least the catalyst in the final selection.

It is not entirely clear what role private or official Americans played in the choice of Diem as Prime Minister up to this point. Surely Washington provided approving backstage noises and a claque in the balcony. Although Diem's devout Catholicism may well have appealed to Secretary Dulles' strong Calvinist character, Dulles probably confined himself to exerting pressure on both the French and Bao Dai to appoint a strong, anti-Communist nationalist Prime Minister who could be a counterweight to Ho Chi Minh. The American Ambassador in Paris, Douglas Dillon, may have indicated to Bao Dai that Diem would be acceptable to Washington. But since Bao Dai was not looking exclusively to Washington for help and since, in any case, the United States was not prepared to offer any military or economic assistance to Bao Dai until Washington had a firmer feel for the final terms of an agreement at Geneva, an American endorsement would probably not have cut much ice if Bao Dai himself had had serious misgivings about Diem.

The question of who would assume the office of Prime Minister in the post-Geneva period was obviously of considerable interest to the French. At least until the fall of Dien Bien Phu, the French hoped to influence Bao Dai to appoint a pliable man who could be induced to preserve French economic and, perhaps, even some political influence in Vietnam. Those French who had business interests in Indochina, especially the bankers, shipping magnates, and owners of the rubber plantations and tin mines, were putting constant pressure on Paris to assure that such a man was, in fact, selected. And the tottering Laniel Government, needing all the support it could muster, was in no position to ignore this powerful lobby. Very much involved in the negotiations with Bao Dai was Laniel himself, Vice Premier Paul Reynaud, Foreign Minister Georges Bidault, and even President Coty. These men were well aware of Diem's attempts a few years earlier to stiffen Bao Dai's demands for complete independence, and they had little confidence in Diem as an instrument for the protection of French interests. As it turned out, they were right.

But French capabilities to influence or shape a post-Geneva Vietnam government were eroding rapidly. On June 6th, two weeks before the fall of Laniel's Government, the French bowed to the realities of the situation and indicated they would not object to the choice of Diem as Prime Minister. Ten days later the post was offered to Diem, and when Prime Minister Buu Loc resigned shortly after, Diem agreed to accept the Bao Dai offer.

As his price for taking office, Diem demanded from Bao Dai full civil and military powers, the authority to determine the future status of the country, Vietnamese control over the country's economy, and the freedom to establish a representative national assembly. In return Diem swore an oath of allegiance to Bao Dai, pledging that "he would submit the monarch's fate to the Vietnamese people rather than use his powers to depose him arbitrarily." [4]

When John Foster Dulles was in Paris in the spring of 1954, he met with Bao Dai in an effort to persuade him to join Diem in Vietnam and help Diem defend the South. The Emperor told Dulles that he would not go back to a partitioned Vietnam; he would not share the country with Ho Chi Minh. If he were to go back, it would be to fight for all of Vietnam. Dulles and Bao Dai agreed that Bao Dai should remain in France and return to Vietnam after Diem had won over the country. This was eminently satisfactory to Bao Dai, since it was his original intent to have Diem do the necessary dirty work in taking over the post-Geneva government of South Vietnam. Bao Dai planned that when some degree of stability had been achieved, he would return to Vietnam and replace Diem with someone more compatible. As part of his strategy Bao Dai hoped to exert remote control over Diem through General Hinh, Chief of the Army. But Bao Dai did not reckon with Diem's own agenda and ambitions.

Diem went to Vietnam determined to establish a strong, anti-Communist government, to eliminate the power of the various religious sects and armed pressure groups, and to eliminate French influence. In the course of this, Bao Dai would have to remain a figurehead and might even be dethroned. But that was the Emperor's problem, not Ngo Dinh Diem's.

*   *   *

Diem arrived in Saigon on June 25, 1954 to find a capital wracked with political intrigue. He was very much on his own. During the early months of his regime, American support was neither robust nor enthusiastic. The Central Intelligence Agency was given the mission of helping Diem develop a government that would be sufficiently strong and viable to compete with and, if necessary, stand up to the Communist regime of Ho Chi Minh in the North. Colonel Edward Lansdale, who had had remarkable success in helping President Magsaysay defeat the Huks in the Philippines and establish a stable and popular government in Manila, was dispatched to Saigon shortly before Diem's arrival. Lansdale, together with a few other Americans, provided considerable moral support and guidance to Diem in his first difficult months of office. But at this point neither the Embassy in Saigon nor the Administration in Washington was entirely sold on Diem as the answer to Ho Chi Minh. It was to be many more months before Diem received unequivocal official American support. But unofficial help was soon on the way.

One aspect of the Geneva Agreements provided Diem with some of his most difficult immediate problems. At Geneva it was agreed that for three hundred days after the signing of the Accords there should be unhampered movement of all Vietnamese who wished to resettle from one zone to the other. Most of the military units loyal to Ho Chi Minh were transferred to the North, but some of the best-trained units made their way to inaccessible jungle and mountain areas in the South from which, in due course, they would operate as guerrilla bands. Also moving north from South Vietnam were approximately 120,000 people— some were carefully selected younger men destined for military training and eventual return to South Vietnam, and others felt so compromised by their political associations with the Viet Minh that they were fearful of retribution.[5] Hanoi selected thousands of trained and well-disciplined party members to remain in their native villages in South Vietnam to await further orders. Arms and ammunition were hidden for future use throughout South Vietnam, and Diem was confronted with a delayed time bomb.

From North Vietnam to the south came a massive flow of people who, now given the choice, were anxious to get out from under the Communist government of Ho Chi Minh. Approximately 85 percent of these refugees were Catholic. In the event, between 850,000 and 900,000 people fled the North—almost seven percent of the total population.

Although there was great uncertainty, even anxiety about their fate under a Communist regime, the vast movement of Catholics to South Vietnam was not spontaneous. The Catholic Church sponsored a campaign shortly after the Geneva Conference to arouse its congregants to the dangers to freedom of worship, and Diem himself went to Hanoi in early August, 1954 to encourage the Catholic hierarchy to move South. The slogans were hardly subtle: "Christ has gone to the South" and "the Virgin Mary has departed from the North." Aside from the purely religious factor there was a demographic one: unless a mass movement to areas south of the 17th parallel could be encouraged, North Vietnam would have a larger population than South Vietnam.

The American International Rescue Committee (IRC)—a group organized during World War II to assist the escape and resettlement of intellectuals from Nazi Germany and later from Soviet occupied areas—was soon seized with the question of whether it should launch a program to assist the refugees from North Vietnam. This was not an easy decision in view of the numbers and kinds of people involved. The Committee had traditionally been Europe-oriented, and it was primarily interested in scholars and professionals rather than rank and file farmers and urban workers. The IRC had remained aloof in two earlier refugee crises in Asia—the flight of anti-Communists from Mainland China to Hong Kong and from North Korea to the South—and perhaps many of the Committee members had some feeling of guilt. In any case, when the refugees from North Vietnam began streaming south in August, 1954, the IRC decided to participate by helping to resettle the intellectuals among them. But Committee representatives found little interest in Washington in either the refugees or in American voluntary assistance programs. The Administration apparently felt it was doing everything necessary by providing Navy transport for the refugee movement. However, the flow from the North increased to such proportions—approximately 40,000 to 50,000 per day at its peak—that it was soon evident Diem's new government would be incapable of handling this vast problem without immediate outside help.

In early August Leo Cherne, Chairman of the IRC, arrived in South Vietnam and met with Ambassador Donald Heath to discuss a possible assistance program. He found Heath "distinctly discouraging." The Ambassador felt that the French still had major responsibility for Vietnam and that the United States role should be minimal. Moreover, in Heath's view the Diem Government was only a temporary and transitional one, and, therefore, the United States, officially and unofficially, should make no commitments to or investments in Diem. Meanwhile Cherne's presence in Saigon came to Diem's notice, probably through Wesley Fishel, a professor from Michigan State University who was in Saigon as a consultant to the American Aid Mission.

Diem attached great importance to Cherne's visit. The IRC concern about the refugee problem was the first evidence Diem had had of any American interest in Vietnam since he had taken office. Cherne came away from his first session with Diem convinced that if Diem could survive the first several months of French obstructionism, internecine Vietnamese opposition, and apparent American indifference he would make an effective leader.

Cherne sent a cable expressing his views on Diem's problems and prospects to his management consultant firm for distribution to its clients. Although the cable was heavily censored by the French who still controlled the post and telegraph service, the thrust of Cherne's perceptive assessment got through.

"According to armistice," Cherne cabled, "Communists supposed to evacuate southern Vietnam. But Communists are retaining complete control of important pockets south of Saigon. Elsewhere government suspects much Red strength, had no way of finding out how much. . . . Success of effort to hold Vietnam from Communists depends on whether all non-Communist Vietnamese can unite for struggle. . . . Political opponents, even while plotting frantically against him, concede Diem completely incorruptible. This his strength and weakness. So far Diem won't even make deals that are normal here to retain power. . . . One point most

Vietnamese leaders agree on: Don't want French. Political and
financial instability must follow unless Vietnamese government
can organize important forces and U.S. continues pouring in substantial help and money. . . . Diem's followers hope Emperor Bao
Dai stays on French Riviera. Even though he appointed Diem
Premier, his return would be viewed undercutting Diem, maybe
replacing him. Bao Dai distrusted as not anti-French enough.
Diem walking a tightrope, trying to persuade Nationalist Vietnamese he is anti-French, and persuading the French he is not too
anti-French. . . . All recognize huge stakes riding on gamble that
Vietnam can survive further Communist penetration and win
election supposed to be held twenty months from now. If free
elections held today, all agree privately Communist would win.
Reason: Effect of Communist military victory plus Indochinese
hatred of previous colonial status. Situation not hopeless. There is
danger, but not paralysis. Future depends on organizing all resources to resettle refugees, sustain near bankrupt government,
give people something to fight for and unite them to resist
communism. . . ." [6]

Cherne returned to New York in late September convinced
that the International Rescue Committee should launch a major
refugee assistance program in South Vietnam. He was also convinced that the United States should disassociate its policies from
the French and commit itself fully to the support of the new
Vietnamese Government.

To administer its program in Vietnam, the Committee sent
Joseph Buttinger to Saigon in October. Buttinger was a former
member of the socialist underground in Austria and had been
highly successful in assisting European refugee intellectuals in
the late '40s and early '50s. He had had no experience in Asia and
initially was unenthusiastic about his assignment. But once in
Vietnam, he did a remarkable job in organizing refugee aid. After
meeting with Buttinger, Diem reportedly was enthusiastic about
the prospects for the program.

Buttinger remained in Vietnam until December, 1954. Like
Cherne he was convinced that Diem represented a major, perhaps
even the only hope for a non-Communist Southeast Asia, and he

was depressed at the lukewarm official American attitude toward Diem. He returned to the United States determined to stimulate interest in a massive program of civil assistance for the Diem Government. "I came to realize," he wrote shortly after his return, "that the information about the hopelessness of the Vietnamese situation was of French origin. For different reasons, before and after Geneva, the French have had a vested interest in maintaining that there wasn't much chance for an independent Vietnam. . . . Because [Diem] is firm, he is called 'rigid'; because he is honest, he is called 'politically inexperienced,' . . . and because he is the first Vietnamese Premier who dares disobey the weakening French, it is said he is 'unable to compromise.' . . . Vietnam . . . needs our help in freeing itself from . . . decaying colonialism. We should send there an Ambassador with sympathy for the people's national aspirations. . . ." [7]

Buttinger buttonholed every one he could find who had known Diem and who might be of some assistance in influencing American policy. Among these were Cardinal Spellman, Senators Mansfield and Kennedy, and Representative Walter Judd. As part of their effort, Cherne and Buttinger induced a group of American intellectuals and businessmen to organize the "American Friends of Vietnam." For many years thereafter, the "American Friends" provided important informational and publications services for the Saigon Government. It was more than an association of scholars and somewhat less than a lobby group. The group continued to be a lively if small claque and pressure group in support of Diem until 1961, when the group virtually disbanded as a result of its disenchantment with Diem. It acquired a brief new lease on life in 1964 after his downfall.

Well before Buttinger and Cherne launched their personal campaign, however, United States policy toward Diem was beginning to turn around. Diem had managed to remain in office much longer than many of the American and French Cassandras had predicted, and it became clear that the Prime Minister was a man to be reckoned with. Given a fair share of luck and some assistance, he might develop South Vietnam into a stable, non-Communist rival to the Communist North.

Senator Mansfield visited Vietnam in the late summer. He found the situation "grim and discouraging," but he returned to Washington convinced that Diem deserved American support. "Saigon is the hub of the political crisis. Since the Geneva agreement that capital city has seethed with intrigue and counterintrigue, with rumors and counter-rumors. The political plotting goes on in army circles, government circles, foreign circles, in party headquarters, in police headquarters, and even in the demimonde of ill-disguised gangsters, pirates, and extortionists." Mansfield commented on Diem's lack of power over both the army and police, but he defended the Prime Minister for his "intense nationalism and equally intense incorruptibility, traits which have been sorely needed in the government of Vietnam." Mansfield further noted that Diem's government was "based on the sound principles of national independence, an end to corruption and internal amelioration. . . ." He implied that the U.S. had no choice but to cast its lot with Diem since, in his words, "the visible alternatives to the Diem government are not promising." These alternatives seemed to Mansfield to be limited to a Communist take-over of the South, or to a weak, pre-1954 type of government dependent on foreign support. The Senator came to a stark conclusion: "In the event that the Diem government falls, therefore, I believe that the U.S. should consider an immediate suspension of all aid to Vietnam and the French Union Forces there. . . ." [8]

Mansfield's report had an important influence on the Administration's decision to move forward with an aid program for the struggling Saigon Government. On October 23, 1954 President Eisenhower sent a letter to Premier Diem, and it was that letter that was cited by members of the Kennedy Administration and even more often by officials in the Johnson Administration to relate the origin and continuity of U.S. policy in support of Diem to the earliest years of the Eisenhower Administration. Eisenhower's letter implied that American aid was forthcoming, but Washington's doubts about Diem's ability to implement an effective political and economic program protruded through the smooth diplomatic rhetoric. Eisenhower told Diem that the White House was "exploring ways and means to permit our aid to Vietnam to be more effective and to make a greater contribution to the welfare and stability of the government of Vietnam. . . ." The American Ambassador, the President said, had been instructed to work out with Diem "an intelligent program of American aid given directly." But Diem was cautioned that American aid would be conditioned on Vietnamese readiness "to give assurances as to the standards of performance it would be able to maintain." The United States expected that its aid would "be met by performance on the part of the government of Vietnam in undertaking needed reforms." [9] In its public announcement of the new American policy, however, Administration officials played down their doubts and concerns. The main point of Eisenhower's letter, they said, was "to make evident U.S. support" and "to strengthen the hand of the Premier and give his regime ammunition to use against his political enemies. . . ." [10]

Eisenhower's letter culminated many weeks of soul-searching in Washington. In the end the President became convinced that the future of South Vietnam rested on continued American support of Diem, on Diem's readiness to take American advice, and on Diem's willingness and ability to "reform" his administration so as to attract a large cross-section of Vietnamese support. Diem was eager to accept the support, resigned to frequent proffers of advice, but resistant to the substance, if not the spirit of reform. It is not surprising, then, that Eisenhower's letter to Diem was carefully hedged with references to Vietnamese "performance." This was to be only the beginning of the American dilemma with respect to Vietnam. Washington's attempt to balance off aid against performance was inherited by Kennedy, later by Johnson, and then by Nixon.

But the immediate, rather than the remote future was what worried President Eisenhower. And he had ample reason to be concerned. Having invested more than $2 billion to assist the French to defeat the Viet Minh, Eisenhower and Dulles now looked with trepidation at what was transpiring during the late summer and autumn of 1954. The future of American policy in Southeast Asia seemed to be resting on one stubborn, difficult, tenacious, and lonely man. Senator Mansfield later recalled how the situation looked to him in 1954: ". . . the Diem Government was in the midst of a crisis that threatened its very existence. Near-chaos reigned in the Capital. Hundreds of thousands of destitute refugees . . . had been brought to the Saigon–Cholon area. . . . All the while, not only the Binh Xuyen [a Vietnamese version of the Mafia] but the Vietnamese army command and certain sect leaders were conducting themselves in open contempt of the President. An orgy of conspiracy and subversion was the order of the day. The teacup speculation centered on predicting the day or hour when the Diem Government would be ousted." [11]

Mansfield's reference to Diem's troubles with the "Vietnamese army command" hardly did justice to the crisis the new Prime Minister was confronting at the very moment of the Senator's visit. By September the issue of whether the flamboyant General Nguyen Van Hinh, Chief of the Army under the previous government, protégé of Bao Dai, and son of a former Prime Minister, would yield to Diem's order to leave the country or would stage a coup was still in doubt. After many weeks of anguished but fruitless correspondence with Bao Dai, Diem removed Hinh from his command in September, but Hinh remained in Saigon taunting the government and presenting a constant, if uncertain, possibility of a coup d'etat. According to General Hinh, "I only had to lift my telephone, and the *coup d'état* would have been over. Nothing could have opposed the army. But the Americans let me know that if that happened, dollar help would be cut off. That would not matter to the military; if necessary, we soldiers could go barefoot and eat rice. But the country cannot survive without American help. We would only have played into the Viets' hands with a revolt." [12] As a last resort American representations were made to Bao Dai, who finally ordered General Hinh's departure from Vietnam—almost two months after Diem had ousted him.[13]

In retrospect Hinh was not a very serious or potent rival to Diem. But at the time, when Diem had the assured loyalty of little more than a battalion of Vietnamese troops and was beset on all sides with problems and crises, it must have seemed to the Prime Minister that Hinh posed a substantial threat. Hinh probably had a fair amount of backing from the French during this period and perhaps some sympathy within the American Embassy itself. Indeed shortly after Diem ousted Hinh, Ambassador Heath declared (probably without advance knowledge or approval from Washington) that the United States could not support a government which was maintained by force.[14]

This is new

As part of the new approach toward Vietnam, it was decided to replace Ambassador Heath. Heath had spent several years working with the French in Vietnam, and his relations with Diem during the past few months did not augur well. On November 3 the White House announced that Heath would be replaced by General J. Lawton Collins. Collins was given two major missions. His first task was to examine in consultation with the Vietnamese "how a program of American aid given directly to Vietnam can best assist that country"; such aid was "to supplement measures adapted by the Vietnamese themselves." Collins' second major task was to "maintain close liaison with the French Commissioner General Paul Ely, for the purpose of exchanging views on how best, under existing circumstances, the freedom and welfare of Vietnam can be safeguarded." [15] As in the Eisenhower letter to Diem, the announcement of Collins' appointment hinted at some nagging doubts in Washington as to the depth of the American commitment. The emphasis on the *supplementary* "nature of American aid" was an attempt to convey to Diem the tentative nature of the American commitment.

Diem wasn't an Army man or corporate attorney

When Collins arrived in Saigon, Diem had weathered the threat posed to his government by General Hinh and the Vietnamese Army. But Diem's troubles were just beginning. For a starter, there was General Collins himself. Immediately upon his arrival, the new Ambassador briskly undertook a series of steps to implement his mission. He worked out with General Ely a schedule for the withdrawal of French troops, and, together with the Vietnamese and the French, he established a program for the training of a new Vietnamese Army. Within three weeks he and Diem were in basic disagreement over some key staff appointments to the Vietnamese Army. To make matters worse Collins found it increasingly necessary to warn Diem of reforms that Washington insisted be implemented if American aid were to continue. Partly because of Collins' insistence, a number of encouraging steps were taken by the Diem Government at the end of 1954. A land reform legislation was worked out, and a provisional assembly was organized to draft a constitution. There was also talk—much talk but little action—by the Prime Minister of substantial and rapid progress in the areas of political and social reform. The relations between Collins and Diem remained correct but cool.

In mid-February Collins returned to Washington to report on Vietnam's problems and prospects. Despite his difficulties with Diem he made a strong and successful case for continued American support. In the face of Bao Dai's attempts through the French in Paris and through his own channels in Vietnam to undercut Diem, the Administration felt it was high time to unequivocally inform Bao Dai of Washington's policy. Eisenhower made the American decision clear to His Majesty shortly after Collins' return to Saigon. "It is gratifying to learn from him [Collins] of the distinct progress that is being made in Viet Nam by Prime Minister Diem and the Government of Viet Nam," Eisenhower wrote to Bao Dai. "The Prime Minister's announced programs of land reform and reorganization of the Armed Forces should, when fully carried out, further increase the stability and unity of the Government. . . . I have concurred in General Collins' recommendation to continue and expand support for Free Viet Nam. . . . The United States Government intends to continue its support of his [Diem's] Government." [16]

The firm commitment of American support came none to soon for the hard-pressed Diem. He needed all the moral and tangible help he could get to weather the crises that lay immediately ahead. An even more serious threat to Diem than the swashbuckling General Hinh were private armies which, in loose combination, controlled large parts of South Vietnam. One of these armies was in the service of the Cao Dai sect (an exotic mixture of Confucianism, Buddhism, spiritualism, and Catholicism). Yet another army was the military army of the Hoa Hao sect (a fundamentalist Buddhist splinter group). Both sects had raised military forces a few years before when the French were desperate for any local military assistance they could get against the Viet Minh. The French had supplied arms and provided troop pay in exchange for a commitment by the Cao Dai and Hoa Hao to defend their own respective areas. Shortly after the end of the war both sects had tried to strengthen their political and economic bargaining positions with the government in Saigon and attempted to seize as much territory in South Vietnam as they could control. Neither army met with much resistance from the local populace or the Vietnamese Army, and it was not long before each group was levying taxes and drafting troops throughout large areas of the countryside. Indeed, like the warlords of China, the sects established virtual sovereignty over the areas they controlled. But not satisfied with the fruits of the hinterland, both sects soon tried to gain control over the Saigon area. In his early months of office Diem was so dependent on the support of the two sects that his Cabinet included several representatives from both the Cao Dai and the Hoa Hao.

The Cao Dai and the Hoa Hao by no means completed the catalogue of monsters waiting to devour the earnest, mystical man in the white suit. Diem was threatened by yet another and more dangerous private army. This force was under the command of the Binh Xuyen, a group already alluded to by Senator Mansfield in his grim description of Diem's problems. The Binh Xuyen group made no claims to lofty religious goals. Rather it was an organization of goons and pirates that had been controlling the river traffic into Saigon and the neighboring Chinese city of Cholon for many years. The Binh Xuyen's stranglehold on Saigon was virtually completed when Bao Dai the year before sold the municipal police to this group for a little over a million dollars.[17] In a burst of magnanimity and good sportsmanship, the Emperor threw in control over gambling, prostitution, and opium for the Saigon and Cholon areas.

By early 1955 the French had stopped their subsidies to the Cao Dai and Hoa Hao armies. The only alternative source of funds for the financially strained sects was the treasury of the Saigon Government. Diem, who seemed to derive some masochistic satisfaction from looking for trouble in large doses, took just this moment to crack down on the rackets of the Binh Xuyen. Perhaps he felt that with their funds drying up the three private armies would simply melt away. But their generals were made of sterner and more materialistic stuff. They submerged their rivalries for the sake of the Greater Cause and insisted that Diem deal them into the big money game. They proposed a Government of National Union which would result in a four-way split of power (and of government revenues). Diem dismissed this proposition out of hand. He gained some time by playing the conspirators off against each other, but this was a delicate and risky enterprise and had a predictably short life-span. For many weeks Saigon was living on the brink of civil war.

Bao Dai and the French, each for different reasons, were not at all displeased by Diem's desperate situation. Hoping to give his Prime Minister the final shove down the slippery slope, Bao Dai took the occasion to order Diem and Diem's Chief of Staff to join him in France for "consultations." Diem refused. The French business community in Vietnam pressed their home offices in Paris to urge the French Government to act now to replace Diem with a more malleable and pro-French Prime Minister. The French Government, hoping to give its problem child the coup de grâce, publicly voiced its lack of confidence in Diem's ability to cope with the problem of internal stability. Diem shrugged.

By April, 1955 most American analysts (this author included) regarded Diem's position as virtually hopeless. The only plausible explanation for Diem's ability to keep going seemed to be that he was so harassed and so deeply involved that he was unable to pause long enough or draw back far enough to realize how hopeless his situation was. To be sure, he had pretty much contained the two religious sects—much to the surprise and consternation of the French and probably of Bao Dai as well—but he still had the tough Binh Xuyen to deal with. It was clear that Diem would be unsuccessful in dividing or buying off the gangster group the way he had done with the disunited and, in some respects, even more venal religious sects. Diem decided to confront the Binh Xuyen head on. And the Binh Xuyen, for its part, seemed ready and eager to do battle.

The French reaction to the Binh Xuyen challenge was not un-expected and Diem probably had already discounted it. He may even have been slightly amused by it. It was a different matter, however, when he learned that General Collins was also opposed to his showdown policy with the Binh Xuyen and had communi-cated his concern to Washington.

After several skirmishes between the forces loyal to Diem and the Binh Xuyen, a truce was arranged in early April by Collins. In the meantime the French garrisons still remaining in Saigon took up posts in strategically important parts of the city, including some positions held by the Binh Xuyen. Vietnamese Army forces were prevented from entering these areas. As a further constraint the French command, which still controlled the logistics for the Viet-namese Army, withheld ammunition and other needed supplies. The truce fell apart after six days and sporadic fighting broke out again. C. L. Sulzberger's article in *The New York Times* of April 18 was fairly typical of the lugubrious view many Americans, both unofficial and official, held of the situation in Saigon at that time. "The chances of saving South Vietnam from chaos and commu-nism are slim. Brooding civil war threatens to tear the country apart. And the government of Ngo Dinh Diem has proven inept, inefficient and unpopular. Almost from the start the French wished to get rid of the little Premier. Now they appear to have sold the idea to General Collins, our special Ambassador. . . . Any objec-tive observer in South Vietnam has known for months that there was no effective government. . . . We tried to insist Diem's popu-larity and strength were gaining. But the only people we fooled were ourselves."

It would have been only a psychopathic optimist who during this latter part of April could reach any conclusion other than that South Vietnam was faced with "chaos." Like Job, Diem seemed to be a man "born to trouble." The latest of his compounding trib-ulations was a crisis within his own government. The Cao Dai and Hoa Hao Ministers had already resigned, but now several of his own hand-picked associates, including his old friend Foreign Minister Tran Van Do, walked out. Diem turned to the only peo-ple he felt he could really trust—his brothers and a handful of

beginning of the end

others. Chief among these was Nguyen Ngoc Tho, who had been Minister of Interior in Diem's first Cabinet and later became Vice President. He continued to serve Diem faithfully until Diem's assassination, although by 1961 his influence had been eroded by Nhu.

General Collins was recalled to Washington for consultations on the 20th of April. *The New York Times* summed up both the event and the Administration's mood in one sentence: Collins was to discuss "the future of the tottering government of South Vietnam." [18] At a press conference several days after his talk with General Collins, President Eisenhower revealed his own uncertainty and concern about the situation in Vietnam. He also took pains to remove any doubts as to where Collins stood. When questioned about the Administration's views "toward the sticky situation in Vietnam and particularly whether . . . there may be the necessity to change the policy of recognition of Premier Diem," Eisenhower hedged, "I can't give you any final answer . . . it is still under discussion. We have called General Collins back here . . . [he] has been supporting, of course, Premier Diem. Now there have occurred lots of difficulties. People have left the Cabinet and so on. . . . it is a strange and it is almost an inexplicable situation . . . but he [Collins] has come back because we have . . . to clarify ideas as to future policy. . . . What the exact terms of our future policy will be I can't say." [19]

A few days later, however, the Administration announced its stand. On the 29th the State Department reaffirmed that "the present head of the legal government of Free Vietnam which we are supporting is Diem." [20]

The last few days in April and the first few days in May were among the most triumphant in Diem's hectic career. His army had put the Binh Xuyen to rout after some wild to-ings and fro-ings that would have done credit to a Far Eastern "Western." Diem could at long last breathe freely.

To put the final gloss on the American decision of April 29, the Administration on May 6 reaffirmed its support for him: "The United States has great sympathy for a nationalist cause that is free and effective. For this reason we have been and are continuing to support the legal government of Ngo Dinh Diem." At least as important to Diem was a final unequivocal American rupture with Bao Dai. Just a few days earlier the Revolutionary Committee Congress in Saigon had demanded the ouster of Bao Dai and had called for the formation of a new government headed by Diem. The U.S. position, according to the May 6 statement, was that it was "up to the Vietnamese to resolve this problem and decide their form of government by whatever constituent process they freely choose." State Department officials added that the U.S. was "likely to recognize any constitutional arrangement . . . as long as it was representative, legally established and genuinely anti-Communist." [21] It was clear that after many months of discussion, officials became convinced that Bao Dai had outlived his usefulness and would be a hindrance to any national Vietnamese government, even in a titular role.

In the clearer light of history one can see that Diem had held a better hand than most of the kibitzers realized at the time. He even had a face card or two. One of these was the economic aid he had been getting directly from the United States. For several months now, the Vietnamese Army had been on Diem's payroll and its loyalties reflected this mundane fact. Neither the French nor Bao Dai could do much about it. Secondly, Diem was in Saigon and Bao Dai was in France; the French were Out and the Americans were In; and the Americans in Saigon, or at least some of them, were giving Diem their support. In the end, these cards, skillfully played with the help of his shrewd brothers and his gutsy sister-in-law, carried the day. By early May, 1955 there was only one boss in Saigon.

VII

Diem, Dulles, and Dominoes

May, 1955 was an historical watershed, not only in terms of Diem's acknowledged authority in Vietnam, but also in terms of the nature and depth of the American commitment to Diem and his government. The statement of American support for Diem on May 6th may have seemed redundant in the light of the similar commitment made only a week or so before, but the Secretary of State had a special purpose in mind: He was about to leave for a NATO meeting in Paris and wished to set the stage for private conversations with the French on the whole question of American support for the government of Prime Minister Diem.

In the American view, only a strong national Army would be able to maintain the fragile independence with which the South Vietnamese non-Communists had come out of Geneva. And time was short—the North Vietnam Government had a well-developed, highly-motivated military force flushed with its sense of victory over the French. Within a few months after the conclusion of the Geneva Conference, Washington was pressing both Paris and Saigon for permission to train the South Vietnamese Army. American pressure increased when, in September 1954, Diem told Paris that all French forces would have to be evacuated from South Vietnam within eighteen months.

Shortly after his arrival in Saigon in mid-November, 1954 Gen-

eral Collins had confirmed that discussions were underway between the United States, France, and Vietnam to work out
arrangements for training the Vietnamese Army by an American
Mission. The American Mission, he announced, "will soon take
charge of instructing the Vietnam Army in accordance with special American methods which have proved effective in Korea,
Greece, and Turkey. . . . The Mission will work under the supervision of General Paul Ely. . . . The aim will be, however, to build
a completely autonomous Vietnam Army." [1] General Collins' statement was somewhat premature; it was to take many more months
of negotiations with the French before the final arrangements
could be worked out. The General was also over-optimistic; the
American training produced an Army totally unsuited to the challenge it was to face.

Thus, long before Dulles' confrontation with the French in
Paris in May, 1955, and long before Diem had consolidated his
power in Vietnam, the United States had made a major, public
commitment to the frail and untested government of South Vietnam. The stage was already set, the prologue had been written,
the plot was starting to unfold.

Secretary Dulles' agenda in Paris included not only reaffirming American economic aid and political support for the Diem
Government, but launching a program of military assistance as
well. He urged the French to begin their military withdrawal
from Vietnam as soon as possible and to hand over the responsibility for training the South Vietnamese Army to the Americans.
Dulles reportedly argued that the American hands were pure and
the French stained with colonialism and, consequently, the United
States could best deal with Vietnamese problems. The French
were outraged. They told Dulles that the American intent to pursue a strong anti-Communist policy in South Vietnam, especially
if accompanied by military support for Diem's Government, would
endanger the Geneva Accords and would trigger a Communist
reaction. In an effort to bring further pressure on the Secretary,
the French sent for the British Prime Minister. Harold Macmillan
also told Dulles that this new step in American policy toward
Vietnam might lead to an abrogation of the agreement reached

at Geneva. Dulles remained unconvinced and unmoved, although in the end he agreed to modify the language in his proposed communique.

Learning of Dulles' conversations with the French, Bao Dai made an attempt to see the Secretary. The Emperor was worried, with good reason, about his own position in the light of the May 6 statement. Moreover he was aware that if the Americans replaced the French military presence in Vietnam, his hopes for removing Diem would vanish. The Secretary refused to see him, although he permitted some deference to His Majesty's role to be incorporated in the final communique. The communique also reflected the British desire to see Diem's government broadened and the French insistence that Diem cool his anti-French campaign. Finally it made only an oblique reference to the French withdrawal —and no reference to the American intent to establish a training mission. According to the London *Times,* the three governments agreed that: "Mr. Diem shall be advised and persuaded to broaden his government . . . including in it men who are more representative of different interests and tendencies. Diem shall be advised and persuaded to desist from his anti-French attitude and propaganda. The representatives of the powers shall help to devise some form of popular consultation . . . in order that the government . . . shall be based to the greatest practicable degree upon popular consent. The French will not withdraw the expeditionary corps at a rate faster than it can be replaced by the Vietnam Army. . . . The Emperor Bao Dai's position as legal head of the State will remain unaltered." [2] (To those with long memories, President Nixon's "Vietnamization" policy provides a sense of déjà vu.)

Two days before the communique was released in Paris, the decision to transfer responsibility for training the Vietnamese Army from a French to an American military mission was made known in Washington. On May 10th the White House announced that "at the request of the government of Vietnam and with the agreement of the government of France, [the United States] had undertaken responsibility for the training of Vietnam national armed forces." [3] The French had apparently been presented with a fait accompli. And so at Paris in the spring of 1955, the long journey started—a journey in which Americans and Vietnamese together were to experience trauma, frustration, and rare moments of fulfillment in pursuit of an ever-elusive victory.

In a cozy little TV chat with the President shortly after he returned from Paris, Secretary Dulles told Eisenhower and the American people about his trip. Dulles reminded the President that, although the reason for his going to Europe was primarily to deal with European and especially NATO problems, "I never forget the fact that we have got Asian problems as well as European problems and I took advantage of this NATO council to talk a bit to them about our Asian problem, because there is a considerable failure to understand the motivation of our Asian policies. . . ." The President interjected, "That is a wonderful way to tell them!" Dulles continued, "The main point I made there was that we had to accept the fact that Vietnam is now a free nation—at least the Southern half of it is—and it does not have a puppet government, it has not got a government that we can give orders to and tell what we want it to do or we want it to refrain from doing. . . . One can only hold free South Vietnam with a government that is nationalistic and has a purpose of its own and is responsive to the will of its own people, and doesn't take orders from anybody outside, whether it be from Paris—or Cannes [where Bao Dai was basking] for that matter—or from Washington. . . . I think we came to a better understanding and that there is more chance of coordination of French policies with ours along sound lines than has been the case heretofore. The government of Diem, which seemed to be almost on the ropes a few weeks ago, I think is re-established with strength." [4]

McCarthy taints the view [handwritten marginal note]

Diem's period of testing was over. To implement its policy of unequivocal support, the Department of State dispatched Ambassador Frederick Reinhardt to Saigon to succeed General Collins shortly after the Paris meeting. Reinhardt was a career Foreign Service Officer who, like most of the regular Ambassadors to Saigon before him, was a graduate of the Department's Office of European Affairs. Despite Washington's new policy, the Office of Far Eastern Affairs had still not captured bureaucratic control of Indochina. Nonetheless, Reinhardt had gotten the message loud

It never got political control [handwritten marginal note]

and clear. Shortly after his arrival the new Ambassador announced, "I came here under instructions to carry out United States policy in support of the legal government of Vietnam under Premier Ngo Dinh Diem." [5]

Paris was now convinced that the restoration of French influence through Bao Dai was a forlorn hope. There seemed little to be gained or even salvaged by maintaining a French military force in Vietnam, and so with little resistance Paris agreed to hand over its military responsibilities to the Americans. On May 20th the French forces left the Saigon area and assembled in a coastal enclave. From there the troops progressively withdrew from Vietnam until about a year later the last soldier departed. The French also abolished their Ministry for the Associated States of Indochina, and transferred its functions to the Ministry of Foreign Affairs. And to put the final end to the old colonial tie, Paris withdrew its High Commissioner from Vietnam (it would take almost a year before an Ambassador from Paris was appointed).

The ink was hardly dry on the Paris communique when Diem took steps to get rid of Bao Dai. Despite the specific reference in the communique to the effect that the Emperor's position would remain "unaltered," Diem felt secure in moving against him. It was the reality of events in Paris, rather than the words of the communique that Diem heeded. And what had transpired there convinced Diem that French influence over developments in Vietnam was now virtually nil. Diem also knew that the disappearance of French influence meant that Bao Dai's own bargaining power had eroded. Nor was Diem unaware that the United States itself had washed its hands of Bao Dai. Not only had Secretary Dulles refused to see him in Paris, but General Collins, at the dinner marking his departure from Saigon, pointedly ignored the Emperor in his toast—a form of diplomatic non-recognition that no Ambassador would take upon himself and, thus, it must have reflected official Washington policy. But Diem would probably have moved against the Emperor in any case; he had good reason to believe that the Vietnamese people had long since become disillusioned with Bao Dai and his entourage.

Diem's first overt step against Bao Dai was to disband the

Imperial Guard and to incorporate its five thousand men into regular units of the Vietnamese Army. This was quickly followed up by an expropriation of the crown lands which Diem later used for the resettlement of refugees and as a basis for his land reform program. The next step, which took place in mid-June of 1955 was even less subtle. A civil disturbance, inspired by the Diem clan, in the ancient capital of Hue was made the occasion for a convocation of the ancient, obsolete Council of the Royal Family. The Council obliged Diem by renouncing Bao Dai's claim to rule and advocating that Diem take over as President. Diem then announced that a referendum would be held on October 23rd to give the Vietnamese people a choice between himself and the Emperor as the ruler of Vietnam.

Shortly after Diem announced the referendum, he told his countrymen (and the world at large) that the election to decide the question of unification with North Vietnam, which had been called for in the Geneva Accords and scheduled for July, 1956, would not be held. (It will be recalled that the election was scheduled to take place two years after the close of the Geneva Conference.) "We did not sign the Geneva Agreements," Diem noted on July 16th. "We are not bound in any way by these Agreements, signed against the will of the Vietnamese people. . . . it is out of the question for us to consider any proposal from the Vietminh if proof is not given that they put the superior interest of the national community above those of Communism. . . ." [6]

Diem's announcement came as an anti-climax. Secretary Dulles had pre-empted Diem two weeks before. Asked at a news conference on June 28th about the position of the United States with respect to the elections, the Secretary said "neither the United States Government nor the Government of Vietnam is, of course, a party to the Geneva Armistice agreements. We did not sign them and the Government of Vietnam did not sign them and, indeed, protested against them. On the other hand, the United States believes, broadly speaking, in the unification of countries which have a historic unity. . . . we are not at all afraid of elections provided they are held under conditions of genuine freedom which the Geneva Armistice agreement calls for." [7]

hedging to look good

In October, Assistant Secretary of State Robertson officially sanctioned Diem's decision. He noted that the refugees from North Vietnam, together with millions of their countrymen in South Vietnam, "aspire toward unification of their country in liberty. These millions are passionately opposed to Communism and to any scheme for unification under Communism. They are consequently highly skeptical of the inter-zonal election scheduled for July 1956. The Free Vietnamese strongly doubt such elections could be held under genuinely free conditions in Viet Minh-held territory. Red-style elections in the more populous north . . . would unquestionably produce a Communist victory, thus achieving by seemingly legal means the subjugation of Free Viet-Nam to Communist slavery." Robertson then put the question, "Is it possible to obtain in North Vietnam the necessary conditions for a free expression of the national will through general elections?" [8] *

Senator Mansfield was dubious about the possibility for free elections in either zone. "Elections should and must play a major part in the unification of Viet Nam if unification is to be achieved by peaceful means. Unless they are to constitute more than mere ritual, however, elections must have as their purpose providing the people of Viet Nam with an opportunity to make a free choice. . . . the conditions for such a choice hardly yet prevail even in the South. Much less do they exist under the ironclad dictatorship of the North." [10]

The New York Times, which ten years later strongly criticized the American involvement in Vietnam, expressed its opposition to an election to decide the unification issue: "The coolness of the South toward the election plan is understandable. . . . If the vote is a straight numerical one the South can expect to be swamped and the so-called 'Geneva settlement' will simply mean the sentencing of 10,000,000 to life under the Communist yoke. . . . The

* Senator John F. Kennedy was even tougher-minded on the election issue than Robertson. In a speech made in June, 1956, at about the time the elections on reunification had been scheduled to take place, he pleaded that "the United States never give its approval to the only nationwide elections called for by the Geneva Agreement of 1954. . . . neither the United States nor Free Vietnam is ever going to be a party to an election obviously stacked and subverted in advance. . . ." [9]

imperatives in the situation are obvious. South Vietnam must be strengthened. And we must not be trapped into a fictitious legalism that can condemn 10,000,000 potentially free persons into slavery. . . ." [11]

There was ample room for the considerable doubts that had been expressed about the possibility of a free election in the North. Shortly after the Geneva Conference, Ho Chi Minh had launched a land reform program that had political rather than economic objectives. It was one of the principal devices to consolidate Communist power throughout the countryside. Although estimates vary, as many as 50,000 peasants may have been executed under the program, with perhaps twice as many arrested and detained in prisons and forced labor camps. The atmosphere in North Vietnam during 1955 and 1956 was hardly one in which the kind of "free elections" envisaged by some of the delegations at Geneva could have been held.

Although the unification election was cancelled, the referendum on Bao Dai was held as scheduled. The guiding genius was Brother Nhu. The "election campaign," the preparation of the ballots, and the counting of the votes cast a pall over any bright hopes that may have been held that this first election under Diem would be a shining example of democracy in action. It was not simply that Diem wound up with an incredible 99 percent of the votes, but that Diem and Nhu permitted and perhaps even encouraged such flagrant violations as "counting" more votes in favor of Diem in the Saigon area than there were registered voters.

Even such ardent admirers of Diem as Joseph Buttinger were appalled and disgusted. "The one-sided 'election campaign,'" Buttinger writes, "and the methods employed to assure an almost unanimous vote for Diem were quite outrageous. . . . The use of these methods to secure the victory of a good cause boded ill for the future of a regime whose leader liked to advertise his acts as morally inspired." [12] This "election" was to be only the first of a train of events which would eventually shatter any illusions that Diem and his family would be able, or even wish, to institute the reality of a democratic process in "Free-Vietnam."

The United States put the best face on the election that it

could. In a press release dated October 26 the State Department noted that "We are glad to see the evolution of orderly and effective democratic processes in an area of Southeast Asia which has been and continues to be threatened by Communist efforts to impose totalitarian control." [13]

By the end of 1955 Diem had achieved most of the objectives he had originally set for himself. The power of the sects was broken; the French influence was virtually eliminated; Bao Dai was deposed. The goal he was not to achieve during 1955 was one he would never achieve—the creation of a strong and popular anti-Communist government.

*   *   *

While Diem's policies and programs from 1956 onward led to inevitable disaster, the trend was not apparent to most observers at the time. When one saw the chaos in other ex-colonial areas of Asia and Africa and the high-handed, corrupt, and inefficient standards of government in much of Latin America, South Vietnam and its leader Ngo Dinh Diem looked very good in comparison. In mid-1956 Senator John F. Kennedy noted that news about South Vietnam had virtually disappeared from the front pages of American newspapers and that "the American people have all but forgotten" Vietnam. This was in part due to "the amazing success of President Diem in meeting . . . the major political and economic crises which heretofore continually plagued Vietnam." Kennedy then read his own fortune, ". . . in my opinion, Vietnam would in all likelihood be receiving more attention from our Congress and administration, and greater assistance under our aid programs, if it were in imminent danger of Communist invasion or revolution." [14]

At that time and for a few years to come, Senator Kennedy's reading of the situation in Vietnam seemed reasonable. To be sure, most of the reports coming out of Saigon were colored by the fervor of a small but prolific band of American experts and observers who tended to look upon Diem as a latter-day Saint Joan. There were, of course, some hints of discontent with Diem's methods of rule, impatience with his tendency to lecture rather than inspire, and unease in the face of Communist forays in the countryside. Some Americans and other foreigners had had a feeling of foreboding with respect to the future as it would unfold under the Saigon regime. As early as mid-1955 Graham Greene had expressed grave concern: "The South, instead of confronting the totalitarian North with the evidences of freedom, has slipped into an inefficient dictatorship; newspapers suppressed, strict censorship, men exiled by administrative order. . . ." [15] But these views were overshadowed by respect for Diem as a hard-working, incorruptible leader. More importantly, there was no one who seemed ready or able to challenge his leadership.

Despite the progress in Vietnam (some of it real and some only apparent) and despite the brisk activity of Diem's public relations touts in the United States (some of them professional and some self-appointed amateurs), there were occasional unpleasant whiffs that made even Diem's supporters feel a bit queasy. The large number of political prisoners in Saigon jails, most of whom were non-Communist nationalists, caused an undercurrent of unease about the Diem regime among some of its friends in the United States. Joseph Buttinger, for example, became increasingly disenchanted, not only because President Diem ignored his advice about releasing the prisoners, but because he found him lying to the American press on this matter during his tour of the United States in May, 1957.

The political prisoner issue, however, stirred very few other Americans. Diem's visit to the United States was a huge success. His speech to a joint session of Congress was enthusiastically received, and the press generally was favorable. His remarks on Capitol Hill had just the right mix of humility, gratitude, and determination and were shrewdly designed to fit the current mood of Congress. Diem thanked the United States for its "generous and unselfish assistance" and he pledged to "continue to fight Communism." He was described by *The New York Times* as "an Asian liberator, a man of tenacity of purpose, a stubborn man . . . bent on succeeding, a man whose life—all of it—is devoted to his country and to his God." [16] But *Life* magazine, normally pro-Diem, was moved to note: "Miraculous though their recovery and progress have been, Diem and Vietnam still have plenty of problems. . . .

For all its electoral and constitutional show, South Vietnam appears in many ways to be as much of a police state as its Vietminh rival to the north, and Diem may easily be mistaken for another dictator." [17]

It soon became evident that despite some advances on the economic and social fronts, Diem lacked two important, ultimately critical, ingredients in the recipe for success. He was unable or not inclined to gain the support of important elements of the urban population, and he seemed incapable of stemming the erosion of security, not only in the countryside, but in Saigon itself. In late October, 1957 there was a portent of the dark days to come—terrorists bombed the United States Information Service Library and an American barracks; thirteen American soldiers were injured.

By 1958 Diem was engaging in the wholesale suppression of Vietnamese newspapers whose editorial line was critical or whose reporting displeased him. By now too the various members of the Ngo family were becoming conspicuously more powerful and increasingly objectionable. Indeed Diem's government had become little more than a facade with the real power exercised by his three brothers, none of whom held any official position: Nhu, the "adviser" in the Presidential Palace; Can, the virtual warlord of Central Vietnam; and Archbishop Thuc, who wielded substantial influence through his authority as the eldest surviving brother and through his control over the vocal and powerful Catholic minority. And behind the men behind the scenes was the beauteous, bitchy, and clever Madame Nhu. Joseph Buttinger tells of a trip he made to Saigon in August, 1958 in a desperate effort to influence Diem to broaden his government and to move ahead with some basic political and economic reforms. Diem, a past master of oral jujitsu, kept him off balance throughout their conversation. Whenever the discussion got to a point where Buttinger felt prepared to make his case, Diem changed the subject. Nhu was present during much of the conversation, although at one point when Nhu became particularly aggressive, Diem sent him from the room. It was then, according to Buttinger, that he realized that even the powerful Nhu could not be used as an instrument to influence the recalci-

trant President, and that the situation in Vietnam was "desperate."
Some time later, when Archbishop Thuc was in New York, Buttinger pleaded that Thuc induce Diem to undertake some major
political and economic improvements. Thuc responded that no one
could wield influence over Diem. He recalled that when his
brother was a child and he had carried him piggyback, "he would
beat on my head and back if I turned to the left and Diem wanted
to go to the right."

At least as important to Diem as the network of supporters he
had built up in the United States, was the group of Vietnamese
experts and technicians he had been able to attract to his government after he became Prime Minister in the summer of 1954. Most
of these were non-Communist nationalists who had either refused
to cooperate with the French or who had actually been members
of the Viet Minh. It was largely through these men that Diem had
been able to construct a government and develop a Civil Service
which could make a start on the gigantic task of rebuilding South
Vietnam. But the first flush of enthusiasm soon wore off. Diem's
stubborn, dictatorial, and sometimes bizarre style and methods
angered and disillusioned many of these much-needed experts.
They quietly faded back to private life (like Tran Van Do, Vietnam's first Foreign Minister), went into active opposition, or
joined the colony of expatriates in Paris.

Diem would have been a fascinating subject for a psychiatrist
or psychologist, and I am neither. What comes through even to a
layman, however, is a man who was almost totally disengaged
from the world around him. He came back to Vietnam a respected
but alien figure. He shared few of the experiences of those non-
Communist nationalists who had remained in Vietnam during the
French–Viet Minh war, and, except for a few old friends or young
technicians, he regarded the professional and political elite of
Saigon with hauteur or suspicion. They returned the compliment.
In the first critical years Diem might have gained the whole-
hearted cooperation of this group if he had given them a stake
and a sense of participation in what he was trying to accomplish.
But he chose to ignore them when they remained aloof and to jail
them when they registered opposing views. The number of his

loyal adherents decreased month by month, until ultimately he felt
that he could rely only on his own family. The effect was to deny
South Vietnam even a thin layer of experienced political leaders.
When Diem and his brothers were overthrown a few years later,
there was no one prepared for effective leadership of South Vietnam; chronic political instability was the inevitable result.

It had become clear by 1959 that the threat to South Vietnam
was not from an invasion of North Vietnamese troops across the
northern border but from small hit-and-run guerrilla and propaganda actions throughout the length and breadth of the land. The
regular South Vietnamese Divisions, in static defense positions
along the 17th parallel, sopped up much of Diem's available military manpower and equipment. In addition, and more importantly,
this conventional deployment (largely a result of the "Korea-
complex" of the American advisers) diverted much-needed protection from the rural areas throughout the country where Communist terrorism was becoming more than the "nuisance" it had
appeared to be a few years earlier. The peasant population, apathetic to a central government of whatever character, was becoming increasingly alienated as a result of Saigon's failure to supply
the only service that every village and hamlet expected of it—
security from attack. Land reform, tax reforms, fertilizer programs
added up only to slogans—which in far too many cases they tended
to be—unless the farmers could plant their seed and harvest
their crops unmolested.

The threat to South Vietnam's domestic tranquillity was given
an added and ominous dimension by the infusion of well-trained
specialists in military and political warfare from North Vietnam.
The young men who had gone North after the Geneva settlement
of 1954 were beginning to come "home." They were sturdy and
strongly motivated and had not been idle during the period they
had spent in North Vietnam. By now they were skilled in the techniques of radio communication, ordnance repair, sabotage, and
agitprop. By the end of 1960 it was estimated that 4,500 ex-South-
erners and some natives of North Vietnam had slipped through the
porous security net along South Vietnam's border. They joined up
with the growing bands of local Communist dissidents and added

substantially to the Communists' discipline and technical capabilities.

*   *   *

Thus a bare five years after Diem's assumption of power, his "miracle" began to show stains of ugly reality. Remarkable economic progress had been made, but much of it was a result of massive infusions of American economic aid ($1.2 billion between 1954 and 1959). The country was relatively stable, but to make it so Diem had to resort to Draconian measures—measures that alienated some people he needed most and which, while temporarily stemming the activities of local Communist activists, ultimately made their task easier by stimulating hatred for the Saigon regime. On Diem's infrequent excursions into the rural areas he relied almost entirely on his courtiers and intelligence officers for information—and they told him only what he wanted to hear. He apparently had no conception of the expanding Communist control over vast areas in the Mekong Delta and in the northern provinces of South Vietnam. When he visited with the farmers, it was Diem who did all the talking. "This and this that I did for you—wasn't it good?" And the chorus of farmers sang out, "Yes, Mr. President, it was wonderful."

By early 1959 the security situation had deteriorated to the point that Diem felt it necessary to establish drumhead courts with authority to sentence to death not only terrorists and members of subversive organizations, but speculators and "rumor spreaders." In an effort to give the peasants in the most troubled areas some measure of security and at the same time tighten Saigon's control over them, the Government, primarily through the efforts and inspiration of Brother Nhu, attempted to resettle large numbers into fortified village-clusters. The scheme was borrowed from one the French had adopted several years before. The affected peasants reacted bitterly to the idea and the enterprise was dropped after a two-month trial. It was followed by an "agroville" scheme borrowed from Malaya where thousands of jungle squatters had been moved away from the centers of guerrilla activity. But Vietnamese farmers are not Chinese jungle squatters and did not take lightly to the idea of abandoning their native hamlets. In any case the program was very costly and was abandoned in its early stages. The next approach was Nhu's "strategic hamlet" idea, which had enthusiastic American backing but which also faded away.

Perhaps in direct challenge to the harsh new government methods, perhaps because the time was ripe in any case, terrorism, sabotage, and subversion increased markedly in the latter half of 1959. At the year's end, large areas of South Vietnam were under Communist control and five thousand hard-core guerrillas were estimated to be at large.

Events moved rapidly and for the worse in 1960. The number of trained guerrillas grew substantially until by the end of the year an estimated ten thousand were raising havoc throughout large areas of the countryside—this despite Diem's increasingly repressive measures. According to the Government of Vietnam, fourteen hundred local government officials and civilians were assassinated and more than seven hundred persons kidnapped during 1960 alone. Even with ample allowance for imprecision and exaggeration, it is evident that South Vietnam was no longer what one writer had called it just two years before, "one of the more stable countries of South Asia." [18]

In September, 1960 Hanoi, through the vehicle of the Third Communist Party Congress, made an official clarion call for the violent overthrow of Diem and the removal of "American imperialist rule." There is evidence to suggest that the North Vietnamese had thus far looked upon the terrorist effort of the Communist activists in South Vietnam as being premature and ill-conceived. Until 1959 Hanoi seemed to have preferred political action leading toward a relatively bloodless reunification. In any case, two years were to elapse between the time terrorism and subversion broke out in earnest in South Vietnam and the time the official green light was flashed on from Hanoi.

Perhaps the guerrilla movement in South Vietnam was sparked by the refusal of the Diem Government to hold the elections for unification in July, 1956—elections which Ho Chi Minh had counted on to give him the victory denied him in Geneva. But if

Ho would have permitted the kind of elections in the North that were envisaged in the Geneva Agreement, he would have been the first Communist in history ready to accept the results of a free election. In any case, Ho consolidated the efforts of the South Vietnamese returnees by establishing in the spring of 1959 a South Vietnamese branch office of the Vietnamese Communist Party. By the following year Hanoi and the National Liberation Front were preparing to move from sporadic guerrilla violence to a much more organized and effective assault at every level against the Saigon Government.[19]

As the grumbling of the population about both Communist terror and Diem's counter-terror increased, Diem turned increasingly inward. In a sense he reverted to the meditative, cloistered style of life that had been so much a part of his recent past. His strong sense of idealism and his confidence in his own political instincts made him even less inclined to listen, let alone accede to American advice and blandishments. It was this stubbornness, at once exasperating and awesome, that planted the seeds of his own destruction.

Personal loyalty to Diem, rather than ability and efficiency, became the criterion for promotion and reward. Catholics, in part because they were better educated, in part because they were considered more reliable, were given the more important and lucrative positions in the Army and Civil Service. The fact that a large number of these Catholics had come down from the North only a few years before and were either ignorant of or insensitive to the problems of the South exacerbated Diem's problems in providing an effective and popular government. This caused further unrest and dissatisfaction among the non-Communist—especially Buddhist—circles in South Vietnam. In April, 1960 a group of distinguished Vietnamese, including ten former Cabinet members, published a proclamation asking Diem to step down. They were all arrested. In November a small group of military officers staged an abortive coup. It failed because Diem was able to outmaneuver them. In February, 1962 two Air Force pilots bombed the Presidential Palace. Although the wing occupied by the Nhus was destroyed, the Nhus and Diem were unharmed.

Perhaps one of Diem's greatest political errors had been his failure on the grounds of security to come to grips with the problem of local government, especially at the village level. By century-old tradition Vietnam's villages were autonomous units with their own elected officials. In June and August, 1956 Diem had arbitrarily replaced all village chiefs and municipal councils with others who were appointed by his hand-picked province chiefs and district advisers. By eliminating the surviving remnants of village democracy and by breaking with a strong political tradition, Diem had alienated a vast number of people in the countryside.

*   *   *

It is easier in retrospect than it was at the time to see how Diem's world turned sour. Perhaps Diem really never had a chance; the events of the preceding decades may have stacked the cards hopelessly against him—or against any non-Communist leader holding power in the wake of the Geneva Accords. The French occupation had sapped vitality from much of the country—intelligent, ambitious men became either enthusiastic sycophants of the French or violent revolutionists. The only course between the two was apathy; there was no place in Vietnamese society for the "moderate," the "liberal," the rational man of action. The arts of accommodation, fence-sitting, and subversion flourished under the Japanese occupation. During the war with the French a whole generation of Vietnamese learned little but violence. For a time Diem could play one self-interested group off against another, and he could restore some semblance of order and create a sense of economic progress with American backing and aid. But by 1960 he required more than this: he needed qualities and resources that he lacked and that the United States could not supply. Somehow he had to develop the talent for establishing positive loyalty; he now had grudging and often superficial obedience. And he had to be able to master the greedy and privileged within his own circles in order to establish a meaningful, sustained effort that could compete in deed with the promises (and sometimes even the performance) of the Communists within South Vietnam. Finally he needed to mus-

ter the necessary self-discipline which would permit him to listen
as well as talk, talk, talk. Sheer dedication and a deep trust in
God were not enough to meet the problems he confronted.

Perhaps no one short of Ho Chi Minh himself could have
licked the problems that the government in Saigon faced on its
fifth anniversary. Ho's methods probably would have created a
"stable" and "secure" Vietnam. In terms of repressing the dissidents,
he would have been infinitely more efficient and thorough than
Diem and Nhu; in terms of searching out the subversives, he would
have been much more successful. And in terms of harnessing or
disposing of the apathetic or the indifferent, Ho would have done
well too. Diem's problem was that he was too much of a mandarin
to be a democrat, too much of a democrat to be a dictator, and too
much of a dictator to attract spontaneous popular support. Ho Chi
Minh had no such inner conflicts.

❋   ❋   ❋

Although the Saigon Government was skidding and careening
down treacherous paths in the autumn of 1960, the issue of Vietnam played a minor role in the American election campaign. The
menacing noises coming out of Castro's Cuba, the rapidly eroding
non-Communist position in Laos, and the growing bellicosity of
the Chinese Communists with respect to the Offshore Islands received much of the attention in a campaign not very noteworthy
for the level of debate on foreign policy.

Vice President Nixon, by inclination and by force of circumstance, played the role of the heavy. And some of his views then
seem particularly ironic in the light of events that have transpired
during the subsequent decade. Speaking of Laos at the Veterans
of Foreign Wars Convention in Detroit on March 24, 1960, Nixon
advocated that the United States should "build our own strength
and be tough at the conference table and let the rest of the world
go hang. . . ." And, "There was a situation in Indochina where
we had a civil war raging—and finally settled without war." [20]
And, "As a result of our taking the strong stand that we did [in
Indochina], the civil war there was ended, and today at least in
the south of Indochina [sic] the Communists have moved out and

we do have a strong free bastion there." [21] So much for Nixon's views on Vietnam in 1960.

Senator Kennedy's campaign statements were even less informative on Asian problems in general, and on Vietnam in particular, than those of Vice President Nixon. He confined himself largely to attacks on Nixon's 1954 recommendation that American troops be sent to Indochina to fight with the French, and on the deteriorating situation in Laos. But with respect to American troops fighting in Vietnam during the French–Viet Minh war, Kennedy's remarks had more relevance than was apparent at the time: "If ever there was a war where we would have been engaged in a hopeless struggle without allies, for an unpopular colonialist cause, it was the 1954 war in Indochina." [22] Implicitly promising more than it turned out his Administration could actually deliver, Kennedy asked an audience in September, 1960, "Are other countries of Asia going to join Laos in the next ten years? What contribution can we make to the cause of freedom . . . ? . . . It is not the questions that have been traditionally before us. . . . Now the problems are new and they require new solutions." [23] And this was as specific as Senator Kennedy was willing to be on where we were and where we should go in Southeast Asia. He would soon find many loose ends to tie up in both Laos and Vietnam.

VIII

Kennedy's Commitment

After several months, it was a special form of purgatory—moving reluctantly out of the bright Geneva sunlight, taking a backward glance at the sailboats on the shimmering lake, trudging up the marble steps of the Palais, listening to Krishna Menon's interminable oration, writhing through the Pathet Lao spokesmen's now-familiar diatribe, sleeping during the consecutive translations in The Language of The Day, trudging down the steps hours later. Each Conference prisoner contrived his own form of escape—crossword puzzles under the shelter of an official document, word games (wait until the first mention of a place name—"I call upon the distinguished representative of Thailand"—then scribble all the place names one can think of beginning with "T": Tunisia, Texas, Tibet . . .). For several days I took my pad of foolscap and neatly inscribed across the page: *Places I would Rather Be and Things I would Rather Be Doing than Sitting in the Palais des Nations at 3 o'clock in the Afternoon of July—1961.* There followed a long list that became more inspired as the days went by. (I abandoned this form of innocent divertissement when my neighbor, the crossworder, looked at my list and pronounced me "a very wicked man.")

The Laos talks, or officially "The Fourteen Nation Conference on Laos," were convened on May 16, 1961. Agreement was finally reached on July 23, 1962, fourteen months and a billion words later. During this period the situation in Laos, which together with Cuba represented President Kennedy's most troublesome international problems, became more or less stabilized. During this period too Hanoi and Washington turned their attention increasingly toward South Vietnam.

*   *   *

International crises are relative phenomena in Washington—as they tend to be in every world capital. Thus during Eisenhower's second term little attention was paid to developments in Vietnam or Laos, until it finally became abundantly and depressingly clear that the regimes of Ngo Dinh Diem and Phoumi Nosavan were both in serious trouble. The Hungarian uprising, the Suez debacle, Castro's take-over of Cuba, the U–2 shoot-down over the Soviet Union, the abortive Summit Conference, the Sputnik launch all overshadowed local jungle wars and diverted the Administration's attention from events in Southeast Asia. Vietnam seemed to be going reasonably well. Indeed a 1960 Senate report concluded "that the U.S. Military Aid Advisory Group can be phased out of Vietnam in the foreseeable future." [1] Few high ranking officials could find Laos on a map, let alone understand what was going on in that complicated, confusing, and remote little Kingdom.

Occasional utterances, warnings, promises, and predictions about Southeast Asia emerged from the White House, but responsibility was pretty much left in the hands of those on watch—the Ambassadors, the Assistant Secretary, desk officers, third-echelon foreign affairs and defense officials. Senator Mansfield, the man on Capitol Hill most interested in and most knowledgeable about the area, had last visited Vietnam in 1955 and was not to make another trip until 1962. The peripatetic Secretary Dulles dropped in on Vietnam in 1955, and Vice President Nixon paid a visit in 1956. Then there was a complete hiatus; no government official above the level of Assistant Secretary made a trip to Saigon until the spring of 1961 when Vice President Johnson went on a factfinding mission for President Kennedy. Press coverage of events was also low-key and spasmodic. Until 1960 there were only three resident American correspondents in Saigon.

I was assigned to our Embassy in London from 1955 to 1958. As part of my responsibilities there I gave regular briefings to American and British officials on international developments. I cannot remember a single occasion during this period when events in Vietnam were regarded as sufficiently important to warrant more than passing mention. Nor do I recall members of the British Foreign Office or the intelligence services even asking for special briefings on Vietnam, despite residual British responsibility as Co-Chairman of the Geneva Conference.

From the Geneva Conference in 1954 until mid-1959, the official U.S. economic and military aid commitment to South Vietnam amounted to approximately $1.8 billion. Beginning in January, 1955, when the United States first began giving aid directly to the Vietnamese government rather than channeling it through France, the aid program was designed to strengthen South Vietnam against the possibility of an armed attack from the North and to keep the war-devastated economy limping along. For the first two years American aid was largely confined to paying the monthly costs of the South Vietnamese Army and assisting in the resettlement of refugees.

During the period 1955–1959 practically all economic aid to South Vietnam was administered through "counterpart fund" financing, a device whereby Vietnamese importers purchased certain essential goods (such as fertilizer, steel, machinery, trucks, and cement) under a commercial import program. The American Government paid the seller of these goods directly; the Vietnamese importer paid for these goods by depositing piasters into a special counterpart fund. These funds were then made available to the South Vietnamese Government to meet internal budgetary requirements, specifically to meet the payroll of the Vietnamese armed forces and much of the civil service. Approximately 80 percent of counterpart funds were used by the Government of South Vietnam for defense expenditures. Reviewing the American aid program for Vietnam, a 1960 Senate report stated that "from the outset, military aid has been the tail that wags the dog; military needs have had first and predominant call on all American aid and much of the nonmilitary aid program has been designed to meet these needs." [2]

The basic philosophy of American aid to Vietnam may seem in retrospect to have been pathetically naive and idealistic. But those with perfect hindsight should bear in mind some fundamental aspects of American thinking about foreign aid during the mid-fifties. Most important perhaps was the factor of sheer inexperience. To be sure, we had developed effective programs and policies in connection with the Marshall Plan for the recovery of Western Europe and with the civilian/military occupation for the reconstruction of Japan. But in each case we were dealing with modern economies with which we had some familiarity. Moreover in each of the recipient countries there was a reservoir of local administrative skills, both at government and industry levels, and there were local economists, engineers, technicians, and statisticians with whom our own administrators and experts could communicate and cooperate. Even as late as 1959 our experience in providing large-scale aid to underdeveloped and, particularly, ex-colonial countries had been limited to a very few nations—the Philippines, where at least there was a common language and where administrative and technical skills were available; South Korea, where we had a substantial military presence that provided some controls and a logistics infrastructure; India, where our program consisted, as it still does, principally of food shipments; and Taiwan, where our program was primarily geared to military assistance. (It is interesting to note that the annual Vietnam program was several times that for the Philippines from 1955–1958.)

Another factor that influenced American thinking and implementation with respect to the Vietnam aid program was a strong desire to maintain for the South Vietnamese the independence they were granted at Geneva. Many Americans felt there was no point in subjecting the Vietnamese to tight American controls to replace those imposed in the recent past by French colonialism. And besides, Diem was regarded as so clearly incorruptible that many of the safeguards that might otherwise have been imposed were not considered necessary in Vietnam. Thus no strings. And thus, as we were soon to learn to our sorrow, no leverage. Although Diem himself was honest, from 1956 on Nhu convinced him that some funds would have to be used to finance the Diemist Can Lao party. At about the same time another brother, Msgr. Thuc, persuaded Diem that economic advantages should be provided to the Catholic clergy. Here, then, was the beginning of officially-sponsored corruption that was to plague Vietnam under Diem.

❀   ❀   ❀

This was Kennedy's inheritance on January 21, 1961: an American commitment in Vietnam which, while less specific in form and smaller in substance than it later became, was nonetheless concrete and substantial enough that American prestige in Asia—and beyond—was intimately tied to the declining fortunes of Ngo Dinh Diem. The new President, however, was not altogether innocent of the nature or the extent of the commitment; as a Senator he was a close and interested observer of American–Vietnamese relations. He had given no indication that he opposed the Eisenhower–Dulles policy; rather, as his speeches amply demonstrated, he was one of the leading advocates in the Senate of strong and tangible American support. But he was also realistic. In 1954, when the United States was contemplating military intervention in Indochina, Kennedy had no quarrel with the basic U.S. objective of preventing Communist domination of the area, but he told the Senate that "no amount of American military assistance in Indochina can conquer an enemy which is everywhere and at the same time nowhere, 'an enemy of the people' which has the sympathy and covert support of the people." After reviewing briefly the optimistic statements on prospects for victory made by the French military commanders, as well as by various U.S. officials, Senator Kennedy went on to say: "The hard truth of the matter is . . . that without the whole hearted support of the peoples of the Associated States, without a reliable and crusading native army with a dependable officer corps, a military victory, even with American support, in that area is difficult if not impossible of achievement." [3]

As early as June, 1956, in a speech to the American Friends of Vietnam, Kennedy went at least as far as Secretary Dulles in emphasizing the importance of Vietnam to the security of the United States and the urgent need for full American support. While his prose may seem somewhat melodramatic from our present vantage point in time, we should remember that Kennedy was speaking against a background of a troubled and troubling Asia. The French, the Dutch, and the British had left unstable and rickety regimes groping for their place in the international sun; China posed an ever-present threat; and Japan was still struggling to its feet after a decade of postwar reconstruction. "Vietnam represents the cornerstone of the Free World in Southeast Asia, the Keystone to the arch, the finger in the dike. Burma, Thailand, India, Japan, the Philippines and, obviously, Laos and Cambodia are among those whose security would be threatened if the red tide of Communism overflowed into Vietnam. . . . Moreover, the independence of Free Vietnam is crucial to the free world in fields other than the military. Her economy is essential to the economy of all of Southeast Asia; and her political liberty is an inspiration to those seeking to obtain or maintain their liberty in all parts of Asia— and indeed the world. The fundamental tenets of this nation's foreign policy, in short, depend in considerable measure upon a strong and free Vietnamese nation." [4] In short, Kennedy may have had many occasions to whistle softly, raise his eyebrows, or swear under his breath as the world he inherited was revealed in the written and oral briefings he was given during his first two weeks behind the big desk in the Oval Room—but the story of Vietnam should have given him no surprise.

Urging or applauding a policy is one thing, having the responsibility for implementing that policy is another. And when Kennedy found that the "keystone to the arch" was not only eroding but that the repair job would be his, he lost no time in trying to assess the dimensions of the job. There was ample information at hand—much of it lugubrious. The gravity of the Communist threat in South Vietnam and the apparent inability of the Diem Government to cope with it came through loud and clear. Ambassador Elbridge Durbrow in particular had made no bones about the situation, nor had he been coy in attempting to get Diem to take action to restore his government's authority. In fact he was so insistent that Diem now regarded Durbrow as having worn out his welcome. Over and above the reporting from our Embassy in Saigon, Kennedy had on his desk a memorandum from Brigadier General Edward Lansdale, who had been sent to Vietnam by the previous Administration to take a close look at the situation.

Lansdale, the Pentagon's leading expert on guerrilla war, returned to Washington in early January after weeks in Vietnam. He brought the news that matters were even worse than Washington had thought. Not only was the situation in the countryside precarious, but Diem's military and civil structure was a shambles. Even more disturbing, the Saigon Government, despite Durbrow's prodding and needling, was unprepared psychologically, militarily, and in every other respect to fight the kind of war it was confronting—and losing. Diem remained incapable of undertaking the kind of programs that would attract the mass of Vietnamese to his side; the South Vietnamese military forces were still largely deployed along the 17th parallel; and those that were not were using large-unit, conventional tactics totally unsuited to the terrain and the enemy they faced. There was apparently no recognition on the part of either the Vietnamese or most of the Americans in Vietnam that current tactics and strategy needed to be revised sharply if Diem with our help was to be able to cope with the Mao-Giap style of guerrilla warfare. Lansdale urged that the South Vietnamese Government would have to fight the insurgents on their terms, not only through unconventional military means but by aggressive political, economic, and social action.

In addition to the Lansdale Report, President Kennedy found awaiting him as he first entered his office an ambitious new program for fighting the war—a Counter-Insurgency Plan for Vietnam that had been worked out in preliminary form by the previous Administration. As the plan evolved, it recommended that Diem be given equipment and supplies to expand South Vietnam's regular army to 170,000 men, an increase of 20,000. In addition the United States should equip and train 32,000 irregular local forces (the Civil Guard) bringing this group up to a total of 68,000 men. In exchange for this new assistance the Diem regime would be required to make an earnest effort to increase its popular support, especially among the urban population, by inviting non-Communist opposition leaders to join the government. In addition Diem was to give the National Assembly power to look into charges of corruption within the government. Finally, the plan called for an ambitious program of "civic action" throughout the rural areas. In short, if the plan were approved, the United States would be making a deal with Diem: he would get financial support for a substantial expansion of his armed forces in exchange for his improving the effectiveness of his government.

The package made sense to the new President and he approved it in late January. Negotiations started with Saigon in mid-February. Despite Diem's frequent protestations that he urgently needed to expand the Vietnamese armed forces, he procrastinated for many months before he even disclosed the terms of the Counter-Insurgency Plan to members of his Cabinet. Meanwhile, the original American conditions on which the additional support would be forthcoming eroded. Ultimately Diem got his expanded army and Civil Guard in exchange for vague promises that he would press efforts to win the support of the peasants; the matter of broadening his government and of giving the Assembly power to investigate corruption was quietly dropped. And from February to May the security situation in Vietnam continued to deteriorate.

*   *   *

But as troubling as the Vietnam problem was during Kennedy's first months in office, it was overshadowed by the collapsing non-Communist position in Laos. Clark Clifford, who was then an adviser to Kennedy, points out that in the transition period before the inauguration the first item on the foreign policy agenda was "the deteriorating situation in Southeast Asia." On the day before he took office Kennedy received a briefing from President Eisenhower and his subordinates. "Most of the time, the discussion centered on Southeast Asia, with emphasis upon Laos." Clifford's notes on this occasion reveal Eisenhower's conviction that "Laos was the key to the entire area of Southeast Asia. . . . if we per-

mitted Laos to fall, then we would have to write off all the area."
Quoting Eisenhower directly, Clifford evokes the depth of Eisenhower's concern: "Our unilateral intervention [in Laos]," Eisenhower said, "would be our last desperate hope in the event we're
unable to prevail upon the other signatories [to the Southeast
Asia Treaty] to join us." [5]

In his first Message to Congress on the State of the Union,
Kennedy voiced his own concern about the situation in Southeast
Asia, particularly in Laos. "In Asia, the relentless pressures of the
Chinese Communists menace the security of the entire area—from
the borders of India and South Viet Nam to the jungles of Laos,
struggling to protect its newly-won independence. We seek in
Laos what we seek in all Asia, and, indeed, in all of the world—
freedom for the people and independence for the government.
And this Nation shall persevere in our pursuit of these objectives." [6]

One curious aspect of Kennedy's remarks was the absence of
any reference to the North Vietnamese, who, even more than the
Chinese Communists, were causing the mischief in Laos and Vietnam. This omission was to be corrected in subsequent pronouncements from Washington as the dimensions of Ho Chi Minh's support to the Pathet Lao and Viet Cong forces became more fully
known during the course of 1961.

As Kennedy's State of the Union Message revealed, Laos
rather than Vietnam was uppermost in the President's mind; it
was to remain so during the months to follow. The Administration
had ample reason to worry. Laos had no government worth mentioning (although even its unmentionable government had ardent
and powerful supporters in the U.S. Embassy in Vientiane); the
Royal Laotian Army seemed unable, despite considerable infusions of American aid, to engage in any form of movement other
than flight; and the Communist Pathet Lao Army, generally reinforced by tough comrades from North Vietnam, seemed to be able
to go anywhere it pleased.* In the face of such heavy weather in

* Governor Harriman tells of a briefing given to him in which an American
officer reported major improvements in the Laos Army: "Only a few months ago,
the Laotians used to retreat without their weapons; now they take their weapons
with them when they run away."

Laos, the gathering clouds in nearby Vietnam did not appear to be as ominous to the new team in Washington as they otherwise would have. As a consequence Vietnam was a residual claimant for the time and attention of a harassed Administration.

By the winter of 1961 Laos was being torn apart by three contesting forces—the Government forces under General Phoumi Nosavan, a neutralist group under Prince Souvanna Phouma, and the Communist Pathet Lao under Prince Souphanouvong. In early January the Communist and Neutralist forces had captured the strategic Plaine des Jarres in central Laos, as well as a key provincial capital. In late January the British, with the support of the United States, responded to a Soviet suggestion for a peace conference on Laos similar to the Geneva Conference of 1954; but the two sides disagreed on whether the neutralist Souvanna or the Prime Minister of the Royal Government should represent Laos at such a conference. By March there was no breakthrough on the diplomatic front, and the fighting had increased. On March 23 President Kennedy, in a televised news conference, affirmed the American desire to see "a neutral and independent Laos" and implied American military steps would be taken to prevent Laos from falling under Communist control.* On the same day the Russians received a joint American–British proposal for a ceasefire in Laos, which would be followed by a conference along the lines Moscow had suggested a few months before. The Russians agreed to this proposal on April 1.

With the start of the Geneva Conference on Laos, President Kennedy could turn his attention to other troubles in other parts

---

* Although Kennedy did not announce any specific military action on the part of the United States, he backed up his statement by moving the Seventh Fleet into the South China Sea, putting U.S. combat troops in Okinawa on an alert, and sending a 500-man Marine Corps helicopter force into an area of Thailand bordering closely on Laos. Some of the President's advisers argued for a limited commitment of American forces to Laos. The Joint Chiefs of Staff all favored some kind of military action but were divided on the extent to which the United States should become involved. Those who were opposed to a limited commitment of forces to Laos drew, according to Arthur Schlesinger, a lurid picture of an all-out Communist response, with thousands of Viet Minh troops pouring into Laos and the ultimate possibility of war with China. Their recommendation was all or nothing; either go in on a large scale, with 60,000 soldiers, air cover, and even nuclear weapons, or else stay out." [7]

of the world. High on his list were Cuba, Berlin, and Vietnam. His problems with Cuba came to an ugly climax with the Bay of Pigs fiasco in April, 1961; the Berlin access issue reached a showdown in August; the situation in Vietman went from bad to worse and was not to be resolved during Kennedy's lifetime.

Between January and June events in Vietnam moved quickly— and not for the better. By mid-year it was reckoned that 12,000 Viet Cong hard-core guerrillas were at large, more than twice the number that had been estimated twelve months earlier. Incidents of violence averaged more than twenty per day, and almost 60 percent of South Vietnam was believed to be under some degree of Communist control.

Developments in Vietnam, as well as in Laos, bore out President Kennedy's concern that the United States had become much too dependent on the Eisenhower Administration doctrine of "massive retaliation." Kennedy had been much impressed with General Maxwell Taylor's arguments for a "flexible response," [8] and during the election campaign Kennedy had emphasized the need for such an American military posture—an arsenal of weapons, a trained soldiery, and a carefully developed doctrine to cope with those threats to our national security that fell below the threshold requiring the use of nuclear weapons, the Strategic Air Command, and massive ground forces.

Kennedy's views on defense problems had been set forth in a review he had written in September, 1960 of a book by Liddell Hart, the British expert on strategic problems. "The central problem we face is clear enough. The Soviet acquisition of nuclear weapons and the means for their delivery . . . now makes certain that a nuclear war would be a war of mutual devastation. The notion that the free world can be protected simply by the threat of 'massive retaliation' is no longer tenable. . . . responsible leaders in the West will not and should not deal with limited aggression by unlimited weapons. . . . the central task of American and Western military policy is to make all forms of Communist aggression irrational and unattractive." [9]

The Communist doctrine of "wars of liberation," which had been so frequently discussed and debated at various Communist conferences during the late 1950s, had made a deep impression on Kennedy. Peking was the principal proponent of the doctrine and made it one of the key issues of the Conference of Communist Parties held in Moscow in November, 1960. Although the final communique was a mishmash of jargon and compromise between the fanatic Chinese and the more realistic Russians, it was clear the two major Communist states were prepared to support local revolutionaries in the underdeveloped areas. Khrushchev's speech on January 6, 1961 promising Soviet support for wars of liberation in Cuba, Vietnam, and Algeria, clinched the President-elect's determination to move ahead on counter-insurgency programs. Kennedy's warning to China in his 1961 State of the Union address indicated his particular concern about international meddling by Peking.

The first few months of 1961 saw the development of a doctrine to counter "wars of liberation." Although the doctrine was described by various names, it generally came to be known as "counter-insurgency warfare." Counter-Insurgency was the "New Thing," and everybody who wished to be somebody in Washington scrambled on the bandwagon. The special training programs at Fort Bragg were vastly expanded, and the Army's "Special Forces" were given greater emphasis (as well as green berets). The disaster at the Bay of Pigs in the spring of 1961 may have added to Kennedy's determination that the United States had to be better prepared to engage in unconventional warfare.

The Department of State, mindful that insurgencies had political and economic roots, organized courses in Counter-Insurgency which were, theoretically at least, required for all civilian personnel going to Asia, Latin America, and Africa. A top level interagency group, "Special Group, Counter-Insurgency" was established, headed by General Maxwell Taylor. And there was unleashed a flood of literature, special studies, doctoral dissertations, think-tank analyses, and personal reminiscences dealing with the philosophy and tactics of this new form of international confrontation.

But the pressing need was not for some general theories to counter Mao's newly-discovered doctrine and precepts, but some ready solutions to the specific problem of insurgency in Vietnam. A Vietnam Task Force, comprising representatives of the White House and other elements of the foreign affairs side of the government but heavily oriented toward the Defense Department, was established in April, largely on the basis of General Lansdale's recommendation. This group's first act was to translate the Counter-Insurgency Plan into specific recommendations for American and Vietnamese action. The Task Force came up with about forty suggested moves. It was hoped that the Task Force report would provide the Administration with some levers to pull in Saigon; somehow the Vietnamese had to be induced to address the Counter-Insurgency Plan which was resting undisturbed on the overflowing desks of Diem and Nhu.

In May, Ambassador Durbrow was replaced by Ambassador Frederick Nolting. Durbrow was by now pretty much persona non grata at the Presidential Palace. Although his blunt and insistent style was what the situation probably required, Diem and his brother found it offensive. Durbrow's real problem, however, was not style but content. His demarches had a hollow ring, since the Ambassador represented no one but himself. Washington was not prepared to back him up and Diem knew it. Nolting, who had been the American Ambassador to NATO, was an able, less flamboyant, more patrician man. He tended toward gentle suggestion rather than tough demands. (Prior to his Saigon assignment Durbrow was Minister at our Embassy in Italy. I had several occasions to be in Rome while he was there and was bemused by Ambassador Clare Boothe Luce's references to her deputy as "Durby Darling." Even Ambassador Luce would not have called Nolting "Fritzy Darling.") Although Diem and Nhu were pleased with the new Ambassador, Nolting was no more successful than Durbrow in getting Saigon to undertake meaningful governmental reforms. By the end of his Ambassadorial assignment in 1963, Nolting's reputation as a friend of Nhu was so well established that no Vietnamese would speak critically of the regime with an American official for fear it would be reported back to Nhu.

It was in May too that President Kennedy sent Vice President Johnson on a factfinding, fence-mending trip to Asia. Both aspects of the mission were urgent. Kennedy was uneasy and of two minds about whether South Vietnam could make any real progress against the increasing strength of the Viet Cong as long as Diem, and especially his brother Nhu, regarded the struggle as a personal, holy war. The information he was getting through official and unofficial channels from Saigon was soft and contradictory. And there was disquieting evidence that some of the governments in the Far East, especially those in Bangkok and Taipei, were beginning to wonder aloud whether the Kennedy–Rusk combination was made of less stern stuff than the Eisenhower–Dulles team. Ngo Dinh Diem had no such doubts. According to those close to him at the time, Diem was so convinced of the importance of Vietnam to the U.S. and to the rest of the free world that he was sure the Americans were disengaging from Laos to concentrate on Vietnam. His expressed concern of a "sellout" was a device to increase his leverage in Washington.

Johnson set forth in early May accompanied by President Kennedy's sister and brother-in-law, Jean and Stephen Smith. In Saigon Johnson had some frank talks with Diem about the need for social progress, both in the urban and rural areas. But if in his private conversations he had been able to convince Diem to listen more readily to American advice, Johnson reduced the effectiveness of his visit by his extravagant public praise of the Vietnamese leader. Diem, he said, was "the Winston Churchill of today." Since the President of Vietnam already regarded himself as a combination of Joan of Arc and George Washington, this added tribute did nothing to give Diem a much-needed sense of humility.

The Vice President returned to Washington impressed with, but vaguely worried about, Diem. "He has admirable qualities, but he is remote from the people, and is surrounded by persons less admirable than he." Johnson was also worried by our apparent inability to get across to the Vietnamese our conditions for continued aid. "It would be useful to enunciate more clearly than we have—for the guidance of those young and unsophisticated nations —what we expect or require of them." [10] President Kennedy was in a chronic state of vacillation as to whether to support Diem or let him fall. Johnson came down on the side of supporting Diem.

And even after he became President, Johnson had lingering doubts *Johnson's* about the policy Kennedy adopted in late 1963 of withdrawing *ethnocen-* support from Diem.   *trism*

The Vice President urged that the Administration undertake prompt moves to reassure and support the people of Southeast Asia. This meant increases in both economic and military aid. The non-Communist governments of Asia were dubious of our long-range commitments in that region, and there was already concern about Washington's readiness to accept a coalition government in Laos. Tangible evidence of American interest had to be forthcoming quickly lest some nations make their own accommodations with Hanoi and Peking. But according to Johnson, American "combat involvement [at the time] . . . was not only unnecessary but undesirable." [11]

Following Johnson's visit to Saigon, Diem agreed to some of the points that had been included in the Vietnam Task Force Report, although subsequent follow-through and performance was half-hearted at best and frequently nonexistent. In June Diem forwarded a letter to Washington requesting American support for Vietnamese Armed Forces, comprising 270,000 men—an increase of 100,000 over the total originally proposed in the Counter-Insurgency Plan. Diem's letter reached Washington at just about the time that a group of American economic and financial experts arrived in Vietnam to explore how Saigon could do more on its own to finance its army. The American team confronted a reluctant, even frightened Diem. He was conscious of his narrow base of popular support and felt he could not risk additional austerity measures to put more resources into the military effort. Finally Kennedy agreed to provide American support for Vietnamese Armed Forces totalling 200,000 (70,000 less than Diem requested but 30,000 more than the United States had proposed in January).

As the dreary spring of 1961 pushed toward its close, there was a growing feeling of fatalism that whatever happened at the Laos Conference the Communists rather than the West would probably come out on top in Laos (a wrong assumption, as it later turned out). But, the reasoning went, the West (i.e., the United States) would nevertheless have to make a strong stand against Communist expansion in Southeast Asia; if the Laotians did not have the courage and determination to warrant American support, the Vietnamese—a tougher, more energetic, and more strongly motivated people—would have to be relied upon. Johnson's report crystallized the Administration's decision to cast its lot with Diem—warts, family, and all. And as a down-payment on Washington's new promise of support, four hundred American Special Forces troops were sent to Vietnam in late spring to expand the training programs for the Vietnamese Army.

The adrenalin that Johnson injected into the Saigon regime had only a temporary effect; lassitude and uncertainty soon again became the dominant symptoms of the deterioration. In September the Viet Cong, in an uncommon act of bravado, seized a province capital about 50 miles from Saigon, decapitated the province chief, and scurried into the jungle before the Government troops arrived. President Kennedy told the United Nations that Vietnam was "under attack" and that Laos was being used as a base for the Communists. A few days later Diem proclaimed that there was a "real war" raging in South Vietnam. Throughout the summer there had been much talk in Washington of sending American combat troops to Southeast Asia, and by October several plans had been worked out for direct U.S. intervention.

It was against this background that President Kennedy announced he was sending his military adviser, Maxwell Taylor, to Saigon to appraise the threat to the security of Vietnam and neighboring countries. Kennedy asked Taylor to return with recommendations that would avoid a further deterioration in Vietnam, but reminded him that maintaining Vietnamese independence was essentially the responsibility of the Vietnamese themselves; American efforts would have to be measured and Taylor's suggestions formulated with this consideration in mind. Finally, Kennedy told Taylor, he should not confine himself to the military aspect of the situation, but should address the "equally significant" economic, political, and social factors.

In the same issue that announced the Taylor Mission, *The New York Times* had a story headlined "500,000 Go Hungry As South Vietnam Is Hit By Floods"—a situation that was to have an interesting effect on the policy discussions that followed the Taylor Mission.[12] (Also gracing the same page of the same issue was a story reporting the arrival of the Pakistani camel driver Vice President Johnson, in a burst of Texas hospitality on his Asian tour, had invited to Washington.)

Taylor arrived in Saigon on October 18 accompanied by Walt Rostow, then deputy to McGeorge Bundy, and General Lansdale. On the same day (possibly, but not necessarily, a coincidence) Diem declared a State of Emergency in Vietnam because of the floods and the increasing gravity of the security situation. The Vietnamese let it be known that their current estimate of Viet Cong forces was 20,000—a third more than had been estimated just a few weeks before. Despite Taylor's constant denials, rumors were rife about an early deployment of American combat troops to Vietnam. This prospect was duly noted by Hanoi's delegation to the Laos Conference. If American troops were sent to South Vietnam, the delegation's spokesman said, the United States "will have to accept all the responsibility and the consequences of such a military adventure." Taylor's trip to Vietnam was another piece of evidence to Hanoi that the United States was attempting to prevent "the peaceful reunification of Vietnam."

*   *   *

General Taylor returned to Washington on November 3. He took a sober view of the situation in Vietnam and in Southeast Asia generally. He told the President that the Communist strategy of gaining control of Southeast Asia through subversion and guerrilla war was well on the way to success in Vietnam. Taylor noted a "double crisis in confidence" in Vietnam. There was doubt about American determination to hold Southeast Asia and there was doubt that Diem's methods could defeat the Communists. American actions, he said, would play a decisive role in determining the final outcome. Small Viet Cong forces were wreaking havoc through Vietnam, and a political crisis would be inevitable unless the Communist threat could be contained.

Taylor suggested that the United States, on the request of the Saigon Government, provide large-scale assistance in coping with the Viet Cong and for flood relief operations. He recommended a "massive joint effort" in which the American representatives would participate "actively" in the fields of government administration, military plans and operations, intelligence, and flood relief. These forces should go beyond "the advisory role" they had played in the past. Specifically he recommended: American administrators should be introduced into Saigon's bureaucracy in types and in numbers approved by Diem; South Vietnamese–American efforts should be undertaken to improve the Saigon Government's intelligence capabilities; a joint comprehensive survey of the conditions in the provinces should be initiated to reach a common judgment on the situation and on the measures to deal with it; a major effort should be made to change Vietnamese Army operations from a static to a mobile character and to promote American support in such technical fields as air surveillance, photography, and airlift; surveillance and control over coastal waters and inland waterways should be established with whatever American assistance that might be necessary; the American Military Assistance Advisory Group (MAAG) should be expanded and reorganized to implement the Taylor recommendations; the American aid program should be reviewed in the light of the flood and the expanded counterinsurgency effort. Finally, the United States should "offer" the South Vietnamese "a military task force to operate under U.S. control" to raise South Vietnamese morale and demonstrate our serious intent, to undertake logistic operations in support of flood relief and military actions, to conduct whatever combat operations that might be required for self-defense and for the security of their base areas, to provide a reserve for the Vietnamese Armed Forces in the event of an emergency, and to act as an advance group for whatever additional American forces might later be required.

Taylor included a paragraph in his report that had special significance a few years hence. "It is my judgment and that of my colleagues that the United States must decide how it will cope with Khrushchev's 'wars of liberation' which are really para-wars of guerrilla aggression. This is a new and dangerous Communist technique which bypasses our traditional political and military

responses. While the final answer lies beyond the scope of this
report, it is clear to me that the time may come in our relations to
Southeast Asia when we must declare our intention to attack the
source of guerrilla aggression in North Vietnam and impose on
the Hanoi Government a price for participating in the current war
which is commensurate with the damage being inflicted on its
neighbors to the south." [13]

In the end, the Administration decided against sending combat troops to Vietnam, although there was a momentary stir of
interest in dispatching engineering and logistical units for the
ostensible purpose of helping the South Vietnamese with flood relief and reconstruction. The decision against sending troops was
taken in part because of concern that the delicate negotiations on
Laos then taking place in Geneva would be upset; in part it was
based on the feeling that, in the last analysis, fighting the Viet
Cong was a South Vietnamese job. Kennedy had no desire to
give Diem a blank check for American aid. But even if he had,
General Taylor's account of administrative and political defects
in Saigon must have strengthened the President's determination
to get Diem to pull up his socks. It was decided, however, that
we should increase our military assistance. A large number of
American advisers and a substantial amount of military equipment, including helicopters with their crews, were sent to Vietnam during November and December. This was accompanied by
an elaborate effort by the Administration to publicize North Vietnamese political and military support for the Viet Cong insurgents.
As part of this campaign, the Department of State in December
published a "White Paper," *A Threat to the Peace,* which documented Hanoi's involvement.

Ambassador John Kenneth Galbraith, who was on his way
back to Delhi from consultations in Washington, was asked by
the President to stop off in Saigon and forward his views as to
whether Diem's government had any potential for reform and
effectiveness. Galbraith, as usual, was blunt and to the point. In a
letter to President Kennedy, he said: "The political reality is the
total stasis which arises from [Diem's] greater need to protect
himself from a coup than to protect the country from the Vietcong.

I am quite clear that the absence of intelligence, the centralization
of Army control, the incredible dual role of the provincial gover-
nors as Army generals and political administrators, the subservient
incompetence of the latter, are all related to his fear of being given
the heave. The desire to prolong one's days in office has a certain
consistency the world around and someday somebody should explain this to the State Department with pictures. I would love to
have come up with the conclusion that our man would be re-
formed and made into an effective military and political
force. . . ." [14] In a private communication to the President, Galbraith also urged dumping the unpopular and inefficient Diem
Government and indicated that an "alternative to the dictatorship
would be acceptable" but should not be initiated by the United
States.

Washington did not take Galbraith's strong medicine but did
inform Diem that any increased military aid would be contingent
on evidence that he was broadening his political base. However,
Diem did receive additional military support and delivered virtually nothing in terms of improvements or reforms.

By the end of 1961 our various attempts to get Diem to shape
up had not only been fruitless but had stirred up an anti-American campaign in Saigon. The keynote set by Diem's brother and
sister-in-law was that the United States, by insisting on political,
economic, and social reforms, was interfering in Vietnamese affairs. The United States, it was charged, was now preparing to
betray the South Vietnamese, just as it had the non-Communists
in Laos.

●   ✿   ●

Meanwhile, the weeks were stretching into months, and the
months ground on in Geneva. While Laos was obviously the focus
of discussion, developments in Vietnam were more often than not
the subject of corridor and dinner conversations. And while the
conference's rules of engagement prevented formal consideration
of Vietnam, Saigon's articulate and aggressive representatives lost
no opportunity to remind the assembled delegates of Viet Cong
atrocities and Hanoi's support of the insurgents.

Represented at Geneva, in addition to Laotians of various political hue, were the British and Russians (who alternated as chairmen of the conference), the Canadians, Indians, and Poles (who comprised the International Control Commission), and the Americans, South Vietnamese, North Vietnamese, Cambodians, Thais, French, Burmese, and Chinese Communists. The Conference had been convened largely as a result of the efforts of Prince Sihanouk of Cambodia, who with admirable skill had arranged a preliminary meeting of the three contending Lao factions and had achieved sufficient agreement among them to permit the conference to go forward. Having accomplished this, however, the Cambodians lost interest in the conference itself, and their participation during the long months of negotiating was pro forma.

The Chinese Communists, as they had in the conference of 1954, fielded more than a hundred delegates and seemed, once again, to be using the occasion as a means for training younger members of their foreign service. A surprising number of the Chinese were apparently able to understand English. Scores of them read such periodicals as the *Saturday Evening Post* during the long periods of consecutive translations. The obvious difficulty they experienced in departing from their prepared texts and in responding to new conference initiatives probably reflected divided responsibility in their delegation among several officials and groupings representing the Communist Party and the Foreign Affairs bureaucracy. It was not unusual to find them in earnest and sometimes acrimonious debate among themselves in the Delegates Lounge over what appeared to be last minute changes in their afternoon's presentation. As the conference dragged on, frictions between the Chinese and their Russian colleagues became increasingly evident. There were many occasions toward the end of the summer of 1961 when one could observe tense, even angry, exchanges between senior members of the Chinese and Russian delegations.

Except for one occasion which was especially noteworthy as far as I was concerned, there was virtually no contact between the Americans and the Chinese. The exception occurred at the very end of the conference when the Chinese, as did the other delegations, held a reception for all the delegates. The American delegation received an invitation, which everyone, including the Chinese themselves, expected to be ignored. But Secretary Rusk, who had arrived for the closing ceremonies, and Governor Harriman decided that it would be courteous and possibly diplomatically advantageous to have a token American presence. William Sullivan (later Ambassador to Laos) and I were designated the sacrificial lambs. Our appearance at the Chinese villa caught hosts and guests by surprise. As we entered, the senior Chinese delegates interrupted their chitchat with their other guests and rushed to the door to greet us. After we had drunk a ceremonial toast to peace and understanding, Foreign Minister Chen Yi overheard me say a few words of restaurant-Chinese to a houseboy. Ignoring the interpreter, he looked squarely at me and asked whether I spoke Chinese. In an apparent seizure of diplomatic madness, I dredged up a Chinese idiom roughly equivalent to *comme ci, comme ça.* This convinced my host that I not only spoke fluently but that I was also a becomingly modest man. Chen Yi dismissed the interpreter and then poured forth a virtual Niagara of rhetoric. He spoke rapidly and earnestly to me for about thirty minutes. I discovered after a moment or two that the time I had spent in trying to learn the language during the war was love's labor lost. To increase my sense of embarrassment and helplessness, scores of guests were carefully observing what must have seemed to them a momentous development in international affairs. I could imagine the juicy tidbits they would be cabling back to their governments later that evening. When Chen Yi finished his discourse, he raised his glass again in a toast. I weakly raised mine, gulped down the strong rice whisky gratefully, and tried to escape the phalanx of questioners from the other delegations who were descending upon me. I collected Sullivan and got back to our hotel as soon as I could. Seeing us return, Rusk and Harriman asked how we had fared. I tried to pass off the whole experience with some light remarks about the food and drink, but I still wonder what, in fact, my host had said. Every six months or so I awaken with the thought that Chen Yi may have been trying to defect, or surrender all of Mainland China to the Americans, or sell me some rare Chinese porcelain.

The Russian delegation headed by G. M. Pushkin, Soviet Vice Minister of Foreign Affairs, played a constructive role. Pushkin took his responsibility as co-chairman seriously, although his interest in reaching a settlement only became apparent after the June, 1961 meeting between Kennedy and Khrushchev in Vienna. One of the crosses the Chinese had to bear was the conspicuously easy-going, professional relationship between members of the American and Soviet delegations. The Chinese seemed worried that the Russians and the Americans were working up a secret deal that would sell Peking down the river. No such deal was made, of course, but this was probably due more, I think, to the fact that no one could think of a good one than to inhibitions on either side.

One young delegate caught my eye very early in the game. He wore well-cut suits circa Brooks Brothers 1960, and he carried himself with an air that my daughter would describe as "cool." What attracted me, however, was his insouciance as he sat in the bar drinking a leisurely martini early each afternoon prior to the plenary session. While some folk tried to induce insomnia by fortifying themselves with black coffee, he was the only person in the bar ready to tempt Morpheus by consorting with Bacchus. To my narrow, puritan mind this seemed not only a rather extravagant act of bravado, but the last thing a junior member of any delegation should be doing on his way into a warm and crowded conference room. I discovered in due course that he was not a stylish member of the Georgetown set within the American delegation —he was a member of the Soviet Delegation's Secretariat. He spoke excellent English and had been stationed in Washington for several years. (In my first encounter with him he introduced himself as "A real live Red Russian.")

The British delegation was headed by Malcolm MacDonald, a long-term Southeast Asian expert and son of a famous Prime Minister. As in 1954, the British had a major part in bringing the conference to a successful conclusion. MacDonald was much less tense and less highly charged than Eden had been. His relaxed manner kept the plenary sessions on an even keel and the more important committee meetings productive. The British chairmanship of the Laos talks may well be regarded by diplomatic historians as one of the last truly international roles England played in the decade of the '60s.

The French fielded a competent delegation whose knowledge of Indochina rivaled that of the Southeast Asian delegations themselves. Unlike 1954, they were free of pressure from their government in Paris, as well as from the trauma of daily, desperate telegrams from Indochina. Perhaps more than any other non-Communist delegates, the French were able to address the problem of Laos objectively and unemotionally. Their knowledge of the background of the 1954 agreements was detailed and accurate, and they did much to sort out the technical snarls that constantly arose.

India held the Chairmanship of the International Control Commission and therefore had a rather special position, but the Indian delegation was more interested in discussing broad international profundities than the technical questions of how the ICC could be more effectively used to implement the terms of any final agreement. Krishna Menon, who blew in and out of Geneva on short notice, was clearly the Super Star of the Geneva Follies and relished his role. He consciously and conspicuously played to an audience well beyond the confines of the Palais des Nations. He was wordy, windy, and exasperatingly oratorical. The Indians provided an occasional oasis of amusement in a desert of dull speeches, and they treated their fellow-conferees to some tidbits of international philosophy. But more often than not they sent most of the long-suffering delegates into spasms of frustration and irritation.

By virtue of its membership in the ICC, Canada was an important participant in the activities of the conference. Its delegation was unusually well informed about technical and legal details that came up in the course of the debates and in the sessions of the conference's drafting committee. Canadian experience in the practical workings of the ICC proved of considerable value.

Poland was the third member of the ICC. Its delegation

tended to echo the Communist line throughout the conference proceedings, but its members were usually cordial, poised, and polite by comparison with the other Communists. The delegation took a particularly active part in the drafting committee—possibly on its own initiative, possibly at Soviet instigation.

The North Vietnamese delegation was tough, truculent, bitter, and rigid. Perhaps the men from Hanoi were in a bad temper because they were forced to spend their days denying what everyone knew was true—the presence of North Vietnamese forces in Laos. Even the Russians admitted, albeit privately, that a substantial number of North Vietnamese troops were engaged in combat in Laos (the Americans and Laotians estimated that there were about 5000), but the North Vietnamese rather stupidly insisted that they had not a single soldier there. (My head still resounds with the ringing cries of "The whole world knows that the United States calls white, black and black, white!" "On the contrary, we and the world know that black is black and white is white and that there are thousands of North Vietnamese fighting in Laos at this very moment!") As the months went by there was more and more evidence that North Vietnamese troops were not only in combat against the Royal Laotian Army, but were improving the network of trails going through Laos into South Vietnam. Already political cadres and military specialists and technicians were moving into South Vietnam to buttress the Viet Cong.

Best that could be gotten?

The Saigon delegates were probably as good a professional team, man for man, as any in Geneva. One of the most impressive things about them was the manner in which they managed to keep their cool even under considerable provocation by the Communists.

The Thais took a dim view of the neutrality formula for Laos which, of course, was a major guide line for the conferees, and as a result the Thais refused to attend during the initial days of the conference; after they did take their seats, they walked out every now and then. However, the Thais performed a useful function as a kind of inner conscience by their frequent and pointed reminders to the non-Communist delegations of the need for a robust stand. The Burmese contribution was neither noteworthy nor

Afraid of Viet hegemony?

constructive. The Acting Chief of their delegation seemed to believe his appointed role was that of conference jester.

The Laotians themselves were divided into three groups, each representing a "political tendency"—right, neutralist, and left. In the final settlement these groups provided the basis for the coalition government. Although representatives of the Laotian Government at first refused to participate in the conference because of their unwillingness to be seated on the same basis as the neutralists and the Communists, after some delay and considerable massaging, the Vientiane Government agreed to be represented by some affable, ineffectual gentlemen from several conservative political parties. They seemed to be totally uninstructed, even ignored by Vientiane, and had little interest in the proceedings. A member of the American delegation, for his many sins, had to spend a considerable amount of time wet-nursing them. It was not unusual on his late-morning call to the Vientiane group's villa to find his friends, bleary-eyed and still in their pajamas, recovering from Geneva's exotic night life.

The principal Neutralist delegate was Quinim Pholsena, a complex, tense, and withdrawn man, who in many respects seemed to be closer to the Communists than to the political group he was representing. As the months went on, however, Quinim seemed to relax, and he eventually played a constructive role in working out the final settlement. He returned to Vientiane as Foreign Minister in the Coalition Government and several months later was shot down by assassins.

The Communist delegation from Laos was nothing less than pathetic. Its leader may (presumably must) have been effective in the shadowy councils of the Pathet Lao, but he was out of his depth in Geneva. He suffered from a severe nervous ailment, possibly palsy, but his shrill, outrageous fanaticism made it hard to sympathize with his physical problem. His remarks were so extravagant, pointless, and insulting that even his comrades among the other Communist delegations were restless and embarrassed when he spoke—or rather shouted. If this was the Pathet Lao, the omens were unfavorable for any coalition government.

To the extent that anything useful emerged from the long

months of dreary discussion, Ambassador Harriman deserves a
large share of the credit. In this assignment Harriman reported
directly to President Kennedy, as well as to Secretary Rusk. The
Ambassador was frequently to remind his delegation, and some of
his kibitzers and hecklers in Washington, that "I work for the
President of the United States. I am here to do what he wants."
His mission, as he understood it from Kennedy, was to stop the
fighting in Laos and to arrange for a negotiated settlement and a
neutral Laos. Harriman had more than his share of difficulties with
a Department of Defense that long persisted in believing that the
proper American policy was to support the right wing government — *not*
of Phoumi Nosavan and that anything short of that would be a *feasible*
sellout. He also had troubles with a Department of State that
frequently sent him instructions either impossible to fulfill or inconsistent with what Harriman thought Kennedy desired. Although Harriman had the complete cooperation of Ambassador
Winthrop Brown in Vientiane, some key officers in our Mission
there found it difficult to adjust to President Kennedy's decision to
dump the rightist General Phoumi for the neutralist Souvanna
Phouma. Eventually these Mission officials had to be replaced.

The was my first direct exposure to Averell Harriman. He was
a tough boss. His single-minded sense of purpose in reaching an
agreement was matched only by his tremendous energy. He was
then 70 years old, yet his day started at 9 in the morning and
ended at midnight. I am told that when he was in his 60s his
working day started at 6 A.M. Lunches were "working lunches";
dinners were "working dinners." He would take a rare Sunday
afternoon off, but he typically worked straight through the week.
He preferred to work with a lean and hungry team and was appalled to discover that at the outset his delegation consisted of
almost a hundred people; two-thirds of them were promptly sent
home, including some of the delegation's most senior members.

The Laos Accords were signed on July 23, 1962, sixteen months
after the delegates had first convened in Geneva. Under the terms
of the Accords, consisting of a Declaration of the Neutrality of
Laos and an attached protocol, the signatories agreed to recognize,
respect, and observe the sovereignty, independence, neutrality,

unity, and territorial integrity of the Kingdom of Laos; to refrain from interfering in Laotian internal affairs; to attach no political strings to any aid offered the country. In addition, Laos was not to be brought into any military alliances, foreign military bases could not be established there, and Laotian territory could not be trespassed upon by outside forces to attack other countries (e.g., Vietnam). The Accords further prohibited the introduction of any foreign troops or military personnel into the country.

The agreement stimulated some hope but few illusions. The hope was based in part on the personality of Souvanna Phouma, an urbane and quietly confident man who had been maligned as a Communist stooge and undermined by some officials in our Embassy at Vientiane and in Washington. Yet another reason for believing that something of value had been achieved was a private deal worked out between the leaders of the American and Soviet delegations—the "Harriman–Pushkin Agreement." In essence the Russians agreed to use their influence on the Pathet Lao, Peking, and Hanoi to assure compliance with the terms agreed upon at the Conference. In exchange for this, the British agreed to assure compliance by the non-Communists. Both Co-Chairmen would keep the other member countries informed of any violations and would reconvene the Conference if necessary. Although this informal arrangement as such was not published nor made part of the official record, the spelling out of the Co-Chairmen's responsibilities was incorporated in the final Accords.*

Whether indeed Pushkin ever informed his own Government of his compact with Harriman will probably never be known for certain; Pushkin died of a heart attack not long after the Laos talks, and Moscow has never admitted to any knowledge of the arrangement. In any case the agreement on troop-withdrawal was ignored by Hanoi. Although the United States was virtually certain that many thousands of North Vietnamese troops were in Laos, the International Control Commission officially counted only a score of them returning to North Vietnam.

The coalition government under Souvanna was not given a

---

* At a break in one of the sessions, Pushkin told Harriman that Laos "would be the last country in the world to go Communist." Harriman reminded him that he had once been assured by Khrushchev that the U.S. would be the last. Pushkin corrected himself: "Laos would be the *next* to last."

realism

very long life-expectancy by most of the delegates—probably including Souvanna himself, who seemed to have mixed feelings
about leaving the pleasant life of southern France for a difficult,
dangerous job in the heat and dust of Vientiane. But even the pes-
simists among the American delegates were ready to give Souvanna six months, and six months would give Washington much-
needed time to shore up Diem. The Kennedy Administration had
long since discovered that Laos was actually a non-country. It
had also become clear that the Laotians in their good-humored
lassitude were reeds too thin to support a heavy American commitment against Communist expansion in Southeast Asia.

Although Souvanna's government has stayed in power ever
since (indeed, it has had a longer life span than virtually any
other of the governments that were represented in Geneva), this
is probably the only remnant left of the Geneva agreement. It is
clear now—indeed it was clear within weeks of the signing—that
neither the Pathet Lao nor the North Vietnamese were going to
honor any of the provisions that were disadvantageous to them.
The Pathet Lao was unwilling to cooperate with the coalition
government, let alone participate in the operations of that government. Moreover, the Pathet Lao continued to run the two provinces under its control as sovereign states, refusing entry to government officials, including Souvanna himself. What emerged
was a de facto partition of the country, with two-thirds of the
population living under government control. Of much more significance in terms of the problems Kennedy was to face in the
ensuing months, Pathet Lao and North Vietnamese troops continued military operations against the Royal Laotian forces, which
by now had incorporated Souvanna's own neutralist units.

But Vietnam was a different story. Despite the troublesome
Diem and the trouble-making Nhus, here was a country of energetic, nationalistic people. If the line was to be held, Vietnam
rather than Laos was the place to hold it.

*   *   *

The trouble was that the line wasn't being held in Vietnam either, despite more and more infusions of American economic and
military aid. Somehow the Administration was unable to find the

combination of ingredients that would lead to political and military recovery. Three high-level missions and a score of lesser ones had made the pilgrimage to Saigon during 1961, and all returned with long lists of prescriptions, many of which were put into effect in Washington and some even implemented in Saigon. But still the situation continued to erode.

At the close of 1961 Diem agreed to make some administrative changes in response to the recommendations General Taylor brought back. The early months of 1962 saw a quickening of American support. In his 1962 State of the Union Message to Congress, the President expressed his hopes and concern about the area. "A satisfactory settlement in Laos would also help to achieve and safeguard the peace in Vietnam—where the foe is increasing his tactics of terror—where our own efforts have been stepped up—and where the local government has initiated new programs and reforms to broaden the base of resistance. The systematic aggression now bleeding that country is not a 'war of national liberation' —for Vietnam is already free. It is a war of attempted subjugation —and it will be resisted." [15]

To demonstrate the seriousness of the Administration's intent to stave off the Communist threat and also to provide a command and administrative channel for military advisers in Vietnam, a new American military headquarters was established in Saigon in early February—"The United States Military Assistance Command, Vietnam." Something between 2000 and 4000 American troops were already admitted to be in Vietnam, although the Administration stressed that they were "not in combat." "MACVee," as it was to become known to the Vietnam aficionados, was conceived in the autumn of 1961 but born only after a spate of conferences in Washington and Honolulu in January, 1962.

The establishment of the new American military headquarters may or may not have genuinely worried the Communists (the reaction from Hanoi and Peking was, of course, predictably hostile), but it did stir up considerable concern in the United States. To many thoughtful Americans this move seemed to confirm their fears that the Administration was now moving down the track of military involvement, rather than mere economic and military assistance. James Reston said in *The New York Times* that America had entered an "undeclared war." On the same day the Republican National Committee raised an issue that would continue to haunt President Kennedy, and even more so, President Johnson. Its publication, "Battle Line," charged that the President had been "less than candid" on the extent of American military involvement in Vietnam and called for a "full report." Specific charges and subtle innuendoes about American troops in combat were to grow in number and shrillness, and Kennedy was to become increasingly defensive on this issue as the months wore on. He had, of course, been less than frank. But a President can never be completely frank in foreign affairs. As Eisenhower's problem with the U–2 affair has shown, frankness may on occasion create more problems than it solves.

contra-diction of democracy

The late winter and early spring of 1962 was an especially tricky period for Kennedy's Asian policymakers. On the one hand, we were exerting considerable pressure on the Laotian right-wing elements to join a neutralist coalition with Souvanna as its head and the Communist Pathet Lao as the third horse in the troika; on the other hand, we were trying to assure the South Vietnamese (and the Thais) that we were determined to help them stand up against Communist expansion in Southeast Asia. In order to convince our allies that we were ready to act as well as talk, thousands of American troops were sent to Vietnam, but it was constantly necessary to remind the American people that their sons and husbands were there to "advise," not to fight. A dilemma that Washington was going to face time and time again during the next several years was illustrated by Ambassador Harriman's statement to the Senate Foreign Relations Committee in mid-February. This was the problem of reassuring the Vietnamese Government without unduly worrying the American people. "It is their war," Harriman told the Committee. But "they have asked for help, and we ought to give it." The Administration, however, had "no present plans for commitment of American combat forces." [16] To complicate Kennedy's problem even more, the United States at that very moment was in a delicate and fragile phase of the negotiations in Geneva, which could be upset by ham-handed political or military moves in Vietnam.

Perhaps no better illustration of the President's problems in trying to cope with these various and inconsistent public demands were two events that took place between mid-February and mid-March. Robert Kennedy, stopping in Vietnam briefly while flying from Thailand to Indonesia, assured the Vietnamese that "we are going to win in Vietnam. We will remain here until we do win." To a correspondent's question as to whether the American people understood and approved "of what is going on" in Vietnam where "American boys are dying," Robert Kennedy replied, "I think the American people understand and fully support this struggle." [17]

But a few weeks later, in the face of reports of fire-fights between American and Viet Cong troops, Defense Secretary Robert McNamara found it necessary to explain just what the American forces in Vietnam were doing and what they were not expected to do. Our military personnel were in Vietnam solely in an advisory capacity and could defend themselves, but they were "not to fire unless fired upon." On the same day the President took pains to point out that although there were "a good many Americans" in Vietnam, they were not "combat troops." If American troops were to go into combat, Kennedy said, "I, of course, would go to Congress." [18]

The issue of whether Americans were merely advising Vietnamese forces or actually participating in combat operations opened a fissure between the American press and the Administration. This was widened further by conflicting interpretations and assessments of political and military developments in Vietnam. As the American involvement grew so did the size, quality and interest of the press corps in Saigon.

The American Mission in Vietnam was soon seized not only with problems of dealing with Diem, and the troublesome Nhus, and corrupt, inffectual Vietnamese civilian and military officials, but with a platoon of high-spirited, skeptical, and sometimes overly-critical American news correspondents. To increase the difficulties of Ambassador Nolting and MACV Commander Harkins, and to ease the problems of the press, the Embassy and the MACV headquarters became the arenas for quarreling among competing agencies and individuals. However tight-lipped or platitudinous or determinedly optimistic the top American officials were, there was always someone in the second or third layer of the Mission who was prepared "to tell it like it was."

In retrospect, at least, the Administration reaped the fruits of its almost compulsive optimism. American agencies in Washington and Saigon were easy prey for bright, cynical reporters with on-the-spot knowledge. "We have full confidence in President Diem," said Robert Kennedy in February; the South Vietnamese have been able to go on the offensive against the guerrillas as a consequence of American aid, said Admiral Harry Felt (Commander, U.S. Forces in the Pacific) in March; the Vietnamese had seized the initiative, said General Harkins in April; he was "tremendously encouraged" and American aid would taper off, said McNamara in May. These were sophisticated men, and each tempered his optimism with a caveat or an obvious crossing of the fingers. But what came through in the large print was their belief that the corner had been turned. And generally speaking, they really believed their own pronouncements.

Doubting voices became increasingly loud and garrulous. At a press conference on February 7th the President was asked, "What are the rights of the American people to know what our forces are doing?" At a news conference a month later one reporter asked, "Mr. President, I wondered if you could tell us how the subterranean war is going there, because the Pentagon won't put out anything. . . ." While the news accounts were frequently straightforward and faithful accounts of what American spokesmen were saying, feature stories tended more and more to reveal deep reservations about the nature of our role and the progress of our enterprise. "The United States has shouldered a sweeping commitment, the future scope, hazards and durations of which are highly uncertain," Tillman Durdin wrote in April.[19] "American officials who 'leak' stories unflattering to the Saigon Government or who depart from the Washington line of 'cautious optimism' on the progress of the war . . . are tracked down by the Embassy and muzzled," wrote Homer Bigart in June.[20]

Many newsmen in Saigon claimed that they were being misled by American officials. Some even charged that they were being told outright lies. Whatever the reasons, there was a total absence of dialogue between the official American community and the public media. At a time when the Administration's policy was beginning to be seriously questioned and Kennedy needed public understanding of his Southeast Asian stance, he confronted a hostile, suspicious press. It was not that Ambassador Nolting and General Harkins generally were trying to deliberately dissemble or fool the correspondents, although on occasion this was true. The problem was at once more simple and more serious: the American Mission had few independent sources of information and had to rely largely on what the Vietnamese told them. Then too with almost childlike faith they believed what they heard and could not understand why the press would not believe what they, in turn, passed on. Many of these same officials had ridiculed their predecessors for having been so gullible as to accept unquestioningly the French reports on the course of the war against the Viet Minh.

The fact was that the war was *not* going well, the Vietnamese Army was *not* taking kindly to American advice, and Diem was *not* following through on his promises to liberalize his regime or increase its effectiveness. Despite increased U.S. aid, and despite the statements of official spokesmen, progress against the insurgents was hardly discernible. High Vietnamese military officers held their jobs because of their personal loyalty to Diem, rather than their professional competence. Diem's captive National Assembly passed a law that had the effect of prohibiting even weddings and funerals unless permission was granted twenty-four hours in advance. (This had been preceded by Mme. Nhu's "public-morality law" that forbade dancing, among other diversions, and by her "family law" that banned divorce.) And to add to the growing Saigon–Washington frictions, Diem turned down an American proposal to circumvent the slow-moving and sticky-fingered Saigon bureaucracy and give aid directly to hard-pressed provincial and district chiefs.

By May the Administration was confronted with two undeclared wars, one with the Viet Cong, the other with the American press. Secretary McNamara returned from Saigon implying that the newsmen were causing trouble in Congress through their exaggerated stories of Americans in combat. The correspondents returned the compliment by charging that the Pentagon was with-holding or delaying news on American casualties in Vietnam. Diem's government did little to help in either war. In September Saigon ousted the local *Newsweek* correspondent, charging that he did not report accurately on the progress of the war (i.e., he was too critical); the American press corps protested to Diem and were told that they themselves were engaging in an "intimidation campaign." In November Madame Nhu endeared herself to the press to an even greater extent than she already had by calling American newsmen in Saigon "worse than Communists." She also took this occasion to level a broadside at Americans generally. She said the Americans were dancing illegally, even in front of the security police, and accused them of not respecting Vietnam-ese laws. "They discuss them, they argue them, they combat them either publicly or privately." [21]

In December Senator Mansfield returned from his first visit to Vietnam since 1955. "It would be a disservice to my country," he wrote to Chairman William Fulbright of the Senate's Committee on Foreign Relations, "not to voice a deep concern over the trend of events in Viet Nam in the 7 years which have elapsed since my last visit. What is most disturbing is that Viet Nam now appears to be, as it was then, only at the beginning of a beginning in cop-ing with its grave inner problems. All of the current difficulties existed in 1955, along with hope and energy to meet them. But it is 7 years later and $2 billion of U.S. aid later. Yet, substantially the same difficulties remain if, indeed, they have not been com-pounded." In the body of his report he noted that "Those who bear responsibility for directing operations . . . are optimistic over the prospects for success. Indeed, success was predicted . . . al-most without exception by responsible Americans and Vietnamese, in terms of a year or two hence. . . . But . . . experience in Viet Nam going back at least a decade recommends caution in predict-ing its rapid achievement. The new strategy is not entirely new. Elements of it have appeared over the past decade or more in various unsuccessful plans for resolving the guerrilla problem in Viet Nam. . . . It is most disturbing to find that after 7 years of the Republic, South Viet Nam appears less, not more, stable than it was at the outset, that it appears more removed from, rather

than closer to, the achievement of popularly responsible and responsive government." The report was especially cautious about
the new "strategic hamlet" program, which was the brainchild of
Brother Nhu and on which both the American and Vietnamese
officials had set great store. "While the plans for the strategic hamlets are cast in a democratic mold, it is by no means certain at this
point how they shall evolve in practice. The evolution of the practices of the Central Government to date, are not reassuring in this
connection." [22]

On December 14, a week or so after Senator Mansfield and his
Committee returned from Vietnam, *The New York Times* reported
from Washington that "United States military and economic programs in South Vietnam were said today to have halted the Communist advance during the last year. . . . There are hopeful signs
in the strategic hamlet program, the authority said. . . . He con-
tended that American diplomatic and military leaders had better
relations with the Government of President Ngo Dinh Diem than
ever before." [23]

President Kennedy had been somewhat more cautious in his
news conference a day or two before. "Mr. President," said a reporter, "it was just a year ago that you ordered stepped-up aid to
Vietnam. There seems to be a good deal of discouragement about
the progress." "Well, we are putting in a major effort in Vietnam,"
responded the President, ". . . we have about 10 or 11 times as
many men there as we had a year ago. We've had a number of
casualties. We put in an awful lot of equipment. We are going
ahead with the strategic hamlet proposal. In some phases the military program has been quite successful. There is great difficulty,
however, in fighting a guerrilla war. . . . So we don't see the end
of the tunnel, but I must say I don't think it is darker than it was a
year ago, and in some ways lighter." [24]

And on this note another year of the United States in Vietnam came to a close. It had been a year of difficult decisions
and few rewards for Vietnam policymakers in Washington. But
compared to what lay ahead, 1962 would seem like the "good old
days."

IX

Death of a Mandarin

The New Year started with a bang in Vietnam—a bang that was heard in the oval office of the White House and echoed throughout the labyrinthine corridors of the State Department and the Pentagon. On January 2 in the Mekong Delta village of Ap Bac, fifty miles from Saigon, a Viet Cong battalion was surrounded by a Vietnamese Army force ten times its size. Despite the desperate urging of the American advisers, the Government forces chose not to engage the enemy. Result: the Viet Cong killed three Americans, shot down five American helicopters and damaged nine more, and then melted away into the night. The United States spokesmen put the best face they could on the debacle. General Harkins even claimed it as a Government victory, junior grade, but the incident sent shivers down the spines of Washington policy-makers and MACV planners.

The events following the trauma of Ap Bac provided a preview of what was to happen on many subsequent occasions when Saigon's forces suffered a major blow. To some, the lesson of Ap Bac was that the United States had to sharply increase its export of military advisers (there were 11,000 in Vietnam at this time), helicopters, and equipment. Others felt that, until there were basic political, economic and social changes, increased military aid would be fruitless. Moreover, the latter group maintained, the

199

Vietnamese Army should first be made into an effective professional force, rather than merely a source of patronage and a means for balancing off rival political elements within the country. And finally, according to this group, there should be a closer look at the American military establishment in Saigon where the number of generals, officers clubs, and the full panoply of aides, staff cars, and war rooms was mushrooming. (By 1968 there were more than eighty American generals in Vietnam—twice as many as General Bradley had on his staff during World War II when he commanded a force five times as large.)

Ap Bac was only a dramatic example of countless similar incidents that preceded and were to follow that sorry performance. The Vietnamese Army was not organized, equipped, or trained for the kind of war it was fighting. It was comprised of standard divisions, was loaded down with heavy crew-served and individual weapons, and was geared to fight a conventional, full-scale invasion from North Vietnam. By 1963 many South Vietnamese officers were politicians in uniform—in the personal service of Diem and Nhu. Any officer who gave evidence of straying from unquestioned personal loyalty to the ruling family was removed. That was bad enough, but even worse was the fact that any officer, no matter how incompetent, was guaranteed a high and safe post in the army providing he played his political cards correctly, or at least carefully. As for the bulk of the army, it just didn't care. The important thing was to live through the morrow. This meant remaining in the barracks instead of patrolling at night, it meant clanging mess kits when on daylight patrol to warn the Viet Cong to get out of the way. It meant staying out of trouble—and trouble meant the sound of shots fired in anger. American advisers could and did wheedle, shout, lead, push, suggest, or demand, but to little avail.

I remember talking in early 1963 to an American colonel who was adviser to a Division in the northern part of South Vietnam. He had heard rumors that helicopters were to be put under the operational control of the Vietnamese Corps Headquarters, rather than remain under American control. He was beside himself. His power to assign or withhold "choppers" was the only leverage he had over his Vietnamese counterparts. Without this he could do nothing to inject his own views into Vietnamese operational planning. In the end, of course, the Vietnamese got their own helicopters.

Despite the experience of Ap Bac, Washington was optimistic about progress in Vietnam. In his State of the Union message to Congress on January 14 President Kennedy affirmed that, "In the world beyond our borders, steady progress has been made in building a world of order. . . . The spear point of aggression has been blunted in Viet-Nam." [1] Two weeks later Secretary McNamara told the House Armed Services Committee that the war in Vietnam was going well. He noted the possibility, however, of "overt aggression from North Vietnam" against South Vietnam that "could require a greater direct participation by the United States." At a news conference on the same day Admiral Henry D. Felt, Commander of American forces in the Pacific, said the Vietnamese Government would achieve victory within three years. Planners in Peking and Hanoi would "hesitate a long time" before sending forces into South Vietnam. "They don't want to fight the United States because they know how strong we are." [2]

These bullish pronouncements and predictions were in no sense an effort to paint a false, sunlit picture. Official reporting from Saigon was encouraging on the new strategic hamlet program. Although some of the more skeptical analysts in Washington felt that the statistics on hamlet construction were a little fishy—too many being completed too fast—most observers were of the opinion that the "oil-spot" approach held promise of stemming the erosion of GVN strength in the countryside. (In all fairness I hasten to add that I was among this group.) Secretary Rusk was not trying to mislead his audience when in a speech on April 22 he noted with satisfaction that "already approximately 7 million Vietnamese live in well over 5000 strategic hamlets. The program calls for the completion of another 3000 by the end of this year." [3] Aside from the apparent progress of the strategic hamlet program, hopes were buoyed by the fact that more American advisers and equipment were flowing into Vietnam each week. Ap Bac seemed to be an embarrassing trough in an upward-moving curve of government progress.

If there was any question about the curve, information—more information than most people felt they wanted to have—was supplied on a daily, weekly, and monthly basis. There was, for example, a dubious statistic falling under the macabre rubric of "Kill Ratios" (how many guys in white hats knocked off compared to guys in black pajamas). There was the equally gruesome and equally questionable statistic, "Actual Body Count" (a post-engagement inventory of Viet Cong corpses—only no one, even if he had the energy and interest left after combat to search and count accurately, could tell the difference between a dead porter and a dead soldier). There were the Weapons/Lost, Weapons/Captured Ratio and the Incident Count. And there were red, white, and blue charts designating with deceptive accuracy the localities under Viet Cong, Saigon, or mixed control. It was all very quantitative, very scientific, and very misleading.

*   *   *

Despite the favorable ratios, there were disquieting portents. In mid-February Ambassador Nolting felt it necessary to give Diem some rare, blunt advice. In a speech to Vietnamese officials he urged more frankness in the relationship between them and the Americans. "I would suggest less touchiness and more of a willingness to face the bad along with the good in the months and years of effort that lie ahead." [4] Throughout early 1963 there was an increasing sense of exasperation in Washington with Diem and his family and it was against this background that I was sent to Vietnam in the spring to search for the answer to "Can we win with Diem?" The very phrasing of the question implied more anxiety about developments in Vietnam than official statements were currently admitting. Secretary Rusk told the press in early February, and again three weeks later, that he thought there was "a turning of the corner" in Vietnam.

Aside from the marathon visits with Diem and Nhu (Chapter VI), in which the question of "frankness" was academic in the face of the flood of monologues, I spent a great deal of time looking at

strategic hamlets. I hovered a hundred feet above them in helicopters, walked around them with province chiefs, and lunched in
them with the local notables. No one suggested that I stay overnight in any of the hamlets, and it was clear that if I volunteered
to do so (which I did not) I would have had little company from
the province chief or members of his entourage. But I must admit
to having been impressed with much that I saw. There were
schools with teachers and children and books, clinics with technicians and patients and medicine, stockades surrounded by sharp-
ened spikes, trenches and barbed wire, and AID-financed fish
ponds, pig pens, and chicken runs. I am not so naive now, nor was
I then, not to know that I could have been seeing a group of
Potemkin villages or that I was being shown the best of the
species, but I did come away with the sense that there were such
things as "strategic hamlets" and that somewhere someone was
showing some initiative in translating a "program" into something
tangible.

Perhaps my most impressive experience was that of visiting a
newly-constructed Montagnard (aborigine) village. I flew into
Dalat, then clattered by helicopter to the nearest district town,
and finally bumped by jeep over some dusty primitive trails to the
settlement. Several hundred families had "voluntarily" moved
from areas where they were exposed to Viet Cong harassment and
blandishment. With its log buildings and stockade, the village
looked very much like a motion picture set for a Grade B Western.
Unlike my other visits, this one was laid on with much ceremony.
The villagers (with the obvious advice and consent of the shrewd
district chief) had made an elaborate crossbow and had woven
some cloth which they wished me to present to President and Mrs.
Kennedy.

I walked through the main gate of the stockade past two lines
of ancient notables, young men with long spears, and pretty young
girls playing high-pitched native instruments or swaying in a
languid sensuous dance. The men wore g-strings, the women were
naked to the waist. I was feeling slightly dizzy, whether from the
culture shock, the hot sun, or not having had any food since an
early breakfast. But worse was yet to come. I was first taken on a

tour of the village—the school, the communal "long house," the primitive outdoor weaving and dying factory. Close behind me trailed the notables, the spear carriers, the bell ringing, flute playing girls, and the dancers. The tour terminated in front of the village headquarters where, it was explained, I would be made an honorary member of the tribe. But first I had to demonstrate my manliness, or some other undefined virtue, by consuming a vast quantity of fermented something-or-other served up in an earthen crock. This gastronomic treat had to be imbibed by vigorous suction through an inadequate bamboo straw. There was no escape; this was too sophisticated a group to use a ploy that sometimes works at diplomatic receptions in Washington—"on the wagon" or "bleeding ulcer" or even a "sick headache" (the last, incidentally, was here becoming quite imminent). Two young, physically precocious girls waited upon me, one holding the straw and the other the jug. I applied powers of suction I never knew I had, and the fermented juice oozed upwards and inwards while the spear carriers chanted and the music soared and the dancing girls swayed and the sun beat down. Taking one last sickening gulp for President Kennedy, I got unsteadily to my feet to murmurs of general approval. I was given a silver bracelet (now lost someplace in a daughter's drawer) to signify my membership in the tribe, and then with great ceremony (or so I was later told), was presented with the cross bow and the cloth and then with a bow for myself. I delivered an awkward little speech, and clutching my treasures made my way out of the village, back to the jeep, back to the helicopter and back to Dalat and some solid food. Much of the last is still very hazy to me. A White House acknowledgment of the gifts, at last report, was hanging proudly on the wall of the long house.

By the time I returned to Washington the late spring air was heavy with uncertainty and controversy. Uncertainty within the White House about which way to turn as far as Diem was concerned, and uncertainty about how to pursue a successful policy in South Vietnam if Diem and his brother remained in power. Con-

troversy between American officials and the American press, and
controversy between the Administration in Washington and the
government in Saigon.

Diem had by now tightened up on his policy of censorship of
books and newspapers. He cut material that could be classified as
pro-Communist, and publications or articles that were regarded as
"anti-Diem." The jails were bursting with political prisoners, some
of whom had never been tried and hundreds of whom were non-
Communist liberals who had been arrested for expressing views
unfavorable to Diem and Nhu.[5] The man behind Diem's internal
security apparatus at this time was a Dr. Tran Kim Tuyen, a diminutive, Machiavellian-minded man who had once been a physician.
The only time I ever saw him was at the home of the CIA Chief in
Saigon. He was pointed out to me by a young American intelligence officer who described him with a mixture of hate and ad-
miration as a "fourteen carat son of a bitch." The little doctor was
fired and exiled when Nhu discovered Tuyen had come to the
conclusion that if Diem were to be able to maintain power it
would have to be without the company of the Nhus.* Upon Tuyen's removal, Nhu and Madame Nhu's brother took over the task
of keeping the indigenous wolves at bay. Whether the brilliant
Tuyen could have handled the events of mid-1963 so as to have
avoided, or at least mitigated, the crises that brought Diem to his
downfall is still a matter of gossip and debate among the Vietnamese.

The tightening of the screws on any form of political expression in Vietnam was disturbing enough, but the fact that the
seething in the cities was accompanied by little or no progress
against the insurgents in the countryside was giving the Administration in Washington many sleepless nights. By April, 1963 the
American press was virtually ignoring the official handouts from
Public Affairs Officers in Saigon and Washington. Although there
was still an occasional brave official pronouncement about "turned
corners" and government "initiatives," the American people were

* Tuyen was packed off to become Consul-General in Cairo in September,
1963, two months prior to the coup that toppled both Diem and Nhu. He returned
to Saigon in mid-November expecting to get a high post with the new regime but
was jailed instead. By this time nobody trusted him.

getting daily doses of bad news and lugubrious predictions from
the press. In late April, Malcolm Brown, the Associated Press correspondent in Saigon, wrote that ten more years of civil war was
possible "if the present pattern continues"; Neil Sheehan, the
United Press correspondent, said that "the authoritarian regime of
Ngo Diem has shown little sign of popular support" or of making
the reforms necessary to win essential peasant backing. David
Halberstam of *The New York Times* told of "major obstacles" that
blocked American and Vietnamese agreement on a program for
fighting the Viet Cong. And a news story, quoting "American
military sources," described "South Vietnam's massive American-
backed military machine" as being "confused and sluggish."

Critical news stories such as these infuriated the increasingly
sensitive and isolated residents of the Presidential Palace. Their
fury was directed at both American correspondents and American
civilians and military officers who were circumventing the official
public relations channels and telling stories out of school. Largely
because of this, Diem and Nhu were having second thoughts about
the desirability of having young, aggressive American officers attached as advisers to the lower echelons of the Vietnamese Army
and to the local political units in the countryside. Such close association at the rice roots level, they felt, would give Americans distorted views of the Vietnamese war effort. The vast majority of
the 12,000 American advisers now in Vietnam were attached to
large headquarters in Saigon and other cities, but about 2000
young officers had been assigned to work with province chiefs
throughout the countryside. The Americans had independent
sources of information on both military and civil developments
outside of Saigon and were venting their frustration to receptive
American reporters. It was obvious that matters could get out of
control, especially since the Americans were pressing for more advisers to give more advice to more people. It was not surprising
that Diem and his brother felt uneasy.

In fairness, Diem and the Nhus were in an awkward situation.
Partly because of the pressures they were under to keep abreast of
plots and counterplots against them, and partly because they had
long since cut themselves off from what was actually taking place

in the countryside and in the fighting units, they were beginning to worry about what they did not know. American officials in the Embassy and MACV displayed an uncomfortable degree of familiarity with the situation on the ground. Generalized requests for "improvements" and "reform" could be met with vague and misty promises, but a specific charge about a listless Division Commander or a corrupt Province Chief was more difficult to deal with. More often than not the man in question turned out to be a cousin of a powerful general whose support was needed in the Presidential Palace.

Aside from the fact that some Americans were beginning to know more about what was happening outside of Saigon than did most Vietnamese government officials, Diem and Nhu had another gripe. This was a more justifiable one. Gung-ho twenty-five-year-old American captains fresh from New York or Kansas City wanted to revolutionize the economy and political structure of the province they were assigned to—and wanted to conclude the process during their one-year tour of duty. The matter of "advising" was an art not a science, and many of the Americans practiced this art in ways that galled or confused their Vietnamese "counterparts." One experienced American military officer aptly summed up the issue: "The U.S. 'arrogance of power' was manifested in an attitude [on the part of many advisers] which as much as said, 'Get out of my way, I'd rather do it myself!' " [6] Diem could legitimately wonder what great knowledge these inexperienced American "short-timers" could pass on to the Vietnamese that would make such a great difference in winning the war. And if, in addition, the Americans were acting as watchdogs for the Embassy or MACV under the cover of their role as advisers, Diem might well have wondered whether the game was worth the candle.

For a brief period during April and May, Diem and Nhu had apparently decided it was not worth it. According to a Reuters account in late April, the "Diem Government is reported to be fighting United States suggestions to increase the influence of American military advisers" and "Diem himself is said to oppose strongly a reported plan for a big increase in the number of United States military advisers." [7] In mid-May Diem and Nhu told some visiting journalists of their doubts about the extent to which Americans really understood the situation in Vietnam. "I don't think the Americans are able to advise us on subversive warfare," Nhu said. "I am afraid the Americans don't know as much as we do." [8]

When asked at a press conference on May 22 about Nhu's views on American troops, Kennedy told the reporter (and the Vietnamese Government) that "we would withdraw the troops, any number of troops, any time the Government of South Viet-Nam would suggest it. The day after it was suggested, we would have some troops on their way home . . . we are hopeful that the situation in South Viet-Nam would permit some withdrawal in any case by the end of the year, but we can't possibly make that judgment at the present time. . . . But I would say that if requested to, we will do it immediately." [9]

The storm blew over as, of course, it was bound to do. For their part, Diem and Nhu had no illusions about the prospects for their survival if they had to stand alone against either the Viet Cong or the plotters within their own Army. As for the Administration in Washington, pulling out American forces would have been by no means as simple a matter as Kennedy implied; the United States, even then, had a tremendous stake in a successful outcome of the war. In short, Diem and Kennedy were stuck with each other in the spring of 1963, and it would take more than sharp oral volleys to break the bond. By early May the Pentagon's chief spokesman, Arthur Sylvester, could say, "the corner has definitely been turned" toward victory in South Vietnam and Defense Department officials were hopeful that the 12,000-man United States force there could be reduced in one to three years. [10]

*   *   *

Almost simultaneously with Sylvester's ebullient pronouncement, the curtain rose on the tragedy that would end six months later with the corpses of Diem and Nhu being dumped out of the back of an army vehicle. And ironically enough, it was not the Viet Cong that proved the Ngo family's undoing (although the Communists almost certainly helped the process along); it was a handful of Buddhist monks. The flash point of the explosion took place in Hue on May 8 when Diem's troops fired indiscriminately into a crowd of Buddhists who were displaying a religious banner in defiance of a government edict. But as George Carver of the CIA notes in an article in *Foreign Affairs*, "Bit by bit a plethora of incidents, events, practices, and policies—many of them almost certainly unintentional or accidental—laid the groundwork for a 'religious issue' on which non-Communist but also non-Catholic opposition to Diem could, and eventually did, focus. This was not something that suddenly happened in the spring of 1963. Instead, it was something that had been gradually building up almost from the day Diem took office." [11] It is hard to believe that Ambassador Nolting was very diplomatic or entirely accurate when he reportedly said, "I myself . . . after almost two and a half years, have never seen any evidence of religious persecution." [12]

The flames of Buddhist revolt against the government spread from Hue to Saigon. Within weeks government troops were raiding pagodas, monks were publicly burning themselves alive, students were rioting, and the government and the Buddhist hierarchy were beyond reconciliation. Madame Nhu's remarks about the monks putting on a "barbecue show" did nothing to enhance the prospects for compromise. There was a temptation at the time, and even more so since, to regard the revolt of the bonzes as a struggle of good against evil. But although the bonzes were holy men, they were by no means angels. "After eight weeks interviewing various members of the hierarchy," wrote one not unsympathetic journalist, "the most lasting impression is one combining equal parts of pettiness and slyness. Buddhist spokesmen have lied outright to the press. . . ." [13]

Hard-pressed American Embassy officers trying to determine what the Buddhists actually wanted in terms of specific government programs despaired of cutting through their obscure, fog-shrouded rhetoric. Finally, the State Department dispatched to Saigon the only Buddhist Foreign Service Officer on the rolls (then serving in Hong Kong) to see if he could penetrate the fog. He had somewhat better luck in communicating with the bonzes, but there was still a yawning abyss between the American officials and the Buddhist activists. The monks had concepts, aspirations, ambitions, hopes, and fears—but no program. They had a clear idea of what they did *not* want but seemed unable to communicate what they *did* want. (Or so it seemed to me—and this may well reflect my own inability to understand.)

As late as 1965, the Buddhist mind was still terra incognita to American policymakers. I spent many hours with students of the Buddhist culture and with Buddhists. I had hoped to discover how we could induce the bonzes to become engaged in the political process of Vietnam in a more constructive way. The air in my office and my home was heady with discussions of Hinayana or Theravada Buddhism (which stressed individual salvation) and Mahayana Buddhism (which emphasized the need to help others as well as oneself to achieve Nirvana). In the course of my pursuit of the elusive key to understanding the bonzes, I was told of a study done by two Thai psychologists for the National Institute of Mental Health. The burden of the study was that Buddhist monks had an alarmingly high incidence of schizophrenia as a consequence of their efforts to bridge the gap between the real world and the world of isolation and meditation.

In spite of its inexperience in practical politics, the Buddhist hierarchy had an instinct for public relations, an uncanny sense of timing, and plenty of guts. This, plus years of being treated as second class citizens in a country where they vastly outnumbered the Catholics,* drove them to the ramparts. And that was the beginning of the end for Diem.

By mid-June the Buddhist crisis was tearing apart the two cities of Hue and Saigon and having major reverberations throughout the rest of Vietnam. Government troops were diverted from military operations against the Communists to cope with street demonstrations, guard government buildings and isolate the pagodas. Hundreds of thousands of Vietnamese, whose contact with Buddhism had been confined to an occasional wedding or funeral, suddenly found common cause with the bonzes. The universities

* The actual number of practicing, as opposed to nominal, Buddhists in Vietnam has always been uncertain, but even the lowest accepted number was still much higher than the Catholic population. One estimate that seems reasonable is that South Vietnamese Catholics comprised about 10 percent of the population and the nominal Buddhists between 70 and 80 percent.

and high schools of Hue and Saigon, which by and large had been non-political and docile, became centers of dissension. The Saigon Government had little time to devote to anything but the Buddhist challenge. Even Nhu's strategic hamlet program was ignored.

❖   ❖   ❖

July and August are hot, humid, unpleasant months in Saigon. Aside from the weather the summer of 1963 was especially unpleasant. In mid-July President Kennedy was asked if the Buddhist problem had hampered American aid in the fight against the Viet Cong. "Yes," said Kennedy, "I think it has. It is unfortunate that this dispute has arisen at the very time when the military struggle has been going better . . . I would hope this would be settled, because we want to see a stable government there. . . . We are not going to withdraw . . . for us to withdraw . . . would mean a collapse not only of South Viet-Nam but Southeast Asia." [14]

The President was more worried than his remarks revealed. He had already decided to replace Ambassador Nolting with Henry Cabot Lodge,* and he ordered the Embassy in Saigon to apply pressure on Diem to come to some arrangement with the Buddhists. Before leaving Saigon in mid-August, Nolting was told by Diem that attacks against the Buddhists would stop. But barely a week had passed when on August 21 Nhu's elite troops raided the principal pagodas in Saigon and elsewhere throughout the country in a night of fire and carnage. The Americans were caught completely by surprise. Lodge arrived in Saigon on the day following the attack to find the conflict between the government and the Buddhists beyond healing. The Foreign Minister, the Vietnamese Ambassador to Washington (Madame Nhu's father), and a host of other officials resigned in protest, some shaving their heads to show support for the bonzes; university and high school students went on a rampage and were arrested by the hundreds;

---

* Lodge had many obvious qualifications for the job, including his fluent knowledge of French and his experience in the United Nations. Moreover his Republican connections were important at a time when Vietnam was already becoming an important domestic issue. And whether President Kennedy was aware of it or not, Lodge prided himself on another asset—his uncle was a Buddhist.

there was an audible murmur of revulsion and disaffection among Diem's erstwhile trusted generals.

In a terse comment immediately following the dark deeds of August 21, the State Department was as angry as its official voice could convey. A statement drafted by Averell Harriman hit the issue on the line: "The action represents a direct violation by the Vietnamese Government of assurances that it was pursuing a policy of reconciliation with the Buddhists. The United States deplores repressive actions of this nature." [15]

Within days after the pagoda raids, Ambassador Lodge was approached through covert, indirect channels by a group of generals who wanted some assurances on the American position in the event of a coup. The American reply to a query from Lodge was carefully drafted by Under-Secretary of State Averell Harriman, Assistant Secretary Roger Hilsman, and White House Staff Assistant Michael Forrestal to cover all contingencies including continued support for Diem if he resolved the Buddhist problem. But the basic thrust of the message was that a stable non-Communist government emerging from a successful coup would have the support of the United States. Secretary Rusk had helped draft the cable from New York where he was attending a meeting at the UN, and Kennedy had personally cleared it from Hyannisport. The only initials on the telegram as it was sent out, however, were those of Acting Secretary of State George Ball, Harriman, Hilsman and Forrestal. General Taylor himself heard about it only after it had been dispatched and Roswell Gilpatric, acting for McNamara who was out of town, was not given an opportunity to see it. When the President later learned that the message had been sent without its being cleared by McNamara and McCone, he was not altogether pleased—especially when McNamara and McCone registered their objections. Kennedy felt that he had been painted into a corner and indicated that he would have preferred to give an even more ambivalent answer to the generals.[16] In the end it didn't make much difference, since the plotters were unable to screw up the necessary courage or to raise sufficient troops to pursue the idea seriously.

Although Kennedy felt that it was premature to imply Amer-

ican support for a coup d'etat, he was nonetheless angry with
Diem and Nhu and took the occasion of an interview with Walter
Cronkite in early September to warn the Saigon regime of his
impatience. "I don't think that unless a greater effort is made by
the [Saigon] Government to win popular support that the war can
be won out there. . . . in the last 2 months, the government has
gotten out of touch with the people. The repressions against the
Buddhists, we felt, were very unwise. Now all we can do is to make
it very clear that we don't think this is the way to win." When
asked if he thought there was still time, the President said, "I do.
With changes in policy and perhaps with personnel, I think it
[Diem's government] can. If it doesn't make those changes, I
would think that the chances of winning it would not be very
good." [17]

Kennedy did not say so, but he had a very clear idea of what
he meant by "changes in personnel." He, McNamara, and Bundy
were coming to feel that the Nhus would have to leave Vietnam
if the situation were to be salvaged. By then very few would have
disagreed privately with Stanley Karnow's description of the family as being a cross between the Borgias and the Bourbons,[18] or
with the flat statement made by Denis Warner in October that
"the Ngo Dinhs are simply despots." [19] But there was a lingering
hope that with his brother and sister-in-law out of the country,
Diem might be able to pull together a government of leading
Catholics and Buddhists, restore order, and create a sense of national purpose.

Diem was outraged by current American views and took every
opportunity to imply that the Buddhists were being actively encouraged by the United States. In response to a demarche from the
Asian and African members of the United Nations protesting his
persecution of the Buddhists, Diem sent a message to U Thant that
"the East and the West" were taking advantage of the growing
pains of the Buddhist movement and were taking the opportunity
"to infiltrate, if not to impose their own cadres who try to take
over the leadership." [20]

By mid-September there was virtually no communication between the American Embassy and the Presidential Palace. Lodge

had told Diem and Nhu what the American Government expected of them. The next move, he felt, was theirs. Neither was to make a move until the end of October when Diem invited Lodge to accompany him to the opening of an atomic energy research laboratory. In the meantime there had been a flood of expletives in the government-controlled press about Lodge, Kennedy, and the United States generally. The American press, in particular, was a favorite target for Diem and the Nhus—and American reporters returned the compliment. During this period there was a "goodwill" tour by Madame Nhu to the United States and Western Europe. The photogenic emissary, who was now being referred to as the "Dragon Lady," lost no chance to appear on television, at women's clubs, or at political meetings. She and her husband must have suspected that matters were taking a dangerous turn in Vietnam, and her departure from Saigon at this time may have been motivated by the desire to get out while there was still a chance to do so. But since she was accompanied by only one of her children (the others were taken out of Saigon in the care of an American Embassy Officer to join her in Rome after Nhu was murdered), a more likely explanation for her trip at this particular moment would be that she and her husband felt there might be one final, desperate chance to turn American policy around. In any case, her mission was not only unsuccessful, but it exacerbated the anti-Diem/Nhu feeling in the United States. Calling American officers "little soldiers of fortune," castigating the American press, and casting aspersions on the steadfastness and integrity of the American Government did little to help Diem's cause.

Madame Nhu was not the only VIP traveling across the Pacific during the early autumn. At a National Security Council meeting in late September it was decided to send Secretary McNamara and General Taylor to Vietnam to get the "facts" on the situation in Saigon. The White House was anxious to avoid, if it could, any speculation that the trip was related to the political crisis in Vietnam. The official announcement made a special point of noting that the Secretary and the Chairman of the Joint Chiefs were going on a "military mission." But efforts to minimize the political implications of the trip beguiled few people either in the

United States or Vietnam. *The New York Times* reported that "The crucial problem facing the Administration was not the temporary state of affairs in the Delta or elsewhere in South Vietnam . . . but a fundamental evaluation of Saigon's capacity to go on with the war in the light of its unsolved political difficulties." McNamara and Taylor were expected to provide the President with views which would "help decide further United States policy in dealing with the regime of President Ngo Dinh Diem." [21]

The McNamara–Taylor report to the President was optimistic with respect to the military situation but full of foreboding with respect to political developments. Indeed, the two emissaries said, there were already signs that the Buddhist crisis and the political tensions in Saigon had created hostility among military officers against the Diem regime. Both McNamara and Taylor favored continuing pressure on Saigon for moderation and reform. But according to one presumably knowledgeable source, Roger Hilsman (at the time Assistant Secretary of State for Far Eastern Affairs), they then insisted that the public National Security Council announcement of their findings refer to the fact that the war was going well and that "the Pentagon was right" in its reports of progress.[22] In the event, the official White House statement acknowledged, "The military program in South Viet-Nam has made progress and is sound in principle, though improvements are being energetically sought." [23]

Hilsman may have been present at the Council meeting (I was not), and his account of McNamara's insistence on a White House stamp of approval for the way the war was going may, therefore, reflect his firsthand observations. But I was in the West Basement of the White House when the meeting adjourned and I reviewed the final draft of the statement with Kennedy's Special Assistant McGeorge Bundy and Deputy Assistant Secretary of Defense William Bundy. I was not troubled by the reference to military progress (such statements were now part of the liturgy) but was surprised and outraged over this one: "Secretary McNamara and General Taylor reported their judgment that the major part of the U.S. military task can be completed by the end of 1965, although there may be a continuing requirement for a limited number of U.S. training personnel." [24]

This sentence was not only gratuitous, but it was loaded with booby traps. For the past several months the press had been making a convincing case that official reporting on the military situation in Vietnam was overly optimistic. The announcement of the McNamara–Taylor findings was too sanguine in any case. The "Bring-the-boys-home-by-1965" flavor would destroy whatever credibility it had. Both Bundys agreed, but Bill had little elbow room. Finally, in utter exasperation Bill said, "Look, I'm under instructions!" In Washington that closes any argument, unless recourse is taken by tackling the Instructor. Mac called Secretary McNamara, but was unable to persuade him to change his mind. McNamara seemed to have been trapped too; the sentence may have been worked out privately with Kennedy and therefore imbedded in concrete. The words remained, and McNamara and the Administration were to pay a heavy price for them. They were not ignored by the waiting press. VIETNAM VICTORY BY END OF '65 ENVISAGED BY U.S. was *The New York Times* headline on October 3.

The dramatic prediction had the effect of submerging the most significant part of the White House announcement, a somber reflection of the Administration's current views and fears: "The political situation in South Viet-Nam remains deeply serious. The United States has made clear its continuing opposition to any repressive actions in South Viet-Nam. While such actions have not yet significantly affected the military efforts, they could do so in the future." [25]

*   *   *

As part of the last gasp effort to apply pressure on Diem in the late summer and early autumn, the Administration cancelled the funding program for Nhu's Special Forces. Although these troops were designed to be an elite combat unit, the regime had been using them as a Palace Guard. (This was the force which reportedly was used to smash the pagodas during the August reprisals against the Buddhists.) After considerable soul searching and with some encouragement from the Senate, Kennedy also cut off American import aid to the Vietnamese Government. This aspect of American economic assistance, known as the Commodity Import Program, amounted to about $150 million a year. It permitted private Vietnamese firms to import subsidized non-military, largely luxury items which were then sold on the open market. The program was designed to soak up the ever-increasing supply of piasters in circulation. There was considerable doubt, however, that a cut in import aid would have any immediate influence on Diem and Nhu —the warehouses in Saigon were then bulging with consumer goods. There was also some concern that cutting off the flow of such commodities as canned milk would entail real sacrifice on the part of the most innocent and helpless of the Vietnamese population. I can remember a lively debate at a White House staff meeting on the issue of whether to continue subsidizing the import of milk and medicine, but I believe these items too were included in the embargo. In order that the Diem regime would have an opportunity to make concessions as gracefully as possible, no publicity was given in Washington to the elimination of import aid. But Nhu himself announced the aid cut and asserted that the Vietnamese were prepared to carry on the good fight without American help.

Although such pressures from Washington had little or no tangible effect on the course of events in Vietnam during the last critical weeks of October, they did have a major psychological effect. For the first time since 1954 the United States had taken a definite step to demonstrate its opposition to the policies of the Saigon regime. It was now clear to Vietnamese officials and the populace generally that Washington would not remain supine if Diem ignored or flouted requests for major changes in policy and improvements in performance. Most importantly, it provided a clear signal to those Vietnamese opposing Diem that the United States was not automatically, irrevocably, and indefinitely committed to supporting the present regime.

The next act of the tragedy was played out with more passion, plot and counter-plot, internecine struggles, and awesome offstage noises than any dramatist could have contrived. The cast featured religious mystics and mad, isolated rulers. There was a pervasive mood of suppressed excitement fed by public announcements of impending doom. There were suicides by fire in the public market place. Offstage sounds emanating from Madame Nhu were becoming more extravagant and hysterical. And in Washington the differences among key personalities and elements within the Administration about how to face up to Scene II were now an open secret. In particular, the problems between Ambassador Lodge and John Richardson, the CIA Station Chief in Vietnam, were beginning to come to a boil.

The "Agency's" man in Saigon had had for years the special responsibility of maintaining contact with Nhu; the Ambassador's task was to work directly with President Diem. Lodge was an all-or-nothing Ambassador; he had made it clear to Kennedy before he left for Vietnam that he expected to control all aspects of American policy there, including the military. When Lodge arrived in Saigon he set about to examine the whole melange of relationships between the Embassy and the Palace. He took a dark view of the separate channels to Nhu. Aside from differences in personality and operational policy between the Ambassador and Richardson, there was a more important reason why the CIA man had to be replaced: as long as Nhu *felt* that he had a private, sympathetic channel to Washington (whether he *actually* did was not so important), the Embassy's contacts with the Palace were even more complicated and byzantine than they would have been otherwise. The CIA Station Chief was called back to Washington for "consultations" early in October.

The denouement took place in the final week of October. But even now, years later, there is some murkiness about just how the plot developed. What actually happened is best known by only one American—a shrewd and shadowy ex-colonel who was the Embassy's contact with the plotters. Although he apparently gave Robert Shaplen much of the story, there are still some gaps.[26] In essence, however, a group of generals and colonels representing most, but not all, of the key elements of the Vietnamese Armed Forces, attacked the Palace during the siesta hour of November 1. Diem and Nhu refused to surrender. Many hours later, after ascer-

taining that the forces they thought they could rely on had either
gone over to the side of the plotters or had been neutralized, the
two brothers escaped through a secret tunnel to a waiting jeep
that took them to a house of labyrinthian design in the Chinese
section of the city. Here they hid for several hours. They gave
themselves up in the early morning of the following day and were
shot while being taken to the generals' headquarters. The people
of Saigon had their happiest day in many years—and since.

The Americans were the popular heroes of the coup, although
Lodge and the White House publicly professed complete innocence of its planning and execution. (Many Vietnamese jokingly
suggested that Ambassador Lodge should run for President of
Vietnam to make up for his failure to gain the American Vice
Presidency in 1960.) Arthur Schlesinger emphasizes that "the
coup of November 1, 1963 was entirely planned and carried out
by the Vietnamese. Neither the American Embassy nor the CIA
were involved in instigation or execution." [27] Sorensen states that
the coup "received no assistance from the United States, nor did
this country do anything to prevent or defeat it." [28]

In a literal sense it was true that Washington played no role.
Planning for the coup had been taking place since the summer
and, although rumors were rife (there were, in fact, at least two
separate groups, one of them led by General Duong Van Minh
("Big Minh"), planning for the disposal of the Diem regime), the
Americans were kept in the dark until early October when the
generals who were involved in the November 1 coup told a trusted
American about their plans. The American was an old Vietnam
hand and had known most of the Vietnamese officers for many
years. He was probably one of the few attached to the Mission
who got to know the Vietnamese outside the cocktail party or
official circuit. He kept the Ambassador closely informed of developments (as the generals knew he would), and the Ambassador
in turn reported the developments through highly secret channels
to the White House. But few other American officials were aware
of what was about to transpire. Admiral Felt, the Commander of
American Forces in the Pacific, paid a courtesy call on Diem the

morning of the coup and was given a ceremonial send-off by one of the key generals not very long before zero hour.

The United States did not overtly encourage the generals, but it must have been very clear to them by September that Washington was not opposed to a change. To be sure, the message sent to Lodge on August 24 in response to an inquiry from some coup-minded generals was hardly a robust or unequivocal commitment of American support. However, the President's television interview a week later, which included a somewhat wistful reference to "changes in personnel" in Saigon, must have given encouragement to those who had designs on Nhu if not on Diem. The removal of Nhu's prime American contact, the curtailment of funds for Nhu's Special Forces, and, most importantly, the cutting off of import aid must have convinced the generals that they could proceed without fear of subsequent American sanctions. What was not contemplated, even by those who were most sympathetic to the idea of a new regime in Saigon, was the execution of Diem and Nhu. The undisguised relief felt in Washington that at long last there would be a New Deal in Vietnam was tempered by disgust and horror at the final act of violence. (But not so in Saigon, where the deaths of the two leaders were either regarded with massive indifference or unrestrained glee.)

The new government in Saigon was headed by General "Big Minh," the hero of the battle against the Binh Xuyen gangsters many years before. Minh was likable and well-meaning, and both the Administration in Washington and the new government in Saigon basked briefly in the sunlight of high hopes and great expectations. Secretary Rusk "was encouraged about the possibilities" but acknowledged that "there is a good deal of unfinished business and some real problems ahead." [29] And President Kennedy went to his fateful appointment in Dallas feeling that the odds were still high against American success in Vietnam.

X

Interregnum: Washington and Saigon

It was early on Saturday morning, November 23rd, and I was hanging around McGeorge Bundy's outer office in the White House West Basement. I didn't know what else to do or where else to go, and I didn't know what to say, even if I felt like saying anything—which I didn't. Bundy's two secretaries were trying to get through the early morning routine—sorting the mail, checking the calendar. I envied them; they had something to do, and they could cry unashamedly. There were several other men standing around aimlessly who were strange to me. I found out later that they were members of Lyndon Johnson's staff—some were to become very familiar, some I never saw again.

John McCone, the Director of CIA, came in. He had been summoned to brief the new President. This was Lyndon Johnson's first exposure as President to the international situation, and the Director had only about twenty minutes to fill him in. He decided to concentrate on the most critical issue—the Soviet nuclear threat and the intelligence collection techniques that had been developed and deployed to keep abreast of it.

Mr. Johnson arrived with Bundy. He was gray and grave, but very much in command. McCone and the President went into

Bundy's office (the Oval office upstairs, with the new red rug that had been laid down during President Kennedy's absence, would not be used for several days); Bundy and I waited outside. Mc-Cone came away from that short meeting tremendously impressed with the new President's self-control. He had listened carefully, and asked some searching questions. He told the Director he would soon ask for another detailed briefing. And a few days later he did.

On Thursday, December 5 President Johnson called his first National Security Council meeting. There was only one item on the agenda—a briefing by John McCone on the world situation, with primary emphasis on the Soviet and Chinese Communist threat to American security interests. The Speaker of the House of Representatives, John McCormack, who would succeed to the Presidency if yet another disaster struck, was invited to attend. But at the last moment it was discovered that he didn't have the necessary clearances to listen to McCone's highly classified report. The Speaker was given the appropriate oaths, vows, and admonitions to read and sign at the guard's desk in the West Basement. It was obvious that he was bemused both by the frenetic formalities and by the discussion that subsequently took place. He was seldom invited again.

The President made two eloquent pleas to the men sitting around the Cabinet Room. He urged that in their approach to international affairs they consider seriously "the other fellow's point of view." And he stressed that he wanted to hear many, even divergent, views around the National Security Council table. Throughout the two-hour meeting, the subject of Vietnam was barely touched upon.

Shortly after he took office the new President expressed his intention to convene regular and frequent meetings of the National Security Council. As Vice President he had had a Foreign Service Officer assigned to his staff to keep him abreast of the international situation, but Johnson had been given little opportunity to participate in or even be exposed to major international policy decisions. He knew little of the Laos negotiations and had been only peripherally involved in the decisions during the Cuban Missile Crisis. As a consequence, Lyndon Johnson succeeded to the Presidency with only a spotty knowledge of the troublesome defense and foreign affairs problems he was about to confront.

The President soon discovered that the number of people who attended Council meetings and the formality of the institution did not suit his style of operation. Although there were more frequent meetings during Johnson's tenure than Kennedy's, more often than not the Council served as a briefing forum, rather than as a vehicle for addressing and thrashing out key issues. More of the meetings, naturally enough, dealt with Vietnam than with any other single subject. The President used these occasions to inform the Council members of decisions reached in smaller, more intimate meetings with the Secretaries of State and Defense, his Special Assistant for National Security Affairs, and a very few other advisers. Johnson also used the Council to assure that all participants were on record as being in agreement with major, sensitive decisions.

The NSC meetings I attended had a fairly standard format: the Secretary of State first presented a short summary of the issues, the Secretary of Defense added his comments, and there was some fairly bland and desultory discussion by the others present. Because many around the table had not participated in, nor indeed been told of the detailed advance discussions, "gut" issues were seldom raised and searching questions were seldom asked.

The President, in due course, would announce his decision and then poll everyone in the room—Council members, their assistants, and members of the White House and NSC Staffs. "Mr. Secretary, do you agree with the decision?" "Yes, Mr. President." "Mr. X, do you agree?" "I agree, Mr. President." During the process I would frequently fall into a Walter Mitty-like fantasy: When my turn came I would rise to my feet slowly, look around the room and then directly at the President, and say very quietly and emphatically, "Mr. President, gentlemen, I most definitely do *not* agree." But I was removed from my trance when I heard the President's voice saying, "Mr. Cooper, do you agree?" And out would come a "Yes, Mr. President, I agree."

❊ ❊ ❊

President Johnson inherited more than "the dirty little war" in Vietnam. He inherited Kennedy's principal advisers on foreign affairs—Rusk, McNamara, Bundy, and Taylor; he found himself with a "commitment" of uncertain specificity and duration, and he fell heir to what the press was already describing as a "credibility gap." But in those days, and indeed for the years to follow, many American military and civilian officials were supremely confident that "victory" was in sight. It seemed inconceivable that the lightly armed and poorly equipped Communist forces could maintain their momentum against, first, increasing amounts of American assistance to the Vietnamese Army and, subsequently, American bombing and combat forces. To those officials (including myself in late 1964 and early 1965), the Saigon-based correspondents were Cassandras and false prophets.

In late 1963, the President had no way of knowing that already present were all the ingredients that would soon combine to tear the fabric of American society apart and eventually lead to his decision not to seek a second term: the strength of the Communists was increasing, our Vietnamese ally was unable to achieve a broadly-based and effective government, and frustration and anxiety were growing among the American people. The optimistic accounts of how the war was going, the lights at the ends of tunnels, the corners being turned, and finally Secretary McNamara's out-by-the-end-of-1965 statement were weighing heavily on an increasingly skeptical and worried American public. Under Johnson the war, the commitment, and the credibility gap were to grow and flourish.

In his first hectic several weeks Lyndon Johnson was able to spare little time for the Vietnam problem. As a holding action, he issued a directive to all agencies and departments having a role in Vietnam. In it Johnson reaffirmed the policy of the previous Administration with respect to support for the government in Saigon. He stressed that all military and economic programs were to be kept at the levels maintained during the Diem regime, although he urged that particular attention be given to the deteriorating situation in the critical Delta area. The President admonished his subordinates that the war was a Vietnamese war and Americans should not attempt to run it for them. He reminded American officials that they should present a united front with respect to United States policy and objectives in Vietnam. Finally, he expected the new government in Saigon to make a major effort to increase its public support. The memorandum reflected the growing concern of Secretary Rusk and General Taylor who had recently returned from a Vietnam policy conference in Honolulu. Viet Cong control was spreading throughout the populous, rice-rich Mekong Delta, and there had been ample evidence of impatient Americans overstepping the fuzzy boundary between giving advice and taking charge.

The worries that were subsumed in President Johnson's memorandum were confirmed when Secretary McNamara made yet another brief trip to Vietnam in the latter part of December. His visit was in large part stimulated by a special report on Long An Province, a rich rice-growing area just south of Saigon. A team of American investigators had found the Viet Cong virtually in control of the province and the strategic hamlet program there had pretty much come to a halt. While recent Embassy reporting, to be sure, had not painted a very rosy picture of the situation in Long An, no one up to this point had suspected it was quite so bad. (When I visited the province capital not long after, the province chief confessed that he would not dare to go very many kilometers beyond the town limits even in broad daylight.) McNamara's report to the President when he returned on December 21 was gloomy indeed. He confirmed the deteriorating situation in the Delta and implied his disquiet about the uncertain and languid approach of General Minh toward the problems posed not only by the Viet Cong but by the still-restive Buddhists. "We observed the results of the very substantial increase in the Viet Cong activity, an increase that began shortly after the new government was formed, and has extended over a period of several weeks. . . . This rapid expansion of activity . . . obviously was intended to take advantage of the period of organization in the new government, a period during which there was a certain amount of confusion—confusion that you might have expected would result from the replacement of the Province Chiefs and other key administrators in the government." [1]

In his State of the Union Message the President gave scant

attention to Vietnam. He mentioned it only in the section on civil rights ("Americans of all races stand side by side in Berlin and in Vietnam") and later, in passing, when he pointed out that the United States would be "better prepared than ever" to defend freedom against "the infiltration practiced by those in Hanoi and Havana." [2] If Johnson fully realized the gravity and dimensions of the Vietnam problem, he apparently decided not to share his worries with the American people. Soon enough he would find Vietnam dominating his every waking hour. There were already some ominous portents—provided not by the Viet Cong but by our South Vietnamese allies.

Many Vietnamese, especially those in the urban areas, felt a tremendous sense of relief following the downfall of Diem and Nhu. To them the new government under General Minh signaled a bright, new era. Popular and highly-motivated though he was, Minh was pathetically lacking in political know-how and administrative competence. Perhaps no one could actually have fulfilled the extravagant expectations of the students or satisfied the unrealistic desires of the Buddhist hierarchy. The situation was grave, and McNamara told the House Armed Services Committee just that when he appeared before them in late January.

On the day following the Secretary's appearance on the Hill, things become even more complicated. After weeks of indecision and inaction, Minh's period of grace had ended. He was turned out of office in a coup led by General Nguyen Khanh, a powerful Corps Commander who thereupon dubbed himself Chief of State and Chairman of the Revolutionary Military Committee. When a week later Minh was restored to office and Khanh became Prime Minister, there was little reason in either Saigon or in Washington to hope for stability.*

Khanh's coup had some interesting implications. A few days before his move, Khanh had hinted privately that he planned to

---

* By August Khanh was Chief of State and Minh was back by September. And so it went; there were seven governments in Saigon in 1964—all, in one form or another, serving at the pleasure of a group of politically-minded generals. It was no wonder the war continued to go badly during the year. Not only did the Communists increase in strength and aggressiveness, but virtually every high-ranking officer in South Vietnam had one eye cocked in the direction of Saigon where he might one day be the boss.

seize power in order to preempt another coup by two "pro-French neutralist" generals. There might have been a temptation to dismiss this as empty rhetoric, except for the fact that a few days later General de Gaulle advanced his proposal for the "neutralization" of Vietnam. It may have been only a coincidence, of course, but a suspicious mind could reasonably speculate that the events were related; the French may have hoped that a "pro-French neutralist" government would be in place at the moment that de Gaulle surfaced his idea.

The Administration's gloom was deepened in early February by the year-end reports from the American Mission in Saigon that were just beginning to reach Washington. The assessments were pessimistic; even the usual Pollyanna-ish reviews of military progress had undertones of concern. The strategic hamlet program, which had been the source of such high hopes just a few months before, had come to a virtual halt. The fortified hamlets were much more vulnerable to Viet Cong attack than most people had expected. Their perimeter defenses seemed formidable, but all too often Viet Cong sympathizers within the hamlet simply opened the front gate to the enemy at nightfall. And the theory that paramilitary or regular forces would rush to the aid of a hamlet under attack proved to be only theory—these forces were frequently too slow, or too busy, or too far away, or too disinterested, or too afraid. The fortified hamlets turned out to be attractive targets, not only because of the psychological effect that stemmed from their being overrun, but because they were rich sources of arms and medicines. Judgments of the political scene were especially lugubrious. The Minh–Khanh combination was a fragile one, and there was an ubiquitous group of lean and hungry generals waiting in the wings for a chance to get into the spotlight and into the treasury. To leaven the already bubbling situation, none of the problems that emerged after Diem's downfall had really been tackled, let alone solved.

The President's press conference on the first of February introduced themes that were to echo through the months and years to follow. ". . . I have received assurances from the new and friendly leaders of Vietnam that they are proceeding immediately to step up the pace of military operations against the Viet Cong. . . . I

think that the present course we are following is the only answer
. . . and I think that the operations should be stepped up there." [3]

A few weeks later the President told Hanoi that it was playing
"a deeply dangerous game" by supporting the Viet Cong [4]—a remark that was described by an Administration spokesman on the
following day "as a deliberate warning" to Hanoi. The implications of this probably did not cause much of a stir in Hanoi (there
was certainly no resulting diminution of support for the South
Vietnamese insurgents), but they troubled many Americans. There
was already concern that the war would be expanded and Johnson's reference to the "dangerous game" led to speculation and
further worry. Asked a week later at a press conference what he
meant, the President obfuscated rather than clarified his earlier
statement. "That is what I said, that is what I meant, and that is a
very dangerous situation there and has been for some time." [5] The
President may have intended to send a clear warning signal to
Hanoi, or may have wished merely to prepare the groundwork for
other words or deeds to follow. Johnson himself may not have
known what precise message he wanted to convey, although various Administration spokesmen subsequently made specific or
veiled references to possible direct American involvement if the
North Vietnamese did not cool down their support of the Viet
Cong. But it would have been too much to ask Hanoi to read such
a signal if, indeed, it was a signal, against the background of conflicting statements and just plain static that characterized American statements about "an expanded war" during the winter and
spring of 1964. (Several months later, on July 31, Secretary Rusk
told reporters that American warnings to Hanoi had "registered."
Forty-eight hours later the North Vietnamese attacked an American destroyer.)

In February an effort was made to rationalize and coordinate
the efforts of the various government agencies and the various parts
of particular agencies involved in making or implementing Vietnam policy. It was the first of many such steps taken during the
Johnson Administration, but this like all the others to follow was
piecemeal and not very effective. An interagency Vietnam Task
Force was established, chaired by William Sullivan, which
in effect cut Assistant Secretary Roger Hilsman's Far East Bureau

out of the direct policy channel; the Bureau would now be just one of many elements within the Department feeding ideas and recommendations into a top-level group with direct access to the Secretary; many of the Bureau's Vietnam specialists were transferred to the Inter-Agency Committee. Hilsman resigned a short time after this decision on the grounds that he was in basic disagreement with the political and military strategy that was being followed or contemplated in Vietnam.* When William Bundy succeeded Hilsman, responsibility for Vietnam was returned to the Bureau. Bundy reported directly to the Secretary.

The public unveiling of the new Task Force was accompanied by an announcement that McNamara and Taylor were to leave soon for yet another trip to Vietnam. Once again they were to get a first-hand sense of the current situation and once again they were to do what they could to shore up the new government in Saigon.

I was sent to Vietnam in advance of the McNamara group to look into the Mission's reporting system. The deluge of statistics, commentary, and "situation reports" that poured into Washington each day evoked visions of the Mississippi River in high-water season. The problem was not that there was too little information but too much—uncoordinated, unreadable ("VC KIA 200 Rpt 200 at 1000Z; ARVN DIV 10 KMS COORDS _____, PREP ATTK VC BN EST AT 300"), and frequently not available in Washington until hours or even a full day behind the press accounts.

The reporting system was soon streamlined and a weekly assessment of progress on the political and economic as well as the military front was instituted. The military operations and intelligence folk were persuaded to put their telegrams into language more understandable to the layman. But we were never able to lick the race with the press. A reporter needed only to send his account of a battle through the regular telegraph, while the official

---

* There would be many more resignations of officials and White House Staff members over the next few years, but even among those who were soon to join the Vietnam Critics Chorus, there were few who did not rationalize their departure from their prestigious Washington offices behind vague references to "personal reasons" or "other opportunities difficult to turn down." One of Johnson's speech writers turned out to be a leading light in the Vietnam protest movement, although there was no criticism of Johnson's Vietnam policy in his resignation statement.

U.S. report had to be cleared by a host of senior officers, encoded, processed, decoded, retyped, and distributed by courier; it was usually well into the day by the time government officials were able to assess the morning newspaper account against the MACV reports. The President, with three press service tickers by his desk was, of course, ahead of the newspapers. I can't recall how many times there were anguished inquiries from the Oval Office about what the Embassy or MACV had said about a battle or a political development; a hapless minion would have to report that nothing was known beyond the AP, UPI or Reuters account. And more often than not, nothing more would be known until after the White House noon press conference, during which awkward questions and empty responses were exchanged.

It was on this trip that McNamara made another diplomatic blunder (his first being the "end-of-1965" statement several months before). The Secretary decided to take special pains to solidify the new government's position by demonstrating American support for the Saigon regime, and on his arrival at the airport he staged a sticky love feast. The schoolchildren, ladies' groups, and other "spontaneous" demonstrators supplied by Saigon's Central Casting Bureau dutifully cheered as McNamara, in the unaccustomed role of ebullient politician, repeatedly joined hands with General Khanh and shouted the Vietnamese equivalent of "solidarity"; Khanh, not surprisingly, assumed as a consequence that he had a blank check from Washington—an assumption that had some awkward consequences many months later when his own position and that of Washington began to diverge on key policy issues. But aside from that, we had identified ourselves so closely with Khanh that when the General was removed from office, several months later, it was almost as much an embarrassment for the United States as it was for Khanh himself.*

*   *   *

* One would have hoped this would be the last time an American official would make a public demonstration of support for an individual Vietnamese politician rather than for the Vietnamese Government as a whole, but both Presidents Johnson and Nixon have made a point of publicly embracing both Thieu and Ky.

The McNamara and Taylor recommendations served as a guideline for the Administration's approach to the war until the North Vietnamese attacked American destroyers in early August. General Khanh was given the official American blessing and American officials were reminded that they were to do whatever they could to discourage further coups. Khanh's plan for concentrating major military resources in the Saigon area and progressively clearing areas radiating outward from the capital (later to be known as the "Hop Tac" plan) was approved, as were the broad outlines of his idea for a general military and civilian mobilization. On the basis of the McNamara and Taylor findings it was decided to shelve the proposals that American combat troops be introduced into Vietnam, that attacks be launched against North Vietnam, and that American dependents be evacuated from South Vietnam. At the same time the Administration reaffirmed its opposition to the neutralization of South Vietnam as proposed six weeks earlier by General de Gaulle.

Shortly after his report to the President and the preparation of the government's policy guidelines, McNamara gave the most articulate account the American people had received thus far of America's purpose and problems in Vietnam. In a speech on March 26 McNamara gave three reasons for American involvement: "To answer the call of the South Vietnamese . . . to help them save their country for themselves; to help prevent the strategic danger which would exist if Communism absorbed Southeast Asia's people and resources; and to prove in the Vietnamese test case that the free world can cope with Communist 'wars of liberation.' . . ." He acknowledged that "the situation in South Vietnam has unquestionably worsened, at least since last fall. . . . Clearly, the disciplined leadership, direction, and support from North Vietnam is a critical factor in the strength of the Viet Cong movement. But the large indigenous support that the Viet Cong receives means that solutions must be as [much] political and economic as military. Indeed, there can be no such thing as a purely 'military' solution. . . . [General Khanh] has demonstrated the energy, comprehension and decision required by the difficult circumstances that he faces." McNamara then went on to describe the choices that confronted the Administration: to withdraw—which "the United States totally rejects"; the "neutralization" of Vietnam— "neutralization would in reality be an interim device to permit Communist consolidation and eventual takeover"; to expand the war outside Vietnam—"whatever ultimate course of action may be forced upon us by the other side, it is clear that actions under this option would be only a supplement to, not a substitute for, progress within South Vietnam's own borders"; to concentrate on assisting the South Vietnamese to win their own battle—"this, all agree, is essential no matter what else is done." [6]

During the weeks that followed the McNamara and Taylor trip, the President had his first meaningful opportunity to undertake a comprehensive look at the situation and to reappraise American policy. Up to this point he had been following a course of action he had inherited; but the reexamination of objectives and policy, which was made against a background of somber reports of the deteriorating situation in Vietnam, provided Johnson with perhaps his first real inkling of the dimensions of the problem he confronted. Now there was a renewed commitment and with it a yet more closely-related identification of American prestige with the outcome of the struggle.

*   *   *

Although Secretary McNamara could give General Khanh assurances of American support and could provide conspicuous evidence of how much we loved him, neither McNamara nor any other American could solve Khanh's problems. Khanh was an active soldier, not a patient statesman. Despite McNamara's public demonstration of confidence, the General seemed unable to translate heroic intentions and brave words into meaningful programs. The Buddhist hierarchy was fussing and the Catholic activists were fuming. Army desertions were on the increase, and so was Viet Cong terror. The pacification program was not making any perceptible progress, nor was Khanh's much-touted "mobilization program." Province chiefs were under-trained and over-worked; they had inadequate staffs in terms of both numbers and ability, and were called upon to cope with everything from animal hus-

bandry to emergency calls from besieged hamlets. To make matters worse for harassed provincial administrators and their desperate American advisers, petty bureaucrats and venal officials in
Saigon were either unable or unwilling to provide them with
sufficient funds to implement even minimal programs.

Despite—or perhaps because of—Khanh's tragic lack of success
in coming to grips with his problems, the Administration was trying to starch up the Vietnamese Government in every way it
could. Throughout the early spring there were repeated assurances
of American support. Secretary Rusk told a Saigon audience in
mid-April that he was optimistic about the prospects for a Communist defeat. But the Viet Cong celebrated the first of May by
sinking a ship in Saigon harbor and followed up the next day by
throwing a bomb into a crowd of Americans.

Khanh was becoming increasingly frustrated. He wanted a
"quick fix" and flailed about until he thought he found one. By
mid-spring he began to circulate the idea of a "March North."
The South Vietnamese, he said, must tackle the insurgency problem at its source. He may have thought he was not straying too far
from McNamara's March 26 speech which, after all, did not unequivocally reject the idea of military operations against North
Vietnam. Ambassador Lodge sent a telegram to Washington that
neither endorsed nor objected to Khanh's plan, but the dead-pan
message had a flavor of "who-can-blame-him?" In as diplomatic
terms as possible—telegrams sent directly from the White House
to Lodge, and later to Ambassadors Maxwell Taylor and Ellsworth Bunker, were drafted with kid gloves, velvet pencils, and
scented stationery—Lodge was informed that the Administration
would have none of the "March North" idea.

In early May McNamara and Taylor once again set off for
Saigon. Khanh was told that the Americans would not support
any attempts by the South Vietnamese Army to cross the 17th
parallel. Moreover McNamara did not hide the Administration's
impatience with Khanh's lackluster performance in getting the
pacification program moving. He also urged Khanh to move supplies and funds out to the provinces so the province chiefs could

implement the social and economic plans that had been lying on the shelf for months. The honeymoon with Khanh was over.

In the meantime Secretary Rusk had gone to a NATO meeting in Brussels where he hoped the United States would get allied support for the effort in Vietnam. Both Secretaries returned from their separate missions depressed with what they had seen and heard.

Rusk brought back some half-hearted expressions of moral support and some free advice from our NATO partners. McNamara brought back recommendations for increases in American aid: more American training personnel were required, the South Vietnamese must be provided with a larger air force. In a special message to Congress, President Johnson requested $125 million in additional military aid funds. Congress came through.

As a result of McNamara's disquieting report, the President felt he needed a full and frank account of progress and prospects, so he ordered Lodge and his principal subordinates to meet with top-level Washington officials in Honolulu. The formulation and implementation of a program for dealing with the Communist threat in the countryside was given priority, as it would be time after time again over the next several years. The first step would be to buttress the woefully weak administration at the province level. As a starter it was decided to increase the number of American civilian and military advisers in seven "key" provinces. Progress, or the lack of it, in the key provinces was to dominate reporting from Saigon for many months. Later there would be fourteen "critical" provinces. Later still the concept of designating particular provinces for special attention was dropped—all provinces were deemed "critical."

During the conference in Honolulu, President Johnson tried to dispel the inevitable public concern that had now become a backdrop to every high-level discussion of Vietnam. To those who were beginning to feel that the United States had embarked upon a new and dangerous course in Vietnam (and with one eye cocked on the Republican Convention now just a few weeks away), Johnson quoted in full the letter sent to Diem by President Eisenhower in October, 1954, adding, "That was a good letter then and it is a good letter now, and we feel the same way." To those worried that the United States might be weakening in its resolve, Johnson reasserted our position: "We are bound by solemn commitments to help defend this area against Communist encroachment. We will keep this commitment." To those worried about an escalation of the hostilities, the President gave his assurances that, "It is others who make war, and we who seek peace"; and in answer to a question, he said that he knew of "no plans" to expand the war to North Vietnam.[7]

Despite the President's efforts, the fears and speculation that the Administration was planning attacks on North Vietnam were not dispelled. Washington and Saigon were full of vague references to widening the war and veiled warnings that this would happen at any time. Just a week before his June 2 press conference, Secretary Rusk warned that the war might be expanded if the Communists continued their aggression. And a few days later General Khanh, in an apparent reply to Rusk, fed the rumor-hungry by announcing that he opposed a "March North" unless the United States provided additional military support, including combat troops. There was, in fact, some substance behind the gossip. By mid-June the Administration was exploring the possibility of a Congressional Resolution that would provide support from Capitol Hill in the event the March North contingency became a necessary course of action. While Congressional authorization, per se, did not seem necessary, it was felt that especially in an election year it would be desirable for the President to have Congress on record as supporting such an action. Several draft resolutions were prepared, but neither the idea of a resolution nor an expanded war strategy was given White House sanction—at least for a while. But the proponents of carrying the war to North Vietnam were becoming increasingly vocal within the various Vietnam policy forums. Such a move was regarded by those officials as the one single step that could restore sagging South Vietnamese morale. They argued that this would not only attack the main source of support for the insurgents, but it would provide incontrovertible evidence to Hanoi, the Viet Cong, and the South Vietnamese public that the United States was fully committed to a Communist defeat.

The fires of speculation about Marching North were given additional fuel by two separate events in the latter part of July. On the 18th General Khanh once again publicly advocated attacking North Vietnam. A few days later General Ky, then chief of the Air Force, confided to the world that there were already covert combat teams north of the 17th parallel and that South Vietnamese pilots were being trained for large-scale attacks against the North.

General Maxwell Taylor, who had taken over the Ambassadorial post from Henry Cabot Lodge only a few weeks before, treated Khanh and his colleague Nguyen Chanh Thi to some old-fashioned man-to-man talk and reminded them that American officials had told them the United States was opposed to an expansion of the war. Stories leaked out that Taylor had given the Generals a tongue-lashing, and President Johnson felt it necessary to deny that there was any major clash between Taylor and Khanh. A week later, however, Secretary Rusk admitted there were "differences" between the Administration and the Saigon Government on the issue of expanding the war. While back-room and second-echelon staffers in Washington secretly applauded this all-too-rare instance of frankness, there was some concern that Taylor might not have the finesse to handle the tricky political and diplomatic problems that lay ahead.

Meanwhile diplomatic events elsewhere were churning President Johnson's troubled waters. In early July UN Secretary-General U Thant suggested the Geneva Conference of 1954 be reconvened. Since military operations by either side appeared unlikely to bring about peace in Vietnam, U Thant urged that "the political and diplomatic method of negotiation" be tried once again. However, a forum along the lines of the 1954 Conference was far from an ideal approach to coping with the complexities that marked the situation ten years later. More importantly the summer of 1964 was far from a propitious time for the Administration to start negotiations; it was an election year, and the Republican candidate was already questioning the strength of the Administration's resolve. To embark on negotiations in the inhospitable atmosphere of a Geneva Conference at a time when the South

Vietnamese Government was politically and militarily at a low ebb, and in the face of a Goldwater campaign slogan, "Why not victory?" did not seem very attractive to Johnson. It is not surprising that Washington's response to U Thant was less than enthusiastic. But as experience would show, Washington did not need to assume such a negative posture; other countries could do it for us. Neither the Russians nor the Chinese were anxious to air their differences in a new Geneva Conference, and the North Vietnamese could be counted on to reject (or ignore, as they did in this case) U Thant's proposals.

De Gaulle entered the picture again in July, not at all daunted by the President's negative reaction to his neutralization proposal earlier in the year ("I do not agree with General de Gaulle's proposals. I do not think that it would be in the interest of freedom to share his view." [8]) Anxious to go U Thant's proposal one better, de Gaulle urged that the Geneva Conference be reconvened for the purpose of ratifying a prior agreement on the part of the United States, the Soviet Union, France, and Communist China to get out and stay out of Vietnam, Laos, and Cambodia. President Johnson gave this suggestion short shrift too. "We do not believe in a conference called to ratify terror, so our policy is unchanged." [9]

The situation on the ground in Vietnam in midsummer offered no more cheer than the diplomatic maneuverings. The United States now had 21,000 military personnel in South Vietnam, but this seemed to have made no discernible difference in the progress of the war. The Viet Cong were becoming increasingly aggressive. Firings on American helicopters were now commonplace and becoming more effective. The South Vietnamese Armed Forces were performing badly and had suffered 200 casualties in a single battle—the largest number of the war to date. There were few Administration spokesmen in the early summer of 1964 who were taking an optimistic view.

The first six months of the Johnson Administration were thus marked by frustration and growing doubts stemming from the daily erosion of the situation in Vietnam. There was a great deal of planning going on against various military contingencies. In line with the findings and recommendations that followed McNamara's various trips to Vietnam, more American advisers were dispatched, more equipment was sent, large numbers of helicopters and pilots were deployed, and an increasingly major effort was mounted to patrol the approaches to Vietnam along the Laos border, the 17th parallel, and the coast of Vietnam. It was this latter enterprise that was to present Johnson with the sharpest crisis thus far in his tenure—one that was to haunt his Administration until the day in 1969 when he boarded the plane for Texas.

On the second of August the American destroyer *Maddox* was steaming in the Gulf of Tonkin, 30 miles off the coast of Vietnam. Although the destroyer was on a routine patrol and was clearly in international waters, this was no ordinary peacetime mission and this was no ordinary body of water. The Gulf is bordered by North Vietnam, the China Mainland, and Hainan Island. Hanoi and Peking looked upon these waters as being a sensitive, virtually private preserve.

As part of the Administration's reappraisal of Vietnam policy following the McNamara–Taylor visit to Vietnam in March, it was decided to institute a program of naval surveillance and intelligence collection ("de Soto patrols") against North Vietnam. The *Maddox* was one of the destroyers assigned to this duty from time to time. The National Security Council policy decisions of the previous March had also included a program of active, armed, covert harassment of North Vietnam by South Vietnamese special ground and naval units. No American participation was authorized, but the United States Military Headquarters in Saigon had a direct role in the planning and approval of these actions north of the 17th parallel.

In early August the *Maddox* was carrying out its assigned surveillance and intelligence collection mission in the Tonkin Gulf when it was fired upon by three North Vietnamese torpedo boats. The destroyer and a few American planes struck back, damaging the attacking craft. When the President heard the news he was enraged not only because of the attack, but also because the Navy had not sunk Hanoi's attacking craft. An eyewitness reported that he virtually "climbed the walls." Nevertheless, the official reaction from Washington was mild and low key. "I have instructed the Navy," the President said on August 3, "1) to continue the patrols . . . 2) to double the force by adding an additional destroyer . . . 3) to provide a combat air patrol . . . 4) to attack with the objective . . . of destroying [attacking forces]." [10] Secretary Rusk played it cool: North Vietnam "got a sting out of this. If they do it again, they will get another sting."

The immediate reaction in the West Basement of the White House and in the offices of the Vietnam specialists around Washington was one of mixed wonder and surprise at the sheer bravado of the North Vietnamese. Their PT boat crews obviously hoped to sink the *Maddox*, and some of us wondered whether Hanoi's policymakers had weighed the consequences of success. The sinking of an American ship on the high seas would have tipped the delicate balance then prevailing in Washington in favor of the advocates of a more vigorous American military posture. But as additional details became available, it appeared that the attack was not a premeditated, carefully considered policy decision made in Hanoi, but rather a local act of retaliation for a raid against a North Vietnamese island (almost 200 miles north of the 17th parallel) made two days before by units of the South Vietnamese Navy. The captain of the *Maddox* was not informed that the raid had taken place, and he was in the area on his unrelated, routine intelligence and surveillance mission. The North Vietnamese torpedo boats sent to investigate the attack on the island probably assumed the *Maddox* had participated directly or had provided naval cover for the South Vietnamese.

Washington's summer air seemed warmer and heavier than usual on August 3rd, but there was still a sense of relief that the President had not moved to expand the war. But the relief was short-lived. On the following day, shortly after nine o'clock in the morning Washington time, the *Maddox* and the *Turner Joy* (the ship sent to reinforce the patrol) reported that North Vietnamese naval forces had been ordered to attack them. Almost two hours later the *Maddox* reported the two destroyers actually under attack.

When these reports of a second attack reached Washington

on the morning of August 4th, there was a general assumption that "they had done it again." But as the hours went by, several officials, Secretary McNamara especially, began to have some doubts. Reports from the two destroyers were unclear. It was night there and, unlike the first episode against the *Maddox,* visual sightings were impossible. But the skippers had apparently been certain that an attack was imminent. Radio, radar, and sonar evidence indicated that the ships were being shadowed and that torpedoes might actually have been launched. But the two ships were thrashing around the area to avoid being hit and this, together with what was later described as the "nervousness" of the ships' radar and sonar technicians, may well have produced confused or confusing signals. McNamara made several calls to the Commander of the American naval forces in the Pacific in an effort to get further and more definite information. But these calls added little to what was being reported from the two destroyers. A retaliatory attack was scheduled for six in the evening against North Vietnam, and the President's mood became more impatient as the day went on. In the end, the attack had to be postponed for several hours until McNamara and Admiral Sharp were convinced to their own satisfaction that the attack on the two destroyers had actually taken place. Then, whether or not Hanoi was looking for "another sting," it got one. The President ordered "air action . . . against gunboats and certain supporting facilities" in North Vietnam. Sixty-four sorties were flown against the torpedo boat bases and an oil storage area nearby.

The punishment seemed clearly to fit the crime. The President had no difficulty in geting a Joint Resolution through Congress on August 7. The Resolution gave blanket authority to the President "to take all necessary measures to repel any armed attack against the forces of the United States and to prevent further aggression. . . . the United States is . . . prepared, as the President determines, to take all necessary steps, including the use of armed force, to assist any member or protocol State of the Southeast Asia Collective Defense Treaty requesting assistance in defense of its freedom. . . ."

There was then, as there is now, a lingering uneasiness that the evidence on which the decision was based was something less than conclusive. Lending weight to the case of those who doubt the second attack actually occurred is the fact that Hanoi, while admitting the firing of August 2, stated that American claims of a second attack were "fabrications." Furthermore, doubts continued to increase when the North Vietnamese decorated only the crews of the PT boats involved in the August 2nd incident—but not those in that of August 4th.

On the night of September 18th, a night of weather and sea conditions strikingly similar to those of August 4, a third incident involving U.S. destroyers occurred in the Gulf of Tonkin. The *U.S.S. Morton* and *U.S.S. Edwards,* on a patrol mission off the coast of North Vietnam, radioed that they were "under attack," but the evidence as reported to Washington was sketchy and inconclusive. Radar reports said that the ships were "menaced by four unidentified vessels which . . . indicated hostile intent. The destroyers, after changing course . . . fired warning rounds . . . [but] the unidentified vessels continued to close. The destroyers then properly opened fire and the approaching craft disappeared. . . ." [11]

Three days after the reported attack of September 18 Johnson was asked if he had any additional information "on what may have happened" in the Gulf. He gave this rather garbled reply. "I have no further information on the incident other than that given you. . . . On Friday morning at around 9 o'clock which was around 9 o'clock in the evening in the Tonkin Gulf, we received a flash information . . . that ships were approaching our destroyers. The ships were unidentified; that a warning shot was being fired; and that they would, pursuant to orders, fire additional shots in order to protect and defend themselves. So I received that information from Secretary McNamara. I asked to be informed immediately upon receipt of any other information. . . . I was later informed that the ships or the unidentified vessels continued to approach our two destroyers and then opened fire. The ships disappeared. . . . Planes had been launched and were in the air to protect the destroyers and to conduct a search, and to contribute anything they could contribute during the darkness of the night. . . . during Friday night the members of our fleet and our planes spent the daylight hours out there . . . attempting to conduct adequate reconnaissance, locate any hostile vessels that might be in the area. Saturday morning . . . they notified us of their reports through the Commander in Chief of the Pacific and CINC-PAC [sic], both of whom evaluated their reports, which were brought to me here in the Cabinet Room. I spent 2 hours reviewing them with the Secretary of Defense, the Chairman of the Joint Chiefs of Staff, the Secretary of State, and my security people. At that time I directed Mr. McNamara and the Chairman of the Joint Chiefs to issue an operational statement giving you all the facts that we had been able to confirm from the first daylight hours surveillance we could make. . . ." [12]

Three and a half years later McNamara testified that "it was decided at both Washington and field command levels that no credible evidence of an attack existed. . . . In view of our unresolved doubts, no retaliatory action was taken." [13]

Controversy has surrounded "Tonkin Gulf" for several years. This has been particularly true in the case of the August 4 episode. Reports of the PT boat attacks on the *Maddox* and the *Turner Joy* were by no means as definitive as those on the *Maddox* two days before, although Secretary McNamara told the Senate Foreign Relations Committee in February, 1968 that he and Admiral Sharp had been convinced on the basis of radio intercepts that the second attack had, in fact, taken place.

In retrospect I have the feeling that if there had not been a confirmed attack in broad daylight on August 2nd, the reports of the night attack on August 4th might have been treated somewhat more cautiously and the reaction in Washington might have been much more judicious. In the light of the August 2nd episode, however, there was a general disposition to believe that the North Vietnamese had apparently discounted the risks of attacking U.S. naval vessels. I was in the White House Situation Room when the messages were coming in on August 4th, and although I remember that the radar and sonar readings seemed to be short of definitive, there seemed little doubt that Hanoi had attacked again. Certainly there was no attempt to fudge or doctor the evidence, and there were many attempts in the course of that day to seek further and more accurate information. We learned a lesson that was applied several weeks later during the third reported attack.

The "Tonkin Gulf Incident" was a watershed for President Johnson, as it gave him virtually unanimous Congressional support for wide-ranging powers—support especially important in an election year. But the circumstances surrounding the whole affair sowed seeds of mistrust that would poison the relations between the President and many members of Congress, as well as between the Administration and a large segment of the American public. There are many honest folk in and out of Congress who feel that the Senate and the House were "conned" by the Administration during those early days of August—conned into passing a Joint Resolution of any type on the basis of the August 4 attack, and conned into giving up substantial influence over the future course of the Administration's policy as a result of the wording of the Resolution. My own feeling is that the Resolution was drafted and requested in good faith by the Administration, but that it was subsequently parlayed into a blank check to rationalize the President's unwillingness to have Congress play a meaningful role in his Vietnam policy.[14]

Few Senators or Congressmen realized in the heat and excitement of the Tonkin Gulf attacks that they would be surrendering so much of their influence on the future course of events in Vietnam by passing the Joint Resolution in the form suggested by the Administration. One who did was Senator Wayne Morse, who referred to it as a "pre-dated resolution of war." On August 7, he said: "I believe that history will record that we have made a great mistake in subverting and circumventing the Constitution of the United States . . . by means of this resolution . . . we are in effect giving the President . . . war making powers in the absence of a declaration of war. I believe that to be a historic mistake."

A sense of the uncertainty of just what the Resolution meant is conveyed by the following dialogue which also took place at the time between Senators John Sherman Cooper and William Fulbright:

> *Cooper*— . . . are we now giving the President advance authority to take whatever action he may deem necessary respecting South Vietnam and its defense. . . .
> *Fulbright*—I think that is correct.
> *Cooper*—Then, looking ahead, if the President decided that it was necessary to use such force as could lead into war, we will give that authority by this resolution?
> *Fulbright*—That is the way I would interpret it. If a situation later developed in which we thought the approval should be withdrawn it could be withdrawn by concurrent resolution.[15]

The Resolution was so comprehensive that eighteen months later, when the question of whether a declaration of war by Congress was necessary, the Legal Advisor of the Department of State concluded that further Congressional action was not required: "Section 2 [of the Resolution] constitutes an authorization to the President, in his discretion, to act—using armed force if he determines that is required—to assist South Vietnam at its request in defense of its freedom. . . . the grant of authority 'as the President determines' is unequivocal." [16] In hearings before the Senate Foreign Relations Committee in August, 1967 Under-Secretary of State Nicholas Katzenbach underscored the Administration's view that a declaration of war was unnecessary: "what could a declaration of war have done that would have given the President more authority and a clearer voice of the Congress of the United States than it did?" [17]

Many Senators and Congressmen have had second thoughts about the Resolution since 1964. In his opening statement during Secretary Rusk's public testimony on March 11, 1968, Senator Fulbright claimed that during the debate on the Joint Resolution "Congress, and certainly I, believed at the time that it was acting not to authorize a bigger war but to prevent one." On June 24, 1970 the Senate repealed the Resolution.

✳   ✳   ✳

The Administration coupled its August 4th request for Congressional support with an effort to raise the problem of the North Vietnamese attacks in the United Nations Security Council. The

Council met in an urgent session and invited Saigon and Hanoi to participate in the debate. The South Vietnamese agreed, but Hanoi rejected the Security Council's competence. The Council adjourned after two fruitless sessions.

The Tonkin Gulf attacks and their aftermath came at a difficult moment for President Johnson. The political campaign was just beginning to warm up, and issues with respect to Vietnam were becoming sharply drawn. Johnson had described the country as going through a "summer of discontent." In his speeches on Vietnam the operative words were "limited," "prudence," "patience," "restraint," "firmness." Goldwater spoke of "lack of strength," "lack of will," "victory," "no appeasement." The North Vietnamese attack on American ships upset Johnson's delicate policy balance; it looked for a few days as though, willy-nilly, the war would be expanded—a prospect that clearly troubled many Americans already disillusioned and frustrated by Saigon's inability to achieve significant political stability and military progress. The Administration's tactic was to bomb those North Vietnamese targets directly related to the torpedo boat attacks—a clear tit-for-tat—to prepare for any further requirement to move against the North (through the Congressional Resolution), and then to revert to the pre-Tonkin strategy of limiting the fighting to south of the 17th parallel.

Officials in Washington, not only from election-year considerations but for broader national security reasons as well, felt comfortable with the decision to return to a relatively low-risk posture. Our Mission in Saigon, on the other hand, felt that the raids against North Vietnam had given the South Vietnamese a shot of adrenaline and that unless the momentum could be maintained the Saigon Government would soon be confronted again with popular malaise and a resurgence of coup plotting. Khanh himself felt that his advocacy of a "March North" strategy had been vindicated and that the attacks against North Vietnamese targets should be continued.

Riding piggyback on the American retaliation for the attacks on the American destroyers, General Khanh ordered a state of emergency in South Vietnam. On August 16 he succeeded in pushing through a new Charter that gave him actual dictatorial power. General Big Minh was removed from his post as Chief of State. Although Minh had been a virtual figurehead for many months, he had a large personal following and his departure narrowed still further the precarious base of popular support on which Khanh's government rested.

Khanh's charter was drafted in panic and was generally regarded, and not without justification, as an instrument for popular oppression. The deep frustration and disillusionment of the articulate Vietnamese could neither be diverted by American retaliatory attacks against the North nor held in check by martial law. It had been nine months since the joyous parades celebrating Diem's downfall and a "New Deal"; little had happened in the intervening period except for the announcement of ambitious but vague programs to further the fight against the Communists and improve the lot of the urban and rural population. Khanh's call for unity had a hollow and self-serving ring that only infuriated the already-restless students, seething Buddhists, and wary Catholics. Communist agents in the urban centers, particularly in Saigon, added to the tension by organizing their own street gangs.

The stage was set for trouble. On August 21 Khanh got a large dose of it. The students took to the streets, first in Saigon and later in other cities. They were soon joined by the Buddhists, Viet Cong-sponsored hoodlums, and Catholic youth groups. Within a few days the Buddhist hierarchy which, to its knowledge or not, had been infiltrated by the Viet Cong, moved to unseat the government. By the 27th the streets of downtown Saigon were in the hands of the mob—or rather several mobs. Buddhists were fighting Catholics, the Viet Cong-hired hooligans were moving against any target of opportunity. Unarmed police and soldiers stood by, helpless and confused by Khanh's orders not to interfere.

Meanwhile, the Generals were trying to work out a formula that would permit the Military Council to retain power, but would yet satisfy the inchoate and conflicting demands of the rebelling religious and student groups. Between August 16th and September 3rd there were three governments in Saigon. Khanh and Minh checked in and out of their offices in the Presidential Palace like traveling salesmen at a commercial hotel. On the 13th of September there was a coup attempt against Khanh by some "out" Catholic generals, but it collapsed within twenty-four hours. Khanh was saved by General Ky, who sent his planes over Saigon and threatened to bomb the city, and by General Thi, commander of a key division, who refused to lend his support to the dissident generals.[18] The failure of the coup gave the young Generals Thi and Ky increased power among the wheelers and dealers of Saigon and led to the organization of a High National Council composed of venerable civilians. The Council was given the task of working out plans for a provisional legislative body that in turn would prepare a permanent constitution.

It would have been too much to expect that the war against the Viet Cong could maintain much momentum during all this political turmoil. The security situation went from bad to worse during the summer and fall of 1964. The high priority "Hop Tac" Program, designed to clear a progressively wider area around Saigon, had drained military units from other parts of South Vietnam. But what the military briefers referred to as the "troop density" in the Hop Tac area was still insufficient to guarantee security even in the first ring around Saigon—a radius of but a few miles. Not long after a division was deployed to the Hop Tac mission from a relatively secure area in the central part of South Vietnam, regular Viet Cong units began to take the initiative there; by late autumn the Commander of the Second Corps area acknowledged that South Vietnam was in danger of being cut in two. During this period too, infiltration from North Vietnam increased, and for the first time a significant number of North Vietnamese soldiers (as opposed to South Vietnamese "returnees") were coming down the trails.

President Johnson was now actively on the campaign trail, and naturally enough he had to put the best face he could on his Vietnam policy. He was being accused by his opponent of having a "no-win" policy and it was, in fact, hard to demonstrate that an early victory in Vietnam was likely. At a meeting in Manchester, New Hampshire in late September, Johnson revealed some of his frustrations. "Some of our people . . . have . . . suggested the possible wisdom of going north in Vietnam. Well, now, before you start attacking someone and you launch a big offensive, you better give some consideration to how you are going to perfect what you have. And [referring to the abortive coup of September 13] when a brigadier general can walk down the streets of Saigon as they [sic] did the other day, and take over the police station, the radio station, and the government without firing a shot, I don't know how much offensive we are prepared to launch." [19]

The Manchester speech was noteworthy in two other respects. There was, once again, the effort to associate President Eisenhower with the present Vietnam policy: "I didn't get you into Vietnam. You have been in Vietnam 10 years. President Eisenhower wrote Premier Diem a letter in 1954 . . . and said, 'We want to help you to help your people keep from going Communist, and we will furnish you advice, we will furnish you assistance, and we will furnish you equipment. . . .'" And then, in an effort to relieve some of the anxiety that the war was going to be expanded, Johnson said, "I have not thought that we were ready for American boys to do the fighting for Asian boys. What I have been trying to do . . . was to get the boys in Viet-Nam to do their own fighting with our advice and with our equipment. . . . We are not going north and drop bombs at this stage of the game. . . ." [20]

President Johnson was given little respite by either the Viet Cong or our South Vietnamese allies in the weeks that followed his Manchester speech. In the critical central highlands area the and religious agitation continued in the urban areas throughout aborigine Montagnards revolted against the Saigon Government; American helicopter losses were mounting alarmingly; political the country; and in Saigon the preparation of a new constitution was in constant jeopardy as the drafters proceeded against a background of popular unrest and political jostling among the generals.

The Administration was cheered in late October, however, by the best news to come from Saigon in a long time. The provisional constitution had been completed and a civilian government was installed. There was more in the picture, to be sure, than could be discerned by the naked eye. The new Chief of State was the elderly, ailing, but generally respected Phan Khac Suu. The new

Prime Minister—also neither young nor robust—was Tran Van Huong, the former mayor of Saigon (later to be Prime Minister under President Thieu). Suu and Huong's principal function was to provide a cosmetic civilian overlay for the ever-present coterie of senior generals who still held the real power. Despite his ups and downs over the previous several months, General Khanh remained the principal manipulator. Nevertheless Washington, thirsting for even the forms of civilian control and political stability, was delighted by the new government.

The Administration's satisfaction was short-lived. At the end of October, virtually on the eve of our elections, the Viet Cong struck its hardest blow to date against American forces. Bien Hoa, the largest United States air base in Vietnam, was attacked. Six American B–57 jet bombers were completely destroyed, and 23 American soldiers were killed or wounded. Ambassador Taylor recommended retaliation against North Vietnam, but he was turned down by Washington.

        ✻   ✿   ✿

With the Presidential elections over, President Johnson could devote his full attention to the mounting problems America was facing—not the least of which were those evolving or overflowing from Vietnam. Shortly after the election McGeorge Bundy, the President's Special Assistant, asked me to serve on his staff and to concentrate on Asian problems. Although "Asia" included an area from the Sino–Soviet border to Indonesia, we both agreed that priority would have to be given to Vietnam. Bundy warned that it would be a "difficult, thankless task." He was right. I began to sense what might be in store when, shortly afterward, one of the President's secretaries—a chipper, charming lady—asked me in all seriousness at lunch one day why I couldn't arrange a personal meeting between the President and Ho Chi Minh. "The President is so good with people. If you could only get the two men alone in one room so that they could reason together!"

The President soon had more urgent matters to worry about than choosing a time and place for reasoning with Uncle Ho. In late November South Vietnam's civilian government headed by

Suu and Huong, for which such high hopes had been expressed just a few weeks before, began to run into trouble. Once again the students and the Buddhists, reinforced by Viet Cong agents and hoodlums, took to the streets. On November 25 Huong declared "a state of siege."

The Buddhists, as was their maddening wont, had vague, undocumented, but strongly-felt complaints: Huong was "pro-Diem"; Huong did not command popular support. Remembering General Khanh's unfortunate experiences during the previous August, Huong was anxious not to use force. But when neither the students nor the Buddhists responded to sweet reason, Huong resorted to martial law. This only served to stimulate further unrest.

In the meantime Ambassador Taylor was in Washington conferring with the President. He presented a somber view of the political and military prospects—and well he might, for there was little room for optimism. Vietnam's government was toppling, the economy was staggering from crisis to crisis, the security situation was deteriorating, and the infiltration from North Vietnam was increasing each month. It was estimated that 10,000 hard-core Viet Cong had entered South Vietnam from the North during 1964, bringing the total to 30,000.

The White House press release following Taylor's Washington visit seems, in retrospect, as inane as a soap-opera script. "The President instructed General Taylor to consult urgently with the South Vietnamese Government as to measures that should be taken to improve the situation in all its aspects." More to the point, the White House reaffirmed the American commitment to South Vietnam and implied that more aid would be forthcoming in accordance with "the terms of the Congressional joint resolution of August 10, 1964 which remains in full force and effect." [21] A few days later Washington announced that it would assist Saigon to increase its armed forces by 100,000 men. This would mean a total South Vietnamese military establishment of over 700,000. There were now almost 23,000 American military advisers in Vietnam.

Taylor returned to Saigon to find that Huong's government was being besieged, and that the Buddhists were taking an ugly anti-American line. They charged the United States with "selling out Vietnam to the anti-Communist right." To add to the political turmoil, the young generals who had backed Khanh when he was within a hair's breadth of being thrown out of power in mid-September now demanded that several of the older generals (including Big Minh) be fired. The civilian High National Council refused, and on December 20 the Young Turks took matters in their own hands. They dissolved the Council and fired the senior generals in one fell swoop.

Once again Ambassador Taylor found himself having to confront the Vietnamese Generals. This time, however, Khanh was not present—he sent Ky, Thieu, and Thi to represent him. In a blistering dressing-down, Taylor told them the United States was mightily displeased with their high-handed dismissal of the civilian High Council. He hinted that Washington might have to reconsider its new aid commitment and indeed its whole position on the war unless the "fabric of legal government" was immediately restored. When the generals reported back to Khanh they got another dose of trouble; Khanh upbraided them for subjecting themselves to such treatment.

In describing the meeting later, General Ky said he felt like a West Point cadet being taken over the coals by the Superintendent. The Vietnamese neither forgot nor forgave Taylor for that session, and relations between the Ambassador and the new junta remained cool and distant.* Khanh took a day or two to bounce back. When he did he accused Taylor of "activities beyond imagination." Moreover, said Khanh, Taylor was "not serving his country well." In an order of the day on December 22 Khanh said that the Vietnamese military made "sacrifices for the country's independence . . . but not to carry out the policy of any foreign country." [22] On the following day Secretary Rusk publicly noted that the United States might cut off aid to Vietnam unless the South Vietnamese Government achieved some semblance of unity in the country.

To add to the strained relations, a bomb exploded in an Amer-

---

* Neither did Ky, Thi, and Thieu forgive Khanh who, they felt, had used them as whipping boys. This may have been one of the reasons they later turned on him.

ican officers' billet on Christmas Eve, killing two Americans and injuring almost one hundred people. This, coming on the heels of the Generals' coup and Khanh's diatribe against American interference, unleashed a wave of "Get-Out" sentiments in Congress, the press, and the universities. Even the Administration had a momentary feeling of uncertainty—there were some who felt the bomb might have been set by South Vietnamese government agents.

On New Year's Eve I received a call from Madame Chuong, wife of the ex-Vietnamese Ambassador and the estranged mother of Madame Nhu. She urged me to see her as soon as possible, and I stopped off at her residence on my way home from the office. The lovely, high-strung lady was distraught. The recent advice of Senator Frank Church and Walter Lippman to "disengage" had kept her awake for many nights. She would not blame us if we did decide to get out, but we should recognize that the Vietnamese considered the American presence as "the only remaining obstacle to complete Communist control." Madame Chuong then went on to the main burden of her message—a message she wished me to "convey immediately to the President." She urged that we dump General Khanh and the Young Turks, who would lead the Vietnamese to disaster, and deal instead with another set of generals (one of whom was General Khiem, who was then in exile as Ambassador to Washington and is now the Prime Minister of South Vietnam). I told Madame Chuong that the United States Government did not wish to intervene in the internal politics of Saigon even if it had the knowledge and ability to do so. "We would be prepared to work with any government that represented the Vietnamese people and wished to work with us." Ambassador Chuong made a passionate plea for us to "intervene." "Your mere presence in Vietnam is intervention. Unless you get a satisfactory government in Saigon all your efforts will be wasted!" We parted with an empty, almost hopeless "Happy New Year" wish.

In retrospect, at least, the confrontation with Khanh was an ideal moment to have taken a hard look at where we were and where we were going in Vietnam. To be sure, Taylor and Rusk hinted that a "reconsideration" was in process, but this apparently made no impression on General Khanh and his colleagues—they had heard it all before. With 1964's seventh government (and the only one with a civilian cast) headed for the junk heap, with variants of the "Yankee-go-home" theme being chanted by the more militant Buddhists and repeated in even more invidious form by General Khanh himself, with virtually no progress being made against the Viet Cong—despite large infusions of American equipment and advisers during the year—and with increasing numbers of Americans raising serious doubts about what we were doing in Vietnam, the time was ripe for a serious reappraisal of American policy. Over and above this, and perhaps most important of all, the President had just won a landslide victory at the polls. Never again in his term of office would he have more political elbowroom to pick and choose among options. But while there was a great deal of rhetoric on the subject of "reconsideration," serious thinking with respect to the choices available was desultory and inconclusive, and a major opportunity was missed.

XI

McNamara's War

It was in 1964 that the fighting in Vietnam was described as "McNamara's War." And there was some truth in the description— Robert McNamara pretty much took charge, if only by default. Well into the year the President was preoccupied with giving his Administration an identifiable Johnsonian stamp, which to him meant far-reaching social and economic legislation rather than foreign policy initiatives. Until the North Vietnamese attacked American destroyers in early August, he was giving international problems, including Vietnam, what remained of his time and attention. In the early period of Johnson's Administration, Secretary Dean Rusk kept in the background in public and it was McNamara who set forth the Administration's views on the Vietnam war in a major speech in March.

Secretary McNamara kept in close touch with all aspects of the war—political as well as military. He had a staff comprised of an aggressive group of civilians and military officers working under a brilliant Assistant Secretary of Defense for International Security Affairs, the late John McNaughton. Through the Joint Chiefs of Staff, with its regiment of planners and briefers, he was provided with virtually instantaneous military estimates, facts, statistics, and trends. All this, added to McNamara's unique ability to grasp and synthesize a vast mass and variety of information, made him the best informed official in Washington. Some hardened bureaucrats claimed that McNamara always "looked good" in the White House Cabinet Room because he had to travel from the Pentagon and consequently had eight extra minutes to do his homework in the back of his limousine.

Although Secretary Rusk had virtually no personal staff, and information on the non-military aspects of Vietnam was served up to him by a variety of individuals and units within the State Department, he was able to keep on top of developments through the Herculean efforts of Benjamin Read, the Executive Secretary of the Department, and William Bundy, the Assistant Secretary of State responsible for Asian problems.

The issue of McNamara vs. Rusk, however, went beyond the personalities and the staffs of the two Secretaries; even on the lower levels of the two great Departments, Defense officials seemed to run the show on both military and non-military matters. One former State Department official has publicly deplored Secretary Rusk's "surrender" of responsibility to Secretary McNamara.[1] But time after time during 1964 and 1965 McNamara and his subordinates seemed to be crying for political guidance and leadership from the State Department. It was slow in coming.

The State Department seemed resigned to playing a reactive, even peripheral, role during the early '60s. The war in Vietnam, it was felt, was Pentagon business. For their part Department of Defense officials were frustrated with the political situation in Saigon, which they felt was responsible for the ineffectiveness of the Vietnamese forces.

By and large the non-defense elements of the government were neither psychologically nor organizationally able to come to grips with an insurgency that was quickly getting out of hand. None of the courses given at the Foreign Service Institute, and none of the experiences of AID specialists and Foreign Service officers elsewhere, seemed relevant to what was going on in Vietnam.

*   *   *

By early 1965 American policy was clearly floundering. In spite of Ambassador Taylor's admonitions, Khanh had fired Big

Minh and the other older generals, and Prime Minister Huong's civilian government was fighting for its life against the "in" group of younger military officers. Despite Secretary Rusk's veiled threat that the United States might have to reconsider its aid policy toward Vietnam if Huong were removed, no such reconsideration was seriously contemplated and none took place. Although Rusk's talk about taking a fresh look at our Vietnam policy reflected genuine anger and frustration, for all practical purposes he was engaging in empty rhetoric. Anyone who actually advanced a program involving a scaling down, let alone a reversal of the American economic or military commitment, would have been given short shrift in the State Department. Within the Defense Department, ironically enough, there was somewhat more tolerance for heresy.

Some officials in Washington were already advocating a political-economic-military strategy that would permit the United States "to lose more slowly," in the hope that a South Vietnamese government could be organized that would eventually be able to compete politically with the National Liberation Front. But the official Administration line was much more positive. The State of the Union Message laid it out: "To ignore aggression now would only increase the danger of a much larger war. . . . What is at stake is the cause of freedom, and in that cause America will never be found wanting." [2]

As soon as the President could free his mind from his State of the Union and Budget Messages, some of his principal subordinates urged him to focus on Vietnam. The Administration seemed to be on dead center and the President was caught between McNamara's pleas for new initiatives and Rusk's reluctance to take any important new steps until the political situation in Saigon could be put in some semblance of order. The President agreed to send a high-level working group including members of his own staff to Saigon in early February for a fresh look. Out of such an examination, he felt, would come recommendations either to move ahead in new and more vigorous ways to gain the initiative against the Viet Cong or to proceed down a path of disengagement. The middle course, "more of the same," was implicitly rejected. McGeorge Bundy and assorted lesser beings, including myself, left for Vietnam on the second of February. It was a fateful coincidence that Premier Kosygin was at that moment preparing to leave for Hanoi.

We arrived during the Vietnamese New Year and this, plus the Saigon Government's elaborate welcoming ceremony, gave the airport a deceptively festive air. Reality took hold almost immediately, however. We were told that a senior AID official had been kidnapped by the Viet Cong an hour or so before. (I was later to spend some of the worst days of my government career in a vain search for Gustave Hertz.)

The Embassy had arranged for us to meet a number of South Vietnamese officials. They were sincere older men of probity and wisdom, but the dynamism and imagination so necessary to get popular support and to move forward on the political, social, and military fronts were certainly not evident among them. Nonetheless, in contrast to the parade of generals who had been marching in and out of office during the past year, a government of civilians, gray and tired as they were, seemed a definite plus if it could restore stability and continuity to the Saigon political scene.

Much more worrisome than the meetings with government officials were those with the dissident Buddhists and students. Bundy came out reeling from a two-hour session with a leading member of the Buddhist hierarchy. His razor-sharp mind just couldn't cut through the ooze of generalities. Two cultures and two educational backgrounds did not directly conflict but rather slid past one another.

I was presented with about a dozen students representing a wide range of interests. They were keen and quick, but even the most articulate of them had a difficult time moving from slogans to programs. I came away knowing what they opposed, but uncertain of what they wanted. Many suggested stepping up the war rather than making compromises with the NLF, but few seemed ready to join the Army; many wanted the Americans to come in and take over the whole business, but some hoped the Americans would get out altogether.

Any remaining illusions we might have had about the security situation, even in the Saigon area, disappeared shortly after our arrival. It was apparent both from official briefings and first-hand evidence that the Viet Cong held the initiative throughout much of the Vietnamese countryside and could mount a considerable campaign of terror within the limits of Saigon itself. The Vietnamese Government, despite all the help it had been given, seemed unable to hold the Communist forces in check, let alone turn the tide. The Viet Cong were roaming at will around the outskirts of the capital, despite the tremendous diversion of resources to the Hop Tac program. When parents of boys in the local Boy Scout troop decided after long debate one night to fetch their sons from their overnight campsite bordering the airport, we didn't need the maps and charts of the MACV briefers to convince us of the proximity of the Viet Cong.

The two alternatives put to the President before our departure from Washington seemed even more stark now: the United States either had to withdraw or to increase its commitment to the Vietnamese. And a greater commitment would entail major changes in American policy. By Saturday, February 6 the general shape of our conclusions began to take form. Clearly, efforts would have to be made to encourage the Saigon Government to establish closer working relationships with the disaffected Buddhist and student groups. In addition the United States should be prepared to respond sharply and quickly to any further Viet Cong attacks on American installations or to major terrorist attacks on Vietnamese civilians. While the North Vietnamese could not be made responsible for every terrorist act in the South, they probably were aware of large-scale, premeditated attacks; therefore major Communist attacks on American installations or Vietnamese civilians should be retaliated for by bombing North Vietnamese military targets. It was felt, however, that bombing should not be initiated until there was a credible and clear-cut provocation. There already was, of course, a contingency plan for the launching of retaliatory strikes against North Vietnam; it was known as "Flaming Dart" and involved the positioning of aircraft carriers within striking distance of North Vietnamese targets. (In early January I had registered doubt that bombing targets in North Vietnam would

force Hanoi to stop its support of the Viet Cong or to become
more amenable to negotiations, as well as my belief that we should
concentrate instead on improving the performance of South Vietnamese military forces. There were many among my colleagues
who shared this doubt and conviction.)

On Sunday, February 7th Bundy had planned to take a trip into
the countryside for a first-hand look at some of the American economic and military assistance programs. But early that morning the
Viet Cong attacked an American military barracks at Pleiku in
Central Vietnam. Eight Americans were killed, and more than 100
were wounded. The conference room at MACV Headquarters was
a busy place. The efforts of military and Embassy officers in Saigon
to piece together the events at Pleiku and to assess Viet Cong
actions taking place elsewhere, as well as the attempts by Bundy's
group to work out a coherent series of recommendations for Washington's consideration, were constantly interrupted by phone calls
from the White House West Wing. Washington wanted a play-by-
play account of developments. The National Security Council had
been called into session, but there was little or no hard information
available. As he dashed out for the fourth call, Bundy was heard
muttering, "If those guys would only leave us alone for an hour,
perhaps we could work things out." (I was reminded of this when
we were back in Washington and badgering the Saigon Mission
for information that could hardly have then been available.)

On our return trip to Washington we heard the White House
statement over the plane's radio.

On February 7, U.S. and South Vietnamese air elements were
directed to launch retaliatory attacks against barracks and staging
areas in the southern area of North Viet-Nam which intelligence
has shown to be actively used by Hanoi for training and infiltration
of Viet Cong personnel into South Viet-Nam. . . .

Today's action by the U.S. and South Vietnamese Governments
was in response to provocations ordered and directed by the Hanoi
regime.

To meet these attacks the Government of South Viet-Nam and
the U.S. Government agreed to appropriate reprisal action against
North Vietnamese targets. The President's approval of this action

was given after the action was discussed with and recommended by the National Security Council. . . .

Today's joint response was carefully limited to military areas which are supplying men and arms for attacks in South Viet-Nam. As in the case of the North Vietnamese attacks in the Gulf of Tonkin last August, the response is appropriate and fitting.

As the U.S. Government has frequently stated, we seek no wider war. Whether or not this course can be maintained lies with the North Vietnamese aggressors. The key to the situation remains the cessation of infiltration from North Viet-Nam and the clear indication by the Hanoi regime that it is prepared to cease aggression against its neighbors.[3]

* * *

Thus in early February, 1965 the die was cast. The war was about to be changed in kind rather than in degree, but the President anxiously tried to reassure the American people that the bombing of North Vietnam was a logical extension of the Vietnam policy he had inherited. In a press conference on March 13 he stressed, "our policy there is the policy that was established by President Eisenhower, as I have stated, since I have been President, 46 different times, the policy carried on by President Kennedy, and the policy that we are now carrying on. . . . Although the incidents have changed, in some instances the equipment has changed, in some instances the tactics and perhaps the strategy in a decision or two has changed. Our policy is still the same, and that is to any armed attack, our forces will reply." [4]

It would have been hard, perhaps impossible, for the President to ignore the February 7th attack and similar ones against American military billets that followed soon after. Against the background of the President's campaign statements in Manchester, New Hampshire that "we are not going north and drop bombs," the passive American reaction to the attack on the Bien Hoa airfield in November and the bombing of the American barracks on Christmas Eve may well have encouraged the Communists to believe they could undertake such attacks with impunity. Unless the President was now prepared to reverse gears and begin a withdrawal from Vietnam, he was bound to respond in a dramatic and forceful way. Whether he should have stopped the bombing after the first few clearly retaliatory blows against North Vietnam is another question. Whether he should have waited to start the bombing until after Kosygin had left Hanoi is yet another matter; the Premier regarded the attack as a personal insult.

The option of reversing gears may never have been accepted, but considering the mood that prevailed in Washington during the early winter of 1965, it might have been given serious consideration. American officials were genuinely angry with the Saigon military junta and were deeply frustrated with the chronic inability of the South Vietnamese to carry out effective political, economic, and military programs. If the Communists had played their cards differently in early February—if, for example, they had attacked only Vietnamese military forces, stirred up Buddhist and student groups in urban areas, and pressed their campaign of propaganda and subversion in the countryside—the Administration might well have entertained the idea of pulling back from Vietnam. But the Viet Cong attacks on American troops in early February eliminated that as a politically feasible option for the President.

For the first week or so after the bombing started, the raids against North Vietnam were described as "reprisals" for Communist atrocities in South Vietnam. For a few weeks an attempt was made to keep a running account of Communist terrorist actions— "railroad from Saigon to Danang mined, busload of civilians attacked in Long An, hamlet in Gia Dinh attacked, school destroyed," etc., etc. Although this gruesome bookkeeping was regarded initially as a useful device to justify our bombing attacks, it was soon found to be more trouble than it was worth. Targets for air attacks could not be found that would make a credible case for a tit-for-tat bombing policy. The terrorism laundry list and the whole concept of reprisal were abandoned by the end of February. In any case, a more sustained program of raids on North Vietnam was deemed necessary in the light of Hanoi's role in the fighting in South Vietnam. "Flaming Dart" (the reprisal program) was abandoned and "Rolling Thunder" (the graduated bombing program) was initiated in early March.

According to General Taylor in testimony before the Senate Foreign Relations Committee in February, 1966, there were three basic reasons for the bombing decision. "The first was to give the people of South Vietnam the assurance for the first time of imposing a direct penalty on the source of aggression. . . . The second reason . . . was . . . to limit and render more difficult the infiltration of the men and supplies from North Vietnam to South Vietnam. . . . The third reason . . . was to provide a sobering reminder to the leaders in Hanoi that progressively they must pay a mounting price for the continuation of their support of the Vietcong insurgency. . . . In a very real sense the objective of our air campaign is to change the will of the enemy leadership." [5]

Tension was high in the White House during the early stages of the bombing campaign. There was, of course, worry about possible Chinese and Soviet military moves. Over and above this, however, was the President's personal concern for the fate of each bombing sortie. He insisted that he be called each night as soon as the planes had returned to their bases. When a plane was shot down he was kept closely informed on the progress of rescue attempts. Vietnam had moved to the front rank of the President's problems —a position it would hold throughout the remainder of his Administration.

As the weeks wore on, the bombing expanded in scale and intensity and became part of the overall military campaign, rather than a separate war. Nonetheless each "package" of targets was carefully reviewed not only within the Pentagon, but in the State Department and White House as well. This review process eroded by late 1966, and it became more and more difficult to get sensitive targets stricken from the list. By then the White House threshold of discrimination had been so lowered that the military would have had to suggest an absolutely outrageous target for the President's staff to veto it. Guidance on bombing restrictions was now derived from broad instructions rather than target-by-target examination (nothing any closer than 10 miles to the Chinese border, for example).

✻   ✻   ✻

The inception of the American bombing campaign created a tremendous outcry, both abroad and at home. One of my responsibilities at the White House was to deal with the increasingly widespread and shrill domestic opposition to the war in general and to the bombing in particular. Before very long many hours of my week were spent receiving a flood of peace advocates who were to inundate the White House during the year.

For most of the period Diem was in power, American administrations were criticized by liberals for supporting him. After November, 1963 there were grumbles from the right that the United States had "abandoned" him. Cutting closer to the bone was the general ridicule of Washington's plight in the face of the succession of post-Diem governments. In March, 1965 popular disagreement began to take an organized form with the first of a series of university "teach-ins." When the Civil Rights movement merged with the anti-Vietnam forces in the summer of 1965, the Administration faced a serious problem in its relations with academic groups and with the liberal community generally.* By the fall there were large-scale sit-ins, draft card burnings, and two suicides. The clergy were now raising the morality issue. Johnson was losing the support of the groups which only a year before had helped to give him his tremendous victory over Goldwater.

Public confusion about American policy and objectives in Vietnam was genuine and justifiable, as many officials in Washington were well aware. There was an urgent requirement for the Administration to articulate a clear-cut policy, not only for the sake of enlightening the American public but to clarify muddy official thinking and work out inconsistencies. One close observer of the public mood noted that the ordinary American could well believe, on the basis of Administration statements, that the United States had gotten involved in South Vietnam because that country was vital to American security interests in Asia and that we would do whatever was necessary to preserve South Vietnam's independence; or he could believe we had gotten involved because the

* Mrs. Martin Luther King has described her husband's attitude toward the war. "As he was the catalyst for the Negro awakening in America, he also reacted as early as 1965 to the Vietnam war—it was America's tragic distraction, he felt." [6]

South Vietnamese had asked us for help and that we would leave whenever they requested us to do so. He might also justifiably believe that a strong central government was of the utmost importance to American interests or, conversely, that since the war was being fought in the countryside developments in Saigon were of peripheral concern. On the basis of some statements out of Washington, he might be convinced that a civilian government in Saigon was fundamental to the achievement of our objectives or, on the other hand, that since the army represented the only real power in Vietnam it was important to have a military government. He was continually told that the new government was better than the last, although prior to the last coup he was told that any shift of power in Saigon would be disastrous. He might believe that infiltration from North Vietnam had a critical effect on the military situation or that even if the infiltration stopped it would be a long and bloody war.

It was hoped that a "White Paper" defining American objectives and documenting the extent of Hanoi's involvement in the war in South Vietnam would promote wide public understanding and support for the Administration's policy. But the White Paper proved to be a dismal disappointment. No such publication could have accomplished the ambitious objectives its proponents (including myself) hoped to achieve. It was impossible to provide sufficient documentary evidence of Hanoi's direction and support of the war to convince the confused non-expert or the sophisticated skeptic. To be sure, some captured documents and information from the interrogation of captured Viet Cong prisoners were declassified and incorported into the White Paper, but certain clinching, critical data were too highly classified to be used.

More important than the problem of establishing the authenticity of the information was the fact that the actual findings seemed pretty frail. "Since 1959, nearly twenty thousand Viet Cong . . . are known to have entered South Vietnam under orders from Hanoi. Additional information indicates that an estimated seventeen thousand more infiltrators were dispatched. . . ." [7] Thus, even if the "known" and "probable" infiltrators were combined, there was an average southward movement of little more than nine thousand per year. When compared with the approximate 500,000 men in Saigon's military establishment and the 23,000 American troops already in South Vietnam, the number of infiltrators did not loom very large. The White Paper was slightly defensive on this point. "To some, the level of infiltration from the North may seem modest in comparison with the total size of the armed forces of the Republic of Vietnam." [8] The Paper went on to point out that it required a large number of friendly troops to cope with each guerrilla, and therefore the figures had much more significance than might first appear to be the case.

The information on enemy weapons was even less earth-shaking. Three 75-millimeter recoilless rifles of Chinese Communist origin, forty-six Soviet-made rifles, forty sub-machine guns and one automatic pistol of Czech origin had been captured. This was hardly the kind of arsenal to lead many people, especially those who were initially skeptical, to feel it was necessary to bomb North Vietnam in order to stop the flow of men and equipment. The fact that since 1961 we had given the Government of South Vietnam over $860 million in military assistance made Hanoi's aid to the Viet Cong seem hardly consequential.

The White Paper created ripples of support for the Administration and tidal waves of opposition. Senator Mansfield noted that "The paper helps to make clear why this Nation has been compelled to take steps which it has in recent weeks. . . . it should satisfy those who have been insisting that the President should address an explanation to the American people as to what is involved in Vietnam." He pointed out, however, almost as a sotto voce warning to the President, that "Despite the serious intensification of the military conflict, the problem . . . is still primarily a Vietnam problem." [9] Senator Gruening had a somewhat less sympathetic view: the White Paper "certainly adds no new facts to the already muddied waters of Vietnam. Of course, North Vietnam is and has been aiding the . . . Viet Cong. That is nothing new. But . . . we have been aiding the South Vietnamese on a scale far surpassing the aid given by the North Vietnamese." [10]

The New York Times was deeply troubled. "The assertion that North Vietnam is a principal supplier of men and munitions to the

Viet Cong is certainly not new, nor is the charge that the extent of its support is increasing. . . . Page after page of . . . miniscule detail . . . merely raises anew the question of whether massive air strikes would accomplish anything except large-scale civilian casualties." [11] But the sharpest criticism of the White Paper, and indeed one that pretty much destroyed its usefulness in intellectual circles, came from I. F. Stone. "The striking thing about the State Department's new White Paper is how little support it can prove." [12]

*   *   *

In addition to its quest for domestic understanding and support, the White House was obsessed with the need to widen international support for the Government of South Vietnam. The "More Flags" campaign had gotten off to a slow start in late 1964. It required the application of considerable pressure for Washington to elicit any meaningful commitments. One of the more exasperating aspects of the search for "More Flags" was the lassitude, even disinterest, of the Saigon Government. In part the reason was that the South Vietnamese leaders were preoccupied with political jockeying; in part too they were unable to take the initiative on almost any matter, whether it concerned the war or a peace. In addition Saigon appeared to believe that the program was a public relations campaign directed at the American people. As a consequence, it was left to Washington to play the role of supplicant in the quest for Free World support.

Even after the program got underway only a few countries came forward with anything very consequential. In an effort to show the extent of Free World backing for the South Vietnamese Government (and our own), Washington periodically published a list of contributions that included a shipload of coffee from Latin America and an X-ray unit from Europe. The only major troop contributor, aside from the United States, was the Republic of Korea, and it would be interesting to calculate the price the United States paid for ROK troops. According to official Administration estimates, the war in South Vietnam provided South Korea with 20 percent of its foreign exchange earnings in 1969.

The Filipino force consisted of a 1,500-man engineering unit, for which the United States paid $39 million between 1967 and 1969 —$26,000 per man. Approximately 10 percent of the Philippines' foreign exchange income is derived from its participation in the Vietnam war. Thailand provided 11,000 troops at an annual cost to the United States of approximately $50 million. Strictly speaking, then, the only non-mercenary third country allies we had in Vietnam were Australia and New Zealand. Their forces were miniscule, however, compared to those they sent abroad during World War II.

The 65,000 third-country troops that were ultimately deployed to Vietnam constituted a significant force, but as far as Washington was concerned it was of greater political than military importance. The military commitment of our allies relieved some of our sense of international isolation, but the Administration was to discover that there would be a political price to pay. The participating governments frequently had major differences about the conduct of the war and about the terms of a settlement. Considerable effort had to be expended to keep a united political front.

The third-country effort was mounted on the Southeast Asia Treaty Organization, a very shaky vehicle indeed. From 1966 onward, our own military involvement was frequently justified by Washington officials in terms of American obligations under this Treaty. But the SEATO rationale was more cosmetic than real. Of the seven member countries, three—Pakistan, France, and the United Kingdom—were not represented in Vietnam, and neither Pakistan nor France were ready to give even moral support to the effort. Moreover, the largest contributor, South Korea, is not a member of SEATO. In May, 1965 the SEATO Council meeting in London published a communique that implied strong support for South Vietnam: ". . . the defeat of this Communist campaign is essential not only to the security of the Republic of Vietnam, but to that of Southeast Asia. . . ." [13] But France declined to send an official representative to that meeting, and Pakistan opposed the Council's views.

Although some experts maintain that American military involvement in Vietnam could not be legally justified unless

SEATO was specifically mentioned, a document prepared by Department of State lawyers after the bombing started in early 1965 explained the American actions without reference to SEATO.[14] A year later, however, the Department put emphasis on SEATO as a major rationale for American policy.[15] (The explanation for this apparent difference in emphasis may lie in the fact that the earlier memorandum attempted to justify the bombing in terms of *international* law, and the later one was put in terms of American *constitutional* law.)

*   *   *

The bombing campaign may have improved the morale of the Vietnamese in Saigon and other urban areas, but in the countryside it probably made little difference. By early 1965 the Viet Cong controlled much of the rural area, and even if the country folk were concerned about events beyond their village, they probably learned little more than the National Liberation Front wished to tell them. Whether or not the bombing improved popular morale, it had little effect on the political situation in Saigon; the generals continued to squabble. In January Prime Minister Huong's government was ousted. After a fragile interregnum, Chief of State General Khanh named Dr. "Jack" Oanh, a Harvard-trained economist, as acting Premier. Oanh lasted all of a week, and then yet another civilian, Dr. Quat, was installed. A day or two later Khanh himself was deposed in a bloodless coup d'etat and left the country on February 21 amidst rumors that he had accumulated a vast fortune during his period of power. Dr. Quat, a capable and honest man, spent the next several months treading the now well-worn but precarious path between the restless Buddhists and students on one side, and the scheming generals and politicians on the other.

Meanwhile the military situation continued to deteriorate. Units of the Vietnamese Army, with few exceptions, were still concentrating on avoiding engagements. When this tactic failed, the Viet Cong won the day more often than not. By late January it was clear that the South Vietnamese needed more and heavier fire support if they were going to confront and maintain contact

with regular Viet Cong units. The United States acceded to a
MACV request to send jet aircraft into battle when ground artillery and helicopter gun ships were inadequate for the task. (The
jet aircraft sent to Vietnam, in clear violation of Article 17 of the
1954 Geneva Accords, first began arriving in South Vietnam within
a few days after the Gulf of Tonkin incidents—50 military jets of
various categories were deployed to South Vietnamese airfields in
August, 1964.) Another major new step up the ladder was the introduction of American and South Korean regular military units.
In late February 600 Korean engineers, with their own security
troops, were assigned to "civic action" duty; in early March an
American Marine Brigade and an Army Military Police unit assumed the responsibility for security at American installations.

The Administration's decision made in early February to evacuate American dependents was not an easy one. The issue had
frequently been raised and then postponed during the preceding
several months. Many of the Mission wives worked in one or another of the various American military and civilian agencies in
Saigon, and their departure would require replacements; morale
among Embassy and AID staffs (who were in Vietnam on longer
tours than military officers) would be lowered if husbands were
separated from their families; recruitment of civilian specialists
for duty in Vietnam would be much more difficult. Perhaps the
most important consideration, as far as the American Embassy
was concerned, was the serious effect evacuation would have on
the morale of the South Vietnamese Government and the population as a whole. But with the bombing of North Vietnam, these
considerations were set aside. The war had now taken a new and
serious turn; it was time to "roll up our sleeves and get down to
business," in the words of John McCone, Director of Central Intelligence and an early advocate of evacuation.

The evacuation took place none too soon. A few weeks after
the last dependent had departed it became clear that the front
was as likely to be in Saigon as in the jungles or the highlands. On
March 30th an attempt was made to blow up the American Embassy. That the building was not totally destroyed, and that there
were not massive American casualties, was a reflection on the skill,

rather than the intent, of the Viet Cong terrorists. As it was, two Americans and twenty Vietnamese were killed, and almost two hundred were wounded. The building itself was heavily damaged. One of the terrorists was apprehended, and the others were killed as they fled the scene.

The reaction in Washington was one of horror and rage. Surely this was one act of terrorism that must have been cleared in advance with the North Vietnamese. Some American officials maintained that Hanoi may even have ordered the bombing as a reprisal for American attacks against North Vietnam, and they urged immediate raids against government buildings in Hanoi. Detailed city maps, with the location of key ministries clearly marked, were drawn up and passed around. Cooler heads prevailed, however, and the American bombing against North Vietnam continued to be confined to military-related targets outside the main population centers. But if the Communists had wanted to do something to strengthen the Administration's determination to press on with the war, they could not have selected a better target for attack.

By the end of March it was plain that the bombing had not changed Hanoi's views about war or peace. Viet Cong military activity, starched up by the presence of regular North Vietnamese regimental-size units, became even more intense.

April turned out to be a fateful month. It began with a White House meeting to consider what could be done to regain the initiative. A wide range of new steps, from psychological warfare to increased American troop deployments, was adopted. Recommendations for extending the bombing to Hanoi itself were rejected. The President agreed to send approximately 20,000 troops and two additional Marine battalions to Vietnam. He also agreed to permit the Marine units guarding major American installations to engage in active combat.

The decision to send the Marines to Danang and its sequel, the agreement that their mission would go well beyond passive security operations, was an important milestone on the journey leading to major war. In a few short weeks the mission of American forces in Vietnam, which had already been transformed from "advisory" to "support," now became one of active combat. It was one of those major policy changes that Washington slithered into almost through inertia, rather than by design. But there were a few who sensed the implications of the President's approval of the deployment and later the expanded mission of the Marine detachment. One of these was Ambassador Taylor, who sent a brilliant message to Washington warning of what might be entailed if American Marines were moved into Danang. His telegram was one paragraph too short; the Ambassador registered his concern but did not specifically advise against the deployment. As a consequence his views had little impact in Washington.

* * *

The early spring of 1965 was not only a time of decision with respect to an American ground force commitment to Vietnam, it also marked country-wide stirrings on the peace front. Influenced by both of these considerations the President started down the peace track on March 25. "The United States will never be second in seeking a settlement in Viet-Nam that is based on an end of Communist aggression. . . . I am ready to go anywhere at any time, and meet with anyone whenever there is promise of progress toward an honorable peace." [16]

Neither Lyndon Johnson nor his advisers were quite sure of the route or even the destination of the new leg of the journey the United States had embarked upon. They did know, however, that the decision to launch American bombers against North Vietnam and the decisions about further escalation that were still confronting them would have to be balanced off with a posture of reason and moderation. This balance would have to be struck, not only to provide assurances to Peking and Moscow ("The United States still seeks no wider war") and to Hanoi ("We threaten no regime and covet no territory"), but to demonstrate to our allies and our own public that the Administration was not mindlessly and compulsively pursuing a rigid military policy. But the statement of March 25 was merely rhetoric, a public relations holding-action. No thought had been given in Washington to the form and not very much to the substance of any possible negotiations. The declaration was heavily insured against any immediate negotiation initiatives on the part of Hanoi. Nonetheless, its tone and content were soothing to an anxious American and foreign public.

The March statement was followed within a week by an appeal from the leaders of seventeen nonaligned nations for a "termination of the conflict . . . through negotiations." [17] Happily the language of the petition was restrained and general, and Washington had no difficulty in "welcoming" the "concern and interest" of the signers. The official reply [18] to the seventeen nation group made on April 8 was cautiously phrased, however: although the Seventeen Nations had made "an urgent appeal to the *parties* concerned to start . . . *negotiations* as soon as possible without . . . preconditions," the American response referred to the "*governments* concerned" (eliminating, by definition, the National Liberation Front) and to "unconditional *discussions*" (hedging the question of negotiations). Despite these quibbles, the affirmative response scored some political points for the Administration both at home and abroad—particularly since Hanoi rejected the overture.

The most important non-military event of these first dismal weeks of spring was the speech the President made in Baltimore on April 7. In his remarks the President indicated the Administration's agreement with the proposal of the Seventeen Nations, emphasized the limited nature of American objectives in Vietnam, warned Hanoi of American determination and restated his readiness to engage in "unconditional discussions" with the "governments concerned." And he invited U Thant "to initiate, as soon as possible . . . a plan for cooperation in increased development" of the countries of Southeast Asia, including North Vietnam. "For our part I will ask the Congress to join in a billion dollar American investment in this effort as soon as it is underway. And I would hope that all other industrialized countries, including the Soviet Union, will join in this effort. . . ." [19]

The speech was a landmark policy statement of the Johnson Administration. The bold approach toward developing Southeast Asia in cooperation with the Soviet Union, the inclusion of North Vietnam as a recipient country, and the implication that a billion dollars would be available were new and dramatic. The speech and the spirit of commitment behind it represented a welcome break from past rhetoric.

Nevertheless the President's remarks on regional economic development raised serious questions within the Washington bureaucracy. While Johnson was undoubtedly sincere in his desire to encourage a major program of development in the region, the idea had not been discussed in advance with the experts and technicians and it took them by surprise. They had been giving some thought to questions of regional economic cooperation and development, but they had found few projects or schemes that could be undertaken and make much sense. The vast sums the President had mentioned seemed clearly beyond the ability of the region to absorb. In the course of preparing the President's speech, the original reference to an American contribution was around $500 million, but the final drafters and the President himself thought "a billion dollars" was a nice, round, dramatic figure. Moreover, there was some uncertainty (not ever resolved) about the precise area covered by the President's proposal: Indochina (North and South Vietnam, Laos, and Cambodia)? Indochina plus Thailand? Plus Burma? Plus Malaysia? Moreover, it was unclear how the United Nations Economic Commission for Asia and the Far East (ECAFE) and the existing program for developing the Mekong basin fitted into the President's plan. Finally, there was an awkward question as to where the "billion dollars" would come from and what the President meant by asking Congress "to join" in the American "investment." Would AID have to turn over a large proportion of its existing budget? (It did not.) Would the President go to Congress for additional funds? (He did not.) But these were relatively petty details which if raised directly with the President would have made him very cross.

The men of Hanoi were not idle during this period. On the day following the Baltimore speech North Vietnam released its proposal for a settlement. It contained four major points: (1) The United States must withdraw its troops, weapons, and bases from South Vietnam and cease its "acts of war" against North Vietnam; (2) Pending unification of the country, both North and South Vietnam must agree that no foreign bases or troops be allowed on their soil and that they will join no military alliances; (3) The internal affairs of South Vietnam must be settled in accordance with the program of the National Liberation Front; (4) The re-unification of Vietnam must be settled by the Vietnamese them-selves without outside interference. The most troublesome part of the statement turned on one word—the word *the* in a wrap-up sentence of the proposal: The Government of the Democratic Re-public of Vietnam is of the view that the stand expounded above is *"the* basis" for a political settlement. Hanoi clinched this point in a concluding paragraph: ". . . any approach contrary to the above-mentioned stand is inappropriate." This Four Point Proposal was the basis of Hanoi's negotiating posture for years.

Washington might even have been able to accept the impli-cations of Hanoi's phrase "the basis," but if so, major modifications would have been necessary in Point Three—the insistence that South Vietnamese problems would have to be resolved "in ac-cordance with the program of the National Liberation Front." * Some of the more flexible officials in Washington felt that with such modifications the North Vietnamese proposal was one the United States probably could live with, or at least could regard as a beginning of a dialogue. But Point Three, as stated, brushed aside the ideas and aspirations of any group other than the NLF. If this were accepted as it stood, there would actually have been no need to negotiate a political settlement; the NLF would have been given carte blanche. Several staff officers in Washington, in-cluding myself, felt we should probe Hanoi's views, and indeed

---

* Hanoi was referring in its Point Three to the National Liberation Front program that had been developed as far back as 1960. In summary form, the NLF Ten Points were (1) Overthrow the camouflaged colonial regime of the American imperialists and . . . Ngo Dinh Diem . . . and institute a government of national democratic union. (2) Institute a . . . liberal and democratic regime. (3) Estab-lish an independent and sovereign economy, and improve the living conditions of the people. (4) Reduce land rent; implement agrarian reform. . . . (5) Develop a national and democratic culture and education. (6) Create a national army de-voted to the defense of the Fatherland and the people. (7) Guarantee equality between the various minorities . . . protect the legitimate interests of foreign citizens established in Vietnam and of Vietnamese citizens residing abroad. (8) Promote a foreign policy of peace and neutrality. (9) Re-establish normal rela-tions between the two zones, and prepare for the peaceful reunification of the country. (10) Struggle against all aggressive war; actively defend universal peace.

this was later done. We felt the United States should push hard
for free elections in which all parties were permitted to contest
freely, protected from terror and compulsion. This would, of
course, have required an international policing mechanism (a
strengthened International Control Commission or some other
body). We argued that if these objectives coincided with the
program of the National Liberation Front, we could accept Point
Three. In short, we felt that, if we chose to make them so, Pham
Van Dong's proposals could provide a basis for exploratory talks,
recognizing, however, that our experience in the Laos negotiations
had shown the Communists to be allergic to effective international
control, and that any progress in this direction would therefore be
slow and tortuous.

*   *   *

With the deployment of American combat troops, policymaking
took on a new complexion. Up to this point the civilians, whether
in the Department of State or Defense, played the leading roles in
all policy discussions. Indeed the Chairman of the Joint Chiefs of
Staff, General Earle D. Wheeler, had frequently been excluded
from many of the high-level meetings. Now that the security of
American forces was involved, military participation in virtually
every facet of our Vietnam involvement was taken for granted
(although the President himself saw little or nothing of any senior
military officers other than the Chairman of the Joint Chiefs and
the commanders of our forces in Vietnam).

Once given a legal hunting license, the Pentagon went after
some big game. In the spring of 1965 the Joint Chiefs of Staff
proposed that the military assume responsibility for a large part of
the American AID programs in Vietnam's rural areas. The proposition was that "Civil Affairs" teams, as in World War II, should
be deployed throughout Vietnam to serve as integral parts of the
provincial governments. Only the military, it was maintained,
could bring together the necessary experts quickly enough to get
the provincial administrations moving. Naturally enough the working levels in State, AID, and the White House strongly opposed
this scheme. Aside from a feeling that the military was trying to

invade sacred civilian territory, there were well-founded substantive concerns. Civil Affairs reservists were not necessarily trained to cope with the delicate political problems that confronted Americans in dealing with provincial officials. More importantly there was a queasy feeling that implicit in the Chiefs' proposal was the assumption that South Vietnam would be treated as an occupied enemy country. There was considerable steam behind the plan, however, and it might have been adopted had Ambassador Taylor not rejected the idea.

Another facet of the new military role in the policymaking process was the direct participation of the Commander of the American forces in the Pacific (CINCPAC). Until the bombing of North Vietnam had started in February, the American military establishment in Vietnam had been only nominally under CINCPAC command. The vast headquarters in Honolulu was hardly more than a post office and a message center for Vietnam operations, and serious consideration had been given during 1964 to eliminating CINCPAC from the chain of command between Washington and Saigon. When in late 1964 a senior military commander in Vietnam was asked for his judgment on whether the MACV should be placed directly under Washington command, he agreed that this made sense. Since CINCPAC was his "boss," however, he could not go on record with this view.

Although virtually every decision on Vietnam, even those affecting day-to-day operations, required Cabinet-level and Presidential approval during this period, one international development became so urgent as to temporarily divert the attention of the President and his senior advisers. This was the crisis in the Dominican Republic in late April, 1965. (The only other major diversion during the Johnson Administration was the Arab–Israeli war two years later.) For the brief period that the Caribbean received top priority, Vietnam specialists at the Department of State, and I at the White House, had a respite from the urgent summonses and the hot breaths of our various bosses, and could reflect on where we were going.

The situation in Vietnam did not stand still while Washington was concentrating on the Dominican Republic. Communist strength had increased substantially during the first few months of 1965. By the end of April it was believed that 100,000 Viet Cong irregulars and between 38,000 and 46,000 main-force enemy troops, including a full battalion of regular North Vietnamese troops, were in South Vietnam. Meanwhile American combat forces were moving into South Vietnam at a rapid rate; in late April more than 35,000 American troops had been deployed and by early May the number had increased to 45,000. It was now clear that the President would have to seek a supplemental defense appropriation to meet the costs of American military operations. On May 4 he went to Congress with a request for an additional $700 million. He used this occasion to assert that he would regard a vote for the appropriation as a vote of approval for the Administration's Vietnam policy. Since the decision to send American combat forces to Vietnam had already been made, and indeed many thousands of troops were already there, it would have been difficult for any legislator to vote against funds for their support. The President had pulled off a neat political ploy. In any case the House approved the new appropriation by a vote of 407 to 7, and the Senate approved it by a vote of 83 to 3. The President promptly interpreted this as he had said he would: ". . . each Member of Congress who supports this request is voting to continue our effort to try to halt Communist aggression." [20] He would refer to this, together with the Tonkin Resolution of the previous August, to document his case that he had given Congress the opportunity to approve or veto his Vietnam policy. The State Department Legal Adviser subsequently used the appropriations vote as well as the Joint Resolution to justify not asking Congress to approve American military involvement in Vietnam: ". . . the legality of United States participation in the defense of South Viet Nam does not rest only on the constitutional power of the President under Article II. . . . the Congress has acted in unmistakable fashion to approve and authorize United States actions in Viet Nam. Following the North Vietnamese attacks in the Gulf of Tonkin . . . Congress adopted . . . a Joint Resolution containing a series of important declarations and provisions of law. . . . Congress in May, 1965 approved an appropriation of $700 million to meet the expense . . . in Viet Nam. . . . The Appropriations Act constitutes a clear Congressional endorsement and approval of the actions taken by the President." [21]

*   *   *

The public outcry against the Administration's Vietnam policy was now reinforced by shrill opposition to the deployment of American troops to the Dominican Republic. It was time once again for the President to assure the country that, despite the deployment of American combat forces and mounting defense expenditures, he was ready to move toward negotiations. It was by now a familiar Administration strategy to balance escalation in Vietnam with declarations and even deeds of moderation. Thus the decision to bomb North Vietnam in February, 1965 was quickly followed by an appeal to the United Nations, and the move to send combat troops to Vietnam in March was followed by the President's speech in Baltimore.

By early May there was considerable pressure on the President, not only from the peace groups but within the Administration, for a "pause" in the bombing of North Vietnam to test Hanoi's readiness to negotiate. Following Congressional approval of the White House request for additional defense funds, the time seemed to be ripe. Hanoi could not have failed to notice evidence of renewed American determination, so a brief halt in the bombing was not likely to be regarded as a sign of weakness. On May 13 the President ordered a bombing pause. The pause lasted five days. The result was negative, although there was a brief flurry of political activity by the North Vietnamese representative in Paris the day the bombing resumed.

The President regarded Hanoi's disinterest in negotiations as sufficient justification to heat up the war. Air attacks intensified against North Vietnam, and in June the giant B–52 bombers were unleashed against the Viet Cong in South Vietnam. Although American troops in Vietnam had now reached more than 70,000, more North Vietnamese regular troops were flowing across the 17th parallel and the situation in South Vietnam was still desperate. To compound the problem the civilian government of Premier

Quat had resigned on a relatively trivial issue, and the generals once more took over in Saigon. This time the government was headed by General Ky, the Air Force Chief who was one of the powerful Young Turks behind the scenes. Another Young Turk, General Nguyen Van Thieu, took over the less powerful but more prestigious post of Chief of State.

Pressure on the President from his military and some of his civilian advisers for more American combat troops in Vietnam continued to grow as the weeks went on. Despite the air strikes against enemy concentrations in South Vietnam and against targets in the North, the Communists continued to hold the military initiative. Westmoreland has reported that "By late spring of 1965 the South Vietnamese Army was losing almost one infantry battalion a week to enemy action. Additionally, the enemy was gaining control of at least one district capital town each week. . . . the Government of Vietnam could not survive this mounting . . . offensive for more than six months unless the United States chose to increase its military commitment. Substantial numbers of U.S. ground combat forces were required." [22]

At a news conference on July 9 the President began to prepare the country for possible new major military steps, and he eliminated the sugar from the unpleasant medicine: "The incidents are going up: that is, the Viet Cong attacks. The casualties are going up. . . . We expect that it will get worse before it gets better. They have had substantial increases in the aggression forces. They are swinging wildly. They are suffering substantial losses in their sneak attacks. Our manpower needs there are increasing, and will continue to do so. . . . Whatever is required I am sure will be supplied." [23]

Secretary McNamara, General Wheeler, and Henry Cabot Lodge (who had just been appointed to serve once again as Ambassador to Saigon) were directed to assess the current political and military situation in Vietnam at first hand. On July 13, the day before the high-level group left for Vietnam, the President warned that "Increased aggression from the North may require an increased American response on the ground in South Viet-Nam. . . . It is quite possible that new and serious decisions will be necessary in the near future. Any substantial increase in the present level of our efforts . . . will require steps to insure that our reserves of men and equipment of the United States remain entirely adequate for any and all emergencies." [24]

McNamara was more explicit on the eve of his departure. If larger numbers of American troops were sent to South Vietnam, "it will be necessary to consider calling up reserves, extending tours, and increasing the draft." This would also require, McNamara said, substantial additional increases in the defense budget. "The Viet Cong are continuing to increase in South Vietnam. They have forces in the country they have not yet assigned to combat. We can expect further increases in Viet Cong operations." [25]

* * *

Physiologists claim that moving rapidly from one time zone to another requires a considerable adjustment of one's "internal clock." They believe it takes about twenty-four hours for the average person to reach his usual proficiency in adding a column of figures after he has experienced a time zone change of several hours. But if McNamara was aware of the physiologists' theory, he ignored it. His typical trip involved leaving Washington in the evening and, after a twenty-four hour journey and a thirteen hour time change, arriving at Saigon at eight in the morning. The Secretary would emerge from the plane and suggest graciously that his fellow-travelers take a half-hour or so to wash up and then join him at a 9 o'clock briefing at MACV Headquarters. There, for the next three hours, they were expected not merely to add up figures but to absorb a rapid-fire series of complicated military briefings liberally seasoned with charts, graphs, maps, and the inevitable sequence of slides. While we less adaptable beings desperately attempted to make sense out of the mass of information, McNamara queried every apparent inconsistency and was usually well ahead of the briefers.

In addition to taking a close look at the security situation, McNamara was anxious to meet the new leaders of the Saigon Government. Stories about Ky had not been reassuring. He was young, flamboyant, and indiscreet—almost a stereotype of the

World War II "Fly Boy." As for General Thieu, little was known
about him except that he was a good soldier and somewhat shy
with Americans. Deputy Ambassador Alexis Johnson arranged a
small shirt-sleeves dinner with the new government leaders on the
night of our arrival. The Vietnamese arrived somewhat late and
Ky made a spectacular entrance. He walked in breezily, wearing
a tight, white dinner jacket, tapered, formal trousers, pointed, pat-
ent leather shoes, and brilliant red socks. A Hollywood central
casting bureau would have grabbed him for a role as a sax player
in a second-rate Manila night club. McNamara, who definitely
would not have gotten the part, seemed momentarily dazed and
bemused at his first sight of Vietnam's new leader. (Somebody
standing near me muttered, "At least no one could confuse him
with Uncle Ho!") General Thieu wore a conservative business
suit and seemed content, or at least resigned, to have Ky remain
in the spotlight—a position Ky appeared eager to hold.

As I reflect upon that evening, it occurs to me that we must
have given Ky and Thieu a difficult and bewildering time. Each of
us used every minute of our conversations with them to press them
to move forward quickly with the whole list of actions we had been
urging on the various Vietnamese governments over the past year—
acceleration of land reform and psychological warfare programs,
elimination of politics from the South Vietnamese Army, steps to
stop inflation, a more constructive approach toward the Buddhists.
The Vietnamese must have left Ambassador Johnson's home that
night with terrible headaches and a feeling that the Americans
were difficult, persistent, even unreasonable allies.

On the following day we met with Ky, Thieu, and senior Vietnamese staff officers. We were first presented with an elaborate
plan for a new country-wide paramilitary and civic action organization. The briefing dealt in detail with such trivia as the uniforms
the new group would wear but lacked any sense of overall conviction. The most important aspect of the session, however, was a
strong plea by the Vietnamese for more American combat troops.
The Vietnamese suggested the additional American forces should
be responsible primarily for the security of the thinly populated
highlands, while the Vietnamese would concentrate on the popu-

lated sections of the country. Their rationale for this division of responsibility was based on the superior mobility of the American forces. But the Vietnamese had another and more serious reason for their proposal, which they alluded to only elliptically. The presence of thousands of American troops was already having inflationary effects on the Vietnamese economy and creating frictions among the Vietnamese population. Clearly the government was anxious to have the Americans deployed away from the cities and towns. The American reaction was polite but critical. McNamara and Wheeler felt that American forces should be where the action was, even though this risked the chance of anti-American incidents. (As matters turned out, we eventually had so many troops in Vietnam that they were deployed not only in the highlands area but throughout the country.)

The following day McNamara inspected American installations outside of Saigon. Lodge and I flew up to Camranh Bay, where a large new port and logistics base were being constructed. We felt a proprietary interest in the project, since we both had long been urging that it be undertaken. Construction had been going on for only a few weeks or so, and the little fishing and coast guard town, with its breathtaking view of the sea, still had much of the charm of a small resort in the south of France. We were given a briefing by the American Colonel in charge of construction, who was frank to say he was rehearsing the presentation he was going to make to McNamara the following day. He had prepared elaborate charts and briefing aids, despite the primitive nature of the facilities available. I was amused at first—and then horrified—as the Colonel began to detail how the area would look when completed. "This," he said, "will be the parade ground, this will be the officers club, and this will be the non-commissioned officers mess." I took him aside later and told him that he had better revise his briefing for McNamara. As a starter, he should change the designation "parade ground" to "drill field" and eliminate the officers and non-commissioned officers clubs, in terminology if not in fact. I had occasion to see the Colonel many months later, and he told me I had probably saved him from committing professional suicide.

At the end of the McNamara visit, an Embassy spokesman told American correspondents that General Westmoreland and the Vietnamese Government had urged a substantial additional build-up of American forces. The spokesman, probably unwittingly, then made a most important revelation—although few reporters picked it up. The rationale for more American troops, he said, was based on the need to achieve a decisive military victory against the Viet Cong. Until now there had been little if any mention of American troops engaging in major offensive ground operations; the emphasis had been on helping the South Vietnamese forces and on protecting American bases.

McNamara returned to Washington on July 21 and promptly met with the President and the National Security Council. This was to be the first in a series of meetings over the next several days dealing with the scale and nature of new military moves in Vietnam. There were agonizing decisions to be made. But we were now in too deep to back out, and it was a foregone conclusion, as the President had already warned, that major new deployments would be made. The only open questions revolved around the size of the new forces to be committed and how they were to be raised and supported.

XII

Johnson's War

The White House meetings that addressed the problem of new troop commitments to Vietnam extended over a period of a week during the latter part of July. This was the most searching examination yet made of where we were and where we should go. The press, with not a little encouragement from the White House, painted a picture of options advanced, carefully examined, retained for further consideration, or dismissed out of hand. According to this portrayal, the final decision represented the best judgment of the President after his exposure to the views and arguments of his key military and civilian advisers. Pains were taken to emphasize that the "dovish" briefs of Under-Secretary George Ball, as well as those of the "hawkish" military, were put forward.

Many government officials close to the developments of that week are convinced that the image of a soul-searching and agonizing examination of alternatives, including the option of cutting our losses and pulling out, was an accurate reflection of what actually occurred. They believe if one or two senior participants had joined George Ball in opposing new troop deployments, the President might have been induced to think through the issue of whether more troops should be sent, rather than simply worrying about how many. There are others who feel the President almost certainly knew by the end of the first day's discussion, and perhaps even before the meeting started, what he planned to do, but it suited his purpose and his style to give the impression that he was engaging in a lengthy and thorough appraisal in which all points of view were advanced and weighed. To back up their position they maintain the decision had been reached earlier by McNamara when he conferred with senior military officers in Honolulu on his way home from Vietnam. It is my belief that the issue of additional deployments was already resolved; the only question was how many troops the President felt he could commit.

The 75,000 American troops then in Vietnam were now a hostage. They represented too large a force to pull out without a tremendous loss of prestige, yet they were too small a combat force (most were engineering or supply troops) to take over the burden of the fighting from the clearly ineffectual South Vietnamese forces. The President lost nothing by letting George Ball play the role of devil's advocate; it was actually useful to give the impression that disengagement was being seriously discussed.

As the meetings went on and the time of decision became more imminent, the number of participants got smaller and smaller. The President, with his deep concern for secrecy, eventually met with only a few of his most senior advisers. On the 27th of July Johnson briefed selected members of Congress on his decision, and on the 28th he revealed it to the American people.

American fighting forces in Vietnam, the President told a nationwide television audience, would be increased from the present level of 75,000 to 125,000 men almost immediately, and further increases would be ordered if the situation required. It would not be necessary, he said, to call up the reserves, but over a period of time draft quotas would be raised from 17,000 to 35,000 a month. The President emphasized that the increase in troop deployments was in response to General Westmoreland's request. "I have asked the Commanding General, General Westmoreland, what more he needs to meet this mounting aggression. He has told me. We will meet his needs." His speech included, once again, a statement of his readiness to negotiate a political settlement, although he reminded his listeners that all his previous efforts had been rejected by North Vietnam and China. "Fifteen efforts have been

made to start these discussions with the help of 40 nations throughout the world, but there has been no answer." [1]

The announced increase to 125,000 men was almost certainly
substantially less than either the Joint Chiefs or Westmoreland
had requested and expected. Johnson was determined to fight the
war with minimum disruption at home, and the troop increase was
not based on the estimated number required, but rather on the
maximum number that could be deployed without having to call
up the reserves. Doling out additional forces with a view to balancing off military requirements in Vietnam and political consequences at home typified the President's approach. He wished to
avoid giving the impression that the United States was, in fact, "at
war." Much later, when there were more than half a million American troops in Vietnam and when casualties approached the level
of the Korean war, he still resisted going to Congress for a Declaration of War.[*] Moreover, he would not agree to any fundamental
changes within the Executive Departments that would have permitted the war to be pursued more effectively.

Johnson accompanied his announcement of additional military
deployments with a dramatic peace gesture. On the day of the
speech, Ambassador Goldberg delivered a letter to U Thant. The
President told the Secretary General, "we hope that the Members
of the United Nations, individually and collectively, will use their
influence to bring to the negotiating table all governments involved in an attempt to halt all aggression and evolve a peaceful
solution. I continue to hope that the United Nations can, in fact,
be effective in this regard." [2] In the light of the history of earlier
efforts to engage the UN, this effort was obviously doomed to
failure. If there was any faint hope, the Soviet Union soon

---

[*] In his televised memoirs of February 6, 1970 ex-President Johnson stated
that the Tonkin Gulf resolution had provided him with a "sky's-the-limit" Congressional approval of his Vietnam policy. He emphasized that he did not ask for
a Declaration of War because he was concerned that a "secret treaty" between
North Vietnam and China or the USSR might have required the Chinese or the
Russians to come to North Vietnam's defense. Mr. Johnson is, of course, the ultimate authority. From my own admittedly limited vantage point, however, I have
no recollection of any White House or State Department concern about a possible
"secret treaty." In any case, one would have thought such concern would have
acted as a constraint on the bombing of North Vietnam, especially the bombing
of Hanoi.

smothered it. In a *Pravda* editorial Moscow indicated it would have no part of any attempt to involve the United Nations in Vietnam.

*   *   *

Several days after the announcement of the new troop deployment the President indicated he would once again ask Congress for additional defense appropriations. The $700 million authorized three months before was already committed and an additional $1.7 billion was requested for the remaining budget year. Congress approved the request on August 18.

The ensuing months of 1965 were cheerless ones. Even in the face of the increasing buildup of American forces in South Vietnam and the intensified bombing of the North, the enemy still seemed unimpressed and unaffected. Admiral Sharp reports that by September, "despite the damage caused by air attacks in North Vietnam there was no indication of North Vietnamese willingness to negotiate or terminate support of the Viet Cong." [3] Meanwhile, General Westmoreland was having his own difficulties. As of August, he notes, an American Special Forces camp in the Central Highlands area had been overrun and "the tactical picture . . . was not encouraging." By October it appeared that the enemy was concentrating its efforts in the Highlands area in the hope of cutting South Vietnam in half.[4]

The one encouraging aspect of the military situation during those dreary days was the impressive performance of American troops in battle. The first major American engagement took place in August when a Marine unit engaged a regiment of Viet Cong and killed hundreds of the enemy. In November the First Cavalry Division successfully engaged major Communist forces and inflicted appalling casualties. But the South Vietnamese forces continued to perform poorly; in November a South Vietnamese regiment was badly mauled by the Viet Cong not far from Saigon.

By the autumn the war began to intrude seriously on the normal life of Americans. Draft calls had increased substantially, American casualties were now beginning to be felt across the country, military funeral corteges moving across Memorial Bridge and among the trees at Arlington Cemetery were a common sight. It was not surprising that during this period opposition to the war became more shrill and more organized.

In late October, three months after the President announced that American troops in Vietnam would be increased to 125,000 men, it was revealed that American forces in South Vietnam had, in fact, reached a total of nearly 150,000. And two weeks later Secretary McNamara announced it would be necessary to deploy additional combat forces.

Some McNamara-watchers claim the Secretary underwent a discernible change in mood in late 1965. It was not so much a transition from "hawk" to "dove" (these observers would say that that metamorphosis took place much later); it was rather a change from overflowing confidence to grave doubts. If this is a correct reading of McNamara, the change can probably be dated from a quick trip he took to Vietnam at the end of November. On this visit he found that American forces were performing well. But he also discovered that despite our new deployments, despite the tremendous military assistance and training programs for the South Vietnamese Army, despite the use of B–52s against enemy bases in South Vietnam and the intensified bombing of North Vietnam, the Communists were increasing the scale and intensity of their military operations; Hanoi's forces in South Vietnam had expanded, and Communist military equipment and supplies continued to flow down from the North. McNamara sounded grim as he left Saigon. He told the press that the Viet Cong actions "expressed a determination to carry on the conflict which can lead to only one conclusion—that it will be a long war."

It would have been surprising if McNamara had not had a change in mood that November; only two years before, he had said most of the American forces would be home from Vietnam by the end of 1965. A hint of McNamara's developing views about the war was revealed in February, 1966 when he met with some American correspondents in Honolulu. The reporters told the Secretary that General Ky felt strongly that the bombing raids against North Vietnam should be intensified. McNamara replied that anyone who thought the bombing campaign would make a major difference in winning the war was dead wrong.

✿   ✿   ✿

The late autumn was marked by a flurry of reported North Vietnamese peace feelers, each followed immediately by a denial from Hanoi. Pressures were building up for the Administration to initiate a major peace effort during the forthcoming holidays. During the Thanksgiving weekend there was a "March for Peace" in Washington, sponsored by the Committee for a Sane Nuclear Policy. When I first discussed the March with the organizers a few weeks before, I reminded them that Washington could not declare peace unilaterally and that our overtures to Hanoi had thus far been met with rebuff and ridicule. I suggested that they put some pressure on Ho Chi Minh and the NLF if they wanted to improve prospects for negotiations. They agreed. Sanford Gottlieb, Executive Director of SANE, sent the following message to President Ho and to Chairman Tho of the NLF:

> Our organization helping to provide leadership for November 27 demonstration in support of cease-fire and negotiated settlement based on 1954 Geneva Accords. Again urge you respond favorably to immediate peace talks. Demonstrations will continue, but will not lead to U.S. pullout.

Dr. Benjamin Spock also urged both of the Communist leaders to respond to any American initiatives:

> We are urging President Johnson to end the bombings of North Vietnam, to seek a cease-fire, and to negotiate an end to the war with all parties concerned, including the National Liberation Front. An indication of your willingness to participate in a cease-fire and in negotiations leading to a peaceful settlement and self-determination by Asian peoples would be welcomed by us in our efforts and by many Americans.

Ho responded to these messages about a month later—on the day before the March:

Thank you for your message dated 26 October. On April 8 the Government of the DRV stated its four point stand. This stand, based on the 1954 Geneva Agreements wherein the Vietnamese people' fundamental national rights are recognized, conforms to the reality of Vietnam. The U.S. imperialists, who have sabotaged the Geneva Agreements, are the aggressors. The Vietnamese people are the victims of the aggression. If the U.S. imperialists stop their aggression, peace will immediately be restored in Vietnam.

This stand is the only correct basis for a settlement of the Vietnam problem in the interest of the Vietnamese people, the American people, and world peace.

I take this opportunity to warmly hail the American people's struggle for the immediate ending of the U.S. Government's criminal war of aggression in Vietnam, the cessation of the air attacks on the territory of the DRV, the withdrawal of U.S. troops, and for democratic liberties and against racial discrimination.

On the day of the March, I met with Doctor Spock, Norman Thomas, Mrs. Martin Luther King, Jr., and Sanford Gottlieb. Norman Thomas acted as the principal spokesman. The essence of his remarks was that his faith in and enthusiasm for the President's views as expressed on July 28 had eroded in succeeding months with our troop build-up and intensification of bombing; he now doubted we were really interested in negotiations; the President had a tremendous opportunity to prove this country's "greatness," and his own as well, by "taking the initiative" for negotiations; this would require the acceptance of the principle of a cease-fire and a pause in the bombing of the North. He did not advocate the immediate withdrawal of U.S. troops. The group urged a bombing pause of at least several weeks during which, they were confident, Hanoi would be receptive to talks leading to a political settlement. I was sure there would be a bombing pause for at least several days starting on Christmas Eve, but for security reasons I was unable to pass this along. The meeting was cordial, if inconclusive.

There were others too who were confident that a bombing pause of two or three weeks would produce results. A highly-respected and well-informed journalist, Robert Kleiman of *The New York Times,* came down from New York to tell me that his

sources among the Russians and Eastern Europeans at the UN
had given him "in confidence" the same information. Other officials, high and low, in the White House and the State Department, were told pretty much the same story, either directly by
Communist diplomats, or indirectly through third parties. Moscow seemed anxious to get the message through. The most
important affirmation came from the Soviet Ambassador, Anatoly
Dobrynin. He called at the White House in mid-December to give
his assurances that the Russians would do their best to induce
Hanoi to react positively if the United States would halt the
bombing for a few weeks.

Christmas Day was marked by a ceasefire on the ground in
South Vietnam and by a pause in the bombing of North Vietnam.
Ground operations resumed on December 26, but the bombing
pause was extended for one more day. Future historians would do
well to ponder over the importance of this extra day.

There is reason to believe that when it was originally decided to
maintain the bombing pause for a day beyond the brief ceasefire in
South Vietnam, no definite time had been set for the resumption
of the bombing. I was in McGeorge Bundy's office on the 27th
when the President called from the Ranch. In the course of exchanging Christmas greetings Johnson inquired when the bombing
was to start up again. Bundy asked me if I had seen any orders
for the resumption. I had not. Bundy then told the President he
would check with Secretary McNamara. He thereupon called Mc-
Namara who too professed innocence of where the matter stood.
It was apparent that, through a failure of communications or
through inadvertence, no specific hour had been decided upon.

In the light of this it seemed to make sense to keep the bombing pause going for a while longer—at least until New Year's Day.
McNamara concurred, and Bundy communicated this suggestion
to the Ranch. Surprisingly, the President agreed to give the matter
"careful" thought. Later that night he reached his decision. The
two Bundy brothers were summoned from a Debutante Ball. Clad
in white ties and tails, they went to the State Department and,
together with Secretary Rusk, dispatched the orders extending the

pause *sine-die.* The President then decided to use the extended pause to mount a major diplomatic offensive.

The next day Averell Harriman received a call from the President. Could he leave for Eastern Europe "immediately"? Harriman reminded the President that his "bag was always packed." He then called McNamara, who was also at the Ranch and had been with the President during the conversation. Did the President literally expect an "immediate" departure? McNamara told him a plane was being prepared for takeoff that afternoon.

Harriman started in Poland and twelve countries, thousands of miles, and many days later he wound up in the Philippines. So hasty had Harriman's departure from Washington been that there had been no opportunity to work out all the necessary advance formalities. Jerzy Michalowski, then Under Secretary of the Foreign Office, was awakened in the middle of the night with a message that Harriman's plane was approaching Poland and needed a special landing clearance. Harriman talked to Foreign Minister Rapacki and to Prime Minister Gomulka. Michalowski departed for Moscow the next morning. He later told Harriman that the Russians had urged him to proceed to Hanoi and to encourage the North Vietnamese to move toward negotiations. Michalowski spent two weeks in Hanoi but met with no success.

Harriman's trip was the longest and probably the most productive of all those undertaken in early 1966, but there were other Super Stars in flight: Vice President Humphrey, Ambassador Goldberg, McGeorge Bundy, Under Secretary of State Mann, and Assistant Secretary G. Mennen ("Soapy") Williams were also dispatched to carry The Word to friendly and neutral countries. The traveling soloists were accompanied by a chorus of Ambassadorial talks in Washington, letters from Johnson to several Chiefs of State, and messages to all the members of the United Nations stressing that the United States was prepared for negotiations "without prior conditions."

When the possibility of a bombing pause was raised earlier in December, I pointed out the distinction between an attempt to improve our image and a genuine peace probe. The tactics would have to vary depending on which option the President chose. I opted for the probe.

While much of the to-ing and fro-ing, the posturing, and the overall atmosphere of conspicuous busyness during late December and January would seem to lead to the conclusion that the efforts were primarily for the purpose of improving the American image rather than finding the key to actual negotiations, there were some meaningful aspects and results. The various high-level visitations must have given many host governments a better idea of American objectives in Vietnam. Probably more important than anything else, however, was a document drawn up in considerable haste on the eve of the departure of the Great Men. Prepared by Secretary Rusk personally, it was a short and straightforward articulation of an American peace package. In one form or another each of the fourteen points had already been mentioned publicly, but this was the first time they had been stripped of smothering rhetoric and assembled in one document:

1. The Geneva Agreements of 1954 and 1962 are an adequate basis for peace in Southeast Asia;
2. We would welcome a conference on Southeast Asia or on any part thereof;
3. We would welcome "negotiations without pre-conditions," as the 17 nations put it;
4. We would welcome unconditional discussions, as President Johnson put it;
5. A cessation of hostilities could be the first order of business at a conference or could be the subject of preliminary discussions;
6. Hanoi's four points could be discussed along with other points which others might wish to propose;
7. We want no U.S. bases in Southeast Asia;
8. We do not desire to retain U.S. troops in South Viet-Nam after peace is assured;
9. We support free elections in South Viet-Nam to give the South Vietnamese a government of their own choice;
10. The question of reunification of Viet-Nam should be determined by the Vietnamese through their own free decision;
11. The countries of Southeast Asia can be non-aligned or neutral if that be their option;

12. We would much prefer to use our resources for the economic reconstruction of Southeast Asia than in War. If there is peace, North Viet-Nam could participate in a regional effort to which we would be prepared to contribute at least one billion dollars;

13. The President has said "The Viet Cong would not have difficulty being represented and having their views represented if for a moment Hanoi decided she wanted to cease aggression. I don't think that would be an insurmountable problem."

14. We have said publicly and privately that we could stop the bombing of North Viet-Nam as a step toward peace although there has not been the slightest hint or suggestion from the other side as to what they would do if the bombing stopped.[5]

Commenting on the package later, Secretary Rusk mused, "We put everything into the basket except the surrender of South Viet-nam."

The President's patience was wearing thin by the end of January. He was under considerable pressure from his military and some of his civilian advisers to resume the bombing. The final straw was a letter from Ho Chi Minh sent on January 24 to the heads of several governments:

> So long as the U.S. army of aggression still remains on our soil, our people will resolutely fight against it. If the U.S. Government really wants a peaceful settlement, it must accept the four-point stand of the DRV Government and prove this by actual deeds; it must end unconditionally and for good all bombing raids and other war acts against the DRV. Only in this way can a political solution to the Vietnam problem be envisaged. . . .
>
> In the face of the extremely serious situation brought about by the United States in Vietnam, I firmly believe that the people and government of the fraternal (recipient country) [sic] will extend increased support and assistance to our people's just struggle, resolutely condemn the U.S. Government's sham peace tricks, and check in time all new perfidious maneuvers of the United States in Vietnam and Indochina.[6]

Although the President had decided to resume the bombing, I pressed for an extension of another two weeks. Prime Minister

Wilson was scheduled to leave for Moscow on February 21, and I thought there might be an outside chance that in the atmosphere of a continued bombing suspension Wilson could persuade the Soviet leaders to exert some influence on Hanoi to agree to negotiations. Bundy gave me a friendly hearing. But bombing resumed on February 1, Saigon time. As it turned out we would have lost little by an extension; the weather during February greatly hampered bombing operations. In February, according to Admiral Sharp, "there was little to report in the way of results." [7]

The resumption was accompanied by an obviously pro forma attempt to get the United Nations Security Council to arrange an international peace conference. The Council agreed by a vote of nine to two (the Soviet Union and Bulgaria opposed, and France and three of the African nations abstained) to put the Vietnam question on its agenda, but the move came to naught since Hanoi formally rejected any UN action.

The pause and the diplomatic offensive that accompanied it had lasted for almost six weeks. Although there had been a brief exchange between our Ambassador and a North Vietnamese representative in Rangoon, there had been no nibbles from Hanoi. Later in a message to its posts abroad, the State Department gave a gloomy summary of Hanoi's reaction: "Hanoi has rejected the peace initiatives. It has refused to respond to our unilateral effort towards peace. It rejects negotiations except on its own terms. It has reiterated its well-known demands and has labeled the recent peace initiatives as an ultimatum, a trick or swindle. It has referred to the President's special emissaries as freaks and monsters who travel around the world peddling false information." [8]

The experience of January, 1966 influenced the President's views on any further bombing cessations or other gestures toward Hanoi for the remainder of his tenure. He has been said to feel that he had been led down the garden path by doves among his advisers. His two close confidants and unofficial advisers, Abe Fortas and Clark Clifford, reportedly told him the January bombing pause was his "worst mistake" in the Vietnam war. He was to refer to his fruitless efforts of early 1966 again and again, privately and publicly, whenever it was suggested there be another pause or a de-escalation of the bombing.

In retrospect the prospects for negotiations were dim in early 1966. Perhaps Hanoi would have been disinterested in any case, but in looking at other situations that gave more promise—or those such as the offer of March 31, 1968 which actually produced results—the style and method adopted in December and January were plainly unsuitable. Where finely tooled instruments were required, we used a sledgehammer. Where confidential and careful advance work was necessary, we proceeded with the subtlety of a Fourth of July parade. Where a dramatic, surprise proposal may have stirred Hanoi's interest, we made a public spectacle of every melodramatic move. Instead of maximizing the effect of our fourteen-point peace package, we buried it in the razzmatazz of sudden, noisy, and florid VIP trips. In short the President was acting like a ringmaster of a three-ring circus, rather than as the focal point of a carefully worked out exercise in diplomacy.

Having said all this, one wonders why Hanoi did not pick up the offer—and what would have happened if it had. Secretary Rusk's fourteen points provided the North Vietnamese with the best summary of American peace objectives that had been made available up to then (and indeed for years hence), the non-Communist situation in South Vietnam was precarious, and the Buddhists were poised to make it even worse. More to the point, however, Washington was unprepared for negotiations. Little work had been done in blocking out a negotiating strategy, very few position papers on the key negotiations issues had been prepared. For its part, the government in Saigon had hardly spent an hour addressing its own negotiations stance.

❖   ❖   ❖

On Thursday, February 4 I left the White House area for my first leisurely lunch in many weeks. I returned to the West Basement at about 2:30 to find Bundy desperately trying to reach me. An American–Vietnamese "summit meeting" had been arranged for the following Saturday in Honolulu. The next few frenetic hours were spent in preparing an agenda of appropriate subjects for dis-

cussion between President Johnson and General Ky and in listing
general matters for discussion among officials of both governments.
Our Embassy in Saigon and the officials of the Vietnamese Government had to be consulted (or rather, informed), briefs prepared, and arrangements made in Honolulu. Since the President
had decided to minimize military aspects of the talks, it was decided to house the delegations in hotels, rather than at our Pacific
Headquarters in Pearl Harbor where security, residence, and communications arrangements would have been infinitely easier to
work out in the time available. This was the height of the tourist
season in Honolulu and one can only guess at the trauma that
seized the front offices of two of the leading hotels when they were
informed that they had twenty-four hours to prepare appropriate
quarters for a Summit Conference.

At almost the last moment on Thursday it was discovered that
the Vietnamese Ambassador to Washington, Vu Van Thai, had not
been told of the conference. A hurried call was made, and he was
told to make his own transportation arrangements. But on Saturday morning, as the President's plane was warming up, it was
agreed that it would be a nice gesture to ask the Vietnamese Ambassador to accompany the President's party. The Ambassador
raced madly from his home in Chevy Chase to Andrews Field and
barely made the plane.

Part of the advance work for most high-level international conferences is the preparation of a draft "Final Communique." Since
most such conferences are fairly predictable in outcome, and since
there is frequently little time to do much drafting once a conference is under way, it is prudent and expeditious to dispose of the
Communique problem well before the meetings start. On this occasion, the communique-drafting chore was postponed until we
were airborne. On the staff plane, free from phone calls, meetings,
and unexpected visitors, we could churn out a considerable
amount of work.

The document in mind for Honolulu was to include more than
just the routine stuff about how "the two leaders met and agreed
that it was their responsibility to preserve and protect, etc., etc."
The haste with which the meeting had been thrown together

should not mask the fact that it was a dramatic occasion; it was the first time the leaders of the United States and South Vietnam were to meet, and they were each traveling thousands of miles to discuss grave matters. On the level of substance rather than public relations, the meeting was important because there were several key issues Washington had been pressing Saigon to address. If they could be clearly enunciated in a solemn statement of purpose, we might at long last get the South Vietnamese to feel a genuine sense of commitment rather than to fob the issues off with the usual bland assurances. Thus on the top of the first page was scribbled the working title "The Pact of Honolulu" (it was subsequently changed to the more felicitous, "Declaration of Honolulu"). The objectives of the United States and the South Vietnamese Governments were then carefully spelled out. Heavy emphasis was placed on South Vietnamese economic, political, and social reforms, the holding of bona fide elections throughout South Vietnam, and a policy of welcoming back to the government's side those who would leave the ranks of the Viet Cong. In discussions with Saigon's representatives after we arrived at Honolulu there was a surprising amount of agreement—or at least acquiescence—with the American draft, and the final document looked very much like the one prepared on the plane.

In accord with the President's original notion of having the Honolulu meeting be a counterpoint to the increasingly dominant theme of military escalation, the emphasis was placed on economic development, social progress, rural reconstruction, and a readiness to negotiate a political settlement. Secretary of Agriculture Freeman and Secretary of Health, Education, and Welfare Gardner had been brought along to add verisimilitude and resonance to the non-military tone.

General Ky was clearly the star performer of the entire show. He made a major speech which expressed determination to proceed with a non-Communist economic and social revolution. He stressed Saigon's readiness to continue "the search for peace" but added that it was "necessary to demonstrate to the Communists that we do not intend to negotiate from a position of weakness."

In a particularly effective passage Ky emphasized the political challenge facing the Saigon Government:

> I do not mean that we have to cure every one of our ills before we go to the peace table. But we must have a record of considerable [sic] more progress than we have been able to accomplish so far. We must . . . create a society which will be able to withstand the false appeals of communism. We must create a society where each individual . . . can feel that he has a future, that he has respect and dignity, and that he has some chance for himself and for his children to live in an atmosphere where all is not disappointment, despair and dejection.[9]

Ky then described an ambitious list of specific projects which were already under way or contemplated. He emphasized the success of the Saigon Government's program to rally defectors from the Viet Cong, and he closed with a gracious acknowledgment of American sacrifices and an expression of gratitude for American support.

It was an excellent speech—the best made at the conference. Ky sold himself to the Americans as a progressive and farsighted statesman. Considering that the speech had been drafted on the way to Honolulu from Saigon, it was a real tour de force. The man who had written Ky's speech was an old friend of mine. Over drinks later that day I congratulated him and then queried him on something I had been musing about for several hours. The speech seemed especially tailored for Johnson's ears; it contained all the right ingredients, from rural electrification to low-cost housing; the approach to negotiations was a judicious balance between a readiness to talk and a need to negotiate from strength. Was Ky's speech based largely on the texts of President Johnson's own speeches? My friend nodded vigorously and triumphantly.

There was a Final Communique as well as the "Declaration." In the Communique, too, emphasis was on non-military problems, especially on the need to move forward with plans for improving the situation in the countryside. Particular reference was made in the Communique to the agreement to concentrate American and Vietnamese resources "in selected priority areas which are properly related to military plans so that the work of rural construction can be protected against disruption by the enemy."

The conference was a success both in terms of reaching significant decisions and of establishing closer working relations between the top levels of the two governments. The Saigon Government, Ky especially, improved its image in the United States. But there was, nevertheless, a persistent feeling in Washington that the Administration had hastily contrived the whole affair to direct public attention from the bombing resumption. In addition many felt the Honolulu meeting had been a gimmick to steal the spotlight from Senator Fulbright, whose Foreign Relations Committee was just about to start a new round of Hearings on the Administration's Vietnam policy. The latter suspicion was given added credibility by the President's sudden decision on the last day of the Honolulu Conference to send Vice President Humphrey on a trip to Asia to "explain" the developments at Honolulu. Although this had the impromptu quality that characterized the decision to convene the conference itself, there was actually a need for some high-level explanations to the many governments in the region that were worried about the Honolulu meeting. This applied particularly to our "third country" allies in Vietnam who were annoyed at not having been invited.

Since Humphrey had not been at the conference, he was given a difficult and awkward assignment. The fact that he had only a few hours notice and that he would be accompanied by two members of the President's personal coterie, Jack Valenti and Lloyd Hand (then Chief of Protocol in the Department of State), and the knowledge that they would be likely to make private reports to Johnson must have added little lustre to the prospects of the trip as far as the Vice President was concerned. The addition of Averell Harriman and Leonard Marks (Chief of USIA) weighted the party down with heavy brass.

The Vice President's plane met "Air Force One" in California where the President gave Humphrey a quick rundown on the talks. Humphrey then proceeded west to Honolulu where he had a few hours sleep, was given another short briefing, and picked up the Honolulu contingent. After a comic opera interlude of confussion and indecision, I was sped to the Vice President's plane (with my baggage hopelessly lost in the pile of luggage destined for Washington) to accompany the Humphrey party. Tempers of the Johnson and Humphrey staffs had gotten pretty short by the time I happily waved goodbye at Bangkok and, I understand, became even more so as the trip progressed.

To those skeptics and spoil-sports who suspected the President's motives in calling the conference, Johnson insisted that a meeting in Honolulu had been planned for several months. He was neither altogether right nor wrong. In the summer of 1965 a colleague and I suggested that the President participate in a ceremony marking the fifth anniversary of the East–West Center in Honolulu and the investiture of its new head, Howard Jones, ex-Ambassador to Indonesia and friend of Sukarno. We felt the President's presence at the ceremony would warrant invitations to all Asian leaders and that the occasion would provide an opportunity for private talks with them, but particularly with Sukarno who was being especially troublesome at the time. Although the President rejected the idea, this was probably the "conference" he had in mind many months later when he parried with reporters about the timing of his meeting with Ky and Thieu.

Whether the President intended it or not, the Honolulu Conference and Humphrey's trip took front-page space away from the Hearings of the Senate Foreign Relations Committee. Senator Fulbright pressed ahead, nonetheless. He mounted a parade of star witnesses, including Secretary Rusk and Ambassador Taylor. On this occasion the Secretary put major emphasis on the Southeast Asia Treaty of 1954 as the legal basis for the American intervention in Vietnam, which did little to enhance the Administration's credibility. Ambassador Taylor's testimony that the United States intended to wage a limited war in Vietnam, followed shortly after by his call for mining Haiphong Harbor—a move that was never taken for the very reason that it would almost certainly risk expansion of the war—did not advance the cause either.

The President's post-Honolulu press conference, Humphrey's trip, and Senator Fulbright's Hearings were giving the American public during the late winter of 1966 more than their usual heavy daily dosage of news and official comment about Vietnam. But even more was soon to come. In a major speech on Vietnam policy, Senator Robert Kennedy kicked up a storm with his recommendation that the National Liberation Front be included in a postwar Vietnamese government. Cries of outrage and anguish from Washington and Saigon followed on the heels of Kennedy's suggestion. From the other side of the world Humphrey sounded the alarm: this would be just the first step in the complete takeover of a Vietnam government by the Communists. At a news conference in Wellington, New Zealand on February 21 he denounced Senator Kennedy's suggestion, saying that the proposal was "a prescription for the ills of South Vietnam which includes a dose of arsenic."

I must admit to having been annoyed myself. Kennedy's remarks may not seem very far-reaching in the light of developments since, but they were mischief-making at the time. The issue of NLF representation had been addressed in the Fourteen Points for Peace prepared by Secretary Rusk a couple of months before: "The President has said 'The Viet Cong would not have difficulty being represented and having their views represented if for a moment Hanoi decided she wanted to cease aggression. I don't think that would be an insurmountable problem.' " Anything more specific could be worked out with the Communists through negotiations. Kennedy encouraged the NLF to believe that their participation in a post-settlement government could now be taken for granted, rather than be a subject for negotiation. He had discarded a high card even before we sat down at the table. Kennedy himself recognized he had made a gaffe and amended his statement a day or two later. What he really meant, he said, was that the Liberation Front should not be "automatically excluded" from sharing power in any postwar regime.

❀   ❀   ❀

Lyndon Johnson's critics have claimed that the escalation of the war was a conscious policy of his Administration. For his part Johnson was at pains to point out that whatever new military moves were made, whether it was the deployment of American combat troops or the use of B–52s, they were not only consistent with his current policy but were a logical extension of the policies of the past three Administrations. Whether this was in fact the case, the war and American policy with respect to it seemed to have had a momentum of their own. Thus on March 2nd, 1966 McNamara announced that there were over 215,000 American troops in Vietnam, and another 20,000 were on the way. South Korea and Australia were sending more troops. Congress approved yet another supplemental appropriation for Vietnam—this time for $4.8 billion.

Despite the allied efforts, General Westmoreland noted that in February "the war in the northern provinces assumed a new and ominous aspect as two North Vietnamese Army divisions threatened invasion across the Demilitarized Zone." [10] There were those who said that this new threat to South Vietnam was a direct result of the six-week bombing pause of late December and January. Others pointed out, with some validity, that even though bombing intensified throughout the spring, with new targets being hit and the area of attack inching northward to include the cities of Haiphong and Hanoi, the movement of men and supplies to the South steadily increased.

By the end of April American officials were estimating that infiltration of North Vietnamese troops into South Vietnam had reached 5,500 men per month, and Secretary McNamara warned that the United States would have to deploy additional forces to keep pace with the increased infiltration. The numbers game went on and on: we attacked North Vietnam with more and more sorties every month; the North Vietnamese continued to increase their flow of men and supplies into the South; the fighting intensified; American forces had to be expanded; Congress was obliged to provide additional funds. And so it went.

But as troublesome as the new North Vietnamese reinforcements were, developments within South Vietnam were even more disturbing. Soon after Vice President Humphrey concluded his visit to South Vietnam, the Buddhist threat to the authority of the Saigon Government became more serious than at any time since the overthrow of President Diem more than two years before. The events of March and April were to some extent a direct aftermath of the Honolulu Conference. General Ky's speech was impressive to Western ears, but "social justice," "land reform," "security in the countryside" were now part of a political liturgy the Vietnamese had heard countless times before. In any case political stability in Saigon could not be achieved through promises of rural electrification. What actually happened was that the Honolulu Conference had fed the rivalries and jealousies within the new group of political-minded generals.

I had a sense of foreboding after I returned to Washington and discussed the conference with my good friend Ambassador Vu Van Thai. He said somewhat cryptically that he wished "all" the key generals had been included in the Vietnamese delegation to Honolulu. His meaning became more clear when General Thi, a leading member of the military junta who had not been invited to Honolulu, began to take an increasingly independent line. As a Corps commander and a native of the key northern part of South Vietnam, he was in a position, much like the old Chinese warlords, to develop an important power base virtually independent of the national capital. He proceeded to do just that. By March the situation reached a point where Ky and his Saigon colleagues decided that a showdown was necessary. Thi was not only ignoring or disobeying orders from the capital, he was also becoming a formidable rival for Ky's own post. The powerful Buddhist hierarchy centered in Hue had long been spoiling for a fight with Saigon. They now found an issue, for Thi had been their champion and patron, and his dismissal by Ky sparked a series of violent confrontations between the Saigon Government and the students and Buddhists.

*   *   *

By mid-1965 I had been feeling increasingly uncomfortable with both the President's general style and the momentum of escalation in Vietnam. I had made up my mind to leave on March 1 but agreed to stay an extra month, because Bundy himself was leaving in March. Thus in early April, 1966 I took what was euphemistically described as a "year's sabbatical." I had little intention of returning to the White House, and I had no illusion that the

White House was panting for my return. One White House staff
member patronizingly assured me that I was "not in the Boss's
Black Book" but that I was in the "Gray Book."

I accepted a research position that gave me an opportunity to
do something unique—think, read, reflect. As a result some of my
views with respect to Vietnam—viscerally reached and perhaps ineffectually articulated during the previous year or two—now began
to take on a somewhat different perspective. An important influence on my thinking was a twice-a-day exposure to the reality of
the war. Each day on the way to and from my new office, I passed
an addition to Arlington Cemetery. The handful of fresh graves I
noticed in early April multiplied to several score before the month
was over. Soon roads and footpaths were being constructed. Before
long there was a battalion of white headstones. The daily drive began to take on the character of a macabre ceremony. I sometimes
tried to bring myself to change my route but at the last moment
compulsively drove by the Cemetery. The morning news, with its
box score of casualties, took on a new significance; here was an
"Actual Body Count" that had real meaning.

About a week after I left the White House I sent a letter to
Walt Rostow (who had taken over Bundy's job) offering some
gratuitous parting advice. I did not expect a reply, and I did not
get one. "The Vietnamese must be reminded in a way that gets
through to them," I wrote, "that this is their war not ours; that we
will continue to help them only if they are ready to help themselves. In the last analysis, the only effective sanction we have is
the ultimate sanction of US withdrawal. But for this sanction to
be effective:

> 1. The sanction must be credible; we must be prepared to fol-
> low through, and the Vietnamese must know we are so prepared,
> if our conditions (a political shape-up, for example) are not met.
> 2. The GVN and politically influential Vietnamese must be
> genuinely interested in carrying on the war, so that the prospect of
> an American withdrawal would be a meaningful and unwelcome
> one.
> 3. We must carefully prepare the way for both the announce-

ment of our terms and our determination—with the Vietnamese, with our allies, with the American people.

4. We must exact a price from the Communists for our withdrawal—if withdrawal is the course we choose (admittedly easier said than done).

"One could make a case that an opportunity to disengage is one that should be planned for rather than planned against; a close examination of the pros and cons might well net out pro. If we left Vietnam under circumstances in which we had clearly demonstrated our fighting superiority over Communist military forces and at the request of a government we had offered to help as long as they wanted us, US prestige would not suffer. In fact, I believe quite the reverse."

❋   ❋   ❋

During most of the spring the Viet Cong received little time and attention from the Saigon Government. Although the Vietnam war was referred to by some (usually those opposed to American policy) as a "civil war," and by others (usually those supporting the President) as a "war against external aggression," there was no question of semantics with respect to the confrontation between the Saigon Government and the Buddhists. That was a civil war. In May a paper, prepared in the State Department, was sent to the President. It set forth the argument that the Buddhist crisis warranted our posing stiff political conditions for the Saigon Government, which if they were not met would give us a justifiable reason for disengaging. The suggestion was given only passing notice. In any case, the Buddhist troubles had subsided by early June, and the war against the Communists was renewed with increased fury.

Although the Buddhist crisis had virtually halted major ground operations, especially in the area north of Saigon, it had had no effect on the air raids on North Vietnam; bombing continued throughout the spring. Nonetheless, as McNamara noted, the number of North Vietnamese units in South Vietnam had doubled between the end of 1965 and June 1966. According to General

Westmoreland, "as enemy forces increased, so too did the quality of enemy arms." [11] To meet this threat the United States by June had deployed 265,000 troops; 18,000 more were on the way. In addition approximately 50,000 American naval personnel were in the area.

McNamara's reference to the increase in infiltration despite American bombing was a signal that major new measures against North Vietnam would be necessary. In late June oil installations in the area of Haiphong and Hanoi were attacked. This new step, which only a month before the Secretary of the Air Force had said had been rejected by the President, brought the bombing to North Vietnam's major population centers. Hanoi claimed large civilian casualties. A letter explaining the reason for the raids, which Ambassador Goldberg attempted without success to deliver to his Soviet colleague at the United Nations, did nothing to dampen the world-wide and domestic outcry. Speaking before it became known that civilian casualties had been remarkably low, Prime Minister Wilson publicly disassociated himself from the American action. Wilson's protestations to the President about his problems in the House of Commons got little sympathy from Johnson, who himself was experiencing mounting trouble with Congress. Wilson's protestations got even less sympathy from the Governments of Australia and New Zealand; having twice sent troops half way around the world to help Britain, they thought the Prime Minister should have sent military forces to Vietnam—or at lease should not prescribe what to bomb.

The President described the raids against the oil installations as extremely successful. According to Johnson the attacks had hit 86 percent of North Vietnam's known oil storage capacity and destroyed 57 percent.[12] This proved to be a highly optimistic claim, and many more attacks had to be mounted against North Vietnam's petroleum storage and distribution facilities. Wags in Washington were soon referring to some targets in North Vietnam as having been "320 percent destroyed." Johnson's claims were characteristic of a new sense of optimism in Washington. Under-Secretary of State George Ball told the Senate Foreign Relations Committee on June 30 that the decision to attack the oil storage areas reflected a sense of "real encouragement" about military progress in South Vietnam and "weakening morale" in the North.[13]

Despite these raids, Hanoi was able to continue to meet its minimum military and civilian needs through improvisation and rationing. The North Vietnamese established underground storage sites and distributed thousands of small oil drums near key industrial and military centers. And despite the attacks on the Haiphong docks, Admiral Sharp noted that "tankers continued to arrive and discharge their cargo into lighters and barges that made deliveries to inland transshipment points and south along the coast." According to Sharp, this pattern continued until the bombing was stopped altogether in 1968.[14]

The optimistic and extravagant claims of previous years had proved to be unfounded and counter-productive, and the bullish statements about the effect of the bombing raids again stimulated public skepticism—all the more so, since Hanoi showed neither an inclination to discuss peace nor a significant diminution in its ability to wage war. American forces were increasingly taking the offensive in Vietnam during the spring of 1966, but the Administration was obliged more and more to take defensive positions at home. With every new request for additional funds to meet the mounting cost of the war, it was more difficult to satisfy members of Congress and a growing number of American people that the Administration's policy was leading to either a political or a military solution. Nonetheless few legislators were prepared to go so far in their opposition to Administration policy as to vote against funds for equipping American troops, and a request by the President for an additional $12.8 billion was approved.

*   *   *

The spring produced a bountiful number and variety of proposals put forward to stimulate a Washington–Hanoi dialogue. Mrs. Ghandi, Tito, Nasser, Wilson, U Thant, Eden, and a host of others were busily engaged in trying to bring the war to an end. Washington greeted virtually all of these efforts with patient forebearance and, on occasion, even active encouragement. But Hanoi would have no part of any of them, although the burden of almost every proposal was that the U.S. should make initial, unconditional, and major concessions.

The President was well aware of the need to project his keen interest in a political settlement. To this end, in the summer of 1966 he appointed Ambassador-at-Large Averell Harriman to be "in charge of peace," in addition to his other duties. The President's handling of the appointment was a classic example of Johnsonian style. He announced that Harriman would be his top peacemaker, but he sent him nothing in writing with respect to his new responsibilities. This neither bothered nor deterred Harriman. In fact, he liked it that way. Once he got a "go" signal, he preferred to work out his own mandate and then to move forward with virtually unlimited energy.

Harriman asked me to assist him. I agreed and moved to the Department of State in August. That was the least I could do for what was now a regiment of silent, daily reminders of the cost of continued fighting.

The Ambassador was not then a member of the White House inner circle, and there were many of the President's principal advisers who would have wished to keep the sensitive issue of negotiations under their own tight control. It was generally acknowledged that Harriman's appointment was good for the Administration's image, but there was some concern that he would not be satisfied to accept a mere cosmetic role. If the task was to assume any meaning, it soon became clear that Harriman would have to do much of the job with little White House help. He was not asked to participate in the President's "Tuesday Lunches" at which, of course, the Vietnam decisions were made. As a consequence many of the initiatives Harriman was attempting to develop were out of phase with military decisions. This arms-length relationship with the White House continued until shortly before Harriman was sent to Paris in May, 1968.

In May, 1966 Harriman had been given the responsibility for dealing with the problem of American prisoners in North Vietnam. During the summer he organized a major diplomatic and propaganda effort to convince the North Vietnamese leaders that their announced intention to try captured American pilots as war criminals would be a dangerous course. Until then Hanoi had virtually ignored international opinion, but the combined efforts of world leaders and the Administration resulted in Hanoi's changing its mind on the prisoner matter. On July 23 Ho Chi Minh, in response to a telegram from the President of the Columbia Broadcasting System, said "no trial was in view for American prisoners."

＊　　＊　　＊

During the summer of 1966 the Thais had advanced the idea of an All-Asian Peace Conference, but the countries of the area had such diverse views and interests that nothing meaningful seemed likely to emerge. President Marcos of the Philippines then put forward the idea of a more limited meeting—one that would concentrate on the immediate problems of Veitnam, with participation confined to those countries assisting the Government of Saigon. This appealed to Washington. With all the pressures—both international and domestic—to move toward negotiations, it was becoming increasingly apparent that it was necessary to achieve high-level coordination on the part of the seven countries fighting in Vietnam. There had been bilateral talks between Johnson and the leaders of the other troop-contributing countries, and the periodic SEATO meetings permitted multilateral talks at the Foreign Minister level, but there had thus far been no opportunity for joint discussions at the top level. It was high time for a summit meeting. And for President Johnson, with Congressional elections imminent, this was an especially propitious time.

After much backstage maneuvering, a scenario was worked out in which President Marcos would "call for" the conference and President Johnson would "accept the invitation." The President was anxious that the United States should not dominate the proceedings. He intended to play his own role in a low key and insisted that the official Washington delegation be kept very small. A large number of White House staff members, along with some personal advisers (including ex-staff member Jack Valenti), would accompany him to Manila but would be kept in the background. In short, the American delegation would be but one among equals. When the President announced he would attend the Manila Conference, he also revealed his plans to tour several countries in the region.

By the eve of the Manila Conference, Hanoi and Washington were both imbedded in concrete on the issue of a bombing halt. We had said that we would not stop the bombing unless we knew in advance precisely "what Hanoi would do" in return—and by this we were then thinking specifically of a halt in the movement of North Vietnamese men and supplies into South Vietnam. Hanoi, however, would give no advance assurances, although it was implied through third parties that "something" would happen. In an informal "working paper" prepared prior to leaving for Manila, I suggested that a possible way out of this impasse might be to separate the two parts of the problem in a way that would give both Washington and Hanoi what they were seeking. In brief, we would stop the bombing on the basis of prior private assurances that shortly thereafter (probably in no less than two weeks but no more than three) Hanoi and Washington would agree to halt reinforcements into South Vietnam. (Subsequent versions of the formula used the more general term "de-escalatory actions," rather than "halting reinforcements.") Under such an arrangement Hanoi would achieve a bombing halt, ostensibly "without conditions"; Washington would swap a no-reinforcement arrangement for a similar commitment on the part of the North Vietnamese. With more than 300,000 American troops and a total allied force of more than a million men already in Vietnam, this would be a prudent deal—especially if negotations could start soon. Granted, there was no guarantee that Hanoi would keep its side of the bargain, but our intelligence was adequate enough to detect consequential cheating.

The question of American bombing was not addressed in Manila. Later in the autumn and in the following winter, however, the "Phase A (we stop bombing)—Phase B (de-escalatory actions)" formula was to play an interesting role in several major attempts to end the war.

The Chiefs of Government of South Vietnam, the United States, Australia, New Zealand, Thailand, and South Korea converged upon Manila on October 24th. The Philippine Government had done a remarkable job in coping with protocol and security arrangements—no simple matter considering that Marcos had six Great Men on his hands. Each VIP was to land at Manila airport at a predesignated moment and would travel an identical route from the airport to his hotel. The landings were spaced carefully so that, after the airport welcome, each motorcade could proceed with equal pomp and ceremony.

President Johnson was one of the early arrivals, and all went according to plan until almost the last moment of his journey from tarmac to Presidential suite. Watching from my window just above the street, I saw the convoy of outriders and limousines turn from the boulevard into the street leading to the hotel. It was right on schedule. The corner was an especially good vantage point for spectators, because the automobiles had to slow down as they rounded the corner and because there was ample parkland on each side of the street for rest and refreshment between delegations. The thousands of people assembled at this point presented too great a temptation for Johnson to resist. He ordered his car to stop and then emerged into the crowd to "press flesh." The police lines and the Secret Service were unable to cope with the mass of spectators who rushed to get a closer view. When police reinforcements eventually got matters back in hand, the somewhat shaken President was returned to his car and the motorcade resumed its journey. Johnson (and presumably the Secret Service) had had his share of Filipino exuberance. Much to the annoyance of the photographers who had been unable to get close enough to the melee for pictures and had returned to wait impatiently at the hotel entrance, the President's car dashed around to the baggage door at the rear. The schedule for the rest of the VIPs, some of whom had been stacked up in the skies above Manila, was thrown into complete disarray. The image the President had hoped to project of the U.S. being just one of the seven participating countries had been somewhat tarnished before the conference started.

The two primary purposes of the Manila Conference were to come to grips with the problems of a negotiated settlement and to project some lofty plans for the economic development of the Pacific area. While at this point in time the latter was more of a vague idea than a substantive matter, the former was by no means a pro forma exercise. Aside from some basic differences among the conferees, there was the problem of inducing the Saigon Government to take the lead in thinking about peace.

The South Vietnamese leaders had thus far done little planning for negotiations. This was hardly surprising, since they had much to lose and little to gain if negotiations started at an early date. Moreover they were so preoccupied with the day-to-day problems of the war that they barely had time to prepare for negotiations even if they wished to do so; even our own government had done little substantive work on the question of a political settlement. Sometime in 1965 Foreign Minister Tran Van Do had announced a South Vietnamese peace program, but after a few days no more was heard of it. Hanoi for its part had kept its four-point plan in the forefront of the news, and the NLF had been able to keep its own program very much alive. It was important, therefore, to develop forthcoming and clear-cut proposals that the Saigon Government could use as its own touchstone.

Since "Point Programs" were in mode (Hanoi's "Four Points," the NLF's "Ten Points," and Washington's "Fourteen Points"), it was decided that the GVN should have its own "x Point Proposal." I had been given the task of preparing a statement which it was hoped the South Vietnamese would take over as their own and with which the other delegations would associate themselves. The draft was prepared between water and sky as the staff plane moved westward.

A series of propositions were worked up which divided rather neatly into "Six Points." The draft attempted to develop a realistic but forthcoming series of proposals that would give the South Vietnamese Government a badly-needed boost in world public opinion and, much more importantly, commit Saigon to a program that would advance the day of political settlement. This was not a simple chore; the Vietnamese leaders were more sensitive than we to the implications of a negotiated settlement. On the rare occasions they talked about this, they revealed their convictions that it would take another five years before the non-Communists could be molded into a group sufficiently strong and cohesive to compete politically with their tightly knit, strongly motivated rivals. If the South Vietnamese were going to do more than pay grudging lip service to a package of peace proposals, it would have to be one they were genuinely ready to accept.

There were three specifics we were anxious to incorporate into the GVN proposal: a commitment to move ahead with a program of "national reconciliation," * a readiness to subscribe to the essence of the Geneva Agreements of 1954, and a recognition that American forces were not going to be in Vietnam indefinitely. The Saigon leadership accepted the first of these as originally drafted (although after months of backing and filling they did nothing to implement it). They rejected the second after a long and bitter argument on the grounds that they did not sign and would not commit themselves to the 1954 Agreements. The United States, Hanoi, and the NLF had already gone on record as subscribing to the "spirit," or the "essence," or the "substance" of the Agreements, and our proposed wording committed Saigon to do little more than genuflect in the direction of Geneva.

The third issue, the withdrawal of American troops, was the most dramatic and difficult of the conference. Throughout the summer of 1966 the Administration became increasingly aware of the need to assure the American public that the flow of Americans to Vietnam would someday be halted and then reversed. The President's constant calls for more troops and more money and the pronouncements about a long war were putting many Democratic Congressmen, especially those from the Northern urban areas, in jeopardy as the November elections approached. But more than this, the President's professed readiness to engage in "mutual withdrawal" seemed now to call for more specific and credible assurances, not only for Hanoi's ears but for those of our critical friends in allied and neutral countries.

The most appropriate way to get this point across would be to

---

* The Joint Statement issued at the conference described "National Reconciliation" as a program "to open all doors to those Vietnamese who have been misled or coerced into casting their lot with the Viet Cong. The Government seeks to bring them back to participate as free men in national life under amnesty and other measures. Former enemies are asked only to lay down their weapons and bring their skills to the service of the South Vietnamese people."

have it come from the South Vietnamese. Thus in the six point draft we prepared for the Saigon Government's consideration, the South Vietnamese were to ask for the withdrawal of American forces and the closing or turnover of American military installations as soon as it became clear that the Communist threat no longer existed or could be handled by the South Vietnamese themselves. As a companion piece an American statement was prepared in which the U.S. promised to close out its military presence. The wording of both draft statements was argued over at some length on the staff plane. The proposal, we felt, had to be direct, simple, and unequivocal. On the other hand, it had to be sufficiently realistic and prudent to be acceptable to the hard-pressed South Vietnamese and to have a ring of credibility to a skeptical world. In due course, someplace over the Pacific we worked out a statement that seemed to meet those requirements.

The first sign of trouble came from a member of the President's personal entourage soon after we had landed in Manila. He had seen our draft and felt that the withdrawal proposal was too long and too cautious to meet the President's needs. Something "short and snappy" that would "get the headlines" was necessary. I protested that the issue of troop withdrawal was a fundamental and tricky one; it would be better to present it in a form we could live with than to try for a brief publicity splash, even if this meant it would have to be dealt with more prosaically. The President's public relations-minded friend shrugged, but I had an uncomfortable feeling that the matter would be raised again. It was.

After the close of the plenary session on the afternoon of the first day, the working level on the American delegation was told to prepare a final draft communique, including the question of troop withdrawal, and then hammer it out later that evening with our colleagues from the other six countries. As we were leaving for our meeting with the other delegations, the President called. The headline hunters had had their day. Johnson wanted something "dramatic" on American troop withdrawals and wished to make a commitment that all American troops would "leave Vietnam within six months" after Hanoi had taken its troops out. I learned later that the period originally suggested was three months, but as a result of some hasty calls to the Pentagon, the President agreed to a time frame of six months as being the shortest practicable period for an orderly withdrawal.

We did not know whether the President had discussed the six-month formula with his senior advisers, but it was obvious that none of the chiefs of the other delegations at Manila had been informed. We had already girded ourselves for some heavy going with our fellow delegates on many aspects of our draft, as we had received some inkling that the South Vietnamese and South Koreans were worried about our wording on negotiations and were even more worried about the issue of troop withdrawals. If we advanced the six-month proposition at this point, we were sure nothing could be gained, since none of the representatives at the level we would be dealing with had authority to accept it. We decided to touch base with Secretary Rusk and urge him to postpone surfacing the new "dramatic" proposal until after we had resolved the other points and had had a chance to explore the six-month gambit more carefully. Moreover we felt this proposal was one the President himself would first have to discuss with the other Heads of Government. Rusk agreed to put the formula on ice until early the following morning and suggested we reach agreement on the communique as it presently stood.

It was just as well that we had postponed confronting our allies with the six-month bombshell. Even our more generalized version of the communique's withdrawal section involved hours of haggling with the Vietnamese, Thais, and South Koreans. Well after midnight, wording along the lines of the original American draft was accepted: The South Vietnamese would ask that the allied forces be withdrawn and their bases be dismantled as the North Vietnamese forces were withdrawn "and peace thus becomes possible in South Vietnam." The paragraph then went on to acknowledge the right of every country to rely on its own resources to maintain peace and security within its borders.

At breakfast the next day we met with Secretary Rusk to consider the new withdrawal proposal. Our instincts of the night before were amply justified; the President's statement had been hastily prepared by someone with a feeling for the dramatic,

rather than an eye to the long-range political and military implications of a commitment that would be hard if not impossible
to meet. We finally arrived at a somewhat improved version:
". . . Allied forces are in the Republic of Vietnam because that
country is the object of aggression and its government requested
support in the resistance of its people to aggression. They shall
be withdrawn as the other side withdraws its forces to the North,
ceases infiltration, and the level of violence thus subsides. Those
forces will be withdrawn as soon as possible and not later than
six months after the above conditions have been fulfilled."

The next problem was to work out the least troublesome way
of presenting the new formula to the six other delegations. It was
the final day of the conference, and the agenda consisted solely
of formal closing speeches and ceremonial remarks. As far as the
other delegations knew, all substantive questions had been dealt
with the night before. The President and Secretary Rusk decided
to request a private meeting of Heads of Government and Foreign Ministers. If there were to be any violent eruptions it would
be best to confine them to the smallest group possible.

As a result of the pre-meeting activities of the American delegation, the plenary session opened well behind schedule and was
adjourned almost immediately so that the restricted talks could
get underway. There was an air of foreboding in the ballroom of
the Palace as those excluded from the executive session hung
around aimlessly and restlessly. The Americans were constrained
from revealing the subject of the high-level conversations and tried
to make idle conversation with irritated colleagues. During the few
minutes I was present at the private meeting to deal with a technical question that had arisen, I was aware of considerable tension
and so was not surprised to learn later that the going had not been
easy for the President. Eventually the Great Men emerged. The
paragraph on Allied troop withdrawals was adopted with the in-
sertion of the phrase "after close consultation." The plenary resumed. The scheduled speeches would have been anticlimactic in
any case, but they were now even more so. Then the closing remarks, then smiling photographs, and Manila Finis.

The President and his advisers were right. The headlines after the conference were devoted to the six-month withdrawal pledge: "U.S. AND ALLIES PLEDGE TO LEAVE SOUTH VIETNAM WITHIN 6 MONTHS AFTER HANOI ABANDONS THE WAR," trumpeted *The New York Times* on October 26.

The six-month formula was easier to expound than to explain. One of its most troublesome aspects was the implication that the American pull-out would be based on the withdrawal of North Vietnamese troops and that Saigon would be left alone to continue the fight with the Viet Cong. Since American forces were originally sent to Vietnam because South Vietnamese government troops were unable to cope with the insurgents, the skeptics asked, would not their withdrawal simply result in status quo ante? No, the government spokesmen said; the key to the whole formula could be found in the word *thus* in the sentence, "[Allied forces] shall be withdrawn as the other side withdraws its forces to the North, ceases infiltration, and the violence thus subsides."

The American delegation itself was never very confident that we would stand aside as Saigon slugged it out with Viet Cong forces. Some members, especially on the working level, felt that in fact we had committed ourselves to do just that. There was a feeling that by this time the South Vietnamese Armed Forces could deal with an insurgency scaled down to the level of 1964. And in any case, it was thought that the mutual pull-out should be regarded primarily as an important step toward negotiations and a political settlement, rather than as a way of continuing the war. No one, of course, was so naive as to think that Hanoi would withdraw the North Vietnamese "fillers" and cadres from the Viet Cong units or that we would even know with confidence how many were left behind in either category.

Adding to the imprecision of the Manila Formula was the absence of any reference to a bombing halt. A realistic and practical way of dealing with this question was the missing link in the projected chain of events from fighting to negotiating. Unless a way was found, the prospect for a mutual withdrawal of Allied and North Vietnamese troops seemed very remote. We were soon to be reminded of this omission by many world leaders.

On the day following the conference, President Johnson made

a quick trip to Vietnam where he visited American forces. He made no reference to the Manila Formula for troop withdrawal. His message was simple and direct. The Americans are going to stay in Vietnam, the President said, until we can "nail the coonskin" to the wall. If this smacked of a return to the military victory track as opposed to a negotiated solution, neither the President nor his audience seemed concerned.

The President then set off for a series of visits to America's Pacific allies. The theme of his journey was already expressed in that part of the Manila communique dealing with regional development and economic growth. His trip was intended to be an earnest of America's stake in the Pacific area. The President was not purveying idle hopes and empty words; some important steps, notably the organization of the Asian Development Bank under Eugene Black, had already been taken. But as sincere the motives, as high-minded the concept, as important the idea, there was difficulty in maintaining momentum of interest and action. The air was so full of rhetoric (and of VIPs flying from one capital to another) that lofty speeches and grand designs had only a brief half-life. The word-merchants rather than the program planners seemed to be in charge. The programs did not (and frequently could not) meet the ambitious goals that had been announced with such flair and color. Some of them, in fact, never got beyond the pencil and foolscap stage: high-level interest waned, costs were out of reach, or the basic concept sounded fine to the ear but was just not realistic (the Pacific "region," for example, is a vast area facing the Pacific Ocean, but it is not a "region" in the sense that practicable regional economic or even political programs could be drawn up and implemented).

In the weeks that followed, the six-month withdrawal formula became more and more convoluted and less credible. "The key word is *thus*," various low-level briefers and high-level officials intoned to the press and government leaders both at home and abroad. If the North Vietnamese forces withdrew, presumably a reduction of the violence would almost automatically take place; if the violence did not subside, allied forces would remain in Vietnam. But maybe not. We would have to see.

Like a passage from Shakespeare, each new reading of the withdrawal formula brought forth hitherto hidden meanings and nuances. American Congressmen and correspondents, to say nothing of foreign audiences, would nod solemnly as they were given the standard explanation, but one could later catch quizzical looks exchanged and shoulders shrugged. *Thus* became the most subtle term in the English language; never had so much been demanded of one four letter word.

A few weeks later, on election eve, Johnson removed some of the uncertainties with respect to *thus*: removal of Hanoi's troops, he implied, would have to result in a "cessation" rather than a "subsidence" of violence. "We have explained that we would pull out just as soon as the infiltration, the aggression, and the violence ceases. We made that statement and we set a time limit on it. Why would we want to stay there if there was no aggression, if there was no infiltration and the violence ceased? We wouldn't want to stay there as tourists. . . ." [15]

As election day approached, Richard Nixon also spoke out on the withdrawal formula. On November 3, in an appraisal of the Manila Conference, Nixon said: "On the surface, a commitment to mutual withdrawal appears to be a reasonable approach toward de-escalation. But, on reflection, mutual withdrawal of North Vietnam and United States troops simply turns back the clock two years and says 'let the South Vietnamese fight it out with the Vietcong.' . . . Does this new Manila proposal for mutual withdrawal by the U.S. and North Vietnam mean that we are now willing to stand aloof and let the future of the South Vietnamese be determined by the victor of a military contest between the Vietcong and the Government of South Vietnam? If this is a proper interpretation of the Manila communique, our endorsement jeopardizes every strategic American objective in Vietnam." [16]

* * *

Immediately following the Manila Conference, Averell Harriman was asked to visit several allied and unaligned capitals to "explain Manila" to the Heads of Government. He was instructed not to visit countries on the President's list, or Japan and Taiwan (Assistant Secretary William Bundy was going there), or the Soviet Union and Eastern Europe. Beyond this he was given no itinerary and no timetable. Harriman selected Singapore, Indonesia, Ceylon, India, Pakistan, Iran, Italy, France, Germany, England, and Morocco—eleven countries to be visited in a little more than two weeks. He talked to Heads of Government, Foreign Ministers, Buddhist priests, the Pope, prominent politicians, our own Ambassadors, and representatives of the local and American press. He explained the reasons for the Summit Conference in Manila, summarized the proceedings, dwelt at length on the limited nature of American objectives and on the President's desire for peace and his determination to stay in Vietnam until peace was attained, and he described the six-month withdrawal formula (expounding on the significance of *thus*). He reminded his European audiences that Washington still cared about them, and he explained why a defeat of Democratic candidates in the forthcoming "off-year" election was to be expected but should not be regarded as a defeat for President Johnson.

I accompanied Harriman on his whirlwind trip. In Delhi we met expected opposition to the bombing of North Vietnam, and were bluntly told that the United States should stop the bombing immediately and without conditions. A ranking Indian official told us that when he was in Moscow a few months before, he was informed by the North Vietnamese Ambassador that if the bombing were stopped "indefinitely and without conditions" Hanoi would encourage the Viet Cong to move toward direct talks with Washington in an effort to reach a settlement. The official reported that the Indian Consul General in Hanoi had independently provided the same message. When Harriman asked why it would not be preferable and more productive to talk directly to the North Vietnamese instead of the Viet Cong, the Indians replied that Hanoi did not admit to having troops in South Vietnam; talks with the Viet Cong would leapfrog this issue. It was hard to take the Indians seriously, not because they were deliberately dissembling or misleading us, but rather because it was so difficult to pin them down on details and documentation. Nevertheless variations on this theme were being passed along by virtually every neutralist statesman and politician we confronted. It was clear that the Communists had launched a widespread diplomatic campaign.

We arrived in Rome at about one a.m. after the longest day of my life: breakfast with Ambassador Bowles in Delhi, lunch in Rawalpindi with President Ayub of Pakistan, tea in Teheran with the Shah, dinner someplace over North Africa. When we touched down in Rome, Italian reporters (who, except for the Japanese and the Filipinos, are probably the most voracious in the world) swooped down on Harriman. Nothing would deter them from dragooning him into the airport waiting room where television cameras were waiting. The Governor was articulate, fresh looking, charming. I cannot say the same about his younger traveling companions.

Although there were several meetings with the Pope, Prime Minister, and Cabinet Members, as far as peace moves were concerned the most important conversation of the entire trip was with an Italian Ambassador on leave in Rome. No one who arranged or participated in this informal tête-à-tête knew at the time its fateful consequences.

Ambassador Giovanni D'Orlandi was the Italian representative to Saigon. He had served there for about three years, and in that transient capital this was long enough to make him Dean of the Diplomatic Corps. In the course of his duties he came to know the Polish Representative on the International Control Commission, Ambassador Janusz Lewandowski, who made frequent trips between Hanoi and Saigon in connection with the Commission's affairs. Ambassador Lodge, who had close personal and professional relations with D'Orlandi, had soon joined the Italian and Polish Ambassadors in informal and highly secret bull sessions. Except for an interruption following the bombing of North Vietnamese oil installations in July, the meetings continued through the summer. By September, Lewandowski was passing along American queries to Hanoi about possible North Vietnamese responses to a bombing pause.

The occasion of my talk with D'Orlandi was a lunch given for Governor Harriman by Foreign Minister Amintore Fanfani at the

elegant Villa Madama outside Rome. The seating arrangement
had been worked out with great subtlety. I was placed between
D'Orlandi and a Foreign Office official who clearly had been instructed to concentrate his attention elsewhere. D'Orlandi did not
waste time on small talk. He was returning to Saigon, he said, on
Friday, November 4th, two days hence. He planned to stop in
Cairo for a few days of sun and rest and would arrive in Vietnam
on the 8th or 9th. Other things being equal he would have postponed his return because of his poor health, but he felt that the
next few months would be "critical."

On his arrival in Saigon he would immediately seek out his
friend Lewandowski, because the Pole was scheduled to depart
for Hanoi on the 11th. He felt that Lewandowski was a reliable
channel and an accurate reporter. He was confident that Moscow
knew of and approved Lewandowski's role as intermediary. Was
it not now time for the United States to provide Lewandowski
with something more meaningful than a series of questions and a
repetition of the same propositions that we had time and again
made in our public statements? Perhaps we could use Lewandowski to inform Hanoi how we envisaged an end to the war and how
we conceived of an ultimate political settlement. Perhaps we
could start with some agreement on the final arrangements and
then negotiate how to get there (Fanfani had made the same
point to us earlier, without mentioning D'Orlandi's views).

I told D'Orlandi that we were unable to do more now than to
report the conversation to the State Department. We would not
return to Washington until November 9th, but immediately after
our arrival we would see what could be done. Could D'Orlandi
ask Lewandowski to postpone his trip to Hanoi for several days
on the possibility that Washington might be ready to pass on some
new message? D'Orlandi agreed and felt that he could persuade
his Polish colleague to wait. In the event, Lewandowski did wait
for a new message, and, as we shall see, he got one.

Another meeting of particular significance was a session with
Prime Minister Wilson and Foreign Secretary Brown in London.
Brown was soon to go to Moscow and was anxious to get back-
ground information on American intentions with respect to Viet-

nam. He seemed confident that the Russians might be induced to inch Hanoi toward negotiations. Wilson noted that Moscow appeared to place more confidence in London's role as an intermediary since he had told Parliament that the British would disassociate themselves from any American attacks on Hanoi and Haiphong. Brown left for Moscow two weeks later, armed not only with his confidence but with a concrete new American proposition.

* * *

In the closing weeks of 1966 the American venture in Vietnam entered a new phase. To be sure, during subsequent months escalation of the ground and air war would continue, more American troops would be deployed, casualties on both sides would increase, the war would exacerbate social, economic, and political problems here at home. But in November, 1966 the Johnson Administration embarked on a sustained search for a way out. The search would not always be whole-hearted and would more often than not be marked by groping and fumbling. It would be accompanied by Byzantine-like conspiracies, bitter—if muted—in-fighting, and soul-searing phases of euphoric hope and deep despair. In the last analysis the goal would be beyond Lyndon Johnson's grasp.

XIII

Tragedy of Errors

The lunch in the Villa Madama started a train of events that led to one of the most dramatic acts in a long melodrama of negotiations. But much had gone on before; some of it was farcical, some tragic, and, as we have seen, some of it was pure carnival. The cast of characters included statesmen and politicians from every continent. Some were skilled diplomats, others were fumbling fools; many were highly motivated, others were simply eager for publicity and the Nobel Peace Prize.

Well before President Johnson's April, 1965 statement in Baltimore, in which he said that the United States was ready for "unconditional discussions," several proposals had been made for international meetings to settle the war. Some called for a Soviet–American summit, others for re-convening the Geneva Conference of 1954, and still others for a special meeting of the United Nations. Most of these initiatives followed on the heels of the American bombing of North Vietnam in early February, 1965.

One of the first serious attempts to establish a private line of communication between Hanoi and Washington took place in the spring of 1964. In a somewhat unorthodox approach, the United States "borrowed" a Canadian diplomat to present its views on the Vietnam war and the outlook for peace to the officials in Hanoi. Blair Seaborn was a bright and sophisticated official whose appointment as the Canadian representative on the International Control Commission provided him the opportunity to shuttle between Hanoi and Saigon. Until this time Washington had been unable to deliver a clear signal to Hanoi through all the verbal static. Nor had we been able to receive one; North Vietnamese propaganda, indirect and inconsistent messages, and transparently fabricated "reports" were confusing Washington analysts and officials, even at this early point.

Seaborn, with the approval of his Prime Minister and with the knowledge of a few Canadian and American officials, agreed to try to cut through the layers of public propaganda and private obfuscation. William Sullivan and I made a quick trip to Ottawa at the end of May to brief Seaborn. Actually we had little of consequence to say. The American bargaining position was just about nil; the South Vietnamese forces were being mauled; there were not enough American advisers in Vietnam to influence the tide of events, but there were more than enough to give us the onus of running the country; opposition to the war was already evident and growing in the United States. Although Seaborn pressed for something nourishing to put before the North Vietnamese, he gracefully accepted the thin gruel he received. In any case, his mission was to find out what the North Vietnamese were thinking, and this Seaborn endeavored to do when he visited Hanoi in the summer.

He was correctly if not cordially received by the North Vietnamese officials, who seemed neither surprised nor impressed to learn that he was acting as an American emissary; perhaps they expected no more, or no less, from the "imperialist camp." Nonetheless, they were frank about their own position. If the United States wanted an end to hostilities, that could be quickly and easily achieved: the American military should simply withdraw from South Vietnam, and the National Liberation Front, which represented the genuine aspirations of the South Vietnamese people, should take over the Saigon government. Seaborn reported his chilly findings to Washington through closely-guarded channels. Although he made a few more visits to Hanoi during subsequent months, he was able to learn little more. The effort was soon dropped.

Another initiative that predated the American bombing attacks turned out to have puzzling, even mysterious aftereffects. In the summer of 1964 U Thant had visited the White House at President Johnson's invitation to tell of his trip to Europe and the Middle East. The conversation naturally led to how peace could be restored to Vietnam. U Thant mentioned that the first necessary step was a secret private meeting between representatives of Washington and Hanoi. He seemed to be convinced that Washington not only agreed to this proposition but encouraged him to go ahead with arrangements for such a meeting. The story now becomes murky. Thant apparently sounded out Ho Chi Minh through the Russians. Ho is said to have agreed. Thant then contacted Adlai Stevenson in early October and told him that he could arrange for a meeting in Rangoon and provide conference facilities, interpreters, and communications.

Stevenson thought the matter so secret that he told only Secretary Rusk—by telephone. Neither his two deputies at the United Nations, Ambassadors Charles Yost and Francis Plimpton, nor the responsible Assistant Secretary in the Department of State, Harlan Cleveland, were informed. Nothing was put in writing. Rusk's reaction was negative, primarily because the proposal excluded the South Vietnamese Government. Apparently hoping he could get Rusk to change his mind, Stevenson did not inform U Thant of the Secretary's reaction. U Thant interpreted the silence from Washington as reflecting pre-election caution and did not press Stevenson. But many weeks later, when Stevenson was on vacation, U Thant asked Yost and Plimpton why he hadn't received any reply to his proposal for a meeting between Americans and North Vietnamese in Rangoon. Ambassador Yost called Assistant Secretary Cleveland from U Thant's office. "What is going on?" he demanded. Cleveland had no idea, but he called Stevenson in the Caribbean and for the first time learned of the Rangoon proposal. Cleveland then called Under-Secretary George Ball (Secretary Rusk was also away at the time). Ball had never heard of Stevenson's call to Rusk. Ball called McGeorge Bundy. Bundy was also uninformed.

Cleveland told Ball that U Thant was in no mood for any further procrastination and was likely to "blow" the story at any moment. A few weeks later the U Thant initiative was mentioned in a front page story in *The New York Times*. Upon reading the news account of U Thant's unanswered initiative, the President was furious. He telephoned the West Basement demanding to know whether such a proposal had actually been made. Since Bundy was away, Bromley Smith, the Executive Secretary of the National Security Council, and I had the hapless chore of providing a quick answer. A hasty search of the files turned up only a terse account of Ball's earlier telephone conversation with Bundy —a sketchy "Did-you-know-that-U Thant-told-Stevenson-that-he-could-set-up-a-meeting-in-Rangoon-with-Hanoi?" This by itself did not seem a very robust initiative, and we told the President so. The unfortunate White House Press Officer had to take the next move. In response to a question, George Reedy said, "There are no authorized negotiations underway with Mr. Thant or any other government. I am not going into any diplomatic chitchat that may be going forth, or way-out feelers. But authorized or meaningful negotiations—no." This, of course, made U Thant even more angry, and as a consequence relations between him and the President were strained for years. The matter came up again a year later when Eric Sevareid publicized U Thant's approach to Stevenson.[1]

It was later charged that the position of the Saigon Government was desperate (which was true); that consequently the United States was unwilling to negotiate seriously at that time (which was probably true); that U Thant was on the verge of settling the war (which, from what is now known of the whole story, was dubious); and that President Johnson not only flatly rejected the Secretary General's initiative but did not even give him the courtesy of a reply (which was false, since Johnson did not even hear of it until much later).

The next major development on the negotiations front was a product of Marshal Tito's efforts. Alarmed by the escalation of the war, he invited seventeen non-aligned governments to Belgrade in early April, 1965 to draft an appeal to the NLF, Hanoi, Saigon, and Washington for immediate negotiations "without preconditions." President Johnson, as we have seen, agreed with the views of "the Seventeen" in his Baltimore speech on April 7, and a formal American acceptance of their proposition was announced on the following day. There was little risk in such a course. The declaration was well-intentioned and harmless. Moreover, the odds were high that Hanoi would reject the petition—which, in a matter of a week or so, it did on April 19th.

The remainder of the spring and early summer was marked by an increase in the fighting and intensified efforts to end it. The British were especially active and singularly unsuccessful during this period. In April a Labour M.P., Mr. Patrick Gordon-Walker, attempted to explore North Vietnamese and Chinese Communist views on a settlement, but he was refused permission even to visit Hanoi and Peking. In June a delegation of Commonwealth Prime Ministers planned to visit the capitals of all the countries involved in the conflict to explore the possibilities of a peace conference, but Hanoi, calling the enterprise a "swindle," refused to see them. In early July a member of the British Government visited Hanoi but was unsuccessful in an attempt to get the North Vietnamese leaders to change their minds.

The prospects for peace were grim that autumn. Hanoi had been inhospitable to every overture from every quarter. In spite of third-hand assurances filtering into Washington from members of American peace movements, as well as from reporters and foreign politicians, it seemed clear that Hanoi's position was based on two tough propositions. The United States must stop the bombing permanently and without conditions; Hanoi might or might not "do something" in return but would not commit itself in advance. If a settlement were to be worked out it would have to be in accordance with Hanoi's "Four Points" as announced in early April and reiterated frequently since then.

The situation was ready-made for any emissary with credible bona fides who could make a case that the North Vietnamese were ready to move even slightly from their rigid position. He was not long in coming.

On a cool, crisp, autumn afternoon in late October, I was on the Eighth Floor terrace of the State Department escaping the crush and smoke of a reception inside. Secretary Rusk motioned me to a temporarily-secluded corner. Hungary's Foreign Minister, Janos Peter, had told him "on authority from Hanoi" that the North Vietnamese would be prepared to negotiate if the bombing stopped. This looked as if it might be significant. Rusk wondered whether Peter really had been to Hanoi in the late summer. I replied that some inquiries had been made in Budapest, but all that was known was that Peter had been out of Hungary "on vacation" for about two weeks. We were unable to learn where he had spent his holiday. If Peter had, in fact, been to Hanoi, he and the North Vietnamese might be anxious to keep his visit a secret. It was clear that the Secretary for the first time felt we might be on a track that could lead to talks with the North Vietnamese. This almost certainly encouraged Rusk to endorse the long bombing pause that started at Christmas. A year later it was discovered that the Hungarian "initiative" was a hoax, pure and simple. Peter had not been to Hanoi, he had no authority to speak for the North Vietnamese, and he had no reason to believe Hanoi was ready to scale down its demands.

If the North Vietnamese were, in fact, receptive to negotiations on any terms but their own and to a political settlement on any terms other than the surrender of the United States, it was not evident from their public statements during 1965 and 1966. Every American offer of negotiations, no matter how forthcoming or unconditional, was called a "swindle," "deceitful," or a "trick." Every reported North Vietnamese "peace feeler" was vigorously denied by Hanoi—a tactic that frequently pulled the rug out from under those who claimed that the United States was ignoring or rejecting Communist overtures. The plain fact of the matter was that by the summer of 1966 the positions of both Washington and Hanoi were non-negotiable.

The next milestone in pursuit of the elusive olive branch occurred in the late summer of 1966. U Thant had returned from a visit to Moscow convinced that the Russians were ready to use their influence to move Hanoi to the conference table, providing he could deliver some "new" message from the Americans. Ambassador Arthur Goldberg came to Washington in early September anxious to squeeze something out of the White House and State Department that would be robust enough for U Thant to pass on to the Russians who then, presumably, would contact Hanoi. The idea was received sympathetically if not enthusiastically. No one was very optimistic that the Russians could, even if they wished, spark a meeting between American and North Vietnamese officials. Nonetheless there was a willingness to try almost anything to get a dialogue going, and there was also a recognition that the Secretary General should be given reason to believe Washington was taking him seriously. Thant was on the verge of resigning his post in the United Nations, and prospects for securing an acceptable replacement were bleak. Both Washington and Moscow were anxious to avoid the trauma of finding a mutually satisfactory successor. Thus U Thant had more leverage on the Great Powers than he had had at any time up to then or, in fact, than he has had any time since.

The basic problem, of course, was that very little could be provided Goldberg that was new and yet acceptable to all the key officials in Washington. However, there was one possibly saleable item that had been kept on the shelf. Since April, 1965, when it first announced its program, Hanoi had been insistent that its "Four Points" would have to be the basis for a political settlement. Attempts to work out with Hanoi some mutually acceptable rewording of the "Four Points" had been unsuccessful. Could some propositions addressed specifically to Hanoi's program unlock the door to a remote and private conference room? Goldberg went back to New York with a promise that his Washington colleagues would endeavor to provide him with the "something new" he needed. After a day or two of stewing, drafting, and "clearing," a paper was sent to Goldberg to pass on to U Thant so that he in turn could move it on to Moscow.

U Thant was reportedly pleased with both the substance and spirit of the American proposal and promised to pass it on to the Russians forthwith. But nothing further was heard from U Thant or the Russians.

Aside from this private attempt, Goldberg was determined to use the occasion of the opening session of the General Assembly to advance some major new views on Vietnam and on American relations with Communist China. When it reached Washington for clearance, the draft of his speech surprised some of the more cautious and muscle-bound inhabitants of the upper levels of the bureaucracy. Considerable reconstruction work had to be performed before the yawning gaps between Goldberg's draft and the Administration's current policy line were narrowed. But despite the toning down by Washington, Goldberg's speech of September 22 put the American case in more understandable and flexible terms than had any other public statement thus far. Goldberg restated all of the points that had already been made publicly with respect to Washington's limited objectives and flexible position on negotiations. He emphasized that the United States was engaged neither in a "holy war" against Communism nor in an attempt to overthrow the Government of North Vietnam. The United States did not seek permanent bases nor a postwar alliance with South Vietnam. We did not wish to keep American troops in South Vietnam any longer than necessary and were ready to engage in immediate discussions with Hanoi to work out a timetable for mutual withdrawal. Washington would abide by the decision of all Vietnamese on the reunification of Vietnam. The United States "was prepared to discuss Hanoi's four points together with any points which other parties may wish to raise." We were ready to negotiate a settlement based on a "strict observance of the 1954 and 1962 Geneva Agreements." As President Johnson had already said, NLF participation in negotiations would not be an "insurmountable problem," and the North Vietnamese leaders should "consider whether this obstacle to negotiations may not be more imaginary than real."

But the most significant part of the speech was Goldberg's formulation of what we sought from Hanoi in exchange for a bombing halt: the United States was "prepared to order a cessation of all bombing of North Vietnam the moment we are assured privately or otherwise that this step will be answered promptly by a corresponding and appropriate de-escalation of the other side." Up to this point the United States had been insisting, or at least strongly implying, that nothing short of a *demonstrable* cut in

infiltration of North Vietnamese to South Vietnam would be the
required quid pro quo for a bombing halt. Now an American
spokesman was saying that private *assurances* that Hanoi would
move toward a "corresponding and appropriate *de-escalation*"
would be sufficient to warrant Washington's stopping the bombing. This statement was internationally regarded as an important
advance, and rightly so.

Within hours after Goldberg's speech I received a half dozen
calls from as many embassies asking if the Ambassador was reflecting a major change in American policy. "Goldberg is an American
official, and unless he's fired in the next twenty-four hours you
can assume that he was speaking for the Administration," was my
reply. Happily, he wasn't, and one could. Nevertheless, there were
many in the Administration who were noticeably relieved when
forty eight hours later both Hanoi and Peking unequivocally rejected Goldberg's proposals.

❂   ❂   ❂

Now we must return to the aftermath of that lunch in Rome. I
arrived in Washington on November 9th to discover that little
had been done in response to the telegram describing the meeting
with D'Orlandi. To be sure, it had aroused a certain amount of
interest in the State Department, but the fallout from the various
post-Manila VIP trips and the preoccupation with the Congressional elections took precedence over moving ahead on the D'Orlandi–Lewandowski track. But D'Orlandi himself had not been
idle. On his return to Saigon he discovered that Lewandowski,
having once postponed his trip to Hanoi, was now ready to leave
within a matter of days. D'Orlandi sought out Lodge, and at a
meeting on November 14 Lodge had to admit he had not yet
received any goodies from Washington. In response to his urgent
request, a statement of the American position was forwarded to
Saigon the next day. The telegram from Washington described the
American views on a settlement, reiterated our determination to
give the Vietnamese a free choice and to abide by the results of
such a choice, emphasized the Administration's intention to with-

draw American troops and close American military installations once the fighting had stopped.

Much of what Washington provided Lodge had already appeared either in Rusk's "Fourteen Points" or in subsequent public statements. But Lodge was also given something new and shiny. It was a statement of the "Phase A–Phase B" proposition that had been lying dormant since it was first advanced in a planning paper prepared for the Manila Conference. Lodge was told that the United States would be ready to stop the bombing of North Vietnam, ostensibly unconditionally. In fact, however, the bombing halt would be based on an advance agreement that Hanoi and Washington would, "after some adequate period," undertake other agreed "de-escalating actions." Thus there would be two separate, seemingly unrelated, but actually closely tied, parts to the agreement. Hanoi could claim, if it wished, that the United States had acceded to the North Vietnamese call for an "unconditional halt" in the bombing. Since Washington intended that Hanoi's "de-escalatory action" would involve stopping infiltration, the United States for its part would have achieved a primary objective.

Lodge met with D'Orlandi and Lewandowski within hours after he received the telegram. He carefully reviewed the American position. Lewandowski expressed satisfaction, took copious notes, and rushed off to Hanoi. The Polish Ambassador returned to Saigon about the first of December and got in touch with Lodge through D'Orlandi. He told Lodge that, on the basis of their conversation prior to his departure for Hanoi, he had reduced Lodge's presentation of the American position to ten major points. He had discussed the ten points with North Vietnamese officials and could now report that Hanoi seemed ready to meet with the Americans on the basis of this statement of the American position. If Washington was interested, such a meeting could take place in Warsaw fairly soon.

Lodge was pleasantly surprised by the pace of events, but he was somewhat concerned that the Lewandowski version of the American position might not, in fact, be one the United States would wish to use as its own. He told Lewandowski that before he made any commitments he would have to examine the ten points and forward them to Washington for review; Lewandowski expressed disappointment at Lodge's "bureaucratic" approach but apparently understood.

As soon as it became apparent that the Lodge–Lewandowski conversations were serious, the President ordered a sharp reduction in the number of people permitted to read the relevant telegrams. At this point the enterprise was given the code name "Marigold." For some who had been keeping abreast of the Lodge–D'Orlandi–Lewandowski meetings, the train of events stopped with the Pole's mid-November trip to Hanoi.

Although Lewandowski had done well in reducing Lodge's oral presentation of November 15th to writing, there were some aspects of his text that were troublesome. In some respects all that was required was a certain amount of editing to make the United States position more clear. In other respects, however, Lewandowski, consciously or not, had distorted the American position. In particular, the questions of American troop withdrawals and Vietnamese elections needed to be clarified. Moreover, there was no reference to the Phase A–Phase B proposal, the single new point we had asked the Pole to pass on to Hanoi. When queried about this, Lewandowski said he had presented it orally to North Vietnamese officials.

There was not only concern as to the precise wording of Lewandowski's presentation but also some unease about what the Polish Ambassador and the North Vietnamese had in mind. Did they regard the ten points as a formal agenda for negotiations, or did they simply consider them an informal record of the American position which could serve as a common starting point for discussion? Lewandowski gave no hint of how the list would be used (he probably did not know), and the North Vietnamese neither publicly nor privately acknowledged its existence. Washington had a visceral feeling, however, that the ten points as Lewandowski had drafted them—and presumably as Hanoi had approved them—would eventually wind up as a firm commitment on the part of the United States and a binding agenda for any meeting.

In an overnight reply Lodge was given certain revisions to

pass on to Lewandowski. When the two Ambassadors next met, there was friction and even controversy over the rewording. Lewandowski claimed we were quibbling if not dissembling, but Lodge made it clear that the United States would not involve itself in an American–North Vietnamese parley without having some control over the wording of its own position. We thought it not unreasonable to insist on editing and correcting his written version of Lodge's oral remarks. But there was more behind Washington's instructions to Lodge than a simple desire to get the record straight.

During the summer and early autumn the prospects that anything would ever come of Lodge's bull sessions seemed very remote. Rostow, Rusk, McNamara, and the President himself had been paying scant attention to the meetings of the three Ambassadors in Saigon. As a general matter, the issue of negotiations was very much a residual claimant on the time of the President's "Tuesday Lunch" group; it was the military track, and especially the bombing targets, that virtually dominated the discussions. But now it appeared that the Lewandowski channel might well bag the elusive North Vietnamese. For the first time since February, 1965 there were signs that Hanoi would talk about a political settlement without first insisting on a bombing cessation. It was clear that the Administration at the highest levels would have to focus carefully on the Polish initiative and particularly on Lewandowski's ten points. It was not a question of drawing back or dissembling. There was an urgent need to assure that the points accurately reflected the United States negotiating position.

Although Lewandowski again implied that we were quibbling and perhaps even acting in bad faith, he indicated the Poles were ready to arrange discussions in Warsaw on a more formal level. He told Lodge that the North Vietnamese would not join the talks immediately, since there were still some modalities to be worked out between the American representative and officials of the Polish Foreign Office. But, Lewandowski implied, Hanoi's men would be waiting in the wings and within a few days would join the talks. At some point soon after, the Poles would bow out.

The first meeting, presumably a preparatory meeting for the

subsequent substantive talks, was scheduled for Monday, December 5. The American representative was Ambassador to Poland, John Gronouski. The choice of Gronouski was not made without agonized discussion in Washington. Gronouski, the former Postmaster General, had established good relations with the Polish Foreign Office during his brief tenure in Warsaw, but he knew nothing about Vietnam and had been unaware of the discussions with Lewandowski in Saigon. Nonetheless, he seemed to be the logical candidate. The North Vietnamese, according to Lewandowski, were insistent that any meeting with the Americans be very closely held. Since Washington was also eager to keep the talks a secret, it made sense to use the least conspicuous American representative available—and he happened to be the American Ambassador on the spot. If talks with the North Vietnamese actually got down to serious business, Washington was prepared to send a small group of experts to join Gronouski.

Gronouski had been given two days to bone up on the background and details of the Lodge–D'Orlandi–Lewandowski conversations and to familiarize himself with the Vietnamese problem generally. By the time he set forth for his first meeting with the Polish Foreign Minister, the Ambassador must have felt very much like a college student who had been cramming for final exams.

While Gronouski was doing his homework in preparation for his preliminary discussions with the Poles, American bombers launched two attacks on Hanoi, one on December 2, the other two days later. These were the first such attacks in more than two weeks. The bombings cast a pall of uncertainty and gloom over the final discussions in Saigon. Lewandowski warned Lodge that the raids would be regarded in Hanoi as a sign that the Americans were disinterested in talking. But far from being a signal one way or another, the attacks were just a piece of unfinished business. The bombing raids had been authorized on November 12 as part of a large package [2] and, as in the case of all scheduled target packages, once approval was given the military could, within a specified period, attack whenever the weather was propitious. The weather had been unfavorable during the latter half of November, but on December 2 the skies cleared over Hanoi and the attack took place as originally approved. Despite Lewandowski's warning after the first raid, the second took place as planned on December 4. Lodge did his best to reassure Lewandowski of Washington's interest in proceeding with the meeting at Warsaw. He explained to Lewandowski that if the raids had been cancelled there would have been widespread suspicion that some diplomatic break was impending and that this was just what Hanoi said it wished to avoid. Ambassadors earn their salaries.

We later heard that Hanoi might have assumed that the United States was, in fact, attempting to send a definite, albeit subtle, message. The fact that bombing attacks on Hanoi and Haiphong had practically ceased from mid-November apparently led some North Vietnamese officials to believe that the United States was signaling its support of Lewandowski's efforts to arrange an American–North Vietnamese meeting. But as we have seen, we, the hapless Lewandowski, and perhaps some wishful thinkers in Hanoi were victimized by two cruel acts of God. The weather became unfavorable for high-level, precision bombing just as Lewandowski was leaving for Hanoi with his message, and it remained bad during the entire period he was there. Shortly after he returned to Saigon the skies cleared and the bombing was resumed. If, in fact, officials in Hanoi were trying to read something into the timing of the raids, they might well have concluded that we were waiting for Lewandowski to return from Hanoi and were dissatisfied with his report. Perhaps the North Vietnamese concluded that the Americans as a consequence had decided to resume attacks on the North Vietnamese capital and major port. Such a rationale would have done American policymakers too much credit. The relationship between major bombing raids and American political decisions was by no means as intimate as the North Vietnamese, or even more sophisticated observers, might have assumed. Another case in point was provided only ten days later.

On December 13 Gronouski was in the midst of a delicate meeting with Polish officials. Rapacki told him that the North Vietnamese wished to postpone the discussions indefinitely, and "Marigold" seemed a very perishable flower indeed. Just at this

moment fierce American bombing attacks were unleashed against
Hanoi, despite Lewandowski's earlier warning, and despite strong
objections by McNamara, Katzenbach and Ambassador Thompson. And there were additional raids on the following day. The
President would not be persuaded or diverted from his conviction
that more pressure was the right prescription for Hanoi.

The attacks would have been hard to justify, even if they had
been executed with the "surgical precision" the bombing advocates boasted about. But on these occasions, either because of bad
weather or sloppy bombsmanship, there was a substantial amount
of what the Pentagon euphemistically described as "subsidiary
damage." To further complicate matters, a large number of
civilians and several structures in Hanoi's diplomatic quarter were
hit. There was a worldwide outcry. Only now was there any
reaction in Washington. Admiral Sharp noted laconically that
"On December 15 restrikes . . . were prohibited. . . ." [3]

Gronouski's early sessions with the Poles were not very promising. If there were any North Vietnamese in the wings they were
extremely quiet and well-hidden. The issue of Lewandowski's
"ten points" vs the American revisions dragged on. We had earlier
agreed to use Lewandowski's ten points as a basis for discussion,
but had reserved the right to interpret several of the points as we,
rather than as Lewandowski, understood them. Rapacki kept
pressing Gronouski for wording we would accept, but before this
could be worked out, the bombing of mid-December occurred.
This seemed to suggest to the Poles, presumably to the North
Vietnamese, and even to a few people in the State Department,
that the United States had little interest in serious discussions.
The Poles broke off the talks.

Those who had objected strenuously to the attacks now had
the bitter and empty pleasure of mumbling, "I told you so." Gronouski was summoned home on December 21 to brief White
House and State Department officials on the current unpromising
state of affairs in Warsaw. Some of the folk in the White House
who had been positive and glib about their superior knowledge
of how to deal with Hanoi were now unusually quiet and humble.
It was clear even to them that something consequential in the

way of getting the bombing under control had to be done if the talks were to be resumed. There were few who had been very optimistic that the North Vietnamese would ultimately emerge from the woodwork, if indeed there were any there. But even the most skeptical and hard-nosed members of the exclusive Marigold Club now seemed anxious to give the talks an extended lease on life. For some it may have been a matter of prickly consciences; for others there was a genuine desire to salvage the talks, if only to test Hanoi's readiness to participate.

The proposition that finally emerged from the frequently heated exchanges was later referred to by some less-reverent inhabitants of the State Department's Seventh Floor as the "Christmas present." Gronouski was authorized to inform the Poles that the United States would forthwith prohibit bombing within a ten-mile radius of Hanoi. After taking this message back to Warsaw, he reported that the Poles would review the state of play and get in touch with him after Christmas. On the 27th there was a call from the Foreign Minister. Gronouski, in a high state of excitement, expected that it was an invitation to resume the talks. But Rapacki simply wanted clarification of the new American proposition. Was the radius of ten miles in "nautical miles" or "statute miles?" Gronouski duly forwarded this technical and seemingly quibbling query. Washington hadn't even considered the question, but in a burst of generosity responded that the radius would be measured in "nautical miles" (a somewhat larger radius than statute miles). On December 30 the Polish Foreign Minister called again. This time he asked Gronouski to meet with him. He told the Ambassador that the talks were over. Hanoi refused to be involved any further. Marigold Finis; *exeunt omnes.* Something of value did emerge from the fiasco, however: the ten-mile bombing sanctuary around Hanoi provided Washington with an opportunity in early January to initiate a contact directly with the North Vietnamese in Moscow.

If "Marigold" proved nothing else, it demonstrated that officials in both Washington and Warsaw could maintain secrecy if they tried hard enough. Not a word of the proceedings had been leaked. Neither America's fighting partners nor even the Saigon

Government had been informed of the three-party conversations in Saigon or the subsequent dialogue in Warsaw. One could safely assume that the Poles had been in constant touch with the Russians during the course of the talks, but there was no indication that any of the other Eastern European nations had been informed.

Shortly after the first of the year the veil of secrecy was broken. The Polish Ambassador to the UN told U Thant, and the Polish Ambassador to Italy told the Pope about the Warsaw meeting. Naturally enough the Poles put the full onus on the Americans for the talks breaking off. According to their account, Hanoi had been ready and eager to join, but despite earlier warnings the Americans continued to bomb Hanoi, undoubtedly in a deliberate effort to sabotage any possibility of negotiations. Thus American spokesmen had the task not only of justifying the attacks on Hanoi ("already scheduled," "bad weather," "good weather," etc.), but of explaining Washington's doubts with respect to Hanoi's ultimate intentions. Officials in the White House and the State Department claimed that the raids only marginally influenced the course of events in Warsaw. "If Hanoi were interested in talking to us they would have appeared on the scene by the 12th. If they were really interested, they would have agreed to talk even though the bombings had taken place."

The Australian Minister to Washington, Robert Furlonger, normally a placid and understanding man, stormed angrily into the State Department early in January. What about these private talks in Warsaw that the Poles had discussed with U Thant? This was the first hint we had that the Poles had breached the understanding about keeping the talks secret. The Minister was given a complete briefing on the talks, the reasons for the secrecy, and the rationale for the bombing. We then informed our other allies in Vietnam, as well as the British and the Canadians.

In retrospect many officials in Washington felt the whole purpose of the Warsaw exercise, as far as the Poles and Hanoi were concerned, was to give Hanoi a breathing spell, and that from the outset the North Vietnamese had no intention of engaging in discussions with American representatives. Even the most charitable among the "Marigolders," myself included, were inclined to believe that at most the North Vietnamese had given Lewandowski a hunting license rather than any definite commitment when he was in Hanoi. This does not, of course, excuse the slipshod, cavalier approach of the U.S. to the bombing of North Vietnam during the talks, especially in the light of the Polish warnings.

That the raids on Hanoi occurred while such sensitive diplomatic discussions were taking place reflected the risks involved in limiting knowledge of the Warsaw talks to just a few people, most of whom were unaware of day-to-day bombing plans. Largely because of this, the alarms were not sounded and the raids on Hanoi proceeded on their inexorable, pre-planned schedules. Two officials who were aware of Marigold and who also would normally have been briefed about the mid-December raids, Secretary Rusk and Assistant Secretary Bundy, were abroad on December 12. Whether either would have urged the White House to stand down the bombing is a moot point. But the whole fiasco must be examined in a broader context: the Administration, as of late 1966 and early 1967, was just not interested in negotiations to the extent necessary to prevent military actions from interfering with or even negating diplomatic initiatives.

*   *   *

When the British learned of the developments in Warsaw their reaction made that of my Australian friend seem mild. Foreign Minister George Brown had gone to Moscow in late November in ignorance of the discussions that were even then under way between Lodge and Lewandowski. The near-certainty that his interlocutors in Moscow knew of these talks did not make the British feel one bit better. Adding insult to injury, as far as Wilson and Brown were concerned, was their discovery that we had provided Lewandowski with the Phase A–Phase B formula in mid-November. As he was setting off for Moscow in November, we had told Brown in a detailed telegram that he could submit this proposition to the Russians and indicate that he had authority from his "friends in Washington" to make the proposal. (For reasons which now escape me, Brown was given a much more precise version of the proposal than had been given earlier to Lewandowski, although the Pole obviously needed at least as much detail as Brown.) Brown had no hint before he took off from London that the formula might already have reached Soviet officials via the Poles.

Sending the Phase A–Phase B proposition to Moscow through Brown was not a capricious idea; it was decided upon after careful deliberation. Washington planners had concluded that the formula would gain in significance and authority if officials in both Hanoi and Moscow felt the United States was serious enough to advance the proposal through two, separate, secret channels pretty much at the same time.

Brown's own reaction, which the British Ambassador in Washington, Sir Patrick Dean, was instructed to transmit to Secretary Rusk, was so irate that even those officials in the White House who had become somewhat cool to Her Majesty's Government's tendency to "meddle" in Vietnam felt the need to soothe our angry ally.

My relations with George Brown dated back to the mid-50s, and over the years I had gotten to know him well. When we first met he held a high post in the Loyal Opposition. Together with the rest of his Labour Party colleagues, he was virtually ignored by the American Embassy during the tenure of Ambassador Winthrop Aldrich. A few of us, however, tried to provide key Labour Party members with some background on United States policy so that when they spoke against American moves in Europe or elsewhere, their opposition would at least not stem from sheer ignorance of the facts. In the decade since, I had had several occasions to work with Brown on such touchy matters as the Cuban Missile Crisis and the Multilateral Force. Our relationship was comprised of mutual affection, respect, and confidence. In part because of this, and in part because of my familiarity with our negotiations policy, I was sent to London to do some fence-mending.

The temperature of both the air outside and the atmosphere within the government buildings in Whitehall was very chilly that January. It took a great deal of talking—some of it pretty undiplomatic—before I could mollify Brown. He swore that his ignorance of the Warsaw exercise had destroyed his bona fides when he was in Moscow. As he looked back on his visit he was sure that the Russians must have been aware that Americans were meeting with Polish officials. To make matters worse, Brown was convinced that the Russians must have thought he was a fool or a charlatan when he presented the Phase A–Phase B formula as his own. Surely they had learned of the proposal earlier through Warsaw or Hanoi. The Americans had given him "a vote of no confidence" by keeping him in ignorance of the Saigon and Warsaw talks, and the Russians, aware of this, had not taken him seriously. He had gone to Moscow with a feeling of optimism. That nothing had been accomplished may well have been a result of Washington's neglecting to inform him of important related developments.

If I had been in Brown's shoes, I would have been angry too. But he had to understand, and I think he eventually did, that it was essential for the Warsaw talks to be kept secret. Wilson recognized this, and later professed to a feeling of relief that he was spared the responsibility of knowing about them while they were in progress; if there had been any leaks, it would have been well for the British to be beyond suspicion. But, according to Wilson, he and the Foreign Minister should have been officially informed about the Warsaw happening after it had been concluded, rather than to have learned about it indirectly and accidentally. Both Wilson and Brown were having serious problems with their own party because of their support for the United States position. By permitting Brown to set off for Moscow innocent of developments taking place simultaneously in Warsaw, Saigon, and Washington we had made their problems in Parliament even more difficult.

Wilson warned that if the British Government was to remain a reliable supporter of American policy in Vietnam, President Johnson would have to keep it closely informed. He sought assurances that Washington would keep him advised of all major diplomatic developments with respect to Vietnam. I argued that no government could make a blanket commitment even to its closest ally to tell it everything, no matter how sensitive. Her Majesty's Government would probably not be prepared to give this commitment to Washington, and it was unfair to expect President Johnson to make such a promise. Nonetheless Washington was now ready, within the rules of reason, to give Wilson and Brown the assurances they sought.

As an earnest of the President's intention to inform them of important recent diplomatic developments, I was permitted to describe two current, closely-held efforts to open a channel to Hanoi. The first of these was based on an elaborate planning paper setting forth the terms on which Washington would be ready to settle the conflict. The paper was prepared in part on the basis of advice Harriman and I had gotten from Italian officials in Rome—advice also received subsequently from other and perhaps even better informed sources. The idea was to provide Hanoi with a firm and full statement of our views on a political settlement in order to get their reaction and, it was hoped, their agreement. Both Hanoi and Washington would then attempt to work out means for reaching the agreed-upon settlement. It was dubbed the "settle first–negotiate later" approach. A wide range of issues was included: a ceasefire, the exchange of prisoners, the political arrangements that might be made following a settlement, the problem of eventual reunification. The draft was submitted first to Harriman's Negotiations Committee, then to the White House for Rostow's clearance and to the Secretary of State for his approval. The paper came back from the White House with the grumble that it was "too soft," but with no specific criticism. It remained in Rusk's "in box" for many weeks, and then dropped from sight. In the light of Rostow's general comment and Rusk's apparent disinterest, the "settle first–negotiate later" paper hovered between life and death. Nonetheless, Llewellyn Thompson, who had just been re-appointed Ambassador to the Soviet Union, took it with him to Moscow. If an opportunity arose to use the paper or pass its contents to Hanoi, we were sure that Dean Rusk and Walt Rostow would come forward with their views.

The second item was a more juicy tidbit. As I was leaving for London, a face-to-face dialogue had already started with the North Vietnamese. Perhaps the aborted Warsaw talks had stimulated Hanoi's curiosity and made the North Vietnamese susceptible to a Soviet suggestion that they at least listen to what we might have to say. Or perhaps the Goldberg–U Thant exchange in late September had paid off. In any case the Russians informed our Embassy in Moscow in early January that if we made an effort to see the chargé d'affaires of the North Vietnamese Embassy, preliminary exchanges might take place which could lead to serious talks. We took the advice and John Guthrie, who was the senior Embassy Officer until Ambassador Thompson's arrival, made a call on his North Vietnamese counterpart on January 10. He was greeted by a startled guardian of the portals, and after many minutes of cooling his heels and staring at a large picture of Ho Chi Minh in the dreary reception room, he was ushered into the presence of the North Vietnamese official. Following his instructions carefully, as all good Foreign Service Officers do, Guthrie explained that the United States was ready to engage in direct conversations with the North Vietnamese Government, and that this might lead to meaningful discussions on how the war could be ended. Guthrie reminded his silent listener that the United States was prepared to order a bombing halt during the Tet holidays, which were to start on February 4, and that Washington had already established a ten-mile sanctuary around Hanoi. It was hoped that serious, substantive, non-polemical meetings could begin very soon at either their level or, if Hanoi wished, at the level of the North Vietnamese and American Ambassadors, both of whom were scheduled to be in Moscow soon. Of course, if the North Vietnamese preferred, discussions need not be held in Mossow but could be arranged at some other mutually agreeable site.

Guthrie reported that his North Vietnamese host appeared extremely nervous. He offered and consumed endless cups of tea, smoked incessantly, and said hardly anything at all. But finally he agreed to a second meeting at which the Americans would submit some specific ideas about what the Americans and Vietnamese might discuss if substantive talks were, in fact, to take place. And this is about where matters stood when I left for London.

At just about the time I was explaining "Marigold" to Prime Minister Wilson and Foreign Minister Brown, Guthrie was back again in the North Vietnamese Embassy. He had with him a detailed list of suggestions to serve as a possible basis for substantive talks. Since Washington desired that its proposals be regarded as informal and flexible, Guthrie was told to make his presentation orally and to avoid giving the impression that he was delivering an ultimatum or a demarche.

Washington's list included such issues as a ceasefire, troop withdrawals, elections, political participation of the NLF, and eventual reunification of North and South Vietnam. In any discussion between American and North Vietnamese representatives, Guthrie said, Hanoi could present its "four points" and any other questions it wished to raise. These would be considered together with the American proposals. The list of topics could be dealt with in any order the North Vietnamese wished. The United States did not regard its proposals as a final, firm agenda; we would like Hanoi's reactions. In short, we hoped that Hanoi would regard the American proposition as sufficiently flexible and attractive to come back with some ideas of its own that might, in turn, lead to a useful exchange of substantive ideas.

Once again the North Vietnamese chargé listened solemnly and took careful notes. A few pleasantries were passed, but Guthrie left no wiser as to how the North Vietnamese felt about the prospects for further meetings.

A week passed before Guthrie received a message that his North Vietnamese contact was ready to see him. Hopes were high that Hanoi had reacted favorably to the American proposal and that, at long last, substantive talks could be arranged. But these hopes were short-lived. Guthrie was treated to a long, insulting polemic. Not once did the chargé refer to the American proposals, nor did he advance any counter-suggestions. There was nothing Guthrie could do but pick up his marbles and go home. For reasons of their own, the North Vietnamese must have decided to discourage any further exploration through this channel. The suggested list of topics for negotiation so carefully worked out in Washington joined the "settle now–negotiate later" package and the Lewandowski–Lodge ten points in the graveyard of forgotten scenarios and buried hopes. But within a few days, in another form, through another channel, Hanoi's Foreign Minister did transmit a reply of sorts to Washington's invitation to talk.

*   *   *

From London I went to Paris where yet another possible approach to Hanoi was being explored. I was following up on a meeting Ambassador Harriman had had with Monsieur Jean Sainteny when he was in Paris on other matters several weeks earlier. The meeting had been suggested by Henry Kissinger, who some years before had met Madame Sainteny at Harvard.

Sainteny was an old Indochina hand, having served there as a French official during the colonial period. During World War II he was a member of the French intelligence service in South China. Shortly after the Japanese surrender, he induced an OSS team to provide him with transportation from Kunming to Hanoi, but when he reached Hanoi he was placed under virtual house arrest. Although it was the Viet Minh who actually kept him confined, he felt then (and probably still does) that Ho's soldiers were encouraged by the OSS group that preferred to deal with the Viet Minh privately and unencumbered by the French. The Americans departed not long after, however, and Sainteny, who was then French Commissioner for Northern Indochina, became the link between the French Government and Ho Chi Minh. It was he who played a critical role in working out a negotiated settlement with Ho in 1946.

Through the years Sainteny had maintained his contacts with the Vietnamese Communists, who regarded him as a "good" Frenchman. Shortly before he and Ambassador Harriman met, he had been a Minister in the de Gaulle Government. Although he no longer held an official position, he remained on close personal terms with de Gaulle, and because of his entree into the Elysée and his contacts with the North Vietnamese Government, it was thought he might provide a bridge between Washington and Hanoi.

Sainteny told Ambassador Harriman of his visit to Hanoi the previous July. He was convinced the North Vietnamese would make an "important gesture" in response to a bombing cessation. Indeed a personal promise had been given to him by Pham Van Dong, the North Vietnamese Prime Minister. He could furnish nothing very specific, however, on what this "important gesture" might be. But he was convinced that Hanoi was ready to adhere to the Geneva Agreements of 1954, and that the North Vietnamese would be interested in the American position with respect to those Agreements. Before negotiations could start the Americans would have to convince Hanoi of their "good faith," which could be done only through secret discussions with people in whom the North Vietnamese had confidence. Sainteny felt that East European leaders could not serve this function because their visits to Hanoi tended to be "too spectacular." The Russians also presented problems, according to Sainteny, because Hanoi was worried about its own relations with Peking. As for the French, he was dubious that de Gaulle would permit any official involvement at this time. Although Sainteny did not actually volunteer, Harriman came away from the meeting with the feeling that he would be willing to make a personal try.

Ambassador Harriman provided me with a letter assuring Sainteny that I had his trust and that Sainteny could speak with frankness. My task was to persuade Sainteny to undertake a personal mission to Hanoi and attempt to establish preliminary contacts between the American and North Vietnamese Governments. I was authorized to tell him that Washington had given careful thought to the terms of a final political settlement, and that we would like to discuss those terms with representatives of Hanoi. I was not permitted to reveal any of the details of our negotiations package, the Phase A–Phase B formula, or the tenuous link we already had established in Moscow.

Sainteny was especially interested in an analysis that had been prepared for our meeting. The study acknowledged that there were many aspects of the Geneva Agreements that would be relevant to a new political settlement; we had placed particular emphasis on prohibition of reprisals, arrangements for the free movement of population, re-establishment of the demilitarized status of an area on each side of the 17th parallel, provisions for a ceasefire, and elections both within South Vietnam and with respect to the unification of the two Vietnams.

Sainteny indicated that, while he was not anxious to undertake another trip to Hanoi, he recognized the importance of ending the war and was convinced that the United States Government was genuinely anxious to enter negotiations. Such a mission would obviously be undertaken on a personal basis, but he felt he would have to get de Gaulle's permission and would try to see the General as soon as possible.

A few days later we met again. Sainteny said ruefully that de Gaulle was unwilling to assume any role or responsibility as a mediator until he felt "the time was ripe." De Gaulle thought that even if Sainteny were to go on his own Hanoi would be likely to interpret his trip as an official French mission. It was clear that de Gaulle was not interested in having the French play a mere exploratory role; he wanted to wait until he could deliver a political settlement. I reminded Sainteny that we had agreed he would go to Hanoi as a private French citizen who had the friendship and trust of both the Americans and the North Vietnamese. As he and de Gaulle knew, many self-appointed, would-be mediators with few bona fides had made the trip with no results. We had confidence that he might be able to carry it off. Sainteny shrugged. One more attempt to establish a channel to Hanoi had failed.

In the spirit of Washington's agreement with Brown and Wilson, I had mentioned upon my departure from London that I was going to Paris to meet with a possible French intermediary. British relations with the French Government were strained, and I sensed some concern that de Gaulle might increase his stature by pulling off a French-sponsored political agreement. Before I left Paris for Washington, I sent word to London that nothing had resulted from my visit to France. I had a feeling my British friends would be secretly relieved.

❋   ❋   ❋

After a brief intermission, the curtain rose on another act of the diplomatic melodrama. The time was about two weeks later, the place was London, the cast included two super-stars—Prime Minister Wilson and Premier Kosygin.

While the principal players and the supernumeraries were reviewing their scripts for their London opening, several developments were taking place off stage—developments which would be of importance in creating atmosphere, and even in influencing the plot. The first was an interview given by North Vietnamese Foreign Minister Nguyen Duy Trinh to Wilfred Burchett, an Australian Communist newspaperman. The North Vietnamese had found Burchett useful in the past not only because of his excellent contacts with Western correspondents and diplomats, but because his reports could be denied if Hanoi had second thoughts or if public reaction was unsatisfactory. But there were no second thoughts, and there was no retraction of the interview Foreign Minister Trinh gave Burchett on January 28th. It is worth noting that the interview took place the day after Guthrie was subjected to the diatribe in Moscow. This may have been Hanoi's answer to Washington's proposals of January 20th, although it was far from the answer Washington was hoping for.

After the standard dose of vitriol, Trinh came to the point: "Only after the unconditional cessation of U.S. bombing and all other acts of war" against North Vietnam "could there be talks." In spite of Trinh's harsh tone and the implied ultimatum, that interview contained considerable food for hungry State Department analysts to digest. This was the first time Hanoi had directly addressed the possibility of an official dialogue between North Vietnamese and Americans. Until now Hanoi's alleged position had been relayed to Washington through second or third-hand sources who, even if well-intentioned, were frequently unreliable. Now, at last, we were being given North Vietnamese views from a high official source. And for whatever it was worth, Trinh had modified the reference to a bombing halt; instead of the usual "finally and unconditionally," he used "unconditionally" only.

And yet there was still reason for doubt. Did the public interview actually represent Hanoi's official policy? After all, the North Vietnamese had had an opportunity to pass their message directly and privately to the United States through their channel in Moscow. One could only speculate that there were considerable differences within the upper echelons of the North Vietnamese Government about the advisability of the clandestine Moscow meetings—differences which may have become increasingly unmanageable as the days went on. Those who had opposed the meetings must have been able to exert their full influence when

Hanoi was pressed for a substantive response to the American proposals. North Vietnamese officials, suspicious of Washington's good faith, may have felt they were being seduced into substantive talks while the bombing of North Vietnam continued. But whatever the reasons, Hanoi had decided to slam the door on Guthrie and to respond to the American proposals publicly, emphatically, and on North Vietnamese terms.

Any doubts among the Hanoi-watchers in Washington that Trinh's remarks should not be taken seriously simply because they had been transmitted through a newspaper interview were dispelled within a few days. Robert Kennedy, meeting with officials of the French Foreign Office on January 31, was told that the French had been officially informed by the North Vietnamese that Trinh's remarks represented a significant policy statement. This was underlined when the interview was published on the front pages of North Vietnamese newspapers (thereby providing a hint, for the first time, to the people of North Vietnam that the regime was even considering talking to the American Government). Within a day or two the Chinese Communist press added further emphasis to Trinh's views by giving them wide publicity.

Surprisingly enough, the interview was initially given little play in Soviet propaganda organs. On the eve of Kosygin's departure for London, however, Soviet media gave it wide coverage. According to Soviet commentators, the Kremlin regarded the North Vietnamese statement as "a new manifestation of the good will of the Democratic Republic of Vietnam." [4] More would be heard along this line when Kosygin came to London.

Even granting that Trinh had made an important, official statement, the conclusion in Washington was that, after all, he did not say anything very constructive. It was unclear whether the North Vietnamese were actually aware of the significance of the word "could" until the interview was translated into English and had been dissected in Washington. The formulation may originally have been put into the "could" form quite innocently by Trinh. Perhaps he meant to convey that, upon a bombing cessation, talks would be likely or even certain; even American spokesmen have been known to be careless of their English grammar. In any case,

Washington chose to interpret Trinh's statement to mean that when bombing stopped, Hanoi would then decide whether there would be talks or not. Possibly because this was the correct interpretation, possibly because he found he had been given some additional leverage thanks to the complexities of the English language, Trinh stuck with the conditional mood.

Whether we would have stopped the bombing at this time if Trinh had used "would" is a moot point. Most American policymakers objected at that time to a trade-off between a bombing cessation and talks. In any case, for almost a year discussions of this issue took on a Talmudic quality, with great attention being paid to the slightest word or tense changes in statements emerging from Hanoi. When finally, late in December 1967, Hanoi changed its formulation from "could" to "will," there was a new flurry of diplomatic activity.

Foreign Minister Trinh and Premier Kosygin were not the only officials using the news media to float official positions on negotiations. On February 2nd President Johnson held a TV news conference. He said he was ready to meet the North Vietnamese "more than half way" in search of a peaceful settlement. The President went even further; he described in detail America's willingness to discuss almost any subject of interest to the North Vietnamese at almost any acceptable site. Johnson virtually repeated the proposal made in the secret meeting with the North Vietnamese chargé two weeks before. American spokesmen took pains to point out during the next day or so that the President's views should be regarded as having particular significance. This too would influence the atmosphere, if not the actual discussions that were to take place in London a few days later.

The final, and the most important, off-stage development was unfolding just before Comrade Kosygin met Mr. Wilson at No. 10 Downing Street. During the latter part of January a secret personal letter from President Johnson to President Ho was being discussed in Washington.

Whether the President approved the idea of a letter to Ho when it was first advanced, I am not sure. He was reported to have registered no objection, but, typically enough, indicated a desire to keep his "options open" until he saw a final draft. Secretary Rusk apparently took a dim view of the enterprise from the very beginning. No precise timing for the dispatch of such a letter had been discussed, although the hope at the staff level was that it would be sent some time during the relatively relaxed period of the Vietnamese New Year. There were at least two or three versions being passed back and forth between the West Basement of the White House and the Seventh Floor of the Department of State. The first draft had the stamp of Walt Rostow's lofty style. The prose was elegant—too elegant. Since the primary purpose was to get Ho to take some action, our propositions should be as easy as possible to translate into Vietnamese. After some fiddling much of the high-flown language was removed. The last version I saw in early February impressed me as straightforward and constructive. It expressed Johnson's conviction that both he and Ho Chi Minh had a heavy responsibility to bring peace to Vietnam. It reiterated the Phase A–Phase B proposition pretty much in the terms that were now standard, but did not go into the kind of detail we had earlier provided George Brown. It emphasized the President's readiness to discuss any subject that had relevance, as well as his flexibility as to the form and site of negotiations. I left Washington for yet another trip to London without knowing whether Johnson had approved—or had seen—this version, or whether he had even decided to communicate directly and personally to Ho Chi Minh.

I arrived in London on February 3rd in response to a request from Prime Minister Wilson for another briefing on the state of play on the diplomatic front. Kosygin was expected on February 6th, and Wilson wanted to insure against any more surprises from Washington before he started his round of important talks. It was originally intended that I spend only a few days in England, returning to Washington on the eve of Kosygin's arrival. However, the Prime Minister requested that I remain throughout the Kosygin visit to serve as a link between London and Washington in the event there were substantive discussions on Vietnam. But it was by no means clear that such discussions were likely. Even the ebullient Harold Wilson was disappointed when he learned of the composition of Kosygin's entourage. The delegation was largely

comprised of experts on trade and on European affairs. Gromyko
was not in the party, nor was any other high-ranking figure from
the Soviet Foreign Ministry. Kosygin's trip seemed designed to
promote Soviet propaganda and trade. When the Premier insisted
on visiting some factories and going to Scotland (he was an admirer of the poet Robert Burns), the British were even more convinced that discussion of Vietnam would be brushed off.

The first two days of my visit were spent telling Wilson and
Brown of the abortive effort in Moscow and describing Washington's view of the Trinh interview. To the Prime Minister alone, I
mentioned the possibility of a personal letter from the President to
Ho. I emphasized that this had not yet been approved by the
President, and warned Wilson that, although I had been authorized to mention it to him, the matter should be held in the strictest
confidence.

I saw Wilson shortly after he had greeted Kosygin at the airport and deposited him in the splendor of Claridges. The Prime
Minister was in high spirits. It was clear, he thought, that despite
the lackluster character of the Soviet delegation Kosygin was
prepared to discuss matters of substance, including Vietnam. Indeed on the way into the city from the airport, Kosygin talked
about almost nothing else but the problems the Russians were having in Asia. Adding to Wilson's optimism that something consequential might emerge during the next several days of discussion
was the fact that the Vietnamese New Year period ("Tet") was
about to start, and with it a ceasefire in South Vietnam and a
bombing suspension in the North. Under such circumstances a
discussion of Vietnam seemed especially propitious.

Wilson's enthusiasm might have been somewhat dampened if
he had known that President Johnson, Walt Rostow, and a few
people in the State Department took a rather dim view of his
eagerness to discuss Vietnam with Kosygin. There was a sense that
the British Government was pushing hard, perhaps too hard, to
undertake the role of mediator. To be sure the British could claim
both a right and responsibility to assume such a role; they and the
Russians were Co-chairmen of the 1954 Geneva Conference and
of the 1961–62 Laos Conference. But some of Wilson's American

cousins felt his underlying motivation was to bolster his own and England's prestige. Several efforts to reconvene the Geneva Conference had already come to naught, but Washington still suspected that both Wilson and Brown were having happy dreams of being in the spotlight of a major international conference. There was another, less articulated but more deeply felt attitude about Wilson's imminent meeting that cooled Washington's interest and perhaps even contributed to the failure of the talks. After all the recent frustrations and disappointments of Warsaw and Moscow, the prospect that Wilson might be able to use American chips to pull off peace talks was hard for the President and some of his advisers to swallow. If the time was now ripe to get Hanoi to talk, Johnson, not Wilson, should get the credit.

It was thus with some concern and reluctance that Washington viewed giving Wilson much latitude in dealing with Kosygin on Vietnam. I suspected too that there was some unease about having an American intimately, albeit indirectly, tied to the Wilson–Kosygin talks—especially one who by personal disposition and professional responsibility was committed to getting negotiations started. In any case, there I was, and it was apparent the British intended to keep me in close touch with the discussions on Vietnam and expected me in turn to keep in close communication with Washington.

In his first session with Wilson on Monday afternoon Kosygin shared his worries about China and, as expected, stressed the importance the Russians attached to Trinh's "initiative." He suggested that Wilson join him in endorsing the North Vietnamese statement.

Virtually the entire meeting the following day was devoted to Vietnam. Kosygin reminded the British again of Trinh's talk with Burchett. It was suggested that Wilson use the "hot line" to the White House to inform the President that he favored Trinh's proposal. Wilson pressed Kosygin as to just what he was supposed to say to Johnson; for example, was he to tell Johnson that Kosygin subscribed to Trinh's proposition that if bombing ended there was a possibility that talks could start? How seriously would Washington regard a British statement which simply suggested that he,

Wilson, had faith in the fact that Kosygin had faith in the fact that Trinh's statement meant more than it seemed to mean? Would this be very meaningful to Washington? Or would Kosygin personally guarantee that talks would actually start if the bombing stopped? Kosygin apparently was unwilling to make such a commitment. Wilson then advanced his own suggestion—reconvening the Geneva Conference. He also put forward an abbreviated version of the Phase A–Phase B formula. Kosygin perked up his ears when he heard this and asked Wilson to let him see the formula in writing. Wilson and Kosygin agreed to spend the next day on trade and European problems and to return to a discussion of Vietnam on Thursday.

I reported this to Washington that night and was instructed the next morning to urge Wilson to try to divert Kosygin from pressing the Trinh formula. Washington was also anxious to play down the idea of reconvening the Geneva Conference, since neither Moscow nor Peking seemed ready to discuss such a delicate issue as Vietnam in a public forum. Instead, Wilson should emphasize the Phase A–Phase B arrangement as the most promising starting point for negotiations. The version Wilson had tabled orally should be made more specific. Washington suggested the following: Phase A—the bombing of North Vietnam will stop; Phase B— the infiltration of North Vietnamese troops into South Vietnam will stop and the augmentation of American forces in Vietnam will stop.

On Wednesday morning Washington also sent information on the movement of North Vietnamese troops and supplies southward toward the 17th parallel. The flow had started within a few hours of the bombing pause. (An American reconnaissance pilot later reported that on the first day of the pause the traffic proceeding south in North Vietnam reminded him of "a Sunday on the New Jersey Turnpike.") Would Wilson tell Kosygin of this and emphasize that it weakened Hanoi's case for a bombing cessation? Wilson raised the matter with Kosygin—the first of three occasions when this was done.

As advertised, the Wednesday meeting between Wilson and Kosygin concentrated on bilateral British–Soviet questions. It looked like a Vietnam-less day. But in a speech to London business and civic leaders on Wednesday afternoon, Kosygin made some cryptic remarks about the Geneva Agreements of 1954 that interrupted the first proper dinner I had had in several days, kept me up most of the night, threw parts of Whitehall into disarray, gave Mrs. George Brown a pounding headache, and complicated Washington's instructions to me.

Just as I had sat down to dinner Wednesday night, there was an excited call from George Brown. Would I meet him at his flat as fast as I could get there? I dashed to the Foreign Secretary's flat and burst into the drawingroom. George was raising unshirted hell with several officials from the Foreign Office. He felt he had been victimized by a breach in protocol as he was leaving an official reception for Kosygin an hour or so before. I retreated into the kitchen where I found Mrs. Brown, and she and I had some tea and biscuits until the storm blew over. When I rejoined the group Brown had calmed down, and he recounted Kosygin's speech of that afternoon. He was convinced that he and Wilson were on the right track in proposing another Geneva Conference—Kosygin's remarks suggested that the Russians were anxious to take this route. My Foreign Office friends and I tried to point out that the Geneva idea was a non-starter; the Russians had never really expressed any interest in it before; the Chinese had clearly indicated their disinterest; the North Vietnamese had rejected the idea even though they professed a readiness to subscribe to the "spirit" of the 1954 Agreements. Long after midnight I went to the Embassy code room to report Brown's conviction that Moscow was interested in reconvening Geneva. The reply from the State Department confirmed my belief that Washington was unenthusiastic about the Geneva track.

The Prime Minister and the Premier met again Thursday morning, but when Wilson raised the possibility of reconvening the Geneva Conference, Kosygin gave the idea short shrift. Kosygin then asked to hear the Phase A–Phase B formula again. Wilson described the proposition as we had gone over it during the past few days. Kosygin asked Wilson to repeat it to him yet again, and slowly. This seemed to be the first time he had really grasped what was involved. He reminded Wilson that he had asked to have the formula in writing. Could he have it before leaving for Scotland the following evening (Friday)? He wanted to give it careful study.

Late Thursday afternoon two Foreign Office officials and I wrote up the Phase A–Phase B proposal. Our statement followed closely the version we had gotten from Washington two days before. Moreover, Secretary Rusk had just called attention publicly to the "Fourteen Points." He pointed out that "We are prepared to order a cessation of all bombing of North Viet-Nam the moment we are assured—privately or otherwise—that this step will be answered promptly by a corresponding and appropriate deescalation of the other side." A key element in the proposition, of course, was the time period between the two phases. This period had always remained fairly vague, but was never less than one week or more than three. As I recall, the version prepared for Wilson to give to Kosygin stated the time between Phases A and B would be agreed upon by both parties before Phase A, the bombing halt, would be implemented.

I cabled the statement to Washington, confident that it required little more than pro forma approval. In terms of all the information we had at hand, our draft seemed fully consistent with the text of a communication from the President to the Prime Minister on February 7, which purported to present the gist of Johnson's letter to Ho. My telegram reminded Washington that Wilson had promised the statement to Kosygin before he took off for Scotland on Friday evening.

Unless something went terribly wrong, the telegram would reach the State Department by about 6:30 P.M. Washington time. This would give Washington ample opportunity to consider the matter, and I felt fairly relaxed. On Friday morning when I found no reply among the incoming telegrams, it occurred to me that the Department might have taken a dim view of my troubling busy people with such a simple question. But, I thought, they could at least send a terse "O.K." I saw Wilson later that morning and warned him of yet further North Vietnamese troop movements toward the 17th parallel. I told him too that I had received no reply to my message of the night before. By 5 o'clock (noon, Washington time), I reckoned the Department had had time to deal with my message, even if no one had paid any attention to it on the previous evening. But there still was not a word out of Washington. When I called Wilson's assistant, he reminded me that his boss was leaving for a reception for Kosygin at the Soviet Embassy within the hour. We agreed that I would stand by until Wilson left so that I could pass along any message that came through. By 7 o'clock I was convinced there would be no reply— and that silence meant consent.

So there I was, with my first free night since I had arrived in London a week before. Wilson and Brown were planning to get some much needed sleep, and Kosygin would be rattling through the British countryside on his way to Scotland. There was nothing between me and twelve hours of peace and quiet. I left word that I could be found at "Fiddler on the Roof," told the theater door- man where I was sitting, warned the usherette that I might be get- ting a phone call, and collapsed into my seat. Midway through the first act there was a tap on my shoulder. The usherette escorted me through a maze of corridors and I found myself at a phone close to the stage door. The stage doorman, a somewhat aged but very distinguished-looking fellow, was beside himself. He shoved the phone at me shouting "It's from Washington—the White House!" Around me were running, shrieking girls from the chorus. Under me the orchestra was pounding away. I had a difficult time getting through. Finally, in exasperation Walt Rostow shouted across 3,000 miles of ocean, "Where the hell are you?" I remember shouting back, "If I told you, you wouldn't believe me!" "How far are you from the Embassy?" Rostow demanded. "About as far as I can possibly get," I answered. "Well, get back damn fast."

I dashed back to Grosvenor Square. When I finally reached him again, Rostow told me that a completely different version of the written message Wilson should pass on to Kosygin was on its way. I was to go to Downing Street where Wilson, who had been alerted over the "hot line," would be waiting. I tried to get across to Walt my horrifying suspicion that Wilson had *already* passed on a message to Kosygin, but I don't think it registered. When I reached Downing Street, I found Wilson, Brown, and a few members of their staff impatiently waiting. We placed a call to Rostow, who in ominously frigid tones said the message was on its way. Indeed it began to come in as we were talking. My heart fell as I saw it. We were in a brand new ballgame.

According to the new version, the U.S. would stop the bombing and the augmentation of our forces in Vietnam *after* Washington was assured that Hanoi had *actually* stopped infiltration. The sequence of Phase A and Phase B had been reversed, and the whole formula had been distorted. In short what we would be saying to the North Vietnamese was that a bombing cessation would be directly conditional on their stopping infiltration—a proposition Hanoi had thrown back to us time and time again, and one that was completely inconsistent with Rusk's elaboration of his "Fourteen Points," as publicly released only a few days before. It was hard to believe that the Washington draftsmen realized the implications of their new formula.*

I called Rostow again to see if the message read the way I thought it did. I was informed that that was precisely the way it read. By now both of us had pretty much lost our cool. The Pres-

---

* There was nothing magic, of course, about the Phase A–Phase B formula. Even if Hanoi had accepted it, considerable negotiation about the details of Phase B would have been necessary. We were never clear, for example, whether we expected the North Vietnamese to stop *all* infiltration or merely stop making *net* additions to their force in the South. Washington opinion was divided on this question, although even the advocates of a complete stop to infiltration agreed that Hanoi could not be expected to continue to suffer heavy losses without attempting to replace them. As far as the American side of the bargain was concerned, we talked about no net increase in U.S. forces; we would merely replace casualties and men whose tours were up. Moreover, we had no intention of halting shipments of weapons, ammunition, petroleum products, etc., although we had not really faced up to the matter of North Vietnamese shipments under Phase B. A more difficult and important question was the question of verifying Hanoi's compliance. Regardless of how Phase B was finally worked out, we would never be absolutely certain Hanoi was not cheating.

Phase B was geared to the flow of North Vietnamese troops southward, not because we were unaware of these complications, but because the top echelon of policymakers had a hang-up on the infiltration issue. The liturgy as of late 1966 and 1967 ran much like this: the bombing would not stop without a significant "reciprocal act" from Hanoi; a qualifying reciprocal act was not merely a promise to talk, but rather something directly related to the fighting on the ground; this meant infiltration. In due course, there would be another, more practical version of Phase B, but it would take more than a year to come to it.

ident had made up his mind. Period. The North Vietnamese troop movements over the past several days had apparently thrown Washington into a panic.

Brown and Wilson were incredulous and irate. As I had feared, Wilson had taken the statement prepared on Thursday afternoon to Kosygin's reception. Not having heard to the contrary, and assuming, largely on the basis of my assurances, that we were in step with Washington, he felt no qualms about handing it over when Kosygin reminded him that he had been promised the written version of Phase A–Phase B before he left for Scotland. By now it was 10:30. A call to Claridges confirmed that Kosygin was already en route to the station.

The Washington version was typed on Downing Street stationery, with an introductory sentence indicating that this was the official Washington position and should be substituted for the statement Kosygin had been given earlier by the Prime Minister. Wilson's Private Secretary, an ingenious, unflappable man, was dispatched to the station. Somehow he was able to break through the throngs of spectators, passengers, and policemen. He handed the envelope directly to Kosygin just as he was boarding the train.

The atmosphere at Downing Street that night was gloomy and hostile. Washington seemed to have pulled the switch on any further conversations about Vietnam between Wilson and Kosygin. There was to be a final meeting at Chequers, the Prime Minister's official country house, on Sunday, but both Wilson and Brown (and I must confess I, as well) felt little could be salvaged. After much stewing and floor-pacing, Wilson called the White House. In the two decades of my diplomatic career I had never seen anyone quite so angry, but Wilson kept himself very much under control as he explained how embarrassing and damaging the Washington message was.

My own feelings were by no means cheery. I walked from Downing Street to my hotel at midnight convinced my career had come to a precipitate end. (I had mixed views about this, and kept rehearsing the line: "You can't fire me, I quit.") But what troubled me most was a sense that somehow I had led Wilson astray.

When I arrived at the Embassy on Saturday morning there

was a telegram from Washington explaining the reasons for the message of the night before. It did little to better the situation, and I had a sinking feeling that when I showed it to Wilson and Brown (as I was instructed to do) they would be even more bewildered and angry. The telegram pointed out that the President's letter to Ho, dispatched two days before, had said the bombing would stop after assurances that infiltration had stopped—a reversal of the Phase A–Phase B formula. (It was now apparent that the brief message to Wilson a couple of days before had given us only a sketchy and imprecise idea of Johnson's letter to Ho.) The telegram also made the fairly limp point that the critical change in the order of Phase A–Phase B was compensated for by our offer to stop the augmentation of American forces—a matter that had always been subsumed in Phase B anyway.

I was relieved when the wise and skilled Ambassador David Bruce joined me at Downing Street later that evening to plan for the critical and final meeting at Chequers. Wilson and Brown were operating on the raw edges of exhaustion. A difficult week had been capped by the traumatic experience of the previous night. Until late Friday night they had thought the prospects were good for some deal with Kosygin; now Kosygin probably would shrug the whole thing off. They were convinced that the substitute letter, so unceremoniously passed on to Kosygin, destroyed British credibility. In short they were nursing the conviction that they had been badly let down. The word "betrayal" was bandied about, and there were some uncomplimentary references to a few high-level American officials.

I thought we would be lucky if we could finish the night's work without some very ugly scenes between the British and the Americans, or among the British themselves. Ten years before, during the Suez crisis, I had had a ringside seat at a major Washington–London squabble. Once again I sensed Anglo–American relations dissolving before my eyes. I did not look forward to the hours ahead.

Bruce brought the discussion away from personalities and back to substance. Kosygin, he said, would surely understand the significance of the new note he received as he was boarding the train. The Premier, after all, was a realistic, pragmatic man. Wilson had passed along two warnings about the possible consequences of the North Vietnamese movement of supplies and personnel. Kosygin would hardly blame Wilson for this last-minute communication from Washington. In any case, Bruce suggested, the problem was to see what could be salvaged at Sunday's session. He was sure Washington would be sympathetic to any constructive initiatives Wilson and Kosygin could work out.

At noon on Sunday I reported to the Foreign Office where a car was waiting to whisk me out to Chequers. I had received yet another telegram that morning with detailed information on North Vietnamese military movements toward the border of South Vietnam. Hanoi had moved two divisions, and possibly a third, and hundreds of tons of supplies to points just north of the 17th parallel. One could now more easily understand Washington's concern.

When I arrived at Chequers the Prime Minister had just come back from a round of golf, and he seemed relaxed and in good spirits. He had been in touch with the President that morning and felt the "air was cleared." He took great delight in showing me where I was to spend the day—the attic room that in 1565 had served as a prison for Lady Mary Grey, whose pathetic graffiti could still be discerned on the walls. The room was small, simply furnished, and perfectly comfortable for a day and evening of watchful waiting. There was a window high above the front courtyard, which provided a view of the surrounding countryside and also permitted me to look down on the assembling British officials. I tested my direct telephone hook-up with Washington, had a quiet lunch, and in due course heard the motorcyle outriders heralding Kosygin's arrival.

As the afternoon wore on, members of the British party trudged up the several flights of stairs to give me the latest state of play. Kosygin had enjoyed Scotland, was relaxed, and had not even mentioned the switch in notes. We discussed the communique on Vietnam, which was a bland recital of lofty hopes. Kosygin did not press the Trinh proposal, agreeing with Wilson that it would be fruitless. The omens seemed better than any of us had dared hope.

Later in the afternoon Burke Trend, the cool and brilliant Cabinet Secretary, came up for a chat and a drink. We discussed the possibility that Wilson might still salvage something of value, and we sketched out a new proposition involving a commitment by Hanoi to keep its forces in place north of the 17th parallel in exchange for an extension of the Tet bombing pause. With the resulting decline of tension there would be diplomatic elbowroom to explore further steps that might lead to talks, even negotiations. Trend took the proposal downstairs, having agreed that if Wilson liked the idea I would test it with the State Department and the White House. Wilson sent up a note asking me to do so.

My contact in the State Department mused that the proposed trade-off sounded eminently reasonable. After Friday night's experience, however, we both agreed I should seek a green light from the White House. He would forward the proposition to Rostow immediately.

The hours sped by. Two or three needling calls produced only assurances that the proposition was under consideration and that I would be informed when the President had made a decision. Dinner was over downstairs—and still no word from Washington. I made yet another call. This time I was told an answer would be coming very shortly; the Prime Minister should try to detain Kosygin. All the business had been done, the joint communique had been approved, coffee, brandy, and cigars had been consumed. Kosygin was becoming increasingly impatient to return to London, and Wilson was practically hanging on to his guest's coattails. I heard the police rev up their motorcycles in the courtyard below. In utter desperation I called Rostow and dangled the telephone as far out of the window as I could get it so that he could hear the sound of the roaring motors. That did it. By about midnight, Walt thought, the Washington version of the new proposition would be ready. Wilson was to ask Kosygin to stand by for an important message after he returned to Claridges. Ambassador Bruce should be contacted, and both of us should join Wilson at Downing Street.

Wilson delivered the message to Kosygin as the Premier was stepping into his car, and then he joined Brown and Trend in my "prison" for a celebration drink. In spite of the events of the past forty-eight hours, British hopes were high that Wilson, with Kosygin's cooperation, would now pull a rabbit out of the hat.

Shortly after we had assembled at Downing Street, the message came in from Washington. Washington agreed that if North Vietnamese troops north of the 17th parallel stood fast, the bombing pause would be extended. But Hanoi would have to give its assurances by 10 A.M. Monday, London time. It was an impossible deadline. Wilson would have to discuss the proposition with Kosygin, Kosygin would have to send the message to Hanoi, Hanoi would have to consider it and then transmit a reply. It seemed inconceivable, however efficient and well-intentioned all parties involved were, that a response could be received within the ten hours at our disposal.

Several days, perhaps even a week, would be needed to close the loop, but in Washington's present mood the most we thought we could ask for was a turn-around time of forty-eight hours. I called Rostow and pleaded for an extension. He finally agreed to try, but he emphasized that "it would be measured in hours, not days." Then Wilson got on the "hot line" (whether he talked to Rostow or the President, I am not sure). We finally squeezed out another two hours. There was a pointed reminder, however, that Tet had already ended and the bombing was scheduled to resume as soon as Kosygin left for Moscow on Monday morning. Wilson, Kosygin and the North Vietnamese were to "work fast."

The Prime Minister decided to settle for what he could get. He dashed off for Claridges where he spent an hour with Kosygin discussing the new proposal. Kosygin complained that less than twelve hours were available, but he promised to do what he could.

Soon after Wilson returned, Ambassador Bruce and I left Downing Street for the Embassy. Bruce called Secretary Rusk and came directly to the point: the deadline was ridiculous, several days were needed. He urged Rusk to see the President and argue for more time. I didn't hear Rusk's reply. I didn't have to. I could read it in the Ambassador's face. The conversation ended with a brusque "good night." Rusk had told Bruce the British had been given all they were going to get, and Bruce was not to call him again on that subject.

Early Monday morning arrangements were made to assure that if a response came through from Hanoi, Washington could be immediately informed. Once again I was sitting with my two constant companions—the telephone and the clock. By 10 o'clock there was no word. I called Washington and pleaded for an extra several hours. Kosygin was leaving at noon. Could we at least give him time to return to Moscow and press Hanoi for a reply? I eked out a few hours more. This meant Kosygin would be removed from the play, but it was better than nothing. But 3 o'clock came and went, and still no word from the Soviet Embassies in London or Washington, from Moscow, or from Hanoi. At 3:30 Hanoi broadcast a letter from Ho Chi Minh to the Pope. It was a sharp and angry demand for an unconditional cessation of bombing. The phone rang at about 4 o'clock. It was the State Department Operations Center. Bombing had resumed. I notified Wilson, who was then in the House of Commons describing the events of the past week. Bitterly disappointed, he told the MPs and the press that "peace was in his grasp." More than two years later he told a television audience that "I believe, we got very near . . . then the whole thing was dashed away." He said a 48-hour extension of the bombing pause might have done it.[5]

Wilson had been overly optimistic from the outset. George Brown, for his part, had been much less so. And the Americans had been much less optimistic than Brown. Wilson may be right when he says two more days might have done the trick. But there would still have been a very long way to go even if Hanoi had agreed to our proposal, which on the basis of Ho's letter to the Pope seemed dubious. Nonetheless, the extra time might have given us a chance, and to that extent I share Wilson's despair.

*   *   *

Many days later I was able to reconstruct what had happened in Washington on that fateful Friday afternoon. It was clear that Washington officials actually had had little real interest in the London episode; they regarded it primarily as a sideshow to the main event they were trying to get under way in Moscow. My message had reached the State Department early Thursday evening; no one seemed to take it seriously enough to address himself to it, or even to flag it for priority attention. Harriman was out of Washington and was unaware of the matter. During most of Friday the people who could have given me an answer were doing other things (other things which, to me at least, did not seem especially important or urgent). When my message was finally brought to his attention, Johnson reportedly blew sky high. A group of advisers was quickly assembled. The meeting was held against a background of concern about the North Vietnamese troop movement. Indeed, Washington had been in a state of near panic during the previous several days. Perhaps this explains why the President's letter to Ho had been drafted in haste by Johnson and a few others at 2 o'clock in the morning.

So far as I can determine no one present at either meeting had a text or remembered the wording of the Phase A–Phase B formula that had been used time and time again during the past several months. Nor, apparently, could anyone recall any of the previous history surrounding the formula. In short, my message from London was regarded as a new, somewhat shoddy, proposal. This is all the more heart-rending, since on that fateful Friday Ambassador Goldberg told an audience at Howard University that "The United States remains prepared to take the first step and order the cessation of all bombing of North Vietnam the moment we are assured, privately or otherwise, that this step will be answered promptly by a tangible response toward peace from North Vietnam." [6]

And so ended several months of initiatives, high expectations, and soul-destroying frustrations. The peace efforts from November through mid-February ended in another pall of smoke over Hanoi.

XIV

End of an Administration;
End of a Policy

The spring and summer months of 1967 were lean ones for those working in the negotiations vineyard. The frustration and trauma of the Wilson–Kosygin meeting left a bitter aftertaste in Washington and London, and probably in Moscow and Hanoi as well. One highly placed White House official told me that the Administration would not again allow itself to be seduced into talks with Hanoi through "third parties." Wilson's public statements, that he and Kosygin had come within inches of working out an agreement only to be frustrated by Washington, did nothing to make the President and his advisers look more kindly toward the London episode. Perhaps Wilson was right. But a more realistic view would lead to the conclusion that in February, 1967 neither President Johnson nor President Ho felt himself able to take the steps necessary for the success of the Kosygin–Wilson talks. In any case, although the ten-mile sanctuary around Hanoi was maintained through April, the bombing of targets elsewhere in North Vietnam proceeded with renewed fury immediately following the London talks.

Clouding the skies still more was Ho Chi Minh's answer to Johnson's letter. It was dated February 15, after the resumption of bombing, and was written with ill-concealed anger. To the President's point that "we both have a heavy obligation to seek earnestly the path of peace" and his invitation to engage in direct talks, Ho replied, "The United States Government has unleashed the war of aggression. . . . It must cease this aggression. That is the only way to the restoration of peace." To the President's offer that he was "prepared to order a cessation of bombing . . . and the stopping of further augmentation of U.S. forces" as soon as he had "assurances that infiltration has stopped," Ho replied: "It is only after the unconditional cessation of the U.S. bombing raids and all other acts of war . . . that the Democratic Republic of Vietnam and the United States could enter into talks. . . ."

The tone of Ho's response was as troubling as the content. Although the President's letter was hardly forthcoming in substance, an effort had been made to preserve the diplomatic niceties. But this was not Ho's style: "The U.S. Government has committed war crimes . . . you apparently deplore the suffering and destruction in Vietnam. May I ask you: who has perpetrated these crimes? It is the United States and satellite troops. . . . The U.S. Government has unleashed the war of aggression. It must cease the aggression." The final straw was Hanoi's publication on March 21 of Ho's reply to Johnson. The timing coincided with a meeting on Guam between Johnson and Thieu at which the President exuded optimism about the course of the war and expressed confidence in Thieu's regime.

The release of this hitherto confidential correspondence signaled North Vietnamese disinterest in any further pen pal exchanges between the two government leaders. Whether this reflected a victory of Hanoi's "hard-liners" or whether the North Vietnamese leadership generally was acceding to Peking's demands, Washington analysts were unable to say. A hint of the pressure the North Vietnamese must have been under from their Chinese comrades was provided by reports of an interview in March between Chou En-lai and a Western news correspondent. According to the correspondent, Communist China had earlier warned Hanoi not to propose negotiations in exchange for a bombing cessation and had threatened to send its armies into North

Vietnam in the event of a "sellout peace." Peking subsequently denied the interview, but the correspondent insisted it had taken place.

To be sure, there were some who tried in the late winter and early spring to keep alive the possibility of negotiations. In early March Senator Robert Kennedy proposed that the United States halt the bombing in exchange for a North Vietnamese commitment to negotiate. This was given short shrift by the Administration, which was still hanging on to the original concept of a "reciprocal act" of a meaningful military nature in exchange for a bombing cessation. The mere promise to "talk," or even to "negotiate," was not considered to be a sufficient trade-off. U Thant in mid-March proposed a "stand–still truce" and the reconvening of the Geneva Conference. It was not clear just what this meant; indeed it was not even clear that U Thant himself knew quite what it meant. Nonetheless, Washington and Saigon (after some American persuasion) agreed to give U Thant's proposal serious consideration. But Hanoi and the National Liberation Front rejected the idea.

By spring Hanoi had become more adamant. The North Vietnamese may have been banking on a successful summer offensive, or Hanoi's Washington-watchers may have been impressed with the evidence of increasing American frustration and war-weariness. There was no question that the Communists were prepared to discount their own mounting losses. But whatever their calculations they pounded away, in both their propaganda and diplomacy, at the theme that even tentative steps toward preliminary talks were out of the question so long as the bombing continued.

This was an inhospitable atmosphere for would-be peacemakers. Even the most sincere seemed to be engaging in practice play until they felt they could have a more receptive audience. Kennedy must have realized his proposal flew in the face of current Administration policy. And U Thant must have known that his proposition was unlikely to have much of a chance; Hanoi was certain to reject it in any case, and reconvening the Geneva Conference was repugnant to virtually all interested parties—especially the Russians and Chinese.

In April the Canadians put forward a sensible, if modest idea. They suggested that both sides agree to respect once again the Demilitarized Zone ("DMZ") along the 17th parallel. This could be a first step toward restoring the terms of the 1954 Agreement and might lead to further de-escalation. Although Ottawa may not have been aware of it, the Canadian proposal had a special appeal for the United States. American troops in the northern part of South Vietnam had been under constant harassment from North Vietnamese ground forces operating out of the DMZ, and they had been suffering heavy casualties from the fire of hidden guns and mortars north of the parallel.* Although there were serious doubts in Washington as to whether they were accomplishing enough to warrant their remaining within range of North Vietnamese guns across the parallel, there was great resistance to a withdrawal lest it appear that Hanoi had forced a retreat. The Administration was receptive to any idea that would permit moving American forces further south without loss of face. Ottawa's proposal regarding the DMZ was acceptable to the Administration, but there were some who felt that it could well be expanded.

On April 19 the State Department formally announced a more ambitious approach that involved widening the buffer zone. It acknowledged that the Canadian concept ". . . offers considerable promise for deescalating the conflict in Viet-Nam and for moving toward an over-all settlement. . . . We believe an important step toward resolving the conflict could be taken if military forces were withdrawn from a significant area on both sides of the 17th parallel. The United States Government and the Government of the Republic of Viet-Nam would be prepared to withdraw their forces to a line 10 miles south of the demilitarized zone if the DRV (North Viet-Nam) were willing to withdraw its forces simultaneously to a line 10 miles north of the DMZ. . . . Upon the separation of forces, the United States Government and the Government of the Republic of Viet-Nam would be ready to undertake talks leading to further deescalation and to an overall settlement. Such talks

---

* Much of the military activity observed during Tet probably had involved the movement, emplacement, and supply of these weapons.

could be public or private and take place at any appropriate level and site that the Government of the DRV might suggest."[1]

Immediately after the public announcement, Ambassador Harriman met with representatives of the British and Soviet Embassies in Washington to explain the proposal. He urged them to inform their governments that the United States regarded this as an important first step toward de-escalation; the withdrawal area could be expanded increasingly in both North and South Vietnam. We then contacted the Canadians and suggested that they meet soon with their Indian and Polish partners in the International Control Commission to explore the implications of an ICC "peacekeeping force," as opposed to a mere monitoring force, in the expanded zone. We also asked Pentagon planners to give us their assessment of what would be required for a peacekeeping force. In short, the concept of an expanded demilitarized area and a de-escalation of hostilities resulting from it was taken seriously—by some.

Within an hour or so after the State Department announcement, I learned that a bombing raid on major new targets in the city of Haiphong was scheduled for that evening. Two hitherto untouched electric power plants inside the city were to be hit. Unlike the closely-held Marigold exercise, the initiative with respect to the Demilitarized Zone was widely known to White House, State, and Defense officials. It was hard to believe that the raid could not be canceled even at this late hour. Secretary Rusk was not in Washington, and no one else in the State Department hierarchy was ready to face up to the admittedly distasteful chore of confronting the President on the touchy bombing issue. I made a few distraught, pleading phone calls to the Pentagon and to the West Basement of the White House—but with no success. The sorties had been scheduled and the President was determined that they would proceed on schedule.

On April 20th the morning newspapers carried the story of the new peace initiative; on April 21 there were accounts of the attack on two new targets in the middle of Haiphong. Soon after, Harriman was visited by the Soviet diplomat who had been briefed on our proposal. The Russian had forwarded the American proposal to Moscow and had told his government that Washington wished it to be regarded seriously and hoped too that the Co-Chairmen would urge its acceptance by Hanoi. According to our visitor, Moscow had taken the American offer at face value, but before Hanoi could be contacted there was a major bombing attack on a principal North Vietnamese city. "How could Moscow now assure the North Vietnamese that the United States was seriously anxious to de-escalate the war?" the Russian asked. Harriman did his best, but it was not easy to answer that one. The North Vietnamese turned down the American offer on the following day. (Early in the Paris negotiations of 1968 the subject of respecting the Demilitarized Zone was revived but was again rejected by Hanoi.)

The American bombing during the same 24-hour period in which we launched a major new negotiations approach did not stem from a conscious high-level decision to sabotage the efforts of the peacemakers. Nor was it a "carrot/stick" attempt to signal Hanoi that, even though we were making a new diplomatic initiative, the pressure was still on. Either of these would at least have had the merit of reflecting some thinking on the subject at high levels of the government. But there was none at this point in time; instead, there was inertia, lethargy, and a reluctance "to upset the President." There was just no interest or effort expended in orchestrating military and diplomatic moves; everyone was doing his own thing.

The bombing raids that were scheduled for April 20 could have been called off, but no one at the State Department would screw up his courage to make the try. The President dug in his heels when presented with any suggestion to modify or delay bombing timetables, let alone to de-escalate the bombing. State Department officials were reluctant to dip into whatever capital they had in the White House bank. Even the most determined optimist was forced to conclude after this miserable performance that there were those at the top–level who had no interest in any new ideas, approaches, or initiatives with respect to negotiations. The current operative concept was "Hit 'em again, but harder."

As the spring wore on, however, a small group in the Pentagon and State Department set quietly and carefully to work on a proposal that could have important implications for the course of the war. It involved cutting back all bombing of North Vietnam to points south of the 20th parallel. The arguments were based on the casualties we had been sustaining as a result of the concentration of anti-aircraft weapons in the area of Hanoi and Haiphong and on the lack of profitable, suitable targets still remaining in north and central North Vietnam. Attacks on the southern part of North Vietnam would be continued in the hope of stemming the flow of men and supplies into South Vietnam.

In addition to noting our heavy losses and lack of lucrative targets north of the 20th parallel, the advocates of the bombing cutback argued that we might induce Hanoi to start the process of negotiations by easing the pressure on North Vietnam. The proposition was sufficiently convincing to gain the support of both Secretaries Rusk and McNamara. A meeting was scheduled at the White House to present the case. Hopes were high for the President's approval, and a telegram was drafted informing Saigon of the new bombing policy. On the night of the White House meeting I waited at the State Department with the draft telegram for the go-ahead signal. In due course I was told to put the draft away. The Joint Chiefs wanted the President first to approve a raid on the one juicy target left in Hanoi. Only then would they be prepared, though with many reservations, to limit all bombing to the area south of the 20th parallel. The President agreed to postpone his decision to limit bombing until the Chiefs had been given their opportunity to "take out" Hanoi's thermal power plant. It would be a simple matter that could be executed with "surgical precision"; one strike would do the job.

The power plant supplied 20 percent of the power requirements of North Vietnam. North Vietnam was not an industrial country, and much of the power even in major cities was used for civilian requirements. Nonetheless, it was claimed that the loss of a major part of Hanoi's electric power would substantially impede North Vietnamese military capabilities and seriously affect North Vietnamese morale. Hanoi would thus be more likely to heed our invitations to negotiate.

On May 19th the Joint Chiefs and the Air Force were given their chance to get the last piece of candy out of the box. The power plant was bombed. But the target was not destroyed with "one strike." Nor was the raid characterized by the precision that had been advertised. Many more attacks over many months were necessary before it was put out of operation; in the process the surrounding area took a beating. The power plant was located in downtown Hanoi and was bounded on two sides by residential areas. "Subsidiary damage" was significant, and it was another case of "sorry about that." Hanoi claimed that the premises of the Rumanian and North Korean Embassies were hit. In time, of course, the lights went out in Hanoi, but the people there used kerosene lamps and candles, and the regime neither softened its stand on negotiations nor relaxed its efforts in the South. The President had been given two pieces of bum advice—by those who claimed the bombers could drop their cargo down the smokestacks of the power plant, and by those who equated the simple and resilient economy of Hanoi with the power-dependent cities of the United States.

The bombing cutback proposal was revived in the Department of State prior to the President's meeting with Soviet Premier Kosygin at Glassboro, New Jersey in late June, but the White House gave it a cool reception. In the end, the idea was dropped.

Very little is known about what transpired in Glassboro. There are indications, however, that at lunch on the first day Kosygin showed the President a message he had just received from Hanoi which in essence said that the North Vietnamese would be ready "to talk" if the Americans stopped the bombing. Reportedly a cautious, tentative, but not unforthcoming American reply was drafted and passed on to Kosygin. Nothing further was heard from either Moscow or Hanoi.

Prospects for changing American military policy toward North Vietnam were dim enough that spring; the Arab–Israeli war that broke out in early June provided the coup de grâce. The attention of virtually every high ranking official at the White House, Pentagon, and State Department was deflected from Vietnam. There was so little interest in negotiations in the spring of 1967 that I was declared "surplus" during and after the "Six Day War" and was assigned to a Middle East Task Force for much of June. Not since the Dominican Republic crisis in 1965 had there been such a diversion. But the spotlight was soon to return to Southeast Asia. July saw the beginning of yet another attempt to contact Hanoi.

*　*　*

After several months of diplomatic hiatus and brisk military activity, it was high time to try to recoup whatever political progress had been made and to recover some of the ground on the negotiations front that had been lost since the events of late 1966 and early 1967. The initiative in the summer of 1967 was in many respects the most bizarre and frustrating of them all. The principal players were earnest and highly-motivated amateurs, and the plot took many surprising turns. In June, 1967 a small group of scholars from several countries gathered in Paris to exchange views on Vietnam and the Middle East. During the discussions two old friends met for a private drink. One of them was a French doctor, M. Marcovich; the other was an American social scientist, Henry Kissinger. It was not a chance meeting, and the subject of conversation had been selected in advance. The two men discussed the possibility of stopping the war in Vietnam.

Marcovich told Kissinger that he had a very good friend, M. Aubrac, who had extended his hospitality to Ho Chi Minh during the abortive French–Viet Minh negotiations in 1946. The two men had become very fond of one another and Ho was godfather to one of Aubrac's sons. Marcovich wondered whether it would be possible to trade on this old friendship to work out a political settlement of the war.

Was there any interest, Kissinger asked the State Department, in using such an informal channel to try to establish contact with Hanoi? Kissinger was urged to contact Marcovich again and to suggest that the two of them, together with Marcovich's friend Aubrac, discuss a possible trip to Hanoi. While the State Department would remain officially aloof at this stage, it would certainly do nothing to discourage the Frenchmen from undertaking such a venture. They should understand, however, that Kissinger was acting, not as an official of the United States Government, but as a man with friends in Washington who were interested in their enterprise. Thus if something went wrong, or if the two men turned out to be charlatans or bunglers, the United States could plausibly deny any association with them.

Aubrac revealed himself to be a practical man with a shrewd sense of politics, very much influenced in manner and outlook by his experience in the French underground resistance during World War II. Marcovich was sincere, honest, somewhat naive, and completely innocent of the skills and wiles of diplomatic maneuvering. Both were anxious to make whatever personal contribution was necessary to help end the war. The two Frenchmen went to Hanoi in late July and met with North Vietnamese officials, including Premier Pham Van Dong and Ho Chi Minh. Then through a pre-arranged James Bond-like code, Kissinger was informed that Aubrac and Marcovich had returned to France and had something of interest for him.

When Kissinger got to Paris, he found that they had indeed brought back interesting news. For the first time in several months Hanoi seemed to be relatively forthcoming. The bombing, of course, was still a key issue, but high North Vietnamese officials implied strongly that a bombing halt would bring early negotiations. They also agreed to secret bilateral discussions with the United States on matters that did not directly affect the internal situation in South Vietnam. They seemed realistic about American forces remaining in South Vietnam until after a political settlement. Finally, they indicated that Hanoi would not press for an early reunification of North and South Vietnam. It now appeared that something significant might possibly emerge from the "French channel."

The next move was up to Washington. It was decided to ask Aubrac and Marcovich to deliver an important new proposal to their high-level contacts in Hanoi. In the light of this, the Frenchmen should have no doubts that Kissinger was acting as an official emissary; I was to accompany Kissinger when he next went to Paris. And so in mid-August we all met in a Left Bank hotel. We stressed the significance of Washington's new proposal. And significant it was. For the first time the United States stated its readiness to stop the bombing in exchange for Hanoi's agreement to negotiate.* We were no longer insisting on a substantial act of military reciprocity, although the message did ask that Hanoi "not take advantage" of a bombing cessation.

Despite the official American interest and the importance of the message the two men were to deliver, the meeting was dominated by a feeling of gloom and uncertainty. The reason was not difficult to divine; a fierce bombing attack had been launched against new targets in North Vietnam. (Admiral Sharp laconically reports: "Beginning in August, a major campaign was launched to isolate Hanoi and Haiphong from each other and from the northern and southern logistic routes." [2]) Aubrac and Marcovich repeatedly pressed us as to how they could convince the North Vietnamese that the United States was seriously interested in negotiations when our bombing had reached record levels of intensity. If they undertook another trip to North Vietnam, could Washington reduce the bombing as a signal to Hanoi that their mission was seriously regarded by the United States? Neither Kissinger nor I was in a position to give any encouragement on this score, but we promised to raise the question in Washington. Aubrac and Marcovich agreed to go ahead. But this time they were denied visas to North Vietnam on the grounds that Hanoi was unsafe for visitors. They were asked, instead, to present their message to Mai Van Bo, the North Vietnamese representative in Paris. Washington had reservations about the Bo channel, suspecting that the North Vietnamese office in Paris was carefully watched by French intelligence and that there would be dangers of leaks to the press. But since the operation had gone this far, approval was given. In due course the two men met with Bo, who promised to forward the message and get in touch with them when he had gotten a reply.

For once the string and percussion sections of Johnson's symphony were playing the same score. In early September, at the time when Hanoi was presumably considering the American offer, the ten-mile sanctuary was re-established around Hanoi. Although

* This foreshadowed an offer the President was to make public a few weeks later in San Antonio.

many weeks went by without any word from Bo, a dialogue of sorts was being conducted elsewhere.

In a speech before the UN General Assembly on September 21 Ambassador Goldberg asked: "Does North Viet-Nam conceive that the cessation of bombing would or should lead to any other results than meaningful negotiations or discussions under circumstances which would not disadvantage either side?" [3]

On September 26, Hanoi replied directly to Goldberg and perhaps indirectly to the message sent through Aubrac and Marcovich: "Goldberg had the cheek to clamor about U.S. good will, to demand meaningful discussions on the part of the Vietnamese people which, he said, would not be to the disadvantage of the United States. This means that the United States would not stop its piratical acts without reciprocity and bargains. This is an insolent and ridiculous allegation. . . . Since the United States is committing illegal acts, it must stop these acts. The Vietnamese people have nothing to bargain. As for talks, whether they would be meaningful or not depends on whether or not the United States gives up its aggressive policy." [4]

It seemed hard to believe that the North Vietnamese would reject outright an American offer which came so close to Foreign Minister Trinh's own proposition. Trinh had said that if the bombing stopped unconditionally, talks "could start"; Washington said that if Hanoi agreed to talks, the bombing would stop. There was, of course, one condition attached to the Washington offer—a not unreasonable one in the light of past experience during the February bombing pause: Hanoi should not "take advantage" of a bombing cessation. And even this "no advantage" condition was defined, as Clark Clifford would soon make public, as infiltration exceeding "normal levels."

In late September the President publicly unveiled the new trade-off of a bombing halt for negotiations. In a speech at San Antonio on September 29 Johnson said, "We and our South Vietnamese allies are wholly prepared to negotiate tonight. . . . As we have told Hanoi time and time and time again, the heart of the matter is really this: The United States is willing to stop all . . . bombardment of North Vietnam when this will lead promptly to productive discussions. We, of course, assume that while discussions proceed, North Vietnam would not take advantage of the bombing cessation." [5] It was a dramatic, if not entirely accurate account. This particular formula had not been advanced "time and time and time again." Hanoi had been informed of this new American position for the first time in the secret letter given to Bo, and the American public was only now informed of it.

The President's offer was brushed aside by Hanoi's official newspaper a few days later on October 3 as containing "nothing new." In due course the North Vietnamese flatly rejected the President's offer on the grounds that it was surrounded with "conditions." According to an October 20th report by the Communist correspondent, Wilfred Burchett, Trinh had told him that Hanoi would not bargain on the terms of a bombing halt. "There is no possibility of talks or even contacts between North Vietnam and the United States," Burchett said. "Hanoi is in no mood for concessions or bargaining. There is an absolute refusal to offer anything except talks for a cessation of the bombardment. The word stressed is 'talks' not negotiations." Burchett quoted Trinh as saying that his offer of late January, 1967 "was still valid" (if the bombing stopped, talks *could* start). Referring to the President's word "productive," Burchett went on to say that the question of whether the talks "would be fruitful or productive depends on the United States." [6]

❋   ❋   ❋

In mid-September I went to a European capital in pursuit of another phantom olive branch. The government involved was sympathetic to, but not entirely in favor of our Vietnam policy. It had agreed that its Ambassador to Peking could visit Hanoi to explore the possibility of direct North Vietnamese–American contacts. There was not much that Washington was prepared to tell the government or its Ambassador. My chore was to encourage the Ambassador to go to Hanoi and to brief him on the overall American position. If he and his government decided to undertake the mission, and if Hanoi agreed to his visit, he could anticipate receiving a meaningful message to pass on to the North Vietnamese.

Washington felt that by the time the Ambassador actually left for
Hanoi, a favorable reply might have been received from Bo and
therefore the Ambassador might be able to move the ball forward.
In the meantime, Washington did not wish to reveal the message
we had already passed through the "French channel."

Washington's view toward "third government" peace efforts
was typically a mix of noblesse oblige, diffidence, and skepticism.
Although the country involved in this initiative regarded its offer
to help as a serious, perhaps politically risky matter, to the Administration in Washington it was just the latest in a long series of
unfruitful efforts. Perhaps this explains Washington's sharp and
angry reaction to the cable in which I reported my first meeting
with the Foreign Minister and Ambassador: If the Ambassador
went to North Vietnam, the Foreign Minister asked, would the
United States suspend the bombing of Hanoi while he was there—
not only for the Ambassador's personal safety, but also to improve
the atmosphere in which he would be carrying out his peace mission? I told the two Foreign Office officials that I was confident
such a bombing suspension could be arranged. What I did not
mention to the Foreign Minister and the Ambassador (because it
was none of their business) and what I did not mention in my
telegram to Washington (because it seemed gratuitous) was that
before I left I had received Secretary Rusk's approval to deal with
this expected question in precisely this manner. But any reference
to any bombing suspension for any length of time touched exposed
nerves in the White House West Basement and the State Department's Seventh Floor. By return telegram I was instructed to go
back to the Foreign Office and clear up any implications that our
bombing of Hanoi might be temporarily suspended during the
Ambassador's trip. I took a long walk in the bright, crisp afternoon,
composing, as I strolled, a telegram to Washington. I worked up
a masterpiece of sarcastic references to the record and haughty
explanations of why the Ambassador's request was perfectly reasonable, even if we had not anticipated and already agreed to
meet it—which we had. But my superiors were spared any verbal
parries and thrusts. Soon after I returned to the Embassy I received a phone call from Washington: Apologies, record shows

acted in accord with instructions, apologies, good work, have fun, apologies, regards to Ambassador. In the event, the Ambassador did not get a visa for Hanoi, and so ended yet another try.

I left the Department shortly after I returned from Europe, and my direct responsibilities ended. There was little prospect of early negotiations. Weeks had passed and there was still no word from the "French channel" (in fact it was not until December that the Department got its answer from Bo—a cold no). Both Hanoi and Washington seemed resigned, perhaps even eager, to slug it out on the battlefield. The diplomatic track was getting dusty from disuse.

That autumn Governor Harriman was asked to head a Presidential delegation to dedicate the great dam at Mangla, Pakistan. Harriman suggested that he take the opportunity to visit Marshal Tito in Yugoslavia, and then proceed to Rumania. Prime Minister Maurer had visited Hanoi in late September, and although he had already informed the American Ambassador in Bucharest of his findings, Harriman wanted to get this information firsthand. Moreover, he thought the Rumanians might be helpful in breathing some life into dormant Hanoi–Washington contacts.

Ambassador Harriman arrived in Rumania in late November. According to Maurer, the North Vietnamese were not opposed to the idea of trading off a bombing cessation for negotiations. But Harriman pointed out that President Johnson needed something more precise from Hanoi; the North Vietnamese had apparently rejected the San Antonio formula, which offered to stop bombing in exchange for negotiations. Maurer agreed to try to obtain a more definite commitment. And in due course the Rumanians, who turned out to be among the most effective of the intermediaries, delivered on their promise.

The year 1967 ended with the diplomats feeling discouraged but with the soldiers having high hopes and great expectations. There were now a half-million American troops in South Vietnam and major, perhaps definitive, military victories were in sight. The Communists' casualties had been high during 1967, and their forces had been unable to maintain either the initiative or the momentum that had characterized their performance in earlier peri-

ods. In mid-November General Westmoreland was "never more encouraged in my four years in Vietnam." A few days later he predicted that Communist strength in Vietnam would be sufficiently
sapped by 1969 to permit the withdrawal of some U.S. troops.
And on New Year's Day he said that "we should expect our gains
of 1967 to be increased many-fold in 1968."

*   *   *

The New Year began with two developments that were to have
crucial influence on prospects for negotiations. On January first,
mid-point in the brief holiday bombing pause, Radio Hanoi broadcast an important speech by Foreign Minister Trinh (made several days earlier at a reception for visiting Mongolian dignitaries).
Trinh said that "after the United States had ended unconditionally the bombing and all other acts of war against the DRV, the
DRV *will* hold talks with the United States on questions of concern." With the change of "could" to "will," Hanoi had launched
a major new diplomatic initiative.

Trinh's speech was examined carefully by State Department
experts in the Vietnamese language to make sure that the change
of tense was not simply a mistranslation. But when it was established that Hanoi had actually changed its formulation, another
gnawing question arose: How long would it take Hanoi to start
talks after the bombing ceased? Even if talks were to take place
within a few days, Washington officials were haunted by the fear
of being trapped into a bombing cessation in exchange for endless,
fruitless, and frustrating discussions like the Panmunjom talks in
Korea. But even the most hard-nosed now acknowledged that
Hanoi had gone a long way toward the President's "San Antonio
Formula." Despite some difference in rhetoric, the American and
North Vietnamese public positions were now very close. Nonetheless, the bombing of North Vietnam once more resumed on January 2.

On January 25th a major step was taken to narrow the gap
even more between the North Vietnamese position and our own.
Secretary of Defense-designate Clark Clifford appeared before the
Senate Armed Services Committee to clarify the President's "San

Antonio Formula." * Asked whether a cessation of North Vietnamese military activities would be expected to follow a cessation of bombing, Clifford replied that he did not "expect them to stop their military activities. I would expect that they would start negotiations promptly and not take advantage of the pause. . . ." Pressed on what he meant by "taking advantage," Clifford responded that "military activity will continue in South Vietnam, I assume, until there is a ceasefire. . . . I assume that they will continue to transport the normal amount of goods, munitions, and men to South Vietnam. I assume that we will continue to maintain our forces and support our forces during that period. . . . In the language of the President . . . he would insist that they not take advantage of the suspension of the bombing." But, Clifford admitted, "there is no way to keep them from taking advantage. If they state that they are going to refrain from taking advantage and then refuse to do so, then they have not met their agreement and the conditions for negotiations have failed." [7]

In essence what Clifford was saying, reportedly without the President's advance knowledge and approval, was that if we suspended bombing, we did not expect Hanoi to stop the flow of men and material into South Vietnam but did expect that the flow would not go beyond "normal" current levels.† The President was re-

* Robert McNamara had announced his resignation on November 29, 1967. Clifford was appointed as McNamara's successor on January 19, 1968 and confirmed by the Senate on January 30. McNamara had become increasingly unhappy with the course of American policy in Vietnam. Early in 1967 he had revealed his doubts about the effectiveness and wisdom of the bombing. By summer his views had become widely known. In late August he told the Senate Preparedness Subcommittee that he opposed extending the scale and nature of bombing targets and doubted that any level of bombing, short of direct strikes on population centers, would affect Hanoi's will to continue the war. The issue, he emphasized, would be decided in South Vietnam. A few days later the Subcommittee, which was Johnson's principal source of support in the Senate, claimed that McNamara had "shackled" the bombing campaign. The President then felt it necessary to deny that there was a "deep division" within the Administration on the bombing question. Johnson must have been relieved to find a graceful way of replacing McNamara.

† One of the problems with the San Antonio Formula, especially as elaborated by Clifford, was that our information on the level of infiltration of men and materials into South Vietnam at any particular time was sketchy and unreliable. There was a lag of many weeks, sometimes months, before reliable data became available. We were able to observe major movements of men and supplies down the main roads of North Vietnam, but the daily flow of people slipping down the jungle-

ported to have been puzzled with this interpretation and it was several days before the State Department announced that Clifford's testimony represented the official Administration view. On the same day that Clifford was appearing on Capitol Hill, Secretary Rusk asked an audience in New York, "Do they really expect us to stop half the war while the other half of the war goes on?"

If Hanoi had any interest in negotiations, it was hard as of late January to explain why the North Vietnamese did not pick up Clifford's offer. Perhaps they felt we were about to cave in and that one more body-blow, either at home or in Vietnam, would put us on the ropes. As it turned out, both body-blows were on their way.

Clifford's statement came shortly before the Vietnamese New Year. There was some optimism that, with the Tet ceasefire in South Vietnam and the bombing halt in the North, and with the Trinh and Clifford statements on the record, the time was ripe for a diplomatic breakthrough. The optimistic reports from Vietnam with respect to the military and pacification programs led many to believe that negotiations might now be more acceptable to Hanoi and the Viet Cong than a continuation of the war. General Westmoreland had described 1967 as "The Year of the Offensive," and even the most cynical observers agreed that the North Vietnamese and the Viet Cong had suffered tremendous casualties during that year. The North Vietnamese may well have lost a whole generation of young fighting men in 1967. As for the Viet Cong, green, young recruits with little or no training were being sent into battles. B-52 raids within South Vietnam had pounded away at those Viet Cong base areas that allied ground forces found difficult to penetrate. It was reasonable to believe in early January that Trinh's change of tense reflected a recognition in Hanoi that the odds were heavily weighted against a Communist military victory, rather than a change of heart with respect to a political settlement. Many hard-liners, both military and civilian, argued that negotiations should be stalled off as long as possible while the

---

canopied Laos trails was almost impossible to observe. It was now evident, however, that the Administration was ready to take the calculated risk that gross violations could be detected.

Allied forces continued to improve our military position and political leverage. Thus Washington was in an optimistic mood—the hawks because they sensed military successes in sight at last, and the doves because they saw few remaining differences standing in the way of early American–North Vietnamese talks.

Some of the bloom was removed in mid-January. Mai Van Bo, Hanoi's man in Paris, told the press that the United States could expect no reciprocity for a bombing halt. And when the President said in his State of the Union message that he was "exploring the meaning" of Trinh's proposal but warned that Hanoi "must not take advantage" of a bombing cessation, the North Vietnamese quickly responded that the San Antonio Formula was a "habitual trick" and was accompanied by "insolent conditions." The mood was to change even more dramatically in the course of a few days.

On January 30, in the midst of the Vietnamese New Year ceasefire, the Communists unleashed a tremendous onslaught on virtually every city and major town in South Vietnam. Saigon and Hue, the modern and ancient capital cities, were especially hard hit. Although Communist forces were finally driven out, large parts of Hue, including some of its historic monuments, were destroyed. The attack on Saigon was accompanied by a suicide raid against the American Embassy itself. According to General Westmoreland, "Even though by mid-January we were certain that a major offensive action was planned by the enemy at Tet, we did not surmise the true nature or the scope of the countrywide attack. . . . It did not occur to us that the enemy would undertake suicidal attacks in the face of our power. But he did just that. . . . Over a long period of time . . . enemy troops in civilian dress . . . slipped into the cities, particularly Hue and Saigon. . . . The Vietnamese National Police were ineffective in stopping or detecting the magnitude of the enemy's effort. The minds of the Vietnamese in Saigon and other cities were preoccupied with the approaching Tet holiday. . . ." [8] Although 1,000 Americans, 2,100 South Vietnamese, and 32,000 Communists were reportedly killed during the first two weeks of the Tet offensive, the most significant casualties were American prestige abroad and self-confidence at home.

It took several days for Washington to come to grips with what had actually happened in Vietnam—and with the effects this sharp turn of events had in the United States itself. One thing came out loud and clear: despite ambitious pacification programs and optimistic claims of progress, the Communists still seemed to have sufficient control over the Vietnamese countryside to come and go virtually at will. It was tragically apparent that the efforts over the past two or three years to strengthen the rural areas against Communist assault or infiltration had been in vain. Even the cities, which up to now were regarded as under firm government control, were vulnerable. In the first few days of February it looked as if the non-Communist position and American policy in Vietnam were both in jeopardy.

While the Tet offensive had traumatic effects in both Saigon and Washington, it subsequently turned out that it was not the complete and unmitigated disaster it first appeared to be. The Communists had demonstrated their ability to move against virtually every part of South Vietnam if they were ready to make a determined effort, but it was never clear just what the enemy's ultimate objective was in this Wagnerian onslaught. In some of the cities and towns it is doubtful they planned to do more than demonstrate their strength and then withdraw; at least this seemed to be their tactic in most of the provincial capitals. In Hue they probably counted on being joined by the chronically restive Buddhists and students, who on so many other occasions had shown antipathy for the government in Saigon, but neither group rose up to assist the invading troops.

In Saigon too the Communist goals were not very clear. Captured prisoners said they had expected the population to rise up against the government and cheer the invaders. Many of them supposed that the city would fall in short order. Some regular Viet Cong units were planning "victory parades." [9] On January 31 a National Liberation Front broadcast stated that the objective of the general offensive was to topple the "Thieu-Ky puppet regime" and restore "national independence, peace, sovereignty, democracy and happiness to the people. . . ." Several days later NLF representatives in Moscow and Algiers echoed the broadcast, saying that their purpose was the destruction of the Saigon Government.

Communist agents and infiltrators found hospitality in parts of Saigon, and large sections of the city were damaged or destroyed by "friendly" artillery and air attacks. Nonetheless, government efforts against the Viet Cong did not have to be diverted to cope with popular uprisings.

In part based on its assumption that the Communists had failed to attain their maximum objectives, and in part because of its natural inclination to counter the sense of despair following the Tet offensive, the Administration announced that the Communists had met with a substantial defeat in February. Some spokesmen even claimed that the Tet offensive turned out to be an American and South Vietnamese victory. President Johnson declared that the Viet Cong suffered "a complete military failure," and added that "when all the facts are known, they will not achieve a psychological victory." * Sometime later Ambassador Bunker declared in an interview that the allies were stronger after the offensive than before.

To be sure, the Communists suffered tremendous casualties and were eventually ejected from the major cities, but most Americans hardly equated this with a military victory for the men in the white hats. The hardest thing to swallow in Washington, Kansas, and California was that just a few short days before, reports from Vietnam were so bullish that an unqualified defeat of the Communist forces seemed within reach during 1968. Now the situation was once more in a shambles.

General Wheeler went to Vietnam on February 23 to make a personal investigation. He met with the President within hours after his return. The General was grim and the President even more so. Wheeler told the President that more troops were needed. The 500,000 American troops already deployed were insufficent to assist South Vietnam in protecting its population centers and still ward off fresh North Vietnamese attacks against key

---

* In his televised reminiscences on February 6, 1970, Johnson described the Tet offensive as being "a disaster, a debacle, and a serious military loss" for the Communists. "I don't think that ever got communicated to the American people."

outposts along the DMZ and the Laos infiltration routes. Although the substance of Wheeler's report was closely guarded, it soon became public knowledge that Westmoreland and Wheeler were thinking of requesting very substantial additional forces. In response to a Washington query as to what might be needed in Vietnam, the military indicated that an early deployment of 30,000 troops was required, and that a total of 200,000 would be needed to buttress our forces in Vietnam and to replenish the strategic reserve. According to some who were present, the President was visibly shaken. He had doled out additional forces for Vietnam bit by bit over the past three years, but the military had been given what they said they needed. And their requests had been granted pretty much on the strength of their own cognizance. But with a half-million troops already in Vietnam, and with no military victory in prospect despite the optimism of a week or so before, the President seemed now, for the first time, to doubt that we were on the right military track.

After a few days of agonized reconsideration, it was announced that 10,500 troops would be airlifted to Vietnam, that there was no intent to raise the total beyond the 525,000 troops already authorized, and that a complete review of our military policy in Vietnam would be undertaken before any decision would be made on new deployments. The atmosphere of urgency and foreboding that accompanied both the official statement and the departure of the additional forces did nothing to reassure an anxious American public. The televised departure of the military airlift evoked a feeling that an emergency relief force was on its way to relieve a besieged garrison.

The President had selected Clifford to succeed McNamara not only because of his obvious talents, but because he was one of Johnson's most trusted advisers. Unlike the increasing number of vacillators and "nervous Nellies" in the Administration, he could be counted on for strong and steady advice on Vietnam. Johnson knew that with Clifford he would have someone close by who, together with his other stalwarts, Secretary of State Rusk, Special Assistant Rostow, and Chairman of the Joint Chiefs of Staff General Wheeler, would support him in his determination to see the

Vietnam war through to a victorious end. Clifford and Abe Fortas regarded the long bombing pause of January 1966 as Johnson's biggest mistake. And accurate or not, it was common gossip that whenever the President rejected suggestions for cutting back the bombing, more often than not it was after these two personal friends had dropped by the White House for an evening chat and a nightcap. For some of us the Clifford-Fortas relationship with the President was a source of frustration and despair. We had no idea how much or how little they read or heard about the situation in Vietnam. But while the in-house hard-liners could at least be written or talked to, there seemed to be no way of reaching these insiders. Clifford himself puts the point well: ". . . it was quickly apparent to me [after he took over the position of Secretary of Defense] how little one knows if he has been on the periphery of a problem and not truly in it." [10]

Clifford's first task as Secretary of Defense was to chair the high-level review of Vietnam policy. A portent of the depth of the review was the presence of the Secretary of the Treasury. His participation reflected the Administration's concern over the impact of the war on the country's international and domestic economic position. Secretary Fowler emphasized that an increase of 200,000 American troops for Vietnam would mean tax increases, federal price and wage controls, and credit restrictions. According to one participant, Fowler's most telling argument against the troop increase was his warning of a devaluation of the dollar that might result.

Aside from the economic effects, the additional manpower requests would involve calling up the reserves, increasing the draft, lengthening the period of service, and sending Vietnam veterans back for second and third tours. Clifford pressed the military on whether the additional troops would make the difference between victory and stalemate. The Joint Chiefs of Staff were unable to assure him that it would. At the end of a week of intense deliberation the group recommended, apparently with Clifford and a few others dragging their feet, that the military should be given a small initial increment, and then described how the remainder of the additional 200,000 troops requested could be delivered. The study was given to the President on March 5th. One of those who participated during that long and arduous week described the product of their work as a "delaying action" rather than a series of recommendations. If that was the intent of those who drafted the paper for the President, they succeeded. Johnson had nagging and agonizing doubts to resolve, and he was in no mood to make a quick decision.

During subsequent days Clifford, reinforced by worried and skeptical members of his own staff and some officials in the Department of State, became convinced that regardless of how many additional troops were sent to Vietnam the prospects for a military victory were dim within a tolerable period of time. But no matter how gradually the new increments were dispatched, the effects on the domestic, political, and economic situation would be grave. Daniel Davidson, a bright and outspoken member of Ambassador Harriman's staff, commenting on the review group's recommendation told his boss that "200 thousand or even 400 thousand" additional troops would probably not improve the military situation by the end of 1968.

The battle over troop augmentation ebbed and flowed for many days. It was fueled by leaks in *The New York Times* and *The Washington Post* on March 10 that the Administration was giving serious consideration to the possibility of deploying as many as 200,000 more troops. Rusk found it necessary on the following day to assure Congress that it would be consulted if, in fact, the Administration felt it necessary to send additional men to Vietnam. By the latter part of March it was clear that the proponents of a minimum military augmentation had carried the day. In the event, it was agreed to ask General Thieu to announce that he did not need additional American troops and that South Vietnam would substantially increase its own forces. An increase of 13,500 American support troops was agreed upon.

But the force augmentation question was only one of several momentous issues that were under microscopic scrutiny. There was the broader and more fundamental question of whether the Administration should move forward on a war or peace track. In a series of dramatic confrontations over a period of ten tense days the issue was ultimately decided by the only man who could turn American policy around—Lyndon Johnson. On March 31 he placed the country, for the first time since we became involved in Vietnam, squarely and unequivocally on the peace track. He also announced that he would not run for re-election.[11]

In retrospect the President's speech of March 31 seems to follow logically from the lessons of his Administration's involvement in Vietnam, from the Tet offensive, and from the burden of the arguments put forward by Clifford and subsequently by a convocation of "Wise Men" (including such formidable advisers as Dean Acheson, General Ridgway, and McGeorge Bundy). But other events, not unrelated to the issue of war or peace, may also have played an important role. By the turn of the year Americans had begun to transform insistent, but inchoate and loosely organized yearnings for an end to the Vietnam war into something much more tangible and significant—a movement that caused politicians and statesmen alike to prick up their ears. The enthusiasm for Senator Eugene McCarthy among moderates and radicals in the various peace movements provided a political outlet for those who wanted to get out of Vietnam—by negotiations if possible, but to get out anyway. His strong showing in the New Hampshire primary on March 12 was regarded by many professional politicians as a fluke, but it became harder for them to dismiss the Senator as an amateur politician surrounded by amateur strategists. The fact that an immediate settlement and withdrawal of American troops from Vietnam was his only campaign issue was not lost on the Administration.

The President may have assumed that he could ignore Eugene McCarthy (after all, many McCarthy supporters were not old enough to vote), but Robert Kennedy was another matter. Kennedy had announced his candidacy on March 16, and while his campaign would clearly involve a broad range of issues, an early settlement of the Vietnam war was high on his list. Indeed there was a story afloat that Kennedy had agreed not to run if Johnson appointed a "Blue Ribbon" group to examine alternatives to the current Vietnam policy. Johnson's review group was probably not quite what Kennedy had in mind, either in terms of the cast of characters or the range of alternatives it was considering. So Kennedy, whose inside sources were good enough to know this (even if Johnson would not tell him), entered the race. The possibility of a tough primary fight began to loom. And if the Kennedy and McCarthy camps joined forces, as it was rumored they might, the Democratic Party's renomination of Lyndon Johnson would not be quite the shoo-in it had appeared to be just a few short weeks before.

Other considerations may also have influenced the President's decision to take this new initiative and to return to private life. On February 28 Governor Romney had withdrawn from the Republican primary race leaving the field wide open for Richard Nixon—a much stronger candidate. And on March 16 the public opinion polls showed Johnson's popularity at its lowest point during the entire period of his Presidency.

Johnson had said that he had long been seriously considering returning to the Ranch. But even his closest advisers admit they were staggered when they heard the last few words of his March 31 speech.

The President's announcement that he would not run again was a surprise dessert at an elaborate banquet of pronouncements. As the first step to de-escalate the conflict, he announced that aerial and naval bombardment of North Vietnam would not take place except "in the area north of the demilitarized zone where the continuing enemy buildup directly threatens Allied forward positions and where the movements of their troops and supplies are clearly related to that threat." The area exempted from the bombing would cover "almost 90 percent of North Vietnam's population and most of its territory." To clinch the point that he had opted for the peace track, he declared that "the United States is ready to send its representatives to any forum, at any time" and designated Ambassador Averell Harriman as his "personal representative for such talks." (Ambassador Llewellyn Thompson was also designated but was soon replaced by Cyrus Vance.) The next move was up to Hanoi.

Many of the State Department's senior officers, including those with the longest experience in dealing with the Communists, had serious doubts that Hanoi would accept a partial bombing halt in exchange for an agreement to start negotiations. Ambassador Harriman himself was initially skeptical that the North Vietnamese would respond favorably to anything but a complete cessation. Up until the last moment he urged the President to commit himself to stopping the bombing altogether once Hanoi sat down to talk. There were others (including myself) who felt that the President's revelation of his future personal plans would induce Hanoi to stall until after the political conventions. This seemed all the more compelling because of McCarthy's and Kennedy's growing strength.*

The doubters were wrong. On April 3 Hanoi offered to meet. The North Vietnamese statement was carefully worded to milk the last drop of propaganda from the President's proposal and from their own reply: North Vietnamese representatives were ready to sit down with American representatives "with a view to determining with the American side the unconditional cessation of the U.S. bombing raids and all other acts of war against the Democratic Republic of Vietnam so that talks may start."

There then followed a full month of volleying on the question of the meeting site. The President's reply to Hanoi had stated that he would be willing to send representatives "to any forum, at any time" to get negotiations started. This, together with his earlier statements that the United States would "go anywhere, anytime" to achieve peace, put the Administration in an awkward position when Washington turned down various suggestions from Hanoi as to a meeting place. General Westmoreland's statement on April 7, a few days after the Hanoi-Washington exchange, that "the spirit of the offensive is now prevalent throughout Vietnam with advantage being taken of the enemy's weakened military position . . . militarily we have never been in a better relative position. . . ." fed speculation that Washington's dickering over a meeting place was a stalling action. The Administration in general, and Vice

* Many months later in Paris, Hanoi's "North American expert" told Daniel Davidson, a member of the American delegation, that the North Vietnamese leaders never took McCarthy seriously and had not expected Kennedy to be nominated.

President Humphrey in particular, began to feel on the defensive.

The location of the conference was not as inconsequential a matter as it might have appeared. Although it was contemplated that the first confrontation with Hanoi's representatives would deal merely with "arrangements," there was genuine concern that this preliminary session would spill over into substantive discussions and that the American delegation would be locked into a site that would be inadequate or awkward. Despite earlier flamboyant expressions of willingness to go "anywhere," the United States had a few minimum, fundamental requirements that would have to be met for any conference other than a most preliminary and superficial one. There was no point, for example, in embarking on a long series of meetings in a country where facilities were insufficient to handle the necessary volume of communications. Not unnaturally, too, we preferred that the conference be held in a country where we had a diplomatic Mission. Finally, the site should be one the Saigon Government would accept. On all these counts, the original North Vietnamese suggestion of Cambodia, with whom we had no diplomatic relations and who recognized the Viet Cong but not the South Vietnamese, was impractical. Still another requirement was that the meetings be held in a country where we could be reasonably confident that personal and official quarters would not be monitored and our people would not be under constant surveillance. This seemed to exclude most Communist capitals. On May 3 it was finally agreed that the representatives of Hanoi and Washington would gather in Paris on May 10.

The American delegation was small and high-powered, able, patient, and imaginative. In addition to Harriman and Vance, there was a gruff, knowledgeable, anti-hero from the State Department, Philip Habib; an ex-newspaperman who came to Walt Rostow's staff by way of the State Department, William Jorden; Harriman's bright Special Assistant, Daniel Davidson; and the highly respected General Andrew Goodpaster (who soon left the delegation to command the NATO forces). There was some early speculation that Cyrus Vance had initially been sent to Paris as the personal eyes and ears of the President, but whether or not this was true, there was little doubt about the mission of the member of Rostow's staff who was assigned to the delegation.

President Thieu gave the negotiators a grim sendoff. On the eve of their meeting he warned Hanoi (and presumably Washington as well) that "we will never cede an inch of land to the northern Communists, we will never set up a coalition government with the NFLSV [National Liberation Front of South Vietnam], and we will never recognize the NFLSV as a political entity equal to us, with which we must negotiate on an equal footing." [12] But Thieu was not the only one in South Vietnam warily watching the Paris negotiations. At the end of April the "Alliance of National Democratic and Peace Forces," which had been organized during the Tet offensive, had met near Saigon and issued a manifesto stating that the Alliance "is prepared to enter into discussions with the U.S. Government." It also noted that the NLF "cannot be absent from the settlement of any problem in South Vietnam." [13] The Alliance was a child, or at least an adopted child, of the NLF and Hanoi and consisted of a mix of obvious, if undistinguished South Vietnam front groups and leftists. The move evoked memories of the Laos Conference of 1961–62 when the Communists successfully pressed for a coalition government built around a neutralist group. Although what emerged in Laos was a disappointment for the Communists, it would appear that they were preparing to try the tactic again in Vietnam. The problem in South Vietnam, of course, was the paucity of card-carrying neutralists—the society was polarized into Communists and anti-Communists. Those in between had fled the country or were remaining very quiet. The creation of the Alliance was a transparent attempt to develop an instant "third force" around which non-Communists, it was hoped, would rally. It turned out to be a frail creature. Although Hanoi, the NLF, and even Peking and Moscow gave the Alliance a propaganda boost during the spring and early summer, it suffered from chronic undernourishment.

Washington, meanwhile, was under considerable pressure to get substantive discussions under way as soon as possible. Now at long last Americans and North Vietnamese were talking, or at least shouting, but the American public was becoming impatient. There were some who even harbored the hope that a settlement could be reached before the November election.

Humphrey found himself in a very uncomfortable spot. It was difficult to carve out a position on Vietnam that would maintain whatever lukewarm support he still had from President Johnson on the one hand, and compete with McCarthy and Kennedy on the other. If substantial progress could be made in Paris in the course of the next few months, however, he would be in an excellent position to capture the nomination and win the election.

But days folded into weeks and weeks into months without any visible movement in Paris. The sessions there had more the characteristics of a "happening" than a negotiation. The central point at issue was a complete bombing cessation and the terms on which it would be made. After much bickering on the question of whether bombing should be limited to the area south of the 20th or the 19th parallel, the decision was made to cut back to the 19th parallel. The bombing cut-back to the 19th parallel permitted the heavily populated areas of North Vietnam to return to some semblance of normal life, but heavy raids continued in the southern part of the country and were interfering with Hanoi's efforts to supply its forces in South Vietnam. During the late spring the Pentagon was privately admitting that the concentration of our bombing south of the 19th parallel and in Laos was producing more effective results in terms of inhibiting infiltration into South Vietnam than did the full-scale bombing of a few months before— a contention that McNamara had strongly maintained. To those who had argued a year before that a bombing cut-back would result in fewer American losses, better military payoff, and possibly even political progress, this belated admission provided some bitter satisfaction.

By late June the American negotiators developed a formula designed to get around the "no advantage" versus "no conditions" impasse. The Americans would stop bombing, and Hanoi would then agree to restore and observe the demilitarized character of the buffer zone along the 17th parallel under the supervision of the International Control Commission. In a sense this was a variant of the old Phase A–Phase B approach. In addition the Amer-

icans would inform the North Vietnamese that the bombing
cessation would be maintained on the "assumption" that the
Communists would not launch indiscriminate attacks on the urban
areas of South Vietnam. It would also be "assumed" that substantive talks which would include Saigon Government representatives would quickly follow.

The Americans in Paris were encouraged to believe that Hanoi
would agree to such a proposal. The North Vietnamese had withdrawn some regular units north across the DMZ and seemed ready
to scale down the fighting in the South. But American forces,
under a strategy of "maximum pressure," continued to hold the
initiative and to maintain an offensive posture. The North Vietnamese have since charged that they demonstrated their good
faith during this period but that we did not follow suit. There are
some, particularly Ambassador Harriman, who feel that we could
have made more, even definitive progress in Paris by the end of
the summer of 1968 if we had completely stopped the bombing
of North Vietnam and had de-escalated our ground-force activity
in South Vietnam toward the end of the previous year when the
Communists seemed to be cutting back.

The new variant of Phase A–Phase B was presented to Hanoi's
representatives in a secret private meeting early in July. By late
in the month there was no response and indeed no hint from the
North Vietnamese that a reply would be forthcoming. The lull in
Viet Cong and North Vietnamese military activity had been continuing for several weeks, but there was evidence that an attack
on Saigon was being planned. Although it was thought that such
an attack might be timed to coincide with a meeting between
Johnson and Thieu in Honolulu on July 20, the meeting took place
without incident.

The North Vietnamese may have been waiting for the results
of the Honolulu tête-à-tête before responding to the American
proposal. That meeting must have given them food for thought.
The Conference Communique affirmed that the Saigon Government "should be a full participant playing a leading role" in negotiations. In short, Honolulu did much to buttress Thieu's stature
(he later confided that "he had gotten more out of Johnson than

he had dared hope for," and that the Communique "was too good to be true"), but it did little to stimulate progress in Paris.

By the end of July Harriman and Vance felt it was time for them to launch an initiative of their own. I was then in Paris. A message was sent to Washington assessing the progress that had been made thus far. Harriman and Vance noted that Hanoi had not responded to the bombing cessation proposal, and they suggested the North Vietnamese might be stalling until after the political conventions. The chilling thought was ventured that Hanoi might try to delay its reply until after the election and possibly until after a change of Administration in January. Thus, Harriman and Vance said, it was conceivable that months could pass in Paris without visible progress. They expressed concern about the political climate in the United States under such circumstances. The disillusionment and the weakening of American resolve that would accompany drawn-out and inconclusive negotiations in Paris might force a new Administration to move toward a precipitate withdrawal from Vietnam. It was suggested that a new tack be taken in Paris immediately: instead of waiting indefinitely for a reply from Hanoi to the new Phase A–Phase B proposal, the United States should return to the essence of the San Antonio Formula. The current Communist military lull in Vietnam could plausibly be interpreted as a signal from Hanoi that it had gone far toward meeting American requirements.* Washington could stop the bombing of North Vietnam altogether, providing Hanoi was informed of certain "assumptions" the United States would make with respect to Communist military actions. It was also suggested that Vance return to Washington to explain the proposed new initiative.

Washington's reaction, which came within hours, was sharp and negative. The President not only disapproved of a complete

---

* In particular, it was felt that Hanoi could be said to meet the conditions the President had publicly announced. At a News Conference on February 2, 1967 the following exchange had taken place:

"Q. Mr. President, we have said in the past that we would be willing to suspend the bombing of North Vietnam in exchange for some suitable step by the other side. Are you prepared at all to tell us what kind of other steps the other side should take for this suspension of the bombing?

"The President. *Just almost any step.*" [14] [Italics mine]

bombing halt at this time, but he was annoyed by references to the political conventions and to a change in the Administration. Any implication that Humphrey needed a major switch in Vietnam policy if he were going to win the Democratic nomination and the Presidency directly touched exposed nerves at the White House. The fact that *The New York Times* also was currently pressing for a bombing halt was the final straw. Johnson was apparently convinced that there was a Humphrey–Paris–*New York Times*–Clifford conspiracy. Paris was to continue on its present track and to wait for a reply from the Hanoi delegation. Vance should not return to Washington to explain the new proposal.

Further evidence of the White House mood was provided in a Presidential press conference on July 31 when Johnson told reporters that 30,000 North Vietnamese had moved into South Vietnam during the month, the highest infiltration rate to date. He noted that the North Vietnamese were preparing for a massive attack, consequently he could not order a bombing cessation. A bombing halt at this time, he implied, would lead "to the loss of heavy American and Allied casualties [sic]" and warned that he might have to move ahead with "additional military measures." It was a fighting, if somewhat exaggerated statement. Most intelligence analysts would have placed the infiltration during July at a lower figure than 30,000. And most non-military analysts did not believe there was a direct relationship between the cessation of bombing of North Vietnam and the number of American casualties in South Vietnam.

Before leaving for Paris in mid-July I had been visited by one of Humphrey's campaign aides. He told me the Vice President had prepared a major speech on Vietnam which he hoped to deliver prior to the meeting of the Democratic Platform Committee. The speech proposed a complete cessation of bombing to be followed immediately by serious discussions of a political settlement. Humphrey was caught between a desire not to prejudice the talks in Paris and a need to establish himself as a candidate with views on Vietnam distinguishable from those of President Johnson. But since he was getting little information regarding the negotiations, and since the slightest departure from the President's Vietnam

line would diminish his White House support (which was hardly
robust as it was), he was painted into a corner. My visitor was
anxious to get assurances from Paris that if Humphrey publicly
advocated a complete bombing cessation the negotiators would
not cut the ground from under him. Would I ascertain whether
Harriman and Vance felt Humphrey's proposal would prejudice or
complicate the current talks?

When I returned to Washington, the Paris proposal had been
rejected by the President, but reconsideration had been given to
the idea of Vance's return. He was to come back for a short "private" visit during which he would brief Presidential Candidate
Nixon on developments in Paris. Vance felt there was still some
slight hope that he could convince the President of the desirability
of stopping the bombing. The prospect of getting Johnson to turn
around on this issue was remote, especially after his July 31
speech, but Humphrey's public advocacy of a bombing cessation
would be the kiss of death. Humphrey agreed that the points he
would score among the liberal Democrats were not worth preju-
dicing whatever chance there was for serious negotiations. In an
impressive act of statesmanship, he shelved his speech.

On August 19, a few days before the Democratic Convention,
Johnson removed whatever maneuvering-room Humphrey had
left. In a speech to the Veterans of Foreign Wars, he said the
United States would not halt the bombing "until it has reason to
believe that the other side intends seriously to join with us in de-
escalating the war and moving seriously toward peace." Since the
Communists did not intend to "move seriously" until we had
stopped all bombing, progress in Paris seemed destined for further
delays.

Throughout the late summer many officials within the Administration continued to urge the White House to stop the bombing.
If the hard-pressed Humphrey was going to win the election, the
stalemate in Paris had to be broken. Clark Clifford was one of the
strongest advocates of this course, much to Johnson's annoyance.
In mid-September the President struck Clifford's name from the
distribution list for "sensitive" telegrams relating to negotiations.

In addition to bargaining over the terms of a bombing cessation, the Paris negotiators confronted the critical issue of the composition and the modalities of the "serious talks" if and when they got under way. The matter of NLF participation had had a long and murky history in terms of American policy discussions. In the early '60s Washington had taken the position that the NLF could not participate in negotiations as an independent party because it was a "creature of Hanoi." As time went on, however, this position softened. In July, 1965 President Johnson, it will be remembered, had noted that "The Viet Cong would have no difficulty in being represented [at a conference] and having their views presented if Hanoi for a moment decides that she wants to cease aggression, and I would not think that would be an insurmountable problem at all. I think that could be worked out." [15] And two years later Arthur Goldberg indicated that the Administration was prepared to agree to participation by the NLF in peace talks.

The Saigon Government had long maintained that it would not talk to the NLF in any forum that implied its recognition as an equal. As we have seen, Thieu reinforced this position on the eve of the Paris meeting. The NLF and Hanoi, for their part, had long insisted that the Saigon Government was a puppet of the United States and therefore had no right to sit at a negotiations table.

Various detours around this impasse had been brooded about in Washington. In 1967 there was some discussion of using a formula by which the "four belligerents" (i.e., Hanoi, the NLF, the United States, and the GVN) would be called to a negotiating table by some outside group such as the Geneva Co-Chairmen or the UN. The State Department legal staff, however, had objected on technical grounds to the use of the word "belligerent," and the idea was dropped. In due course a new approach was worked out, and this was the one the American negotiators proposed in mid-July at a private meeting. The idea was simply to refer to "two sides," leaving it to each "side" to work out its own composition. Thus if the Hanoi delegation wished to regard the NLF as a separate body it could do so, and the United States could do the same with the GVN. On the other hand, the United States need not recognize the NLF as being an independent group but only as a member of "the other side"; the Communists could interpret the composition of our "side" any way they wished. Thus was fashioned the "Our Side–Your Side" creature—a new entrant in the international conference parade of horribles.

By October it seemed that the two road blocks to "serious talks" were close to being removed. With the Soviet Ambassador in Paris applying fuel or lubrication whenever the process stalled, the American and North Vietnamese representatives pressed toward agreement on the terms of a bombing cessation and the modalities of the "Our Side–Your Side" solution to Saigon and NLF participation.

It was at about this point that McGeorge Bundy at De Pauw University advocated a bombing cessation and a troop reduction. As he had done at the council of "Wise Men" held in late March, Bundy acknowledged that a negotiated settlement was the only prudent course. "There is no prospect of military victory against North Vietnam by any level of U.S. ɪ ɪlitary force which is acceptable or desirable." Although there was a flurry of speculation that Bundy was a chosen instrument for signaling a major change in the Administration's course, this was not the case. The President had seen an advance copy of the De Pauw speech but had made no comment. In any case there was a sense of movement, real or imagined, and attention was focused on Paris where some dramatic new development was expected. The hopeful were soon to be rewarded.

On October 31 Johnson announced that "all air, naval, and artillery bombardment of North Vietnam" would stop as of 8 a.m., Washington time, on November 1. The Americans and North Vietnamese had evidently reached agreement in Paris on the "assumptions" and "Our Side–Your Side." At last the negotiators could get down to business. But could they? Within hours of the President's statement there were ominous noises out of Saigon. President Thieu pronounced that "the American Government has unilaterally decided to stop the bombing on the whole territory of North Vietnam." And from a member of the South Vietnamese Government came the candid remark: "We were informed last night, but we didn't go along with it. We are very unhappy."

Presidential Candidate Nixon was reportedly also unhappy; the timing of the bombing halt, just a few days before the election, seemed more than merely a coincidence.

Clark Clifford and other Defense Department officials were once more given access to information on the negotiations. After he became abreast of what had been going on in Paris over the previous five weeks, Clifford told the President that he was convinced the Saigon Government had discounted a Democratic victory in the elections. They were obviously stalling off their participation in the Paris talks until the Republicans, from whom they expected a tougher approach, took over.

On November 1 Hanoi's delegation issued a communique announcing that "a meeting including the representatives of the Democratic Republic of Vietnam, the South Vietnam National Liberation Front, the United States and the Republic of Vietnam will be held in Paris not earlier than November 6, 1968." But on the following day the Saigon Government announced that it would not attend the November 6 session; its conditions were not fulfilled. Either the Administration had goofed, or the South Vietnamese Government had double-crossed the Administration. In any case, whatever advantage Humphrey would be able to gain from the bombing cessation now looked very thin.

Some State Department experts feel that Thieu and Ky never really understood the "Our Side–Your Side" formula when Embassy representatives had explained it to them many weeks before. There are others who claim that the South Vietnamese did understand it but reneged at the last minute. According to this view, some over-eager and possibly self-appointed emissaries from the Republican Party had urged the South Vietnamese to stall going to Paris until after the election and a predicted Republican victory. The argument reportedly made to Saigon was that the South Vietnamese Government would get a better deal after the Republicans came into office. Behind this high-minded stint of foreign policymaking was an underlying suspicion among some Republicans that Humphrey's chances would be significantly improved if it appeared that the negotiations were to get down to business on November 6. Clifford's hunch with respect to Republican maneuvering seemed to be right.

In any event, the South Vietnamese held to their position, the first session of the talks was postponed, and Humphrey lost the election. Relations between Washington and Saigon were more strained during November than they had been since December, 1964 when the South Vietnamese military junta purged the government and dissolved the civilian High National Council. Thieu proposed on November 8 that the composition of the conference consist of two delegations; the non-Communist delegation would be headed by South Vietnam, and would include the United States. This suggestion did nothing to soothe Washington's ire. The American negotiators were beside themselves. After all the months of stewing and steaming, of clandestine meetings and spotlighted plenary sessions, of substantive proposals and verbal manipulations, Harriman and Vance felt they were now on the one yard line. It seemed inconceivable that Thieu and Ky could block them. With a considerable assist from Clifford they argued that substantive talks should start as soon as possible after November 6, with or without representatives of the Saigon Government. Clifford told the press on November 12 that "we should make every reasonable effort to demonstrate to Saigon why it should come in and join the talks. At the same time, if they choose not to, I believe the President has the constitutional responsibility of proceeding with the talks." Later that day, when asked whether Clifford was speaking for the President, White House Press Secretary George Christian said Mr. Clifford "was expressing his views as he sees things." However, according to *The New York Times*, it was understood the White House had cleared Clifford's remarks. In any case, the President refused to permit the American delegation to meet alone with the representatives of Hanoi and the NLF, hoping somehow that Saigon could be brought around.

A few days later the South Vietnamese grudgingly agreed to attend. But now yet another major issue had to be addressed: how would the "sides" be seated? And so was born (or rather re-born, because in the bizarre world of International Conferences the seating question was not an uncommon one) the shape-of-the-

table caper. If it had been left to the American and North Vietnamese delegations, agreement would have been reached on an oval
table early in the game. The Saigon group had much more arcane
tastes in interior decoration. Somehow the furniture too had to
evoke the political mystique that the NLF representatives did not
really exist as separate entities from the Hanoi delegation.

American diplomats in Washington and Saigon were irritated
and chagrined. The Vietnamese Ambassador to Washington, Bui
Diem, confided to a friend that the South Vietnamese were
amazed during this period that the United States could be so
tough. It was the first time in a long time that Washington exerted the kind of leverage that its relative strength and national
interests warranted. On November 27, after precious weeks had
been lost haggling about the shape of a table and similar momentous questions, the Saigon Government agreed that its conditions
for participating had been met "in their essential aspects."

With a change in Administration on the horizon, the starch
was removed from the Johnson team. Indeed it was not until January 16, a few days before the new President took office, that official
word came out of Paris that the procedural matters had been
settled. "Under the terms of the agreement, representatives of the
United States, South Vietnam, North Vietnam and the National
Liberation Front, or Vietcong, will sit at a circular table without
nameplates, flags or markings. Two rectangular tables, measuring
about 3 feet by 4½ feet, will be placed 18 inches from the circular
table at opposite sides." [16]

Substantive talks were, at long last, to start. And with that
Ambassador Averell Harriman returned to Washington and private life. A new American team headed by Henry Cabot Lodge
took over in Paris. It would be his task to rid the Nixon Administration of the Vietnam albatross, hopefully with dignity and honor
—a not inconsiderable responsibility, especially for a man who
a few years before maintained that the war would not end with a
negotiated settlement but by the Communists simply "fading
away." Lodge's tenure in Paris lasted less than a year, during
which time the Communists neither negotiated nor faded away.

XV

No More Vietnams

Time is essential for healing, and the healing process has not yet begun in America. No current bedside report can dispassionately discuss the nature of our Vietnam illness, nor its therapy. The thoughtful American is still groping for reasons, explanations, assurances. "Why did it happen to us?" But it will be a long time before the perplexed will have a truly cool, objective, historical analysis of the complex story of the United States and Vietnam. For now, the observer can only provide grist for the historian's mill.

One hopes that when the historian tries to fathom how the United States wandered into the jungles of Vietnam in the first instance, his story will reach out well beyond the borders of Indochina, even beyond the lands of Asia. One hopes that he will take at least passing note of what was transpiring, or what was perceived to be transpiring, in places remote from Hanoi and Saigon and Washington—in Paris, Athens, Berlin, Seoul, Moscow, Peking. For our involvement in Vietnam was more a result of a mood fashioned by people and events in the United States, Europe, and Northeast Asia than any particular event in Vietnam.

✻   ✻   ✻

It is tempting in our bitter exasperation to marshal all the arguments now available and to rail against the stupidity and chicanery of those American leaders who led us down the jungle path. In our superior wisdom we wonder how Eisenhower and Dulles could have been so blind as not to have seen what we can so clearly see in our perfect hindsight. It is difficult enough for those of us who lived through the late 1940s and early 1950s to recapture the sense and the spirit of that period; it is impossible to evoke the mood of the country during the first decade after V-J Day for those who were not directly touched by it.

The world has become a very different place and poses very different problems from the uncomplicated years following World War II. The issue of the "Free World vs. International Communism" made decisions about international relations seem simple and, what is more, cast a mantle of morality and righteousness over all our actions abroad. The Soviet Union and its friends, by their deeds and their words, provided the spark that launched an American crusade to save the world from Communism.

Moscow and Peking, so far as could then be seen, were staunch allies; the Soviet Union had produced an atomic weapon; Eastern Europe was mute and terror-stricken; the "Iron Curtain" was a popular cliché but an appropriate metaphor. Communist-backed revolts, civil wars, and insurgencies were either freshly put down or still continuing in Greece, Malaya, Burma, Indonesia, and the Philippines. Communist parties were threatening the stability of France, Italy, and India. And here in the United States the trauma of Chiang Kai-shek's defeat had barely been absorbed before hundreds of thousands of American troops were dispatched to Korea to hold off Communist aggression. Senator Joseph McCarthy, exploiting the Communist advance abroad and magnifying the Communist threat at home, wreaked havoc with the lives and careers of officials, diplomats, or civil servants he considered "soft" on Communism.

This was the background against which the decision was made by President Eisenhower and Secretary Dulles to preserve a non-Communist government in Vietnam. While there were some who may have approached the challenge with less zeal and more prudence, there were few who disagreed with the decision.

President Kennedy's policy in Vietnam was to a considerable

extent a legacy of the Eisenhower Administration, but it was also greatly influenced by international events emerging at the time he took office. Asia seemed frighteningly vulnerable and highly explosive; Laos was tottering; the new Federation of Malaysia was taking its first uncertain, faltering steps; Indonesia's Sukarno was already displaying his paranoia and his weaknesses; India was lurching to the left; Japanese leftists were a source of trouble and concern. American indecision in Vietnam might encourage the troublemakers elsewhere. While the "domino theory" was part of the liturgy of the previous Administration, Kennedy had himself used an analogy that was no less strong in describing Vietnam's importance to non-Communist Asia—Vietnam, he had said, was "the Keystone to the arch."

Kennedy assumed the Presidency confident that he could establish constructive, realistic relations with the Soviet leadership. The Bay of Pigs debacle in 1961 and his confrontation with Khrushchev in Vienna soon after were soul-searing, sobering experiences. From them came a determination to stand firm in Berlin during the autobahn crisis of 1961. And from them too came the decision to settle the war in Laos on the best possible terms and then to make a stand against further Communist expansion in Vietnam by increasing American assistance to the Saigon Government. Kennedy's foreign policy stance was given an added fillip in late 1962 following his dramatic success in inducing Moscow to remove its missiles from Cuba. He, and Western statesmen generally, were confident that the danger of global war had now passed. After teetering on the verge of nuclear destruction, many observers believed the Soviet Union would now be likely to conduct its foreign policy with more circumspection and less risk. The only remaining obstacle to an East-West modus vivendi was the announced Communist aim to aid and foster "wars of liberation." Vietnam provided an opportunity for the Kennedy Administration to prove to Peking and Moscow that such a policy was dangerous and unpromising.

As part of the new doctrine of "flexible response," increasing attention was given to the American capability to wage "limited war." For Kennedy this was the key to dealing with Communist expansion in the emerging countries of Asia, Africa, and Latin America. Special Forces, counter-insurgency schools, expanded troop-lift capabilities, and more flexible military tactics were the principal elements of the new strategy. Vietnam provided both a challenge and an opportunity to test the new doctrines. But neither our non-Communist ally nor our Communist enemy in Vietnam was cooperative. The essence of dealing with insurgents, as the British so often reminded us on the basis of their successful experience in Malaya, was to "win the hearts and minds of the people." But such an approach was far removed from the style and experience of President Diem; he so isolated himself that he knew little and perhaps cared less about what his people felt and thought. As for the Viet Cong and the North Vietnamese, they moved progressively along the route from small-scale insurgency to large-scale war before the United States—even if it knew how— and the Government of South Vietnam—even if it were willing —could effectively apply the doctrines of guerrilla warfare. But even if we had had the answer to the problem of coping with insurgencies, we were dealing not with an insurgency in the United States but in a foreign country and an alien society. When the situation in Vietnam could still be called an "insurgency" our admittedly limited expertise could be applied only through the Vietnamese, whether at the level of President Diem himself or of a district chief. By the time we had enough Americans in Vietnam so that we could directly implement our own ideas, hostilities had escalated well beyond the stage of guerrilla war. At the point at which President Johnson took over from President Kennedy, few people referred to the "counter-insurgency in Vietnam." It was, even if there was a reluctance to admit it, an honest-to-God war.

❖   ❖   ❖

In Lyndon Johnson's most anguished moments he drew comfort from a reminder that the abuse and ridicule heaped upon him also characterized Lincoln's tenure in the White House, and, Johnson noted with satisfaction, Lincoln was vindicated and glorified by history. Passing years may indeed soften the sharp and raw memories of the American experience in Vietnam, but at this moment one gropes for a convincing rationale for how we got into the morass. Did it make sense at the time, does it make sense now? Is it possible to extricate ourselves with "honor," or at least with "dignity"?

Vietnam presented the United States with an infinitely complex problem. Lyndon Johnson is an infinitely complex personality. Confront Lyndon Johnson every day for almost six years with Vietnam, and the patterns of action and reaction become kaleidoscopic. There are, however, a few themes that come through the changing shapes and colors: Johnson was too much the "hawk" to do what had to be done to make peace, and too much the "dove" to permit the kind of military action that would have risked a world war. Johnson had a "consensus" hang-up; if he could not embark on a policy that clearly satisfied his perception of the consensus, he would compulsively try to manipulate public opinion. The President was a victim of an unfortunate coincidence of events—the Vietnam war was the most unpopular and complex war the United States has ever been engaged in, and it was covered by the mass media in greater detail than any other war in American history.

When President Johnson succeeded President Kennedy he knew and cared little about foreign affairs. For months important American and foreign ambassadors would cool their heels and control their tempers as they waited to present credentials or problems. Visits by foreign dignitaries were regarded in the White House with barely-disguised distaste. The outside world, Communist and non-Communist alike, was regarded with suspicion. (One of Johnson's top personal aides prided himself on never having been abroad, never having worn imported clothing, never having eaten foreign food, never having had the inclination to learn a foreign language.) The priority was the United States, not the world. Work would start where Franklin Roosevelt left off before World War II. And there was much work to be done—civil rights, education, conservation, health, housing, economic growth. This was where Lyndon Johnson's heart was, this was where his talents lay, this would be his claim to an honored place in history.

The Vietnam war was not Lyndon Johnson's invention. He

might have been able to contain it or even to stop it—but he didn't
start it. The war was going on, and with hefty American involvement, well before Johnson lost his first night's sleep over it. Even
at the stage at which he had inherited the war, the rationale for
the original American commitment had begun to lose its credibility, the original level of our involvement had begun to climb
sharply, and the American people were becoming increasingly
skeptical and restless about an insurgency which, almost without
our notice, had boiled over into a major war.

Lyndon Johnson did not want to fight a war, much less declare
one. Much of the official rhetoric, consciously or subconsciously,
was convoluted so as to skip over, fuzz, or sidle around the fact
that the *United States* as well as South Vietnam was at war.
Throughout his Administration there was no Vietnam "high command" through which military, political, economic, intelligence
and information programs could be coordinated. Nor, even in the
Pentagon, was there a single focal point—a "Mr. Vietnam." Until
very late in the game the AID program for Vietnam, which involved sums several times that of the State Department operating
budget, was the responsibility of a low-ranking official. Within
the State Department, day-to-day responsibility for Vietnam was
assumed by a Deputy Assistant Secretary responsible to an Assistant Secretary who had many other difficult and important
countries to worry about. Within the White House Vietnam was
one of several matters under the aegis of a single member of
McGeorge Bundy's (and later Walt Rostow's) staff.

The President's approach was a mixture of tight personal control and loosely structured organization. He kept most of his cards
close to his chest, but he permitted—indeed encouraged—a fluid,
in-and-out, bird-of-passage style of operation among a wide sector
of policymakers and policy kibitzers in the Administration. It was
difficult even for White House staffers to know at any given moment of play which players were in the game and which were not.
Sometimes the players themselves could not tell if they were sitting on the bench or were in the scrimmage.

The stock answer to this, of course, is that the *President* was in
charge of Vietnam; as his immediate staff he had the Secretaries

of State and Defense, the Chairman of the Joint Chiefs of Staff, the Director of Central Intelligence and the President's Special Assistant for National Security Affairs; a "Staff Meeting" was held weekly (the "Tuesday Lunch"), and the participants kept in constant touch by telephone or in person. But the arrangement did not work, indeed could not work. Each member of this elite group had a full schedule of competing demands ranging from ceremonial appearances to problems with Congress to other major and substantive problems. During the Dominican Crisis in 1965 and the "Six Day War" in the Middle East in 1967, Vietnam was virtually ignored by the President and his high-level staff.

Even if the Vietnam problem could have been managed by the President of the United States acting as the Vietnam Desk Officer, the system would soon have broken down from sheer lack of communication. It is one thing for Great Men to make policy, it is another to implement it, monitor it, coordinate it with existing policies and programs, and undertake the advance planning to meet foreseeable problems and possible contingencies. The Tuesday Lunch had much of the character of a cabal: no agenda, no minutes, no regular subsequent communication or follow-up with staff officers and subordinate officials. The President's almost pathological fear of "leaks" had the effect of sowing uncertainty and confusion among those who had the day-to-day burdens of carrying on the fighting, the aid programs, the diplomatic activity, congressional relations, negotiations, policy planning, public information. The problem was not made any easier when participants in the Tuesday Lunch came away with differing perceptions of what had been decided.

In a brief effort to pool ideas and coordinate programs, officials from various agencies met under the chairmanship of Under-Secretary of State Katzenbach. But here too the operative concept was secrecy rather than communication. The very existence of the group was closely guarded. No minutes were kept, no decisions were made; it served primarily as a discussion group. On the State Department's Seventh Floor it was referred to as "The Non-Group."

Various efforts were made, of course, to live with the system.

When highly motivated and charged with important tasks, Washington bureaucrats are ingenious and dogged in the pursuit of the necessary minimum of information that will permit them to handle their assignments. Sometimes the techniques were clandestine and intricate, sometimes buttons were pushed to activate the "Old Boy Net." It was great sport, but it also involved considerable time and energy in the chase.

The President's compulsion to keep as many people in the dark about as many things and for as long as possible spilled over and trickled down to every layer of Washington's Vietnam policy community. I once asked the member of the State Department's Vietnam Desk who was most involved in negotiations for a weekly report on the status of current diplomatic initiatives. Since he was not permitted to see the sensitive telegrams, his list was so incomplete that we dropped the effort. This problem was even more serious for the State Department's Research and Policy Planning staffs. These folk saw so few important communications on Vietnam that their assistance to policymakers was minimal. This was especially unfortunate, since those who had the necessary access tended to be so imprisoned in day-to-day operations and chronic crises that they had little time themselves for contemplative or innovative analysis.

As we have seen, at one period in the early stages of the war the Chairman of the Joint Chiefs himself was excluded from discussions at the highest level. Even after American combat troops were deployed, it was only on rare occasions that other members of the Joint Chiefs were summoned to participate in top level meetings, including those involving decisions on further deployments. When, as we have also seen, the President in the late summer of 1968 was displeased with Clark Clifford's views on bombing, he restricted him and all other officials of the Department of Defense from receiving telegrams relating to the Paris talks. It was not unusual for the Deputy Assistant Secretary of State in the Far East Bureau, the highest ranking State Department official exclusively concerned with Vietnam, to be kept in the dark about important diplomatic moves. The Director of the State Department's Bureau of Intelligence and Research was privy to so few important and therefore sensitive developments that he had to be dropped from Ambassador Harriman's Negotiations Committee. Others of the highest ranking officials in the State Department were kept isolated from many important negotiations initiatives. What, if anything, President Johnson discussed with Kosygin about Vietnam at the Glassboro meeting in 1967 was fully revealed to no one dealing with the subject—including Harriman. An automatic information retrieval system for Vietnam was developed within the Department so that officials would not have to rely for critical information on the files or the memories of junior staff members. But the system was virtually useless, because so much key material was contained in the closely-held "No Distribution" telegrams and therefore not included in the system.

All this served to create an atmosphere of uncertainty and confusion. One might be confident that he could discuss "Ohio" with a colleague, but could he get some advice on "Primrose" or "Packers" or "Pennsylvania"? Since the control of "distribution" and access to telegrams was frequently based on whether a particular official was judged to be "on the team" or whether he was close enough to the top members of the hierarchy to be "trusted," unpopular or off-beat ideas could be easily dismissed on the grounds that their advocates "didn't know what was going on." *

This compulsive secrecy was not so much a conscious conspiracy as it was a reflection of the President's personal style—a style that favored a "closed" rather than "open" system of policy making. Nothing pleased him more than to "surprise"; nothing angered him more than to have a "surprise" spoiled by premature exposure. It was common knowledge that the President would change his mind on a pending policy decision or personnel appointment if there was advance, accurate speculation in the press. Beleaguered White House spokesmen would explain to an impatient and angry press that the President desired to keep his "options open"—options on bombing policy, on the appointment of a deputy commissioner, on whether he would go to a baseball

---

* Lest this seem self-serving, I should emphasize that with very few exceptions, such as the Glassboro discussions of Vietnam, I had all the information necessary to deal with my negotiations portfolio.

game on a particular evening. A description of Henry the Second is surprisingly apt. "Sudden as a pestilence, Henry was wont to appear, here, there, and everywhere, when he was least expected. Even his own clerks bringing him news of importance could not find him or catch up with him. . . . It pleased his humor to vex his stewards with the pandemonium and uncertainty of his plans. The royal household, from chamberlain to scullion, often numbered at least two hundred souls, equipped with chapel, bed furnishings, kitchen utensils, plate, treasure, garments, vestments, documents, and all the services thereunto pertaining. If Henry announced his departure for sunrise and kept his courtiers and servants all night in a turmoil of preparation, he was almost, but not quite certain, upon some shallow pretext, to delay his departure until ten o'clock or noon."[1]

But regardless of the President's motives and intentions, his manner of operation had effects that went well beyond the boundaries of the bureaucratic community in Washington. The American public had the gnawing feeling that the government was not "leveling" on Vietnam. Official promises of lights at the ends of tunnels and corners about to be turned were inevitably premature and ill-founded. Distinctions between a "civil war" and a "war of aggression" became blurred, not only in the public mind but in the official liturgy as well. The reasons for our being in Vietnam and the terms on which we would leave slithered and slid erratically, depending on which high-level official was speaking and the day he spoke.

❊   ❊   ❊

There is a favorite parlor game in Washington that has as its starting signal: "Do you think we would have been in this mess in Vietnam if Kennedy had lived?" The game becomes especially lively if there are visitors from out of town—say, from New York or Cambridge. They open the play with an emphatic and confident "We would not!" There is no final score; the game usually ends with a grudging, "Well, maybe."

Theodore Sorensen is confident that President Kennedy would have been much more prudent than President Johnson: ". . . I am convinced that JFK would have acted during 1964, as he had in West Berlin and elsewhere and as his strategy on Vietnam clearly intended, to avoid being confronted with so limited a choice. By developing diplomatic as well as military alternatives not unlike those forced upon President Nixon in 1969, he would not have permitted this country to be placed in a bind where it had no acceptable alternative to massive escalation in 1965. . . . I believe he would have kept our participation [in Vietnam] at a much lower level, sending no combat divisions to South Vietnam and no missions to bomb North Vietnam." [2]

But those of us who are not skilled in the ouija board school of historical analysis have some serious doubts whether President Kennedy would have been able to stay on the high ground— whether he would have been able to pull off an early political settlement or a quick military success. This has nothing to do with whether he would have conducted the enterprise with more grace and finesse than did President Johnson; he probably would have. Once immersed in a swamp, however, it makes little difference whether one slid into it stylishly or not.

Kennedy had put himself squarely behind Ngo Dinh Diem years before Johnson could have found Vietnam on an outline map of Asia. As early as 1956 Vietnam was the "keystone" and the "finger in the dike." And for more than two years after he took office, Kennedy temporized with Diem and tolerated his procrastination and dissembling on the issue of political reform and improved overall performance. By the autumn of 1963 there were 18,000 American military personnel in Vietnam—a sizeable hostage to and a substantial earnest of the American commitment. And by then there was apparent, if not real, confusion in the Administration, as well as growing unease among Americans generally, about our objectives and the means of achieving them. Up until the moment of his death there was no perceptible indication that President Kennedy was prepared to move in any direction other than doing more of the same in Vietnam.

In April, 1962 Ambassador John Galbraith warned Kennedy that the "growing American military commitment" to a "weak," "ineffectual" government could lead into a "major, long drawn-out, indecisive military involvement." Galbraith urged that the President "open the door for a political solution" and "measurably reduce our commitment to the particular leadership of the government of South Vietnam."[3] But if Kennedy read Galbraith's advice, he gave it little heed: in April, 1962 the United States had 5,000 military personnel in Vietnam; in December of that year there were 11,000; a year later there were almost 20,000.

Perhaps Kennedy was trapped by forces over which he had little control—just as Johnson and later Nixon were trapped. Congress was hostile to him and, at that point, would almost certainly have opposed any sign of a weakening "American resolve"; the Laos settlement was regarded by many Congressmen as an American retreat; and there was a built-in conviction among some in the Administration that Vietnam provided a proving ground for the doctrine of "flexible response." Finally, in 1964 Kennedy, like Johnson later, would have faced an election campaign which would have required from him, just as it did from Johnson, the need to walk the middle ground between a pullout and a major escalation of the war. Having said all this, we might surmise that faced with the situation that confronted Johnson from 1965 onward, Kennedy would probably have exercised more imagination and subtlety in relating military and diplomatic strategies.

This still leaves two major questions unresolved: would Kennedy have launched the bombing against North Vietnam in the first place? Would he have put American combat troops into South Vietnam? I personally haven't the least idea, and I am fairly confident that no one else does either.

✻   ✻   ✻

Since 1960 our Presidents and their principal advisers have given various explanations of why we were in Vietnam: To stop Communist aggression in Southeast Asia; To contain Communist China; To prevent the progressive, rapid fall of neighboring countries to the Communists; To give the South Vietnamese an opportunity to choose their own government; To show that "Wars of Liberation" cannot succeed; To make the North Vietnamese "stop what they are doing"; To show that aggression across internationally recognized lines will not be successful; To show friend and foe that America would keep its commitments; To keep the Communist threat far from "Hawaii and California." This was not putting the same objective into different words; these were different objectives, each calling for separate tactics and strategies, each having its own mix of costs, risks, and prospects for success. No wonder the American people were confused. In response to a Harris poll in late December, 1967, 45 percent of those questioned thought our objective in South Vietnam was "to stop communist aggression once and for all in Southeast Asia," and another 24 percent felt that American forces were in Vietnam "to force North Vietnam to withdraw from South Vietnam completely and eliminate all communist influence." Neither of these was remotely achievable nor, for that matter, were they the stated objectives of the Administration.

The confusion of objectives at the official level may have been more apparent than real. Quiet, relaxed conversation with top Administration officials would have revealed considerable agreement among them as to what our objectives were. But the problem was that there was no time or opportunity for quiet conversation or even for quiet contemplation. Exhausted, harassed, besieged men found it necessary to concentrate on tactics rather than strategy, on micro-problems rather than macro-solutions, on today's crises rather than tomorrow's opportunities. New bombing target "packages" rather than diplomatic or political initiatives tended to be the typical menu for the President's "Tuesday Lunch." Someone once said as he watched the Secretary of State dashing off to the White House, "If you told him right now of a sure-fire way to defeat the Viet Cong and to get out of Vietnam, he would groan that he was too busy to worry about that now; he had to discuss next week's bombing targets." By 1967 the feeling was widely held that there were no more new ideas with regard to either fighting the war or finding the peace. And if there were, it would have been difficult to find an audience for them.

The frenetic pace and sustained tension in Washington was compounded by a growing feeling that Vietnam was turning out to be the Administration's war rather than America's war. As a

consequence there were renewed efforts to describe the current
state of affairs as a logical, inevitable extension of Eisenhower's
original commitment in 1954 to Premier Ngo Dinh Diem, and of
Kennedy's decision in 1961 to send military assistance to the South
Vietnamese. Each additional step up the scale of involvement—
bombing North Vietnam, deploying combat troops, using B-52's—
was referred to both publicly and even within Administration
circles as a "continuation of current policy." There was some truth
in this claim, of course. Eisenhower had left Kennedy with a commitment to Diem and an eroding non-Communist position in Laos
and Vietnam; Kennedy had left Johnson with an even firmer
commitment, as well as a deteriorating position in Vietnam and
a fragile situation in Laos. But despite frequent reminders of all
this in public speeches and background press conferences, it was
during Johnson's tenure that the war became very real and very
close to most Americans. Increasing draft calls, increasing casualties, increasing domestic tensions all took their toll on the popu
larity and credibility of the Johnson Administration and on the
physical health and mental resiliency of its top officials.

As months and years passed there was an increasingly pervasive sense within the Administration of being in an isolated
fortress—a sense of desperate aloneness. The public did not or
would not understand why America could not suddenly disengage
on the one hand, or quickly defeat the forces of a small and weak
military power on the other. The press seemed eager to criticize
and slow to appreciate the efforts of hard-working, underpaid,
sincere officials. Congress was becoming increasingly hostile, our
allies increasingly uncooperative. High-ranking government officials were literally in physical danger when they appeared in
public to explain American policy.

One effect of this criticism was to give the President and his
principal advisers a feeling that they had to take personal charge
of the war if only to vindicate themselves. The Commander of
American forces in the Pacific (CINCPAC) at Pearl Harbor, the
nominal chief of all military operations in the Far East, was virtually ignored. The Ambassador in Saigon and the commander of
American forces in Vietnam were expected to keep Washington

informed of practically every political, military, and economic step taken. The hot breath of the Administration was felt twenty-four hours a day. There was hardly a week when a Cabinet officer, Congressional Committee, or personal representative of the President was not in Saigon on a "fact-finding" trip.* Embassy officials were bombarded with cables from Washington giving new priorities, new targets, new programs. General Taylor described the problem he had: "On our books at the embassy in Saigon were twenty-one military, forty-two non-military, and twelve intelligence programs for which we were required to furnish progress reports to Washington." [4]

The "progress report" to Washington was another symptom of the anxiety complex that infected Vietnam policymakers. Critical statistics on priority programs in key provinces, graphs, slides and charts, regression curves. Numbers! There was a number mill in every military and AID installation in Vietnam. Numbers flowed into Saigon and from there into Washington like the Meking River during the flood season. Sometimes the numbers were plucked out of the air, sometimes the numbers were not accurate. Sometimes they were accurate but not relevant. Sometimes they were relevant but misinterpreted. The emphasis on quantification started very early in the game. In 1962 McNamara was at the American Pacific Headquarters in Honolulu, and after a briefing by General Harkins he said, "Now General, show me a graph that will tell me whether we are losing or winning in Vietnam." By 1967 the numbers may have been accurate, relevant, and correctly interpreted, but few really believed them. The "briefees" had become numbers numb. Some skeptic suggested that we could destroy all the critical targets in North Vietnam by dumping on them the chart books accumulated in Washington over any six-month period.

We must have driven our South Vietnamese friends to the outer edges of despair with demands for quantitative measurement of progress. To oblige us, or at least to get us out of their hair, a flow of "data" gushed forth in torrents from the capital and

* When Senator Edward Kennedy was in Vietnam in 1967, he asked a young AID officer in the provinces whether there was anything he could do to help his operation. The reply was forthright—stop the VIP visits.

the countryside. Surely the Vietnamese must have been playing a huge joke when they submitted "Ninety-eight Criteria for Pacification"! One can just picture them in the privacy of their tea houses, or alone with their wives at night, shaking with laughter as they described how their American counterparts nodded seriously when told that "Village X met 67 out of the 98 criteria." But fun and laughter aside, one has a troubled feeling that this apparently compulsive need for a daily temperature reading was not simply a fetish for charts and graphs but reflected instead a deep sense of anxiety and self-doubt in Washington. The Vietnamese themselves seemed much less interested in the question of "how are we doing today?" A sense of fatality and futility pervaded their outlook; the war had become very personal—Will I be safe in taking this bus? Will my husband be drafted? Where is my daughter? Will I live through the day? Will I get my rice ration? Will my deal go through?

Preoccupation with day-to-day progress continued to divert attention and energy from the fundamental questions of objectives and strategy. President Johnson's review of March 1968 was probably the only thorough examination of fundamental premises and uninhibited probing of available options since the autumn of 1961 when Kennedy addressed himself to the Taylor–Rostow report. In the years between these two major appraisals—the first took us to the edge of the slippery slope and the second began the painful process of extrication from the mire—there were searches for quick fixes, made with one eye on the morning headlines.

It would be unfair to over-stress the emphasis on "crash" programs, the "blowtorch" approaches, the desperate, crisis-ridden mood. There were many first-class minds coolly addressing long-range military, economic, and intelligence problems; academic treatises on various subjects were sought; seminars were held. But this was at the staff levels; decisionmaking in the upper reaches was largely dominated by "operational" considerations. There were many reasons, some of which we have already discussed, that influenced Washington to conduct its Vietnam policy on the run; but one not yet mentioned may have been the most important.

For a long time—indeed through the entire Kennedy Administration and for all but the last several months of the Johnson tenure—many senior policymakers were convinced that the Vietnam mess would not, *could* not last very long. This was especially true after February, 1965 when the bombing of North Vietnam started and American combat forces were introduced. The optimistic predictions that flowered from time to time were not the result of Administration perfidy; they reflected genuinely-held beliefs. While occasional doubts crossed the minds of some, perhaps all, the conviction that the war would end "soon" and favorably was clutched to the breast like a child's security blanket. Views to the contrary were not favorably received; reports to the contrary were unlikely to be included in the President's "night reading" list.

Because the war was likely to be over "soon," there was a reluctance to do anything here at home that might rock the boat, break the china, upset the apple cart—like calling up the reserves, like declaring war, like putting the American economy on a war footing. Competing requirements between the demands of the war and the booming domestic economy were largely ignored (AID was recruiting nurses for Vietnam at a point when Medicare was confronting American cities with a nursing crisis); competing requirements between government agencies for goods and skills in short supply were belatedly addressed (AID and the Pentagon were bidding against each other in Vietnam for construction materials and labor); when President Johnson was told in 1966 that a tax increase was necessary he brushed the idea aside. We thought we could handle Vietnam without any noticeable effect on our economy or society. In early 1966 General Taylor could say, "with over 300,000 men in action, we have not called up a reservist; we have not imposed any economic controls in the U.S.; we have not initiated mobilization; we are paying our bill out of a growing gross national product. . . ." [5]

Because the war was likely to be over "soon," there was also a reluctance to make any substantial changes in the bureaucratic structure. There would be no special institutional arrangements for staffing the war, for implementing or following up decisions. There would be no "Mr. Vietnam," no single place in the White

House complex to coordinate the Vietnam effort. Vietnam would continue to be handled within the Department of State by a regional bureau and Governor Harriman's small staff, and by existing arrangements in the Pentagon. If special attention was needed there would be "working groups," "task forces," "special committees." No one in the White House other than the President, or in the State Department or Pentagon other than the Secretaries, could say (truthfully) with confidence that he was completely on top of the Vietnam problem as it was being handled in his institution. But no one was very troubled by this—the war was going to be over "soon." Why wrench the system?

✿   ✿   ✿

Even if the United States had been able to work out the strategy and the tactics for an early victory, we would still have had to persuade the South Vietnamese to adopt them; it was their war, not ours. How to work out effective bilateral relations between the United States and South Vietnam, or even between our Saigon Mission and the Saigon Government, is a missing chapter in all the learned treatises on counter-insurgency warfare. This war was a new experience for the United States, since it involved being more than an ally and less than a colonizer. None of the theoreticians was able to provide meaningful guidance and none of the practitioners was able to work out anything more useful than his personal solution to the narrow range of problems he confronted.

Americans, in and out of official life, became disillusioned as our initial investment in Vietnam grew but did not prosper. And as we witnessed the limited extent to which we were able to affect the course of events there, disillusionment became despair. It was difficult enough to adjust to the gap between our vast power and our ability to bring it effectively to bear against a third-rate enemy force. In many ways it was even harder to witness the yawning chasm between the resources we devoted to Vietnam and our inability to exert meaningful influence on our ally. One of the most burning questions in the whole murky story of our involvement in Vietnam revolves around this matter of "leverage."

The historical landscape of our involvement in Vietnam is

dotted with the burial mounds of carrots, sticks, demarches, aides-mémoire, presidential letters, and ambassadorial confrontations. But our ability to get a South Vietnamese Army unit to advance, a dishonest province chief removed, a minister to move expeditiously on a major economic problem or to move more cautiously on a delicate political matter has been at best marginal. Throughout the years we have been the junior partner in the enterprise. In the last analysis, the only "stick" we had available to influence a troublesome government in Saigon was the threat of total American withdrawal. And as the size of our forces, and therefore the extent of our commitment to our commitment, increased, this sanction became less and less credible. In short, our leverage declined as our involvement deepened.

It was John Foster Dulles, I believe, who once characterized the United States as being subjected to "the tyranny of the weak." The historian A. J. P. Taylor graphically described the relationship between France and the Papacy during the early nineteenth century: "When one state is completely dependent on another, it is the weaker which can call the tune: it can threaten to collapse unless supported, and its protector has no answering threat to return." [6] Our own relationship with the Government of Vietnam would qualify for such a description. It is not hard to see why. The American stake in Vietnam has been very high; indeed there have been times, as in the recurrent Buddhist crises and the near-civil wars, when our stake in preserving a non-Communist South Vietnam seemed higher than that of the non-Communist South Vietnamese themselves. But the Diems and Kys and Thieus are not the first nor will they be the last to parlay their weakness into a form of strength. Konrad Adenauer, Chiang Kai-shek, and Syngman Rhee are charter members of the club.

New nations of Asia and Africa regard terms like "independence" and "sovereignty" seriously, even literally. And while among most of the developing nations Western technology is still held in high esteem, Western political omniscience is no longer taken for granted. Nigerians and Guatemalans and Vietnamese are convinced (and why should they not be?) that they know better than outsiders how to handle their own affairs. This means: Ad-

vice, yes; "interference," no! Aid, yes; "strings," no! It means too
that a great power's relations with weaker nations tend (even
within the Communist orbit) to be conducted on a government-to-
government basis, rather than by the old-style metropole-to-colony
or master-to-satellite arrangement. Thus the United States must
now persuade rather than demand, request rather than insist. It is
under such circumstances that the application of "leverage" requires consummate skill.

The successful use of leverage is an art. The matter at issue
must be sufficiently important, the timing must be right, the implied sanctions must be credible, the application must be stylish—
firm but not bullying. The true artist knows that maximum leverage comes prior to actual commitment to another's cause. Afterward leverage can only be obtained through one of two uncertain
courses—the carrot of promising to increase the commitment, or
the stick of threatening to break it off. But even these cannot
guarantee significant influence over the subsequent course of
events; when the commitment has been as complete as ours in
Vietnam, for example, the carrot will be assumed to be always
available and the stick too heavy to wield.

In the many years we have been involved in Vietnam, there
have been few instances when the United States has been able to
deal effectively with Saigon's procrastination or defiance on issues
which Washington regarded as important. To be sure, in the fall
of 1968, under direct pressure from President Johnson and with
prodding by Ambassadors Harriman and Vance in Paris, the South
Vietnamese Government grudgingly agreed to send its representatives to the peace talks in Paris. The stick had been wielded: Saigon
was made well aware that we were prepared to conduct peace
negotiations without them. But that was an exceptional case. Time
after time American Administrations either humored various Saigon governments in their non-cooperation, or hinted at sanctions
the Vietnamese knew would not be adopted.

In retrospect there seem to have been a few brief moments in
the history of our involvement that could have provided opportunities for re-examining the terms of the basic Washington–
Saigon contract, for checking on the performance to date, and for

reassessing the risks and the prospects for success in the enterprise. Having done this we then could have decided whether to proceed, whether to revise the terms, or whether to opt out.

In 1954, on the eve of our commitment to Vietnam, President Eisenhower attempted to relate American assistance to Diem's performance. Eisenhower told Diem that he wished to assist Vietnam, "provided that your government is prepared to give assurances as to the standards of performance. . . . The Government of the United States expects that this aid will be met by performance on the part of the Government of Viet-Nam in undertaking needed reforms." Diem ignored the performance clause but got his aid.

President Kennedy's first move in Vietnam was to press Diem to accept a Counter-Insurgency Plan that involved political and military reforms in exchange for major new American assistance. There were no significant reforms, but the help was sent. The Taylor–Rostow report of late 1961 emphasized the need for economic, political, and social action. Although General Taylor had made Diem aware of Kennedy's views on that score, Kennedy did not press the point and Diem ignored the whole issue. In 1963, when Diem and Nhu carried South Vietnam to the brink of civil and religious warfare, the Kennedy Administration withheld some economic aid and threatened to withdraw some of the American advisers, but the two brothers correctly calculated that Washington would not go beyond the pinprick stage. When the new regime took over in Saigon after Diem's assassination, Washington could have made clear the terms on which further American support would be forthcoming. While there were some mild admonitions, however, the momentum of support was so strong that the new Saigon government could safely assume the aid would continue and even increase.

President Johnson had several brief opportunities when, theoretically at least, he could have turned the situation around. The first was immediately after he had taken over the Presidency in 1963. Vietnam was his most serious international problem, and the American people would have regarded it as entirely appropriate if he had taken a close new look and had conditioned continued American support on tough standards of South Vietnamese performance. But the Kennedy policies continued without significant modification for almost six months—and the strategic moment was lost. When Johnson won the election in 1964 by an overwhelming majority, there was another and perhaps even more opportune occasion to take bearings and to change course if necessary. Then there was the moment in early 1965, before we started the bombing of North Vietnam and the Buddhists were once again attacking the government, when frank talk with the Saigon regime might have been effective. And finally, in the spring of 1966, when entire provinces of South Vietnam were caught up in a Buddhist revolt, the threat of American withdrawal (which a few American officials then actually advocated) might have been used to get the South Vietnamese to undertake some long-delayed reforms.

The parade of generals who have held power in Saigon has been successful in staring down several Washington Administrations. For many years they were confident (and rightly so) that when all was said, not much would be done; Washington would not apply its only effective sanction—pulling out American forces. Since American troops would remain, there was no real danger that Washington would take any other steps to weaken the strength and resolve of the South Vietnamese Government or military establishment lest this endanger the security of American troops or jeopardize the prospects for a military victory.

The beginning of negotiations in 1968 provided a new element in Washington–Saigon relations. It meant that the United States was prepared to see the war end at an early date—much earlier than the Saigon Government might desire. It implied a readiness to work out some political compromises. The American elections in the fall of 1968 gave the South Vietnamese leaders a brief opportunity to play in the arena of American domestic politics, but despite some backdoor assurances by shadowy Republican emissaries, Saigon quickly became aware that even the new Administration was ready for serious negotiations to end the war. More palatable options were now available to Washington than either an open-ended commitment or a precipitate withdrawal. And since the Saigon regime knew this as well as we did, the balance of bargaining power tended to shift toward Washington. But even so there were still instances, as during the tacit de-escalation immediately following the death of Ho Chi Minh, when we had to dance to Saigon's tune. "Thieu Defies U.S. and Makes It Pay," was the headline of a story on the South Vietnamese attitude toward a ceasefire.[7]

It is more often true than not that the relationship between allies is less difficult during the course of fighting a war than during the process of bringing hostilities to a close. This is certainly true in the case of Washington and Saigon (and, incidentally, in the case of Washington and the other allies fighting in Vietnam, especially the South Koreans and the Thais). Although, as we have seen, problems have emerged on how to fight the war, these have not caused as much bitterness and ill will as the question of how (and how early) to end it. The relationship between Hanoi and the NLF may be going through similar strains, and for much the same reason.

Since the early years of the Diem regime, South Vietnamese leaders have regarded the war as a means not only of defeating the insurgency but also of providing an opportunity to build a strong anti-Communist political base. Members of various Saigon governments have estimated that it would take "at least five years" to develop sufficient strength among the non-Communists to confront the highly-motivated and ruthlessly organized National Liberation Front in a political contest for control over Vietnam. President Thieu reportedly put it somewhat differently and more dramatically: in the late summer of 1969 he was reputed to have told his delegation in Paris that it would take "twenty or thirty years" before the Vietnamese Communists would be acceptable to the South Vietnamese Government. It is no wonder that the representatives of the Saigon Government were dragged kicking and screaming to Paris and have subsequently sulked their way through the discussions.

❖   ❖   ❖

The bombing of North Vietnam and its follow-up, the deployment of American combat forces to South Vietnam, convinced the South Vietnamese for a brief moment that Washington had decided to fight the war side by side with them until sweet victory had been achieved. Saigon was not alone in this conviction; most of the rest of the world, including that part enclosed within the walls of the White House, State Department, and Pentagon, had arrived at this conclusion. The bombing did not accomplish nearly as much as its most enthusiastic advocates claimed it would. But it did have one major, unanticipated result—a political rather than a military one.

It was only after the bombing of North Vietnam started in early 1965 that a negotiated settlement was regarded as a serious question in Washington. There was a widespread feeling within the Administration that the United States had better keep one eye peeled for an exit as it moved farther and faster down the expressway to full-scale war—thus the President's Baltimore speech of April, 1965 in which he expressed his readiness to begin peace talks. With each announced major increment in American troop deployments or step-up in bombing, the Administration felt more on the defensive at home. The President's desire to "discuss," "talk," "negotiate," "go anywhere," "go anytime," "go more than half-way," became a familiar accompaniment to each act of military escalation.

By early 1967 we had the worst of both worlds—*our* troops were pouring in and *our* bombs were pouring down, and yet *we* were asking for peace talks. We appeared so anxious for negotiations that the North Vietnamese may well have come to believe their inflated estimates of American losses. But despite our pleas and threats, it was to take three years before Hanoi responded. Why? In large part because Hanoi distrusted the very process of negotiations. Their experience in 1946, when they thought—rightly or wrongly but nevertheless sincerely—they were betrayed by the French after an agreement had been reached, did much to make them negotiations-shy. This feeling was intensified at the Geneva Conference in 1954. There they were convinced that the combined machinations of their friends and their enemies led to an agreement far less favorable than Ho Chi Minh had expected. The Laos Conference of 1961–1962 must have been disappointing too; the Chinese and the Russians squabbled openly, and the neutralist government of Souvanna Phouma turned out to be anti-Communist. It would take a skillful combination of carrots and sticks to get Hanoi to a negotiating table again.

Washington was not very skillful. Important American diplomatic initiatives were neutralized by ill-timed bombing raids. Sometimes, as in the case of the abortive Warsaw talks in late 1966, because of sheer stubbornness on Pennsylvania Avenue the bombing continued or intensified in the midst of sensitive conversations. Sometimes, as in the case of the April, 1967 proposal to re-institute the Demilitarized Zone, attacks against new targets were pressed in a clumsy attempt to prove to Hanoi (and ourselves) that the mere fact of our having launched a proposal for negotiations did not mean we were unwilling to carry on the war. Senior military officers, Walt Rostow, Secretary Rusk, and General Taylor, among others in Lyndon Johnson's Administration, seemed to have a bombing hang-up: raids had to continue because of their damage to the physical plant and morale of North Vietnam and because they were inhibiting the movement of North Vietnamese forces to the South—or so it was said and believed. I had a heated argument with Walt Rostow one afternoon about a scheduled raid on targets close to the Hanoi airport; a high-level Polish delegation was scheduled to arrive on the day the bombs were to be dropped. I lost. The bombs fell. The Poles, luckily, arrived the next day.

Over and above the psychological-military argument, many of the bombing advocates, civilian and military, had another, unstated rationale. Stopping or moderating the bombing, even temporarily and even as a logical or necessary accompaniment to a diplomatic initiative, was regarded as an American admission of weakness and failure. Between the long bombing pause in January, 1966 and the Tet offensive in February, 1968 the advocacy of a temporary halt or a major cutback in the bombing—let alone a bombing cessation—would draw down one's capital in the White House bank, or so many genuinely believed. It was no great mystery why, despite American protestations in favor of a political rather than a military solution, the North Vietnamese were wary and skeptical. And to compound their suspicions, many of Washington's plans for a "political solution" involved, for all practical purposes, a negotiated surrender by the North Vietnamese. One ceasefire proposal, which originated in Rostow's staff during 1967, required that the Viet Cong and North Vietnamese stack their arms in designated enclaves. They would, however, be permitted to receive food and medicine from the outside.

But Hanoi was hardly a graceful partner in the pre-negotiations mating dance. Ho and his colleagues made life much easier for the hawks than for the doves in Washington. Time after time North Vietnamese diplomats in Stockholm, Algiers, Rangoon, or Cairo would confide that Hanoi was ready to modify its rigid "Four Points" or to relax somewhat on another major obstacle to negotiations; and time after time—upon rechecking with the same officials or with other presumably responsible North Vietnamese in Paris, Warsaw, Phnom Penh, or Moscow—a different and contradictory account would emerge. Well-meaning Americans returned from unofficial visits to Hanoi with "messages" to pass on to Washington that turned out to be clearly inconsistent with "messages" given to the last and to the next visitors. False leads, confusing signals, and awkward missteps were consciously or unconsciously part of the North Vietnamese choreography. It was not surprising that Washington and Saigon were suspicious of reported North Vietnamese overtures.

In this atmosphere of pervasive mistrust, neither Ho Chi Minh nor Lyndon Johnson felt secure in making the first definitive, unmistakable move toward peace—until the President's speech of March 31, 1968. Whether, despite all the alarums and excursions, hints and rumors, Hanoi would have agreed to the March terms at some earlier point in time is debatable. Probably not. Johnson's March offer with respect to a bombing cutback was actually not as favorable from Hanoi's point of view as the one made in the autumn of the previous year when the North Vietnamese were offered a complete bombing cessation in exchange for a commitment to start negotiations.* Perhaps Hanoi was hurting badly by the early spring of 1968, despite the bravado of the Tet offensive. Or

* According to the "San Antonio Formula" of September 29, 1967, the United States would stop the bombing of North Vietnam "when this will lead promptly to productive discussions. We would assume that while discussions proceed, North Vietnam would not take advantage of the bombing cessation or limitation."

perhaps Johnson's surprise announcement that he was pulling out
of the Presidential race induced Hanoi to pick up the offer. In any
case "talks" got under way. It would be a very long time, however,
before the two sides were to get down to serious business, despite
coy hints out of Washington that much was "going on" in Paris
from February 1969 onwards, and despite President Nixon's plea
to members of the United Nations in September 1969 to use their
"best diplomatic efforts to persuade Hanoi to move seriously into
negotiations which could end this war."

*   *   *

It is hard to believe that Richard Nixon needs daily reminding by
critics of American policy that the war should be ended as soon as
possible. This is a matter of political life or death for him; he has
said so, and he may genuinely believe it to be so. If he still is
uncertain on this score he need only look over his shoulder: Lyndon Johnson has provided both the problem and the lesson.

The lesson was not lost on President Nixon. In late July 1969
at Guam, he told correspondents at a background press conference that the United States would provide military and economic
assistance "as appropriate" to a friend threatened by a neighbor,
but that "we shall look to the nation directly threatened to assume the primary responsibility of providing the manpower for
its defense." A day or two later the White House released this
declaration of intent and then pronounced it the "Nixon Doctrine." It has since been widely interpreted as a clear indication
of a progressive U.S. withdrawal from Asia and as an omen of
future American isolationism.

Why, then, Cambodia? If there were lingering doubts in the
White House that millions of Americans felt strongly about "No
More Vietnams," the countrywide sense of disquiet and despair in
the aftermath of the April 30 announcement that American troops
were moving into Cambodia must have dispelled them. The decision could not have been an easy one for President Nixon and
one can only wonder how he calibrated the pros and cons. Sixteen
Hundred Pennsylvania Avenue could not be so isolated and insulated from the mood of the country that the President and his

advisers were completely innocent of the domestic political reaction that would follow an invasion of Cambodia and even a momentary resumption of the bombing of North Vietnam. Reportedly Secretary Rogers reminded the President that his natives
were restless and that his Vietnam honeymoon was over. But
Nixon's speech of April 30 made it clear that he had decided to
ride out any domestic flak in exchange for a major stroke against
what he described as "the headquarters of the entire communist
military operation in South Vietnam." His military advisers must
have served up golden promises of quick success.

The Pentagon had ample information to realize that the Communist military command—"Central Office of South Vietnam" or
"COSVN"—was not directing operations in Vietnam from an installation in the jungles of Cambodia as elaborate and densely populated with generals as the MACV Headquarters in Saigon. Surely
the President must have been made aware of this. But to many
in his audience that night the President's words implied that the
American attack would result in the early capture of the major
Communist command center complete with General Giap, top
secret maps and hot lines to Hanoi, Peking, and Moscow. Nixon's
grandiloquent formulation of the American military objective in
Cambodia is all the more curious in the light of the private briefing his chief aide gave just prior to the TV speech. Henry Kissinger told a few members of the press that the major targets would
be Communist supply depots and ammunition dumps.

President Johnson, during his tenure, typically rationalized the
escalation of the war on the grounds that each additional action
would shorten the conflict. He said and was probably convinced
that the Communists would have to be driven rather than led toward negotiations. Can we draw no lessons even from the recent
past? Must history always start on Inauguration Day? At least
since early 1968 impatient and frustrated Americans have not
accepted promises of early military victories in Vietnam as a
medium of exchange for buying time. Perhaps the Nixon Administration was mesmerized by an apparent lull in the storm of criticism on Vietnam and a shifting of the winds in the direction of
domestic environmental problems. If so, the President quickly

learned that the grudging tolerance his Vietnam policy had enjoyed reflected a wary watchfulness of his every move and that "Disengagement" was the name of the game.

A judicious observer would take some issue with those, including some members of the Johnson Administration, who grant the current Administration full and wholehearted credit for the Vietnam war. President Nixon should be given his due: it was he, not his predecessor, who turned the troop deployments around. American soldiers are not coming home in the numbers or at the rate many of us would wish, and one suspects that the "Vietnamization" program is comprised of one part hokum, one part wishful thinking, and one part genuine policy. But withdrawals are in process, and we have been told they are "irreversible." On a "pass-fail" rating Mr. Nixon would have squeaked through—until his test in the spring of 1970. This was one that Johnson passed and Nixon flunked.

Time and time again during the late sixties American and South Vietnamese military commanders requested, urged and pleaded that they be permitted to attack Communist sanctuaries in Cambodia. The requests were consistently turned down by President Johnson or his advisers because the advocates could not demonstrate that the military advantages would outweigh the political risks. In April 1970 the military must have presented their case with much more force or had a more receptive audience than the civilians. And the President gave apolitical critics, very political opponents, and a host of just plain worried people a "Nixon's War."

If the Cambodian operation had been successful even in terms of the bullish objectives Nixon originally set forth, Hanoi would have won a major victory. Several years ago when the criticism in the United States of Johnson's Vietnam policy was just coming to a boil, the North Vietnamese exaggerated American war weariness. In the eyes of Hanoi, Washington, like Paris a decade earlier, would soon have to placate domestic public opinion by doing whatever was necessary to close out the war. Hanoi was wrong, or at least premature—then. There is now more reason for Hanoi to be confident that it can wait for Washington to make additional major concessions in any negotiations or to withdraw without a political settlement. Indeed, on June 30, the day of President Nixon's Cambodian deadline, a State Department spokesman hinted at a new concession. He told the press that Washington was now willing to accept a coalition government in South Vietnam without national elections.

The Cambodian side of the Vietnamese border has been a tempting target for American and South Vietnamese military operations since 1965. Sihanouk may well have been a "neutralist," but to speak of Cambodia as having been "neutral territory" is to give credence to but one of the many myths of the Vietnam war. Under a dense jungle canopy Viet Cong and North Vietnamese troops and political cadres have, for years, operated supply bases and staging areas, training camps, prisoner stockades, hospitals and rest centers. Military supplies have filtered into South Vietnam and rice has been smuggled out. Along the long South Vietnamese Cambodian border Viet Cong and North Vietnamese troops have attacked villages and ambushed Allied forces and then melted across the border into Cambodia where, except in isolated cases, they were immune from pursuit. Depending on his mood at any particular time, Sihanouk would grudgingly admit or vehemently deny that his territory was being used by Communist forces. Even if he wanted to do anything about it, he knew the Communist forces were too elusive, the area in question was too remote, and his own forces were too weak. Attempts by curious newsmen and sluggish ICC officials to find evidence of consequential Viet Cong or North Vietnamese forces were singularly unsuccessful. But the Viet Cong and North Vietnamese soldiers were there—hidden and scattered—and the self-righteous anger emerging from Peking and Hanoi about American violations of Cambodia's neutrality would be amusing if it were not so unbefitting coming from them.

Administration spokesmen can argue, not without justification, that the situation in Cambodia in the spring of 1970 was very different from the one prevailing during Johnson's tenure. When in mid–March Lon Nol, a professed anti-Communist, took advantage of Sihanouk's absence from the country to take over the government in Phnom Penh, one of the major inhibitions against crossing the Cambodian border in force no longer applied; it was now unnecessary to help Sihanouk preserve his seventh veil of neutrality.

At various times during the early sixties Prince Sihanouk sought international guarantees for Cambodia's neutrality. In September, 1960 he proposed to the UN General Assembly that Cambodia and Laos be formally established as a neutral bloc in Southeast Asia, but neither Moscow nor Washington was interested and the idea was stillborn. In late 1963 Sihanouk tried again, this time asking the Geneva Co-Chairmen to call an international conference. This effort almost succeeded. The British, Russians, Chinese, and Americans all agreed in principle, but Washington had second thoughts and cited American–Cambodian "tensions" as standing in the way of a useful meeting. Spurred on rather than deterred by American reluctance, the Russians promptly proposed that a conference be held in Geneva in April. In February, 1964 a Cambodian village was bombed by South Vietnamese pilots. Sihanouk demanded that a conference be convened by May of that year or he would break Cambodia's diplomatic relations with the United States. Within a week the Prince changed his mind about both the conference format and breaking relations.* Instead, he asked that South Vietnam, Thailand, and the United States meet with Cambodia at an early date to discuss Cambodia's neutrality and territorial integrity. The United States agreed, but Thailand did not. In any case, his four-nation conference proposal was given a short run for its money. In March the American and British Information Offices were seized by Cambodian mobs and Sihanouk, with Soviet and French backing, again pressed for a Geneva Conference. After several months of desultory diplomatic maneuvering and a deteriorating situation on his borders, Sihanouk dropped the whole idea of an international conference. The matter has rested uneasily ever since.

Over the years it has been easy to be exasperated with Sihanouk's quixotic temperament, but hard not to admire his political

* Relations were in fact broken in May 1965 but restored four years later during the Nixon Administration.

adroitness. Cambodia was the only Indochinese state participating in the 1954 Conference that emerged politically unscathed. Vietnam was carved up in 1954 and Laos in 1962, but Cambodia was left intact; a French general signed the 1954 ceasefire agreement on behalf of Laos and South Vietnam, but the Cambodians themselves signed their own. In the years since 1954 Sihanouk had managed, in a manner belying Cambodia's almost nonexistent military and economic strength, to maintain a flamboyant if slightly threadbare neutral stance in the face of strong and unfriendly Communist and non-Communist forces around him. While Laos and Vietnam were being torn asunder, the Cambodians were able to carry on their simple, sleepy, and amiable lives in peace and quiet. In short, Prince Sihanouk *was* Cambodia and his impressive and sometimes breathtaking balancing act kept hostile forces at bay. Without him the constraints quickly fell away.

Perhaps this was one of the underlying if subconscious elements in Nixon's decision. Perhaps, too, Nixon felt compelled to act lest the Communists return Sihanouk to power, this time under their direction and control. It is one thing for Cambodia to be a Communist sanctuary, the President may well have reasoned; it would be another to have a Communist Cambodia bordering beleaguered South Vietnam and Laos. On April 24 the Cambodian Prime Minister made an impassioned plea for American military assistance. Nixon was placed in the position politicians and even statesmen dread—he was being asked to put up or shut up. And so President Nixon did one of the things that the Johnson Administration had regarded as unthinkable—he "widened the war" beyond the boundaries of Vietnam.

Although Mr. Nixon may yet emerge with some painful, but not fatal, wounds, he will long bear deep scars from his jungle foray. The lovely Washington spring of 1970 turned out to be a nightmare not only for him but for millions of others—many old enough to vote in the November elections. To be sure, American forces were withdrawn after their sweep, and, to be sure, large quantities of enemy supplies were uncovered and destroyed. But the precious months gained in terms of setting back Communist timetables will almost certainly be lost in terms of the Administration's maneuver-time here at home. At best, Nixon will break even.

American military operations in Cambodia provide a graphic example of the narrow confines within which Washington has recently had to conduct its Vietnam policy. The metes and bounds and the firm deadline for the operations were announced by Administration officials in an ex-post facto attempt to mute domestic wrath. These constraints have an interesting history. The "21.7 mile" limit for the penetration of Cambodia was arrived at through an arithmetic error; after the opposition to the invasion became manifest, it was decided that American forces would not advance more than 30 kilometers inside the border. But when some harried aide converted this into miles, he came out with 21.7 instead of 18.7. So "21.7 miles" it is. The time limit was part of the original operational plan, although President Nixon did not mention it on April 30. In his "background briefing" to some correspondents on the night of the speech, however, Kissinger pointed out that the American forces had only eight weeks to accomplish their mission because after July 1 the rains would make operations very difficult.* But whatever the reason, the United States is indeed now waging a *limited* war! As a result, President Nixon is reaping all the disadvantages and none of the advantages from his decision of April 30; he received a full measure of lumps, and he shortchanged himself on what he hoped to buy with the attack across the border.

One fundamental lesson that every wise diplomat, CIA spook, politician, and husband has learned is that it is easier to get into than out of trouble. And Cambodia is now trouble. Vietnamese Communists and non–Communists can be counted on to keep the pot boiling. The political situation in Phnom Penh will remain fragile and in doubt and a Cambodian civil war, with the Viet Cong and North Vietnamese backing pro-Sihanouk forces and the Saigon Government assisting the anti-Sihanouk groups, looms as

---

* The first public hint of this came from one of the President's daughters who told some irate ex–schoolmates that American troops *would* be withdrawn by the President's July 1 deadline because the rainy season started then.

an ugly possibility. It may be a long time before the Cambodians can return to their rice fields, teahouses, and hammocks.

❖   ❖   ❖

Meanwhile, developments in Laos continue to be ominous. Although American military support to Prince Souvanna has been one of the worst-kept secrets of the past decade, it was Mr. Nixon's lot to be presiding when the full story was blown. And it will be Nixon's elbowroom in foreign affairs that will be constricted as Congress vents its wrath on what was essentially Kennedy's and, later, Johnson's decision to provide large-scale, covert, and hopefully deniable support to the government in Vientiane. This decision was not made because either President wanted to play fun and games with Congress or the American people. Rather, it was made in deference to the strongly-stated desire of Prime Minister Souvanna Phouma whose neutralist government was being threatened by the Communist Pathet Lao and their North Vietnamese comrades from the moment in 1962 when they agreed in Geneva to preserve Laos' "sovereignty, independence, neutrality, unity and territorial integrity." There is good reason to believe that Moscow accepted the American role with equanimity as long as the Communists in Laos had freedom of movement in areas they controlled and the American military assistance was kept in the background. As for Peking, it contented itself with occasional angry noises while Chinese military engineers busily constructed a strategic road through Laotian territory. It was a bizarre arrangement, but Laos is a bizarre corner of the world.

This Gentlemen's Agreement was upset in late 1969 when the Communists began to move into new areas of Laos, when American-trained tribal forces were driven out of their hitherto stable if precarious base areas, and when American air attacks against North Vietnamese infiltration trails and Communist troops became so intense that they could no longer be denied. By the spring of 1970 Vientiane as well as Phnom Penh became vulnerable to Communist seizure.

And so, once again, the world is graced with an Indochina war.

In the unforeseeable, paradoxical way that international forces seem to operate, this may yet prove to be Mr. Nixon's and America's salvation. For too many years Washington and Moscow, Saigon and Peking have regarded Vietnam as a separable, soluble problem. Now that it is no longer possible to sweep Laos and Cambodia aside, the sterile Paris "talks" should be replaced by meaningful international negotiations that will result in a neutral, hopefully *genuinely* neutral Indochina. But to *say* "a Geneva Conference" is easier than to convene one. There is little in the record thus far to give one confidence that the Nixon Administration has the zeal or the imagination to achieve a negotiated settlement for Indochina. But Ambassador David Bruce, a man of great skill and no illusions, may be just the man to bring this off.

*   *   *

The outcome of the war, or more accurately, the outcome as it is perceived by the American people, has grave implications for Richard Nixon and for American foreign and domestic policy. It is for this reason that a negotiated settlement with robust international endorsement if not formal guarantees would be the ideal solution. Even in the aftermath of the violent spring of 1970, it is too simple to say that all that counts is that we get out of Vietnam, period. Even less convincing is the argument that only an ignominious retreat from Vietnam will exculpate our original sin. The issues and circumstances are not that clear cut. The analogy with the Soviet Union at the time of the Cuban missile crisis is a good debating point, but not very helpful to American officials seized with the awful responsibility of liquidating a policy and a commitment now fifteen years old.

The aftermath in the United States of an exit from Vietnam that smacked and smelled of a major political and military defeat cannot be brushed aside. Such a defeat is alien to our history and our national personality; it would be a bruising and traumatic experience. It will not be any easier for a Nixon than for a Johnson to accept (and it would not have been very easy for a McCarthy). If there cannot be any visible, approximate facsimile of "victory," Americans will at least have to perceive that something of value

was accomplished in Vietnam. And that gets us back to Square
One. What were our objectives in the first instance, and how close
did we get to achieving them? On the answers to these questions
will hang Johnson's place in history, Nixon's political future, and
quite conceivably the character of American foreign policy for
years to come.

During the past decade, statements of what the United States
hoped to achieve in Vietnam have ricocheted from one elusive,
frequently unobtainable objective to another. Our presence in
South Vietnam has not "contained" Chinese Communist expansion
in Southeast Asia; Peking's own trouble-ridden domestic policies
and its difficulties with Moscow on the long Sino–Soviet border
have had a greater influence on "containing" Red China than has
American policy. The lofty goals of the 1966 Honolulu Declaration
and the 1966 Manila Communique, goals that were designed to
improve life for the Vietnamese people, have been all but forgotten in Vietnam, although our efforts to achieve them have done
much to wrack American society. We now know that even a most
unlikely clear-cut military defeat for the Communists in Vietnam
will not prevent a "domino" from falling elsewhere in Asia if the
governments there do not come to grips with their own political
and social problems. Nor would a defeat for the Communists destroy their faith in "wars of liberation." Is there any significant
objective yet achievable? The short answer is yes.

When all things have been said and when all that could be
done has been done, one consistent theme emerges through the
cacophony of American pronouncements and proclamations about
Vietnam. In its most abbreviated form it is "to permit the Vietnamese to choose freely their future course." This theme has
sometimes been degraded by cheap and corny rhetoric. It has
frequently been distorted by dissembling and quibbling about
whether we would actually accept the outcome of such a choice.
It has often been obscured by our own actions or by our approval
of those of Saigon's actions that would tend to prevent or negate
free choice, such as the constitutional law that excludes Communists and neutralists from the political process. But despite noisy
rhetoric and dissonant deeds, this theme is still discernible.

It took a long time for the "free choice" idea to break through the dominant passages of containment and its many variants. Even in the last months of the Johnson Administration there occasionally were wistful counterpoints to the original Eisenhower–Dulles theme. As late as October, 1968 Secretary of State Rusk noted, "The threat to Southeast Asia is not mitigated by the fact that the Communist world may not be any longer monolithic or that Hanoi may not be a puppet of Peking. For Mao and Ho have both preached the same doctrine of militant communism and have promised the same techniques of expansion through so-called 'wars of national liberation.' We believe that the place to halt these mutually reinforcing expansionist pressures is the Republic of Viet-Nam." [8]

The concept of "free choice" at last came through loud and clear several months after President Nixon took office. In his speech to the United Nations General Assembly on September 19, 1969 Nixon said, ". . . we cannot . . . accept a settlement that would arbitrarily dictate the political future of South Vietnam and deny to the people of South Vietnam the basic right to determine their own future free of outside interference. . . . To secure this right . . . is our one limited, but fundamental objective." In a press conference on September 27 the President left no doubt as to where he stood: ". . . we will accept the results of those [internationally supervised] elections and the South Vietnamese people will as well, even if it is a Communist government. . . . What is not negotiable is the right of South Vietnam to choose their own leaders without outside opposition . . . that limited goal must be one that we must insist on." In his two Vietnam speeches of November 3 and December 15, 1969 President Nixon reaffirmed his view that "anything is negotiable except the right of the people of South Vietnam to determine their own future." And in his Report to the Nation on June 30, 1970, he pledged "to abide by the outcome of the political process agreed upon by the South Vietnamese."

Now at last we know the object of the exercise. Although this goal is indeed "limited," it is nonetheless consequential. It is at once both idealistic and realistic and therefore consistent with the traditions of American foreign policy. But pronouncing it and attaining it are very different things. The achievement of this objective would permit the United States to emerge from Vietnam with some semblance of grace—a matter of no small importance, despite the deprecations of the cynics and the skeptics. But to achieve it Nixon will have to overcome three basic, interrelated difficulties: he will have to convince the American people that this goal was worth the costs; he will have to convince the Saigon Government that it must risk permitting the South Vietnamese people a free choice and then *abide by the choice;* he will have to convince the Communists to do the same. None of these will be easy, and the President is not likely to get much help from either our Vietnamese allies or our enemies.

To the American people the issue of "free choice" tends to be equated with elections—*free* elections. No matter that Asians, especially those living outside the urban areas, may regard Western-style elections as a quaint and unnecessarily complicated arrangement for registering their desires. And no matter that Communists, whether Asian or European, have a different definition of both "free" and "elections." (Averell Harriman recounts a conversation he had with Khrushchev in June, 1959 on the question of "free elections." Khrushchev brought out the long needle: "Do you expect to convince me that the voters of New York State had 'free elections,' when their only choice for Governor was between a Rockefeller and a Harriman?") Somehow the American people will have to be convinced that when we have withdrawn our last military unit and have pronounced "Mission Accomplished," the Vietnamese choice was made through a process that was credible. Regardless of the result, but especially if a Communist government emerges, the modalities of the election and the standards for counting the ballots will have to pass muster in the United States. Which is not to say that more should be expected of Vietnamese than, say, of Bostonians. But it *is* to say that the Nixon Administration and Americans generally have a tremendous stake in how the Vietnamese elections are conducted—a higher stake, probably, than do the Vietnamese themselves.

The election required by the South Vietnamese constitution

to be held in the late summer of 1971 seemed very remote when the negotiators first met in Paris in May, 1968. It does not seem so now. It has been largely ignored in the Paris negotiations and in Washington's political planning. But this election may be the first chance for *all* South Vietnamese to select their leaders through the democratic process, and neither Washington nor Saigon should lose the opportunity by default. The National Liberation Front may choose neither to run nor to vote, but that option should remain open to the Front. In order for such an election to take place, Washington must be ready to conceive of *a* Government of South Vietnam rather than *the* Government of South Vietnam. This means that, somehow, the present regime in Saigon must be induced to revise the current election laws to permit universal voting, to allow any candidate to run for office, and to ensure that the elections are conducted fairly and the results are accepted. If we are serious about "free choice" we can do no less. This may be the last chance for the United States to exert "leverage," and we must be prepared to take it if necessary.

In thinking about the 1971 elections it would be well to ruminate on the last occasion that Thieu and Ky were elected to office. The most recent national elections in Vietnam were held in the late summer of 1967, largely as a result of American urging. It was an impressive accomplishment. Indeed there have been few instances when a country savagely rent by war has moved from a junta toward some form of constitutional government. Critics argue that the rules prohibited Communists and neutralists from running for office. It is hard to see why the government should have been expected to let its enemy run, and in fact peace advocates did run and did well.

Judging that election against the standards of Scandinavia or the United States, Vietnam would have gotten a passing grade; judging it against what transpires in many emerging nations, even those currently blessed with peace and stability, it would have gotten high marks; and judging it against the leadership selection process in North Vietnam, or for that matter in Czechoslovakia or the USSR, the election in South Vietnam in September, 1967 was a model of Jeffersonian democracy. Nonetheless, the election of 1967 may have opened more fissures in Vietnam than it closed. President Thieu and Vice President Ky can rightly say that more Vietnamese wanted them to assume the leadership than any other particular team; but it was also true that more Vietnamese did not want them than did. To many Vietnamese, however, the key point was not only that the new government came to office as the choice of one out of three voters, but that the military candidates won against all civilian aspirants. To these people the election merely continued—"legalized," if you will —the junta. They felt that our efforts to coax and push the democratic process along, idealistic as they might have been, were a heavy-handed attempt to keep the generals in power beneath the cosmetic of a constitutional government. The Administration in Washington would have preferred a civilian instead of General Ky as Vice President, but Washington felt relieved that a split within the armed forces was avoided. While some Buddhists and students were upset by the results, this was less troublesome than if rival military factions had lined up behind Thieu and Ky in the aftermath of a bitter contest between them.

For us and, it is hoped, for the South Vietnamese leaders, the election provided an important lesson. South Vietnam with its myriad religious, regional, political, and ethnic groupings cannot achieve political stability by an election process that allows its leaders to be chosen by a minority of those voting. Moreover, it also would be wise to permit groups receiving a significant proportion of the vote to participate in the government. Surely if the Communists or the Montagnards or the right-wing military or any of the other groups that have been fighting for more than two decades are to have a stake in the government, the present arrangement whereby "winner-takes-all" does not appear to be a fair one. If this adds up to a "coalition," so be it; it may be the only way to persuade the National Liberation Front to participate in the political process rather than operate with violence outside it. The Nixon Administration has apparently recognized this and seems ready to accept such an arrangement.

Clearly, the American hand must be unobtrusive. Perhaps we and the South Vietnamese would be best off if the United States, once having induced the present regime to move ahead along the route of genuine free choice, stayed out of the election altogether. Some international body—the United Nations, the International Control Commission, the two Geneva Co-Chairmen, or almost any other in which confidence could be placed—should play the major outside role in assuring a free, fair election. But all this cannot be done as a last-minute, frenetic exercise. Careful advance planning will be the key to success.

This would seem a large order. But unless the Nixon Administration magnifies or defaults on its stated objective, a fair, universal election in 1971 or before will be a necessary way station on the route to complete American military withdrawal. One hopes that by the time these words are read, the necessary arrangements will have been worked out.*

* * *

In discussing the general proposition of elections, some officials of the Nixon Administration have made the point that the President will need "four or five years of grace" in Vietnam. Translated into political English, this means that a Communist takeover must not occur before President Nixon is at least well into his second term of office. But this period of "grace" may not be in the cards— if what the Administration is worried about is a takeover of South Vietnam by the NLF rather than an outright invasion by Hanoi. An invasion after a settlement is not likely; an NLF takeover may

---

* In November, 1969 a few experienced Vietnam negotiating hands developed a "Peace Package" designed to clear away some of the obstacles on the Washington–Hanoi diplomatic track. It was also designed to expedite American withdrawals and to face up to Vietnamese elections. The proposal was submitted to, but rejected by, the White House. In essence the plan pointed out that the Christmas–New Year–Tet period (1969–70) could be exploited to achieve a breakthrough on the negotiations front and to permit major withdrawals of American forces from Vietnam. It noted that the holiday period was one occasion during the year when, by long-standing practice, military and diplomatic initiatives could be taken by both sides without ostensible political overtones and implications prejudicial to "face."

The proposal involved several distinct but closely related steps: a *de-escalation of* hostilities in early December; a *ceasefire* starting on Christmas Eve and having no fixed termination date; a dramatic *formula for withdrawal of American forces;* a series of *political steps* to be taken in Saigon to broaden the government; and a *negotiations approach* that involved first reaching agreement on broad principles and then working out the specific modalities.

well, but not necessarily, occur. In any case, Nixon has already discounted his period of "grace" by announcing that he would abide by the results of a free election. A Communist victory through ballots rather than bullets will, of course, give a hollow ring to his claims of having accomplished America's objectives. But even in those circumstances, the Administration would be on high ground if the American people are truly convinced that the election represented a "free choice."

It is possible, of course, that the non-Communist forces in Vietnam will overcome their chronic disarray and self-serving manipulations and form a united front against the Communists before the fighting stops and the political competition begins. Surely there is at least a theoretical basis for such cooperation among many elements in South Vietnamese society. There are a host of organizations and groups that seem to have more to gain than to lose under a stable, non-Communist regime—labor unions, veterans, university faculties and students, religious groups, the military, nationalists, urban intellectuals, landowners, small farmers. What is missing is the yeast to stimulate interaction among these ingredients and the glue to bind the resulting amalgam. One of the principal obstacles to developing a lively, cohesive non-Communist movement, and the one that might prevent it from taking place at all, is the present regime in Saigon. Because of the difficulty posed by the Saigon regime, these groups, or elements of them, may form a third force under remote but strong NLF control.

The issue of free choice goes well beyond the scope envisioned by Generals Thieu and Ky. It is not a simple question of the present Saigon Government or the NLF; rather it is a question of the present Saigon Government, some other non-Communist government, a coalition-type government, or the NLF. It is worth noting again that Thieu himself was elected by a minority of the Vietnamese people. Of those who actually cast ballots, 65 percent voted *against* him and Ky by voting instead for civilian candidates, all but one of whom ran on "peace" platforms. Of the *total* adult South Vietnamese population, only 18 percent voted *for* the present government in Saigon. Thieu and Ky obviously are not unaware of this, and their approach to both the negotiations in Paris and the political situation in Vietnam is dictated by a not unnatural desire to hang on to power. A continuation of the war provides one way of doing that, since it permits them to exercise control over their domestic opposition.

It is all very well for President Nixon to say that both the Americans and the South Vietnamese "will accept the results of elections . . . even if it is a Communist Government." [9] But Thieu reportedly told his delegation in Paris that he was opposed to direct Communist participation in South Vietnam's political future. Clearly, if the one objective that President Nixon claims to seek in Vietnam is to be achieved, at least as much diplomatic energy and political leverage will have to be exerted in the Presidential Palace in Saigon as in the Hotel Majestic in Paris. While the American people may be ready to look with sympathy and forbearance on Administration efforts to negotiate the modalities of a free election with the NLF and the North Vietnamese, there is likely to be little patience or understanding if American negotiators have to engage in tough bargaining with our Vietnamese allies on this issue. Our side is *supposed* to be fighting for democracy, free choice, unfettered elections. If not, what are we doing there anyway? This is the stuff of which national disillusionment and domestic political divisions are made. And this is the stuff that gives substance to the vow "No More Vietnams!" and adds to the more general determination to look inward and to avoid further involvement anywhere in the world.

XVI

Crusades, Commitments, and Constraints

Regardless of how our involvement in Vietnam comes out, regardless of whether President Nixon gets several years of grace, or whether the Communists observe the terms of a political settlement, or even whether the Saigon Government successfully weathers the trials of Vietnamization, the cry "No More Vietnams!" conveys a shade too much certainty and finality. It is a slogan more than a statement of policy. In a literal sense it is a self-fulfilling prophecy; the United States will probably never send ground troops to Indochina again. Administration officials themselves have said the process of withdrawal is "irreversible." (Yet—suppose a progressive, non-Communist government emerged in Saigon and turned South Vietnam into a land of milk and honey, full of happy people who loved us. And suppose this shining light of Southeast Asian democracy and progress were to be invaded—not "infiltrated," but *invaded*—by the forces of reaction and darkness. Would we go back in? We just might.) But this literal interpretation is probably an unfair one. Those in or out of the Administration who earnestly believe in the idea of No More Vietnams are thinking in much broader terms; they are opposed to any more American military interventions in situations *like*

Vietnam—insurgencies, civil wars, local revolutions—shadowy forms of conflict where good guys are of dubious character and ineffectual, and bad guys are highly-motivated and gutsy.

As we consider the solemn vow "No More Vietnams!" or ponder the anxious query "No More Vietnams?" one question immediately arises: If we had it to do all over again, should we? Two dissimilar observers imply their support for the original American decision: Arthur Schlesinger does "not see that our original involvement in Vietnam was *per se* immoral," although he quarrels with the means by which we implemented our policy.[1] General Maxwell Taylor believes that "our government did the right thing," although he can find no evidence "that our leaders had a clear understanding of what the consequences of involvement might be."[2] There are many others, of course, who would vehemently claim that we should have kept hands off from the very outset.

A Gallup poll, published in *The New York Times* on June 28, 1970, would support the conclusion that Americans have changed their minds about the wisdom of our commitment. "In view of the developments since we entered the fighting in Vietnam," the pollsters asked, "do you think the U.S. made a mistake sending troops to fight in Vietnam?" Fifty-six percent of those interviewed felt that America had made a mistake. (Twenty-four percent believed we were mistaken in August, 1965 at the time of our first major troop deployments.)

As we look back on the past fifteen years, it is worth reminding ourselves that an inexperienced, weak, ineffectual, shaky regime in Saigon was part of what we bargained for as we successively renewed and increased our commitment to South Vietnam. So were the steaming jungles and mangrove swamps, the porous borders, and the vast distance from American ports, airfields, and bases. In retrospect we should have been more prudent and have insisted upon some minimum standards of stability, appeal, and effectiveness before committing major resources to South Vietnam's aid—no matter how assiduous the Prime Minister, no matter how attractive the people.

But climate and terrain are constants. Governments are not. Shifts and changes in Saigon became more frequent under the very stresses that prompted the original American commitment of aid. South Vietnam at war was not the United States or England or Germany or the Soviet Union—or even, as we know to our sorrow, North Vietnam—at war. Government stability and efficiency were early casualties. The tenuous bonds that held the South Vietnamese Government together loosened rather than tightened; the ties between the government and the people fell away rather than becoming stronger. This was the first evidence, had we had the prescience to realize it, that something was terribly, fundamentally wrong and that we were headed for trouble.

Once we became involved in Vietnam we found ourselves fighting on many fronts. Battles against inflation, corruption, and disease were as critical to the success of our enterprise as the war against the Viet Cong. The non-military battles required a reasonably stable government with a continuing and sustained policy-making and policy-implementing capability. Indeed even the use of raw military force required at least some governmental medical, welfare, and reconstruction skills. The United States, short of undertaking a military occupation, was unable to compensate fully for an ineffective government or an inadequate Civil Service in Vietnam. We have not, thus far at least, demonstrated the ability or knowledge to administer effectively a society at once strange and complex. So even if we had chosen to "run" South Vietnam, we probably would have failed.

Is there a lesson or a moral to all of this? If there is, we need not wait to hear from a scholar in the future. The wily seventeenth century Spanish Jesuit philosopher, Gracian, had some useful guidance for present-day policymakers: "One ought not to give way in everything nor to everybody. To know how to refuse is therefore as important as to know how to consent. This is especially the case with men of position. All depends on the *how*. Some men's No is thought more of than the Yes of others; for a gilded No is more satisfactory than a dry Yes. . . . Your refusal need not be point-blank: let the disappointment come by degrees.

Nor let the refusal be final; that would be to destroy dependence; let some spice of hope remain to soften the rejection."

❖   ❖   ❖

Our experience in Vietnam probably created greater tension in American society than any event since our own Civil War. But unlike the Civil War, the Vietnam war directly involved only a small part of our people, and the scars if not healed are likely to be hidden under more urgent current domestic and international problems. Even with the generous helping of additional fuel that Mr. Nixon provided by the invasion of Cambodia, the fires of opposition to American policy in Indochina are likely to be banked as more urgent foreign (the Middle East) and domestic (environment) problems seize the headlines and attract the interest of articulate American public opinion. The world has crowded in on us with such force and intensity over the past quarter century that even the most traumatic events seem to have a very short half-life in our national memory. December 7th comes and goes with little or no ceremony, but for years Pearl Harbor Day gave members of my generation nightmares. Who remembers Corregidor or Anzio? What was the Berlin airlift? Where is Inchon? Who was Syngman Rhee? Who, for that matter, was Ngo Dinh Diem? And what, who, or where is Lon Nol?

This is not to say that Vietnam will soon be regarded as an incidental, if unfortunate foreign adventure. For a long time to come the decade of the '60s and the Administration of President Lyndon Johnson will evoke unpleasant, bitter memories of bombast and bombing. And President Nixon's miscalculations in the spring of 1970 will not soon be forgotten. But the United States will continue to have international interests and responsibilities, at least during the period of our and our children's lifetimes, and these are not likely to be shucked or shrugged off at the first cry of "Remember Vietnam!"

Thus the memory of Indochina in general and Vietnam in particular will not by itself change American policy from internationalism to isolationism. We would be understating the case, however, if we did not recognize the influence of Indochina on future major foreign policy decisions. Over the remainder of this century, no American President weighing the risks and costs of American military intervention abroad will pass off lightly the experiences of Lyndon Johnson and Richard Nixon. And each Administration for at least the next decade will want to take steps to ensure that the threshold of involvement in a conflict abroad will be higher than it was in the case of Vietnam. President Nixon has already implied in his "Doctrine" that overt aggression by a power unfriendly to the United States against an ally would probably trigger American military assistance, but even in such cases the threat to our national security will have to be clear-cut and credible to the American people. Pleas for help from regimes and nations in trouble are likely to be met with a higher degree of discrimination. Finally, a greater effort will have to be made to enlist popular support and understanding. In the last analysis, these considerations may make for more cautious, possibly more rational international commitments.

* * *

Gracian provides prudent advice for a rash leader, but a Great Power cannot always say "no," regardless of how gilded the refusal may be. There will be circumstances when it will have to say "yes." The measure of a statesman is to choose with wisdom the time, place, and extent of commitment.

The United States has typically been reluctant to become militarily involved in Europe—even when the threat to our friends and to our own interests has been grave and urgent. Assistance to our European allies in the First and Second World Wars was tardy— indeed almost too tardy. We indulged in brave talk but avoided action during the Hungarian uprising in 1956, despite the fact that "the liberation" of Eastern Europe was part of the current official American liturgy. More recently we have stood aside from the Soviet invasion of Czechoslovakia and the rightist coup in Greece. Whether our stance in each case was sensible or unwise is not the question here; the fact is that with respect to the affairs of Europe we have tended to be deliberate, pragmatic, hesitant, aware of risks.

In Asia, however, particularly during the past two decades, Americans have moved quickly to provide military help to nations and governments we hardly knew. To some extent this may reflect the inertia of the old "Open Door" China policy, and to some extent it may be a romantic throwback to our national urge to go ever farther Westward in search of frontiers. More practically and perhaps more importantly, it is a manifestation of John Foster Dulles' original "containment" doctrine. And as a gloss over it all is a missionary zeal that still evokes memories of the "white man's burden" and "the little brown brother." Thus our approach to Laos, Korea, Vietnam, Cambodia, and China itself has all too often been emotion-laden, naive, and impetuous—especially when compared with the prudence we have exercised elsewhere.

This is not only a matter of historical and current interest; it has significance for the future. Confrontations between the United States and the Soviet Union have shifted more and more from the sensitive international core of Europe to less vital, and therefore less dangerous, peripheral parts of the globe—the "third world." Threats to American national security interests in these areas are likely to be less immediate, less direct, and less credible. All the more reason for careful assessments of costs, risks, requirements, and opportunities.

As we survey the third world and the likely points of confrontation there, the Near East and Asia rank high. Asia presents special problems as a consequence of its vast areas and distances. But its more unique characteristic in terms of future American policy stems from the presence and the uncertain future role of giant, groping China. That these adjectives pretty much sum up our knowledge about China is worrisome, but we must recognize that we have been confronting this vast and vexing part of the world with a modicum of experience and expertise. Until World War II Southeast Asia was left to the French, British, and Dutch; Korea and Japan were by and large left to the missionaries. China was another and somewhat different story. Many Americans performed many roles. There were Marines at the Tientsin Garrison, businessmen in the International Quarter of Shanghai, teachers at Yale-in-China, diplomats in Peking, employees of the international cartels in Canton, and missionaries everywhere. But few learned much about the fast currents and strong tides that were sweeping over the length and breadth of the land, and as we moved in to help Chiang Kai-shek the United States found itself in almost total ignorance about China. When the chips were down very few of the Old China Hands knew what made China tick; missionaries had done good works, traders had made good money, and all had led a good life.

There were some exceptions, of course. Many Foreign Service Officers in the Embassy and Consulates gained valuable experience during the fast-moving events of the 1930s and '40s. These China specialists represented an elite group within the State Department and, unlike some of their colleagues, were usually kept in the area instead of being "rotated" from country to country and continent to continent. They spoke the language, participated in the great events, were knowledgeable—albeit sometimes sentimental—about the Chinese people. Two coinciding forces virtually eliminated this precious resource during the early 1950s when we needed it desperately: the fanatical anti–Communist movement in the United States headed by Joseph McCarthy, and the fanatical Communist movement in China headed by Mao Tse-tung. McCarthy's purge cost the United States many of its China experts. Mao's policy (which, of course, simply reinforced our own) prevented those still remaining in the government, and the generation to follow, from acquiring a firsthand exposure to Mainland China.* As a result, there have been no towering Mr. Asias or Mr. Chinas in the forums of high policy in Washington—no equivalents to Bohlen or Harriman or Thompson or Kohler. There has been no one to whom a President or Secretary of State could almost instinctively turn for advice and guidance on Asian policy. Second-echelon and working-level specialists on China, some of whom are brilliant Sinologists, rarely have access to top policy-

---

* It is worth noting, however, that foreign diplomats in Peking are so bottled up that they know little more, if not less, about developments in China than the American Consul General in Hong Kong does.

makers. And other Asian specialists are either wrapped up in day-to-day problems (if, say, they are involved in Vietnam, Laos, or Cambodia) or are far removed from the center of decision-making. Searching analyses and mid-range projections, if they are made at all, are likely to shrivel and perish from neglect.

One of the fruits of the Cambodian venture is an increase of Chinese Communist influence on the course of developments in Indochina. Prince Sihanouk and the forces that endeavor to return him to power in Phnom Penh now report directly to Peking. Since Cambodia and its future will almost certainly be part of any meaningful settlement of the Indochina war, the Chinese are bound to play a key role and our negotiating problem will become even more complicated. This is a matter that must be disquieting to many gentlemen in Hanoi and Moscow, as well as in Washington. The North Vietnamese, even if they wished to resume secret bilateral talks with the Americans, are unlikely to have the freedom of action they had prior to April, 1970. And the Russians, who in the early stages of the Paris talks were able to exert quiet but effective leverage, will probably be somewhat more constrained.

One salubrious effect of Peking's increased influence in Indochina may be that Moscow will press forward more vigorously with its own variant of the "containment" of China. While this may pose challenges for Washington, it offers opportunities as well. Thus there is some probability of Washington–Moscow cooperation in Asia that could mitigate or mute superpower rivalries. The most immediate test of the likelihood of such cooperation will come in Southeast Asia, and especially in Indochina.

If this area is ever to see peace and tranquillity, the Vietnamese, Loatians, and Cambodians must work out a *modus vivendi* among themselves; and outside powers—particularly the United States, the Soviet Union, and China—must let the Indochinese alone. In spite of the history of the past decade, or perhaps because of it, the United States once disengaged is unlikely again to permit itself to be locked into Indochinese internal politics. As the Soviet Union becomes less concerned about ideological rivalries with China in remote areas and more preoccupied with its security along its China border, Moscow's interest in the countries of Indochina will wane, and Japan and North Korea will assume prime importance for Soviet policymakers.

There are those who believe that Ho could have become the Tito of Southeast Asia; that given an opportunity the North Vietnamese would develop an Asian-type of independent communism. Because of their long, cruel subjection to China in the distant past, and because of their fear of being smothered by the sheer weight of China in the future, the Vietnamese—North and South alike—will almost certainly attempt to maintain a significant degree of ideological, economic, and political independence from their giant northern neighbor. But the American bombing of North Vietnam may have increased Hanoi's dependence on Peking,* and the death of Ho Chi Minh may have strengthened the hand of the pro-China wing in the North Vietnamese leadership. China, other things being equal, would obviously prefer to see a satellite regime in Vietnam than a truly independent one. The short-term omens are thus not propitious for a Tito-type regime in Hanoi. It is conceivable, however, that a Communist regime in Vietnam might for a time maintain substantial independence of Peking. The Chinese leadership may continue for several years to be preoccupied with other international or domestic problems, and under these circumstances it may be willing to tolerate what would otherwise be an undesirable degree of latitude and freewheeling on the part of a Vietnamese regime.

The subject of future Hanoi Peking relations, however, should be treated with humility by an amateur. American "Hanoiologists" rank far behind "Kremlinologists" and "Pekingologists" in the level of their precision and sophistication. We have been at war with the North Vietnamese for many years, but we know very little about the personalities of Hanoi's leaders and the relations among them. Who are "doves" and who are "hawks"? Who are "pro-Peking" and who are "pro-Moscow" and who are neither?

* One of my more far-out brainstorms during 1965 was a proposal for some kind of secret arrangement that would allow the United States to finance rice sales to the Soviet Union so that Moscow could then provide the North Vietnamese with the much needed food Hanoi was being forced to obtain from China.

Who are genuine nationalists and who are zealous Communists? These are matters of speculation rather than knowledge.

Out of this one thing at least seems clear: China will have to be reckoned with in any calculation about the future of Vietnam and its neighbors. We would do well to develop long-range policies for the contingency that Southeast Asia will develop the same relationship with China that Eastern Europe has with the Soviet Union. Does this mean that a decade hence we will have "lost" Vietnam? To the extent that we ever "had" Vietnam, the answer is probably yes. And what of Laos, Cambodia, even Thailand? The answers are yes, yes, and maybe.

And yet there are factors in the equation that are not constant and others that are not known. Perhaps the answers should be more tentatively stated. A strong Japan is eager to expand its export of skills, capital, and goods and desirous of stability in the region. The growing hostility between China and the Soviet Union, and Peking's seemingly unending struggle to reorder its own house, may preoccupy the Chinese Communist leaders and thus provide needed time for the independent regimes of Southeast Asia to strengthen their societies and economies. However tacit they may be, there are pragmatic imperatives for some cooperative effort between Moscow and Washington to maintain a working if imperfect neutrality in the region.

❋   ❋   ❋

The President of the United States who takes his oath of office in January 1973 (Richard Nixon if we are well out of Indochina by then—probably another man if we are not) will be able to look back on the Decade of Vietnam with more perspective than President Nixon can now. Even if we are not entirely disengaged, the new President, with the flexibility available to him during his first year in office, is likely to finish the task with dispatch. What then? Surely he will be inclined to shy away from distant crusades in pursuit of an elusive infidel. In any case, neither the American people as a whole nor the Congress are likely to be very enthusiastic about any more such adventures. Congress, at least in this generation, is unlikely to permit any President once more to lurch or to slide into war by executive decree. The Tonkin Resolution will not soon be forgotten; there will be no more blank checks. The ploy of using Appropriations Bills as a means of exacting *ex post facto* Congressional approval of major Presidential decisions is a device of the past; conceivably it may be resorted to in the long-term future, but it will not be part of any President's kit in the '70s.

President Johnson confronted growing hostility in Congress from the outset of our direct involvement in Vietnam, but, thanks to a Democratic majority in both Houses and to his unrivaled ability to manipulate and persuade the power structure on Capitol Hill, he rode out his term of office without major Congressional revolt. The Nixon Administration has had neither the luck nor the skill to avoid a head–on clash. Even before the invasion of Cambodia, it was evident that President Nixon would have to conduct his foreign policy under much less permissive circumstances.

The Senate has demonstrated that it will cast a jaundiced eye on any new military involvements abroad that may be made through unilateral Executive decision. American actions and commitments in Laos, Cambodia, and Thailand have already been subjected to close and critical scrutiny. No President in the foreseeable future is likely to go very far in the use or even positioning of American troops abroad without making sure that his Congressional flanks are covered. Congress has incorporated a provision in the Defense Appropriations Bill for Fiscal Year 1970 that the funds shall not be used "to finance the introduction of American ground troops into Laos and Thailand." Legislation sponsored by Senators Church and Cooper, and by Senators McGovern and Hatfield, carries the same intent with respect to Cambodia and Vietnam.

Late in 1969 Senators Mathias and Mansfield introduced a joint resolution that would wipe the slate clean by repealing the Formosa, Middle East, Cuba, and Gulf of Tonkin Resolutions. The Senators also hoped to terminate the state of national emergency proclaimed by President Truman in 1950 at the start of the Korean conflict. According to Senator Mathias, "All these resolutions are based on an essentially negative view of the American world mission. In each instance, we imply the principle that military containment of international communism is the chief function of our foreign policy. . . . All these resolutions . . . are based on assumptions of dubious validity today. . . . I am fully aware that it may become necessary in the future for the United States to employ military force in fulfilling treaty commitments. If we do, however, it will become imperative that we have a clearer understanding of international politics than was manifested in Vietnam. The slogans of the fifties . . . will never again suffice to persuade our young people to risk their lives in war." [3]

Lyndon Johnson's televised reminiscences to the contrary, Joseph Goulden may well be right when he says "the Tonkin Gulf affair ranks high" among the factors resulting in President Johnson's decision not to seek re-election.[4] Johnson's interpretation of the August, 1964 Joint Resolution may have cost him important support during the critical debates of March, 1968. In any case, it is apparent that the lesson has been driven home: the United States is not likely to go to war again without a clear mandate from Congress, and the role of the Congress in major questions of war or peace cannot be fudged, hedged, or dissembled.＊ Senator Javits has warned the Executive Branch of the Government that "it must adjust itself psychologically and procedurally to a new reality—the reality that the Senate will not again shrink from its responsibilities or yield its constitutional power with respect to national security issues and the solemn undertaking of national commitments." [5] In a startling demonstration of legislative overkill, the Senate repealed the Tonkin Gulf Resolution not once, but twice (June 24, and again on July 10, 1970).

On June 30, 1970 the Senate approved the Church–Cooper Amendment to the Foreign Military Sales Bill. In essence, the Senate refused to approve the expenditure of funds for the support of American military actions in Cambodia after July 1. Despite its academic deadline for the removal of American forces

---

＊ A straw in the wind is the bill passed by the Massachusetts Legislature in April, 1970 permitting Massachusetts residents to refuse combat duty in the Armed Forces unless there has been a declaration of war by Congress.

and its disclaimers with respect to the President's constitutional responsibilities as Commander-in-Chief, the Senate provided the President with a firm reminder that it can exercise a strong, if indirect veto on American international commitments.

In the equable and simplistic decades prior to World War II, the distinction between the President's constitutional responsibilities as Commander-in-Chief and Congress' power to declare war seemed clear–cut and unquestioned. In the more complex years since 1945, the distinction has become fuzzy around the edges; the President has been able to send American troops into battle abroad without resorting to a Declaration of War. Clearly Congress plans to take a more serious and literal view of its responsibilities in the realm of foreign affairs. The effect may not be altogether salutary; the pendulum may swing too far away from the White House toward Capitol Hill, and the President may thus be unnecessarily constrained or inhibited in his conduct of foreign policy.

Yet another matter the President and the Departments of State and Defense must come to grips with is the influence of public debate on the conduct of foreign policy, particularly when the issues involved are emotional but sensitive, complex but subtle. There is and should be no argument with such propositions as "The public must be kept informed" or "The people have a right to know" or "Open covenants, openly arrived at." But how much can and should the President and his principal advisers rely for short-term policy guidance on the Gallup Poll, a March on Washington, an American Legion Convention, or a "Meet the Press" program? The art of the foreign policymaker must be practiced in a different way from that of the investor; decisions in the realm of international affairs cannot be based on the same day-to-day whiffs and omens that determine whether one puts or calls, buys or sells.

To say this is not to say that a government, or at least the Government of the United States, should conduct its international affairs insulated from the views and the mood of its society. Despite the increasing use and sophistication of public opinion polls, we have been laggard and ineffectual in being able to sense the

nature and depth of American public opinion on complex international issues. It is one thing to be guided by a poll that asks
"Who is your choice for President? Check one of the following."
It is another matter to divine meaning from one that poses "Do
you think the President is doing a good job in Vietnam? Yes. No.
Don't know." Consider this exchange between Mr. Gallup and a
"representative sample." On the heels of President Nixon's speech
of April 30, 1970 in which he announced he was sending American troops into Cambodia, the pollsters asked, "Do you approve
or disapprove of the way President Nixon is handling the Cambodian situation?" Fifty-one percent of those polled "approved."
But when asked whether "we should send U.S. troops to help
Cambodia, or not," fifty-eight percent said "we should *not*."

"Public Opinion" is a derivative of a host of factors, some of
which may be only remotely affected by the merits of a particular
issue. But surely one of the major elements in the mix should be
at least a minimal degree of knowledge about the issue. What
Washington must strive to obtain and then tune into is an *informed* public opinion. The interplay between public opinion and
foreign policy promises to remain a lively issue. A report published
by the UN Association in January, 1970 stresses the need for more
careful polling of American attitudes toward complex foreign
policy questions and recommends that a "National Polling Commission" be established to assess American public opinion. In
effect, such a polling could represent a plebiscite on major issues.

Washington has not done very well in its efforts to understand
and influence the public mood, in spite of a regiment of official
spokesmen, public affairs officers and press secretaries. In desperation various Administrations have used such devices as large
and small press conferences, "backgrounders" by high officials to
carefully selected reporters, "fireside chats," television panel appearances, official leaks, "press-guidance memoranda," "White
Papers" and the quiet lunch. But on issues that are many-faceted
and touch emotional chords, issues such as Vietnam, the system
breaks down. The failure of communication between the Johnson
Administration and the American public with respect to Vietnam
resulted not from too little information but from an excessive attention to detail, spot news, and conflicting, frequently trivial

data. The daily doses of horror stories, body counts, ambushes, and bombing raids diverted the Administration from explaining, and the American people from understanding, the Big Picture: Why are we there? What are we trying to accomplish? How do we plan to get out? What would happen if we did? To be sure, there was a plethora of rhetoric on these subjects, but it soon became clear to an increasing number of people that Washington was engaged in a public relations exercise rather than an expository one. News "management"—or at least news manipulation—has become an increasingly accepted weapon for Washington officials to use in their confrontations with the press.[6]

In the last analysis, Americans became confused by an Administration that was itself uncertain about objectives, about progress, about where we were, where we came from, where we were going. The Johnson Administration became lost in its own maze. It was deemed necessary to put the best gloss possible on a rapid succession of ineffectual governments in Saigon, on corruption among Vietnamese officials, on staggeringly high desertion rates from the Vietnamese Army, on the effect of bombing raids on the North Vietnamese will and ability to aid the Viet Cong. The intent was to hold the domestic front until, with American help and guidance, the Vietnamese would pull up their socks. The hope was that with heavier bombing the men in Hanoi would come to the negotiating table. The expectation was that with more and more American troops deployed Communist attrition would become unacceptable to Hanoi. But the public image eroded, and the earnest hopes boomeranged in large part because the ugly realities became submerged in the minds of many of the policymakers themselves. It was genuinely believed that another series of raids, 100,000 more troops, the newest government in Saigon, the new pacification plan would do the trick. The efforts of the President were complicated, and the public was made even more confused by Administration officials who took one position within the policy councils and another when talking "privately." Some were able to have their cake by avoiding confronting the President head-on with unpopular opinions, and to eat it too by revealing their doubts among their colleagues, friends, and selected journalists.

With little attention paid to research, analysis, planning, and policy formulation, the Johnson Administration had little right to expect that it could present a convincing case for either its short-term progress or long-term objectives. No press conference, no backgrounder, no televised speech could provide the kind of enlightenment that would produce a truly informed public. In the spring of 1970 President Nixon began to fall into this trap as announced American objectives in Cambodia bounced from "helping the Cambodian Government," to "capturing COSVN," to "destroying enemy supplies," to "saving American lives." Fifty-one percent of a polling sample might "approve" the President's policy in Cambodia, but what proportion really understood what it was?

*   *   *

The decade of the seventies will be characterized by more rather than fewer of the kinds of problems we have been addressing here. Technological advances will continue to make the globe more closely-knit, but they will also favor continuing economic growth in the rich rather than the poor nations of the world; population will press hard on available resources everywhere, but particularly in countries already buffeted by problems of too many people and too few amenities. The polarization between the "Free World" and the "Communist Bloc" is likely to continue to become blurred, especially as closer ties develop between Eastern and Western Europe. But this is far from saying that Wendell Wilkie's "One World" is within our grasp. New polarizations are on the horizon that are likely to take the form of economic and color divisions rather than ideological ones. And the United States and the Soviet Union may find themselves, willy-nilly, working in close if tacit cooperation in the face of the demands from the Have-Not nations for liberal trade and aid concessions. Under these circumstances the issues of involvement or withdrawal will be slippery to grapple with and thorny to explain. It will be difficult to mount an international crusade in the seventies, even if an Administration in Washington were so long on zeal and so short on memory as to try.

But if international crusades are out, American international obligations and responsibilities will still be very much with us—economic, political, and even military. The United States has a network of treaties, pacts, and arrangements that can neither be shrugged off nor precipitately liquidated. More than forty nations are covered by solemn defense treaties; almost seventy countries receive some form of American economic or technical assistance. The shadow of Indochina will be cast not so much over existing American commitments, although the *interpretation* of some of them may be questioned from time to time, but over new ones. The mood of Congress may make it difficult to maintain the present commitments for economic and technical assistance to underdeveloped nations; with the exception of some expansion of aid for the postwar reconstruction of South Vietnam, and possibly of North Vietnam as well, the question of new economic aid programs will probably remain academic in the foreseeable future. The case of political military commitments is another matter, however. Congressional appropriations are not involved here and, short of the conclusion of formal treaties, there is wide room for independent action by the Executive Branch. Because of this the White House, State Department, and Pentagon will find themselves under continuing surveillance by Congress and the American people.

*   *   *

The immediate challenge for Washington policymakers is to learn how to cope with threats that are less urgent and cataclysmic than the menace of strategic war. And "to cope with" means having the readiness, skills, and patience to work out non-military solutions. We have long known that no one will "win" an all-out war; we have only recently learned that no one wins a Vietnam-type war either. In the last analysis, national security can be attained only in a peaceful and ordered world. To achieve even a realistic approximation of such a world will require undertaking close consultations with the Soviet Union and developing effective, non-polemic channels with Communist China so that we can avoid, insofar as possible, misunderstandings and miscalculations about objectives and intentions. It will mean an expansion of American aid programs and a liberalization of our trade policies lest we find ourselves psychologically and politically besieged by the unfulfilled, bitter, restless populations of Latin America, Africa, and Asia. It will involve a serious quest for knowledge and understanding of, and communication with, vast areas of the world about which we still know little. Finally, it will demand a realization that we must use military force if necessary to protect ourselves against genuine and clear-cut threats to our security, and also a recognition that such action will first require full public understanding and support.

In the short term the American venture in Vietnam may be judged a lost crusade; for a more profound view we must await the considered analysis of the historian. He may discover that the lessons of the sixties produced a more measured and thoughtful American approach to the international problems of the seventies and beyond. He may discover too that as a result of the crusade in Vietnam, the conduct of American foreign policy, and in particular the development of American international commitments, was no longer the sole concern of the Department of State in Washington and the Council on Foreign Relations in New York. A new and broad constituency of awakened and informed people throughout the country has begun to play an important and instructive role. Like the crusades of the Middle Ages, our own crusade in Asia may send important political and social ripples across the space of time. The observer can only hope that the experience of Indochina will help America meet the challenges ahead more effectively and less traumatically. This observer finds comfort in the confidence of a wise and seasoned statesman: "For my part, I have no doubt that in our free institutions we have a wealth of initiative and creative talent to meet these challenges which no totalitarian society can muster." [7]

Glossary

Alliance of National Democratic and Peace Forces A South Vietnamese pro-Communist, anti-government political group established at a meeting in Saigon in April, 1968. Although many of its members were reported to be non-Communist, the Alliance favored a coalition government with the NLF and pledged support for the Viet Cong.

American Friends of Vietnam An organization founded in the fall of 1955 to assist Ngo Dinh Diem in developing Vietnam as a "showcase of democracy." Its announced purpose was "to extend more broadly a mutual understanding of Vietnamese and American history, cultural customs, and democratic institutions." In actuality, it was concerned with the political objective of committing the United States to a massive aid program on Diem's behalf.

Annam A former French protectorate in central Indochina; its area is now divided between North and South Vietnam.

ANZUS A security treaty signed by Australia, New Zealand, and the United States on September 1, 1951.

Can Lao—Revolutionary Workers' Party A pro-government party headed by Ngo Dinh Nhu.

Cao Dai—"Third Amnesty of God" A political-religious sect, divided into a number of branches, with a wide nationalist following in the south.

CINCPAC—Commander-in-Chief, Pacific The Commander of American forces in the Pacific area, headquartered in Honolulu.

Cochinchina A former French colony in Indochina; its area conformed roughly with what is now the southern part of South Vietnam.

Communist Party of Indochina A party established in 1930 by Ho Chi

469

Minh (then known as Nguyen Ai Quoc) and formally dissolved by him in 1945.

Demarcation Line The line dividing South and North Vietnam, established by the Geneva Agreements of 1954. It does not coincide exactly with the 17th parallel but approximates it closely enough that the terms are used interchangeably in many contexts.

DMZ—De-Militarized Zone An area on either side of the demarcation line, established by the Geneva Agreements of 1954 as a buffer zone between North and South Vietnam.

DRV—Democratic Republic of Vietnam The government of North Vietnam, established in September, 1945 with Ho Chi Minh as President.

EDC—European Defense Community A plan for the establishment of a Western European military alliance put forward in 1950 and dropped in 1954.

Elysée Agreement An exchange of letters during 1949 between Emperor Bao Dai, Chief of the State of Vietnam, and President Auriol of France, outlining the general principles affecting French–Vietnamese relations.

Geneva Conference of 1954 A conference convened to discuss problems of Korea and Indochina. For the Indochina portion there were delegates from Great Britain and the Soviet Union (who acted as Co-Chairmen), France, the United States, Communist China, Cambodia, Laos and Vietnam, and the Vietminh regime. The "Agreements," or "Accords," were signed in July, the only signatories being representatives of the French Union Forces in Indochina and the People's Army of Vietnam (Vietminh). The Agreements included the establishment of the Demarcation Line, the De-Militarized Zone, and the International Control Commissoin.

GRV—Government of the Republic of Vietnam The government of South Vietnam, established in 1954 with Ngo Dinh Diem as Prime Minister.

Guam Doctrine See *Nixon Doctrine*.

GVN Another term for the government of South Vietnam.

High National Council A Council set up after an unsuccessful coup against General Khanh in October 1964. It was composed of a group of venerable civilians and charged with the task of working out plans for a provisional legislative body that in turn would prepare a permanent constitution.

Hoa Hao A political-religious sect dominant in provinces located southwest of Saigon.

Honolulu Conference of 1966 The first meeting between U.S. and South Vietnamese leaders to discuss the war in Vietnam with primary emphasis on socio-economic development.

Hop Tac A plan instituted by General Khanh in 1964 for concentrating major military resources in the Saigon area for the purpose of progressively clearing and securing areas spreading outward from the capital.

ICC—International Control Commission   A body set up under the Geneva Agreements of 1954, composed of representatives of Canada, India, and Poland and presided over by the Representative of India. The purpose of the Commission was to supervise the implementation of the Agreements.

Indochina   The area, formerly French Indochina, which now includes North and South Vietnam, Laos, and Cambodia.

Laos Conference   "The Fourteen Nation Conference on Laos" was convened in Geneva in May, 1961, with delegates from Great Britain and the Soviet Union (who again acted as Co-Chairmen), Laos, Canada, India, Poland, the United States, South Vietnam, North Vietnam, Cambodia, Thailand, Burma, France, and Communist China. In July, 1962 the signatories of the Accords agreed "to recognize the sovereignty, independence, neutrality, unity and territorial integrity of Laos." The discussions resulted in the formation of a coalition government headed by Prime Minister Souvanna Phouma.

MAAG—Military Assistance Advisory Group   A U.S. organization set up in several allied countries, which provides military equipment and American personnel to train forces of the host country in the use and maintenance of the equipment.

MACV—U.S. Military Assistance Command, Vietnam   A Command established in 1962, with headquarters in Saigon.

Manila Conference of 1954   See SEATO.

Manila Conference of 1966   A summit conference convoked by President Marcos of the Philippines to bring leaders of the United States, South Vietnam, Australia, New Zealand, Korea, Thailand, and the Philippines together for a review of Allied military, political, and economic programs in South Vietnam. (Notable for President Johnson's six-month formula for the withdrawal of American and Allied forces from South Vietnam.)

Montagnards   Collective name for tribal peoples of various ethnic origin living in the highland regions of both North and South Vietnam.

National Liberation Front—National Front for the Liberation of South Vietnam   The political arm of the Communist subversive effort in South Vietnam, said to have been founded in December, 1960, sometimes referred to as the NLF, NLFSV or NFLSV. Its leaders, who are South Vietnamese, claim to be non-Communist.

Negotiations Committee   An interagency committee called together by Ambassador-at-Large W. Averell Harriman in 1966 after he was asked by President Johnson to develop initiatives for a peaceful solution of the war in Vietnam.

Nixon Doctrine   A general statement of U.S. foreign policy made by President Nixon at a press conference on Guam in July, 1969 and cited in his 1970 State of the Union speech. While reaffirming the U.S. intent to honor all treaty commitments and to provide "appropriate" military and economic assistance to a threatened friendly nation, the Doctrine indicates a shift in the nature of American support by emphasizing that the United States would expect the threatened nation to provide the manpower necessary for its own defense.

OSS—*Office of Strategic Services*   The intelligence organization established during World War II under the command of General William Donovan, USA.

Pathet Lao   The name given by the Communists to a state in northern Laos formed in 1950 and sponsored by the Viet Minh of North Vietnam; it is headed by Prince Souphanouvong.

"*San Antonio Formula*"   A reference to an offer made by President Johnson in a speech at San Antonio, Texas on September 29, 1967. In the President's words, "The heart of the matter is really this: The United States is willing to stop all . . . bombardment of North Vietnam when this will lead promptly to discussions."

SEATO—Southeast Asia Collective Defense Treaty Organization   An alliance established by the Manila Conference of 1954; the member nations (U.S., Great Britain, France, Thailand, Australia, New Zealand, the Philippines, and Pakistan) are committed to resist aggression in the treaty area.

Seventeenth Parallel   See Demarcation Line.

"*Seventh Floor*"   The area within the Department of State building where the Secretary of State, his Under Secretaries, and other high ranking State Department officials have their offices.

Tet—Vietnamese New Year   The New Year holiday is generally celebrated in late January or early February, the date being based on the Buddhist lunar calendar.

Tonkin   A former French protectorate in Indochina; its area conformed roughly with what is now the northern part of North Vietnam.

"*Tuesday Lunch*"   A function instituted by President Johnson and attended by the Secretaries of State and Defense and a few of Johnson's principal advisers. The Lunch was a forum for discussion and decision on many of the most urgent and sensitive foreign affairs problems. Vietnam was a primary, and frequently the exclusive subject on the informal agenda.

U.S. Mission   The Embassy personnel and economic and military advisers who report directly to the Ambassador.

Viet Cong   A derogatory contraction of "Vietnamese Communist." It is used, except by the Communists, to describe the Communist subversive movement in the South after 1954.

Viet Minh—Revolutionary League for the Independence of Vietnam   A Communist-led organization, represented as a coalition of nationalist groups. It actively opposed the French and Japanese during World War II and spearheaded Vietnamese resistance to French rule.

"*West Basement*"   The location in the White House of the office of the Special Assistant to the President for National Security Affairs.

Chronology

February 19   U.S. Consulate General in Saigon raised to Legation; Donald Heath becomes Minister.

May 8   U.S. sends economic and military aid to Indochina (through France).

May 25   U.S. sets up STEM (Special Technical-Economic Mission) headed by Robert Blum.

June 27   President Truman orders military aid increased to France for Vietnam war.

August 2   *U.S. Military Assistance Advisory Group established in Saigon (MAAG).*

December 23   *U.S. signs Mutual Defense Assistance Agreement with France and the Associated States of Indochina* (Vietnam, Laos and Cambodia).

December 23   France grants Associated States independence within the French Union.

1951

September 7   U.S. signs bilateral economic aid agreements with Vietnam, Laos, and Cambodia for direct economic assistance.

1952

June   U.S. supplying about one-third of total war cost.

July   *U.S. raises Legation in Saigon to Embassy.* Donald Heath remains as Ambassador. Vietnamese Embassy established in Washington, D.C.

1953

May 5   Dulles in Congressional Committee warns of chain reaction in Southeast Asia if Indochina is lost.

July 27   Korean Armistice.

                 U.S. aid to France for Vietnam war expenses increases.

August 4   President Eisenhower stresses need to block Communist aggression to save rest of free Asia.

November 1	Vice President Nixon tours war front—urges greater war effort.
November 29	Ho Chi Minh offers to negotiate truce.

1954

February 18	Big Four agree at Berlin to hold Geneva Conference on Korea and Indochina.
March–May	Battle of Dien Bien Phu.
	U.S. weighs issue of intervention.
April 26	*Geneva Conference begins.*
April 28	France declares Vietnam independent.
May 6	French defeated at Dien Bien Phu.
May 8	Discussions on Indochina open at Geneva.
June 14	*Bao Dai appoints Ngo Dinh Diem as Premier of Vietnam.*
June 25	Diem arrives in Saigon.
July 21	*Geneva Agreement signed.*
September 7	*Southeast Asia Collective Defense Treaty signed.*
October 11	Viet Minh formally take over control of North Vietnam.
October 23	*Eisenhower letter to Diem*—U.S. aid to be given directly to SVN, not through France.
November 3	President Eisenhower appoints General J. Lawton Collins as Special Representative in South Vietnam replacing Ambassador Heath.

1955

February 12	*U.S. MAAG takes over training of South Vietnamese Armed Forces.*
May	U.S. support for Premier Diem solidifies. French agree to support him and withdraw their forces.
June 6	Viet Minh demand talks to prepare for July, 1956 elections to unify country.

July 16	Premier Diem declares South Vietnam will not participate in elections unless there are also free elections in the North.
October 23	National referendum in South Vietnam; Bao Dai deposed, Diem elected Chief of State by 98 percent of voters.
October 26	*Diem proclaims South Vietnam a republic— becomes President.*

1956

March 4	General elections for Constituent Assembly held in South Vietnam.
July 4	Constituent Assembly approves draft Constitution—gives President wide powers.
July 6	Vice President Nixon visits South Vietnam— hails Diem, declares U.S. support—says "militant march of communism has been halted."
October 26	South Vietnam's Constitution promulgated.

1957

May 5–19	President Diem visits United States—pledges to continue fight against communism. Eisenhower pledges continued aid.

1958

February	International Control Commission moves its headquarters from Hanoi to Saigon.
March	President Diem in Manila reports Communist subversion in South Vietnam increasing.

1959

April	Communist sabotage and terrorism increases in South Vietnam.
July 8	Two U.S. military advisers killed in terrorist raid at Bien Hoa military base. First American casualties.

1960

April 17	North Vietnam protests to Great Britain and Soviet Union against a "formidable" increase in U.S. MAAG personnel in South Vietnam, accusing the U.S. of turning the country into "a U.S. military base for the preparation of a new war."
April 30	A group of 18 Vietnamese notables, including 10 former Ministers, ask President Diem to liberalize regime by adopting economic, administrative, and military reforms.
May 5	*U.S. announces that the MAAG will be increased from 327 to 685 members.*
June–October	Communist terrorist activities in South Vietnam increase.
October 26	President Eisenhower congratulates Diem on South Vietnam's 5th anniversary, assures him of continued U.S. assistance.
November 10	South Vietnam charges North Vietnam with direct aggression—says regular North Vietnamese Army forces infiltrated through Laos.
November 11	Colonel Nguyen Chanh Thi leads paratroopers in coup against President Diem, demanding end to autocratic rule.
November 12	Diem crushes coup—rebels surrender.
November 16	Diem and Nhu announce government plans reforms and new government.
December	U.S. military personnel in Vietnam total 900.
	Establishment of National Front for Liberation of South Vietnam (NFLSV).

1961

January 29	Radio Hanoi praises establishment of NLFSV.
March 29	SEATO Ministers Council notes with concern efforts of armed minority supported from the outside to destroy South Vietnam.

April 9   President Diem and Vice President Tho re-
                           elected by overwhelming majority in presiden-
                           tial elections.

May 5   President Kennedy at news conference an-
                           nounces Vice President Johnson to visit South
                           Vietnam. Says decision to send U.S. troops will
                           depend on Johnson's report.

May 11–13   *Vice President Johnson visits South Vietnam,
                           pledges additional U.S. aid.*

May 16   Fourteen-nation conference on Laos convenes
                           in Geneva.

                           Staley mission in South Vietnam to examine
                           economic conditions.

September 25   President Kennedy warns in speech at U.N.
                           that South Vietnam is under attack.

October 1   Military experts of SEATO meet in Bangkok to
                           discuss guerrilla war in South Vietnam. U.S.
                           considers sending troops.

October 2   President Diem in speech to National Assembly
                           says struggle has grown into a real war.

October 11   President Kennedy announces at press confer-
                           ence that he is sending General Maxwell D.
                           Taylor to personally investigate situation in
                           Vietnam; decision on sending U.S. combat
                           troops to be based on his report.

October 18–25   General Taylor and Rostow visit South Viet-
                           nam.

October 26   President Kennedy renews pledge to help
                           South Vietnam resist Communists.

November 16   *President Kennedy, following recommendations
                           of Taylor, and with approval of National Se-
                           curity Council, decides to send additional mili-
                           tary advisers and equipment but no combat
                           units now.* Kennedy and Taylor hope military
                           reforms in South Vietnam will enable country
                           to halt communist threat.

December 8   State Department publishes "White Paper"—"A

Threat to the Peace"—documenting North Vietnam's effort to take over South Vietnam.

President Kennedy pledges additional economic and military aid.

U.S. military forces in South Vietnam reach 3,200.

1962

January 4	U.S. and South Vietnam jointly announce program of economic and social aid based on Staley report recommendations.
February 7	Additional U.S. forces arrive in South Vietnam, increasing total to 4,000.
February 8	U.S. reorganizes military command in Saigon, sets up U.S. Military Assistance Command, Vietnam under General Paul D. Harkins.
February 18	Robert Kennedy in Saigon says U.S. troops will remain until Viet Cong defeated.
February 26	Two dissident South Vietnamese Air Force officers bomb and strafe Presidential Palace in attempt to assassinate Diem.
March	U.S. press criticism of Diem regime intensifies.
April	U.S. military force in Vietnam increases to 5,400.
April 20	National Assembly supports Diem's strategic hamlet program.
May 9–11	McNamara makes Vietnam inspection tour; says U.S. aid will level off, doubts U.S. military forces will be increased, encouraged by developments but acknowledges it will take years before Vietnam is secure.
May 15	*President Kennedy orders military forces to Thailand due to deteriorating situation in Laos.*
May 28	President Diem refuses to allow direct U.S. assistance to Montagnards. Americans in Saigon criticize "sink or swim" with Diem attitude on part of Administration.

July 22–24   McNamara confers with General Harkins and Ambassador Nolting in Honolulu—says U.S. military aid paying off, pleased at progress.

July 23   *Laos Conference ends—declaration of neutrality signed in Geneva.*

September 11–13   General Taylor, Chairman JCS, confers in Saigon; generally pleased with SVN's progress, hails strategic hamlet program.

November   Mme. Nhu criticizes American press as "worse than communists."

December   *U.S. military strength in South Vietnam reaches 11,300.*

                                    1963

January 2–3   South Vietnam forces badly defeated in battle of Ap Bac—3 Americans killed. Total U.S. death toll at 30 since start of aid.

January 9–11   Admiral Felt, CINCPAC, confers with General Harkins, sees "inevitable" defeat of Viet Cong, confident Vietnamese will win war. Felt, in Washington, sees South Vietnam victory in three years.

February 12   Ambassador Nolting urges frankness between United States and Vietnamese.

February 24   Senator Mansfield in report after trip to Vietnam in late 1962 says situation there appears less stable than in 1955 despite $2 billion in U.S. aid.

March 8   Secretary of State Rusk says SVN troops have initiative in most areas.

April 17   President Diem announces "Chieu Hoi" (open arms) campaign, appealing to Viet Cong to surrender.

                      12,000 U.S. advisers now in Vietnam; Diem wants number cut.

May 6   Defense spokesman says "corner has definitely been turned toward victory."

May 8	Riots break out in Hue after GVN bars flying of flags and processions on Buddha's birthday.
May 22	President Kennedy says U.S. will withdraw advisers if suggested by SVN.
June 3	Buddhist demonstrations break out in Hue and other cities.
	Martial law imposed. Government uses troops to halt riots.
June 11	Buddhist monk, Thich Quang Duc, commits suicide by self-immolation in Saigon to dramatize protest of government's policies towards Buddhists. Further riots in Saigon by Buddhists. Government troops use force to suppress rioters.
June 27	President Kennedy announces appointment of Henry Cabot Lodge as Ambassador.
July 11	President Kennedy reaffirms U.S. support for Diem but warns that "internal dissension" must not weaken "unity of purpose and purpose in action."
July 17	Buddhist protestors in Saigon beaten back by armed policemen. Most violent attack in Buddhist crisis. President Kennedy in news conference says war effort is impaired by crisis, hopes for early agreement between Diem and Buddhist leaders.
August 4	Second Buddhist priest burns self to death.
August 20–21	Government troops and police raid Saigon's Xa Loi pagoda—arrest hundreds of monks. President Diem declares nationwide martial law.
August 22	Foreign Minister Vu Van Mau and Ambassador to U.S. Tran Van Chuong (father of Mme. Nhu) resign in protest of government's treatment of Buddhists.
	Ambassador Lodge arrives in Saigon.
August 25	Students demonstrate in Saigon—hundreds arrested.

August 29   President de Gaulle in policy statement offers
                     French help to unify country and rid itself of
                     foreign influences. Says Vietnam should be in-
                     dependent and neutral.

September 2   President Kennedy, in TV interview with Wal-
                     ter Cronkite, reminds SVN leaders it's their war
                     and requires support of people—says govern-
                     ment "has gotten out of touch with people."

September 9   U.S. decides to cut aid unless government insti-
                     tutes reforms.

                     Mme. Nhu leaves for Belgrade.

September 11   Lodge tells Diem Nhu must go.

September 12   President Kennedy says U.S. not in Vietnam
                     "to see a war lost," implies aid might be cut if
                     Diem doesn't change policies.

September 16   President Diem lifts martial law, curfew, and
                     censorship.

September 21   President Kennedy sends McNamara and Tay-
                     lor to South Vietnam to review military situa-
                     tion.

October 2   McNamara and Taylor report to Kennedy and
                     National Security Council. Say SVN political
                     situation serious, but war can be won by end
                     of 1965 unless political crisis hampers war
                     effort.

October 4   Kennedy recalls CIA Station Chief in Saigon,
                     John Richardson—highlights rift in Administra-
                     tion over Vietnam policy.

October 7   U.S. suspends some economic aid to SVN.

                     Mme. Nhu arrives in New York for unofficial
                     visit to U.S.

October 8   U.N. agrees to send fact-finding mission to SVN
                     to investigate Buddhist situation. Team arrives
                     October 24.

October 23   *U.S. troop level at 16,500.*

October 27   Seventh Buddhist monk burns self to death in
                     Saigon.

October 31	General Harkins says 1,000 American troops to be withdrawn by December 31.
November 1	*Military coup led by high-ranking military officers deposes Diem. Diem and Nhu assassinated.* Military junta headed by General Duong Van Minh says aims are to vigorously prosecute war.
November 2	U.S. welcomes coup but denies direct involvement.
	Junta establishes provisional government headed by former Vice President Nguyen Ngoc Tho as Premier.
November 7	U.S. recognizes new regime.
	Government lifts curfew, ends censorship.
November 20	McNamara, Rusk confer in Honolulu with Lodge and Harkins on U.S. policy.
November 22	President Kennedy assassinated. President Johnson on November 24 affirms U.S. support for SVN.
December 3	U.S. begins withdrawal of 1,000 support troops from SVN.
December 19–20	McNamara and other U.S. officials visit South Vietnam to evaluate new government. Assure General Minh that U.S. will back war effort as long as help is wanted and needed.

1964

January 6	Junta reorganizes—military triumvirate to rule: General Duong Van Minh named Chief of State, Tran Van Don—Commander in Chief of Armed Forces, General Le Van Kim—Chief of Staff.
January 27	McNamara testifies before House Armed Services Committee—says situation in South Vietnam is grave.
January 30	*Military junta overthrown by General Nguyen Khanh.*

January 31	De Gaulle proposes neutralization of all Southeast Asia nations backed by international guarantees.
February 1	President Johnson pledges greater war effort in South Vietnam.
February 7	Rusk rules out neutralization as solution.
February 8	General Khanh names General Duong Van Minh as titular Chief of State—himself Premier.
February 21	President Johnson warns "those engaged in external direction and supply" in South Vietnam are playing a "deeply dangerous game"; remarks seen as warning to North Vietnam.
March 8–12	McNamara and Taylor in Saigon; promise aid for as long as it takes to win war; laud General Khanh.
April 13–15	SEATO Ministers meeting, Bangkok—communique declares defeat of Viet Cong is "essential" to security of Southeast Asia. Rusk makes two day visit to Saigon after SEATO Conference, optimistic on Communists' defeat, pledges continued U.S. support to General Khanh.
May 2	Viet Cong terrorists sink U.S. transport ship *Card,* Saigon harbor. Next day Viet Cong terrorist throws bomb into crowd of Americans inspecting *Card.*
May 11–13	McNamara and Taylor on 5th Vietnam inspection trip; pledge more aid to bolster war effort.
May 18	*President Johnson asks $125 million additional economic and military aid for war effort* because of increased Viet Cong terrorism; convinced General Khanh can defeat Communists. U.S. to send additional training pilots and airplanes to Vietnam.
May 22	Secretary Rusk says war may be expanded if Communists persist in aggression.
June 1–2	Top military and diplomatic officials meet in Honolulu to review war, conclude situation is very serious, U.S. must increase aid.

June 20	General Westmoreland formally takes over command of MACV from General Harkins.
June 23	*President Johnson announces resignation of Henry Cabot Lodge as Ambassador to Vietnam; to be succeeded by General Taylor.*
July 8	U.N. Secretary General U Thant proposes Geneva Conference to be reconvened to negotiate peace in Vietnam.
July 19	General Khanh backs expansion of war to North Vietnam; General Ky, Air Force commander, says SVN pilots are being trained for attacks against North.
July 27	U.S. to add 5,000 military advisers to MACV bringing total to 21,000.
August 2	*U.S.S. Maddox attacked by North Vietnamese PT boats in Tonkin Gulf.*
August 4	*U.S.S. Maddox and U.S.S. Turner Joy reportedly attacked by North Vietnamese PT boats. President Johnson orders retaliatory bombing of gunboats and supporting facilities in North Vietnam.*
August 5	President Johnson asks Congress to approve joint resolution "to promote the maintenance of international peace and security in Southeast Asia" pledging full support for U.S. forces.
August 7	Congress approves Southeast Asia Resolution: House vote, 416–0; Senate vote, 88–2.
August 11	*LBJ signs Southeast Asia (Gulf of Tonkin) Resolution into law.*
August 16	SVN Military Revolutionary Council elects General Khanh President, ousts General Minh as Chief of State, and votes new Constitution.
August 25	Revolutionary Council withdraws new Constitution following student demonstrations.
August 27	Revolutionary Council agrees on triumvirate of General Nguyen Khanh, General Duong Van Minh and Tran Thien Khiem to lead nation; Council disbands.

August 28   Nguyen Xuan Oanh named Acting Premier; Khanh reportedly suffering from nervous breakdown.

September 3   General Khanh resumes Premiership, dissolves military triumvirate and restores General Minh to position as Chief of State. U.S. encouraged by Khanh's return.

September 13   Abortive coup against General Khanh led by General Lam Van Phat and other dissident military officers; forces loyal to Khanh backed by General Nguyen Cao Ky and General Nguyen Chanh Thi resume control of government.

September 18   U.S.S. *Morton* and *Edwards* reportedly attacked by NVN PT boats in Tonkin Gulf. LBJ decides not to retaliate.

September 19   SVN Military Command changed by coup effects. Generals Ky and Thi get high positions.

September 26   South Vietnam formally inaugurates High National Council to prepare new Constitution and institutions to govern nation. Transitional government to be replaced by civilian government. Phan Khac Suu elected Chairman of Council.

November 1   Tran Van Huong formally named Premier. Names civilian cabinet; pledges to press war against Communists. Viet Cong mortar Bien Hoa airbase.

November 22   Thousands riot against Huong government.

November 25   Premier Huong declares "state of siege."

November 25–December 6   Ambassador Taylor returns to Washington for consultations—speculation on expansion of war. U.S. reaffirms commitment to Premier Huong.

December 11   U.S. to increase economic and military aid to South Vietnam.

December 19   Military leaders dissolve High National Council, U.S. concerned. Taylor clashes with Generals Khanh, Thi, and Ky.

December 21	General Khanh backs military leaders, says Vietnamese will not fight to carry out policy of any foreign country. Situation continues tense between U.S. and SVN.
December 23	Rusk says U.S. may cut off aid; Khanh says aid not essential to SVN.
December 24	Viet Cong bomb Brink Hotel (U.S. BOQ Saigon)—kill 2, wound 52 Americans, 13 Vietnamese also injured.
	U.S. military strength in South Vietnam at 23,300.

1965

January 8	South Korea sends 2,000 troops to South Vietnam.
January 22–23	Buddhist demonstrators attack USIS libraries in Saigon and Hue to protest U.S. support for Huong regime.
January 26	Armed Forces Council ousts government of Tran Van Huong and Phan Khac Suu. General Khanh appointed to solve political crisis. General Khanh names Nguyen Xuan Oanh to be Acting Premier.
February 3–7	McGeorge Bundy and other U.S. officials on Vietnam inspection trip.
February 6	USSR Premier Alexi Kosygin visits Hanoi.
February 7	*Viet Cong attack Pleiku base and airfield*—8 Americans killed, 109 wounded. Heavy damage to aircraft.
	President Johnson orders air attacks on North Vietnamese military targets in response to provocations; U.S. dependents to be evacuated from Vietnam, sends Marine anti-aircraft battalion to Danang.
February 10	Viet Cong bomb U.S. military barracks at Qui Nhon, killing 23 and wounding 21 Americans.

February 11	U.S. and SVN bomb military installations in North Vietnam.
February 15	Armed Forces Council announces new government headed by Dr. Phan Huy Quat as Premier and Phan Khac Suu as Chief of State.
February 18	Military stage coup in Saigon, oust General Khanh as head of Armed Forces Council.
February 19	U.S. begins bombing VC concentrations inside SVN with jet airplanes.
	General Khanh temporarily regains control of Council.
February 20	Armed Forces Council demands resignation of General Khanh.
February 21	General Khanh accepts demand of Armed Forces Council. Tran Van Minh becomes Acting Commander of Armed Forces; Nguyen Van Thieu is top man on Armed Forces Council.
February 24	U Thant urges informal negotiations and withdrawal of U.S. troops.
February 25	North Vietnam informs Thant that it is receptive to informal talks.
	South Korea sends 600-man engineering unit to SVN.
February 27	State Department issues "White Paper" documenting North Vietnamese aggression against South Vietnam.
February 28	South Vietnam and U.S. say President Johnson has decided to open continuous limited air attacks against North Vietnam to bring about negotiated settlement.
March 2	*Institution of Rolling Thunder bombing campaign against North Vietnam.*
March 6	*Marine Corps sends two battalions to Danang for limited security duty.* U.S. forces now total 27,000.
March 8	U Thant proposes 7-power preliminary conference as step toward ending the war.

March 9	U.S. rejects Thant's peace offer unless NVN stops aggression.
March 24	U.S. and SVN bomb North Vietnam radar and communications station and harbor.
March 25	President Johnson hints of economic and social aid to North Vietnam if peace is restored.
March 30	Bomb explodes outside U.S. Embassy in Saigon, causing extensive damage, 2 Americans killed.
April 1	Seventeen nonaligned nations meeting in Belgrade demand immediate negotiations without preconditions to end war.
April 2	U.S. decides to increase military troops to SVN by several thousand.
April 7	*President Johnson in speech at Johns Hopkins University says U.S. is ready to begin talks to end war;* offers $1 billion aid program for Southeast Asia.
April 11	North Vietnam rejects LBJ's peace plan.
April 13	*Hanoi offers four-point peace plan.*
May 3–12	*Additional U.S. troops arrive in Vietnam bringing total to 46,500.*
May 4	LBJ requests $700 million supplemental appropriation for war effort. House approves request on May 5 (408–7); Senate passes bill on May 6 (88–3).
May 7	Armed Forces Council disbands.
May 13	U.S. *halts bombing of North Vietnam* reportedly to survey damage; later acknowledged purpose was to sound out Hanoi on conditions for peace.
May 15	National teach-in on Vietnam policy held.
May 19	U.S. *resumes bombing of North Vietnam.*
June 1	President Johnson requests $89 million for economic aid to Southeast Asia.

June 7   *U.S. military strength at 51,000.*

                  U.S. Senate passes amendment to foreign aid
                  bill adding $89 million for Southeast Asia
                  (42–26).

June 9   *White House confirms U.S. ground troops au-*
                  thorized to give combat support to ARVN
                  forces, but insists mission of forces has not
                  changed.

June 10   *Additional U.S. forces arrive—total now 53,500.*

June 12   Premier Quat forced to resign following intense
                  political crisis.

June 16   *Secretary of Defense McNamara announces*
                  21,000 additional troops to be sent to SVN
                  bringing total to 74,500.

June 17   British Commonwealth Ministers form four-
                  nation peace mission to find an end to Vietnam
                  war.

June 18   *Nguyen Cao Ky becomes new Premier; Gen-*
                  eral Nguyen Van Thieu is Chief of State.

June 24   Soviet Union refuses to meet with Common-
                  wealth peace mission.

June 25   Communist China rejects visit of Common-
                  wealth peace mission to Peking.

                  LBJ appeals to U.N. to help settle war.

                  U.S. makes air raids north of Hanoi.

                  Viet Cong bomb Saigon floating restaurant—
                  kill 9 Americans.

June 28   *U.S. troops participate in first major "search*
                  and destroy" mission.

July 1   North Vietnam rejects Commonwealth peace
                  mission's request for talks.

July 8   *White House announces resignation of Max-*
                  well D. Taylor as Ambassador to Vietnam; to
                  be replaced by Henry Cabot Lodge.

July 14–20	Secretary McNamara makes Vietnam inspection trip to study troop requirements.
July 15	Ambassador W. Averell Harriman begins informal conversations with Kosygin in Moscow.
July 20	Secretary McNamara, on leaving Vietnam, says situation has deteriorated since Diem's overthrow.
July 21–27	Johnson and top aides review Vietnam situation.
July 28	*President Johnson, in televised news conference, says U.S. will send 50,000 more troops to Vietnam,* bringing total strength up to 125,-000. Draft calls to increase, more troops will be needed later; stresses U.S. desire for negotiations. LBJ also asks U.N. to help bring about peace in Vietnam.
August 18	Senate approves supplemental defense appropriation bill of $1.7 billion for military operations in SVN as requested by LBJ.
October 15–16	National Coordinating Committee to End the War in Vietnam organizes mass demonstrations in U.S. cities. David J. Miller burns draft card in front of federal agents in New York—arrested three days later.
October 23	*U.S. announces military strength in Vietnam at 148,300* (89,000 Army; 8,000 Navy; 37,000 Marine Corps; 14,000 Air Force; 300 Coast Guard).
November 2	Pacifist burns self to death in front of Pentagon.
November 9	Pacifist burns self in front of U.N. headquarters.
November 11	Secretary McNamara following meeting at LBJ Ranch with President Johnson, Secretary Rusk and top advisers says President has decided to send more troops to Vietnam to meet needs of military commanders.
November 27	National Committee for a Sane Nuclear Policy (SANE) sponsors March on Washington.

November 28–29   McNamara and top aides confer in Saigon. Military authorities request U.S. forces be increased to 350,000 and 400,000.

December 3   U.S. intensifies bombing of Laos to curb infiltration along Ho Chi Minh trail.

December 15   U.S. bombs thermal power plant in North Vietnam—first raid on major industrial target.

December 24–25   *U.S. and Viet Cong agree to 30-hour Christmas truce. U.S. suspends bombing of North Vietnam.*

December 26   U.S. resumes ground action in South Vietnam, but continues suspension of bombing of North.

December 29   *With bombing halt continuing, U.S. sends high-ranking officials to various world capitals to discuss possibilities for negotiations.*

                  U.S. troop strength in South Vietnam jumps to 180,000.

1966

January 12   LBJ in State of Union Message says U.S. will remain in Vietnam until aggression ceases.

January 15   Premier Nguyen Cao Ky says Government will hold referendum to determine new Constitution leading to national elections in 1967 for civilian government. Also says rural construction will be one of top tasks facing government in 1966.

January 19   *President Johnson requests supplemental funds of $12.76 billion for Vietnam war expenses.*

January 24   Ho Chi Minh says U.S. must accept Hanoi's four points as basis for ending the war, sends letter to world Communist leaders.

January 31   *President Johnson announces resumption of bombing* after 37-day pause due to failure of Hanoi to reply to peace drive. Asks United Nations Security Council to seek international conference to end the war and establish peace in Vietnam and Southeast Asia.

February 1	U.N. Security Council meets on U.S. draft resolution calling for conference to end the war.
	North Vietnam rejects any action by Security Council.
February 4	Senate Foreign Relations Committee begins broad open hearings on U.S. Vietnam policy.
	President Johnson announces he and top aides will confer in Honolulu with South Vietnamese officials.
February 6–8	*Honolulu Conference*—stress on non-military issues, especially pacification and economic and social reforms. Johnson, Thieu, and Ky, in joint communique and Declaration of Honolulu, pledge to continue defense against aggression through joint military action and civic reforms. Vice President Humphrey to go on to South Vietnam to look into economic and social programs.
February 12	LBJ disavows desire to escalate the war, but says additional troops will be sent as needed by military commanders.
February 17	General Taylor, testifying before Senate Foreign Relations Committee, says U.S. intends to wage limited war in Vietnam.
February 18	Secretary Rusk, before Senate Foreign Relations Committee, stresses SEATO as legal basis for U.S. involvement in Vietnam.
February 19	Senator Robert F. Kennedy suggests U.S. offer Viet Cong share of power in South Vietnam— later says Viet Cong should not be automatically excluded from holding power.
March 1	President Johnson renews peace appeal, again offers aid to North Vietnam.
	Congress passes $4.8 billion supplemental funds bill for Vietnam war.
March 2	*McNamara announces U.S. troop strength in Vietnam is 215,000 with 20,000 additional forces enroute*, expects General Westmoreland will request still more forces.

March 5   General Maxwell D. Taylor proposes mining
                                 of Haiphong harbor.

March 10–16   South Vietnamese government ousts General
                                 Nguyen Chanh Thi as Commander of I Corps.
                                 Protests begin in Hue, Danang, and Saigon,
                                 criticizing Saigon government's dismissal of
                                 General Thi and demanding civilian rule. On
                                 March 23, general strikes erupt in Hue and
                                 Danang.

March 25   Premier Ky announces new Constitution will
                                 be drafted within two months; general elec-
                                 tions to follow.

March 25–April 5   Political crisis continues following anti-Govern-
                                 ment demonstrations in Hue, Danang, Saigon,
                                 and other cities. Nguyen Cao Ky threatens to
                                 use force to "liberate" Danang from demon-
                                 strators. Sends SVN Marines and riot policemen
                                 to Danang.

April 6   Premier Ky withdraws government troops from
                                 Danang, decides to seek accommodation with
                                 demonstrating Buddhists, agrees to hold refer-
                                 endum on new Constitution.

April 12   *U.S. starts to use B–52's to bomb North Viet-
                                 nam on regular basis.*

April 12–14   National Political Congress called by Govern-
                                 ment to make arrangements for Constitutional
                                 Convention, assembles in Saigon, agrees on
                                 program to hold elections for Constituent As-
                                 sembly, accepts Buddhist demands. Demon-
                                 strations cease. Elections to be held in August.

April 20   *Secretary McNamara says American forces in
                                 South Vietnam now total 245,000,* supple-
                                 mented by 50,000 naval forces in area.

April 26   State Department spokesmen reiterate U.S. po-
                                 sition that enemy aircraft will be pursued be-
                                 yond borders of North Vietnam.

                                 North Vietnam's news agency reports on
                                 speeches of Ho Chi Minh and Pham Van Dong

before National Assembly reiterating Hanoi's four points as conditions for peace in Vietnam.

May 2

Premier Ky signs decree setting up committee to draft election law and procedures. Militant Buddhists and students continue mass demonstrations.

May 6

Premier Ky announces that his military government will stay in power "at least for another year" and that he and others will fight if new government is neutralist or Communist.

May 14–15

Loyal government troops regain control of Danang from anti-government soldiers and Buddhists, also crackdown on demonstrations in Hue and Saigon. Rebel soldiers take refuge in Danang Buddhist pagodas, vow to continue fight against junta.

May 15–23

Political crisis between government and Buddhists continues with fighting erupting in Hue and Danang. Government continues to use force against demonstrators. War effort hampered; LBJ deplores crisis as diversion from war and from efforts to establish Constitutional government.

May 26

Buddhist students in Hue sack and burn USIS library and cultural center.

May 31

Buddhist leaders and Saigon military junta begin talks on resolving political crisis.

Rioting Buddhist students attack and burn US consulate and residence in Hue.

June 6

Ambassador Lodge begins series of secret meetings with Polish ICC representative Lewandowski and Italian Ambassador D'Orlandi in Saigon to explore positions on negotiations and political settlement.

June 11

U.S. continues military build-up in South Vietnam; Secretary McNamara reports total will soon reach 285,000.

June 18

SVN troops finally recapture city of Hue from Buddhists.

June 18   President Johnson calls on North Vietnam and
                           Viet Cong to stop aggression; if they do not,
                           U.S. will continue using "ground, naval and
                           air strength required to achieve our objective";
                           hints of intensification of air and ground war.

June 20   Nguyen Cao Ky signs decree setting September
                           11 for election of Constituent Assembly.

June 29   *U.S. escalates air war by bombing oil installa-*
                           tions on outskirts of Hanoi and Haiphong.
                           Secretary McNamara says air strikes are related
                           to increasing North Vietnamese infiltration of
                           South Vietnam.

June 30   President Johnson says air strikes against North
                           Vietnamese military targets "will continue to
                           impose a heavy burden and a high price on
                           those who wage war against the freedom of
                           their neighbors," and calls for unconditional
                           peace talks. U.S. air raids against fuel storage
                           areas near Hanoi continue.

July 7   Prime Minister Gandhi of India proposes Ge-
                           neva Conference co-chairmen, Great Britain
                           and the Soviet Union, arrange a conference to
                           end the war; appeals to the U.S. to halt the
                           bombing.

July 8   General Nguyen Van Thieu, Chief of State of
                           South Vietnam, says North Vietnam should be
                           invaded with ground forces if necessary to win
                           the war, calls for more air action against North
                           Vietnam.

July 10   *The Department of Defense announces U.S.*
                           troop strength in South Vietnam will be in-
                           creased to 375,000 by the end of 1966 and to
                           425,000 by the spring of 1967.

July 12   U.S. voices concern over fate of captured air-
                           men after hearing reports North Vietnam in-
                           tends to try prisoners as war criminals.

July 16   U.N. Secretary General U Thant appeals to
                           North Vietnam not to put POW's on trial,
                           urges both sides to comply with the 1949 Ge-

	neva Convention concerning treatment of prisoners.
July 16	India's Prime Minister Gandhi, ending her visit to Moscow, states that U.S. must cease bombing before North Vietnam will negotiate.
July 20	President Johnson, at his news conference, states that the American people would regard trials of POW's as "revolting and repulsive" and warns Hanoi U.S. would "react accordingly."
July 23	Ho Chi Minh, in response to telegram from CBS President, declares there is "no trial in view" for U.S. POW's.
	President Johnson, speaking in Indiana, reaffirms U.S. commitment to South Vietnam and declares "we will persist until the Communists end the fighting or negotiate an honorable peace."
July 25	South Vietnam's Premier Nguyen Cao Ky urges an invasion of North Vietnam even at the risk of Communist Chinese intervention.
July 30	U.S. B–52 bombers begin series of air raids on North Vietnamese troop concentrations in and around the demilitarized zone.
July 31	Premier Ky says he will not be a candidate for President in the 1967 elections.
August 3	Thailand proposes an all-Asian peace conference to end the war in Vietnam; most other nations express approval. Philippines President Marcos offers Manila as site for Conference.
August 13–14	General Westmoreland meets with President Johnson in Texas. LBJ says Communist military takeover of South Vietnam is impossible but warns there will be no quick victory. Stresses U.S. willingness to prosecute the war until the Communists stop fighting or seek a peaceful settlement.
August 18	North Vietnam calls the proposed Asian peace conference "a cheap farce."

August 24

At his news conference, President Johnson supports the proposed Asian peace conference but says U.S. would not try to "hard sell it"; also states U.S. willingness to attend a reconvened Geneva Conference.

September 1

President de Gaulle, speaking in Cambodia, declares U.S. must withdraw its forces from Vietnam before a negotiated settlement is possible. He proposes the U.S. establish a timetable for military withdrawal as a prelude to international negotiations.

September 5

President Johnson says he will publish his timetable for withdrawal of U.S. troops when the Communists offer a similar timetable. On September 11 North Vietnam rejects U.S. offer for mutual withdrawal of troops.

September 11

South Vietnamese voters elect 117-man Constituent Assembly to draft new Constitution and prepare for civilian government in 1967. Eighty-one percent of eligible voters participate in election. U.S. pleased at large turnout. Several days later, LBJ interprets vote to mean Vietnamese approval of U.S. policy in Vietnam.

September 21

President Johnson welcomes peace offers by Pope Paul and U Thant but doubts North Vietnam will respond favorably.

September 22

Speaking before the U.N. General Assembly, U.S. Ambassador Arthur Goldberg proposes a step-by-step de-escalation of the war by both sides; says the U.S. will halt the bombing of North Vietnam when it is assured that North Vietnam will correspondingly and appropriately de-escalate its effort. The U.S. would then withdraw its forces as the other side withdraws theirs.

September 24

North Vietnam and Communist China both reject Goldberg's peace proposals.

September 27

President Johnson accepts Philippine President Marcos' invitation to attend a conference of allied leaders in Manila in October to discuss the Vietnam conflict.

October 3	The Soviet Union announces a new economic and military aid agreement with North Vietnam.
October 13	President Johnson announces U.S. will not suspend the bombing of North Vietnam until Hanoi reduces its military activity in the South. President Johnson says a bombing halt would leave U.S. troops fighting "with their hands behind their backs."
October 24–25	*Manila Conference.* In the Conference Communique, the U.S. and the third-country troop contributors pledge to withdraw their troops "as the other side withdraws its forces to the north, ceases infiltration and the level of violence thus subsides . . . as soon as possible and not later than six months" after Hanoi disengages itself from the war.
October 26	President Johnson makes surprise visit to U.S. installation at Camranh Bay, hails troops and pledges full support.
October 27	North Vietnam and Communist China reject Manila Conference withdrawal offer.
November 4	President Johnson in his news conference says U.S. forces will be withdrawn from South Vietnam when "infiltration, aggression and violence" cease; is reluctant to suspend the bombing without reciprocal action by North Vietnam, but may consider a holiday truce.
November 5	Secretary McNamara, following consultations with President Johnson, says North Vietnamese can no longer achieve a military victory; he also states U.S. troop levels in South Vietnam will increase in 1967 but at a substantially lower rate than 1966.
November 15	Lodge provides Lewandowski with U.S. position to be passed on to Hanoi.
	White House approves expanded list of bombing targets.

November 18	Secretary Rusk says U.S. might agree to halt the bombing for a short period at Christmas, but will not agree to an extended pause. He reiterates U.S. position that Hanoi must engage in reciprocal action in response to cessation of bombing.
November 24–25	British Foreign Secretary George Brown confers in Moscow with Kosygin and Gromyko.
November 25	The Viet Cong offers to observe 48-hour holiday cease-fires at Christmas and New Years. South Vietnam announces cease-fires will be observed at these holidays and at Tet (February 8–12).
December 2–5	U.S. bombers begin a series of intensive air raids on military targets in immediate area of Hanoi, concentrating on truck depots, railroad yards, and fuel storage dumps.
December 5	On basis of Lodge–Lewandowski conversations, Ambassador Gronouski begins series of meetings with Polish Foreign Minister Rapacki in the expectation of establishing direct contact with NVN diplomats in Warsaw ("Marigold" exercise).
December 8	Pope Paul appeals for extension of truces into armistice and beginning of negotiations.
December 13–14	U.S. bombs military targets in Hanoi area. Soviet Union accuses U.S. of bombing residential sections, but U.S. denies they were deliberately hit. On December 16 Communist China charges U.S. bombed its embassy in Hanoi. Rumania follows suit on December 17.
December 15	Polish officials inform Gronouski there will be no talks with North Vietnamese because of U.S. bombings of Hanoi on December 13 and 14.
December 19	Ambassador Goldberg asks U Thant to take whatever steps he considers necessary to bring about cease-fire talks in Vietnam, promising full U.S. cooperation.

December 23	In an effort to salvage the Warsaw talks, the U.S. commits itself not to bomb within a 10 mile radius of Hanoi.
December 25	Harrison Salisbury of *The New York Times* visits North Vietnam. U.S. officials acknowledge pilots have accidentally bombed civilian areas.
December 30	British Foreign Secretary Brown invites U.S., North and South Vietnam to meet on British territory for talks on ending the war.
December 31	President Johnson says U.S. will do "more than our part in meeting North Vietnam halfway in any possible cease-fire, truce or peace conference negotiations."

U Thant, in response to an appeal by the U.S. to bring about a settlement in Vietnam, urges the U.S. to take the first step towards peace by unconditionally halting the bombing of North Vietnam.

U.S. troop strength in South Vietnam reaches 389,000. U.S. combat deaths total 6,644, total wounded reaches 37,738.

1967

January 3	North Vietnam's Premier, Pham Van Dong, in an interview with Harrison Salisbury, says Hanoi's "four points" constitute a "basis for settlement" rather than conditions for peace talks. U Thant informs U.S. that North Vietnam's willingness to negotiate hinges on unconditional cessation of U.S. bombing of North Vietnam.
January 5	Mai Van Bo, North Vietnam diplomat in Paris, states that Hanoi will "examine and study proposals" for negotiations if U.S. will "definitely and unconditionally" halt the bombing of North Vietnam.
January 8	Ambassador Lodge predicts "sensational military gains" by allied forces in 1967, doubts peace talks will ever take place, and believes war will fade out eventually.

January 10   President Johnson, in State of the Union Mes-
                      sage, defends U.S. involvement in Vietnam and
                      says we will persevere in war despite "more
                      cost, more loss and more agony."

                      Embassy official begins series of meetings with
                      NVN chargé in Moscow.

January 28   North Vietnamese Foreign Minister, Nguyen
                      Duy Trinh, in an interview with Australian
                      journalist Burchett, says "it is only after the
                      unconditional ending of the bombing and other
                      acts of war being carried out by the United
                      States against North Vietnam that there could
                      be talks." He also reiterated Hanoi's four points
                      as a basis for a political settlement.

January 31   The State Department declares it could see no
                      change in Hanoi's position despite Trinh's com-
                      ments three days earlier. Two days later Presi-
                      dent Johnson says he is unaware of any serious
                      North Vietnamese effort to stop the fighting
                      and move toward negotiations, and says he
                      would stop the bombing if Hanoi took "almost
                      any step."

February 6   Soviet Premier Kosygin arrives in London for
                      talks with British officials.

February 8   *President Johnson, in a letter to Ho Chi Minh,
                      offers to stop the bombing of North Vietnam
                      and the augmentation of U.S. forces in South
                      Vietnam if North Vietnam ceased infiltration.*
                      The President further proposed an extension
                      of the *Tet* cease-fire to be negotiated by North
                      and South Vietnam and suggested secret diplo-
                      matic talks between Washington and Hanoi. Ho
                      Chi Minh replied talks could occur if the U.S.
                      "definitely and unconditionally" halted the
                      bombing. He also demanded the withdrawal
                      of U.S. forces from Vietnam and recognition of
                      the NLF.

                      Vietnam's New Year (Tet) truce begins.

                      Kosygin, speaking in London, says U.S. must
                      unconditionally stop the bombing in order to

start peace talks, cites recent statement by North Vietnamese Foreign Minister Trinh as significant signal Hanoi will take reciprocal action.

President Johnson in a letter to Pope Paul hopes *Tet* truce can be extended and open the way for negotiations.

February 9

Secretary Rusk in a news conference reports the U.S. will not stop the bombing until Hanoi shows a willingness to reduce its military effort in South Vietnam; he accuses the Communists of trying to bring about a bombing halt without taking any reciprocal action. In London, Kosygin urges the U.S. to halt the bombing in exchange for peace talks with Hanoi.

February 10

The State Department expresses concern over reports that North Vietnam is taking advantage of the Tet cease-fire to increase its supplies to forces operating in South Vietnam. Ambassador Goldberg reaffirms U.S. negotiating position is flexible and stresses U.S. willingness to negotiate without preconditions.

February 12

Tet cease-fire ends as allies resume ground operations, but continue bombing pause to give Wilson chance to persuade Kosygin to exact North Vietnamese promise of reciprocal military de-escalation.

February 13

Kosygin ends visit to London. In communique both countries pledge to make every possible effort for peace. Wilson contacts President Johnson in an effort to continue bombing pause to give Kosygin more time to persuade Hanoi to reduce infiltration and resupply effort in South Vietnam.

February 14

Kosygin returns to Moscow: U.S. resumess air action over North Vietnam. Prime Minister Wilson says, "peace was almost within our grasp" last weekend; further says, "one simple act of trust could have achieved it." President Johnson justifies resumption of bombing on basis of Hanoi's extensive resupply efforts during truce period. U.S. officials acknowledge privately allies also resupplied their own troops during cease-fire.

February 15   Secretary McNamara says war cannot be won by bombing alone, must be won in South Vietnam.

February 22   Mai Van Bo reiterates Hanoi's peace offer of peace talks in exchange for unconditional and permanent bombing halt; says Foreign Minister Trinh made a gesture of goodwill to which U.S. responded in bad faith.

February 27   President Johnson decides to order new types of military action to hasten the end of the war.

March 10   U.S. begins to bomb North Vietnamese heavy industrial targets previously on restricted target list.

March 15   *President Johnson announces Ellsworth Bunker will replace Henry Cabot Lodge as U.S. Ambassador to South Vietnam.*

March 18   South Vietnam's Constituent Assembly unanimously approves the new Constitution.

March 20–21   *President Johnson meets with U.S. and South Vietnamese officials on Guam* to discuss economic and political aspects of the war. LBJ tells Ky and Thieu U.S. will support South Vietnam until an honorable peace is achieved. U.S. places emphasis on reshaping Vietnamese society, while South Vietnam stresses efforts to escalate the war.

March 21   North Vietnam publishes texts of letters exchanged in February between Presidents Johnson and Ho Chi Minh on peace talks. On February 8, Johnson proposed private, direct talks; Ho rejected talks until U.S. stops bombing.

April 1   South Vietnam sets date for Presidential and Senatorial elections for September 1; lower house elections to be held October 1.

April 19	U.S. proposes both sides withdraw their military forces 10 miles from DMZ as first step toward peace talks. The day before, Saigon, acting on a Canadian proposal, had suggested that both sides might withdraw from the DMZ as a possible means of bringing about peace. Hanoi had previously rejected the Canadian offer.
April 20	The U.S. bombs two power plants in Haiphong for the first time. U.S. and Asian allies hold strategy conference in Washington.
April 24	U.S. begins bombing of North Vietnamese MIG airfields, also strikes at Hanoi railroad yards and electric transformer.
	General Westmoreland says antiwar protests give enemy hope that he can win politically what he can't accomplish militarily.
April 28	General Westmoreland addresses a Joint Session of Congress, predicting U.S. troops will "prevail over the Communist aggressor"; says the only way to defeat the enemy "is one of unrelenting but discriminating military, political and psychological pressure . . . at all levels."
May 1	Secretary Rusk says Hanoi does not want peace, lists 28 proposals for peace made by United States and others which North Vietnam has turned down.
May 2	*The New York Times* reports General Westmoreland, during visit to U.S., asked President Johnson to authorize an increase to 600,000 on ceiling of U.S. troops in Vietnam and to send reinforcements as soon as possible. The Administration declines comment. *U.S. strength in Vietnam stands at 436,000.*
May 5	U.S. Marines capture Hill 881 after days of heavy fighting.
May 8	Administration officials state that the United States did not bomb the immediate Hanoi area from December 1966 to April, 1967 in an effort to open negotiations with Vietnam.

May 10   Secretary General U Thant again appeals to
                  the U.S. to "take a calculated risk" and halt the
                  bombing. He believes such a step would result
                  in peace talks within "a few weeks time."

May 11   Premier Nguyen Cao Ky informs his Cabinet
                  he will run for President in the September
                  election. General Nguyen Van Thieu says it is
                  "entirely possible" he will run against Ky.

May 14–June 11   Local elections take place in 4,612 South Viet-
                  namese hamlets.

May 15   South Vietnam's Constituent Assembly decides
                  military men can run for President without re-
                  signing from the armed forces. Assembly rules
                  that President will be elected by plurality, no
                  run-off will be held if a candidate fails to get
                  less than 30 percent of votes.

May 18–19   *U.S. and South Vietnamese forces, for the first
                  time in the war, move into the DMZ.* U.S.
                  planes bomb Hanoi power plant located one
                  mile north of the center of the city.

May 22   President Johnson, in his Memorial Day procla-
                  mation, urges enemy leaders to help find a way
                  "out of this bloody impasse," pledges to con-
                  tinue to resist aggression, but says door is
                  always open to peace.

May 24   Former South Vietnamese Premier Tran Van
                  Huong announces he will be a candidate for
                  President.

June 2–3   Following a U.S. bombing raid over the North
                  Vietnamese port of Campha, the Soviet Union
                  charges the U.S. with bombing a USSR mer-
                  chant vessel. The United States rejects the
                  charge, saying that the damage was due to
                  enemy anti-aircraft.

June 15   Premier Ky announces 600,000 U.S. troops are
                  needed in South Vietnam.

June 18   The Department of Defense acknowledges that
                  U.S. planes may have inadvertently bombed
                  the Soviet ship on June 2. Two days later the

United States, in a note to the Russian Embassy, regrets the bombing, and says efforts will be made to "insure that such incidents will not occur."

June 22

U.S. military strength in South Vietnam reaches 463,000. Other third-country troops increase to 54,000. South Vietnam's armed forces total over 600,000. Communist strength is estimated at 294,000 including 50,000 North Vietnamese regulars.

June 23–25

President Johnson meets with Soviet Premier Kosygin at Glassboro, New Jersey. In a news conference following the talks, Premier Kosygin demands the immediate withdrawal of the U.S. from Vietnam and the unconditional cessation of the bombing.

June 30

Premier Ky withdraws from the Presidential race; will run as Vice President on ticket headed by General Nguyen Van Thieu.

July 6–11

Secretary McNamara visits U.S. officials in South Vietnam to study military commanders requests for additional U.S. troops. General Westmoreland sees need for 70,000 more troops to increase the pressure on the enemy. McNamara wants to hold increase to a minimum and make better use of troops already there.

July 12

South Vietnam's Chief of State Thieu says his country needs more U.S. troops to exploit recent military gains, but rules out general mobilization in South Vietnam as disruptive to the economy.

July 13

Following a meeting with his military advisers, including McNamara and Westmoreland, President Johnson announces "the troops that General Westmoreland needs and requests—as we feel it necessary—will be supplied."

July 18

At his news conference, President Johnson says U.S. is ready to negotiate, but North Vietnam shows no interest in talks. The same day Secretary Rusk predicts a "long, tough job ahead" in Vietnam, even though enemy forces are "hurting badly." Rusk also rules out a bombing halt, saying, "We are not prepared to stop half the war while the other half goes on unrestricted, unimpeded, and with maximum violence."

July 18–19   South Vietnam's Constituent Assembly approves 11 slates of candidates for the Presidential elections.

July 21–25   Herbert Marcovich and Raymond Aubrac, two French scientists, meet with NVN leaders in Hanoi to transmit a State Department-approved message given to them by Henry Kissinger.

July 22   President Johnson sends two advisers, General Maxwell D. Taylor and Clark M. Clifford on tour of Far East to solicit additional troops from allies fighting in South Vietnam.

July 27   Following talks with Taylor and Clifford, Premier Ky announces South Vietnam will increase the size of its armed forces to approximately 685,000. Ky also promises a drastic reorganization of the army and hopes for better leadership.

August 3   *President Johnson announces he has authorized ceiling on U.S. troops in South Vietnam to be raised to 525,000 and plans to send 40,000 to 50,000 more troops.*

August 5   Clifford and Taylor return from tour of Far Eastern capitals; report allies agree on value of bombing and of necessity to increase and maintain military pressure on the enemy.

August 8   President Johnson authorizes increase in scope of bombing by adding additional North Vietnamese targets.

August 9   Senate Preparedness Subcommittee hears secret testimony from Admiral Ulysses G. Sharp, CINCPAC, on air war. Senator Stennis discloses Admiral Sharp testified bombing should be expanded to include more valuable military targets.

August 17

General Earle Wheeler testifies on air war before Senate Preparedness Subcommittee; says North Vietnam has shown "marked ability" to recuperate from effects of bombing, and notes U.S. has had to bomb targets repeatedly to insure sufficient destruction.

Senate Foreign Relations Committee holds hearings on national commitments. *Under Secretary of State Nicholas Katzenbach testifies Gulf of Tonkin Resolution gave President authority to use armed forces making formal declaration of war unnecessary.*

August 19–24

U.S. engages in heavy bombing of Hanoi area.

August 23

President Johnson appoints a 20-man commission to check on fairness of South Vietnamese campaign and elections.

August 25

Secretary McNamara, in testimony before Senate Preparedness Subcommittee, says there is no reason to believe North Vietnam can be "bombed to the negotiating table" and argues against expansion of the air war.

Marcovich and Aubrac present new U.S. peace proposal to Mai Van Bo, NVN diplomat in Paris.

August 31

Senate Preparedness Subcommittee publishes report after 3 weeks of hearings urging President Johnson to intensify the air war against North Vietnam and follow the advice of military commanders in the selection of targets. The next day President Johnson defends his policy of controlled bombing, denying any rift within the Administration.

September 1

NLF states its political objectives are to overthrow the Saigon government and to establish a "national union democratic government" composed of representatives of various groups.

September 3   *Nguyen Van Thieu wins South Vietnam's Pres-
                          idential election by 35 percent of the vote.*
                          Peace candidate Truong Dinh Dzu comes in
                          second with 17 percent of vote. U.S. acclaims
                          election as a "major step forward."

September 6   President Johnson's election panel observes
                          South Vietnam's elections were generally fair.

September 21   Ambassador Goldberg asks the Soviet Union
                          and other friends of North Vietnam to use their
                          influence toward obtaining a peaceful resolution
                          of the war. In a speech before the U.N., Gold-
                          berg also calls on Hanoi to give assurances if
                          the U.S. halted the bombing that peace talks
                          would be meaningful and not be used as an
                          occasion for military or political exploitation.

September 26   An editorial in North Vietnam's official newspa-
                          per rejects Ambassador Goldberg's proposal,
                          saying the U.S. must unconditionally halt the
                          bombing before peace talks are possible.

September 27   Canada presents a four-stage peace proposal
                          to the United Nations.

September 29   *In a speech at San Antonio, President Johnson
                          declares the United States will stop the bomb-
                          ing of North Vietnam "when this will lead
                          promptly to productive discussions. We would
                          assume that, while discussions proceed, North
                          Vietnam would not take advantage of the
                          bombing cessation or limitation."*

October 2   South Vietnam's Constituent Assembly con-
                          firms the Presidential election results by a vote
                          of 58–43.

October 4   North Vietnam rejects President Johnson's San
                          Antonio formula for peace talks, saying it con-
                          tains "nothing new."

October 12   Secretary Rusk declares U.S. cannot abandon
                          its commitments to South Vietnam and warns
                          of dangers posed by Communist China.

October 21   Elections for South Vietnamese lower house
                          take place, resulting in good representation
                          for the military, civil service, and Buddhists.

October 31

Generals Thieu and Ky inaugurated as President and Vice President of South Vietnam. Thieu appoints Nguyen Van Loc as Premier.

November 11

President Johnson says he would be willing to meet with North Vietnam's leaders on a neutral ship in neutral waters. President Thieu announces allies will observe cease-fires during holiday periods.

November 13

Ambassador Bunker says progress is being made on Vietnam's political and military fronts and expresses optimism on outlook for future progress.

November 14

North Vietnam rejects President Johnson's offer to conduct negotiations at sea.

November 15

General Westmoreland confers with top U.S. officials in Washington. Upon arrival, he tells the press "I have never been more encouraged in my 4 years in Vietnam" but indicates his opposition to a bombing halt except for short periods of time. Ambassador Bunker also declares that a prolonged bombing pause would be "very unfortunate" unless there are indications it would be productive.

November 16

Senate Foreign Relations Committee approves two "sense of the Senate" resolutions: (1) calling on the President not to commit U.S. troops in future foreign wars without "affirmative action" by the Congress in accordance with the Constitution, and (2) urging the President to place the Vietnam issue before the United Nations Security Council.

U.S. bombers strike Haiphong shipyards for first time.

November 19

General Westmoreland, in a TV interview, says U.S. may be able to begin withdrawing some of its troops in 1969 if bombing and military progress on the ground continue, but adds that troop withdrawals would be contingent on South Vietnam's ability to assume a greater burden of the fighting.

The Viet Cong announces it will observe holiday cease-fires at Christmas, New Years, and Tet.

November 27   President Johnson nominates Secretary McNamara as the President of World Bank.

November 30   The Senate, by a vote of 82–0, passes Senator Mansfield's resolution urging President Johnson to bring the Vietnam question before the U.N.

Senator Eugene McCarthy announces he will oppose President Johnson in 5 or 6 primaries and hopes his campaign will persuade the Administration to move toward a negotiated settlement.

December 5   The State Department announces the U.S. would not oppose a U.N. invitation to the NLF to appear before the Security Council; South Vietnam declares it would be opposed to an appearance by the NLF at the U.N.

December 7   Ambassador Goldberg says NLF had asked if it could send envoys to the U.N. and were told U.S. would grant visas if they were invited by the Security Council or the General Assembly.

December 9   Secretary General U Thant tells the press the NLF had sought to send representatives to the U.N., but it was Thant's impression the NLF did not want to appear before the Security Council.

December 12   The official Cambodian radio states the Viet Cong "have used Cambodia as a haven," but denies Cambodia has permitted North Vietnam to use its territory for infiltration of men and supplies.

December 19   President Johnson, in a major TV interview, urges South Vietnam to go ahead with informal talks with the Viet Cong, saying such talks "could bring good results." However, he also states he will not stop the bombing without reciprocity from the enemy.

December 20	President Thieu tells the press his government would never recognize the NLF as a political party, but he would be willing to talk with individual NLF members who come over to the South Vietnamese government's side.
December 21	President Johnson and President Thieu meet in Canberra, Australia following the funeral of Australian Prime Minister Holt. They issue a joint communique in which President Thieu expressed his willingness to discuss relevant issues with anyone associated with the NLF.
December 22	Pope Paul calls for peace without victory and asks the United States to suspend the bombing and North Vietnam "to give a sign of serious will for peace."
	President Johnson visits U.S. troops at Camranh Bay promising the American people won't fail them.
December 23	President Johnson confers with Pope Paul in Rome and says the U.S. is ready to stop the bombing if the enemy would offer a guarantee it will move toward peace talks.
December 26	South Vietnam's Foreign Minister Tran Van Do says ARVN forces will pursue Communist troops into Cambodia if they use country as a sanctuary from which to infiltrate South Vietnam.
December 27	Cambodia's Prince Sihanouk says he might seek volunteers from Communist China and other Communist countries if U.S. troops cross over into Cambodia. But on December 29, Sihanouk indicated he would not stop U.S. troops from entering Cambodia in hot pursuit of enemy forces if enemy entered Cambodia illegally and were in remote sections of the country.
December 29	Communist China pledges support to Cambodia if the U.S. extends the war into that country.
December 30–31	In response to an appeal from Pope Paul, the allies extend the 24-hour New Years truce for an additional 12 hours.

1968

January 1

Radio Hanoi broadcasts a December 24 statement by North Vietnam's Foreign Minister Nguyen Duy Trinh that Hanoi *"will* hold talks with the United States on relevant questions" after the United States "unconditionally" halts the bombing of North Vietnam.

President Johnson is pleased by Prince Sihanouk's offer to permit U.S. troops to enter Cambodia in hot pursuit of enemy forces.

January 2

U.S. resumes bombing of North Vietnam after New Years truce.

January 4

Secretary Rusk says U.S. is trying to learn whether North Vietnam is serious about talks in exchange for a bombing halt.

January 12

Following five days of talks between Cambodia's Prince Sihanouk and Chester Bowles, President Johnson's special envoy, both countries agree on measures to insulate Cambodia from the war.

January 15

President Thieu declares that South Vietnam "should have the central role in any developments relating to the events in Vietnam" and that Saigon should initiate peace efforts. In Washington, Secretary Rusk says no decisions on negotiations will be made without fully consulting the South Vietnamese government.

January 16

Mai Van Bo, Hanoi's diplomatic representative in Paris, reiterates North Vietnam's position that before talks could be held the U.S. must stop the bombing of North Vietnam.

January 17

In his State of the Union Address, President Johnson says Hanoi must not take advantage of our restraint if the U.S. stopped the bombing.

January 21

An editorial in North Vietnam's official newspaper describes LBJ's San Antonio formula as "very insolent conditions" for negotiations, adding U.S. cannot ask for reciprocity in exchange for a bombing cessation.

January 25	Clark M. Clifford, Secretary of Defense designate, testifies before Senate Armed Services Committee, stating his assumption that if the U.S. halted the bombing of North Vietnam, Hanoi would continue to resupply its forces in the South, but would not take advantage of the bombing halt to carry out a military buildup. In addition, Clifford says he would oppose a bombing pause under the present military and political circumstances.
January 29	The Allies cancel the scheduled Tet truce in I Corps due to massive Communist buildup near Khe Sanh.
January 30	Administration officials say Hanoi has not responded to secret U.S. offer that bombing would stop and peace talks open if North Vietnam did not increase its infiltration of men and supplies beyond normal and current levels.
January 30–31	*The Tet offensive begins with Communist attacks on major South Vietnamese cities.* In Saigon, the Viet Cong temporarily invade the grounds of the U.S. Embassy. President Thieu cancels Tet cease-fire throughout the country and declares martial law. Viet Cong continue attacks on cities and Allied military bases.
February 1	Secretary McNamara presents his final military posture statement to Congress and states that ultimate success in Vietnam depends on the ability of the Saigon government to reestablish its authority throughout the country. McNamara also says the bombing of North Vietnam cannot halt the flow of men and supplies into the South.
February 2	President Johnson declares the Communists failed to achieve their objective of sparking a general uprising in the South during recent offensive.
February 4	Secretary Rusk interprets Communist attacks on cities as showing North Vietnam's lack of interest in negotiations. He also mentions that

the U.S. had been showing restraint in the bombing of the North while exploring meaning of Trinh's recent statement.

February 8   North Vietnam's Foreign Minister Trinh reiterates Hanoi's position on talks and an unconditional bombing halt.

February 10   U.S. planes resume bombing of Haiphong after a month-long restriction.

February 13   The Pentagon announces 10,500 additional U.S. troops will be airlifted to South Vietnam to meet the needs of General Westmoreland.

February 14   Secretary Rusk announces Hanoi has rejected all U.S. terms for peace talks and has given no indication it would refrain from taking military advantage of a bombing cessation. Two days later President Johnson declares North Vietnam is no more ready to negotiate now than it was one, two, or three years ago.

February 23   General Earle Wheeler, Chairman of JCS, arrives in Saigon to review the military situation and to study requests for additional U.S. troops.

February 24   After 25 days of heavy fighting, ARVN forces recapture the palace grounds of the citadel at Hue.

U Thant reports on his recent peace mission to various world capitals stating that, if the U.S. halts the bombing, meaningful talks will take place within a few weeks. Thant is "reasonably assured" Hanoi will deal in good faith with the issue of not taking advantage of the halt at the talks. In reply to Thant's statement, the United States says it "would welcome confirmation from Hanoi that talks would start promptly where we could reasonably assume that North Vietnam would not take military advantage of the cessation."

February 25   *General Westmoreland indicates he will probably require additional troops. U.S. troop strength stands at 495,000.*

March 9	*The New York Times* reports General Westmoreland has asked for an additional 206,000 U.S. troops.
March 11	Secretary Rusk tells Senate Foreign Relations Committee the Administration is re-examining its Vietnam policy "from A to Z" and is considering all alternatives.
March 12	Senator McCarthy wins 40 percent of vote in New Hampshire's Presidential primary. The following day, Senator Robert F. Kennedy says he is reconsidering his previous decision not to seek the Democratic Party's Presidential nomination. On March 16, Senator Kennedy announces he will seek the nomination because the nation's Vietnam policies can be changed only if the leadership also changes.
March 18	President Johnson says U.S. must make total effort to win the war and the peace in Vietnam and indicates recent Communist military successes will not cause him to change his Vietnam policy.
March 22	President Johnson states U.S. plans for war are still under review.
March 31	*President Johnson announces he has ordered cessation of all air and naval bombardment of North Vietnam* except in the area around the DMZ up to the 20th parallel and states pause covers 90 percent of North Vietnam's population. He adds a complete bombing halt could come if Hanoi matches U.S. restraint. The President calls on Hanoi to respond positively to the bombing halt by agreeing to peace talks during which it would be assumed Hanoi would not take advantage of the bombing halt.
	President Johnson also announces he will neither seek nor accept the Presidential nomination, stressing he will devote his time toward the search for peace.
April 3	North Vietnam offers to meet with U.S. representatives "with a view to determining with

the American side the unconditional cessation of the U.S. bombing raids and all other acts of war against the Democratic Republic of Vietnam so that talks may start."

May 3

After a month of contact with North Vietnam, President Johnson announces the U.S. has accepted Hanoi's offer to meet in Paris for preliminary talks on or about May 10. North Vietnam names Xuan Thuy as chief negotiator. On May 7 the U.S. announces its delegation will be headed by Averell Harriman and Cyrus Vance.

May 13

Delegates of United States and North Vietnam hold their first formal negotiating session in Paris.

May 18

President Thieu appoints Tran Van Huong as Premier of South Vietnam to replace Nguyen Van Loc who resigned.

May 27

Paris talks continue to be deadlocked after five sessions.

June 18

Secretary General Thant predicts Paris talks will remain deadlocked because both sides continue to seek a military victory. Thant proposes a complete bombing halt, de-escalation of military actions by both sides and peace talks involving all participants in the war.

June 19

President Thieu signs law authorizing general mobilization for the first time, stating South Vietnam intends to take over more responsibility for the war.

June 27

U.S. forces begin to withdraw from Khesanh after surviving intensive siege which began in January, 1968.

July 18–20

President Johnson meets with President Thieu in Honolulu. In their joint communique, both men call on Hanoi to respond to the partial bombing halt. President Johnson pledges the U.S. will continue to support South Vietnam as long as help is needed and desired. He also

	states the U.S. would not impose a coalition government on the people of South Vietnam and endorses Saigon's policy offering full political participation to all who agree to uphold the Constitution of Vietnam. Both leaders agree South Vietnam should play a leading role in negotiating a political settlement.
August 8	Richard M. Nixon receives Republican Party's Presidential nomination; will run on platform based on progressive de-Americanization of the war and honorable peace.
August 19	President Johnson states the U.S. will not halt all the bombing until it believes North Vietnam "intends seriously to join with U.S. in de-escalating the war and moving seriously toward peace." He asserts a complete bombing halt would jeopardize American troops along the DMZ.
August 27	President Thieu says South Vietnam will not talk to the NLF.
August 28	Vice President Hubert H. Humphrey nominated by Democratic Party, whose Vietnam platform urges bombing halt along lines of that proposed by President Johnson.
October 31	*President Johnson announces the U.S. will cease "all air, naval, and artillery bombardment of North Vietnam" as of November 1.* President Thieu states the U.S. has taken this action unilaterally.
November 1	At the Paris talks, North Vietnam announces a meeting of representatives of North Vietnam, the U.S., South Vietnam, and the National Liberation Front will be held in Paris no earlier than November 6. In Washington, Secretary Rusk urges North Vietnam to enter into serious talks; he also says bombing was halted on the basis of developments in Paris and "on the expectation . . . the action will bring about a de-escalation of the fighting."
November 2	President Thieu says his government will not attend the November 6 negotiating session until

North Vietnam agrees not to include the NLF as a separate delegation.

November 6

Richard M. Nixon wins U.S. presidential election.

November 8

President Thieu proposes the expanded Paris talks consist of two sides—the Allies (headed by South Vietnam and including the U.S.) and the Communists (headed by North Vietnam and including the NLF). North Vietnam's delegate Xuan Thuy rejects the proposal on the basis Hanoi cannot accept the concept of a single Communist delegation.

November 26

After weeks of discussion on the subject of expanded peace talks, the Department of State issues a statement saying the allied side will consist of the separate delegations of the United States and South Vietnam and the Communist side for "practical purposes" will be treated as a single delegation. The statement also indicates that the presence of the NLF at the Paris talks will not be interpreted to imply recognition of the NLF as a separate entity.

November 27

South Vietnam's Foreign Minister announces Saigon will participate in the expanded Paris peace talks since the United States has satisfied its earlier objections.

1969

January 5

President-elect Nixon names Henry Cabot Lodge Chief negotiator at the Paris talks replacing Ambassador Harriman.

January 16

After weeks of discussion and argument, the United States and North Vietnam announce agreement has been reached on the shape of the conference table and other procedural matters for the expanded Paris peace talks.

January 25

The first substantive session of the Paris peace talks takes place, with each side presenting its terms for a settlement.

February 23	Enemy units launch long-expected general offensive in South Vietnam.
March 4	President Nixon declares U.S. "will not tolerate" continued enemy attacks and warns appropriate responses will be made.
March 6	*The Department of Defense announces U.S. troop strength in South Vietnam totals 541,500 with third country troop levels at 72,000.*
May 17	President Thieu calls for a meeting with President Nixon to coordinate future U.S. and South Vietnamese policies.
May 20	President Nixon agrees to meet President Thieu on Midway Island in June.
May 29	President Thieu says he will never agree to a coalition government with the NLF.
June 8	*President Nixon and President Thieu meet for talks on Midway. Nixon announces 25,000 American troops will be withdrawn from South Vietnam before the end of August* and emphasizes South Vietnam will take on additional responsibilities for the war. Upon his arrival in Washington on June 10, President Nixon declares the Midway meeting has opened the door to peace.
July 25	President Nixon in Guam gives background news conference indicating that the U.S. will in the future tend to avoid situations like Vietnam by limiting its assistance to economic and military aid rather than active combat involvement ("Nixon Doctrine").
July 30	President Nixon, while on his Asian tour, makes a quick stopover in South Vietnam to confer with President Thieu and General Abrams on the future U.S. troop withdrawals and on changes in military tactics. President Nixon declares "we have gone as far now as we can or should go in opening the door to peace, and now it is time for the other side to respond."

August 23   President Thieu names Deputy Premier Tran
                           Thien Khiem to be Premier, replacing Premier
                           Huong who has stepped aside in order to per-
                           mit Thieu to broaden the base of his govern-
                           ment.

September 3   *North Vietnam's President, Ho Chi Minh, dies.*

September 16   *President Nixon announces the second round of
                           U.S. troop withdrawals involving approximately
                           35,000 men,* saying the authorized ceiling on
                           U.S. troops will be reduced to 484,000 by mid-
                           December.

November 15   *Large crowds assemble for the moratorium
                           against the war in Washington, D.C. and other
                           major U.S. cities* demanding a rapid withdrawal
                           of all U.S. forces from South Vietnam.

November 20   *Ambassador Lodge resigns as chief of the
                           American delegation to the Paris peace talks.*

December 1   *U.S. troop strength in Vietnam stands at 479,-
                           500 of which 300,000 are combat troops.*

December 15   *President Nixon announces a third withdrawal
                           of U.S. troops from South Vietnam. This incre-
                           ment of 50,000 men will be withdrawn by
                           April 15, 1970.*

                           1970

January 22   President Nixon in State of the Union address
                           declares end of Vietnam war to be major goal
                           of U.S. foreign policy.

January 29   U.S. command announces bombing of anti-air-
                           craft missile base 90 miles inside North Viet-
                           nam.

February 13   Secretary of Defense Laird says U.S. will con-
                           tinue to withdraw troops from SVN despite
                           stalemate at peace table in Paris. Says "Vietna-
                           mization" program progress warrants with-
                           drawals.

March 18   Cambodia's Prince Norodom Sihanouk over-
                           thrown in coup headed by Lon Nol.

April 13	*U.S. troop strength in SVN down to 429,900.*
April 20	President Nixon announces plan to withdraw 150,000 additional U.S. troops over course of next year.
April 30	*President Nixon announces he is sending U.S. combat troops into Cambodia* to destroy enemy sanctuaries and supplies.
May 2	U.S. bombs supply dumps and other targets in North Vietnam.
May 4	Defense Department announces termination of "large scale" air attacks against NVN but says small raids may be conducted if U.S. reconnaissance planes continue to be attacked.
May 8	President Nixon declares most American troops will be out of Cambodia by mid–June.
May 11	Senate Foreign Relations Committee approves Cooper–Church amendment to cut off funds for future U.S. military operations in Cambodia.
May 27	President Thieu says ARVN troops will continue operations in Cambodia after U.S. troops are withdrawn.
June 3	Nixon calls Cambodia operation successful and announces he will resume withdrawals of U.S. forces from SVN.
June 24	*Senate repeals Gulf of Tonkin Resolution.*
June 30	*Senate passes (58–37) Cooper–Church amendment* barring future U.S. military operations in Cambodia and aid to Lon Nol government without Congressional approval.
	President Nixon reports on Cambodian operation proclaiming it successfully completed. Future U.S. action in Cambodia will be limited to air support and other aid.
July 1	President Nixon names Ambassador Bruce chief U.S. delegate to Paris talks.

Chapter Notes

I. The Decade of Vietnam

1. *Department of State Bulletin*, June 19, 1961, p. 956.
2. Irving Kristol, "We Can't Resign as 'Policeman of the World,'" *The New York Times Magazine*, May 12, 1968, p. 109.
3. For a full account of this confrontation see Arthur M. Schlesinger, Jr., *A Thousand Days* (Boston: Houghton Mifflin Company, 1965), pp. 343–378.
4. For a thoughtful discussion of the question of American international commitments see Graham Allison, Ernest May, and Adam Yarmolinsky, "Limits to Intervention," *Foreign Affairs*, January 1970, pp. 245–61.
5. Hans J. Morgenthau, *A New Foreign Policy for the United States* (New York: Frederick A. Praeger, 1969), p. 16.

II. The Colonial Legacy

1. Henry J. Waterman, "Saigon—The Pearl of the Orient," *Export Trade and Finance*, November 1932, p. 39.
2. U. S. Department of State, *Papers Relating to the Foreign Relations of the United States, 1931–1941* (Washington, D.C.: Government Printing Office, 1943), II *(Japan)*, p. 297.
3. *ibid.*, pp. 320–321.
4. Cordell Hull, *Memoirs* (New York: The Macmillan Company, 1948), II, p. 1598.

5. See Robert Shaplen, "The Enigma of Ho Chi Minh," *The Reporter*, January 27, 1955, p. 13.

6. Maj. Gen. Claire Lee Chennault, *Way of a Fighter: The Memoirs of Claire Lee Chennault* (New York: G. P. Putnam's Sons, 1949), p. 343.

7. William D. Leahy, *I Was There* (New York: McGraw-Hill, 1950), p. 338.

8. U. S. Department of State, *Foreign Relations of the United States, Diplomatic Papers, 1944* (Washington, D.C.: Government Printing Office, 1965) V, *(Japan)*, p. 1206. Hereinafter referred to as *Diplomatic Papers*.

9. Leahy, *op. cit.*, p. 44.

10. Hull, *op. cit.*, p. 1596.

11. *ibid.*, p. 1597.

12. *Diplomatic Papers, 1944*, III *(The British Commonwealth and Europe)*, (GPO, 1965), p. 780.

13. *ibid.*, *1945*, VI *(The British Commonwealth, The Far East)*, (GPO, 1969), p. 293.

14. *ibid. Conferences at Malta and Yalta, 1945* (GPO, 1955), p. 770.

15. Samuel I. Rosenman, ed., *The Public Papers and Addresses of Franklin D. Roosevelt, Victory and the Threshold of Peace* (New York: Harper & Brothers, 1950), pp. 556–57.

16. *Diplomatic Papers, The Conferences at Cairo and Teheran, 1943* (GPO, 1961), pp. 325 and 485.

17. U.S. Congress, Senate, Committee on Armed Services and Committee on Foreign Relations, Hearings, 82nd Congress, 1st Session, June 1951), *Military Situation in the Far East, 1951* (Washington, D.C.: Government Printing Office, 1951), p. 2891.

18. Elliott Roosevelt, *As He Saw It* (New York: Duell, Sloan and Pearce, 1945), pp. 71, 76–77, 114–116.

19. *Diplomatic Papers, 1945*, I *(General: The United Nations)*, (GPO, 1967), p. 124.

20. Albert C. Wedemeyer, *Wedemeyer Reports!* (New York: Henry Holt & Company, 1958), p. 340.

21. *Diplomatic Papers, The Conference of Berlin (The Potsdam Conference), 1945*, 2 Vols., I (GPO, 1960), p. 917.

22. *ibid.*, pp. 918–19.

23. *ibid.*, p. 919. (Also documented U.S. Senate, Committee on Armed Services and Committee on Foreign Relations, *op. cit.*).

24. *ibid.*, p. 920.

25. U.S. Senate, Committee on Armed Services and Committee on Foreign Relations, *op. cit.*, pp. 2892–93.

26. *ibid.*, p. 2891.

27. *Diplomatic Papers, 1945*, VI (GPO, 1969), p. 307.

28. *ibid.*, p. 568.

29. Bert Cooper, *et al, Case Studies in Insurgency and Revolutionary Warfare: Vietnam, 1941–1954* (Washington, D.C.: Special Operations Research Office [American University], 1964), p. 112.
30. Jean Sainteny, *Histoire d'une Paix Manquée* (Paris: Librairie Fayard, 1967), p. 137.
31. Robert Trumbull, *The Scrutable East* (New York: David McKay Company, 1964), p. 195–96.

III. Passing the Baton

1. Charles de Gaulle, tr. by Richard Howard, *The War Memoirs: Salvation, 1944–1946* (New York: Simon & Schuster, 1960), p. 242.
2. *ibid.*, p. 258.
3. U.S. Department of State, *Foreign Relations of the United States, Diplomatic Papers, The Conference of Berlin (The Potsdam Conference), 1945* (Washington, D.C.: Government Printing Office, 1960), II, p. 377. Hereinafter referred to as *Diplomatic Papers*.
4. *ibid.*, p. 84.
5. *Diplomatic Papers, 1945* (GPO, 1969), VI *(The British Commonwealth, The Far East),* p. 313.
6. John Carter Vincent, "The Post-War Period in the Far East," *Department of State Bulletin*, October 21, 1945, p. 646.
7. Ellen J. Hammer, *The Struggle for Indochina* (Stanford, Cal.: Stanford University Press, 1954), p. 13.
8. General Douglas MacArthur as quoted by Edgar Snow, *The Other Side of the River: Red China Today* (New York: Random House, 1961), p. 686.
9. Hammer, *op. cit.*, p. 202.
10. Harold R. Isaacs, *No Peace for Asia* (Cambridge, Mass.: The MIT Press, 1967), pp. 172–73.
11. *The New York Times*, January 1, 1946.
12. *The New York Times*, April 2, 1947.
13. *The New York Times*, February 8, 1947.
14. *The New York Times Book Review*, October 12, 1969, p. 30.
15. William C. Bullitt, "The Saddest War," *Life*, December 29, 1947, p. 68.
16. Lucien Bodard, *The Quicksand War: Prelude to Vietnam* (Boston: Little, Brown & Co., 1967), p. 223.
17. *The New York Times*, June 22, 1949.
18. New China News Agency, November 23, 1949.
19. See George Tanham, *Communist Revolutionary Warfare: The Viet Minh in Indochina* (Frederick A. Praeger, 1961), pp. 68–69.
20. *Department of State Bulletin*, February 13, 1950, p. 244.
21. *Journal Officiel*, Assemblee de Union Francaise, January 19, 1950, p. 32.
22. *Department of State Bulletin*, February 20, 1950, p. 291.

23. *Department of State Bulletin,* April 10, 1950, p. 565.
24. *Department of State Bulletin,* May 22, 1950, p. 821.
25. John F. Cady, "The Historical Background of United States Policy in Southeast Asia," *Southeast Asia: Problems of United States Policy,* ed. by William Henderson (Cambridge, Mass.: The MIT Press, 1963), p. 21.
26. *Public Papers of the Presidents of the United States, Harry S. Truman, June 1 to December 31, 1950* (Washington, D.C.: Government Printing Office, 1965), p. 492. Hereinafter referred to as *Public Papers.*
27. John Foster Dulles, *War Or Peace* (New York: The Macmillan Company, 1950), p. 231.
28. *The New York Times,* January 28, 1953.
29. *Public Papers, Dwight D. Eisenhower, 1953* (GPO, 1960), p. 16.
30. Melvin Gurtov, *The First Vietnam Crisis* (New York: Columbia University Press, 1967), pp. 14–15.
31. Bernard B. Fall, *The Two Viet-Nams: A Political and Military Analysis* 2nd rev. ed. (New York: Frederick A. Praeger, 1967), pp. 122–24.
32. Hammer, *op. cit.,* p. 312.
33. Dwight D. Eisenhower, *The White House Years: Mandate for Change, 1953–1956* (Garden City, N.Y.: Doubleday & Company, 1963), pp. 340–41.
34. *ibid.,* p. 342–43.
35. *ibid.,* p. 344.
36. *ibid.,* pp. 343–44.
37. *The New York Times,* February 23, 1954.
38. *The New York Times,* February 25, 1954.
39. Eisenhower, *op. cit.,* p. 347.
40. *ibid.*
41. *The New York Times,* March 30, 1954.
42. As quoted by Gurtov, *op. cit.,* p. 136.
43. Eisenhower, *op. cit.,* p. 350.
44. *ibid.,* p. 351.
45. *ibid.*

IV. Blueprint for a House of Cards: Geneva, 1954

1. *The New York Times,* April 25, 1954.
2. Anthony Eden, *Memoirs, Full Circle* (Boston: Houghton Mifflin Company, 1960), p. 124.
3. See Jean Lacouture and Philippe Devillers, *La Fin d'une Guerre: Indochine, 1954* (Paris: Editions du Seuil, 1960), p. 174.
4. See Donald Lancaster, *The Emancipation of French Indochina* (London: Oxford University Press, 1961), p. 321.
5. *Department of State Bulletin,* May 17, 1954, p. 744.
6. *Department of State Bulletin,* May 24, 1954, p. 781.

7. Eden, *op. cit.*, p. 141.
8. *ibid.*, p. 142.
9. *ibid.*, pp. 142–43.
10. *ibid.*, p. 144.
11. Dwight D. Eisenhower, *The White House Years: Mandate for Change, 1953–1956* (Garden City, N.Y.: Doubleday & Company, 1963), p. 366.
12. Eden, *op. cit.*, p. 145.
13. *The New York Times*, June 10, 1954.
14. *The New York Times*, June 23, 1954.
15. Lacouture and Devillers, *op. cit.*, p. 231.
16. Denise Folliot, ed., *Documents on International Affairs, 1954* (London: Oxford University Press, 1957), p. 151.
17. See Victor Bator, *Vietnam—A Diplomatic Tragedy: The Origins of the United States Involvement*, (Dobbs Ferry, N.Y.: Oceana Publications, 1965), p. 109. See also Coral Bell, "Crisis in Asia," *Survey of International Affairs, 1954* (London: Oxford University Press, 1957), pp. 57–58.
18. *Department of State Bulletin*, June 28, 1954, p. 990.
19. Eden, *op. cit.*, pp. 148–150.
20. *Congressional Record*, June 30, 1954, p. 9352.
21. *Department of State Bulletin*, July 26, 1954, p. 123.
22. *ibid.*
23. For a fuller account of the proceedings during these dramatic days, see Lacouture and Devillers, *op. cit.*, pp. 252–268.
24. Eden, *op. cit.*, p. 144.
25. *The New York Times*, July 24, 1954.
26. William P. Bundy, "The Path to Vietnam: Ten Decisions," *Orbis*, Fall 1967, p. 649.

V. Forging a Double-edged Sword: Manila, 1954

1. *Public Papers of the Presidents of the United States, Dwight D. Eisenhower, 1954* (Washington, D.C.: Government Printing Office, 1960), p. 642. Hereinafter referred to as *Public Papers*.
2. *Department of State Bulletin*, August 23, 1954, p. 261.
3. *Department of State Bulletin*, June 7, 1954, p. 863.
4. John Foster Dulles, "Security in the Pacific," *Foreign Affairs*, January 1952, pp. 182–83.
5. *Public Papers, Dwight D. Eisenhower, 1953* (GPO, 1960), p. 50.
6. Dwight D. Eisenhower, *The White House Years: Mandate for Change, 1953–1956* (Garden City, N.Y.: Doubleday & Co., 1963), pp. 346–47.
7. Anthony Eden, *Memoirs, Full Circle* (Boston: Houghton Mifflin Co., 1960), pp. 121–122.
8. *Department of State Bulletin*, May 24, 1954, p. 782.
9. *Department of State Bulletin*, June 7, 1954, p. 863.

10. *Department of State Bulletin*, June 21, 1954, p. 948.
11. Eden, *op. cit.*, p. 148.
12. *Department of State Bulletin*, July 12, 1954, p. 50.
13. *Department of State Bulletin*, September 20, 1954, pp. 391–92.
14. *ibid.*, p. 395.

VI. Birth of a Non-Nation

1. See Robert Scheer and Warren Hinckle, "The Vietnam Lobby," *Ramparts*, July 1965, pp. 15–23, and Robert Scheer, *How the United States Got Involved in Vietnam* (Santa Barbara, Cal.: Center for the Study of Democratic Institutions, July 1965).
2. William O. Douglas, *North from Malaya* (New York: Doubleday & Company, 1953), pp. 180–81.
3. See Sol Sanders, "Crisis in Indo-China," *The New Leader*, March 21, 1955, p. 4.
4. Wesley R. Fishel, "Problems of Democratic Growth in Free Vietnam," *Problems of Freedom: South Vietnam Since Independence*, ed. by Wesley R. Fishel (Glencoe, Ill: The Free Press of Glencoe, 1961), p. 16.
5. Bernard B. Fall, "Commentary on Bui Van Luong, "*Vietnam: The First Five Years*, ed. by Richard W. Lindholm (East Lansing, Mich.: Michigan State University Press, 1959), p. 57.
6. Radiogram from Saigon: "To Members Research Institute from Leo Cherne, Exec Dir," September 13, 1954.
7. Joseph Buttinger, "An Eyewitness Report on Vietnam," *The Reporter*, January 27, 1955, pp. 19–20.
8. U. S. Congress, Senate, Committee on Foreign Relations, 83rd Congress, 2d Session, *Report on Indochina, Report of Senator Mike Mansfield on a Study Mission to Vietnam, Cambodia and Laos, October 15, 1954.* (Washington, D.C.: Government Printing Office, 1954).
9. U. S. Department of State, *American Foreign Policy, 1950–1955, Basic Documents* (Washington, D.C.: Government Printing Office, 1957), II, pp. 2401–02.
10. *The New York Times*, October 25, 1954.
11. U. S. Congress, Senate, Committee on Foreign Relations, 84th Congress, 1st Session, *Vietnam, Cambodia, and Laos, Report by Senator Mike Mansfield, October 6, 1955* (Washington, D.C.: Government Printing Office, 1955), p. 2.
12. Peter Schmid, "Free Indo-China Fights Against Time," *Commentary*, January 1955, p. 28.
13. See Brian Crozier, "The Diem Regime in Southern Vietnam," *Far Eastern Survey*, April 1955, p. 51.
14. See *The New York Times*, September 22, 1954.
15. U. S. Department of State, *op. cit.*, II, pp. 2398–99.

16. *Public Papers of the Presidents of the United States, Dwight D. Eisenhower, 1955* (Washington, D.C.: Government Printing Office, 1959), pp. 315–16. Hereinafter referred to as *Public Papers.*
17. Wesley R. Fishel, ed., *Vietnam: Anatomy of a Conflict* (Itasca, Ill.: F. E. Peacock Publishers, 1968), p. 84.
18. *The New York Times,* April 22, 1955.
19. *Public Papers, op cit.,* pp. 436–37.
20. *The New York Times,* April 30, 1955.
21. *The New York Times,* May 7, 1955.

VII. Diem, Dulles, and Dominoes

1. *The New York Times,* November 18, 1954.
2. *The Times* (London), May 13, 1955.
3. *Public Papers of the Presidents of the United States, Dwight D. Eisenhower, 1955* (Washington, D.C.: Government Printing Office, 1959), p. 316.
4. *Department of State Bulletin,* May 30, 1955, pp. 872–73.
5. *The New York Times,* May 30, 1955.
6. Embassy of Vietnam, Washington, D.C. Press and Information Service, July 22, 1955.
7. *Department of State Bulletin,* July 11, 1955, p. 50.
8. *Department of State Bulletin,* October 31, 1955, p. 693.
9. John F. Kennedy, "American's Stake in Vietnam," *A Symposium on America's Stake in Vietnam* (New York: American Friends of Vietnam, 1956), p. 13.
10. U. S. Congress, Senate, Committee on Foreign Relations, 84th Congress, 1st Session, *Vietnam, Cambodia, and Laos, Report by Senator Mike Mansfield, October 6, 1955* (Washington, D.C.: Government Printing Office, 1955), p. 12.
11. *The New York Times,* July 21, 1955.
12. Joseph Buttinger, *Vietnam: A Dragon Embattled* (New York: Frederick A. Praeger, 1967), pp. 890–91.
13. *Department of State Bulletin,* November 7, 1955, p. 760.
14. Kennedy, *op. cit.,* pp. 8 & 9.
15. Graham Greene, "Last Act in Indo-China," *The New Republic,* May 16, 1955, p. 10.
16. *The New York Times,* May 10, 1957.
17. John Osborne, "The Tough Miracle Man of Vietnam," *Life,* May 13, 1957, p. 164.
18. John T. Dorsey, Jr., "South Viet Nam in Perspective," *Far Eastern Survey,* December 1958, p. 177.
19. See George A. Carver, Jr., "The Faceless Viet Cong," *Foreign Affairs,* April 1966, pp. 347–72.

20. "Nixon Tonight," CBS–TV, November 2, 1960.
21. "Face-to-Face, Nixon–Kennedy," TV–Radio Broadcast, October 13, 1960. Documented in U. S. Congress, Senate, Committee on Commerce, Subcommittee of the Subcommittee on Communications, *Freedom of Communications* (Washington, D.C.: Government Printing Office, 1961), Part III.
22. John F. Kennedy, Remarks to Democratic National and State Committees, New York, October 12, 1960. Documented *ibid.*, Part I.
23. John F. Kennedy, Mansfield, Ohio, September 27, 1960. Documented *ibid.*, Part I.

VIII. Kennedy's Commitment

1. U. S. Congress, Senate, Committee on Foreign Relations, 86th Congress, 2d Session, February, 1960, *United States Aid Program in Vietnam, Report* (Washington, D.C.: Government Printing Office, 1960), p. 9.
2. *ibid.*, p. 2.
3. *Congressional Record*, Vol. 100, Part 4 (April 6, 1954), pp. 4672–74.
4. John F. Kennedy, "America's Stake in Vietnam," *A Symposium on America's Stake in Vietnam* (New York: American Friends of Vietnam, 1956), p. 10.
5. Clark M. Clifford, "A Viet Nam Reappraisal," *Foreign Affairs*, July 1969, p. 604.
6. *Public Papers of the Presidents of the United States, John F. Kennedy, 1961* (Washington, D.C.: Government Printing Office, 1962), p. 23. Hereinafter referred to as *Public Papers*.
7. Arthur M. Schlesinger, Jr., *A Thousand Days* (Boston: Houghton Mifflin Company, 1965), p. 332.
8. See Maxwell D. Taylor, *The Uncertain Trumpet* (New York: Harper & Brothers, 1960).
9. John F. Kennedy, Book Review of *Deterrent and Defense*, B. H. Lidell Hart, *Saturday Review of Literature*, September 3, 1960, p. 17.
10. Schlesinger, *op. cit.*, pp. 542–43.
11. *ibid.*, p. 543.
12. *The New York Times*, October 16, 1961.
13. Letter from President Johnson to Senator Henry M. Jackson, quoting the "Taylor Report," *The New York Times*, March 3, 1967.
14. John Kenneth Galbraith, *Ambassador's Journal* (Boston: Houghton Mifflin Company, 1969), p. 267.
15. *Public Papers, John F. Kennedy, 1962* (GPO, 1963), pp. 12–13.
16. *The New York Times*, February 14, 1962.
17. *The New York Times*, February 19, 1962.
18. *The New York Times*, March 16, 1962.
19. *The New York Times*, April 22, 1962.

20. *The New York Times,* June 3, 1962.
21. *The New York Times,* November 28, 1962.
22. U. S. Congress, Senate, Committee on Foreign Relations, 88th Congress, 1st Session, 1963, *Viet Nam and Southeast Asia, Report of Senator Mike Mansfield et al* (Washington, D.C.: Government Printing Office, 1963).
23. *The New York Times,* December 15, 1962.
24. *Public Papers, John F. Kennedy, 1962,* p. 870.

IX. Death of a Mandarin

1. *Public Papers of the Presidents of the United States, John F. Kennedy, 1963* (Washington, D.C.: Government Printing Office, 1964), p. 11. Hereinafter referred to as *Public Papers.*
2. *The New York Times,* January 31, 1963.
3. *Department of State Bulletin,* May 13, 1963, p. 727.
4. *The New York Times,* February 13, 1963.
5. Robert Shaplen, *The Lost Revolution,* rev. ed. (New York: Harper & Row, 1966), p. 157.
6. William R. Corson, *The Betrayal* (New York: W. W. Norton & Co., 1968), p. 96.
7. *The New York Times,* April 27, 1963.
8. *The New York Times,* May 14, 1963.
9. *Public Papers, op. cit.,* p. 421.
10. *The New York Times,* May 8, 1963.
11. George A. Carver, Jr., "The Real Revolution in South Viet Nam," *Foreign Affairs,* April 1965, p. 394.
12. *The New York Times,* August 1, 1963.
13. Robert Karr McCabe, "The Swamps of Saigon," *The New Leader,* August 19, 1963, p. 4.
14. *Public Papers, op. cit.,* p. 569.
15. *Department of State Bulletin,* September 9, 1963, p. 398.
16. Arthur M. Schlesinger, Jr., *A Thousand Days* (Boston: Houghton Mifflin Company, 1965), p. 991. See also Roger Hilsman, *To Move A Nation* (Garden City, N.Y.: Doubleday & Company, 1967), p. 487 and Marguerite Higgins, *Our Vietnam Nightmare* (New York: Harper & Row, 1965), p. 192.
17. *Public Papers, op. cit.,* p. 652.
18. See Stanley Karnow, "Edge of Chaos," *Saturday Evening Post,* September 28, 1963, pp. 27–37.
19. Denis Warner, "Agony in Saigon: The Lady and the Cadaver," *The Reporter,* October 10, 1963, p. 39.
20. *The New York Times,* September 25, 1963.
21. *The New York Times,* September 24, 1963.

22. Hilsman, *op. cit.*, p. 510.
23. *Public Papers, op. cit.*, p. 759.
24. *ibid.*, pp. 759–60.
25. *ibid.*, p. 760.
26. See Shaplen, *op. cit.*, pp. 197–212, and David Halberstam, *The Making of a Quagmire* (New York: Random House, 1964), pp. 291–99.
27. Schlesinger, *op. cit.*, p. 997.
28. Theodore C. Sorensen, *Kennedy* (New York: Harper & Row, 1965), p. 660.
29. *Department of State Bulletin*, November 25, 1963, p. 814.

X. Interregnum: Washington and Saigon

1. *Department of State Bulletin*, January 13, 1964, p. 46.
2. *Public Papers of the Presidents of the United States, Lyndon B. Johnson, 1963–1964* (Washington, D.C.: Government Printing Office, 1965), Bk. I, p. 116. Hereinafter referred to as *Public Papers*.
3. *ibid.*, I, p. 254 ff.
4. *ibid.*, I, p. 304.
5. *ibid.*, I, p. 328.
6. Address by Secretary of Defense Robert S. McNamara, "United States Policy in Vietnam," *Department of State Bulletin*, April 13, 1964, pp. 562–570.
7. *Public Papers, op. cit.*, I, pp. 733–740.
8. *ibid.*, I, p. 259.
9. *ibid.*, II, p. 888.
10. *ibid.*, II, pp. 926–927.
11. *The New York Times*, September 20, 1964.
12. *Public Papers, op. cit.*, II, pp. 1098–99.
13. U. S. Congress, Senate, Committee on Foreign Relations, Hearings, 90th Congress, 2d Session, February 20, 1968, *The Gulf of Tonkin, The 1964 Incidents* (Washington, D.C.: Government Printing Office, 1968), p. 17.
14. For a full account of the Gulf of Tonkin incidents, see Joseph C. Goulden, *Truth Is the First Casualty: The Gulf of Tonkin Affairs—Illusion and Reality* (New York: Rand McNally, 1969).
15. *Congressional Record*, Vol. 110, Part 14, August 6, 1964, p. 18409.
16. U. S. Department of State, *The Legality of United States Participation in the Defense of Vietnam*, Publication 8062 (Washington, D.C.: Government Printing Office, 1966), p. 41.
17. U. S. Congress, Senate, Committee on Foreign Relations, Hearings, 90th Congress, 1st Session, August–September 1967, *U. S. Commitments to Foreign Powers* (Washington, D.C.: Government Printing Office, 1967), p. 82.

18. For an excellent account of the events of August 1964, see Robert Shaplen, *The Lost Revolution,* rev. ed. (New York: Harper & Row, 1966), Chapter IX.
19. *Public Papers, op. cit.,* II, p. 1164.
20. *ibid.*
21. *Department of State Bulletin,* December 21, 1964, p. 870.
22. *The New York Times,* December 22, 1964.

XI. McNamara's War

1. For an interesting account of the State/Defense rivalry, see Roger Hilsman, *To Move A Nation* (Garden City, N. Y.: Doubleday & Company, 1967).
2. *Public Papers of the Presidents of the United States, Lyndon B. Johnson, 1965* (Washington, D.C.: Government Printing Office, 1966), Bk. I, p. 3. Hereinafter referred to as *Public Papers.*
3. *Department of State Bulletin,* February 22, 1965, pp. 238–39.
4. *Public Papers, op. cit.,* I, p. 278.
5. U. S. Congress, Senate, Committee on Foreign Relations, Hearings, 89th Congress, 2d Session, 1966, *Supplemental Foreign Assistance, Fiscal Year 1966—Vietnam* (Washington, D.C.: Government Printing Office, 1966), p. 437.
6. Coretta Scott King, *My Life with Martin Luther King* (New York: Holt, Rinehart & Winston, 1969), p. 69.
7. U. S. Department of State, *Aggression from the North: The Record of North Viet-Nam's Campaign to Conquer South Viet-Nam* (Washington, D.C.: Government Printing Office, 1965), p. 3.
8. *ibid.*
9. *Congressional Record,* March 1, 1965, p. 3685.
10. *ibid.,* p. 3713.
11. *The New York Times,* February 28, 1965.
12. "A Reply to the White Paper," *I. F. Stone's Weekly,* March 8, 1965, pp. 1–4.
13. *Department of State Bulletin,* June 7, 1965, p. 924.
14. U. S. Department of State Memorandum, March 8, 1965, "Legal Basis for United States Action Against North Vietnam." Reprinted in U. S. Congress, Senate, Committee on Foreign Relations, *Background Information Relating to Southeast Asia and Vietnam,* 5th rev. ed. (Washington, D.C.: Government Printing Office, 1969), pp. 161–164.
15. U. S. Department of State, *The Legality of United States Participation in the Defense of Vietnam,* Publication 8062 (Washington, D.C.: Government Printing Office, 1966). Hereinafter referred to as *Legality of United States Participation.*
16. *Public Papers, op. cit.,* I, p. 319.

17. *Department of State Bulletin*, April 26, 1965, pp. 611–612.
18. *ibid.*, pp. 610–611.
19. *Public Papers, op. cit.*, I, pp. 394–99.
20. *ibid.*, I, p. 485.
21. U. S. Department of State, *Legality of United States Participation*, pp. 39 & 46.
22. Commander-in-Chief Pacific and Commander, U. S. Military Assistance Command, Vietnam, *Report on the War in Vietnam* (Washington, D.C.: Government Printing Office, 1968), p. 98.
23. *Public Papers, op. cit.*, II, p. 725.
24. *ibid.*, II, pp. 735–36.
25. *The New York Times*, July 15, 1965.

XII. Johnson's War

1. *Public Papers of the Presidents of the United States, Lyndon B. Johnson, 1965* (Washington, D.C.: Government Printing Office, 1966), Bk. II, pp. 795–96. Hereinafter referred to as *Public Papers.*
2. *ibid.*, II, p. 804.
3. Commander-in-Chief Pacific and Commander, U. S. Military Assistance Command, Vietnam, *Report on the War in Vietnam* (Washington, D.C.: Government Printing Office, 1968), p. 18. Hereinafter referred to as *Report on the War in Vietnam.*
4. *ibid.*, pp. 109–110.
5. *Department of State Bulletin*, February 14, 1966, p. 225. Also noted in *The Washington Post* and elsewhere, December 29, 1965.
6. Richard P. Stebbins, ed., asst. by Elaine P. Adam, *Documents on American Foreign Relations, 1966* (New York: Harper & Row, 1967, for the Council on Foreign Relations), p. 202.
7. *Report on the War in Vietnam*, p. 24.
8. Department of State Airgram from Department to All Diplomatic and Consular Posts (Unclassified), "The United States and Vietnam: A Summary," March 9, 1966, p. 7.
9. Republic of Vietnam, Ministry of Psychological Warfare, "The Historic Honolulu Conference," (Saigon, 1966), p. 18.
10. *Report on the War in Vietnam*, p. 123.
11. *ibid.*, p. 115.
12. See *Public Papers, Lyndon B. Johnson, 1966* (GPO, 1967), Bk. II, p. 706.
13. *The New York Times*, July 1, 1966.
14. *Report on the War in Vietnam*, p. 26.
15. *Public Papers, op. cit.*, II, p. 1324.
16. *The New York Times*, November 4, 1966.

XIII. Tragedy of Errors

1. See Eric Severeid, "The Final Troubled Hours of Adlai Stevenson," *Look*, November 30, 1965, pp. 81–86.
2. See Commander-in-Chief Pacific and Commander, U. S. Military Assistance Command, Vietnam, *Report on the War in Vietnam* (Washington, D.C.: Government Printing Office, 1968), p. 25.
3. *ibid.*
4. *Tass*, February 4, 1967.
5. *The Washington Post*, July 26, 1969.
6. Arthur J. Goldberg, "United States Peace Aims in Vietnam," *Department of State Bulletin*, February 27, 1967, p. 313.

XIV. End of an Administration; End of a Policy

1. *Department of State Bulletin*, May 15, 1967, p. 750.
2. Commander-in-Chief Pacific and Commander, U. S. Military Assistance Command, Vietnam, *Report on the War in Vietnam* (Washington, D.C.: Government Printing Office, 1968), p. 36. Hereinafter referred to as *Report on the War in Vietnam.*
3. *Department of State Bulletin*, October 16, 1967, p. 484.
4. *Nhan Dan*, (Saigon), September 26, 1967.
5. *Public Papers of the Presidents of the United States, Lyndon B. Johnson, 1967* (Washington, D.C.: Government Printing Office, 1968), Bk. II, p. 879.
6. *The New York Times*, October 21, 1967.
7. *The New York Times*, January 26, 1968.
8. *Report on the War in Vietnam*, p. 158.
9. *ibid.*
10. Clark M. Clifford, "A Viet Nam Reappraisal," *Foreign Affairs*, July 1969, p. 609.
11. For a more complete account of the events of March 1968, see Clark M. Clifford, *op. cit.*, pp. 601–622; Henry Brandon, *Anatomy of Error: The Inside Story of the Asian War on the Potomac, 1954–1969* (Boston: Gambit, 1969), pp. 118–139; Townsend Hoopes, *The Limits of Intervention* (New York: David McKay Company, 1969); and Townsend Hoopes, "LBJ's Account of March, 1968," *The New Republic*, March 14, 1970, pp. 17–19.
12. *The New York Times*, May 10, 1968.
13. *The New York Times*, April 29, 1968.
14. *Public Papers, Lyndon B. Johnson, 1967*, I, p. 131.
15. *Public Papers, Lyndon B. Johnson, 1965* (GPO, 1966), Bk. II, p. 803.
16. *The New York Times*, January 17, 1969.

XV. No More Vietnams

1. Amy Kelly, *Eleanor of Aquitaine and the Four Kings* (Cambridge, Mass.: Harvard University Press, 1950), pp. 94–95.
2. Theodore C. Sorensen, *The Kennedy Legacy* (New York: The Macmillan Company, 1969), p. 204.
3. John Kenneth Galbraith, *Ambassador's Journal* (Boston: Houghton Mifflin Company, 1969), pp. 342–43.
4. Maxwell D. Taylor, *Responsibility and Response* (New York: Harper & Row, 1967), p. 50.
5. *ibid.*, p. 37.
6. A.J.P. Taylor, *The Struggle for Mastery in Europe, 1848–1918* (London: Oxford University Press, 1954), pp. 29–30.
7. *The Washington Post*, September 13, 1969.
8. *Department of State Bulletin*, November 4, 1968, p. 463.
9. *The New York Times*, September 28, 1969.

XVI. Crusades, Commitments, and Constraints

1. Arthur M. Schlesinger, Jr., "Vietnam and the End of the Age of Superpowers," *Harper's Magazine*, March 1969, p. 44.
2. Maxwell D. Taylor, *Responsibility and Response* (New York: Harper & Row, 1967), pp. 48–53.
3. *Congressional Record*, Vol. 115, December 8, 1969, p. S 16028.
4. Joseph C. Goulden, *Truth Is the First Casualty: The Gulf of Tonkin Affairs—Illusion and Reality* (New York: Rand McNally, 1969), p. 244.
5. Jacob K. Javits, "The Congressional Presence in Foreign Relations," *Foreign Affairs*, January 1970, p. 234.
6. For an interesting account of the press and foreign policy see Phil G. Goulding, *Confirm or Deny: Informing the People on National Security* (New York: Harper & Row, 1970).
7. Averell Harriman, *Peace With Russia?* (New York: Simon & Schuster, 1959), p. 174.

Selected Bibliography

BOOKS

Acheson, Dean. *Present At the Creation: My Years in the State Department.* New York: W. W. Norton & Company, 1969.

Bator, Victor. *Vietnam—A Diplomatic Tragedy: The Origins of the United States Involvement.* Dobbs Ferry, N.Y.: Oceana Publications, 1965.

Bell, Coral. *Survey of International Affairs, 1954.* London: Oxford University Press, 1957.

Beloff, Max, ed. *Soviet Policy in the Far East, 1944–1951.* London: Oxford University Press, 1953.

Black, Eugene R. *Alternative in Southeast Asia.* New York: Frederick A. Praeger, 1969.

Bodard, Lucien. *The Quicksand War: Prelude to Vietnam.* Boston: Little, Brown & Company, 1967.

Bouscaren, Anthony Trawick. *The Last of the Mandarins: Diem of Vietnam.* Pittsburgh, Pa.: Duquesne University Press, 1965.

Brandon, Henry. *Anatomy of Error: The Inside Story of the Asian War on the Potomac, 1954–1969.* Boston: Gambit, 1969.

Bromke, Adam and Philip E. Uren, eds. *The Communist States and the West.* New York: Frederick A. Praeger, 1967.

Brown, Malcolm W. *The New Face of War.* rev. ed. Indianapolis, Ind.: Bobbs-Merrill Company, 1968.

Buttinger, Joseph. *The Smaller Dragon: A Political History of Vietnam.* New York: Frederick A. Praeger, 1958.

————. *Vietnam: A Dragon Embattled*. New York: Frederick A. Praeger, 1967.

Chennault, Maj. Gen. Claire Lee. *Way of a Fighter: The Memoirs of Claire Lee Chennault*. New York: G. P. Putnam's Sons, 1949.

Cooper, Bert et al. *Case Studies in Insurgency and Revolutionary Warfare: Vietnam, 1941–1954*. Washington, D.C.: Special Operations Research Office (American University), 1964.

Corson, William R. *The Betrayal*. New York: W. W. Norton & Company, 1968.

Critchfield, Richard. *The Long Charade: Political Subversion in the Vietnam War*. New York: Harcourt, Brace & World, 1968.

De Gaulle, Charles, tr. by Richard Howard. *Memoirs: Salvation, 1944–1946*. New York: Simon & Schuster, 1960.

Devillers, Philippe. *Histoire du Vietnam de 1940 à 1952*. Paris: Editions du Seuil, 1952.

Douglas, William O. *North from Malaya*. New York: Doubleday & Company, 1953.

Draper, Theodore. *Abuse of Power*. New York: The Viking Press, 1967.

Dulles, John Foster. *War or Peace*. New York: The Macmillan Company, 1950.

Duncanson, Dennis J. *Government and Revolution in Vietnam*. London: Oxford University Press, 1968.

Eden, Sir Anthony. *Memoirs: Full Circle*. Boston: Houghton Mifflin Company, 1960.

Eisenhower, Dwight D. *The White House Years: Mandate for Change, 1953–1956*. Garden City, N.Y.: Doubleday & Company, 1963.

Fairbairn, Geoffrey. *Revolutionary Warfare and Communist Strategy: The Threat to Southeast Asia*. London: Faber & Faber, 1968.

Fall, Bernard B. *Last Reflections on a War*. Garden City, N.Y.: Doubleday & Company, 1967.

————. *Le Viet Minh, 1945–1960*. Paris: Librairie Armand Colin, 1960.

————. *Street Without Joy: Insurgency in Indochina, 1946–1953*. 3rd rev. ed. Harrisburg, Pa.: The Stackpole Company, 1963.

————. *The Two Viet-Nams: A Political and Military Analysis*. 2nd rev. ed. New York: Frederick A. Praeger, 1967.

————. *Viet-Nam Witness*. New York: Frederick A. Praeger, 1966.

Fifield, Russell H. *Southeast Asia in U.S. Policy*. New York: Frederick A. Praeger, 1963.

Fishel, Wesley R., ed. *Vietnam: Anatomy of a Conflict*. Itasca, Ill.: F. E. Peacock Publishers, 1968.

————. *Problems of Freedom: South Vietnam Since Independence*. Glencoe, Ill.: The Free Press of Glencoe, 1961.

Folliot, Denise, ed. *Documents on International Affairs, 1954*. London: Oxford University Press, 1957.

Galbraith, John Kenneth. *Ambassador's Journal*. Boston: Houghton Mifflin Company, 1969.

Gettleman, Marvin E., ed. *Vietnam: History, Documents, and Opinions on a Major World Crisis*. New York: Fawcett, 1965.

Goulden, Joseph C. *Truth Is the First Casualty: The Gulf of Tonkin Affair—Illusion and Reality*. New York: Rand McNally & Company, 1969.

Goulding, Phil G. *Confirm or Deny: Informing the People on National Security*. New York: Harper & Row, 1970.

Gurtov, Melvin. *The First Vietnam Crisis*. New York: Columbia University Press, 1967.

Halberstam, David. *The Making of a Quagmire*. New York: Random House, 1964.

Hammer, Ellen J. *The Struggle for Indochina*. Stanford, Cal.: Stanford University Press, 1954.

Harriman, Averell. *Peace With Russia?* New York: Simon & Schuster, 1959.

Henderson, William, ed. *Southeast Asia: Problems of United States Policy*. Cambridge, Mass.: The MIT Press, 1963.

Higgins, Marguerite. *Our Vietnam Nightmare*. New York: Harper & Row, 1965.

Hilsman, Roger. *To Move a Nation*. Garden City, N.Y.: Doubleday & Company, 1967.

Hoang Van Chi. *From Colonialism to Communism: A Case History of North Vietnam*. New York: Frederick A. Praeger, 1964.

Honey, P. J. *Genesis of a Tragedy: The Historical Background to the Vietnam War*. London: Ernest Benn, 1968.

Hoopes, Townsend. *The Limits of Intervention: An Inside Account of How the Johnson Policy of Escalation Was Reversed*. New York: David McKay Company, 1969.

Hull, Cordell. *Memoirs*. New York: The Macmillan Company, 1948.

Isaacs, Harold R. *New Cycle in Asia: Selected Documents on Major International Developments in the Far East, 1943–47*. New York: The Macmillan Company, 1947.

———. *No Peace for Asia*. Cambridge, Mass.: The MIT Press, 1967.

Just, Ward S. *To What End: Report from Vietnam*. Boston: Houghton Mifflin Company, 1968.

Kahin, George McTurnan and John W. Lewis. *The United States in Vietnam*. New York: The Dial Press, 1967.

Kraslow, David and Stuart H. Loory. *The Secret Search for Peace in Vietnam*. New York: Random House, 1968.

Lacouture, Jean. *Ho Chi Minh: A Political Biography*. New York: Random House, 1968.

———. *Vietnam Between Two Truces*. New York: Random House, 1966.

——— and Philippe Devillers. *La Fin d'une Guerre, Indochine, 1954*. Paris: Editions du Seuil, 1960.

————. *End of a War.* Translated by Alexander Lieven and Adam Roberts. New York: Frederick A. Praeger, 1969.

Lancaster, Donald. *The Emancipation of French Indochina.* London: Oxford University Press, 1961.

Leahy, William D. *I Was There.* New York: McGraw-Hill, 1950.

Lindholm, Richard W., ed. *Vietnam: The First Five Years.* East Lansing, Mich.: Michigan State University Press, 1959.

Lohbeck, Don. *Patrick J. Hurley.* Chicago: Henry Regnery Company, 1956.

McAlister, John T., Jr. *Viet Nam: The Origins of Revolution.* New York: Alfred A. Knopf, 1969.

Mecklin, John. *Mission in Torment.* Garden City, N.Y.: Doubleday & Company, 1965.

Morgenthau, Hans J. *A New Foreign Policy for the United States.* New York: Frederick A. Praeger, 1969.

————. *Vietnam and the United States.* Washington, D.C.: Public Affairs Press, 1965.

O'Ballance, Edgar. *The Indo-China War, 1945–54.* London: Faber & Faber, 1964.

Pfeffer, Richard M., ed. *No More Vietnams?: The War and the Future of American Foreign Policy.* New York: Harper & Row, 1968.

Pike, Douglas. *The Viet Cong.* Cambridge, Mass.: The MIT Press, 1966.

Raskin, Marcus G. and Bernard B. Fall. *The Viet-Nam Reader: Articles and Documents on American Foreign Policy and the Viet-Nam Crisis.* New York: Vintage, 1965.

Romanus, Charles F. and Riley Sunderland. *Time Runs Out in CBI.* Vol. 9, Part 3, *The U.S. Army in World War II.* Washington, D.C.: Office of the Chief of Military History, Department of the Army, 1959.

Roosevelt, Elliott. *As He Saw It.* New York: Duell, Sloan and Pearce, 1945.

Rosenman, Samuel I., ed. *The Public Papers and Addresses of Franklin D. Roosevelt: Victory and the Threshold of Peace.* New York: Harper & Brothers, 1950.

Sainteny, Jean. *Histoire d'une Paix Manquée.* Paris: Librairie Fayard, 1967.

Schlesinger, Arthur M., Jr. *A Thousand Days.* Boston: Houghton Mifflin Company, 1965.

————. *The Bitter Heritage: Vietnam and American Democracy, 1941–1966.* Boston: Houghton Mifflin Company, 1966.

Scigliano, Robert. *South Vietnam: Nation Under Stress.* Boston: Houghton Mifflin Company, 1963.

Shaplen, Robert. *The Lost Revolution.* rev. ed. New York: Harper & Row, 1966.

Smith, Ralph. *Viet-Nam and the West.* London: Heinemann, 1968.

Sorensen, Theodore C. *Kennedy.* New York: Harper & Row, 1965.

————. *The Kennedy Legacy.* New York: The Macmillan Company, 1969.

Starobin, Joseph R. *Eyewitness in Indo-China.* New York: Cameron & Kahn, 1954.

Stebbins, Richard P., ed. *Documents on Foreign Relations, 1966.* New York: Harper & Row, 1967, for the Council on Foreign Relations.

Survey of International Affairs, 1939–1946. Vol. VII: *The Far East, 1942–1946.* London: Oxford University Press, 1955.

Tanham, George. *Communist Revolutionary Warfare: The Viet Minh in Indochina.* New York: Frederick A. Praeger, 1961.

Taylor, Maxwell D. *Responsibility and Response.* New York: Harper & Row, 1967.

——. *The Uncertain Trumpet.* New York: Harper & Brothers, 1960.

Thompson, Sir Robert. *Defeating Communist Insurgency: The Lessons of Malaya and Vietnam.* New York: Frederick A. Praeger, 1966.

——. *No Exit from Vietnam.* New York: David McKay Company, 1969.

Trager, Frank N. *Why Viet Nam?* New York: Frederick A. Praeger, 1966.

Truman, Harry S. *Memoirs.* Garden City, N.Y.: Doubleday & Company, 1956 & 1958.

Trumbull, Robert. *The Scrutable East.* New York: David McKay Company, 1964.

Warner, Denis. *The Last Confucian.* New York: The Macmillan Company, 1963.

Watt, Sir Alan Stewart. *Vietnam: An Australian Analysis.* Canberra: F. W. Cheshire, 1968.

Wedemeyer, General Albert C. *Wedemeyer Reports!* New York: Henry Holt & Company, 1958.

ARTICLES

"A Reply to the White Paper," *I. F. Stone's Weekly,* March 8, 1965, pp. 1–4.

Brandon, Henry. "The Unwinnable War," *The Sunday Times* (London), Part I: April 13, 1969; Part II: April 20, 1969; Part III: April 27, 1969.

Bullitt, William C. "The Saddest War," *Life,* December 29, 1947, pp. 64–69.

Bundy, William P. "The Path to Viet Nam: Ten Decisions," *Orbis,* Fall 1967, pp. 647–63.

Buttinger, Joseph. "An Eyewitness Report on Vietnam," *The Reporter,* January 27, 1955, pp. 19–20.

——. "Are We Saving South Vietnam?" *The New Leader,* June 27, 1955, Section two, pp. S1–S15.

Carver, George A., Jr. "The Faceless Viet Cong," *Foreign Affairs,* April 1966, pp. 347–372.

——. "The Real Revolution in South Viet Nam," *Foreign Affairs,* April 1965, pp. 387–408.

Clifford, Clark M. "A Viet Nam Reappraisal," *Foreign Affairs,* July 1969, pp. 601–622.

Clubb, O. Edmund. "Trap in Vietnam," *The Progressive*, April 1962, pp. 16–20.

"Conférence de Gèneve: Problèmes Coréen et Indochinois," *Chronique de Politique Étrangère*, September 1954, pp. 506–563.

Cooper, Chester L. "Vietnam: The Complexities of Negotiation," *Foreign Affairs*, April 1968, pp. 454–466.

Cousins, Norman. "How the U. S. Spurned Three Chances for Peace in Vietnam," *Look*, July 29, 1969, pp. 45–48.

Crozier, Brian. "The Diem Regime in Southern Vietnam," *Far Eastern Survey*, April 1955, pp. 49–56.

Dorsey, John T., Jr. "South Viet Nam in Perspective," *Far Eastern Survey*, December 1958, pp. 177–182.

Dulles, John Foster. "Security in the Pacific," *Foreign Affairs*, January 1952, pp. 175–187.

Dunn, William B. "How the West Could Win Vietnam's Support," *Foreign Policy Bulletin*, May 15, 1954, pp. 1–2.

Fall, Bernard B. "Ho Chi Minh, Like It or Not," *Esquire*, November 1967.

Farley, Miriam S. "Vietnam Kaleidoscope," *Far Eastern Survey*, May 1955, pp. 77–78.

Fishel, Wesley R. "Free Vietnam Since Geneva," *Yale Review*, Autumn 1959, pp. 68–79.

———. "Vietnam's Democratic One-Man Rule," *The New Leader*, November 2, 1959, pp. 10–13.

———. "Vietnam's War of Attrition," *The New Leader*, December 7, 1959, pp. 16–21.

Greene, Graham. "Last Act in Indo-China," *The New Republic*, May 16, 1955, pp. 9–11.

Halberstam, David. "McGeorge Bundy," *Harper's Magazine*, July 1969, pp. 30–36.

———. "Return to Vietnam," *Harper's Magazine*, December 1967, pp. 47–50.

Henderson, William. "South Viet Nam Finds Itself," *Foreign Affairs*, January 1957, pp. 283–294.

Holmes, John W. "Geneva: 1954," *International Journal* (Canadian Institute of International Affairs), Summer 1967, pp. 457–483.

Hoopes, Townsend. "The Fight for the President's Mind," *Atlantic*, October 1969, pp. 97–114.

Hughes, Emmet John. "A Man for All Nations," *Newsweek*, December 12, 1966, pp. 62–63.

Javits, Jacob K. "The Congressional Presence in Foreign Relations," *Foreign Affairs*, January 1970, pp. 221–234.

Just, Ward S. "Notes on Losing a War," *Atlantic*, January 1969, pp. 39–44.

Kissinger, Henry A. "The Viet Nam Negotiations," *Foreign Affairs*, January 1969, pp. 211–234.

Kristol, Irving. "We Can't Resign as 'Policeman of the World,'" *The New York Times Magazine*, May 12, 1968, p. 109.

Lacouture, Jean. "How to Talk to Mr. Ho," *Ramparts*, October 1966, pp. 42–46.

———. "Uncle Ho Defies Uncle Sam," *The New York Times Magazine*, March 28, 1965, pp. 25–26.

Ladejinsky, Wolf. "Vietnam: The First Five Years," *The Reporter*, December 24, 1959, pp. 20–23.

Landon, Kenneth P. "The 1954 Geneva Agreements," *Current History*, February 1966, pp. 79–84.

Lansdale, Edward G. "Viet Nam: Do We Understand Revolution?" *Foreign Affairs*, October 1964, pp. 75–86.

Mansfield, Senator Mike. "Reprieve in Vietnam," *Harper's Magazine*, January 1956, pp. 46–51.

McCabe, Robert Karr. "The Swamps of Saigon," *The New Leader*, August 19, 1963, pp. 3–5.

McCulloch, Frank. "Peace Feelers: This Frail Dance of the Seven Veils," *Life*, March 22, 1968, pp. 32–38.

Nixon, Richard M. "Asia After Viet Nam," *Foreign Affairs*, October 1967, pp. 111–125.

Osborne, John. "The Tough Miracle Man of Vietnam," *Life*, May 13, 1957, pp. 156–176.

Radványi, János. "Peace Feelers: 'A Bizarre Adventure in Make-Believe Diplomacy,'" *Life*, March 22, 1968, pp. 60–74.

"Recontres Diplomatiques a Paris en Mai 1955," *Chronique de Politique Étrangère*, July 1955, pp. 341–345.

Sanders, Sol. "Crisis in Indo-China," *The New Leader*, March 21, 1955, pp. 3–5.

Scheer, Robert and Warren Hinckle. "The Vietnam Lobby," *Ramparts*, July 1965, pp. 15–23.

Schemmer, Benjamin F. "Former Under Secretary Speaks Out on Vietnam," *Armed Forces Journal*, September 20, 1969, pp. 20–21.

Schlesinger, Arthur M., Jr. "Vietnam and the End of the Age of Superpowers," *Harper's Magazine*, March 1969, pp. 41–49.

Schmid, Peter. "Free Indo-China Fights Against Time," *Commentary*, January 1955, pp. 18–29.

Severeid, Eric. "The Final Troubled Hours of Adlai Stevenson," *Look*, November 30, 1965, pp. 81–86.

Shaplen, Robert. "A Reporter At Large—Until the Chairs Rot," *The New Yorker*, July 12, 1969, pp. 36–57.

———. "A Reporter in Vietnam," *The New Yorker*, September 22, 1962, pp. 103–131.

———. "Letter from Saigon—Attack on Hue," *The New Yorker*, March 2, 1968, pp. 44–81.

————. "Letter from Saigon—Communist Strategy At Home and in Paris," *The New Yorker*, January 11, 1969, pp. 66–87.

————. "The Enigma of Ho Chi Minh," *The Reporter*, January 27, 1955, pp. 11–19.

Sharp, Lauriston. "Paradoxes in the Indochinese Dilemma," *The Annals*, July 1954, pp. 89–98.

Smith, Hedrick. "Harriman Suggests a Way Out of Vietnam," *The New York Times Magazine*, August 24, 1969.

Smith, Hedrick with William Beecher. "The Vietnam Policy Reversal of 1968," *The New York Times*, March 6 and 7, 1969.

Stone, I. F. "The Supineness of the Senate," *The New York Review of Books*, February 13, 1969, pp. 3–5.

Taylor, Milton C. "South Viet-Nam: Lavish Aid, Limited Progress," *Pacific Affairs*, Fall 1961, pp. 242–56.

"The Implacable Man Named 'He Who Enlightens,'" *Life*, March 22, 1968, pp. 22–31.

Thomson, James C., Jr. "How Could Vietnam Happen?: An Autopsy," *Atlantic*, April 1968, pp. 47–53.

Warner, Denis. "Agony in Saigon: The Lady and the Cadaver," *The Reporter*, October 10, 1963, pp. 39–42.

————. "Vietnam: A Dynasty in Disorder," *The Reporter*, September 12, 1963, pp. 34–35.

White, Theodore H. "Indo-China—The Long Trail of Error," *The Reporter*, June 22, 1954, pp. 8–15.

PUBLIC DOCUMENTS, UNITED STATES

Commander-in-Chief Pacific and Commander, U.S. Military Assistance Command, Vietnam. *Report on the War in Vietnam.* Washington, D.C.: Government Printing Office, 1968.

Public Papers of the Presidents of the United States, Harry S. Truman, June 1 to December 31, 1950. Washington, D.C.: Government Printing Office, 1965.

Public Papers of the Presidents of the United States, Dwight D. Eisenhower, 1953. Washintgon, D.C.: Government Printing Office, 1960.

Public Papers of the Presidents of the United States, Dwight D. Eisenhower, 1954. Washington, D.C.: Government Printing Office, 1960.

Public Papers of the Presidents of the United States, Dwight D. Eisenhower, 1955. Washington, D.C.: Government Printing Office, 1959.

Public Papers of the Presidents of the United States, John F. Kennedy, 1961. Washington, D.C.: Government Printing Office, 1962.

Public Papers of the Presidents of the United States, John F. Kennedy, 1962. Washington, D.C.: Government Printing Office, 1963.

Public Papers of the Presidents of the United States, John F. Kennedy, 1963. Washington, D.C.: Government Printing Office, 1964.

Public Papers of the Presidents of the United States, Lyndon B. Johnson, 1963–1964 (2 Bks.). Washington, D.C.: Government Printing Office, 1965.

Public Papers of the Presidents of the United States, Lyndon B. Johnson, 1965 (2 Bks.). Washington, D.C.: Government Printing Office, 1966.

Public Papers of the Presidents of the United States, Lyndon B. Johnson, 1966 (2 Bks.). Washington, D.C.: Government Printing Office, 1967.

U. S. Department of State. *Aggression from the North: The Record of North Viet-Nam's Campaign to Conquer South Viet-Nam.* Washington, D.C.: Government Printing Office, 1965.

———. *American Foreign Policy, 1950–1955, Basic Documents.* Washington, D.C.: Government Printing Office, 1957.

———. *A Threat to the Peace: North Viet-Nam's Effort to Conquer South Viet-Nam.* Washington, D.C.: Government Printing Office, 1961.

———. *Foreign Relations of the United States, Diplomatic Papers, 1940.* Vol. IV, *The Far East.* Washington, D.C.: Government Printing Office, 1955.

———. *Foreign Relations of the United States, Diplomatic Papers, 1943.* Vol. III, *The British Commonwealth, Eastern Europe, The Far East.* Washington, D.C.: Government Printing Office, 1963.

———. *Foreign Relations of the United States, Diplomatic Papers, 1944.* Vol. III, *The British Commonwealth and Europe.* Washington, D.C.: Government Printing Office, 1965.

———. *Foreign Relations of the United States, Diplomatic Papers, 1944.* Vol. V, *Japan.* Washington, D.C.: Government Printing Office, 1965.

———. *Foreign Relations of the United States, Diplomatic Papers, 1945.* Vol. I, *General, The United Nations.* Washington, D.C.: Government Printing Office, 1967.

———. *Foreign Relations of the United States, Diplomatic Papers, 1945.* Vol. VI, *The British Commonwealth, The Far East.* Washington, D.C.: Government Printing Office, 1969.

———. *Foreign Relations of the United States, Diplomatic Papers, The Conference of Berlin (The Potsdam Conference), 1945* (2 Vols.). Washington, D.C.: Government Printing Office, 1960.

———. *Foreign Relations of the United States, Diplomatic Papers, The Conferences at Cairo and Teheran, 1943.* Washington, D.C.: Government Printing Office, 1961.

———. *Foreign Relations of the United States, Diplomatic Papers, The Conferences at Malta and Yalta, 1945.* Washington, D.C.: Government Printing Office, 1955.

———. *Papers Relating to the Foreign Relations of the United States, Japan,*

1931–1941 (2 Vols.). Washington, D.C.: Government Printing Office, 1943.

——. *Vietnam: Search for Peace.* (undated).

——. "The Legality of United States Participation in the Defense of Vietnam." Publication 8062. Washington, D.C.: Government Printing Office, 1966.

CONGRESSIONAL DOCUMENTS

U.S. Congress, Senate. Committee on Armed Services and the Committee on Foreign Relations. Hearings, 82nd Congress, 1st Session, June 1951. *Military Situation in the Far East.* Washington, D.C.: Government Printing Office, 1951.

U. S. Congress. Senate. Committee on Foreign Relations, 91st Congress, 1st Session, 1969. *Background Information Relating to Southeast Asia and Vietnam.* (5th rev. ed.) Washington, D.C.: Government Printing Office, 1969.

——. 83rd Congress, 2d Session, 1954. *Report on Indochina, Report of Senator Mike Mansfield on a Study Mission to Vietnam, Cambodia and Laos, October 15, 1954.* Washington, D.C.: Government Printing Office, 1954.

——. Hearings, 89th Congress, 2d Session, January–February, 1966. *Supplemental Foreign Assistance Fiscal Year 1966–Vietnam.* Washington, D.C.: Government Printing Office, 1966.

——. Hearings, 90th Congress, 2d Session, February 20, 1968. *The Gulf of Tonkin, The 1964 Incidents.* Washington, D.C.: Government Printing Office, 1968.

——. 90th Congress, 2d Session, 1968. *The Gulf of Tonkin, The 1964 Incidents,* Part II, Supplementary Documents. Washington, D.C.: Government Printing Office, 1968.

——. Hearings, 86th Congress, 1st Session, July 1959. *The Situation in Vietnam.* Washington, D.C.: Government Printing Office, 1959.

——. Hearings, 83rd Congress, 2d Session, November 11, 1954. *The Southeast Asia Collective Defense Treaty.* Washington, D.C.: Government Printing Office, 1954.

——. Hearings, 88th Congress, 2d Session, August 6, 1964. *The Southeast Asia Resolution.* Washington, D.C.: Government Printing Office, 1966.

——. 89th Congress, 2d Session, January 6, 1966. *The Vietnam Conflict: The Substance and the Shadow.* Report of Senator Mansfield et al. Washington, D.C.: Government Printing Office, 1966.

——. 86th Congress, 2d Session, February 1960. *United States Aid Program in Vietnam,* Report. Washington, D.C.: Government Printing Office, 1960.

————. Hearings, 90th Congress, 1st Session, August–September, 1967. *U. S. Commitments to Foreign Powers.* Washington, D.C.: Government Printing Office, 1967.

————. 88th Congress, 1st Session, 1963. *Vietnam and Southeast Asia*, Report of Senators Mansfield, Boggs, Pell and Smith. Washington, D.C.: Government Printing Office, 1963.

————. 84th Congress, 1st Session, 1955. *Vietnam, Cambodia and Laos*, Report by Senator Mike Mansfield, *October 6, 1955.* Washington, D.C.: Government Printing Office, 1955.

PUBLIC DOCUMENTS, GREAT BRITAIN

Documents Relating to British Involvement in the Indo-China Conflict, 1945–1965. Miscellaneous No. 25 (1965), Command 2834. London: Her Majesty's Stationery Office, 1965.

Documents Relating to the Discussion of Korea and Indo-China at the Geneva Conference, April 27–June 15, 1954. Miscellaneous No. 16 (1954), Command 9186. London: Her Majesty's Stationery Office, 1954.

Further Documents Relating to the Discussion of Indo-China at the Geneva Conference, June 16–July 21, 1954. Miscellaneous No. 20 (1954), Command 9239. London: Her Majesty's Stationery Office, 1954.

Recent Exchanges Concerning Attempts to Promote a Negotiated Settlement of the Conflict in Viet-Nam. Viet-Nam No. 3 (1965), Command 2756. London: Her Majesty's Stationery Office, 1965.

MISCELLANEOUS

A Symposium on America's Stake in Vietnam. New York: American Friends of Vietnam, 1956.

Lessons from the Vietnam War, Report of a Seminar Held at the Royal United Service Institution, February 12, 1969. London: Royal United Service Institution, 1969.

Republic of Vietnam, Ministry of Psychological Warfare. *The Historic Honolulu Conference.* Saigon, 1966.

Sacks, I. Milton. "Communism and Nationalism in Vietnam, 1918–1946." Ph.D. dissertation, Yale University, 1960.

Scheer, Robert. *How the United States Got Involved in Vietnam.* Santa Barbara, Cal.: Center for the Study of Democratic Institutions, July 1965.

Index